ACCA

PAPER F7

FINANCIAL REPORTING
(UNITED KINGDOM)

In this new syllabus first edition approved by ACCA

- We **discuss** the **best strategies** for studying for ACCA exams
- We **highlight** the **most important elements** in the syllabus and the **key skills** you will need
- We **signpost** how each chapter links to the syllabus and the study guide
- We **provide** lots of **exam focus points** demonstrating what the examiner will want you to do
- We **emphasise key points** in regular **fast forward summaries**
- We **test your knowledge** of what you've studied in **quick quizzes**
- We **examine your understanding** in our **exam question bank**
- We **reference all the important topics** in our **full index**

BPP's **i-Learn** and **i-Pass** products also support this paper.

FOR EXAMS IN DECEMBER 2007 AND JUNE 2008

LEARNING MEDIA

First edition June 2007

ISBN 9780 7517 3293 1

British Library Cataloguing-in-Publication Data
A catalogue record for this book
is available from the British Library

Published by

BPP Learning Media Ltd
BPP House, Aldine Place
London W12 8AA

www.bpp.com/learningmedia

Printed in Great Britain by
Hobbs the Printer

Your learning materials, published by BPP Learning
Media Ltd, are printed on paper sourced from
sustainable, managed forests.

We are grateful to the Association of Chartered Certified
Accountants for permission to reproduce past
examination questions. The suggested solutions in the
exam answer bank have been prepared by BPP Learning
Media Ltd.

Contents

The BPP Learning Media Effective Study Package

Distance Learning from BPP Professional Education

You can access our exam-focussed interactive e-learning materials over the **Internet**, via BPP Learn Online, hosted by BPP Professional Education.

BPP Learn Online offers **comprehensive tutor support**, **revision guidance** and **exam tips**.

Visit www.bpp.com/acca/learnonline for further details.

Learning to Learn Accountancy

BPP's ground-breaking **Learning to Learn Accountancy** book is designed to be used both at the outset of your ACCA studies and throughout the process of learning accountancy. It challenges you to consider how you study and gives you helpful hints about how to approach the various types of paper which you will encounter. It can help you **focus your studies on the subject and exam**, enabling you to **acquire knowledge**, **practise and revise efficiently and effectively**.

BPP
LEARNING MEDIA

How the BPP ACCA-approved Study Text can help you pass

How the BPP ACCA-approved Study Text can help you pass

Tackling studying

We know that studying for a number of exams can seem daunting, particularly when you have other commitments as well.

- We therefore provide guidance on **what you need to study efficiently and effectively** – to use the limited time you have in the best way possible

- We explain the **purposes** of the **different features** in the BPP Study Text, demonstrating how they help you and improve your chances of passing

Developing exam awareness

We never forget that you're aiming to pass your exams, and our Texts are completely focused on helping you do this.

- In the section **Studying P1** we introduce the key themes of the syllabus, describe the skills you need and summarise how to succeed

- The **Introduction** to each chapter of this Study Text sets the chapter in the context of the syllabus and exam

- We provide specific tips, **Exam focus points**, on what you can expect in the exam and what to do (and not to do!) when answering questions

And our Study Text is **comprehensive**. It covers the syllabus content. No more, no less.

Using the Syllabus and Study Guide

We set out the Syllabus and Study Guide in full.

- Reading the **introduction to the Syllabus** will show you what **capabilities** (skills) you'll have to demonstrate, and how this exam links with other papers.

- The topics listed in the **Syllabus** are the **key topics** in this exam. By quickly looking through the Syllabus, you can see the breadth of the paper. Reading the Syllabus will also highlight topics to look out for when you're reading newspapers or *student accountant* magazine.

- The **Study Guide** provides the **detail**, showing you precisely what you'll be studying. Don't worry if it seems a lot when you look through it; BPP's Study Text will carefully guide you through it all.

- Remember the Study Text shows, at the start of every chapter, which areas of the Syllabus and Study Guide are covered in the chapter.

Testing what you can do

Testing yourself helps you develop the skills you need to pass the exam and also confirms that you can recall what you have learnt.

- We include **Questions** within chapters, and the **Exam Question Bank** provides lots more practice.

- Our **Quick Quizzes** test whether you have enough knowledge of the contents of each chapter.

- Question practice is particularly important if English is not your first written language. ACCA offers an **International Certificate in Financial English** promoting language skills within the international business community.

BPP
LEARNING MEDIA

Example chapter

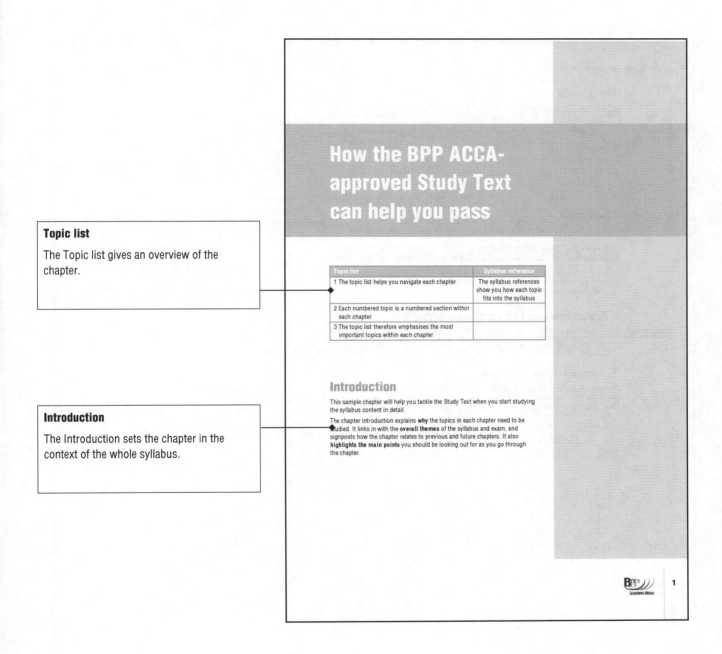

Topic list

The Topic list gives an overview of the chapter.

Introduction

The Introduction sets the chapter in the context of the whole syllabus.

Within the image:

How the BPP ACCA-approved Study Text can help you pass

Topic list	Syllabus reference
1 The topic list helps you navigate each chapter	The syllabus references show you how each topic fits into the syllabus
2 Each numbered topic is a numbered section within each chapter	
3 The topic list therefore emphasises the most important topics within each chapter	

Introduction

This sample chapter will help you tackle the Study Text when you start studying the syllabus content in detail.

The chapter introduction explains **why** the topics in each chapter need to be studied. It links in with the **overall themes** of the syllabus and exam, and signposts how the chapter relates to previous and future chapters. It also **highlights the main points** you should be looking out for as you go through the chapter.

Study guide

	Intellectual level
We list the topics in ACCA's Study guide that are covered in each chapter	The intellectual level indicates the depth in which the topics will be covered

Exam guide

The Exam guide highlights ways in which the main topics covered in each chapter may be examined.

> Knowledge brought forward from earlier studies

Knowledge brought forward boxes summarise information and techniques that you are **assumed to know** from your earlier studies. As the exam may test your knowledge of these areas, you should **revise** your previous study material if you are unsure about them.

1 Key topic which has a section devoted to it

> FAST FORWARD   Fast forwards give you a **summary** of the content of each of the main chapter sections. They are listed together in the roundup at the end of each chapter to allow you to review each chapter quickly.

1.1 Important topic within section

The headings within chapters give you a good idea of the **importance** of the topics covered. The larger the header, the more important the topic is. The headers will help you navigate through the chapter and locate the areas that have been highlighted as important in the front pages or in the chapter introduction.

BPP LEARNING MEDIA   2

Study guide

The Study guide links with ACCA's own guidance.

Exam guide

The Exam guide describes the examinability of the chapter.

Knowledge brought forward

Knowledge brought forward shows you what you need to remember from previous exams.

Fast forward

Fast forwards allow you to preview and review each section easily.

BPP LEARNING MEDIA

Example

Examples show you how theory is put into practice.

Key term

Key terms are the core vocabulary.

Exam focus point

Exam focus points provide specific links to the exam.

Formula to learn

You must remember these formulae in the exam.

Question

Questions provide vital practice of what you've learnt.

Case Study

Case Studies link what you've learnt with the business environment.

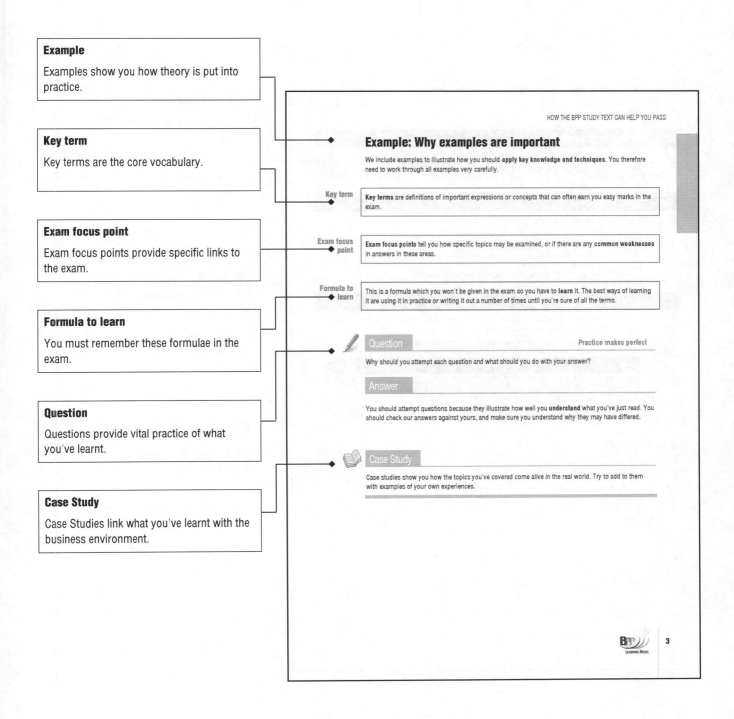

Example: Why examples are important

We include examples to illustrate how you should **apply key knowledge and techniques**. You therefore need to work through all examples very carefully.

Key term | **Key terms** are definitions of important expressions or concepts that can often earn you easy marks in the exam.

Exam focus point | **Exam focus points** tell you how specific topics may be examined, or if there are any **common weaknesses** in answers in these areas.

Formula to learn | This is a formula which you won't be given in the exam so you have to **learn** it. The best ways of learning it are using it in practice or writing it out a number of times until you're sure of all the terms.

Question — Practice makes perfect

Why should you attempt each question and what should you do with your answer?

Answer

You should attempt questions because they illustrate how well you **understand** what you've just read. You should check our answers against yours, and make sure you understand why they may have differed.

Case Study

Case studies show you how the topics you've covered come alive in the real world. Try to add to them with examples of your own experiences.

BPP LEARNING MEDIA   3

BPP LEARNING MEDIA   11

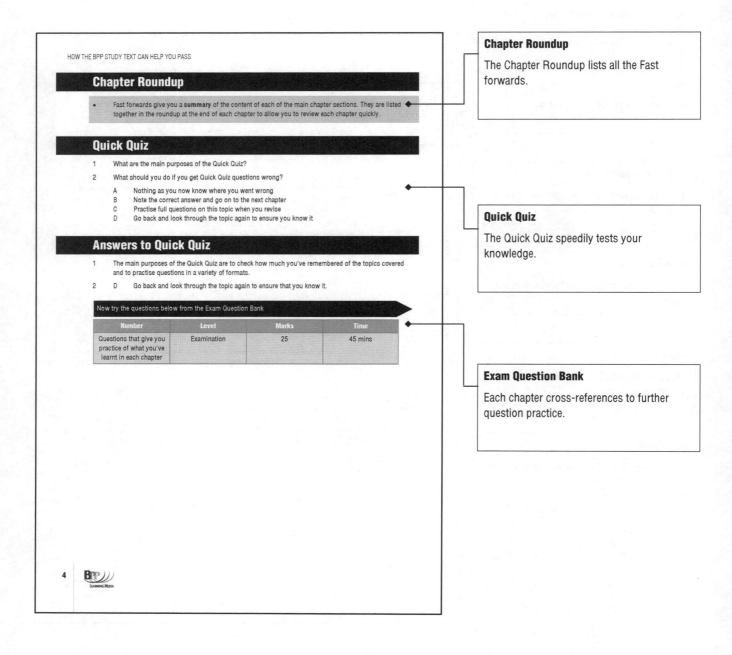

Chapter Roundup

The Chapter Roundup lists all the Fast forwards.

Quick Quiz

The Quick Quiz speedily tests your knowledge.

Exam Question Bank

Each chapter cross-references to further question practice.

Learning styles

BPP's guide to studying, *Learning to Learn Accountancy*, provides guidance on identifying how you learn and the variety of intelligences that you have. We shall summarise some of the material in *Learning to Learn Accountancy*, as it will help you understand how to you are likely to approach the Study Text:

If you like	Then you might focus on	How the Study Text helps you
Word games, crosswords, poetry	Going through the detail in the Text	Chapter introductions, Fast forwards and Key terms help you determine the detail that's most significant
Number puzzles, Sudoku, Cluedo	Understanding the Text as a logical sequence of knowledge and ideas	Chapter introductions and headers help you follow the flow of material
Drawing, cartoons, films	Seeing how the ways material is presented show what it means and how important it is	The different features and the emphasis given by headers and emboldening help you see quickly what you have to know
Attending concerts, playing a musical instrument, dancing	Identifying patterns in the Text	The sequence of features within each chapter helps you understand what material is really crucial
Sport, craftwork, hands on experience	Learning practical skills such as preparing a set of accounts	Examples and question practice help you develop the practical skills you need

If you want to learn more about developing some or all of your intelligences, *Learning to Learn Accountancy* shows you plenty of ways in which you can do so.

Studying efficiently and effectively

BPP
LEARNING MEDIA

What you need to study efficiently and effectively

Positive attitude

Yes there is a lot to learn. But look at the most recent ACCA pass list. See how many people have passed. They've made it; you can too. Focus on all the **benefits** that passing the exam will bring you.

Exam focus

Keep the exam firmly in your sights throughout your studies.

- Remember there's lots of **helpful guidance** about F7 in this first part of the Study Text.
- Look out for the **exam references** in the Study Text, particularly the types of question you'll be asked.

Organisation

Before you start studying you must organise yourself properly.

- We show you how to **timetable** your study so that you can ensure you have enough time to cover all of the syllabus – and revise it.
- Think carefully about the way you take **notes**. You needn't copy out too much, but if you can summarise key areas, that shows you understand them.
- Choose the notes **format** that's most helpful to you; lists, diagrams, mindmaps.
- Consider the **order** in which you tackle each chapter. If you prefer to get to grips with a theory before seeing how it's applied, you should read the explanations first. If you prefer to see how things work in practice, read the examples and questions first.

Active brain

There are various ways in which you can keep your brain active when studying and hence improve your **understanding** and **recall** of material.

- Keep asking yourself how the topic you're studying fits into the **whole picture** of this exam. If you're not sure, look back at the chapter introductions and Study Text front pages.
- Go carefully through every **example** and try every **question** in the Study Text and in the Exam Question Bank. You will be thinking deeply about the syllabus and increasing your understanding.

Review, review, review

Regularly reviewing the topics you've studied will help fix them in your memory. Your BPP Texts help you review in many ways.

- Important points are emphasised **in bold**.
- **Chapter Roundups** summarise the **Fast forward** key points in each chapter.
- **Quick Quizzes** test your grasp of the essentials.

BPP Passcards present summaries of topics in different visual formats to enhance your chances of remembering them.

Timetabling your studies

As your time is limited, it's vital that you calculate how much time you can allocate to each chapter. Following the approach below will help you do this.

Step 1	## Calculate how much time you have

Work out the time you have available per week, given the following.

- The standard you have set yourself

- The time you need to set aside for work on the Practice & Revision Kit, Passcards, i-Learn and i-Pass

- The other exam(s) you are sitting

- Practical matters such as work, travel, exercise, sleep and social life

Hours

Note your time available in box A.   A [   ]

Step 2	## Allocate your time

- Take the time you have available per week for this Study Text shown in box A, multiply it by the number of weeks available and insert the result in box B.   B [   ]

- Divide the figure in box B by the number of chapters in this Study Text and insert the result in box C.   C [   ]

Remember that this is only a rough guide. Some of the chapters in this Study Text are longer and more complicated than others, and you will find some subjects easier to understand than others.

Step 3	## Implement your plan

Set about studying each chapter in the time shown in box C. You'll find that once you've established a timetable, you're much more likely to study systematically.

Short of time: Skim study technique

You may find you simply do not have the time available to follow all the key study steps for each chapter, however you adapt them for your particular learning style. If this is the case, follow the **Skim study** technique below.

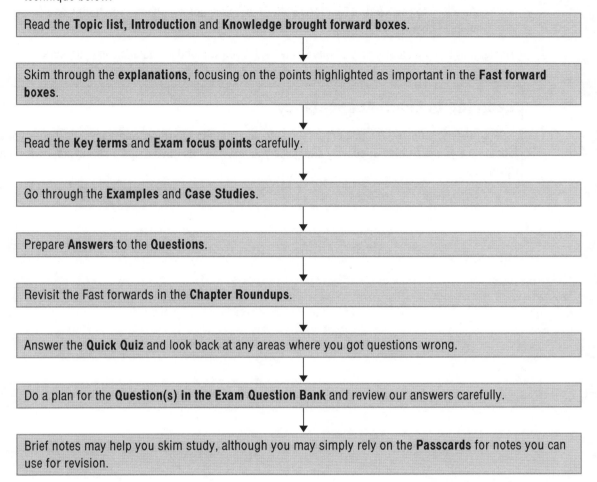

Read the **Topic list, Introduction** and **Knowledge brought forward boxes**.

Skim through the **explanations**, focusing on the points highlighted as important in the **Fast forward boxes**.

Read the **Key terms** and **Exam focus points** carefully.

Go through the **Examples** and **Case Studies**.

Prepare **Answers** to the **Questions**.

Revisit the Fast forwards in the **Chapter Roundups**.

Answer the **Quick Quiz** and look back at any areas where you got questions wrong.

Do a plan for the **Question(s) in the Exam Question Bank** and review our answers carefully.

Brief notes may help you skim study, although you may simply rely on the **Passcards** for notes you can use for revision.

Revision

When you are ready to start revising, you should still refer back to this Study Text.

- As a source of **reference** (you should find the index particularly helpful for this)
- As a way to **review** (the Fast forwards, Exam focus points, Chapter Roundups and Quick Quizzes help you here)

Remember to keep careful hold of this Study Text – you will find it invaluable in your work.

Learning to Learn Accountancy

BPP's guide to studying for accountancy exams, **Learning to Learn Accountancy**, challenges you to think about how you can study effectively and gives you lots and lots of vital tips on studying, revising and taking the exams.

BPP
LEARNING MEDIA

Studying F7

Approaching F7

F7 is a demanding paper covering all the fundamentals of financial reporting. It has five main sections:

(1) The conceptual framework of accounting
(2) The regulatory framework
(3) Preparation of financial statements which conform with FRS
(4) Preparation of consolidated financial statements
(5) Analysis and interpretation of financial statements

All of these areas will be tested to some degree at each sitting. Sections 3 and 4 are the main areas of application and you must expect to have to produce consolidated and single company financial statements in your exam.

Some of this material you will have covered at lower level papers. You should already be familiar with accounting for stocks and fixed assets and preparing simple profit and loss accounts, balance sheets and cash flow statements. You should know the basic ratios.

F7 takes your financial reporting knowledge and skills up to the next level. New topics are consolidated financial statements (which you may have covered if you did the old 1.1), long-term contracts, financial instruments and leases. There is also coverage of the substance of transactions and the limitations of financial statements and ratios. The examiner wants you to think about these issues.

If you had exemptions from lower level papers or feel that your knowledge of lower level financial reporting is not good enough, you may want to get a copy of the study text for F3 Financial Accounting and read through it, or at least have it to refer to. You have a lot of new material to learn for F7 and basic financial accounting will be assumed knowledge.

The way to pass F7 is by practising lots of exam-level questions, which you will do when you get onto revision. Only by practising questions do you get a feel for what you will have to do in the exam. Also, topics which you find hard to understand in the text will be much easier to grasp when you have encountered them in a few questions. So don't get bogged down in any area of the text. Just keep going and a lot of things you find difficult will make more sense when you see how they appear in an exam question.

Syllabus

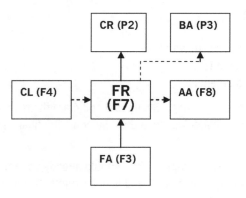

AIM

To develop knowledge and skills in understanding and applying accounting standards and the theoretical framework in the preparation of financial statements of entities, including groups and how to analyse and interpret those financial statements.

MAIN CAPABILITIES

On successful completion of this paper, candidates should be able to:

A Discuss and apply a conceptual framework for financial reporting

B Discuss a regulatory framework for financial reporting

C Prepare and present financial statements which conform with UK accounting standards

D Account for business combinations in accordance with UK accounting standards

E Analyse and interpret financial statements.

RELATIONAL DIAGRAM OF MAIN CAPABILITIES

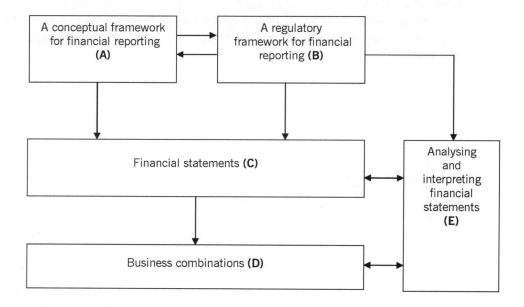

RATIONALE

The financial reporting syllabus assumes knowledge acquired in Paper F3, *Financial Accounting*, and develops and applies this further and in greater depth.

The syllabus begins with the conceptual framework of accounting with reference to the qualitative characteristics of useful information and the fundamental bases of accounting introduced in the Paper F3 syllabus within the Knowledge module. It then moves into a detailed examination of the regulatory framework of accounting and how this informs the standard setting process.

The main areas of the syllabus cover the reporting of financial information for single companies and for groups in accordance with generally accepted accounting practice and relevant accounting standards.

Finally, the syllabus covers the analysis and interpretation of information from financial reports.

DETAILED SYLLABUS

A   A conceptual framework for financial reporting

1.   The need for a conceptual framework

2.   Relevance, reliability, comparability and understandability

3.   Recognition and measurement

4.   The legal versus the commercial view of accounting

5.   Alternative models and practices

6.   The concept of 'true and fair view' ('faithful representation')

B   A regulatory framework for financial reporting

1.   Reasons for the existence of a regulatory framework

2.   The standard setting process

3.   Specialised, not-for-profit, and public sector entities

C   Financial statements

1.   Cash flow statements

2.   Tangible fixed assets

3.   Intangible assets

4.   Stock

5.   Financial assets and financial liabilities

6.   Leases

7.   Provisions, contingent liabilities and contingent assets

8.   Impairment of assets

9.   Taxation

10.   Regulatory requirements relating to the preparation of financial statements

11.   Reporting financial performance

D   Business combinations

1.   The concept and principles of a group

2.   The concept of consolidated financial statements

3.   Preparation of consolidated financial statements including an associate

E   Analysing and interpreting financial statements

1.   Limitations of financial statements

2.   Calculation and interpretation of accounting ratios and trends to address users' and stakeholders' needs

3.   Limitations of interpretation techniques

4.   Specialised, not-for-profit, and public sector entities

25

APPROACH TO EXAMINING THE SYLLABUS

The syllabus is assessed by a three-hour paper-based examination. All questions are compulsory. It will contain both computational and discursive elements. Some questions will adopt a scenario/case study approach.

Question 1 will be a 25-mark question on the preparation of group financial statements and/or extracts thereof, and may include a small discussion element. Computations will be designed to test an understanding of principles.

Question 2, for 25 marks, will test the reporting of non-group financial statements. This may be from information in a trial balance or by restating draft financial statements.

Question 3, for 25 marks, is likely to be an appraisal of an entity's performance and may involve cash flow statements.

Questions 4 and 5 will cover the remainder of the syllabus and will be worth 15 and 10 marks respectively.

An individual question may often involve elements that relate to different subject areas of the syllabus. For example, the preparation of an entity's financial statements could include matters relating to several accounting standards.

Questions may ask candidates to comment on the appropriateness or acceptability of management's opinion or chosen accounting treatment. An understanding of accounting principles and concepts and how these are applied to practical examples will be tested.

Questions on topic areas that are also included in Paper F3 will be examined at an appropriately greater depth in this paper.

Candidates will be expected to have an appreciation of the need for specified accounting standards and why they have been issued. For detailed or complex standards, candidates need to be aware of their principles and key elements.

Study Guide

A A CONCEPTUAL FRAMEWORK FOR FINANCIAL REPORTING

1. The need for a conceptual framework

a) describe what is meant by a conceptual framework of accounting. [2]

b) discuss whether a conceptual framework is necessary and what an alternative system might be. [2]

2. Relevance, reliability, comparability and understandability

a) discuss what is meant by relevance and reliability and describe the qualities that enhance these characteristics. [2]

b) discuss the importance of comparability to users of financial statements. [2]

c) discuss what is meant by understandability in relation to the provision of financial information. [2]

d) distinguish between changes in accounting policies and changes in accounting estimates and describe how accounting standards apply the principle of comparability where an entity changes its accounting policies. [2]

e) recognise and account for changes in accounting policies and the correction of prior period errors. [2]

3. Recognition and measurement

a) define what is meant by 'recognition' in financial statements and discuss the recognition criteria. [2]

b) apply the recognition criteria to: [2]
   i) assets and liabilities
   ii) income and expenses

c) discuss what is meant by the balance sheet approach to recognition; indicate when income and expense recognition should occur. [2]

d) demonstrate the role of the principle of substance over form in relation to recognising sales revenue. [2]

e) explain the following measures and compute amounts using: [2]
   i)   historical cost
   ii) fair value/current cost
   iii) net realisable value
   iv) present value of future cash flows.

4. The legal versus the commercial view of accounting

a) explain the importance of recording the commercial substance rather than the legal form of transactions – give examples of previous abuses in this area. [2]

b) describe the features which may indicate that the substance of transactions differs from their legal form. [2]

c) apply the principle of substance over form to the recognition and derecognition of assets and liabilities. [2]

d) recognise the substance of transactions in general, and specifically account for the following types of transaction: [2]
   i)   goods sold on sale or return/consignment stock
   ii) sale and repurchase/leaseback agreements
   iii) factoring of debtors.

5. Alternative models and practices

a) describe the advantages and disadvantages of the use of historical cost accounting. [2]

b) discuss whether the use of current value accounting overcomes the problems of historical cost accounting. [2]

c) describe the concept of financial and physical capital maintenance and how this affects the determination of profits. [1]

6. The concept of 'true and fair view' ('faithful representation')

a) describe what is meant by financial statements achieving a faithful representation. [2]

b) discuss whether faithful representation constitutes more than compliance with accounting standards.[1]

c) indicate the circumstances and required disclosures where a 'true and fair' override may apply.[1]

B A REGULATORY FRAMEWORK FOR FINANCIAL REPORTING

1. Reasons for the existence of a regulatory framework

a) explain why a regulatory framework is needed.[2]

b) explain why accounting standards on their own are not a complete regulatory framework.[2]

c) distinguish between a principles based and a rules based framework and discuss whether they can be complementary.[1]

2. The standard setting process

a) describe the structure of the UK regulatory system including the role of the Financial Reporting Council (FRC), the Accounting Standards (ASB), the Financial Reporting Review Panel (FRRP) and the Urgent Issues task Force (UITF).[2]

b) describe the ASB's Standard setting process including revisions to and interpretations of Standards.[2]

c) explain the relationship between UK standard setters and the International Accounting Standards Board (IASB).[2]

3. Specialised, not-for-profit and public sector entities

a) distinguish between the primary aims of not-for-profit and public sector entities and those of profit oriented entities.[1]

b) discuss the extent to which Financial Reporting Standards (FRSs) are relevant to specialised, not-for-profit and public sector entities.[1]

C FINANCIAL STATEMENTS

1. Cash flow statements

a) prepare a cash flow statement for a single entity (not a group) in accordance with relevant accounting standards using the direct and the indirect method.[2]

b) compare the usefulness of cash flow information with that of a profit and loss account.[2]

c) interpret a cash flow statement (together with other financial information) to assess the performance and financial position of an entity.[2]

2. Tangible fixed assets

a) define and compute the initial measurement of a fixed (including a self-constructed) asset.[2]

b) identify subsequent expenditure that may be capitalised (including borrowing costs), distinguishing between capital and revenue items.[2]

c) discuss the requirements of relevant accounting standards in relation to the revaluation of fixed assets.[2]

d) account for revaluation and disposal gains and losses for fixed assets.[2]

e) compute depreciation based on cost and revalued amounts and on assets that have two or more significant parts (complex assets).[2]

f) apply the provisions of relevant accounting standards in relation to accounting for government grants.[2]

g) discuss why the treatment of investment properties should differ from other properties.[2]

h) apply the requirements of relevant accounting standards for investment property.[2]

3. **Intangible assets**

a) discuss the nature and accounting treatment of internally generated and purchased intangibles. [2]

b) distinguish between goodwill and other intangible assets. [2]

c) describe the criteria for the initial recognition and measurement of intangible assets. [2]

d) describe the subsequent accounting treatment, including the principle of impairment tests in relation to goodwill. [2]

e) indicate why the value of purchase consideration for an investment may be less than the value of the acquired identifiable net assets and how the difference (negative goodwill) should be accounted for. [2]

f) describe and apply the requirements of relevant accounting standards to research and development expenditure. [2]

4. **Stock**

a) describe and apply the principles of stock valuation. [2]

b) define a long-term contract and discuss the role of accounting concepts in the recognition of profit. [2]

c) describe the acceptable methods of determining the stage (percentage) of completion of a long-term contract. [2]

d) prepare financial statement extracts for long-term contracts. [2]

5 **Financial assets and financial liabilities**

a) explain the need for an accounting standard on financial instruments. [1]

b) define financial instruments in terms of financial assets and financial liabilities. [1]

c) indicate for the following categories of financial instruments how they should be measured and how any gains and losses from subsequent

measurement should be treated in the financial statements: [1]
   i) fair value through profit and loss
   ii) held to maturity (use of amortised cost, interest to income)
   iii) available for sale (carried at fair value with changes to equity, but dividends to income)
   iv) loans and receivables

d) distinguish between debt and equity capital. [2]

e) apply the requirements of relevant accounting standards to the issue and finance costs of: [2]
   i) equity
   ii) redeemable preference shares and debt instruments with no conversion rights (principle of amortised cost).

6. **Leases**

a) explain why recording the legal form of a finance lease can be misleading to users (referring to the commercial substance of such leases). [2]

b) describe and apply the method of determining a lease type (i.e. an operating or finance lease). [2]

c) discuss the effect on the financial statements of a finance lease being incorrectly treated as an operating lease. [2]

d) account for assets financed by finance leases in the records of the lessee. [2]

e) account for operating leases in the records of the lessee. [2]

7. **Provisions, contingent liabilities and contingent assets**

a) explain why an accounting standard on provisions is necessary. [2]

b) distinguish between legal and constructive obligations. [2]

c) state when provisions may and may not be made and demonstrate how they should be accounted for. [2]

d) explain how provisions should be measured. [1]

e) define contingent assets and liabilities and describe their accounting treatment.[2]

f) identify and account for: [2]
   i) warranties/guarantees
   ii) onerous contracts
   iii) environmental and similar provisions
   iv) provisions for future repairs or refurbishments.

8. Impairment of assets

a) define an impairment loss.[2]

b) identify the circumstances that may indicate impairments to assets.[2]

c) describe what is meant by an income generating unit.[2]

d) state the basis on which impairment losses should be allocated, and allocate an impairment loss to the assets of an income generating unit.[2]

9. Taxation

a) account for current taxation in accordance with relevant accounting standards.**[2]**

b) record entries relating to taxation in the accounting records.[2]

c) explain the effect of timing differences on accounting and taxable profits.[2]

d) compute and record deferred tax amounts in the financial statements.[2]

10. Regulatory requirements relating to the preparation of financial statements

a) describe the structure (format) and content of financial statements presented under the Companies Acts and accounting standards.[2]

b) prepare an entity's financial statements in accordance with the prescribed structure and content.[2]

11. Reporting financial performance

a) discuss the importance of identifying and reporting the results of continuing and discontinued operations.[2]

b) define and account for discontinued operations.[2]

c) indicate the circumstances where separate disclosure of exceptional items is required.[2]

d) prepare and explain the contents and purpose of the statement of total recognised gains and losses and of reporting changes in equity.[2]

e) prepare statements for the reconciliation and movement in shareholders funds (changes in equity).[2]

f) earnings per share (eps)
   i) calculate the eps in accordance with relevant accounting standards (dealing with bonus issues, full market value issues and rights issues) [2]
   ii) explain the relevance of the diluted eps and calculate the diluted eps involving convertible debt and share options (warrants) [2]
   iii) explain why the trend of eps may be a more accurate indicator of performance than a company's profit trend and the importance of eps as a stock market indicator [2]
   iv) discuss the limitations of using eps as a performance measure.[3]

D BUSINESS COMBINATIONS

1. The concept and principles of a group

a) describe the concept of a group as a single economic unit.[2]

b) explain and apply the definition of a subsidiary within relevant accounting standards.[2]

c) describe why directors may not wish to consolidate a subsidiary and the circumstances where this is permitted.[2]

d) explain the need for using coterminous year ends and uniform accounting polices when preparing consolidated financial statements.[2]

e)   explain why it is necessary to eliminate intra-group transactions.[2]

2.   **The concept of consolidated financial statements**

a)   explain the objective of consolidated financial statements.[2]

b)   indicate the effect that the related party relationship between a parent and subsidiary may have on the subsidiary's entity statements and the consolidated financial statements.[2]

c)   explain why it is necessary to use fair values for the consideration for an investment in a subsidiary together with the fair values of a subsidiary's identifiable assets and liabilities when preparing consolidated financial statements.[2]

d)   describe and apply the required accounting treatment of consolidated goodwill.[2]

3.   **Preparation of consolidated financial statements including an associate**

a)   prepare a consolidated balance sheet for a simple group (parent and one subsidiary) dealing with pre and post acquisition profits, minority interests and consolidated goodwill.[2]

b)   prepare a consolidated profit and loss account for a simple group dealing with an acquisition in the period and minority interest.[2]

c)   explain and account for other reserves (e.g. share premium and revaluation reserves).[1]

d)   account for the effects (in the profit and loss account and balance sheet) of intra-group trading.[2]

e)   account for the effects of fair value adjustments (including their effect on consolidated goodwill) to: [2]
    i)   depreciating and non-depreciating fixed assets
    ii) stock
    iii) monetary liabilities
    iv) assets and liabilities not included in the subsidiary's own balance sheet, including contingent assets and liabilities.

f)   account for goodwill amortisation and impairment.[2]

g)   define an associate and explain the principles and reasoning for the use of equity accounting.[2]

h)   prepare consolidated financial statements to include a single subsidiary and an associate.[2]

E   **ANALYSING AND INTERPRETING FINANCIAL STATEMENTS**

1.   **Limitations of financial statements**

a)   indicate the problems of using historic information to predict future performance and trends.[2]

b)   discuss how financial statements may be manipulated to produce a desired effect (creative accounting, window dressing).[2]

c)   recognise how related party relationships have the potential to mislead users.[2]

d)   explain why balance sheet figures may not be representative of average values throughout the period for example, due to: [2]
    i)   seasonal trading
    ii) major asset acquisitions near the end of the accounting period.

2   **Calculation and interpretation of accounting ratios and trends to address users' and stakeholders' needs**

a)   define and compute relevant financial ratios.[2]

b)   explain what aspects of performance specific ratios are intended to assess.[2]

c)   analyse and interpret ratios to give an assessment of an entity's performance and financial position in comparison with: [2]
    i)   an entity's previous period's financial statements
    ii) another similar entity for the same reporting period
    iii) industry average ratios.

d)   interpret an entity's financial statements to give advice from the perspectives of different stakeholders.[2]

e)   discuss how the interpretation of current value based financial statements would differ from those using historical cost based accounts.[1]

3.   Limitations of interpretation techniques

a)   discuss the limitations in the use of ratio analysis for assessing corporate performance.[2]

b)   discuss the effect that changes in accounting policies or the use of different accounting polices between entities can have on the ability to interpret performance.[2]

c)   indicate other information, including non-financial information, that may be of relevance to the assessment of an entity's performance.[1]

4.   Specialised, not-for-profit and public sector entities

a)   discuss the different approaches that may be required when assessing the performance of specialised, not-for-profit and public sector organisations.[1]

The exam paper

The exam is a three hour paper with five compulsory questions.

Question 1 will be on consolidated financial statements.
Question 2 will be on single company financial statements.
Question 3 is likely to be a cash flow statement or on interpretation of accounts
Questions 4 and 5 will be on other areas of the syllabus

A certain number of FRSs will be tested in questions 1 and 2. Others will appear in questions 4 and 5.

Analysis of pilot paper

		Number of marks
(1)	Consolidated balance sheet including associate	25
(2)	Single company profit and loss account, balance sheet and statement of movement in share capital and reserves	25
(3)	Interpretation of financial statements	25
(4)	Explain qualitative characteristics of financial statements and apply to scenarios	15
(5)	Calculate amounts related to long-term contract	10
		100

Pilot paper

Paper F7

Financial Reporting (United Kingdom)

Time allowed

Reading and planning: 15 minutes
Writing: 3 hours

All FIVE questions are compulsory and MUST be attempted

Do NOT open this paper until instructed by the supervisor.

During reading and planning time only the question paper may be annotated. You must NOT write in your answer booklet until instructed by the supervisor.

This question paper must not be removed from the examination hall.

Warning

The pilot paper cannot cover all of the syllabus nor can it include examples of every type of question that will be included in the actual exam. You may see questions in the exam that you think are more difficult than any you see in the pilot paper.

ALL FIVE questions are compulsory and MUST be attempted

1   On 1 October 2005 Pumice acquired the following fixed asset investments:
- 80% of the equity share capital of Silverton at a cost of £13.6 million
- 50% of Silverton's 10% loan notes at par
- 1.6 million equity shares in Amok at a cost of £6.25 each.

The summarised draft balance sheets of the three companies at 31 March 2006 are:

	Pumice		Silverton		Amok	
	£'000	£'000	£'000	£'000	£'000	£'000
Tangible fixed assets		20,000		8,500		16,500
Investments		26,000		nil		1,500
		46,000		8,500		18,000
Current assets	15,000		8,000		11,000	
Creditors: amounts falling due within one year	(10,000)		(3,500)		(5,000)	
Net current assets		5,000		4,500		6,000
Total assets less current liabilities		51,000		13,000		24,000
Creditors: amounts falling after more than one year						
8% Loan note		(4,000)		nil		nil
10% Loan note		nil		(2,000)		nil
		47,000		11,000		24,000
Capital and reserves						
Equity shares of £1 each		10,000		3,000		4,000
Profit and loss account		37,000		8,000		20,000
		47,000		11,000		24,000

The following information is relevant:

(i) The fair values of Silverton's assets were equal to their carrying amounts with the exception of land and plant. Silverton's land had a fair value of £400,000 in excess of its carrying amount and plant had a fair value of £1.6 million in excess of its carrying amount. The plant had a remaining life of four years (straight-line depreciation) at the date of acquisition.

(ii) In the post acquisition period Pumice sold goods to Silverton at a price of £6 million. These goods had cost Pumice £4 million. Half of these goods were still in the stock of Silverton at 31 March 2006. Silverton had a balance of £1.5 million owing to Pumice at 31 March 2006 which agreed with Pumice's records.

(iii) The net profit after tax for the year ended 31 March 2006 was £2 million for Silverton and £8 million for Amok. Assume profits accrued evenly throughout the year.

(iv) Consolidated goodwill is to be written off over a five-year life using time apportionment in the year of acquisition.

(v) No dividends were paid during the year by any of the companies.

Required:

(a) Discuss how the investments purchased by Pumice on 1 October 2005 should be treated in its consolidated financial statements. (5 marks)

(b) Prepare the consolidated balance sheet for Pumice as at 31 March 2006. (20 marks)

(25 marks)

2   The following trial balance relates to Kala, a publicly listed company, at 31 March 2006:

	£'000	£'000
Land and buildings at cost (note (i))	270,000	
Plant – at cost (note (i))	156,000	
Investment properties – valuation at 1 April 2005 (note (i))	90,000	
Purchases	78,200	
Operating expenses	15,500	
Loan interest paid	2,000	
Rental of leased plant (note (ii))	22,000	
Dividends paid	15,000	
Stock at 1 April 2005	37,800	
Trade debtors	53,200	
Turnover		278,400
Income from investment property		4,500
Equity shares of £1 each fully paid		150,000
Profit and loss reserve at 1 April 2005		112,500
Investment property revaluation reserve at 1 April 2005		7,000
8% (actual and effective) loan note (note (iii))		50,000
Accumulated depreciation at 1 April 2005 – buildings		60,000
– plant		26,000
Trade creditors		33,400
Deferred tax		12,500
Bank		5,400
	739,700	739,700

The following notes are relevant:

(i)   The land and buildings were purchased on 1 April 1990. The cost of the land was £70 million. No land and buildings have been purchased by Kala since that date. On 1 April 2005 Kala had its land and buildings professionally valued at £80 million and £175 million respectively. The directors wish to incorporate these values into the financial statements. The estimated life of the buildings was originally 50 years and the remaining life has not changed as a result of the valuation.

Later, the valuers informed Kala that investment properties of the type Kala owned had increased in value by 7% in the year to 31 March 2006.

Plant, other than leased plant (see below), is depreciated at 15% per annum using the reducing balance method. Depreciation of buildings and plant is charged to cost of sales.

(ii)   On 1 April 2005 Kala entered into a lease for an item of plant which had an estimated life of five years. The lease period is also five years with annual rentals of £22 million payable in advance from 1 April 2005. The plant is expected to have a nil residual value at the end of its life. If purchased this plant would have a cost of £92 million and be depreciated on a straight-line basis. The lessor includes a finance cost of 10% per annum when calculating annual rentals. (Note: you are not required to calculate the present value of the minimum lease payments.)

(iii)   The loan note was issued on 1 July 2005 with interest payable six monthly in arrears.

(iv)   The provision for corporation tax for the year to 31 March 2006 has been estimated at £28.3 million. The deferred tax provision at 31 March 2006 is to be adjusted to a credit balance of £14.1 million.

(v)   Stock at 31 March 2006 was valued at £43.2 million.

Required, prepare for Kala:

(a)   A profit and loss account for the year ended 31 March 2006.   (9 marks)

(b)   A statement of the movement in share capital and reserves for the year ended 31 March 2006.   (5 marks)

(c)   A balance sheet as at 31 March 2006.   (11 marks)

(25 marks)

Note: A statement of total recognised gains and losses is NOT required.

3 Reactive is a publicly listed company that assembles domestic electrical goods which it then sells to both wholesale and retail customers. Reactive's management were disappointed in the company's results for the year ended 31 March 2005. In an attempt to improve performance the following measures were taken early in the year ended 31 March 2006:

- a national advertising campaign was undertaken,
- rebates to all wholesale customers purchasing goods above set quantity levels were introduced,
- the assembly of certain lines ceased and was replaced by bought in completed products. This allowed Reactive to dispose of surplus plant.

Reactive's summarised financial statements for the year ended 31 March 2006 are set out below:

Profit and loss account	£million
Turnover (25% cash sales)	4,000
Cost of sales	(3,450)
Gross profit	550
Operating expenses	(370)
Operating profit	180
Profit on disposal of plant (note (i))	40
Finance costs	(20)
Profit before taxation	200
Taxation	(50)
Profit for the financial year	150

Balance Sheet	£million	£million
Tangible fixed assets		
Property		300
Plant and equipment (note (i))		250
		550
Current assets		
Stock	250	
Debtors	360	
Bank	nil	
	610	
Creditors: amounts falling due within one year		
Bank overdraft	10	
Trade creditors	430	
Taxation	40	
	(480)	130
Creditors: amounts falling due after more than one year		
8% loan note		(200)
		480
Capital and reserves		
Equity shares of 25 pence each		100
Profit and loss account reserve		380
		480

Below are ratios calculated for the year ended 31 March 2005.

Return on year end capital employed (profit before interest and tax over total assets less current liabilities)	28.1%
Net asset (equal to capital employed) turnover	4 times
Gross profit margin	17 %
Net profit (before tax) margin	6.3 %
Current ratio	1.6:1
Closing stock holding period	46 days
Debtors' collection period	45 days
Creditors' payment period	55 days
Dividend yield	3.75%
Dividend cover	2 times

Notes:

(i) Reactive received £120 million from the sale of plant that had a carrying amount of £80 million at the date of its sale.

(ii) the market price of Reactive's shares throughout the year averaged £3.75 each.

(iii) there were no issues or redemption of shares or loans during the year.

(iv) dividends paid during the year ended 31 March 2006 amounted to £90 million, maintaining the same dividend paid in the year ended 31 March 2005.

Required:

(a) Calculate ratios for the year ended 31 March 2006 (showing your workings) for Reactive, equivalent to those provided. (10 marks)

(b) Analyse the financial performance and position of Reactive for the year ended 31 March 2006 compared to the previous year. (10 marks)

(c) Explain in what ways your approach to performance appraisal would differ if you were asked to assess the performance of a not-for-profit organisation. (5 marks)

(25 marks)

4 **(a)** The qualitative characteristics of relevance, reliability and comparability identified in the ASB's *Statement of principles for financial reporting* are some of the attributes that make financial information useful to the various users of financial statements.

Required:

Explain what is meant by relevance, reliability and comparability and how they make financial information useful. (9 marks)

(b) During the year ended 31 March 2006, Porto experienced the following transactions or events:

(i) entered into a finance lease to rent an asset for substantially the whole of its useful economic life.

(ii) a decision was made by the Board to change the company's accounting policy from one of expensing the finance costs on building new retail outlets to one of capitalising such costs.

(iii) the company's profit and loss account prepared using historical costs showed a loss from operating its hotels, but the company is aware that that the increase in the value of its properties during the period far outweighed the operating loss.

Required:

Explain how you would treat the items in (i) to (iii) above in Porto's financial statements and indicate on which of the Statement's qualitative characteristics your treatment is based. (6 marks)

(15 marks)

5 SSAP 9 *Stocks and long-term contracts* deals with accounting for long-term contracts whose durations usually span at least two accounting periods.

Required:

(a) **Describe the issues of revenue and profit recognition relating to long-term contracts.** (4 marks)

(b) Beetie is a construction company that prepares its financial statements to 31 March each year. During the year ended 31 March 2006 the company commenced two construction contracts that are expected to be completed in the accounting period ended 31 March 2007. The position of each contract at 31 March 2006 is as follows:

Contract	1	2
	£'000	£'000
Agreed contract price	5,500	1,200
Estimated total cost of contract at commencement	4,000	900
Estimated total cost at 31 March 2006	4,000	1250
Certified value of work completed at 31 March 2006	3,300	840
Contract billings invoiced and received at 31 March 2006	3,000	880
Contract costs incurred to 31 March 2006	3,900	720

The certified value of the work completed at 31 March 2006 is considered to be equal to the revenue earned in the year ended 31 March 2006. The percentage of completion is calculated as the value of the work completed to the agreed contract price.

Required:

Calculate the amounts which should appear in the profit and loss account and balance sheet of Beetie at 31 March 2006 in respect of the above contracts. (6 marks)

(10 marks)

The conceptual framework

Topic list	Syllabus reference
1 A conceptual framework of accounting	A1
2 The ASB *Statement of Principles*	A1
3 The objective of financial statements	A2
4 Qualitative characteristics of financial statements	A2
5 Elements of financial statements	A3
6 Recognition in financial statements	A3
7 Measurement in financial statements	A3
8 True and fair view	A6

Introduction

The ASB's *Statement of Principles for Financial Reporting* represents the **conceptual framework** on which all FRSs are based.

A conceptual framework for financial reporting can be defined as an attempt to codify existing **generally accepted accounting practice** in order to reappraise existing standards and to produce new standards.

Study guide

		Intellectual level
A	**A CONCEPTUAL FRAMEWORK FOR FINANCIAL REPORTING**	
1	**The need for a conceptual framework**	
(a)	Describe what is meant by a conceptual framework of accounting	2
(b)	Discuss whether a conceptual framework is necessary and what an alternative system might be	2
2	**Relevance, reliability, comparability and understandability**	
(a)	Discuss what is meant by relevance and reliability and describe the qualities that enhance these characteristics	2
(b)	Discuss the importance of comparability to users of financial statements	2
(c)	Discuss what is meant by understandability in relation to the provision of financial information	2
3	**Recognition and measurement**	
(a)	Define what is meant by 'recognition' in financial statements and discuss the recognition criteria	2
(b)	Apply the recognition criteria to:	2
	(i) Assets and liabilities	
	(ii) Income and expenses	
(c)	Discuss what is meant by the balance sheet approach to recognition' indicate when income and expense recognition should occur.	2
(d)	Demonstrate the role of the principle of substance over form in relation to recognising sales revenue.	2
(e)	Explain the following measures and compute amounts using:	2
	(i) Historical cost	
	(ii) Fair value/current cost	
	(iii) Net realisable value	
	(iv) Present value of future cash flows.	
6	**The concept of 'true and fair view' ('faithful representation')**	
(a)	Describe what is meant by financial statements achieving a faithful representation.	2
(b)	Discuss whether faithful representation constitutes more than compliance with accounting standards.	1
(c)	Indicate the circumstances and required disclosures where a 'true and fair' override may apply.	1

Exam guide

You are unlikely to get a full question on the material in this chapter but it is important that you read through and understand the content of this chapter. It provides you with many of the vital building blocks you will need in the exams.

BPP
LEARNING MEDIA

1 A conceptual framework of accounting

There are advantages and disadvantages to having a conceptual framework.

1.1 The search for a conceptual framework

A **conceptual framework**, in the field we are concerned with, is a statement of generally accepted theoretical principles which form the frame of reference for financial reporting.

These theoretical principles provide the basis for the development of new accounting standards and the evaluation of those already in existence. The financial reporting process is concerned with providing information that is useful in the business and economic decision-making process. Therefore a conceptual framework will form the **theoretical basis** for determining which events should be accounted for, how they should be measured and how they should be communicated to the user. Although it is theoretical in nature, a conceptual framework for financial reporting has highly practical final aims.

The **danger of not having a conceptual framework** is demonstrated in the way some countries' standards have developed over recent years; standards tend to be produced in a haphazard and fire-fighting approach. Where an agreed framework exists, the standard-setting body act as an architect or designer, rather than a fire-fighter, building accounting rules on the foundation of sound, agreed basic principles.

The lack of a conceptual framework also means that fundamental principles are tackled more than once in different standards, thereby producing **contradictions and inconsistencies** in basic concepts, such as those of prudence and matching. This leads to ambiguity and it affects the true and fair concept of financial reporting.

Another problem with the lack of a conceptual framework has become apparent in the USA. The large number of **highly detailed standards** produced by the Financial Accounting Standards Board (FASB) has created a financial reporting environment governed by specific rules rather than general principles. This would be avoided if a cohesive set of principles were in place.

A conceptual framework can also bolster standard setters **against political pressure** from various 'lobby groups' and interested parties. Such pressure would only prevail if it was acceptable under the conceptual framework.

1.2 Advantages and disadvantages of a conceptual framework

Advantages

(a)   The situation is avoided whereby standards are developed on a patchwork basis, where a particular accounting problem is recognised as having emerged, and resources were then channelled into **standardising accounting practice** in that area, without regard to whether that particular issue was necessarily the most important issue remaining at that time without standardisation.

(b)   As stated above, the development of certain standards (particularly national standards) have been subject to considerable **political interference** from interested parties. Where there is a conflict of interest between user groups on which policies to choose, policies deriving from a conceptual framework will be **less open to criticism** that the standard-setter buckled to external pressure.

(c)   Some standards may concentrate on the **income statement** whereas some may concentrate on the **valuation of net assets** (balance sheet).

Disadvantages

(a) Financial statements are intended for a **variety of users**, and it is not certain that a single conceptual framework can be devised which will suit all users.

(b) Given the diversity of user requirements, there may be a need for a variety of accounting standards, each produced for a **different purpose** (and with different concepts as a basis).

(c) It is not clear that a conceptual framework makes the task of **preparing and then implementing** standards any easier than without a framework.

Before we look at the ASB's attempt to produce a conceptual framework, we need to consider another term of importance to this debate: generally accepted accounting practice; or GAAP.

1.3 Generally accepted accounting practice (GAAP)

FAST FORWARD

GAAP is taken to be all the rules, from whatever source, which govern accounting. This varies from country to country and changes over time as new regulations are issued and others are withdrawn or superseded.

This term has emerged in recent years and it **signifies all the rules**, from whatever source, **which govern accounting**. In the UK this is seen primarily as a combination of various sources.

(a) **Company law** (mainly CA 1985)
(b) Financial reporting **standards**
(c) **Stock exchange requirements**

Although those sources are the basis for UK GAAP, the concept also includes the effects of non-mandatory sources such as:

(a) **International** financial reporting **standards**
(b) **Statutory requirements in other countries**, particularly the USA.

In the UK, **GAAP** does **not have** any **statutory or regulatory authority** or definition (unlike other countries, such as the USA). The term is mentioned rarely in legislation, and only then in fairly limited terms.

GAAP is in fact a **dynamic concept**: it **changes constantly as circumstances alter through new legislation, standards *and* practice.** This idea that GAAP is constantly changing is recognised by the ASB in its *Statement of Aims* where it states that it expects to issue new standards and amend old ones in response to:

'Evolving business practices, new economic developments and deficiencies identified in current practice.'

The emphasis has shifted from 'principles' to 'practice' in UK GAAP.

The problem of what is '**generally accepted**' is **not easy to settle**, because new practices will obviously not be generally adopted yet. The criteria for a practice being 'generally accepted' will depend on factors such as whether the practice is addressed by UK financial reporting **standards** or **legislation**, their international equivalents, and whether other companies have **adopted the practice**. Most importantly perhaps, the question should be whether the practice is consistent with the **needs of users** and the **objectives of financial reporting** and whether it is consistent with the **'true and fair' concept**.

From January 2005 UK listed companies have been preparing their group accounts under IFRS. This is the first stage in the transition from UK GAAP to IFRS.

2 The ASB Statement of Principles

FAST FORWARD

The *Statement of Principles* is the ASB's conceptual framework. Key points to note are:

- It is not an accounting standard.
- It affects accounting practice by influencing the standard-setting process.
- 'True and fair' is important.
- Current cost accounting is **not** on the agenda.
- The balance sheet and P&L are equally important.

Exam focus point

You must understand and learn the material covered here. You are most likely to be asked to link it to a particular FRS or given set of circumstances.

The statement consists of eight chapters.

(1) The objective of financial statements
(2) The reporting entity
(3) The qualitative characteristics of financial information
(4) The elements of financial statements
(5) Recognition in financial statements
(6) Measurement in financial statements
(7) Presentation of financial information
(8) Accounting for interests in other entities

2.1 Purpose of the Statement of Principles

The following are the main reasons why the Accounting Standards Board (ASB) developed the Statement of Principles.

(a) To assist the ASB by providing a basis for reducing the number of alternative accounting treatments permitted by accounting standards and company law

(b) To provide a framework for the future development of accounting standards

(c) To assist auditors in forming an opinion as to whether financial statements conform with accounting standards

(d) To assist users of accounts in interpreting the information contained in them

(e) To provide guidance in applying accounting standards

(f) To give guidance on areas which are not yet covered by accounting standards

(g) To inform interested parties of the approach taken by the ASB in formulating accounting standards

The role of the Statement can thus be summed up as being to provide **consistency, clarity and information**.

3 The objective of financial statements

FAST FORWARD

The main objective of financial statements is to provide information that is useful to users.

The main points raised here are as follows.

(a)   'The objective of financial statements is to provide information about the reporting entity's **performance and financial position** that is useful to a wide range of users for assessing the stewardship of management and for making economic decisions.'

(b)   It is acknowledged that while all not all the information needs of users can be met by financial statements, there are needs that are common to all users. Financial statements that meet the needs of providers of risk capital to the entity will also meet most of the needs of other users that financial statements can satisfy.

Users of financial statements include the following.

(i)   Investors
(ii)   Lenders
(iii)   Suppliers and other creditors
(iv)   Employees
(v)   Customers
(vi)   Government and their agencies
(vii)   The public

(c)   The limitations of financial statements are emphasised as well as the strengths.

(d)   Investors are the defining choice of user because they focus on the entity's cash-generation ability or financial adaptability.

Financial statements allow users to assess:

(a)   Financial performance
(b)   Financial position
(c)   Cash generation and use
(d)   Financial adaptability

In this way users an:

(a)   Assess the stewardship of management
(b)   Make economic decisions
(e)   The information required by investors relates to: Financial performance

4 Qualitative characteristics of financial statements

FAST FORWARD

The qualitative characteristics of useful financial information are **relevance**, **reliability**, **comparability** and **understandability**. **Materiality** exerts a **quality threshold**.

Key term

The ASB *Statement of Principles* states that in deciding which information to include in financial statements, when to include it and how to present it, the **aim** is to ensure that **financial statements yield information that is useful**.

(a)   Qualitative characteristics that relate to **content** are **relevance** and **reliability**.

(b)   Qualitative characteristics that relate to **presentation** are **comparability** and **understandability**.

4.1 Materiality

For information to be useful it must also be material. The **materiality test** asks whether the **information** involved is of **such significance** as to **require** its **inclusion** in the financial statements. It exerts a **quality threshold** on financial information.

> An item of information is **material** to the financial statements if its **misstatement** or **omission** might reasonably be expected to **influence** the **economic decisions** of users of those financial statements, including their assessments of **management's stewardship**.

Immaterial information can result in **clutter** that **impairs** the **understandability** of the other information provided.

The principal factors to be taken into account are set out below. It will usually be a **combination of these factors**, rather than any one in particular, that will **determine materiality**.

(a)   The item's **size** is judged in the **context** both of the **financial statements** as a **whole** and of the **other information available** to users that would affect their evaluation of the financial statements. This includes, for example, considering how the item affects the evaluation of **trends** and **similar considerations**.

(b)   Consideration is given to the **item's nature** in relation to:

(i)   the **transactions** or other **events giving rise** to it

(ii)   the **legality, sensitivity, normality** and **potential consequences** of the event or transaction

(iii)   the identity of the **parties involved**

(iv)   The particular **headings** and **disclosures** that are affected

If there are **two or more similar items**, the materiality of the items in **aggregate as well as** of the items **individually** needs to be considered. In practice, accountants often keep separate sheets of adjustments that have not been processed to the financial statements. This should be reviewed and evaluated to ensure that the combined effect of supposedly immaterial items do not, when considered together, represent a material misstatement.

4.2 Relevance, reliability, comparability and understanding

These characteristics may be summarised as per the following table.

Characteristic	Qualities
Relevance	
• Ability to influence economic decisions • Provided in time to influence decisions	• **Predictive value**. To evaluate/assess past, present or future events • **Confirmatory value**. Helps to confirm past evaluations/ assessments • **Both** of the above should be maximised

Characteristic	Qualities
Reliability	
• Entails information that is a complete and faithful representation	• **Faithful representation.** Reflecting the substance of transactions • **Neutral.** Free from bias, not overstating or understating • **Complete.** Free from material omissions or errors • **Prudent.** Exercising due caution where uncertainty exists
Comparability	
• Similarities and differences can be discerned and evaluated	• Enables identification of **trends** in financial position and performance **over time** for an entity • Helps compare **financial performance** between entities • Achieved through **consistency** and **disclosure**
Understandability	
• The significance of the information can be perceived	Depends on various factors. • How transactions are **characterised, aggregated** and **classified** • Way in which information is **presented** • Capability of user – assumed **reasonably knowledgeable** and diligent

5 Elements of financial statements

FAST FORWARD

Transactions and other events are grouped together in broad **classes** and in this way their financial effects are shown in the financial statements. These broad classes are the **elements** of financial statements.

Key terms

Assets are rights or other access to **future economic benefits** controlled by an entity as a result of **past transactions** or events.

Liabilities are **obligations** of an entity to **transfer economic benefits** as a result of **past transactions** or events.

Ownership interest is the residual amount found by **deducting** all of the entity's **liabilities** from all of the entity's **assets**.

Gains are **increases** in **ownership interest**, other than those relating to contributions from owners.

Losses are **decreases** in **ownership interest**, other than those relating to distributions to owners.

Contributions from owners are increases in ownership interest resulting from **investments** made by owners in their **capacity as owners**.

Distributions to owners are **decreases** in ownership interest resulting from **transfers** made to owners in their **capacity as owners**.

Any item that does not fall within one of the definitions of elements should not be included in financial statements.

Note that the primary definitions from which the others proceed, are **asset** and **liability**. This is the ASB's **balance sheet approach** to defining the elements of financial statements

These definitions are important but do not cover the **criteria for recognition** of any of these items, which are discussed in the next section. Whether an item satisfies any of the definitions above will depend on the **substance and economic reality** of the transaction, not merely its legal form. For example, consider finance leases (See Chapter 15).

6 Recognition in financial statements

Recognition involves deciding whether, and at what point, assets and liabilities should be included in the financial statements. There must be **sufficient evidence** of the existence of an asset or liability and it must be capable of **reliable measurement.**

If a transaction or other event has created a new asset or liability or added an existing asset or liability, that effect will be **recognised** if:

(a)   Sufficient evidence exists that the new asset or liability has been created or that there has been an addition to an existing asset or liability.

(b)   The new asset or liability or the addition to the existing asset or liability can be measured at a monetary amount with sufficient reliability.

In a transaction involving the provision of services or goods for a net gain, the recognition criteria described above will be met on the occurrence of the critical event in the operating cycle involved.

An asset or liability will be wholly or partly **derecognised** if:

(a)   Sufficient evidence exists that a transaction or other past event has eliminated a previously recognised asset or liability.

(b)   Although the item continues to be an asset or a liability the criteria for recognition are no longer met.

The objective of financial statements is achieved to a large extent through the recognition of elements in the primary financial statements – in other words, the depiction of elements both in words and by monetary amounts, and the inclusion of those amounts in the primary financial statement totals. Recognition is a process that has the following stages.

(a)   **Initial recognition**, which is where an item is depicted in the primary financial statements for the first time.

(b)   Subsequent **remeasurement**, which involves changing the amount at which an already recognised asset or liability is stated in the primary financial statements.

(c)   **Derecognition**, which is where an item that was until then recognised ceases to be recognised.

In practice, entities operate in an uncertain environment and this **uncertainty** may sometimes make it necessary to delay the recognition process. The uncertainty is twofold.

(a)   **Element uncertainty** – does the item exist and meet the definition of elements?
(b)   **Measurement uncertainty** – at what monetary amount should the item be recognised?

Even though matching is not used by the Statement to drive the recognition process, it still plays an important role in the approach described in the draft in allocating the cost of assets across reporting periods and in telling preparers where they may find assets and liabilities.

Question

Consider the following situations. In each case, do we have an asset or liability within the definitions given by the Statement of Principles? Give reasons for your answer.

(a)   Pat Ltd has purchased a patent for £20,000. The patent gives the company sole use of a particular manufacturing process which will save £3,000 a year for the next five years.

(b)   Baldwin Ltd paid Don Brennan £10,000 to set up a car repair shop, on condition that priority treatment is given to cars from the company's fleet.

(c)   Deals on Wheels Ltd provides a warranty with every car sold.

(d)   Monty Ltd has signed a contract with a human resources consultant. The terms of the contract are that the consultant is to stay for six months and be paid £3,000 per month.

(e)   Rachmann Ltd owns a building which for many years it had let out to students. The building has been declared unsafe by the local council. Not only is it unfit for human habitation, but on more than one occasion slates have fallen off the roof, nearly killing passers-by. To rectify all the damage would cost £300,000; to eliminate the danger to the public would cost £200,000. The building could then be sold for £100,000.

Answer

(a)   This is an asset, albeit an intangible one. There is a past event, control and future economic benefit (through cost savings).

(b)   This cannot be classified as an asset. Baldwin Ltd has no control over the car repair shop and it is difficult to argue that there are 'future economic benefits'.

(c)   This is a liability; the business has taken on an obligation. It would be recognised when the warranty is issued rather than when a claim is made.

(d)   As a firm financial commitment, this has all the appearance of a liability. However, as the consultant has not done any work yet, there has been no past event which could give rise to a liability. Similarly, because there has been no past event there is no asset.

(e)   The situation is not clear cut. It could be argued that there is a liability, depending on the whether the potential danger to the public arising from the building creates a legal obligation to do the repairs. If there is such a liability, it might be possible to set off the sale proceeds of £100,000 against the cost of essential repairs of £200,000, giving a net obligation to transfer economic benefits of £100,000.

The building is clearly not an asset, because although there is control and there has been a past event, there is no expected access to economic benefit.

7 Measurement in financial statements

A number of different measurement bases are used in financial statements. They include:

- Historical cost
- Current cost
- Realisable (settlement) value
- Present value of future cash flows

A monetary carrying amount needs to be assigned so an asset or liability can be recognised. There are two measuring bases that can be used: **historical cost** or **current value**.

(a) Initially, when an asset is purchased or a liability incurred, the asset/liability is recorded at the transaction cost, that is historical cost, which at that time is equal to current replacement cost.

(b) An asset/liability may subsequently be 'remeasured'. In a historical cost system, this can involve writing down an asset to its recoverable amount. For a liability, the corresponding treatment would be amendment of the monetary amount to the amount ultimately expected to be paid.

(c) Such re-measurements will, however, only be recognised if there is sufficient evidence that the monetary amount of the asset/liability has changed and the new amount can be reliably measured.

Current value measurement involves a number of different measurement bases:

(a) **Current cost**

Assets are carried at the amount of cash which would have to be paid to acquire the same or an equivalent asset at current prices.

Liabilities are carried at the amount of cash that would be required currently to settle the obligation.

(b) **Realisable or settlement value**

Realisable value is the amount that could currently be obtained by selling the asset in an orderly (not forced) disposal.

Settlement value is the amount currently required to settle a liability in the normal course of business.

(c) **Present value** is the discounted present value of the expected future cash flow arising from use of the asset.

Some of these are commonly used, for instance stock is valued at the lower of cost and net realisable value.

The *Statement* explains that historical cost and current value are **alternative measures**. It envisages that the approach now adopted by the majority of the larger UK listed companies will continue to be used. This involves carrying some categories of balance sheet items at historical cost and others at current value.

Question — Purpose

What is the purpose of the ASB's Statement of Principles?

Answer

The following are the main reasons why the ASB developed the Statement of Principles.

(a)   To assist the ASB by providing a basis for reducing the number of alternative accounting treatments permitted by accounting standards and company law

(b)   To provide a framework for the future development of accounting standards

(c)   To assist auditors in forming an opinion as to whether financial statements conform with accounting standards

(d)   To assist users of accounts in interpreting the information contained in them

(e)   To provide guidance in applying accounting standards

(f)   To give guidance on areas which are not yet covered by accounting standards

(g)   To inform interested parties of the approach taken by the ASB in formulating accounting standards

The role of the Statement can thus be summed up as being to provide consistency, clarity and information.

8 True and fair view

FAST FORWARD

The overriding requirement for financial statements is that they should present a 'true and fair view'. This concept has not been formally defined.

8.1 Interpretation of true and fair

Section 226 of CA 1985 states that:

> 'the balance sheet shall give a true and fair view of the state of affairs of the company as at the end of the financial year, and the profit and loss account shall give a true and fair view of the profit or loss of the company for the financial year.'

The balance sheet and profit and loss account should also comply with the requirements of the Fourth Schedule (s 226(3) CA 1985).

Key term

> **'True and fair view'** has no set definition. Broadly speaking it means 'reasonably accurate and not misleading'.

The term 'true and fair view' is **not defined** in the **Companies Acts**, nor in **SSAPs** or **FRSs**, which also claim to be authoritative statements on what is a true and fair view. Moreover, the **courts** have **never tried to define it**.

In view of the ASB's policy of **reviewing** and, if necessary, **altering** or **replacing existing accounting standards**, a question **arises** as to whether the concept defined by '**true and fair view**' is constant or is **evolving** over a period of years.

The ASC has sought Counsel's opinion on this question. Very briefly, Counsel's opinion included the following key points:

(a)   **Accuracy** and **completeness** are two key ingredients that contribute to a true and fair view.

(b)   There might **not** be **consensus** amongst reasonable businessman and accountants as to the degree of accuracy and completeness required.

(c)   The concept of **true and fair is dynamic**.

(d)   **Judges** will look for **guidance** to the **ordinary practices** of **professional accountants.**

A later opinion obtained by the ASB, confirms the above views. This opinion also provides further clues on how to interpret the expression true and fair. The opinion suggests that the courts are **unlikely** to **look for synonyms** for the words **'true'** and **'fair'**. **Instead**, the courts will take an approach of trying to **apply** the **concepts implied** by the expression **'true and fair'**.

The **Statement of Principles** echoes the above, but carefully avoids providing a formal definition of **true and fair**.

(a)   The true and fair view is a **dynamic concept** and evolves in **response** to changes in **accounting** and **business practice.**

(b)   **Relevance** and **reliability** and **prime indicators** of the **quality** of **financial information.**

8.2 True and fair override

Important!

> S 226 (5) CA 1985 makes an important statement about the need to give a true and fair view. It states that if, in **special circumstances**, compliance with any of the Act's provisions would be inconsistent with the requirement to give a true and fair view, then the directors should depart from that provision to the extent necessary to give a true and fair view. This is the **true and fair override.**

If a balance sheet or profit and loss account drawn up in compliance with these other requirements of the Act would not provide enough information to give a true and fair view, then any **necessary additional information** must **also** be **given.**

The overriding priority to give a true and fair view **has in the past been treated as an important 'loophole' in the law,** and has been a cause of some argument or debate within the accounting profession. For example, the CA 1985 permits only realised profits to be recognised in the profit and loss account, whereas SSAP 9 requires unrealised profits on long-term contracts to be credited to profit and loss. Such a policy can only be justified by **invoking** the **overriding requirement** to show a true and fair view.

If companies do depart from the other requirements of the Act in order to give a true and fair view, they **must explain the particulars of and reasons for the departure, and its effects on the accounts**, in a note to the accounts. As already stated, the **Fourth Schedule** also requires a statement in a **note to the accounts** that the accounts have been prepared in accordance with **applicable accounting standards** and **particulars of any material departure from** those **standards and the reasons** (s 36A Sch 4).

8.3 True and fair override disclosures

As we saw above, where the directors depart from provisions of CA 1985 to the extent necessary to give a true and fair view, the Act required that 'particulars of any such departure, the reasons for it and its effect shall be given in a note to the accounts'. **FRS 18** *Accounting Policies* seeks to clarify the meaning of that sentence. Any **material departure** from the Companies Act, an accounting standard or a UITF abstract should lead to the following information being disclosed.

(a)   **A statement that there has been a departure** from the requirements of companies legislation, an accounting standard or a UITF abstract, and that the departure is **necessary to give a true and fair view.**

(b)   **A description of the treatment normally required** and also a description of the **treatment actually used.**

(c)   An explanation of why the **prescribed treatment would not give a true and fair view.**

(d) **Its effect**: a description of how the position shown in the accounts is different as a result of the departure, with quantification if possible, or an explanation of the circumstances.

The disclosures required should either be **included in or cross referenced** to the note required about **compliance with accounting standards**, **particulars** of any material departure from those standards and the **reasons** for it (Paragraph 36A Sch 4).

If the departure occurs in **subsequent accounting periods**, the above disclosures should be made in **subsequent financial statements including** the **corresponding amounts** for previous years. If the departure only affects the corresponding amounts then the disclosure should relate to the corresponding amounts.

Chapter Roundup

- There are advantages and disadvantages to having a conceptual framework

- GAAP is taken to be all the rules, from whatever source, which govern accounting. This varies from country to country and changes over time as new regulations are issued and others are withdrawn or superseded.

- The main objective of financial statements is to provide information that is useful to users.

- The qualitative characteristics of useful financial information are **relevance**, **reliability**, **comparability** and **understandability**. **Materiality** exerts a **quality threshold**.

- Transactions and other events are grouped together in broad **classes** and in this way their financial effects are shown in the financial statements. These broad classes are the **elements** of financial statements.

- A number of different measurement bases are used in financial statements,. They include:
  - Historical cost
  - Current cost
  - Realisable (settlement) value
  - Present value of future cash flows.

- **Recognition** involves deciding whether, and at what point, assets and liabilities should be included in the financial statements. There must be **sufficient evidence** of the existence of an asset or liability and it must be capable of **reliable measurement**.

- The *Statement of Principles* is the ASB's conceptual framework. Key points to note are:
  - It is not an accounting standard.
  - It affects accounting practice by influencing the standard-setting process.
  - 'True and fair' is important.
  - Current cost accounting is **not** on the agenda.
  - The balance sheet and P&L are equally important.

Quick Quiz

1   *Tick the appropriate box to indicate your response.*

To meet user needs, financial statements should yield information that is:

(a)   Interesting ☐

(b)   Correct ☐

(c)   Useful ☐

(d)   Objective ☐

2   For financial information to be relevant what two values should it possess?

3   The application of *prudence* requires that

(a)   Where alternative accounting treatments are available, the most cautious or conservative should be selected ☐

(b)   Unrealised gains should never be recognised in financial statements ☐

(c)   Where profits are volatile from year to year, provisions may be used to smooth out reported earnings ☐

(d)   Where uncertainty exists, caution must be exercised in preparing accounting estimates ☐

4   The financial accounting recognition process involves two types of uncertainty. State what these are:

(a)   .... uncertainty

(b)   .... uncertainty

5   Explain the concept of neutrality.

6   Fill in the five missing words below.

An item of information is material to the financial statements if its .... or .... might reasonably be expected to .... the economic .... of users of those financial statements, including their assessments of management's ....

7   Explain what the ASB means by the expression 'asset'. Use no more than 25 words in your answer.

8   What two conditions must be satisfied before an asset or liability may be derecognised?

9   Name **five** of the **six** user groups identified in the Statement of Principles.

10   A **gain** as defined by the Statement of Principles is an increase in the net assets of the entity.

True ☐

False ☐

11   The Statement favours current cost accounting. *True or false?*

Answers to Quick Quiz

1   C. To meet user needs, financial statements should yield information that is **useful**.

2   For financial information to be relevant it should have

    A   Predictive value
    B   Confirmatory value

3   D. The application of *prudence* requires that **where uncertainty exists, caution must be exercised in preparing accounting estimates**.

4   The financial accounting recognition process involves two types of uncertainty.

    (a)   **Element** uncertainty
    (b)   **Measurement** uncertainty

5   Neutral means free from **deliberate** or **systematic bias**. Financial information should not be selected or presented in such a way as to influence the making of an **economic decision** so as to achieve a **predetermined results** or **outcome**.

6   An item of information is material to the financial statements if its **misstatement** or **omission** might reasonably be expected to **influence** the economic **decisions** of users of those financial statements, including their assessments of management's **stewardship**.

7   Assets are rights or other access to future economic benefits by an entity as a result of past transactions or events.

8   (a)   Sufficient evidence exists that a transaction or other past event has eliminated a previously recognised asset or liability.

    (b)   Although the item continues to be an asset or a liability the criteria for recognition are no longer met.

9   See paragraph 3

10   False. A **gain** is an increase in ownership interest, other than one relating to contribution from owners.

11   False. The **Statement** favours historical cost accounting, with certain items carried at current value.

Now try the question below from the Exam Question Bank

Number	Level	Marks	Time
Q1	Examination	10	18 mins

The regulatory framework

2

Topic list	Syllabus reference
1 The need for a regulatory framework	B1
2 The regulatory system	B2
3 Overall regulatory framework	B2
4 ASB standard setting process	B2
5 International Accounting Standards	B2

Introduction

In this chapter, the current financial reporting environment is examined, including the process leading to the creation of Financial Reporting Standards (FRSs). The role and structure of the major bodies involved in the financial reporting regime are discussed, particularly the Accounting Standards Board (ASB).

The work of the ASB in securing convergence with international standards is also covered.

Study guide

		Intellectual level
B	A REGULATORY FRAMEWORK FOR FINANCIAL REPORTING	
1	**Reasons for the existence of a regulatory framework**	
(a)	Explain why a regulatory framework is needed.	2
(b)	Explain why accounting standards on their own are not a complete regulatory framework.	2
(c)	Distinguish between a principles based and a rules based framework and discuss whether they can be complementary.	1
2	**The standard setting process**	
(a)	Describe the structure and objectives of the UK regulatory systems including the role of the Financial Reporting Council (FRC), the Accounting Standards (ASB), the Financial Reporting Review Panel (FRRP) and the Urgent Issues Task Force (UITF).	2
(b)	Describe the ASB's Standard setting process including revisions to and interpretations of Standards.	2
(c)	Explain the relationship of national standard setters (eg. FASB and ASB) to the IASB in respect of the standard setting process.	2

Exam guide

Both this chapter and Chapter 3 are extremely important. Make sure that you understand and learn their contents before going on to look at individual items and standards in the following chapters

1 The need for a regulatory framework

1.1 Introduction

The regulatory framework is the most important element in ensuring relevant and reliable financial reporting and thus meeting the needs of shareholders and other users.

Without a single body overall responsible for producing financial reporting standards (the ASB) and a framework of general principles within which they can be produced (the *Statement of Principles*), there would be no means of enforcing compliance with GAAP. Also, GAAP would be unable to evolve in any structured way in response to changes in economic conditions.

1.2 Principles-based versus rules-based systems

FAST FORWARD

A **principles-based** system works within a set of laid down principles. A **rules-based** system regulates for issues as they arise. Both of these have advantage and disadvantages.

The *Statement* provides the background of principles within which standards can be developed. This system is intended to ensure that standards are not produced which are in conflict with each other and also that any departure from a standard can be judged on the basis of whether or not it is keeping with the principles set out in the *Statement*. This is a **principles-based** system.

In the absence of a reporting framework, a more **rules-based** approach has to be adopted. This leads to a large mass of regulations designed to cover every eventuality, as in the US. As we have seen over the past few years, a large volume of regulatory measures does not always detect or prevent financial irregularity.

1.3 Problems of a principles-based system

The principles-based system also has its drawbacks. The *Statement* was produced in 1999 by the ASB, modelled on the IASB's *Framework*. It is now eight years old and in danger of becoming out of date as constant changes take place in financial reporting. FRSs are being drafted based on IFRSs and the main influence on FRSs is the convergence program, rather then the principles of the *Statement*.

For instance, the 'fair value' concept is now an important part of many IFRSs and FRSs, but is not referred to in the *Framework* or the *Statement*. So the IFRSs are running ahead of the *Framework*, and the FRSs are attempting to keep up with the IFRSs. In this regard, a rules-based system, while more unwieldy, at least has the merit of keeping pace with what is happening.

If it is accepted that the *Statement* should be subject to a continuous process of review and updating, then some machinery will have to be set up to do this, and a rules-based approach could be used to deal with issues which arise between reviews.

2 The regulatory system

The UK regulatory system derives from:

FAST FORWARD

- Company law
- Stock exchange requirements
- Accounting standards and financial reporting standards
- International accounting and financial reporting standards

2.1 Unincorporated businesses

In the UK these can usually prepare their **financial statements** in **any form** they choose (subject to the constraints of specific legislation, such as the Financial Services Act 1986 for investment businesses, for example).

2.2 Companies

All **companies** must **comply** with the provisions of the Companies Act 1985 in preparing their financial statements and also with the provisions of *Statements of Standard Accounting Practice* (**SSAPs**) and *Financial Reporting Standards* (**FRSs**). From 2008 they will have to comply with the provisions of the Companies Act 2006 which replaces most of the 1985 Act and makes a large number of changes – most of them, fortunately not in your syllabus.

In its *Foreword to Accounting Standards* the Accounting Standards Board states that **accounting standards are applicable to all financial statements whose purpose is to give a true and fair view**. This necessarily includes the financial statements of every company incorporated in the UK. Obviously if the financial statements of an unincorporated undertaking needs to show a true and fair view, they should also satisfy the requirements of the accounting standards.

The **regulatory framework** over **company accounts** is based on **several sources**.

    (a)   **Company law**.

    (b)   **Accounting** or **financial reporting standards** and other related pronouncements.

    (c)   **International accounting standards** (and the influence of other national standard setting bodies).

    (d)   The requirements of the **Stock Exchange**.

2.3 Role of company law

The Companies Act 1985 (CA 1985) consolidated the bulk of previous company legislation which is relevant to your syllabus. This was substantially amended by the Companies Act 1989 (CA 1989), and all references in this text are to CA 1985 as amended by CA 1989.

The CA 1985 has various key impacts on financial reporting requirements.

    (a)   Every UK registered company is required to prepare a balance sheet and profit and loss account for each financial year which gives a true and fair view.

    (b)   The financial statements must comply with Schedule 4 to CA 1985 as regards format and additional information provided by way of note.

    (c)   Where a company is a parent company, group accounts are also required.

    (d)   Accounting standards are accorded legal definition as 'statements of standard accounting practice by such body or bodies as may be prescribed by regulators', ie the Accounting Standards Board.

2.3.1 Companies Act 2006

The Companies Act 2006 received the Royal Assent in November 2006 and comes into force in November 2008.

The key changes are:

(a)   Company formation is simplified

(b)   Shareholders can form a plc

(c)   Private companies are subject to less regulation

(d)   It is now easier for private companies to re-purchase their own shares

(e)   Shareholder's rights extended

(f)   A statutory code of director's duties is to be set out

(g)   Auditors are now allowed limited liability

(h)   Quoted companies must include in their business review details of:

    (i)   factors likely to affect future business

    (ii)   environment, employee, social and community issues

The net effect is deregulation for private companies and increased regulation for quoted companies. The main changes do not require existing companies to take any action.

2.3.2 The Stock Exchange

In the UK there are two different markets on which it is possible for a company to have its securities quoted:

(a)   The Stock Exchange
(b)   The Alternative Investment Market (AIM)

Shares quoted on the main market, the Stock Exchange, are said to be 'listed' or to have obtained a 'listing'. In order to receive a listing for its securities, a company must conform with Stock Exchange regulations contained in the Listing Rules or Yellow Book issued by the Council of The Stock Exchange. The company commits itself to certain procedures and standards, including matters concerning the disclosure of accounting information, which are more extensive than the disclosure requirements of the Companies Acts. **The requirements of the AIM are less stringent** than the main Stock Exchange. **It is aimed at new, higher risk or smaller companies.**

Many requirements of the Yellow Book do not have the backing of law, but the ultimate sanction which can be imposed on a listed company which fails to abide by them is the withdrawal of its securities from the Stock Exchange List: the company's shares would no longer be traded on the market.

2.4 Influence of EC directives

Exam focus points

Although your syllabus does not require you to be an expert on EU procedure, you should be aware that the form and content of company accounts can be influenced by international developments.

Also remember the role of the EU in driving the implementation of *International financial reporting standards*.

Since the United Kingdom became a member of the European Union (EU) it has been obliged to comply with legal requirements decided on by the EU. It does this by enacting UK laws to implement EU directives. For example, the CA 1989 was enacted in part to implement the provisions of the seventh and eighth EU directives, which deal with consolidated accounts and auditors.

Remember EU directives are only mandatory when enacted into legislation by Parliament. Other EU directives only hold advisory status.

EU directives have influenced the UK financial reporting regime in various key areas.

(a)   Implementation of prescribed formats and detailed disclosure requirements for financial statements.

(b)   Definition of a subsidiary and permission of various exemptions from Companies Act requirements.

(c)   Introduction of various exemptions from Companies Act requirements in respect of small and medium sized companies.

3 Overall regulatory framework

The Financial Reporting Council (FRC) with its subsidiaries, the Accounting Standards Board (ASB) and Financial Reporting Review Panel (FRRP) together make up an organisation whose purpose is to promote and secure good financial reporting. Although the FRC is the parent of the ASB and the FRRP, they are independent of the FRC, and of each another, in the performance of their functions.

The ASB has various committees including:

(a)   Urgent Issues Task Force (UITF)

(b)   Committee on Accounting for Smaller Entities (CASE)

The structure can be depicted in the following diagram.

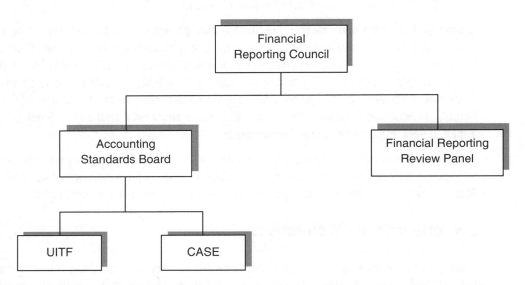

The FRC, ASB and FRRP enjoy strong governmental support but are not government controlled. **They are a part of the private sector process of self-regulation.**

3.1 Financial Reporting Council

The remit of the FRC is to provide support to the ASB and FRRP and to encourage good financial reporting generally. In meeting its remit, the FRC carries out various functions.

(a)   From time to time, making **representations to Government** on the current working of legislation and any desirable developments.

(b)   Providing **guidance** to the **ASB** on **work programmes** and on **broad policy issues**.

(c)   Verifying new arrangements are constructed with **efficiency** and **cost effectiveness**, as well as being adequately funded.

Each year the FRC publishes:

(a)   An annual review describing the activities during the year of the ASB and the FRRP

(b)   Report and financial statements, as required by the Companies Act

(c)   Press releases

(d)   Other relevant information

3.2 The Accounting Standards Board

3.2.1 Role

The role of the ASB, as recognised by the Companies Act, is to **issue accounting standards**. It took over this role from its predecessor, the Accounting Standards Committee (ASC) in 1990.

Unlike the ASC, the ASB can **issue accounting standards** on its **own authority**, without the approval of any other body.

ASB accounting standards are developed having regard to the ASB's *Statement of Principles*.

3.2.2 Membership

The ASB has a **maximum membership** of ten (plus three observers) which may be depicted as follows.

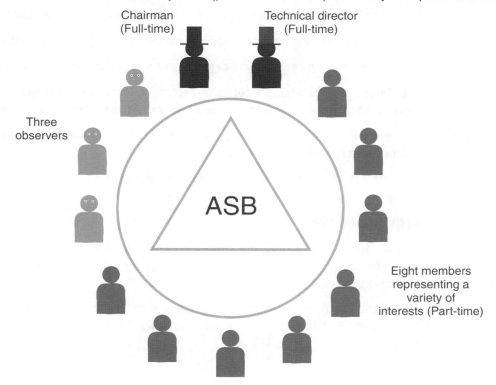

3.2.3 Voting criteria

Any decision to **adopt, revise** or **withdraw** an accounting standard usually requires the **vote** of **seven** members, (**six** when there are fewer than ten members).

3.2.4 Objectives of the ASB

The objectives of the ASB as set out in its *Statement of aims* are to **establish** and **improve standards of financial accounting and reporting**, for the **benefit** of:

(a) **Users**
(b) **Preparers**
(c) **Auditors**

The ASB states that it intends to achieve its objectives by:

(a) **Developing principles** to guide it in establishing standards and to provide a **framework** within which others can **exercise judgement** in **resolving accounting issues**.

(b) **Issuing new accounting standards**, or amending existing ones, in **response** to evolving **business practices**, new **economic developments** and deficiencies being identified in **current practice**.

(c) **Addressing urgent issues promptly**.

Accounting standards developed by the ASB are contained in *Financial Reporting Standards* (FRSs). The ASB has adopted the *Statements of Standards Accounting Practice* (SSAPs) issued by the ASC, so that they also fall within the **legal definition** of accounting standards. Some of the SSAPs have been superseded by FRSs, others remain in force.

Key term

> The *Foreword to Accounting Standards* explains the authority, scope and application of accounting standards.
>
> (a) It will normally be necessary to **comply** with the **standards** to show a **true and fair view**.
>
> (b) In applying the standards, the **user** should be **guided** by their **spirit** and **reasoning**.
>
> (c) **In rare cases** it may be necessary to **depart** from a standard to show a fair view.
>
> (d) **Departures** should be dealt with **objectively** according to the '**economic and commercial characteristics** of the circumstances'; the departure and its financial effect should be **disclosed**.
>
> (e) The **Review Panel** and the **DTI** have powers and procedures to **investigate departures** and to require a **restatement** through the **court**.
>
> (f) Accounting standards **need not** be **applied** to **immaterial items**.

3.2.5 Activities of ASB

The ASB collaborates with accounting standard-setters from other countries and the International Accounting Standards Board (IASB) in order to ensure that its standards are developed with due regard to international developments.

The ASB publicises its activities through press releases and its quarterly newsletter *Inside Track* which provides a broad, non-technical report on the ASB's activities. The ASB also runs a website at www.asb.org.uk.

4 ASB standard setting process

The ASB standard setting process can be best viewed in the diagram set out below, which is based on information shown in the ASB's own website.

STEP 1

Identify topic based on own research or input from outside

STEP 2

Set up management structure and identify project resources and expertise

---

STEP 3

Publish a *Discussion Paper*. The objective here is to canvas the views of the interested public on the possible approaches

---

STEP 4

Analyse and publish feedback received

STEP 5

Publish *Financial reporting exposure draft* (FRED) for further public comment. Sometimes comments on alternative approaches might be invited

---

STEP 6

Conduct any necessary further research or field-test possible procedures

---

STEP 7

Analyse and consider further feedback received from interested parties

---

STEP 8

Issue final pronouncement in the form of a *Financial Reporting Standard* (FRS) or other publication, which specifies the date on which it becomes effective

---

Exam focus point

The December 2005 old syllabus exam had a 25-mark discussion question on the ASB and the standard setting process.

4.1 Accounting standards

Some accounting principles (such as valuation of assets) **are embodied in legislation, while others** (for example cash flow statements) **are regulated by accounting standards**.

> An **accounting standard** is a rule or set of rules which prescribes the method (or methods) by which accounts should be prepared and presented. These 'working regulations' are issued by a national or international body of the accountancy profession.

Accounting standards interact with company law in several ways.

(a) **'Realised' profits** and **losses** are determined by reference to **generally accepted accounting practice**, ie SSAPs and FRSs: s 262 (3).

(b) The **accounts must state** whether the provisions of **accounting standards** have been **followed** or give reasons for, and disclosures of any **material departures**: para 36A, Sch 4.

4.1.1 Authority of accounting standards

As discussed above, accounting standards are intended to **apply** to all **financial accounts** which were '**intended to give a true and fair view** of the financial position and profit and loss'. This includes overseas companies included in UK group accounts. A standard can, however, specify (ie restrict) the 'scope' of its application. For example, FRS 14 on earnings per share applies only to the audited accounts of **publicly traded** companies (companies whose shares are listed on the Stock Exchange).

The **Stock Exchange** requires **listed companies** to **comply** with **accounting standards**. Failure to comply will also usually lead to the auditors qualifying their report, which the company will want to avoid.

Although there are some areas where the contents of accounting standards overlap with provisions of company law, standards are detailed working regulations within the framework of government legislation, and **they cover areas in which the law is silent**. In addition, standards are not intended to override exemptions from disclosure which are allowed to special cases of companies by law.

The Companies Act 1985 states that a departure from its provisions is permissible if that provision is inconsistent with the true and fair view. This may lead to situations in which an accounting standard recommends departure from the legal rules. For example, SSAP 19 *Accounting for investment properties* sanctions such a departure by stating that investment properties need not be depreciated. Other areas of possible conflict between accounting standards and statute will be covered in later chapters.

Members of the Consultative Committee of Accounting Bodies (CCAB), of which the ACCA is a member, are expected to observe accounting standards in their roles either as preparers or auditors of financial information.

4.2 Current accounting standards

The standards in the list are extant at the date of writing. The SSAPs which were in force at the date the ASB was formed have been adopted by the Board. They are gradually being superseded by the new Financial Reporting Standards.

On 7 December 2004, the ASB issued five new accounting standards based on IASs, as part of its strategy for convergence with IFRS.

(a) FRS 22 (IAS 33) *Earnings per share*
(b) FRS 23 (IAS 21) *The effect of changes in foreign exchange rates*
(c) FRS 24 (IAS 29) *Reporting in hyperinflationary economies*
(d) FRS 25 (IAS 32) *Financial instruments: presentation*
(e) FRS 26 (IAS 39) *Financial instruments: measurement*

FRSs 22, 25 and 26 are part of your syllabus and are covered in this text.

These were followed by FRS 27 *Life Assurance* (not part of your syllabus), FRS 28 *Corresponding Amounts*, which is explained in Chapter 3 and FRS 29 *Financial Instruments: disclosure* which incorporates and expands upon the disclosure requirements previously in FRS 25.

UK accounting standards

Title		*Issue date*
	Foreword to accounting standards	Jun 93
FRS 1	Cash flow statements (revised Oct 96)	Sep 91
FRS 2	Accounting for subsidiary undertakings	Jul 92
FRS 3	Reporting financial performance	Oct 92
FRS 4	Capital instruments	Dec 93
FRS 5	Reporting the substance of transactions	Apr 94
FRS 6	Acquisitions and mergers	Sep 94
FRS 7	Fair values in acquisition accounting	Sep 94
FRS 8	Related party disclosures	Oct 95
FRS 9	Associates and joint ventures	Nov 97
FRS 10	Goodwill and intangible assets	Dec 97
FRS 11	Impairment of fixed assets and goodwill	Jul 98
FRS 12	Provisions, contingent liabilities and contingent assets	Sep 98
FRS 13	Derivatives and other financial instruments: disclosures	Sep 98
FRS 15	Tangible fixed assets	Feb 99
FRS 16	Current tax	Dec 99
FRS 17	Retirement benefits	Nov 00*
FRS 18	Accounting policies	Dec 00
FRS 19	Deferred tax	Dec 00
FRS 20	Share-based payment	Apr 04*
FRS 21	Events after the balance sheet date	May 04
FRS 22	Earnings per share	Dec 04
FRS 23	The effect of changes in foreign exchange rates	Dec 04*
FRS 24	Reporting in hyperinflationary economies	Dec 04*
FRS 25	Financial instruments: presentation	Dec 04
FRS 26	Financial instruments: recognition and measurement	Dec 04
FRS 27	Life assurance	Dec 04*
FRS 28	Corresponding amounts	Oct 05
FRS 29	Financial instruments: disclosures	Dec 05
FRSSE	Financial Reporting Standard for Smaller Entities	Dec 99
SSAP 4	Accounting for government grants	Jul 90
SSAP 5	Accounting for value added tax	Apr 74
SSAP 9	Stocks and long-term contracts	Sep 88
SSAP 13	Accounting for research and development	Jan 89
SSAP 19	Accounting for investment properties	Nov 81
SSAP 21	Accounting for leases and hire purchase contracts	Aug 84
SSAP 25	Segmental reporting	Jun 90*
RS1	Operating and financial review	May 05

*These standards are not in your syllabus.

Question

In between now and your examination, make sure you set aside time *every* week or month to read the *Students' Newsletter* and either the *Financial Times, The Economist* or any other equivalent publication. Look for news about the actions of the Accounting Standards Board and the other bodies we have discussed in this chapter and read about the accounts of individual companies as they are discussed in the press. It is a good idea to keep in touch on a regular basis, eg once every few weeks, with the ASB website.

4.3 Financial Reporting Review Panel

The role of the Review Panel is to **examine departures** from the accounting requirements of the Companies Act 1985, including applicable accounting standards, and if necessary to **seek** an **order** from the **court** to **remedy** them.

By agreement with the Department of Trade and Industry the normal ambit of the Panel is **public** and **large private companies**, the Department dealing with all other cases.

The Panel is concerned with an examination of **material departures** from accounting standards with a view to considering whether the accounts in question nevertheless meet the statutory requirement to give a **true and fair view**. While such a departure does not necessarily mean that a company's accounts fail the true and fair test it will raise that question. Remember that the Companies Act 1985 requires large companies to **disclose** in their accounts any such **departures** together with the **reasons** for them, thus enabling them to be readily identified and considered.

The Panel does **not scrutinise on a routine basis all companies accounts** falling within its ambit. Instead it **acts on matters drawn to its attention, either directly or indirectly.** (*Note.* Under the new structure being discussed, the FRRP may become more proactive in searching itself, for cases that might have a market impact.

The Panel normally aims to discharge its tasks by **seeking voluntary agreement** with the directors of a company on any **necessary revisions** to the accounts in question. But if that **approach fails** and the Panel believes that revisions to the accounts are necessary, it will seek:

(a)   A **declaration from the court** that the **annual accounts** of the company concerned do **not comply** with the requirements of the Companies Act 1985

(b)   An order requiring the directors of the company to **prepare revised accounts**. If the court grants such an order it may also require the directors to meet the **costs** of the proceedings and of revising the accounts.

Where accounts are revised at the instance of the Panel, either voluntarily or by order of the court, but the company's **auditor** had **not qualified his audit report** on the **defective accounts** the Panel will draw this fact to the **attention** of the **auditor's professional body**.

4.4 The Urgent Issues Task Force (UITF)

The main role of the UITF is to **assist the ASB** in areas where an accounting standard or Companies Act provision exists, but where **unsatisfactory** or **conflicting interpretations** have developed or seem likely to develop.

Its **consensus pronouncements** are issued as UITF Abstracts, which the ASB expects be regarded as **accepted practice** in the area in question, and part of the collection of practices forming the **basis** for what determines a **true and fair view**.

A UITF Abstract may be taken into **consideration** by the **FRRP** in deciding whether a company's financial statements **call for review**.

The UITF abstracts tend to become effective within approximately one month of publication date. The UITF has so far issued twenty two abstracts. Abstracts 1, 2, 3, 7, 8 and 14 have all been superseded by new FRSs and Financial Reporting Exposure Drafts (FREDs). **Only Abstracts 4, 5 and 15 are included in the ACCA's list of examinable documents**. These are discussed briefly here and they are mentioned in the relevant parts of this text when necessary.

4.4.1 Abstract 4 Presentation of long-term debtors in current assets

Where the figure of debtors due after more than one year is material in the context of the total net current assets then it should be **disclosed on the face of the balance sheet**, rather than just by way of a note (as has been the practice in the past where long-term debtors were included in current assets). The figure would be material in relation to net current assets if its non-disclosure on the balance sheet would cause readers to misinterpret the accounts. You should bear this in mind when considering the Companies Acts formats, given in Chapter 3.

4.4.2 Abstract 5 Transfers from current assets to fixed assets

This abstract requires transfers from current assets to fixed assets to be made **at the lower of cost and net realisable value**. This prevents the practice of transfers being made at a value higher than NRV. This avoids charging the profit and loss account with any diminution in value of what are, in effect, unsold trading assets. Once transferred to fixed assets, the CA 1985 alternative accounting rules could be used to take the debit reflecting the diminution in value to a revaluation reserve. This abstract follows the statement of Principles and was triggered by a Review Panel Judgement on Trafalgar House's 1991 accounts. In that incidence, commercial properties were transferred out of current assets into tangible fixed assets, thereby avoiding a £102 million hit to pre-tax profits in the original accounts. Fixed assets are dealt with in Chapter 5.

4.4.3 Abstract 15 Disclosure of substantial acquisitions

This clarifies the threshold for **disclosure of substantial acquisitions** under the Stock Exchange Listing Rules.

The UITF is currently considering another topic, marking current asset investments to market.

4.4.4 Abstract 40 Revenue recognition and service contracts

Abstract 40 applies the provisions of Application Note G to FRS 5 to all contracts for services. It requires that unbilled revenue relating to service contracts should be accrued as per SSAP 9 where a point has been reached at which an invoice could be raised. This is explained further in Chapter 14, para 3.7.

4.4.5 Foreword to UITF Abstracts

This foreword was issued in February 1994. It is closely associated with the *Foreword to accounting standards* in its scope and application and users are asked to 'be guided by the spirit and reasoning' behind the abstracts.

Most importantly, the document sets out the following criteria for compliance with the UITF abstracts.

'The Councils of the CCAB bodies expect their members who assume responsibilities in respect of financial statements to **observe UITF Abstracts until they are replaced by accounting standards or otherwise withdrawn** by the ASB.'

The scope of and compliance with the abstracts are similar to those associated with accounting standards (accounts which show a true and fair view, non-compliance must be justified and disclosed etc).

4.4.6 The effectiveness of the UITF

There is no doubt that the prompt action of the UITF has **closed many loopholes** as soon as they have become apparent. Some of the abstracts have been triggered by the accounts of individual companies, whereas others reflect concern which has arisen over a period of time. Another aspect of the success of the UITF is the **relative speed** with which the abstracts have been included in new standards, or exposure drafts. In other words, the topics were obviously important enough, not only for the attention of the UITF, but also for the ASB.

In combination with the Review Panel, the UITF can halt abuses in financial reporting as soon as they occur. This will also act as a preventative measure, causing many companies and their auditors to hesitate before breaking (or even bending) the rules.

5 International Accounting Standards

FAST FORWARD

> International Accounting Standards (IASs) and International Financial Reporting Standards (IFRSs) are ultimately intended to be **global** standards. There is currently a process of **convergence** taking place between UK and International standards.

International Accounting Standards (IASs) were originally produced by the **International Accounting Standards Committee** (IASC), now the **International Accounting Standards Board** (IASB). The IASB **develops accounting standards through an international process that involves the world-wide accountancy profession, the preparers and users of financial statements, and national standard setting bodies.**

The objectives of the IASB are to:

(a) **Develop**, in the public interest, a **single set** of high quality, understandable and **enforceable global accounting standards** that require high quality, transparent and comparable information in financial statements and other financial reporting to help participants in the various **capital markets** of the world and other users of the **information** to make **economic decisions**

(b) **Promote** the use and **rigorous application** of those standards

(c) Work actively with national standard-setters to bring about **convergence** of national accounting standards and International Financial Reporting Standards (IFRSs) to **high quality solutions**

A substantial number of **multinational companies** now prepare financial statements in accordance with IASs. IASs are also endorsed by many countries as their own standards, whether unchanged or with minor amendments.

A great many **stock exchanges** now **accept IASs** for **cross-border listing purposes** (ie when a company in one country wishes to list its shares on another country's stock exchange), but Canada, Japan and the United States are exceptions.

In May 2000, the Presidents Committee of the International Organisation of Securities Commissions (IOSCO) recommended the IOSCO members permit **incoming multi-national issuers** to use the **IASC core standards** to prepare their financial statements for **cross-border offerings and listings**. The core standards include all IASs except for IAS 15, IAS 26 and the recently issued IASs 40 and 41.

On 25 May 2000, the US Securities and Exchange Commission recommended that IASs should now be accepted for use in **cross-border listings** in the United States, without reconciliation to results under US GAAP.

As the use of IASs grew, the role of the IASC expanded and as a result, the member bodies approved the restructuring of the IASC. As a result, on 1 April 2001, the new IASB assumed the IASC's standard-setting responsibilities. Current standards issued by the IASB are known as *International Financial Reporting Standards* (IFRSs). Existing IASs and SICs were adopted by the IASB.

5.1 The use and application of IASs

IASs have helped to both **improve** and **harmonise** financial reporting around the world. The standards are used:

- (a) As national requirements, often after a national process
- (b) As the basis for all or some national requirements
- (c) As an international benchmark for those countries which develop their own requirements
- (d) By regulatory authorities for domestic and foreign companies
- (e) By companies themselves

5.2 Effects of IASs on UK regulation

Before the ASB came into existence, the effect of IASs and other IASC publications on UK standard setting was limited and haphazard. Many SSAPs and IASs were in agreement, but some were not, and some covered completely different topics.

In its FRSs, usually in an appendix, the ASB identifies where the UK standards are in agreement with or are different from IASs or IAS exposure drafts. The ASB sees itself as closely aligned with the IASC, now the IASB. However, it seems that the ASB will only follow the relevant IAS if it fits in with the desired UK practice. The IASB is revising and improving its current IASs and one of the reasons is the elimination or reduction of alternative accounting treatments.

5.3 Harmonisation in Europe

In June 2000, the European Commission proposed that all **publicly listed companies** should be required to implement IASs and IFRs for their **consolidated financial statements** with **accounting periods beginning on 1 January 2005**.

The objective of the European Commission is to build a fully integrated, **globally competitive capital market**. A key element of this is the establishment of a level playing field for EU financial reporting, supported by an effective enforcement regime.

Harmonised financial reporting standards are intended to provide a variety of benefits.

- (a) A platform for **wider investment choice**
- (b) A more efficient capital market
- (c) Lower cost of capital
- (d) Enhanced business development

In March 2002, the European Parliament voted to endorse the use of international standards for publicly limited companies in the EU in respect of their group accounts.

In August 2002, the UK Department of Trade and Industry (DTI) set into motion processes to **extend** the **use** of international financial reporting standards in the UK **beyond publicly listed companies**. The EU would also like to implement IFRSs for all companies.

5.4 The ASB's convergence policy

The following statement is taken from the Convergence Handbook.

> 'The ASB is working with the IASB and other national standard setters in order to seek improvements in IFRS and convergence of national and international standards. The ASB is one of several national standard setters that have a formal liaison relationship with the IASB. This relationship involves regular meetings and other consultations as well as several joint standard setting projects, including the ASB's joint project with the IASB on reporting financial performance.
>
> The ASB intends to **align UK accounting standards** with IFRS whenever practicable. It proposes to do this, in the main, by a **phased replacement** of existing UK standards **with new UK standards based on the equivalent IFRS**.'

Exam focus point

Consider the likelihood of small general discursive question on how the work of the ASB, IASB, EU etc link into the process of globalisation.

Chapter Roundup

- A **principles-based** system works within a set of laid down principles. A **rules-based** system regulates for issues as they arise. Both of these have advantages and disadvantages.

- The UK regulatory system derives from:

  - Company law
  - Stock exchange requirements
  - Accounting standards and financial reporting standards
  - International accounting and financial reporting standards

- International Accounting Standards (IASs) and International Financial Reporting Standards (IFRSs) are ultimately intended to be **global** standards. There is currently a process of **convergence** taking place between UK and international standards.

BPP LEARNING MEDIA

Quick Quiz

1   The Financial Reporting Council (FRC) draws its strength from the fact that it reports to the Department of Trade and Industry (DTI). *True or false?*

2   *Fill in the six missing words at the end of the following sentence.*

Accounting standards apply to all companies, and other kinds of entities that prepare accounts that are intended to

....

....

3   Because the FRC is the parent undertaking of the ASB, FRSs produced by the ASB must be sanctioned by the FRC. *True or false?*

4   *Fill in the two missing words below.*

In applying financial reporting standards, users should be guided by their .... and

....

5   Explain when it is permissible to depart from the requirements of a financial reporting standard.

6   The Review Panel has a monitoring unit that reviews the published financial statements of listed companies to identify any material departures from accounting standards. *True or false?*

7   How are international standards required to be implemented by companies in the European Union?

8   Describe the process by which the FRRP enforces the revision to financial statements that it requires.

9   UITF Abstracts should not be taken into consideration by the FRRP in deciding whether a company's financial statements call for review. *True or false?*

10   Describe the steps the ASB takes in developing and issuing financial statements.

Answers to Quick Quiz

1   False. The FRC enjoys strong government support but is **not government controlled**. It is part of the private sector process of self-regulation.

2   Accounting standards apply to all companies, and other kinds of entities that prepare accounts that are intended to **provide a true and fair view**.

3   False. The ASB can issue accounting standards on its own authority. It does not need to obtain the approval of any other body.

4   In applying financial reporting standards, users should be guided by their **spirit** and **reasoning**.

5   It is permissible to depart from the requirements of a financial reporting standard where this is necessary to ensure the true and fair view is maintained.

6   False. The FRRP in effect has a 'watching brief'. It reacts to matters brought to its attention.

7   All EU publicly-listed companies are required to implement IASs and IFRSs for their consolidated financial statements with accounting periods beginning on 1 January 2005.

8   The FRRP will initially try to get the company to voluntarily agree to make the necessary revisions to their accounts. Failing that the FRRP will seek a court order.

9   False. UITF *Abstracts* **should be** taken into consideration by the FRRP in deciding whether a company's financial statements call for review.

10   **ASB standards setting process**

The following is a summary drawn from the ASB website.

(a)   **Identify topic** based on ASB research or input from outside.

(b)   Set up **project management structure** and identify project resources and expertise.

(c)   Publish a *Discussion Paper.* The objective here is to canvass the **views** of the **interested public** on possible approaches.

(d)   Analyse and publish **feedback** received.

(e)   Publish *Financial reporting exposure draft* (FRED); sometimes comments on alternative approaches might be invited.

(f)   Analyse and consider **further feedback** received from interested parties.

(g)   Issue **final pronouncement** in the form of a *Financial Reporting Standard* (FRS) or other publication, which specifies the date on which it becomes effective.

Now try the question below from the Exam Question Bank

Number	Level	Marks	Time
Q2	Examination	10	18 mins
Q3	Examination	10	18 mins

Presentation of published financial statements

Topic list	Syllabus reference
1 FRS 18 *Accounting policies*	A2
2 Published accounts	C10
3 The format of accounts	C10
4 Notes to the accounts	C10

Introduction

This chapter lays out the Companies Act formats for the balance sheet and profit and loss account as well as the disclosures required in the notes to the accounts. These are fundamental to the study of financial accounting.

Before we look at the Companies Act, we will refresh your memory of the accounting standard which lays out some of the basic premises upon which accounts are based, FRS 18 *Accounting Policies*.

Study guide

		Intellectual level
A	**A conceptual framework for financial reporting**	
2	**The standard setting process**	
(d)	Distinguish between changes in accounting polices and changes in accounting estimates and describe how accounting standards apply the principle of comparability where an entity changes its accounting policies.	2
(e)	Recognise and account for changes in accounting policies and the correction of prior period errors.	2
C	**Regulatory requirements relating to the preparation of financial statements**	
(a)	Describe the structure (format) and content of financial statements presented under the Companies Act and accounting standards.	2
(b)	Prepare an entity's financial statements in accordance with the prescribed structure and content.	2

Exam guide

FRS 18 is an important standard. Make sure you understand how to use it. Practise the format of the accounts until you can quickly lay out a proforma in the exam.

Knowledge brought forward from earlier studies

- The **'accruals' concept:** revenue and costs are accrued (that is, recognised as they are earned or incurred, not as money is received or paid).

- The **'consistency' concept:** there is consistency of accounting treatment of like items within each accounting period and from one period to the next.

- The **concept of 'prudence':** revenue and profits are not anticipated, but are recognised by inclusion in the P&L a/c only when realised in the form either of cash or of assets, the ultimate cash realisation of which can be assessed with reasonable certainty.

There is always a presumption that these concepts have been observed. If this is not the case, the facts should be explained.

1 FRS 18 Accounting policies

FAST FORWARD

FRS 18 emphasises **accruals** and **going concern** as **bedrocks** of accounting. Prudence and consistency are simply 'desirable features'.

FRS 18 *Accounting policies* replaced SSAP 2 *Disclosure of accounting policies.* It builds on the concepts outlined in SSAP 2 (issued almost 30 years ago) and attempts to align them with the ASB *Statement of Principles.* FRS 18 can be said to provide a '**bridge**' between the ideas and concepts envisaged by the *Statement of Principles* and enshrined in SSAP 2 for a long time in the past.

The CA 1985 requires the following:

(a) **Accounting policies should be applied consistently** from one financial year to the next.

(b) If accounts are prepared on the basis of assumptions which differ in material respects from any of the generally accepted fundamental accounting concepts (principles) the details, **reasons for and the effect of, the departure from the fundamental concepts must be given in a note to the accounts**.

(c) The **accounting policies** adopted by a company in determining the (material) amounts to be included in the balance sheet and in determining the profit or loss for the year **must be stated by a note to the accounts**.

The objective of FRS 18 is to ensure that for all **material items**:

(a) An entity adopts the accounting policies **most appropriate** to its particular circumstances for the purpose of giving a **true and fair view**

(b) The accounting policies adopted are **reviewed regularly** to ensure that they remain appropriate, and are changed when a new policy becomes more appropriate, and are changed when a new policy becomes more appropriate to the entity's particular circumstances

(c) **Sufficient information** is disclosed in the financial statements to enable users to **understand** the accounting policies adopted and how they have been implemented.

1.1 Desirable features

The most obvious change is the relegation of two fundamental accounting concepts

(a) **Prudence**
(b) **Consistency**

These concepts are now **desirable features** of financial statements. This mirrors their **role** within the *Statement of Principles.*

1.2 Pervasive concepts

The bedrocks of accounting are

(a) **Accruals** basis of accounting
(b) **Going concern** assumption

FRS 18 places great **importance** upon these concepts. Although these are on the face of it, similar to the previously matching and going concern concepts, there are subtle but important differences.

1.3 Accruals

Within FRS 18, the accruals concept goes to the heart of the definition of assets and liabilities, and plays an important role in the way these items are recognised.

Basic requirement

> The accruals basis of accounting requires the **non-cash impact** of transactions to be reflected in the financial statements for the **period in which they occur**, and not, for example, in the period any cash involved is received or paid.

From the above, it can be seen that FRS 18 adopts a slightly different approach to SSAP 2 on the accruals concept. Together with the definitions of assets and liabilities set out in FRS 5, *Reporting the Substance of Transactions*, FRS 18 in effect provides a discipline within which the old SSAP 2 matching process can operate.

Key terms

> - **Asset**: right to **future economic benefits** controlled by an entity as result of past events.
> - **Liability**: entity's **obligation** to **transfer economic benefits** as result of past events.

FRS 18, like CA 1985, does not refer to matching.

1.4 Example

How would you assess whether expenditure such as unexpired advertising or unused stationery should be carried forward to the next year?

Solution

Under the old SSAP 2 regime, the decision on whether to carry expenditure forward into next year would involve the matching concept and whether there is a reasonable expectation of future revenue.

Under the new FRS 18 regime, the **decision to carry forward** depends on whether the item being considered meets the **definition of an asset**.

FRS 18 effectively updates SSAP 2 within the ambit of the **Statement of Principles** and FRS 5.

CA 1985 only allows realised profits to be recognised in the **profit and loss account**. However, CA 1985 does not adequately define the expression 'realised'. Neither does FRS 18 define 'realised'. What FRS 18 does do is to link realisation with the **creation of new assets and liabilities** and hence with the **concept of accruals**.

1.5 Going concern

1.5.1 Criteria

FRS 18 requires financial statements to be prepared on a going concern basis, except where:

    (a)   An entity is being liquidated and has ceased trading
    (b)   The directors have no realistic alternative but to cease trading or liquidate the business.

In these circumstances, the **directors have an option** to prepare its financial statements on a **basis other than that of a going concern**. Remember, where the criteria are met, the **decision is discretionary** rather than mandatory, to prepare the financial statements on a non-going concern basis.

The going concern hypothesis assumes that the entity will **continue** in **operational existence** for the **foreseeable future**. The justification for this is that financial statements prepared on a **break up basis** do **not provide** users with much **useful information**, such as on financial adaptability and cash generation ability.

1.5.2 Directors responsibilities

The directors have an obligation to **assess** whether there are **significant doubts** about an entity's ability to continue as a **going concern**, when preparing financial statements.

FRS 18 suggests that directors should review the following factors:

(a)   History of company's profitability
(b)   Access to financial resources
(c)   Debt repayment schedules

Such considerations also govern the **length of time** for which the going concern assessment should be made.

1.5.3 Disclosures

The following information should be disclosed in the financial statements in relation to the going concern assessment required by FRS 18.

(a)   Any material uncertainties, of which the directors are aware in making their assessment, related to events or conditions that may cast significant doubt upon the entity's ability to continue as a going concern.

(b)   Where the foreseeable future considered by the directors has been limited to a period of less than one year from the date of approval of the financial statements, that fact.

(c)   When the financial statements are not prepared on a going concern basis, that fact, together with the basis on which the financial statements are prepared and the reason why the entity is not regarded as a going concern.

1.5.4 Statement of Principles

As you will have gathered from the above, FRS 18 is designed to sit alongside the *Statement of Principles* framework. This helps explain the downplaying of the previously important prudence and consistency concepts.

FRS 18 can be said to provide a **'bridge'** between the ideas and concepts envisaged by the *Statement of Principles* and the concepts enshrined in SSAP 2 for a long time.

The preparers of financial statements must now consider the following **objectives** and constraints in **assessing** the appropriateness of **accounting policies:**

(a)   Relevance
(b)   Reliability
(c)   Comparability
(d)   Understandability

1.5.5 Relevance

Information is **relevant** if it possess **certain qualities**.

(a)   Ability to **influence economic decisions** of users
(b)   Is sufficiently **timely** to influence the decision
(c)   Has **predictive** or **confirmatory** value, or both.

Eg the FRS 3 requirement for separate analyses of the results of discontinued operations can be said to improve the predictive value of a set of financial statements.

1.5.6 Reliability

Financial information is reliable if:

(a)   It can be depended upon by users to **represent faithfully** what it either purports to represent or could reasonably be expected to represent, and therefore reflects the **substance of the transactions** and other events that have taken place

(b)   It is **free** from deliberate or systematic **bias** (ie it is **neutral**)

(c)   It is **free** from **material error**

(d)   It is **complete** within the bounds of **materiality**

(e)   Under conditions of **uncertainty**, it has been **prudently prepared**

1.5.7 Prudence

In terms of FRS 18, **prudence** relates to the **uncertainty** that may be associated with the **recognition** and **measurement** of **assets** and **liabilities**.

FRS 18 suggest different levels of confirmatory evidence regarding the recognition of assets and liabilities, where uncertainty exists. In such circumstances, the existence of an **asset or gain** requires **stronger confirmatory evidence** than that required to acknowledge the existence of a liability or loss.

FRS 18 emphasises that prudence may only be called upon to justify setting up a provision if uncertainty exists. **Prudence** should **not** be **invoked** to **justify setting up hidden reserves, excessive provisions** or **understating assets**. Prudence should not be seen as a tool for smoothing profits in financial statements.

FRS 18 emphasises that **if financial statements are not neutral they cannot be reliable**. Neutrality means that the information is **free from deliberate** or **systematic bias**. Financial information cannot be neutral if it has been selected or presented in such a way so as to influence the making of a decision so as to achieve a predetermined result or outcome.

Tension often exists between neutrality and prudence. This should be reconciled by finding a balance that ensures that the deliberate and systematic understatement of assets and gains, and overstatement of liabilities and losses, does not occur.

Several recent FRSs, especially FRS 12, have adopted a more **'even-handed'** approach to the challenge of **measuring** and **recognising** income, expenses, assets and liabilities in financial statements.

1.5.8 Comparability

FRS 18 suggest that this is achieved through:

(a)   Consistency
(b)   Disclosure

Hence, consistency, no longer a fundamental accounting concept it its own right, is subsumed under the objective of comparability. Under the old SSAP 2 regime, **consistency implied** a *status quo* approach to financial reporting.

In practice, **comparability** will often be achieved through **consistency**. However, there may be circumstances where a change in the method of presenting financial information increases the usefulness of the financial report for users.

1.5.9 Understandability

FRS 18 stipulates that information provided by financial statements should be capable of being understood by users who have

(a) A **reasonable knowledge** of business and economic activities.

(b) A willingness and **reasonable diligence** to study the information provided.

There can be tensions between the different objectives set out above. In particular, sometimes the accounting policy that is most relevant to a particular entity's circumstances is not the most reliable, and vice versa. In such circumstances, the most appropriate accounting policy will usually be that which is the **most relevant of those that are reliable**.

Generally, FRS 18 encourages an approach that leads to the most appropriate policies for the company. Note also that FRS 18 does not use the word 'conflict' but prefers a process of resolving 'tensions' between different objectives.

The relationship between pervasive concepts, desirable features and accounting policy objectives may be summarised briefly in the following diagram.

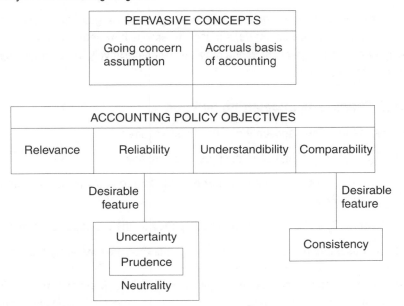

1.6 Accounting policies

FRS 18 prescribes the **regular consideration of the entity's accounting policies**. The **best** accounting policy should be adopted at all times. This is the major reason for downplaying consistency (and to a lesser extent prudence). An entity **cannot retain** an **accounting policy** merely **because** it was **used last** year **or** because it **gives a prudent view**.

However, the entity should consider how a **change** in accounting policy may affect **comparability**. Essentially a **balance** must be struck between selecting the **most appropriate policies** and presenting **coherent and useful** financial statements. The **overriding guidance** is that the financial statements should give a **true and fair view** of the entity's business. Chopping and changing accounting policies year on year is likely to jeopardise the true and fair view but so too is retaining accounting policies which do not present the most useful information to the users of the accounts.

FRS 18 suggests that the need to balance the cost of providing information should be balanced with the likely benefit of such information to the users of the entity's financial statements. However, FRS 18 also cautions against the use of cost and benefit considerations to justify the adoption of an accounting policy that is inconsistent with the requirements of accounting standards, UITF Abstracts and CA 1985.

1.6.1 Disclosure

FRS 18 requires the disclosure of

(a) A **description of each accounting policy** which is material to the entity's financial statements

(b) A description of any significant estimation technique

(c) **Changes** to accounting policies

(d) The effects of any material change to an estimation technique

1.6.2 Estimation techniques

An estimation technique is material **only where a large range** of monetary values may be arrived at. The entity should **vary** the **assumptions** it uses, to **assess** how **sensitive** monetary values are under that **technique**. In most cases the range of values will be relatively narrow (consider the useful life of motor vehicles for example).

1.6.3 Changes to accounting policies

The disclosure of new accounting policies also requires

(a) An explanation of the **reason for change**

(b) The **effects of a prior period adjustment** on the previous years results (in accordance with FRS 3)

(c) The **effects of the change in policy** on the previous year's results

If it is **not possible** to disclose the last two points then the **reason** for this should be disclosed instead.

The most complex aspect to FRS 18 is the **application of the terms and definitions** within the standard. SSAP 2 defined accounting policies and accounting bases. There was some confusion as to what an accounting base was. FRS 18 has dispensed with the term accounting base. However, the term which seems to replace it**, estimation technique**, may prove difficult to apply in practice.

It is essential that you **understand the following definitions** so you can apply them in an examination situation.

Key term

Accounting policies. The principles, conventions, rules and practices applied by an entity that prescribe how transactions and other events are to be reflected in its financial statements.

Accounting policies are **not** estimation techniques.

An accounting policy includes the

(a) Recognition
(b) Presentation
(c) Measurement basis

... of assets, liabilities, gains, losses and changes to shareholders funds.

Key term

> **Estimation technique.** The methods used by an entity to establish the estimated monetary amounts associated with the measurement bases selected for assets, liabilities, gains, losses and changes to shareholder's funds.

Estimation techniques are used to **implement the measurement basis** of an accounting policy. The accounting policy specifies the measurement basis and the estimation technique is used when there is an uncertainty over this amount.

The method of **depreciation is an estimation technique**. The accounting policy is to spread the cost of the asset over its useful economic life. **Depreciation** is the **measurement basis**. The **estimation technique** would be, say, **straight line** depreciation as opposed to **reducing balance**.

A change of estimation technique should **not** be accounted for as a prior period adjustment unless the following apply.

(a) It is the correction of a fundamental error

(b) The Companies Act, an accounting standard or a UITF Abstract **requires the change to be accounted** for as a prior period adjustment.

1.7 Application of FRS 18

FRS 18 gives a number of examples of its application in an appendix to the standard. When a change is required to an accounting policy then **three criteria** must be **considered** to ensure that the change is affecting the accounting policy and not an estimation technique.

1 Recognition
2 Presentation
3 Measurement basis

If **any one of the criteria apply** then a change has been made to the accounting policy. If they do **not** apply then a change to an estimation technique has taken place.

You should note that where an **accounting standard gives a choice** of treatments (i.e. SSAP 9 states that stock can be recognised on a FIFO or weighted average cost basis) then adopting the alternative treatment is a **change of accounting policy.** Also note that FRS 15 states that a **change in depreciation method is not** a change in accounting policy.

	Example	Recognition	Change to Presentation	Change to Measurement basis?	Change of Accounting Policy
1	Changing from capitalisation of finance costs associated with the construction of fixed assets to charging them through the profit and loss	Yes	Yes	No	Yes
2	A reassessment of an entity's cost centres means that all three will have production overheads allocated to them instead of just two	No	No	No	No

	Example	Recognition	Change to Presentation	Change to Measurement basis?	Change of Accounting Policy
3	Overheads are reclassified from distribution to cost of sales	No	Yes	No	Yes
4	Change from straight-line depreciation to machine hours	No	No	No	No
5	Reallocate depreciation from administration to cost of sales	No	Yes	No	Yes
6	A provision is revised upwards and the estimates of future cash flows are now discounted in accordance with FRS 12. They were not discounted previously as the amounts involved were not material	No	No	No	No
7	Deferred tax is now reported on a discounted basis. It was previously undiscounted	No	No	Yes	Yes
8	A foreign subsidiary's profit and loss account is now to be translated at the closing rate. It was previously translated at the average rate	No	No	Yes	Yes
9	Fungible stocks are to be measured on the weighted average cost basis instead of the previously used FIFO basis	No	No	Yes	Yes

1.8 Fungible assets

Key term

> **Fungible assets** are similar assets which are grouped together as there is no reason to view them separately in economic terms. Shares and items of stock are examples of fungible assets.

The last example (example 9) is based on a **change to fungible assets**. The standard states that when fungible assets are considered in **aggregate** a change from weighted average cost to FIFO (or vice versa), is a change to the **measurement base**. The standard also recommends that fungible assets should **always be considered in aggregate** in order to enhance **comparability** of financial statements.

Question   **Accounting policies 1**

The board of Sarah plc decide to change the depreciation method they use on their plant and machinery from 30% reducing balance to 20% straight line to better reflect the way the assets are used within the business. Is this a change of accounting policy ?

Answer

No. This is a change to the **estimation technique**. The same measurement basis is used. The historic cost is allocated over the asset's estimated useful life.

Question

The board of Sarah plc also decide to change their stock valuation. They replace their FIFO valuation method for an AVCO method to better reflect the way that stock is used within the business. Is this a change in accounting policy?

Answer

Yes. This is a change to the **measurement basis**. The paragraphs on fungible assets discuss this further.

Question

The board of Sarah plc decide in the following year that the development costs the business incurs should not be capitalised and presented on the balance sheet. Instead they agree that all development expenditure should be expended in the profit and loss account. Is this an accounting policy change?

Answer

Yes. The choice to capitalise or not is given in SSAP 13. The criteria affected by this decision are **recognition and presentation.**

Question

Sarah plc's board are also considering reallocating the depreciation charges made on its large fleet of company cars to administration expenses, they were previously shown in cost of sales. Is this an accounting policy change?

Answer

Yes. Sarah plc would be changing the way they **presented** the depreciation figure.

Exam focus point

In the current financial reporting climate, companies may be tempted to utilise a change of accounting policy or estimation technique to give more favourable reported results. Be prepared for a question in the area perhaps linked to accounting ratios and the interpretation of financial statements.

1.9 Summary

FRS 18 requires an entity to conduct a review on an annual basis in order to ensure that it is using the most appropriate accounting policies.

(a) The three criteria
(b) Recognition
(c) Presentation
(d) Measurement basis

Are considered in order to establish whether there has been a change of accounting policy or merely a change of measurement basis. The objectives of

(a)   Reliability
(b)   Relevance
(c)   Comparability
(d)   Understandability

The above must be fulfilled by the accounting policies adopted. This requirement helps prevent entities from changing accounting policies too often.

FRS 18 introduces subtle changes into the meaning of accruals and going concern. Whereas matching was driven by the need to ensure completeness in the profit and loss account, the accruals basis approaches recognition from the need to ensure the validity of assets and liabilities.

Prudence and consistency have a lesser role in the accounting policy framework. There may be tension between prudence and neutrality. Prudence should not be used as an excuse for setting up excessive provisions or understating assets. The use of prudence must be linked to uncertainty.

FRS 18 provides a bridge between the standards setting process and the *Statement of Principles*.

2 Published accounts

FAST FORWARD

Statutory accounts are part of the price to be paid for the benefits of limited liability. **Limited companies must produce such accounts annually and they must appoint an independent person to audit and report on them.**

Once prepared, **a copy** of the accounts **must be sent to the Registrar of Companies**, who maintains a separate file for every company. The Registrar's files may be inspected for a nominal fee by any member of the public. This is why the statutory accounts are often referred to as *published accounts*.

It is the responsibility of the company's directors to produce accounts which show a true and fair view of the company's results for the period and its financial position at the end of the period (see Section 3 of this chapter). The board evidence their approval of the accounts by the signature of one director on the balance sheet. Once this has been done, and the auditors have completed their report, the accounts are laid before the members of the company in general meeting. When the members have adopted the accounts they are sent to the Registrar for filing.

The requirement that the accounts show a true and fair view is paramount; although statute lays down numerous rules on the information to be included in the published accounts and the format of its presentation, any such rule **may be overridden** if compliance with it would prevent the accounts from showing a true and fair view.

2.1 Documents included in the accounts

The documents which **must be included by law** in the accounts laid before a general meeting of the members are:

(a)   A **profit and loss account** (or an income and expenditure account in the case of a non-trading company).

(b)   A **balance sheet** as at the date to which the profit and loss account is made up.

(c)   A **directors' report**.

(d)   An **auditors' report** addressed to the members (not to the directors) of the company.

In addition, FRS 1 requires a cash flow statement to be given. FRS 3 has also introduced the Statement of Total Recognised Gains and Losses. Here we will look at the profit and loss account and balance sheet.

2.2 The accounting reference period

The Companies Act 1985 contains the following rules about the length of a company's accounting period and the frequency with which it may be altered (ss 223 to 225).

(a) **Accounts must be prepared for an accounting reference period** (ARP), known as the 'financial year' of the company (whether it is a calendar year or not).

(b) **The profit and loss account should cover the ARP or a period ending not more than seven days before or after the accounting reference date.** Subsequent accounts should cover the period beginning on the day following the last day covered by the previous profit and loss account, and ending as specified above.

(c) **The balance sheet should give a true and fair view** of the state of affairs of the company as at the end of the financial year.

(d) **A company can decide its accounting reference period by giving notice to the Registrar of the date on which the accounting period will end each year.** This date will be the accounting reference date. S 225 makes provisions for the alteration of the accounting reference date.

2.3 The laying and delivery of accounts

S 241 CA 1985 specifies that the directors shall lay before the company in general meeting and also deliver to the Registrar, in respect of each accounting reference period, a copy of every document comprising the accounts for that period. However, the CA 1989 has amended the CA 1985 to allow the members of private companies to elect unanimously to dispense with general meetings. This does *not*, however, exempt the company from providing accounts to members.

Unlimited companies (with some exceptions) are exempt from the duty to deliver copies of their accounts to the Registrar.

The **period allowed for laying and delivering accounts** varies, and (s 244):

(a) For **private companies**, it is **ten months** after the end of the accounting reference period.

(b) For **other (public etc) companies**, it is **seven** months.

2.4 Accounting records

S 221 requires that every company's **accounting records must:**

(a) Be sufficient to show and explain the company's transactions.

(b) Disclose with reasonable accuracy at any time the financial position of the company at that time.

(c) Enable the directors to ensure that any profit and loss account or balance sheet gives a true and fair view of the company's financial position.

S 221 also specifies that accounting records **should contain:**

(a) Day-to-day entries for money received and paid, with an explanation of why the receipts and payments occurred (ie the nature of the transactions).

(b) A record of the company's assets and liabilities.

(c) Where the company deals in goods:

    (i) Statements of stocks held at the financial year end.

    (ii) Statements of stocktakings on which the figures in (c)(i) are based.

    (iii) With the exception of goods sold on retail, statements of all goods bought and sold identifying for each item the suppliers or customers.

S 222 specifies that the **accounting records are to be kept at the registered office** of the company or at such other place as the directors think fit, and they **should be open to inspection at all times by officers of the company.**

Also in s 222 is a **requirement for companies to preserve their accounting records:**

(a) **Private** companies, for **3 years**.

(b) **Other** companies, for **6 years**.

2.5 The classification of companies

A company is considered to be private unless it is registered as a public company. A major advantage for a public company is that it can raise new funds from the general public by issuing shares or loan stock; s 81 CA 1985 prohibits a private company from offering shares or debentures to the public.

2.6 Related party transactions

It is generally agreed that separate disclosure of transactions between a company and related parties may be needed if the user of the accounts is to be able to gain a full understanding of the results for the accounting period.

Two parties are considered to be related when:

(a) One party is able to exercise control or significant influence over the other party.

(b) Both parties are subject to common control or significant influence from the same source.

For example, companies within the same group will be related parties, or a company and its directors will be related parties.

3 The format of accounts

FAST FORWARD

The CA85 sets out balance sheet and profit and loss account proformas for **published accounts**. Learn the main headings so that you can write them out quickly in the exam.

Exam focus point

If you are in a hurry or revising, skip or skim the explanations in Paragraph 3.1 and go straight to the proformas in Paragraphs 3.2 and 4.

3.1 The form and content of the balance sheet

The Companies Act 1985 sets out **two formats** for the balance sheet, one **horizontal and** the other **vertical. Once a company has chosen a format it must adhere to it for subsequent financial years** unless, in the opinion of the directors, there are special reasons for a change. Details of any change and the reason for it must be disclosed by note to the accounts.

Each item on the balance sheet format is referenced by letters and roman and Arabic numbers. These reference labels do not have to be shown in a company's published accounts but are given in the Act for the guidance of companies and are relevant in identifying the:

(a) Extent to which information may be combined or disclosed by note (rather than on the face of the accounts).

(b) Headings and sub-headings which may be adapted or re-arranged to suit the special nature of the company.

(c) Items which do not need to be disclosed in modified accounts for small and medium-sized companies.

The following points should be borne in mind.

(a) Any item preceded by letters or roman numbers **must** be shown on the face of the balance sheet, unless it has a nil value for both the current and the previous year.

(b) Items preceded by arabic numbers **may** be amalgamated:

(i) If their individual amounts are not material.

(ii) If amalgamation facilitates the assessment of the company's state of affairs (but then the individual items must be disclosed by note).

(c) Items preceded by arabic numbers **may** be:

(i) Adapted (eg title altered)
(ii) Re-arranged (in position)

In any case where the special nature of the company's business requires such an alteration.

(d) Any item required to be shown **may** be shown in greater detail than required by the prescribed format.

(e) A company's balance sheet (or profit and loss account) **may** include an item not otherwise covered by any of the items listed, except that the following must not be treated as assets in any company's balance sheet:

(i) Preliminary expenses.
(ii) Expenses of and commission on any issue of shares or debentures.
(iii) Costs of research.

Schedule 4 includes the following notes about the balance sheet format.

(a) **Concessions, patents, licences, trademarks**, etc (Item B I 2) may only be shown if:

(i) They were acquired at a purchase cost, and do not consist of goodwill
(ii) Or they are assets created by the company itself.

(b) **Goodwill** (Item B I 3) should be included only to the extent that it is purchased goodwill.

(c) **Own shares** (Item B III 7). CA 1985 allows a company to purchase or acquire its own shares.

(d) **Debtors** (Items C II 1 – 6). Any amounts not falling due until after more than one year should be disclosed separately.

(e) **Debenture loans** (Items E1 and H1). Convertible loans should be shown separately from other debenture loans.

(f) **Payments received (in advance) on account** (Items E3 and H3). These should be shown unless they are accounted for as deductions from the value of stocks (as in the case of progress payments for work in progress on long-term contracts).

3.2 The form and content of the profit and loss account

The Companies Act 1985 sets out two **horizontal and** two **vertical formats** for the profit and loss account. The rules applying to the balance sheet formats described above also apply to the profit and loss account.

The two different formats are distinguished by the way in which expenditure is analysed. Format 1 analyses costs by type of operation or function, whereas Format 2 analyses costs by items of expense.

The following points should be borne in mind.

(a) Every profit and loss account **must show the company's profit or loss on ordinary activities before taxation**, no matter what format is used nor how much it might be amended to suit the circumstances of a particular case.

(b) Every profit and loss account must also show, as additional items:

(i) Amounts to be **transferred to reserves**, or amounts to be withdrawn from reserves.

(c) Amounts representing income may not be set off against items representing expenditure (just as assets and liabilities may not be 'netted off' in the balance sheet).

Below are proforma balance sheets and profit and loss accounts.

PROFORMA BALANCE SHEET (VERTICAL FORMAT)

				£	£	£
A	CALLED UP SHARE CAPITAL NOT PAID*					X
B	FIXED ASSETS					
	I	Intangible assets				
		1	Development costs	X		
		2	Concessions, patents, licences, trade marks and similar rights and assets	X		
		3	Goodwill	X		
		4	Payments on account	X		
					X	
	II	Tangible assets				
		1	Land and buildings	X		
		2	Plant and machinery	X		
		3	Fixtures, fittings, tools and equipment	X		
		4	Payments on account and assets in course of construction	X		
					X	
	III	Investments				
		1	Shares in group undertakings †	X		
		2	Loans to group undertakings †	X		
		3	Associated undertakings †	X		
		4	Loans to associated undertakings	X		
		5	Other investments other than loans	X		
		6	Other loans	X		
		7	Own shares	X		
					X	
						X

C   CURRENT ASSETS

    I   Stocks

1	Raw materials	X		
2	Work in progress	X		
3	Finished goods and goods for resale	X		
4	Payments on account	X̲		
			X	

    II Debtors

1	Trade debtors	X		
2	Amounts owed by group undertakings †	X		
3	Amounts owed by associated undertakings	X		
4	Other debtors	X		
5	Called up share capital not paid*	X		
6	Prepayments and accrued income**	X̲		
			X	

    III Investments

1	Shares in group undertakings †	X		
2	Own shares	X		
3	Other investments	X̲		

    IV Cash at bank and in hand   X̲

                                                 X

D   PREPAYMENTS AND ACCRUED INCOME**   X

E   CREDITORS: AMOUNTS FALLING DUE WITHIN ONE YEAR

1	Debenture loans	X	
2	Bank loans and overdrafts	X	
3	Payments received on account	X	
4	Trade creditors	X	
5	Bills of exchange payable	X	
6	Amounts owed to group undertakings †	X	
7	Amounts owed to associated undertakings	X	
8	Other creditors including taxation and social security	X	
9	Accruals and deferred income ***	X̲	
			(X)

F   NET CURRENT ASSETS (LIABILITIES)   X̲

G   TOTAL ASSETS LESS CURRENT LIABILITIES   X

H   CREDITORS: AMOUNTS FALLING DUE AFTER MORE THAN ONE YEAR

1	Debenture loans	X	
2	Bank loans and overdrafts	X	
3	Payments received on account	X	
4	Trade creditors	X	
5	Bills of exchange payable	X	
6	Amounts owed to group undertakings †	X	
7	Amounts owed to associated undertakings	X	
8	Other creditors including taxation and social security	X	
9	Accruals and deferred income***	X̲	
			(X)

PROFORMA BALANCE SHEET (VERTICAL FORMAT)

			£	£	£
I	PROVISIONS FOR LIABILITIES				
	1	Pensions and similar obligations †	X		
	2	Taxation, including deferred taxation	X		
	3	Other provisions	X̲		
				(X)	
J	ACCRUALS AND DEFERRED INCOME ***			(X̲)	
					(X̲)
					X̲
K	CAPITAL AND RESERVES				
	I	Called up share capital			X
	II	Share premium account			X
	III	Revaluation reserve			X
	IV	Other reserves			
		1 Capital redemption reserve			X
		2 Reserve for own shares			X
		3 Reserves provided for by the articles of association			X
		4 Other reserves			X̲
					X
	V	Profit and loss account			X
					X̲

(*), (**), (***). These items may be shown in either of the positions indicated.

Both vertical formats of the profit and loss account are reproduced below.

PROFORMA PROFIT AND LOSS ACCOUNT: FORMAT 1

		£	£
1	Turnover		X
2	Cost of sales *		(X)
3	Gross profit or loss *		X
4	Distribution costs *	(X)	
5	Administrative expenses *	(X)	
			(X)
			X
6	Other operating income		X
			X
7	Income from shares in group undertakings †	X	
8	Income from shares in associated undertakings †	X	
9	Income from other fixed asset investments	X	
10	Other interest receivable and similar income	X	
			X
			X
11	Amounts written off investments	(X)	
12	Interest payable and similar charges	(X)	
			(X)
	Profit or loss on ordinary activities before taxation		X
13	Tax on profit or loss on ordinary activities		(X)
14	Profit or loss on ordinary activities after taxation		X
15	Extraordinary income	X	
16	Extraordinary charges	(X)	
17	Extraordinary profit or loss	X	
18	Tax on extraordinary profit or loss	(X)	
			X
			X
19	Other taxes not shown under the above items		(X)
20	Profit or loss for the financial year		X

* These figures will all include depreciation.

Note. This is the most common form of the profit and loss account, and the form you are most likely to meet in the exam.

PROFORMA PROFIT AND LOSS ACCOUNT: FORMAT 2

			£	£	£
1	Turnover				X
2	Change in stocks of finished goods and work in progress			(X) or	X
3	Own work capitalised				X
4	Other operating income				X
					X
5	(a) Raw materials and consumables		(X)		
	(b) Other external charges		(X)		
				(X)	
6	Staff costs:				
	(a) wages and salaries		(X)		
	(b) social security costs		(X)		
	(c) other pension costs		(X)		
				(X)	
				(X)	
7	(a) Depreciation and other amounts written off tangible and intangible fixed assets **		(X)		
	(b) Exceptional amounts written off current assets		(X)		
				(X)	
8	Other operating charges			(X)	
					(X)
9	Income from shares in group undertakings †			X	
10	Income from shares in associated undertakings †			X	
11	Income from other fixed asset investments			X	
12	Other interest receivable and similar income			X	
					X
					X
13	Amounts written off investments			(X)	
14	Interest payable and similar charges			(X)	
					(X)
	Profit or loss on ordinary activities before taxation				X
15	Tax on profit or loss on ordinary activities				(X)
16	Profit or loss on ordinary activities after taxation				X
17	Extraordinary income			X	
18	Extraordinary charges			(X)	
19	Extraordinary profit or loss			X	
20	Tax on extraordinary profit or loss			(X)	
					X
					X
21	Other taxes not shown under the above items				(X)
22	Profit or loss for the financial year				X

** This figure will be disclosed by way of a note in Format 1.

Note that because the captions have Arabic number references, they do not have to be shown on the face of the profit and loss account but may instead be shown in the notes.

<table>
<tr><td>**Exam focus point**</td><td>Do not worry about memorising these formats. During your revision phase you will do a lot of exam-standard questions and you will get very used to the formats.</td></tr>
</table>

3.3 FRS 28 Corresponding amounts

Corresponding amounts for the previous financial year **must be shown for items in the primary financial statements and the notes. Where** a corresponding amount for the previous year is **not properly comparable** with an amount disclosed for the current year, **the previous year's amount should be adjusted** and the basis for adjustment disclosed in a note to the financial statements.

3.4 Some items in more detail

In the balance sheet, item A and item CII5 are 'called up share capital not paid'. This item is more relevant to other countries in the EU than to Britain (remember that the Fourth Directive applies to all EU countries). However, if at the balance sheet date a company has called up some share capital and not all the called up amounts have been paid, these will be a short-term debt (see Chapter 12 on the issue of shares). This would probably be shown (if material) as item CII5. Item A should not be expected in the accounts of British companies.

Item BIII7 in the balance sheet, investments in 'own shares', refers to shares which have been bought back by the company, but which have not yet been cancelled.

'Turnover' is defined by the 1985 Act as **'the amounts derived from the provision of goods and services, falling within the company's ordinary activities, after deduction of:**

    (a)   **Trade discounts.**
    (b)   **Value added tax.**
    (c)   **Any other taxes based on the amounts so derived'.**

'Cost of sales' (format 1) is **not defined**, nor are 'distribution costs', nor are 'administrative expenses'. The division of costs between these three categories is based on accepted practice.

Format 1, unlike Format 2, does not itemise depreciation and wages costs, but:

    (a)   Provisions for depreciation charged in the year
    (b)   Wages and salaries, social security costs and other pension costs

Must be disclosed separately in notes to the accounts.

The Act extends the requirements of FRS 3 about extraordinary profits or losses (see later chapters). The extraordinary profit or loss must be shown as the gross amount, with taxation on it separately disclosed. **Extraordinary items are now extremely rare**.

The profit and loss account must show profit or loss for the financial year. Statutory Instrument 2947 now brings UK practice into line with International, in that dividends paid are no longer shown on the face of the profit and loss account. They will be shown in the reconciliation of movements in shareholders' funds. Proposed dividends are no longer accounted for.

In itemising staff costs, wages and salaries consist of gross amounts (net pay plus deductions) and social security costs comprise employer's National Insurance contributions.

4 Notes to the accounts

Part III of the Fourth Schedule deals with notes to the balance sheet and profit and loss account. These are sub-divided into:

    (a)   Disclosure of accounting policies.
    (b)   Notes to the balance sheet.
    (c)   Notes to the profit and loss account.

A note to the accounts must disclose the accounting policies adopted by the company (including the policy used to account for depreciation or the fall in value of assets). This gives statutory backing to the disclosure requirement in FRS 18. Companies must also now state that all relevant accounting standards have been complied with and if not, what the departures are and the reasons for the departure.

The following example shows a *pro forma* profit and loss account and balance sheet with the required notes covering your syllabus. These notes are expanded in the subsequent chapters on different accounting standards and disclosures.

STANDARD PLC
PROFIT AND LOSS ACCOUNT FOR THE YEAR ENDED
31 DECEMBER 20X5

	Notes	£'000	£'000
Turnover	2		X
Cost of sales			X
Gross profit			X
Distribution costs			X
Administrative expenses			X
Operating profit	3		X
Income from fixed asset investments			X
			X
Interest payable and similar charges	6		X
Profit before taxation			X
Taxation	7		X
Profit for the period			X

STANDARD PLC
BALANCE SHEET AS AT 31 DECEMBER 20X5

	Notes	£'000	£'000
Fixed assets			
Intangible assets	9		X
Tangible assets	10		X
Fixed asset investments	11		X
			X
Current assets			
Stocks	12	X	
Debtors	13	X	
Cash at bank and in hand		X	
		X	
Creditors: amounts falling due within one year	14	X	
Net current assets			X
Total assets less current liabilities			X
Creditors: amounts falling due after more than one year	16		X
Accruals and deferred income	17		X
			X
Capital and reserves			
Called up share capital	18		X
Share premium account	19		X
Revaluation reserve	19		X
General reserve	19		X
Profit and loss account	19		X
			X

Approved by the board on .... Director

The notes on pages XX to XX form part of these accounts.

NOTES TO THE ACCOUNTS

1   **Accounting policies**

(a)   These accounts have been prepared under the historical cost convention of accounting and in accordance with applicable accounting standards.

(b)   Depreciation has been provided on a straight line basis in order to write off the cost of depreciable fixed assets over their estimated useful lives. The rates used are:

Buildings	X%
Plant and machinery	X%
Fixtures and fittings	X%

(c)   Stocks have been valued at the lower of cost and net realisable value.

(d)   Development expenditure relating to specific projects intended for commercial exploitation is carried forward and amortised over the period expected to benefit commencing with the period in which related sales are first made. Expenditure on pure and applied research is written off as incurred.

Notes

(a)   Accounting policies are those followed by the company and used in arriving at the figures shown in the profit and loss accounts and balance sheet.

(b)   CA 1985 requires policies in respect of depreciation and foreign currency translation to be included. Others are required by accounting standards insofar as they apply to the company.

2   **Turnover**

Turnover represents amounts derived from the provision of goods and services falling within the company's ordinary activities, after deduction of trade discounts, value added tax and any other tax based on the amounts so derived.

	Turnover	Profit before tax
Principal activities	£'000	£'000
Electrical components	X	X
Domestic appliances	X	X
	X	X
Geographical analysis		
UK	X	
America	X	
Europe	X	
	X	

Notes

(a)   Directors are to decide on classification and then apply them consistently.

(b)   Geographical analysis must be by destination of sale.

(c)   If the directors believe this disclosure to be seriously prejudicial to the business the information need not be disclosed.

(d)   The profit after tax figures are only required by SSAP 25 (see Chapter 14) for larger companies.

3   **Operating profit**

Operating profit is stated after charging:

	£'000
Depreciation	X
Amortisation	X
Hire of plant and machinery (SSAP 21: see Chapter 6)	X
Auditors' remuneration	X
Exceptional items	X
Directors' emoluments (see note 4)	X
Staff costs (see note 5)	X
Research and development	X

Notes

Separate totals are required to be disclosed for:

(a)   Audit fees and expenses
(b)   Fees paid to auditors for non-audit work

This disclosure is not required for small or medium-sized companies.

Question

Auditors' remuneration

Alvis Ltd receives an invoice in respect of the current year from its auditors made up as follows.

	£
Audit of accounts	10,000
Taxation computation and advice	1,500
Travelling expenses: audit	1,100
Consultancy fees charged by another firm of accountants	1,600
	14,200

What figure should be disclosed as auditors' remuneration in the notes to the profit and loss account?

Answer

	£
Audit of accounts	10,000
Expenses	1,100
Taxation computation and advice	1,500
	12,600

The consultancy fees are not received by the auditors.

4   **Directors' emoluments**

New requirements for the disclosure of directors' remuneration were introduced by *The Company Accounts (Disclosure of Directors' Emoluments) Regulations 1997* (SI 1997/570). A distinction is made between listed/AIM companies and unlisted companies.

5   **Employee information**

(a)   The **average number of persons** employed during the year.

(b)   **Employment costs**

	£'000
Aggregate wages and salaries	X
Social security costs	X
Other pension costs	X
	X

6   **Interest payable and similar charges**

	£'000
Interest payable on:	
Bank overdrafts and loans	X
Other loans	X
Lease and HP finance charges allocated for the year	X
	X

Note

Similar charges might include arrangement fees for loans.

7   **Taxation**

	£'000
UK corporation tax (at x% on taxable profit for the year)	X
Transfer to/from deferred taxation	X
Under/over provision in prior years	X
Unrelieved overseas taxation	X
	X

Note

The rate of tax must be disclosed.

8   **Dividends**

These are no longer shown on the face of the profit and loss account.

9   **Intangible fixed assets**

	Development expenditure £'000
Cost	
At 1 January 20X5	X
Expenditure	X
At 31 December 20X5	X
Amortisation	
At 1 January 20X5	X
Charge for year	X
At 31 December 20X5	X
Net book value at 31 December 20X5	X
Net book value 31 December 20X4	X

Note

The above disclosure should be given for each intangible asset.

10 Tangible fixed assets

	Freehold land and Buildings £'000	Leasehold land and Buildings		Plant and machinery £'000	Fixtures and fittings £'000	Total £'000
		Long leases £'000	Short leases £'000			
Cost (or valuation)						
At 1 Jan 20X5	X	X	X	X	X	X
Additions	X		X		X	X
Revaluation	X					X
Disposals	(X)			(X)	(X)	(X)
At 31 Dec 20X5	X	X	X	X	X	X
Depreciation						
At 1 Jan 20X5	X	X	X	X	X	X
Charge for year	X	X	X	X	X	X
Revaluation	(X)					(X)
Disposals	(X)			(X)	(X)	(X)
At 31 Dec 20X5	X	X	X	X	X	X
Net book value						
At 31 Dec 20X5	X	X	X	X	X	X
At 31 Dec 20X4	X	X	X	X	X	X

Notes

(a) Long leases are $\geq$ 50 years unexpired at balance sheet date.

(b) Classification by asset type represents arabic numbers from formats.

(c) Motor vehicles (unless material) are usually included within plant and machinery.

(d) Revaluations in the year: state for each asset revalued:

(i) Method of valuation

(ii) Date of valuation

(iii) The historical cost equivalent of the above information as if the asset had not been revalued

11 Fixed asset investments

	£'000
Shares at cost	
At 1 January 20X5	X
Additions	X
Disposals	(X)
At 31 December 20X5	X

The market value (in aggregate) of the listed investments is £X.

Note

An AIM investment is *not* a listed investment. All stock exchanges of repute allowed. Aggregate market value (ie profits less losses) to be disclosed if material.

12   Stocks

	£'000
Raw materials and consumables	X
Work in progress	X
Finished goods	X
	X

The replacement cost of stock is £X higher than its book value.

13   Debtors

	£'000
Trade debtors	X
Other debtors	X
Prepayments and accrued income	X
	X

14   Creditors: amounts falling due within one year

	£'000
Debenture loans: 8% stock 20X9	X
Bank loans and overdrafts	X
Trade creditors	X
Other creditors including taxation and social security (see note 15)	X
Accruals and deferred income	X
	X

The bank loans and overdraft are secured by a floating charge over the company's assets.

Notes

(a)   Give details of security given for all secured creditors.

(b)   Include the current portion of instalment creditors here.

15   Other creditors including taxation and social security

	£'000
UK corporation tax	X
Social security	X
	X

Notes

(a)   Liabilities for taxation and social security must be shown separately from other creditors.

(b)   Dividend liabilities to be disclosed separately.

16   Creditors: amounts falling due after more than one year

	£'000
8½% unsecured loan stock 20Y9	X

Notes

(a)   Very long-term creditors:

(i)   Disclose the aggregate amount of debentures and other loans:

(1)   Payable after more than five years

(2)   Payable by instalments, any of which fall due after more than five years

(ii)   For (1) and (2) disclose the terms of repayment and rates of interest.

(b) Debentures during the year, disclose:

    (i)   Class issued

    (ii)   For each class

        (1)   Amount issued

        (2)   Consideration received

(c) As per FRS 25, redeemable preference shares will now appear under long-term creditors.

17 Accruals and deferred income

	£'000
Government grants received	X
Credited to profit and loss account	(X)
	X

Note

Alternative presentation if not included as part of creditors, which saves dividing the accruals or deferred income amount between within and greater than one year.

18 Called up share capital

	£1 ordinary shares £'000	10% preference Shares (non-redeemable) £'000
Authorised		
Number	X	X
Value	X	X
Allotted		
Number	X	X
Value	X	X

Notes

(a) Disclose number and nominal value for each class, both authorised and allotted.

(b) *Shares issued during the year*, disclose:

    (i)   Classes allotted

    (ii)   For each class

        (1)   Number and aggregate nominal value allotted

        (2)   Consideration received

(c) Only non-redeemable preference shares are now included under equity

19 Reserves

Reserve movements are no longer shown on the face of the profit and loss account. They will be shown in the **reconciliation of movements in shareholders funds**.

	Share premium £'000	Revaluation £'000	General £'000	Profit and loss £'000
At 1 January 20X5	X	X	X	X
Retained profit for the year				X
Revaluation		X		
Transfers			X	X
At 31 December 2095	X	X	X	X

BPP
LEARNING MEDIA

20 **Contingent liabilities**

Note: governed by FRS 12.

21 **Events after the balance sheet date**

Note: governed by FRS 21.

22 **Capital commitments**

	£'000
Amounts contracted but not provided for	X

Note

This figure is not included in the balance sheet as it is simply a note of future obligations to warn users of likely future capital expenditure.

Question
Formats

The best way to learn the format and content of published accounts and notes is to practice questions. However, you must start somewhere, so try to learn the above formats, then close this text and write out on a piece of paper:

(a)   A standard layout for a balance sheet and profit and loss account

(b)   A list of notes to these accounts which are generally required

4.1 Filing exemptions for small and medium-sized companies

Small and medium-sized entities (SMEs) are allowed certain 'filing exemptions': **the accounts they lodge with the Registrar of companies, and which are available for public inspection, need not contain all the information which must be published by large companies.**

This concession allows small and medium-sized companies to reduce the amount of information about themselves available to, say, trading rivals. It **does *not* relieve them of their obligation to prepare full statutory accounts, because all companies,** regardless of their size, **must prepare full accounts for approval by the shareholders.**

Small and medium-sized companies must therefore balance the expense of preparing two different sets of accounts against the advantage of publishing as little information about themselves as possible. Many such companies may decide that the risk of assisting their competitors is preferable to the expense of preparing accounts twice over, and will therefore not take advantage of the filing exemptions.

A company qualifies as a **small or medium sized** company in a particular financial year **if**, for that year, **two or more** of the following **conditions are satisfied**.

	Small	Medium
(a) **Turnover** (must be adjusted proportionately in the case of an accounting period greater than or less than 12 months)	≤ £5.6m	≤ £22.8m
(b) **Balance sheet total** (total assets before deduction of any liabilities; A-D in the statutory balance sheet format)	≤ £2.8m	≤ £11.4m
(c) **Average number of employees**	≤ 50	≤ 250

Public companies can never be entitled to the filing exemptions whatever their size; nor can banking and insurance companies; nor can companies which are authorised persons under the Financial Services Act 1986; nor can members of groups containing any of these exceptions.

The form and content of the abbreviated accounts are contained in separate schedules of the Act: Schedule 8A for small companies and Schedule 245A for medium-sized companies. **Small companies may file an abbreviated balance sheet** showing only the items which, in the statutory format, are denoted by a letter or Roman number. They are **not required to file either a profit and loss account or a directors' report. No details need be filed of the emoluments of directors. Only limited notes to the accounts are required.**

The only exemptions allowed to medium-sized companies are in the profit and loss account. Turnover need not be analysed between a company's different classes of businesses, or its different geographical markets. The profit and loss account may begin with the figure of gross profit (or loss) by amalgamation of items 1, 2, 3 and 6 in Format 1, or of items 1 to 5 in Format 2.

If a small or medium-sized company files 'abbreviated accounts' a statement by the directors must appear above the director's signature on the balance sheet. The statement must be that the financial statements have been prepared in accordance with the special provisions of Part VII of the Act relating to small or (as the case may be) medium-sized companies.

Abbreviated accounts **must be accompanied by a special report** of the company's auditors stating that, in their opinion, the directors are entitled to deliver abbreviated accounts and those accounts are properly prepared. The text of the auditors' report on the full statutory accounts must be included as a part of this special report. A true and fair view is still required, however; if the shorter-form financial statements fail to give a true and fair view because of the use of exemptions, or for any other reason, the auditors should qualify their audit report in the normal way.

The requirements of the Companies Acts regarding SMEs are now incorporated into the 'one stop shop' FRSSE (Chapter 2).

4.2 Directors' report

FAST FORWARD

> The directors' report provides additional information regarding the directors and their holdings in the company, details of share capital transactions and other significant matters of interest to shareholders and others.

Attached to every balance sheet there must be a directors' report (s 234 CA 1985). (The Companies Act 1985 allows small companies exemption from delivering a copy of the directors' report to the Registrar of companies.) CA 1985 states specifically what information must be included in the directors' report (as well as what must be shown in the accounts themselves or in notes to the accounts as we saw above).

The directors' report is **largely a narrative report**, but certain figures must be included in it. **The purpose of the report is to give the users of accounts a more complete picture of the state of affairs of the company**. Narrative descriptions should help to 'put flesh on' the skeleton of details provided by the figures of the accounts themselves. However, in practice the directors' report is often a rather dry and uninformative document, perhaps because it must be verified by the company's external auditors, whereas the chairman's report need not be.

The directors' report is **expected to contain a fair review of the development of the business of the company during that year and of its position at the end of it.** No guidance is given on the form of the review, nor the amount of detail it should go into.

S 234 CA 1985 also requires the report to **show the** amount, if any, **recommended** for **dividend**.

4.3 The auditors' report

The annual accounts of a limited company must be audited by persons independent of the company. In practice, this means that the members of the company appoint a firm of Chartered Accountants or Chartered Certified Accountants to investigate the accounts prepared by the company **and report as to whether or not they show a true and fair** view of the company's results for the year and its financial position at the end of the year. **The audit report is governed by auditing regulations**.

When the auditors have completed their work they must prepare a report explaining the work that they have done and the opinion they have formed. In simple cases they will be able to report that they have carried out their work in accordance with auditing standards and that, in their opinion, the accounts show a true and fair view and are properly prepared in accordance with the Companies Act 1985. This is described as an **unqualified audit report**.

4.4 The chairman's report

Most large companies include a **chairman's report** in their published financial statements. This is **purely voluntary** as there is no statutory requirement to do so.

The chairman's report is not governed by any regulations and is often unduly optimistic. Many listed companies now include an Operating and Financial Review (OFR) in the annual report. This has been introduced to encourage more meaningful analysis.

Question		Company accounts

In between now and your examination obtain as many sets of company accounts or annual reports as you can. (You may like to use the Financial Times Free Annual Report Service for this purpose – look for the advert on the share price pages of the FT for information.) Read through the whole of each report and compare the format of the accounts and the disclosure of the notes with the contents of this chapter, and with the rest of this Study Text.

Chapter Roundup

- FRS 18 emphasises **accruals** and **going concern** as **bedrocks** of accounting. Prudence and consistency are simply 'desirable features'.

- The overriding requirement for financial statements is that they should present a 'true and fair view'. This concept has not been formally defined.

- Statutory accounts are part of the price to be paid for the benefits of limited liability. **Limited companies must produce such accounts annually and they must appoint an independent person to audit and report on them.**

- The CA85 sets out balance sheet and profit and loss account proformas for **published accounts**. Learn the main headings so that you can write them out quickly in the exam.

- The directors' report provides additional information regarding the directors and their holdings in the company, details of share capital transactions and other significant matters of interest to shareholders and others.

Quick quiz

1   The two bedrocks of accounting are:

    A   Accruals, prudence
    B   Prudence, consistency
    C   Consistency, accruals
    D   Going concern, accruals

2   An estimation technique is the method used to establish the estimated monetary amounts associated with the selected measurement bases.

    True   ☐

    False   ☐

3   What does CA 1985 say about a 'true and fair view'?

4   What points are made by the legal opinions sought regarding a 'true and fair view'?

5   The period allowed for layout and delivery of accounts.

    •   Private companies .... months

    •   Public companies .... months

6   Turnover is defined by the Companies Act as the amounts derived from the provision of goods and services falling within the company's ordinary activities after deduction of which of the following.

    A   Carriage inwards
    B   Trade discounts
    C   VAT
    D   Carriage out
    E   Other sales taxes
    F   Stock losses

7

	Small company	Medium company
Turnover	....	....
Total assets	....	....
Average number of employees	....	....

8   List eight disclosures required in the directors' report.

9   Companies must disclose their creditor payment policy in the financial statements.

    True   ☐

    False   ☐

10   The chairman's report is a statutory requirement.

    True   ☐

    False   ☐

11   Explain the accruals basis of accounting in no more than fifty words.

Answers to Quick Quiz

1   Going concern and accruals

2   True

3   CA 1985 does not define a 'true and fair view' (see para 3.1)

4   Accuracy and completeness are required. It is a dynamic concept. Judges will have regard to the practices of professional accountants, but acknowledge there may be no consensus among them.

5   Ten, seven

6   B, C and E

7

	Small company	*Medium company*
Turnover	≤£5.6m	≤£22.8m
Total assets	≤£2.8m	≤£11.4m
Average number of employees	≤50	≤250
		(5.7)

8   See paragraph 4.3

9   False, Only if they are a public company or they fail to meet the requirements for small or medium companies.

10 False.

11 The accruals basis of accounting requires the **non-cash impact** of transactions to be reflected in the financial statements for the **period in which they occur** and not, for example, in the period any cash involved is received or paid.

Now try the question below from the Exam Question Bank

Number	Level	Marks	Time
Q4	Examination	25	45 mins

Fixed assets

4

Topic list	Syllabus reference
1 Statutory provisions relating to all fixed assets	C2
2 FRS 15 *Tangible fixed assets*	C2
3 Revaluation	C2
4 SSAP 19 *Accounting for investment properties*	C2
5 SSAP 4 *Accounting for government grants*	C2

Introduction

In Section 1, before we look at individual accounting standards, we will review the **Companies Act disclosure requirements** relating to fixed assets. Refer back to Chapter 3 to put these requirements into context. Remember that these provisions apply to *all* fixed assets.

You should already have examined the principles of **depreciation** in your earlier studies. If you are in any doubt about the possible methods of depreciation, refer back to your earlier study material.

The other two standards covered in this chapter are on **investment properties** and **government grants**. These are quite straightforward. Develop a sound knowledge of their main provisions and make sure that you can do the relevant exercises.

Study guide

		Intellectual level
C	**FINANCIAL STATEMENT**	
2	**Tangible fixed assets**	
(a)	Define and compute the initial measurement of a fixed (including a self-constructed) asset.	2
(b)	Identify subsequent expenditure that may be capitalised (including borrowing costs) distinguishing between capital and revenue items.	2
(c)	Discuss the requirement of relevant accounting standards in relation to the revaluation of fixed assets.	2
(d)	Account for revaluation and disposal gains and losses for fixed assets	2
(e)	Compute depreciation based on cost and revalued amounts and on assets that have two or more significant parts (complex assets).	2
(f)	Apply the provisions of relevant accounting standards in relation to accounting for government grants.	2
(g)	Discuss why the treatment of investment properties should differ from other properties.	2
(h)	Apply the requirements of relevant accounting standards for investment property.	2

Exam guide

This is a key area and quite straightforward. Tangible fixed assets may come up as part of a question or subject matter from two or more sections of this chapter may be tested in a full question.

1 Statutory provisions relating to all fixed assets

FAST FORWARD

A number of accounting regulations on the valuation and disclosure of fixed assets are contained in the **Companies Act 1985**.

The standard balance sheet format of CA 1985 divides fixed assets into three categories:

(a) **Intangible assets** (BI in the CA 1985 format).
(b) **Tangible assets** (BII).
(c) **Investments** (BIII).

In this chapter we will deal with the general rules of the CA 1985 relating to *all* fixed assets. These may be considered under two headings.

(a) **Valuation:** the amounts at which fixed assets should be stated in the balance sheet.
(b) **Disclosure:** the information that should be disclosed in the accounts regarding:

- Valuation of fixed assets
- Movements on fixed asset accounts during the year.

1.1 Valuation of fixed assets

1.1.1 Cost

The two key ways of acquiring a tangible fixed asset are either by purchase or by self-production.

Purchased asset: Its cost is simply the purchase price plus any expenses incidental to its acquisition.

Asset produced by a company for its own use: This should be included at 'production cost' which *must* include:

(a)   **Cost of raw materials**
(b)   **Consumables** used
(c)   Other **attributable direct costs** (such as labour)

Production cost **may** additionally **include**:

(a)   **A reasonable proportion of indirect costs**
(b)   **Interest** on any capital borrowed to **finance production** of the asset.

The amount of **capitalised interest** must however be disclosed in a note to the accounts.

1.1.2 Depreciation

The **'cost'** of any fixed asset having a limited economic life, whether purchase price or production cost, **must be reduced by provisions for depreciation** calculated to write off the cost, less any residual value, **systematically over the period of the asset's useful life**. This very general requirement is supplemented by the more detailed provisions of FRS 15 *Tangible fixed assets* which is dealt with in the next section.

Any provision for **impairment** should be disclosed on the **face of the profit and loss account or by way of note**. Where a provision becomes **no longer necessary**, because the conditions giving rise to it have altered, it should be **written back**, and again **disclosure** should be made.

1.2 Fixed assets valuation: alternative accounting rules

Although the Companies Act 1985 maintains **historical cost** principles as the **normal basis** for the preparation of accounts, **alternative bases** allowing for **revaluations** and **current cost accounting are permitted provided that**:

(a)   The **items affected** and the **basis of valuation** are **disclosed** in a note to the accounts;

(b)   The **historical cost** in the current and previous years is **separately disclosed** in the balance sheet or in a note to the accounts. Alternatively, the difference between the revalued amount and historical cost may be disclosed.

Key term

> Using the **alternative accounting rules**, the appropriate value of any fixed asset (ie its **current cost or market value**), rather than its purchase price or production cost, **may be included in the balance sheet**.

Here is a diagram to help clarify the options available under CA 1985, schedule 4.

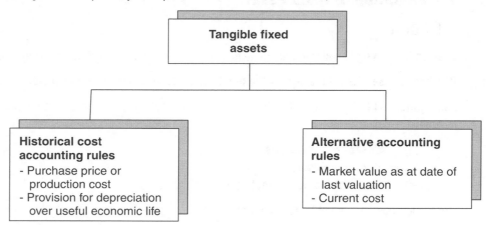

Where appropriate, depreciation may be provided on the basis of the new valuation(s), such depreciation being referred to in the Companies Act 1985 as the 'adjusted amount' of depreciation. For profit and loss account purposes, **FRS 15** (see below) specifically states that depreciation must be charged on the **revalued amount** and that the *whole* charge must be taken to the **profit and loss account**.

1.3 Revaluation reserve

Key term

> Where the value of any fixed asset is determined by using the **alternative accounting rules**, the amount of **profit or loss arising** must be credited or (as the case may be) debited to a separate reserve, the **revaluation reserve**. (Revised asset value – Net book value prior to valuation = Transfer to revaluation reserve)

1.3.1 Uses of revaluation reserve

The Companies Act 1985 states that an amount may be transferred from the revaluation reserve to the profit and loss account ie debit revaluation reserve and credit profit and loss reserve, if the amount:

- (a) was previously charged to profit and loss account
- (b) represents realised profit
- (c) relates to taxation on a profit or loss taken to the revaluation reserve, or
- (d) is no longer necessary for the valuation method used.

The revaluation reserve may also be used for a **bonus issue** of shares. No other debits to revaluation reserve are allowed.

The revaluation reserve must be **reduced** to the extent that the amounts standing to the credit of the reserves are, in the opinion of directors of the company **no longer necessary** for the purposes of the accounting policies adopted by the company.

The amount of a revaluation reserve must be shown under a **separate sub-heading** in **position KIII** on the **balance sheet**. However, the reserve need not necessarily be called a 'revaluation reserve'.

 Question   Revaluation

Studivation Ltd revalued a freehold building on 31 March 20X5 to £300,000. The original purchase cost 10 years ago was £180,000. Studivation Ltd depreciates freehold buildings over 40 years.

Show the accounting entries for the revaluation and the depreciation charge for the year ended 31 March 20X6.

Answer

(a)	*Revaluation*	£	£
	DEBIT Fixed asset cost (£300,000 – £180,000)	120,000	
	DEBIT Accumulated depreciation (£180,000 ÷ 40 × 10)	45,000	
	CREDIT Revaluation reserve		165,000

(b)	*Depreciation charge*		
	DEBIT Depreciation (£300,000 ÷ 30)	10,000	
	CREDIT Accumulated depreciation		10,000

1.4 Fixed assets: companies act disclosures

Notes to the accounts must show, for **each class** of **fixed assets**, an analysis of the **movements** on both **costs** and **depreciation provisions**. Refer back to the note on fixed assets in Chapter 3.

Where any **fixed assets** of a company (other than listed investments) are included in the accounts at an alternative accounting valuation, the **following information** must also be given:

(a) The **years** (so far as they are known to the directors) in which the assets were **severally valued** and the **several values**.

(b) In the case of assets that have been **valued** during the **financial period**, the **names** of the **persons** who valued them or particulars of their **qualifications** for doing so and (whichever is stated) the **bases of valuation** used by them.

A **note to the accounts** must **classify land and buildings** under the headings of:

(a) **Freehold property**.

(b) **Leasehold property**, distinguishing between:

   (i) **Long leaseholds**, in which the **unexpired term** of the lease at the balance sheet date is **not less than 50 years**.

   (ii) **Short leaseholds** which are all leaseholds other than long leaseholds.

2 FRS 15 Tangible fixed assets

FAST FORWARD

In the case of **tangible fixed assets**, Companies Act requirements are supplemented by the provisions of FRS 15 *Tangible fixed assets*.

Key term

Tangible fixed assets have physical substance and are held for:

- use in the production or supply of goods or services
- rental to others
- administration purposes

on a **continuing basis** in the **reporting entity's activities**.

They are held to **earn revenue** by their **use**, **not** from their **resale**.

2.1 Objective

FRS 15 deals with accounting for the initial measurement, valuation and depreciation of tangible fixed assets. It also sets out the information that should be disclosed to enable readers to understand the impact of the accounting policies adopted in relation to these issues.

2.2 Initial measurement

Exam focus point

> Initial measurement and capitalisation of subsequent expenditure were tested in the December 2001 paper.

A tangible fixed asset should **initially be measured at cost**.

Key term

> **Cost** is purchase price plus any costs directly attributable to bringing the asset into working condition for its intended use.

2.3 *Directly attributable costs*

Directly attributable costs include:

(a) **Direct labour** costs of using **own employees**

(b) **Acquisition costs**, eg stamp duty, import duties

(c) Cost of **site preparation** and clearance

(d) Initial **delivery and handling** costs

(e) **Installation** costs

(f) **Professional fees** eg legal and architect's fees

(g) The estimated cost of **dismantling and removing** the asset and restoring the site, to the extent that it is recognised as a provision under FRS 12 *Provisions, contingent liabilities and contingent assets* (discussed in Chapter 11). The fact that the prospect of such decommissioning costs emerges only some time after the original capitalisation of the asset (eg because of legislative changes) does not preclude their capitalisation.

Administration and other general overhead costs and employee costs not related to the specific tangible fixed asset are not directly attributable costs.

In general terms, directly attributable costs can be regarded as incremental costs that would have been avoided only if the tangible fixed asset had not been constructed as required.

2.3.1 Abnormal costs

Costs such as those arising from design error, wasted materials, industrial disputes, idle capacity or production delays are considered to be **abnormal** and **not directly attributable** to bringing the asset into **working condition** and its **intended use**. This approach is consistent with SSAP 9. They should therefore should **not be capitalised** as part of the cost of the asset.

2.3.2 Time frame for capitalisation

Capitalisation of **directly attributable costs** should **cease** when substantially all the activities that are necessary to get the tangible fixed asset ready for use are complete, even if the asset has not actually been brought into use. A tangible fixed asset is considered to be ready for use when its **physical construction is complete**.

2.3.3 Start-up or commissioning period

The costs associated with a **start-up** or **commissioning period** should be **included** in the cost of the tangible fixed asset **only where** the **asset is available for use** but **incapable** of operating at **normal levels without** such a **start-up** or **commissioning period**.

The costs of an **essential commissioning period** are included as part of the **cost of bringing the asset up to its normal operating potential**, and **therefore** as **part** of its **cost**.

However, there is no justification for regarding costs relating to other start-up periods, where the asset is available for use but not yet operating at normal levels.

Question   Start-up period 1

Halliday Inn has been is being built and opens for business in January 20X9. Demand is expected to build up slowly and high levels of room occupancy are only likely to be achieved over a period of several months.

Should any of the costs incurred in the run up to optimal occupancy of hotel be capitalised.

Answer

No. The hotel is able to operate at normal levels immediately on opening without necessarily having to go through a start up period in a slack season.

Question   Start-up period 2

Duncan Donatz Ltd has constructed a high speed machine for making holes of different shapes in doughnuts.

The machine is to be commissioned in two stages:

(a)   *Test run phase.* This phase is designed to ensure that the shapes are punched properly and the process operates smoothly and efficiently. During this run in phase, output will be restricted to test runs.

(b)   *Demand building phase.* During this phase output is expected to be low because the company is trying to achieve product acceptance of a different innovative type of doughnut. However, the machine is capable of operating at a normal level of output.

How should the costs relating to these two start up phases be treated?

Answer

Phase 1.   The relevant costs should be capitalised together with the cost of machine because the machine is **not capable** of operating at normal levels without such a start up or commissioning period.

Phase 2.   Costs associated with this period should be written off to profit and loss account. The machine is now capable of operating at normal levels and the low volumes are due to market factors.

From the above, it is important to be aware of the **practical distinction** between **two phases**:

(a) **Essential start-up** and **commissioning** phase, without which the asset is **incapable** of operating at normal levels.

(b) **Demand building phase** when output is built up to **full utilisation**.

2.3.4 Suspension of a revenue activity during construction

Operating losses that occur because a revenue activity has been suspended during the construction of a tangible fixed asset are not directly attributable costs. For example, if a restaurant closes for rebuilding, the revenue losses and other costs arising from the suspension of trading are not part of the cost of the new restaurant. Such losses are considered to be **too indirect** and **not linked sufficiently closely** with the **future economic benefits** to be obtained from the new asset.

Question   Suspension of trading

Café Edmondo Ltd has to close its restaurant for rebuilding.

Should the revenue losses and other costs arising from the suspension of trading be capitalised?

Answer

No. These losses are too indirect and not linked sufficiently closely with the economic benefits to be derived from the rebuilt restaurant.

Remember that the FRS 15 approach differs from the SSAP 9 approach to initial recognition. FRS 15 works on an **incremental cost approach,** whereas **SSAP 9** is based on **total absorption costing basis** and therefore does not prohibit recognition of general overheads.

2.4 Borrowing costs

Finance costs directly attributable to the construction of a fixed asset **may be capitalised** if it is **company policy** to do so. However, this **policy must be applied consistently**.

All finance costs that are **directly attributable** to the construction of a tangible fixed asset should be **capitalised** as part of the **cost of the asset**.

Key term

> **Directly attributable finance costs** are those that would have been **avoided** if there had been **no expenditure on the asset**.

If finance costs are capitalised, capitalisation should start when:

(a) Finance **costs** are being **incurred**
(b) Expenditure on the **asset** is being **incurred**
(c) **Activities** necessary to get the **asset ready** for use are **in progress**

Capitalisation of finance costs should cease when the asset is ready for use.

Sometimes construction of an asset may be completed in parts and each part is capable of being used while construction continues on other parts. An example of such an asset is a retail park consisting of several units. In such cases capitalisation of borrowing costs relating to a part should cease when substantially all the activities that are necessary to get that part ready for use are completed.

Sometimes **active development** on a tangible fixed asset might be **interrupted** for extended periods. During such periods, **capitalisation** of finance costs should be **suspended**.

The following disclosures are required in respect of capitalisation of borrowing costs.

(a) The accounting policy adopted
(b) The amount of borrowing costs capitalised during the period
(c) The amount of borrowing costs recognised in the profit and loss account during the period
(d) The capitalisation (interest) rate used to determine the amount of capitalised borrowing costs

Question

Capitalisation

On 1 January 20X6 Stremans plc borrowed £1.5m to finance the production of two assets, both of which were expected to take a year to build. Work started during 20X6. The loan facility was drawn down and incurred on 1 January 20X6, and was utilised as follows, with the remaining funds invested temporarily.

	Asset A	Asset B
	£'000	£'000
1 January 20X6	250	500
1 July 20X6	250	500

The loan rate was 9% and Stremans plc can invest surplus funds at 7%.

Required

Ignoring compound interest, calculate the borrowing costs which may be capitalised for each of the assets and consequently the cost of each asset as at 31 December 20X6.

Answer

		Asset A	Asset B
		£	£
Borrowing costs			
To 31 December 20X6	£500,000/£1,000,000 × 9%	45,000	90,000
Less investment income			
To 30 June 20X6	£250,000/£500,000 × 7% × 6/12	(8,750)	(17,500)
		36,250	72,500

	Asset A	Asset B
	£	£
Cost of assets		
Expenditure incurred	500,000	1,000,000
Borrowing costs	36,250	72,500
	536,250	1,072,500

2.5 Recoverable amount

The **amount recognised** when a tangible fixed asset is acquired or constructed should **not exceed its recoverable amount**. If it does, it should be written down accordingly to its recoverable amount.

Recoverable amount is defined as being the higher of

(a) Net realisable value (NRV)
(b) Value in use (VU)

It is not necessary to review tangible fixed assets for **impairment** when they are acquired or constructed. They need to be **reviewed for impairment** only if there is some **indication** that impairment has occurred. Such indications are specified in the current FRS 11 *Impairment of fixed assets and goodwill*. We will look at impairment in more detail later.

2.6 Subsequent expenditure

After a tangible fixed asset has been brought into use, in practice, there is likely to be **further money spent**.

(a)   **Revenue expenditure** which should be **written off** to the profit and loss account.

(b)   **Capital expenditure** which should be debited to **tangible fixed assets**.

2.6.1 Expenditure to be written off to profit and loss account

General rule

> Subsequent expenditure to ensure that a tangible fixed asset maintains its previously assessed standard of performance should be written off to profit and loss account as it is incurred.

Question

Yummy Foods Ltd has to regularly service and overhaul its labelling machines to ensure that the labels are properly aligned and the tins roll off the production line efficiently, in accordance with the company's production targets.

How should these cost be treated?

Answer

Such expenditure ensures that the machinery sustains its originally assessed standard of performance. Without such expenditure, the useful economic life or residual value is likely to be reduced and in consequence the depreciation charge would increase.

Hence the expenditure is effectively 'repairs and maintenance' to be expensed in the profit and loss account.

2.6.2 Expenditure to be capitalised

FRS 15 specifies three scenarios where subsequent expenditure should be capitalised.

(a)   It **enhances** the **economic benefits** over and **above previously assessed standards of performance**.

(b)   A **component** of an asset that has been treated **separately** for **depreciation purposes** (because it has a substantially different useful economic life from the rest of the asset) has been **restored** or **replaced**.

(c)   The expenditure related to a **major inspection** or **overhaul** that **restores economic benefits** that have been consumed and reflected in the depreciation charge.

2.6.3 Enhancement of economic benefits

FRS 15 offers two ways of **enhancing** the **economic benefits** that a tangible fixed asset might deliver:

(a) Mod**ifying the asset** to increase its capacity.

Eg a hotel reduces its non-productive communal areas to give it more bedrooms.

(b) **Upgrading the asset** to achieve a substantial **improvement** in the **quality** of the product or service provided to customers.

Eg a hotel re-upholsters its fabric furniture with leather to improve the quality of service provided to its guests.

2.6.4 Replacement of separately depreciated component

In these circumstances, the component is disposed of and replaced by a new asset.

| Question | Separate component 1 |

Safeair Ltd treats its aircraft engines separately for depreciation purposes. The engine on one of its aircraft caught fire on take off and has had to be replaced.

How should the cost of the replacement engine be treated?

| Answer |

The new engine should be capitalised as a fixed asset addition with the destroyed engine taken to disposal account and expensed via the profit and loss account.

General rule

Each component is depreciated over its **individual** useful life, so that the depreciation profile over the whole asset **more accurately reflects** the **actual** consumption of the asset's economic benefits.

2.6.5 Major overhauls and inspections

In addition to routine repairs and maintenance, some assets also require substantial expenditure every few years on major overhauls or inspections. Some examples found in practice are aircraft airworthiness inspections, ocean liner refits, theme park ride overhauls, refurbishment of kiln linings and replacing roofs of buildings.

| Question | Overhauls |

Safeair Ltd is required by law to overhaul its aircraft once every three years. Unless the overhauls are done, the aircraft cannot be flown.

How should the costs of the overhauls be treated?

| Answer |

The cost of the overhaul is capitalised when incurred because it restores the economic benefits flowing from the tangible fixed assets. The carrying amount representing the cost of benefits consumed is removed from the balance sheet.

The need to undertake an overhaul or inspection is acknowledged in the accounts by depreciating an amount of the asset that is equivalent to the inspection or overhaul costs over the period until the next inspection or overhaul. Hence, a **new asset** is **treated**, **in effect**, as being made up of **two elements**.

(a) **The core asset**. This is depreciated over its expected useful economic life.

(b) **The built-in overhaul cost**. This is depreciated over the period until the first actual overhaul takes place.

2.6.6 Decision to identify several economic lives

The **decision** whether to **identify separate components** or **future expenditures** on **overhauls** or **inspections** for **depreciation** over a **shorter useful economic life** than the rest of the tangible fixed asset is likely to **reflect various factors**.

(a) Whether the **useful economic lives** of the components are, or the period until the next inspection or overhaul is, **substantially different** from the useful economic life of the remainder of the asset

(b) The **degree of irregularity** in the **level of expenditures** required to restate the component or asset in different accounting periods

(c) Their **materiality** in the context of the financial statements.

The decision may be not to account for each tangible fixed asset as several different asset components or to depreciate part of the asset over a different timescale from the rest of the asset. In these circumstances, the cost of replacing, restoring, overhauling or inspecting the asset or components of the asset is not capitalised, but instead is recognised in the profit and loss account as incurred.

2.7 Depreciation

You need to have a good working knowledge of FRS 15.

The important point to note is that depreciation is the allocation of cost (or revalued amount), less estimated residual value, over expected useful life. It is not intended as a process of valuing assets.

Depreciation is consistent with the FRS 18 accruals basis of accounting. The cost is spread over the periods to which the cost relates, rather than being charged to the period in which the payment is made. This is in keeping with what the ASB *Statement of principles* refers to as 'time matching'.

2.7.1 Purpose of depreciation

As noted earlier, the Companies Act 1985 requires that all fixed assets having a limited economic life should be depreciated. **FRS 15** provides a useful discussion of the **purpose of depreciation** and supplements the statutory requirements in important ways.

Key term

Depreciation is defined in FRS 15 as the measure of the cost or revalued amount of the **economic benefits** of the tangible fixed asset that have been **consumed during the period**.

Consumption includes:

- wearing out
- using up
- other reduction in the useful economic life

Key term

of a tangible fixed asset, whether arising from:

- use
- effluxion (passage) of time
- obsolescence through either:
  - changes in technology
  - reduction in demand for the goods and services produced by the asset.

This definition includes

(a) **amortisation** of **assets** with a **pre-determined life**, such as a **leasehold**

(b) **depletion** of **wasting assets** such as **mines**.

2.7.2 General requirements

FRS 15 specifies the following general rules regarding depreciation.

(a) The depreciable amount of a tangible fixed asset should be allocated on a **systematic basis** over its **useful economic life**

(b) The depreciation method used should **reflect** as fairly as possible the **pattern** in which the asset's **economic benefits** are **consumed** by the company

(c) The depreciation charge for each period should be recognised as an **expense** in the profit and loss account unless it is permitted to be included in the carrying amount of another asset.

The general requirements of FRS 15 entail three key issues.

(a) Selecting a method which reflects the pattern of consumption

(b) Estimating the useful economic life and residual value

(c) Dealing with the impact of subsequent expenditure on depreciation

2.8 Methods of depreciation

A **variety of methods** can be used to allocate the depreciable amount of a tangible fixed asset. No specific method is stipulated.

FRS 15 mentions two common methods of depreciation.

(a) **Straight-line**. This method assumes that equal amounts of economic benefit are consumed in each year of the asset's life. Therefore the asset is written off in **equal instalments** over its **estimated useful economic life**.

(b) **Reducing balance**. Here the **depreciation rate** is applied to the **opening net book value**. This method charges more depreciation in the early years of an asset's life than in later years.

The closest FRS 15 gets to making a recommendation is to suggest that where the pattern of consumption of an asset's economic benefits is uncertain, straight-line method of depreciation is usually adopted. In practice this is the most widely used method.

2.9 Factors affecting depreciation

FRS 15 outlines the factors to be considered in determining the useful economic life, residual value and depreciation method of an asset.

(a) The **expected usage** of the asset by the entity, assessed by reference to the asset's **expected capacity** or **physical output**

(b) The **expected physical deterioration** of the asset through use or **effluxion of time**; this will depend upon the **repair and maintenance programme** of the entity both when the asset is in **use** and when it is **idle**

(c) Economic or technological obsolescence, for example arising from changes or improvements in production, or a change in the market demand for the product or service output of that asset

(d) Legal or similar limits on the use of the asset, such as the expiry dates of related leases

2.10 Review of useful economic life

General rule

> The **useful economic life** of a tangible fixed asset should be **reviewed** at the **end of each reporting period** and revised if expectations are significantly different from previous estimates.

If **useful economic life** is **revised**, the **carrying amount** (ie book value) of the tangible fixed asset at the date of revision is **depreciated** over the **revised remaining useful economic life** from that point onwards.

Remember that the useful economic life of a tangible fixed asset is an **accounting estimate**, not an accounting policy. In such cases, the standard accounting practice is **not to restate previous years' figures** when estimates are revised.

The approach is to depreciate the carrying amount of the tangible fixed asset over the remaining useful economic life, beginning in the period in which the change is made.

However, if future results could be materially distorted, the adjustment to accumulated deprecation should be recognised in the accounts in accordance with FRS 3 (normally as an exceptional item).

2.10.1 Example: review of useful economic life

B Ltd acquired a fixed asset on 1 January 20X2 for £80,000. It had a useful economic life of ten years and no residual value.

On 1 January 20X5 the total useful economic life was reviewed and revised to seven years.

What will be the depreciation charge for 20X5?

Solution

	£
Original cost	80,000
Depreciation 20X2 – 20X4 (80,000 × $^3/_{10}$)	(24,000)
Carrying amount at 1 January 20X5	56,000
Remaining useful economic life (7-3) =	4 years
Depreciation charge years 20X5 – 20X8 (56,000/4)	14,000

2.11 Revision of residual value

General rule

> Where residual value is material, it should be reviewed at the end of each period to take account of **expected technological changes**, but still based on prices prevailing at the date of acquisition (or revaluation).

A change in estimated residual value is **accounted for prospectively** over the asset's remaining useful economic life, except where the asset is impaired. If an impairment occurs, the asset should be written down immediately. (Impairment will be covered in more detail later in this text.)

When an asset is revalued, the residual value should also be reassessed, based on prices at the date of revaluation.

2.12 Revision of method of depreciation

General rule

> A change in depreciation method is permissible only on the grounds that the new method will give a **fairer presentation** of the results and of the financial position.

The depreciation method is an **accounting estimate**. Therefore, a change of method is not a change of accounting policy.

The carrying amount (ie book value) of the asset is depreciated on the new method over the remaining useful economic life, beginning in the period in which the change is made.

2.13 Two or more components of a fixed asset

General rule

> Where the tangible fixed asset comprises two or more major components with substantially different useful economic lives, each component should be accounted for separately for depreciation purposes and depreciated over its useful economic life.

Examples include:

    (a)   Land and buildings
    (b)   The structure of a building and items within the structure, such as general fittings

Freehold land usually has an indefinite life, unless subject to depletion (eg a quarry). Buildings have a limited life and are therefore depreciated.

Question   **Separate component 2**

What about the trading potential associated with a property valued as an operational entity, such as a hotel, pub or club? Should this be treated as a separate component?

Answer

No. The value and life of any trading potential is inherently inseparable from that of the property.

In effect, the asset is treated as though it were several different assets for depreciation purposes. FRS 15 also requires component depreciation if subsequent expenditure on replacing a component is to be capitalised.

2.14 Impact of subsequent expenditure

In calculating the useful economic life of an asset it is assumed that **subsequent expenditure** will be undertaken to **maintain** the **originally assessed standard of performance** of the asset (for example the cost of servicing or overhauling plant and equipment). Without such expenditure the depreciation expense would be increased because the useful life and/or residual value of the asset would be reduced. This type of expenditure is **recognised as an expense when incurred**.

In addition, subsequent expenditure may be undertaken that results in a **restoration** or **replacement** of a component of the asset that has been depreciated or an **enhancement** of **economic benefits** of the asset in excess of the originally assessed standard of performance. This type of expenditure may result in an extension of the **useful economic life of the asset** and represents **capital expenditure**.

Important!

> Subsequent expenditure does not obviate the need to charge depreciation.

2.15 Non-depreciation

General rule

> For tangible fixed assets other than non-depreciable land, the **only grounds** for not charging depreciation are that the depreciation charge and accumulated depreciation are **immaterial**.
>
> The depreciation charge and accumulated depreciation are immaterial if they would **not reasonably influence** the **decisions** of a **user** of the accounts.

An entity must be able to justify that the uncharged depreciation is not material in **aggregate** as well as for **each tangible fixed asset**. Depreciation may be immaterial because of **very long useful economic lives** or **high residual values** (or both). A high residual value will reflect the remaining economic value of the asset at the end of its useful economic life to the entity. These conditions may occur when **all the following are met**:

(a) The entity has a policy and practice of **regular maintenance and repair** (charges for which are recognised in the profit and loss account) such that the asset is kept to its previously assessed **standard of performance**

(b) The asset is **unlikely** to **suffer** from economic or technological **obsolescence** (eg due to potential changes in demand in the market following changes in fashion)

(c) Where estimated residual values are material:

    (i) The entity has a policy and practice of disposing of similar assets well before and end of their economic lives

    (ii) The **disposal proceeds** of similar assets (after excluding the effect of price changes since the date of acquisition or last revaluation) have **not** been **materially less than** their **carrying amounts**.

The above rules come into play in relation to what are known as **'trophy assets'**.

(a) **Top quality** buildings in desirable areas
(b) **Antique** fixtures and fittings
(c) **Historic** buildings

This approach was also advocated by the hotel, catering and public house industry on the grounds that their assets were regularly maintained and refurbished and therefore their useful economic life were not restricted.

However, where entities have avoided changing depreciation on the grounds of immateriality, they will nevertheless be required to perform impairment reviews under FRS 11. In practice, the **impairment review route** may prove **costly** and **counter-productive**, when the profit and loss account has nevertheless and **inevitably to suffer a hit** resulting from an impairment loss.

2.16 Impairment requirements

The application of impairment reviews in relation specifically to trophy assets has been touched on above. **Generally** tangible fixed assets other than non depreciable land, should be **reviewed for impairment** at the **end of the reporting** period where:

(a)   **No depreciation** is charged on the **grounds** that it would be **immaterial**.

(b)   The **estimated remaining useful economic life exceeds 50 years**.

The review should be in accordance with FRS 11 *Impairment of fixed assets and goodwill,* which will be discussed in more detail in the **next chapter**

2.17 Depreciation on revalued assets

Many companies **carry fixed assets** in their balance sheets at **revalued amounts**, particularly in the case of freehold buildings. When this is done, the **depreciation charge** should be calculated **on the basis of the revalued amount** (not the original cost).

As discussed above where the **residual value is material**, it should be **reviewed** at the **end of each reporting period** to take account of reasonably **expected technological changes**. A **change** in the **estimated residual value** should be **accounted for prospectively** over the asset's remaining useful economic life, **except** to the **extent** that the asset has been **impaired** at the **balance sheet date**.

2.18 Renewals accounting

Key term

> Where **renewals accounting** is adopted, the level of annual expenditure required to maintain the operating capacity of the infrastructure asset is treated as the depreciation charged for the period and is deducted from the carrying amount of the asset (as part of accumulated depreciation). Actual expenditure is capitalised (as part of the cost of the asset) as incurred.

Definable major assets or components within an infrastructure system or network with determinable finite lives should be treated separately and depreciated over their useful economic lives. For the remaining tangible fixed assets within the system or network, renewals accounting may be used if:

(a)   The infrastructure asset is a system that as a whole is intended to be maintained at a specified level of service by the continuing replacement and refurbishment of its components.

(b)   The level of annual expenditure required to maintain the operating capacity or service capability of the infrastructure asset is calculated from an asset management plan certified by a qualified, independent person.

(c)   The system or network is in a mature or steady state.

2.19 Disclosure requirements of FRS 15

The following information should be disclosed separately in the financial statements for each class of tangible fixed assets.

(a) The depreciation methods used

(b) The useful economic lives or the depreciation rates used

(c) Total depreciation charged for the period

(d) Where material, the financial effect of a change during the period in either the estimate of useful economic lives or the estimate of residual values

(e) The cost or revalued amount at the beginning of the financial period and at the balance sheet date

(f) The cumulative amount of provisions for depreciation or impairment at the beginning of the financial period and at the balance sheet date

(g) A reconciliation of the movements, separately disclosing additions, disposals, revaluations, transfers, depreciation, impairment losses, and reversals of past impairment losses written back in the financial period

(h) The net carrying amount at the beginning of the financial period and at the balance sheet date

2.20 Adverse feedback on FRS 15

FRS 15 has been largely welcomed, particularly the rules on revaluations (see below). However, some commentators have found problematic the treatment of subsequent expenditure where there is a major overhaul. As mentioned previously, the treatment has been described as 'contrived'.

3 Revaluation

> **FAST FORWARD**
>
> FRS 15 lays down detailed requirements concerning the revaluation of fixed assets. Directors can no longer choose to revalue certain assets and not others.

3.1 Policy basis

Before FRS 15, companies could pick and choose which of their assets they wished to revalue and when. This allowed companies to massage their balance sheet figures through the inclusion of meaningless **out of date valuations**, thereby **hindering comparability** between companies from year to year. FRS 15 puts a stop to this 'cherry picking'.

Basic requirements

An entity may adopt a policy of **revaluing tangible fixed assets**. Where this policy is adopted **it must be applied consistently** to all assets of the same class.

Where an asset is revalued its carrying amount should be its **current value** as at the balance sheet date, current value being the **lower of replacement cost and recoverable amount**. The recoverable amount, in turn, is the **higher** of **net realisable value** and **value in use**.

A **class of fixed assets** is 'a category of tangible fixed assets having a similar nature, function or use in the business of an entity'. (FRS 15)

Key terms

Replacement cost. The cost at which an **identical asset** could be **purchased** or **constructed**.

Depreciated replacement cost. Replacement cost with appropriate **deduction** for **age, condition and obsolescence**.

Recoverable amount. The higher of net realisable value and value in use.

Net realisable value. The **amount** at which an **asset could be disposed of**, less any **direct selling costs**.

Value in use. The **present value** of **future cash flows** obtainable as result of an asset's **continued use**, **including** those resulting from **ultimate disposal**.

Open market value. The **best price** that could be obtained between a **willing seller** and a **knowledgeable buyer**, assuming **normal market conditions**.

Existing use value. As for **open market value**, except that value is based on the **assumption** that the property can be used for the **foreseeable future** only for its **existing use**.

The above basic requirements can be summarised by the following diagram.

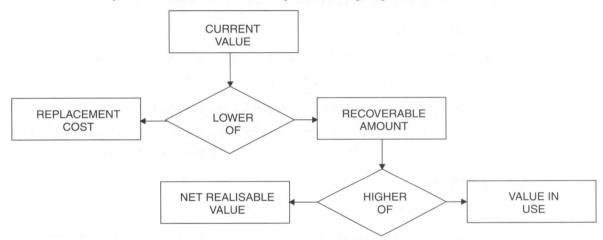

Remember the decision to adopt a policy of revaluation of tangible fixed assets is discretionary. Do not confuse this with other scenarios where the carrying value of a fixed asset should be adjusted:

(a) **FRS 15 rule** that:

'if the amount recognised when a tangible fixed asset is acquired or constructed exceeds its recoverable amount, it should be written down to its recoverable amount.'

(b) FRS 11 response to indications of impairment that requires:

'A review for impairment of a fixed asset (or goodwill) should be carried out if events or circumstances indicate that the carrying amount of the fixed asset (or goodwill) may not be recoverable.'

You may find the following diagram helpful in clarifying the scenarios where, in addition to annual depreciation, the carrying value of a tangible fixed asset needs to be adjusted.

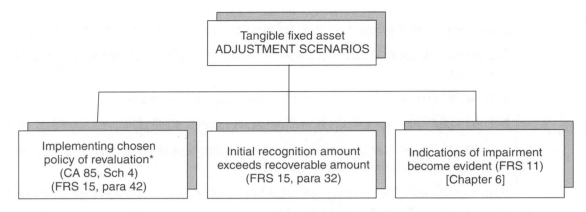

* We shall see later that in certain circumstances, a loss arising on revaluation is effectively tantamount to an impairment loss. However, you must remember that this arises from the revaluation policy route rather than the indications of impairment route.

3.2 Frequency of valuation

3.2.1 General rule

The valuation of properties should be carried out on the basis of a 5 year cycle.

(a)   A **full valuation** every **5 years**

(b)   An **interim valuation** in **year 3 of the five-year cycle**.

(c)   An **interim valuation also in years 1, 2 and 4** of the five-year cycle should also be done where it is likely that there has been a **material change in value**.

3.2.2 Valuers

FRS 15 specifies who may carry out a **full valuation**.

(a)   A qualified external valuer (eg a surveyor, who is independent of the company), or
(b)   A qualified internal valuer, but subject to review by a qualified external valuer.

An **interim valuation** may be done by an internal or external, qualified valuer.

3.2.3 Other tangible fixed assets

For certain types of assets (other than properties) eg company cars, there may be an **active second hand market** for the asset or **appropriate indices** may exist, so that the directors can establish the asset's value with **reasonable reliability** and therefore avoid the need to use the services of a qualified valuer.

For an index to be appropriate:

(a)   It must be appropriate to the class of asset, its location and conditions.
(b)   It must take into account the impact of technological change.
(c)   It must have a proven track record of regular publication.
(d)   It is expected to be available in the foreseeable future.

Such valuations must be performed **every five years**, and also in the **intervening years** where there has been a **material change in value**.

3.3 Valuation basis

The following valuation bases should be used for properties that are not impaired.

TYPE	BASIS
Specialised properties	• These should be valued on the basis of **depreciated replacement cost**. • Specialised properties are those which, due to their **specialised** nature, there is **no general market** in their existing use or condition, except as part of a sale of the business in occupation. Eg oil refineries, hospitals, chemical works, power stations, schools, colleges and universities where there is no competing market demand from other organisations using these types of property in the locality. • The objectives of using depreciated replacement cost is to make a realistic estimate of the current cost of constructing an asset that has the same service potential as the existing asset.
Non-specialised properties	• These should be valued on the basis of **existing use value** (EUV), plus notional directly attributable acquisition costs where material.
Properties surplus to an entity's requirements	• These should be valued on the basis of open market value (OMV) less expected direct selling costs where these are material. They may be specialised or non-specialised properties. • The **assumption** supporting the specified accounting treatment is that they **will be sold**.

Where there is an indication of impairment, an impairment review should be carried out in accordance with FRS 11. The asset should be recorded at the lower of revalued amount (as above) and recoverable amount.

Tangible fixed assets other than properties should be valued using market value or, if not obtainable, depreciated replacement cost.

3.4 Reporting gains and losses on revaluations

3.4.1 General points

A revaluation gain or loss arises when there is a difference between the valuation of a tangible fixed asset when compared to its carrying amount.

Revaluation gains and losses are dealt with through either:

(a)   Profit and loss account; or
(b)   Statement of total recognised gains and losses

This will depend on the underlying scenarios, which are explored below.

3.5 Tangible fixed asset revalued upwards

Gain	Treatment of gain
Asset not previously revalued	• Gain credited to revaluation reserve. • Reported in STRGL.
Asset previously revalued upwards	• Gain credited to revaluation reserve. • Reported in STRGL.

Gain	Treatment of gain
Asset subjected to previous revaluation loss	• Portion of gain that in effect reverses the prior revaluation losses should be credited to profit and loss account, ie restores the asset to its depreciated historical cost. • Any gain in excess of the above should be credited to revaluation reserve and reported via STRGL.

The above points are covered in the example 3.24, below.

3.6 Tangible fixed asset revalued downwards

Loss	Treatment of loss
Loss clearly due to consumption of economic benefits eg physical damage or deterioration in quality of goods or services provided by the asset.	All of the loss must be debited to profit and loss account. It does not matter that the asset involved might have been previously revalued upwards. (FRS 15 suggests that this is really an impairment loss)
Losses owing to other causes than the above. Asset previously revalued upwards.	These losses should be recognised in the following order. (a) In STRGL until the carrying amount reaches depreciated historical cost. (b) In the profit and loss account.
Losses owing to other causes than top item above. Asset not previously revalued upwards.	These losses should be recognised in the profit and loss account.

3.7 Depreciation on revalued assets

Basic requirements

Where an asset has been revalued, the depreciation charge is based on the revaluation amount, less residual value, from the date of revaluation.

The asset's residual value should also be re-estimated on revaluation, based on values prevailing at that date.

This approach entails two different and conflicting issues.

(a)   The profit and loss account bears the cost of the economic benefits consumed, as measured by the enhanced depreciation charge based on the revalued figure for the tangible fixed asset.

(b)   Distributable profits should not be prejudiced by the additional depreciation caused by the revaluation.

The remedy to this problem is to make an annual transfer from revaluation reserve to profit and loss account covering the amount for the additional depreciation caused by the revaluation. This is permitted by Companies Act 1985 and also represents best practice. This is illustrated in the example below.

3.8 Example: impact of revaluation on depreciation

Kevin Ltd acquires a buffing machine costing £100,000 on 1 July 20X4, which it depreciates at 10% straight line. The company policy is to charge a full year's depreciation in the year of acquisition but none in the year of disposal.

When the directors came to prepare the accounts for the year ended 31 December 20X7, the directors decided to obtain a full professional valuation, to be incorporated into the financial statements.

Yasmin, Nicole and Associates valued the asset at £108,000. There was no change in the estimated life.

It is now 31 December 20X9. Show the entries in the relevant accounts in the book of Kevin Ltd.

Solution

PLANT AND EQUIPMENT

		£			£
1.7.X4	Cost of buffing machine	100,000	31.12.X7	Balance c/d	108,000
31.12.X7	Revaluation reserve (W3)	8,000			
		108,000			108,000
1.1.X8	Balance b/d	108,000			

PROVISION FOR DEPRECIATION

		£			£
1.7.X7	Revaluation reserve (W3)	40,000	31.12.X4	Charge for year (W1)	10,000
			31.12.X5	Charge for year (W1)	10,000
			31.12.X6	Charge for year (W1)	10,000
			31.12.X7	Charge for year (W1)	10,000
		40,000			40,000
			31.12.X8	Charge for year (W2)	18,000
			31.12.X9	Charge for year (W2)	18,000

DEPRECIATION CHARGE

		£			£
31.12.X4	Provision (W1)	10,000	31.12.X4	Tfr to P+L a/c	10,000
31.12.X5	Provision (W1)	10,000	31.12.X5	Tfr to P+L a/c	10,000
31.12.X6	Provision (W1)	10,000	31.12.X6	Tfr to P+L a/c	10,000
31.12.X7	Provision (W1)	10,000	31.12.X7	Tfr to P+L a/c	10,000
31.12.X8	Provision (W2)	18,000	31.12.X8	Tfr to P+L a/c	18,000
31.12.X9	Provision (W2)	18,000	31.12.X9	Tfr to P+L a/c	18,000

REVALUATION RESERVE

		£			£
31.12.X8	Add'l depn to P+L a/c	8,000	31.12.X7	Adj. On buffing machine (W3)	48,000
31.12.X9	Add'l depn to P+L a/c	8,000			
Note: These adjustments go directly to P+L reserve, avoiding the current year's P+L account.			*Note:* This adjustment will be done via STRGL.		

PROFIT AND LOSS RESERVE (depreciation adjustments only)

		£
31.12.X8	Depn adj	8,000
31.12.X9	Depn adj	8,000

Workings

1   £100,000 ÷ 10 years = £10,000 per annum.

2   £108,000 ÷ 6 years = 18,000 per annum.

3   *Revaluation of buffing machine*

	£
Cost	100,000
Accumulated depreciation to 31.12.X7	(40,000)
Net book value at 31.12.X7	60,000
Revaluation increase	48,000
Valuation as at 31.12.X7	108,000

Note that the concept of 'split depreciation' is not acceptable ie. the charge for the year may not be split between a portion based on historical cost and a portion based on the revaluation increase with these being debited to profit and loss account and revaluation reserve, respectively.

3.9 Example: Revaluation movements

The following details relate to Moggy Ltd which has a December year end.

• *Year ended 31 December 20X0:*	Acquired a building for £100 million Depreciation; 5% straight line
• *31 December 20X5:*	A professional valuation was obtained in the amount of £42 million.
• *31 December 20X8:*	Due to improved economic circumstances, the value of the building increased to £132 million.

Identify the adjustments required and indicate what statements would be affected.

Solution

20X0 to 20X5

• Annual depreciation charge £5m (£100m × 5%)
• Recognised via the profit and loss account.

31 December 20X5

	£m
Cost	100
Accumulated depreciation (£5m × 6 years)	(30)
Net book value	70
Revalued amount 20X5	42
Revaluation loss charged to profit and loss account	28

20X6 to 20X8

• Annual depreciation of £42m ÷ 14 = £3m
• Processed through the profit and loss account.

31 December 20X8

	£m
Previous revalued amount	42
Accumulated depreciation (£3m × 3 years)	(9)
Carrying value before 20X8 valuation	33
New valuation 20X8	132
Revaluation gain 20X8	99

The portion of the gain that in effect reverses the prior revaluation loss should be credited to profit and loss account, ie restores the asset to depreciated historical cost.

	£m
Historical cost	100
Less depreciation (£5m × 9 years)	(45)
Depreciated historical cost 30.12.X8	55

Hence:

	£m
Depreciated historical cost 30.12.X8	55
Carrying value before 20X8 revaluation	(33)
Portion of gain credited to profit and loss	22
Remainder of gain credited to revaluation reserve via STRGL	77
Revaluation gain 20X8, as above	99

Reconciliation of movements in reserves:

	£m
Depreciation – £5m × 6 years	30
– £3m × 3 years	9
Depreciation 20X0 to 20X8	39
Revaluation loss 31.12.X5	28
Revaluation gain 31.12.X8	(22)
Total debits to profit and loss account 20X0 to 20X8	45
Credit to revaluation reserve 31.21.X8	(77)
Net movement 20X0 to 20X8	(32)

Being:

	£m
Historical cost 20X0	100
Valuation 20X8	(132)
Net amount written up	(32)

3.10 Gains and losses on disposal

Basic requirements

> Gains or losses on disposal of revalued tangible fixed assets should be accounted for in the profit and loss account of the period in which the disposal occurs.
>
> The profit or loss is calculated as the difference between the
>
> - net sale proceeds
> - carrying amount, whether accounted for or
>   - the historical cost accounting rules
>   - alternative accounting rules

3.11 Credit balance on revaluation reserve

Where this relates to an asset which has been sold, this now becomes realised. It should therefore be transferred to profit and loss account.

Question   Disposal

Refer back to the Moggy Ltd example above in 3.9.

How would you account for the disposal if the building had been sold on 1 January 20Y1 for £35 million?

Answer

	£m
Valuation at 31.12.X8	132
Accumulated depreciation (£12m × 2*years)	24
Carrying value at 31.12.Y0	108
Proceeds of sale disposal 1.1.Y1	(35)
Loss on disposal	73

* No charge in year of disposal

- This loss should be processed to disposals account in the usual way.

- In addition, the balance on the revaluation reserve is now realised and can be taken to profit and loss account.

Adjustments

		DEBIT £m	CREDIT £m
DEBIT	Bank – proceeds of sale	35	
DEBIT	Accumulated depreciation	24	
DEBIT	Loss on disposal of fixed assets	73	
CREDIT	Fixed assets		132

Standard journal entry for disposal

		DEBIT £m	CREDIT £m
DEBIT	Revaluation reserve (W1)	63	
CREDIT	Profit and loss reserve		63

Transfer of gain, now realised, to profit and loss reserves.

Working

REVALUATION RESERVE

		£m		£m
31.12.X9	Release to P+L a/c	7	31.12.X8 Revaluation gain	77
31.12.Y0	Release to P+L a/c	7		
31.12.Y1	Realised gain transferred to P+L a/c	63		
		77		77

Proof:

	£m
Profit realised per revaluation reserve	63
Loss on carrying value	(73)
Net loss	(10)

Being:

	£m
Historical cost	100
Less depreciation (£5m × 11 years)	(55)
Depreciation historical cost 1.1.Y1	45
Proceeds of disposal 1.1.Y1	(35)
Net loss, as above	10

4 SSAP 19 Accounting for investment properties

FAST FORWARD

SSAP 19 conflicts with the statutory requirement to depreciate all fixed assets with a finite useful economic life, by stating that **investment properties** need not ordinarily be depreciated.

The introduction of SSAP 12, with its requirement that all fixed assets including freehold buildings (though excluding freehold land) should be depreciated, caused a stir amongst property investment companies who feared that their reported profits would be severely reduced. The lobby was sufficiently strong to result in the publication of a separate standard for such properties.

4.1 Definition of investment properties

SSAP 19 defines an investment property as follows.

Key term

> '.... An **investment property** is an interest in land and/or buildings:
>
> (a)   In respect of which **construction** work and **development** have been **completed**
>
> (b)   Which is held for its **investment potential**, any **rental income** being **negotiated** at **arm's length**.
>
> '....The following are **exceptions** from the definition:
>
> (a)   A property which is **owned** and **occupied** by a company for its **own purposes** is not an investment property.
>
> (b)   A property **let to** and **occupied** by **another group company** is not an investment property for the purposes of its own accounts or the group accounts.'

Question
Investment properties

Lucy Limited and its subsidiaries are engaged in manufacturing of sweets and confectionery in Luton. It owns three properties which are held in a different ways.

(a)   **Broadacres** is its factory and office building.

(b)   **Kandikorna** is a retail premises let to Darren Limited a subsidiary which deals directly with the public.

(c)   **High Standards** is an office block which is let to a firm of accountants on an arms length rental basis.

Identify which properties are investment properties.

Answer

(a)   Broadacres is **not** an **investment property** because it is owned and **occupied** by Lucy Limited for its **own purposes**.

(b)   Kandikorna is **not** an **investment property** because it is let and **occupied** by **another group company**.

(c)   High Standards is an **investment property** because it **meets the criteria** for being classified as an investment property.

4.2 Justification for special approach to investment properties

Investment properties, as defined, are **not held** to be **consumed within** the **operations** of an enterprise, but instead for their **investment potential**.

The sale of an investment property is also unlikely to materially impact on the manufacturing trading operations of an enterprise.

What is of **prime importance** to users of accounts, regarding investment properties, is their **current value** and any **charges in their current value**, rather than a systematic calculation of annual depreciation.

4.3 Accounting treatment

Per **SSAP 19**, investment properties should not be depreciated. Instead they should be **revalued annually** at their **open market value** and the aggregate **surplus** or **deficit** arising transferred to **investment revaluation reserve** (IRR) via the STRGL.

There may be circumstances where the **deficit** relating to an **individual investment property** is expected to be **permanent**. In such case, the deficit should be charged in the **profit and loss account** for the period.

Sometimes an investment property is held on a **lease** with a relatively **short unexpired term**, ie 20 years or less. Here the **carrying value** of lease must be **depreciated** over its **useful economic life** in accordance with the approach set out in **FRS 15**, the charge going to profit and loss account. The objective is to avoid the situation whereby the rentals received for such short leases are credited to profit and loss accounts whilst on the other hand any annual movements arising from revaluations are processed to investment revaluation reserve via STRGL. Under these requirements, both debit (depreciation) and credit (rental income) would be processed to the profit and loss account.

SSAP 19 specifies various criteria for determining open market value.

(a)   The valuation **need not** be made by **qualified** or **independent valuers**.

(b)   However, **disclosure** is required regarding:

   (i)   The **names** and **qualifications** of the valuers
   (ii)   The **basis** of valuation used
   (iii)   **Whether** the person making the valuation is an **employee** or **officer** of the company.

(c)   Sometimes investment properties represent a **substantial proportion** of the **total assets** of a **major enterprise** (eg a listed company). In these instances, their **valuation** would normally be carried out:

   (i)   **Annually** by a **qualified person** having **recent experience** of valuing **similar properties**

   (ii)   At least every **five years** by an **external valuer**.

 Question | Revaluation reserve

Kikaround Limited acquired two investment properties in Manchester on 31 December 20X6.

	Keegan Towers £'000	Ferguson Towers £'000	Total £'000
Cost 31.12.X6	100	100	200
Valuation			
31.12.X7	70	140	210
31.12.X8	85	145	230
31.12.X9	120	70	190

The deficits on Keegan Towers arising on 31 December 20X7 and 20X8 are expected to be temporary whereas the deficit on Ferguson Towers arising on 31 December 20X9 is expected to be permanent.

Show the investment revaluation reserve for the years ended 31 December 20X7, 20X8 and 20X9.

Answer

INVESTMENT REVALUATION RESERVE

			£'000				£'000
31.12.X7	Keegan Towers		30	31.12.X7	Ferguson Towers		40
31.12.X7	Balance	c/d	10				
			40				40
31.12.X8	Balance	c/d	30	1.1.X8	Balance b/d		10
				31.12.X8	Keegan Towers		15
				31.12.X8	Ferguson Towers		5
			30				30
31.12.X9	Ferguson Towers*		75	1.1.X9	Balance b/d		30
31.12.X9	Balance	c/d	20	31.12.X9	Keegan Towers		35
				31.12.X9	Transfer to P+L a/c (Ferguson)		30
			95				95

* This could have been debited directly to profit and loss account with a transfer of £45,000 credits from IRR, to give effect to the £30,000 permanent deficit in respect of Ferguson Towers.

The carrying value of investment properties and investment revaluation reserve should be disclosed prominently in the accounts.

Investment properties can be owned by **ordinary trading companies as well as property investment companies**. If the assets of a company consist wholly or mainly of investment properties, this fact should also be disclosed.

Further points to note about SSAP 19 are as follows.

(a) SSAP 19 acknowledges that exemption from depreciation for investment property is **contrary** to the depreciation rules in the **Companies Act 1985**. This departure is considered permissible because the Act states that compliance with the rules is a subordinate requirement to the **'overriding purpose of giving a true and fair view'**.

Where the true and fair override is invoked the notes to the accounts must disclose particulars of that departure, the reasons for it, and its effect. (See Chapter 3.)

(b) SSAP 19 **does not apply to immaterial items**.

4.4 Disposals

SSAP 19 does not deal with the problem of accounting for the disposal of investment properties. However, FRS 3 *Reporting financial performance* **states the following** in relation to the disposal of any revalued fixed assets.

(a) The **profit or loss** on **disposal** of an **asset** should be accounted for as the **difference** between the **sale proceeds** and the **net carrying amount**.

(b) Any **revaluation surplus** remaining is now **realised**, so FRS 3 requires this to be transferred to the **profit and loss reserve**.

4.5 Diminution in value: Amendment to SSAP 19

Previously, under SSAP 19, any deficit on the IRR had to be taken to the profit and loss account. In other words, where the value of one or more investment property fell so far that the total IRR was insufficient to cover the deficit, then the excess was taken to the profit and loss account. SSAP 19 has now been amended as follows.

(a) **Any diminution in value which is considered permanent should be charged to the profit and loss account.**

(b) **Where diminution is temporary, a temporary IRR deficit is allowed.**

Question   **Investment properties**

Compare the accounting treatment of land and buildings as laid down by FRS 15 with the accounting treatment of investment properties as laid down by SSAP 19 and explain why a building owned for its investment potential should be accounted for differently from one which is occupied by its owners.

Answer

FRS 15 requires that all fixed assets should be depreciated, including freehold buildings. The only exception to this is freehold land which need only be depreciated if it is subject to depletion, for example, quarries or mines.

Where a property is revalued, depreciation should be charged so as to write off the new valuation over the estimated remaining useful life of the building.

SSAP 19, by contrast, recognises that there is a **conceptual difference** between *investment properties* and other fixed assets. Such properties are not depreciated and are carried in the balance sheet at open market value, re-assessed every year. An external valuation should be made at least once every five years.

Changes in the value of an investment property should not be taken to the profit and loss account. In other words, a company **cannot claim profit** on the **unrealised gains on revaluation** of such properties. The revaluation should be disclosed as a movement on an 'investment revaluation reserve'. Should this reserve show a **debit balance** (a loss) the **full amount** of the balance should be removed by charging it to the **profit and loss account**, unless the loss in value is considered to be temporary.

SSAP 19 acknowledges that there is a difference between investment properties and other fixed assets, including non-investment properties. Investment properties are held 'not for consumption in the business operations but as investments, the disposal of which would not materially affect any manufacturing or trading operations of the enterprise'.

It follows from this that the item of prime importance is the current value of the investment properties and changes in their current value rather than a calculation of systematic annual depreciation should be reported.

5 SSAP 4 Accounting for government grants

FAST FORWARD

Government grants can be **revenue-based** or **capital-based**. **Revenue grants** are credited to revenue in line with the revenue costs which they are intended to cover. **Capital grants** are credited to revenue over the useful life of the fixed asset for which they have been granted.

Key term

Government grants are assistance provided by government to an entity.

(a)   In the form of **cash** or **transfers** of **other assets**.

(b)   In **return** for compliance with **certain conditions** relating to the operating activities of the entity.

Note: (Items such as free consultancy services are not grants)

In practice, the range of grants available is quite wide and may change regularly, reflecting changes in policy introduced by various governments. You therefore need to understand the general principles included in SSAP4 and be able to apply them to any scenario you encounter in your exams.

Note that for these purposes, government includes local, national or international government, agencies and similar bodies.

Basic requirements

(a)   Government grants should be recognised in the profit and loss account so as to match them with the expenditure towards which they are intended to contribute.

(b)   Government grants should not be recognised in the profit and loss account until the conditions for this receipt have been compiled with and there is reasonable assurance that the grant will be received.

5.1 Revenue-based grants

These are given to **cover** some of the costs of various categories of **revenue expenditure**.

No particular problems arise in respect of revenue grants as they can be **credited** to **revenue** in the **same period** in which the **revenue expenditure** to which they **relate** is charged.

5.2 Capital-based grants

These are given to **cover** a **proportion** of the **costs of certain** items of **capital expenditure** (for example buildings, plant and machinery), and may be **treated** in a **number of ways**.

(a)   **Credit** the **full amount** of the capital grant to **profit and loss account**.

(b)   **Credit** the **full amount** of the capital grant to a **non distributable reserve**.

In (a) there is an immediate impact on earnings and in (b) there is no impact on earnings. In both cases the concept of matching costs and revenues is not applied. The grant, like the depreciation cost of fixed assets, should apply to the full life of the assets and so should be spread over that period of time.

SSAP 4 states that grants relating to fixed assets should be credited to revenue over the expected useful life of the assets and this can be done in one of two ways:

(a)   **By reducing the acquisition cost of the fixed asset** by the amount of the grant, and providing depreciation on the reduced amount.

(b)   By **treating** the amount of the grant **as a deferred credit and transferring a portion of it to revenue** annually.

5.3 Example: accounting for government grants

Needham Limited receives a government grant towards the cost of a new grinder.

- Cost £100,000.

- Grant = 20%

- Expected life = four years

- Residual value = Nil.

- Expected profits of the company, before accounting for depreciation on the new machine or the grant = £50,000 per annum over expected life of the grinder.

The two alternative approaches outlined in SSAP 4 would give different accounts presentations.

Solution

(a)   *Reducing the cost of the asset approach*

	Year 1 £	Year 2 £	Year 3 £	Year 4 £	Total £
Profits					
Profit before depreciation	50,000	50,000	50,000	50,000	200,000
Depreciation*	(20,000)	(20,000)	(20,000)	(20,000)	(80,000)
Profit	30,000	30,000	30,000	30,000	120,000

*The depreciation charge on a straight line basis, for each year, is ¼ of £[100,000 – 20,000 (20%)] = £20,000.

Balance sheet at year end (extract)

	£	£	£	£
Fixed asset at cost	80,000	80,000	80,000	80,000
Accumulated depreciation	(20,000)	(40,000)	(60,000)	(80,000)
Net book value	60,000	40,000	20,000	–

(b)   *Treating the grant as a deferred credit approach*

	Year 1 £	Year 2 £	Year 3 £	Year 4 £	Total £
Profits					
Profit before grant & dep'n	50,000	50,000	50,000	50,000	200,000
Depreciation	(25,000)	(25,000)	(25,000)	(25,000)	(100,000)
Grant	5,000	5,000	5,000	5,000	20,000
Profit	30,000	30,000	30,000	30,000	120,000

Balance sheet at year end (extract)

	Year 1	Year 2	Year 3	Year 4
Fixed asset at cost	100,000	100,000	100,000	100,000
Accumulated depreciation	(25,000)	(50,000)	(75,000)	(100,000)
Net book value	75,000	50,000	25,000	–
Deferred income				
Government grant				
deferred credit	15,000	10,000	5,000	–

Exam focus point

A government grant may arise as part of an accounts preparation question.

5.4 Assessment of alternative approaches

The annual profits under both methods are the same, and both methods apply the matching concept in arriving at the profit figure. Reducing the cost of the asset is simpler since, by reducing the depreciation charge, the amount of the grant is automatically credited to revenue over the life of the asset.

The **deferred credit method has the advantage of recording fixed assets at their actual cost, which allows for comparability and is independent of government policy**.

However, the netting off **method** may be in **conflict with the Companies Act 1985** in that the asset would no longer be carried at its purchase price or production cost.

Legal opinion confirms the unacceptability of the netting off approach and hence the credit method is preferable.

Where the second method is used then **the amount of the deferred credit, if material, should be shown separately in the balance sheet**. SSAP 4 states that it should not be shown as part of the shareholders' funds and it is suggested that the amount should appear under the heading of **'Accruals and deferred income'** in the balance sheet.

The SSAP requires the **disclosure of the accounting policy** adopted for government grants **and** also requires disclosure of:

(a) The impact of government grants on the **company's profits** in the period **and/or** on its **financial position** generally.

(b) Any **potential liability** to repay grants.

(c) The nature of **government aid other than grants** which has materially affected profits in the period and an estimate of the impact, where possible.

A grant may be awarded to assist the financing of a project as a whole, where both capital and revenue expenditure are combined. In such cases the accounting treatment should be to match the grant with the relative proportions of revenue and capital expenditure incurred in the total project cost. For example, if two thirds of a project's costs are capital in nature and one third is revenue in nature, then any grant awarded against the whole project cost should be treated as one-third revenue-based and two thirds capital-based.

Exam focus point

> You may be asked to discuss whether a given company's policy for the treatment of government grants accords with the ASB *Statement of principles*.

Question — Government grant

Kaytal plc is to receive a relocation grant of 30% of total expenses incurred. In 20X8 the company incurred the following costs associated with the relocation.

	£'000
Capital cost of factory	2,000
Training costs	200
Removal/relocation costs	300
	2,500

Required

Show the treatment of the government grant for 20X8.

Answer

		£'000
Grant received = 30% × 2,500 =		750
Capital expenditure		2,000
Revenue expenditure		500
		2,500

Revenue grant = $\dfrac{500}{2,500} \times 750 =$ 150

Capital grant = $\dfrac{2,000}{2,500} \times 750 =$ 600

750

		£'000	£'000
DEBIT	Cash	750	
CREDIT	P&L account		150
CREDIT	Deferred income		600

Section summary

The following accounting treatments apply.

    (a)   *Revenue-based grants*

        DEBIT   Cash
        CREDIT   P & L account

        In the period in which the revenue expenditure to which the grant relates is charged.

    (b)   *Capital-based grants*

        DEBIT   Cash
        CREDIT   Accruals and deferred income

        When the grant is received.

        DEBIT   Accruals and deferred income
        CREDIT   P & L account

        Over the useful life of the related fixed asset.

Disclosure will be as follows.

    (a)   *Balance sheet: deferred income note*

	£
Balance at 1.1.20X0	X
Grants received during year	X
Transferred to profit and loss account	(X)
Balance at 31.12.20X0	X

    (b)   *Profit and loss account*: credit under 'other operating income'.

Exam focus point

> A full question on tangible fixed assets might combine two or even all three of the standards covered here.

Chapter Roundup

- A number of accounting regulations on the valuation and disclosure of fixed assets are contained in the **Companies Act 1985**.

- In the case of **tangible fixed assets**, Companies Act requirements are supplemented by the provisions of FRS 15 *Tangible fixed assets*.

- FRS 15 lays down detailed requirements concerning the revaluation of fixed assets. Directors can no longer choose to revalue certain assets and not others.

- **SSAP 19** conflicts with the statutory requirement to depreciate all fixed assets with a finite useful economic life, by stating that **investment properties** need not ordinarily be depreciated.

- Government grants can be **revenue-based** or **capital-based**. **Revenue grants** are credited to revenue in line with the revenue costs which they are intended to cover. **Capital grants** are credited to revenue over the useful life of the fixed asset for which they have been granted.

Quick Quiz

1   Which of the following elements can be included in the production cost of a fixed asset?

    A   Labour
    B   Raw materials
    C   Electricity and fuel used
    D   Interest on loan taken out to finance production of the asset

2   Define depreciation.

3   When the method of depreciation is changed this constitutes a change of accounting policy and an adjustment should be made to the depreciation charged in previous year.

    True ☐

    False ☐

4   When are investment properties (as defined by SSAP 19) subject to depreciation?

5   In which two ways can fixed asset grants be credited to revenue?

Answers to Quick Quiz

1   All of them. (see Paras 2.2 – 2.3)

2   See Paragraph 2.7 for the FRS 15 definition.

3   False. This is a change of **accounting estimate**.

4   When the property is subject to a lease which has 20 years or less to run.

5   By reducing the cost of the asset, and therefore the depreciation, or by treating the grant as a **deferred credit** (see 5.2)

Now try the question below from the Exam Question Bank

Number	Level	Marks	Time
Q6	Examination	25	45 mins
Q7	Examination	10	18 mins

Intangible assets

Topic list	Syllabus reference
1 Intangible assets: Companies Act 1985 requirements	C3
2 SSAP 13 *Accounting for research and development*	C3
3 Goodwill: Introduction	C3
4 FRS 10 *Goodwill and intangible assets*	C3

Introduction

We will look at intangible assets in this chapter, the main categories of which are R & D costs and goodwill.

Accounting for research and development according to SSAP 13 is relatively straightforward, and has been covered in your lower level studies.

The study material on goodwill is closely connected with the later chapters on group accounts. When you reach these chapters you should refer back to the coverage here on goodwill.

Study guide

		Intellectual level
C	**FINANCIAL STATEMENTS**	
3	**Intangible assets**	
(a)	Discuss the nature and accounting treatment of internally generated and purchased intangibles.	2
(b)	Distinguish between goodwill and other intangible assets.	2
(c)	Describe the criteria for the initial recognition and measurement of intangible assets.	2
(d)	Describe the subsequent accounting treatment, including the principle of impairment tests in relation to goodwill.	2
(e)	Indicate why the value of purchase consideration for an investment may be less than the value of the acquired identifiable net assets and how the difference (negative goodwill) should be accounted for.	2
(f)	Describe and apply the requirements of relevant accounting standards to research and development expenditure.	2

Exam guide

Goodwill is certain to feature in the group accounting questions in the exam. You need to be able to account for goodwill but also understand the reasons for its accounting treatment; FRS 11 could come up as the second part of a question.

1 Intangible assets: Companies Act requirements

FAST FORWARD

The Companies Act sets out the **statutory accounting requirements** relating to **intangible fixed assets** and **investments**. These requirements are supplemented in the case of **development costs** by SSAP 13, in the case of **goodwill** by FRS 10 and in the case of **impairment** by FRS 11.

The **statutory balance sheet** format lists the following intangible fixed assets (item BI in the format).

    (a)   **Development costs**
    (b)   **Concessions, patents, licences, trade marks** and similar rights and assets
    (c)   **Goodwill**
    (d)   **Payments on account**

1.1 Patents and trade marks

Concessions, patents, licences, trade marks etc should only be **treated,** and **disclosed,** as **assets** if they were **either:**

    (a)   **Acquired** for **valuable consideration**
    (b)   **Created** by the **company itself.**

1.2 Development costs

Development costs, may only be treated as an asset in the balance sheet (rather than being written off immediately) in 'special circumstances'. The Act does not define these circumstances and this is a case where a SSAP goes further than statute. SSAP 13 (see below) lays down strict criteria for determining when such expenditure may be treated as an asset. The Act merely states that, if it is so treated, the following disclosures must be made by way of note:

(a)   The period over which the amount of the costs originally capitalised is being or is to be written off

(b)   The reasons for capitalising the development costs

1.3 Goodwill

The Act implicitly makes a distinction between inherent goodwill and purchased goodwill. The distinction will be explained when we review FRS 10 *Goodwill and intangible assets.* For now, please remember that the Act does not permit inherent goodwill to be included as an asset in the balance sheet. The difficulties of valuing inherent goodwill are in any case so great that very few companies have ever carried it in their balance sheets. However, several listed companies have capitalised brands which were developed in-house.

Purchased goodwill may be treated as an asset in the balance sheet. If it is so treated (rather than being written off immediately):

(a)   It must be written off systematically over a period chosen by the directors

(b)   The period chosen must not exceed the useful economic life of the goodwill

(c)   Disclosure should be made of the period chosen and of the reasons for choosing that period.

This statutory requirement to amortise any goodwill capitalised does not extend to goodwill arising on consolidation. Even so, companies have to amortise consolidation goodwill to comply with the stricter requirements of FRS 10. You should note that FRS 10 is stricter than the Companies Act in the case of goodwill on acquisition, as we will see below.

2 SSAP 13 Accounting for research and development

SSAP 13 is a standard which has been around for some time and is generally accepted and well understood. It distinguishes between research expenditure and development expenditure and lays down strict criteria for the capitalisation of development expenditure.

In many companies, especially those which produce food, or 'scientific' products such as medicines, or 'high technology' products, the expenditure on research and development (R & D) is considerable. When R & D is a large item of cost, its accounting treatment may have a significant influence on the profits of a business and its balance sheet valuation.

Exam focus point

SSAP 13 might feature as part of a consolidation or accounts preparation question, or it could be the subject of the 10-mark or 15-mark question in your exam.

Knowledge brought forward from earlier studies

SSAP 13 Accounting for research and development

Definitions

- **Pure/basic research** is experimental/theoretical work with no commercial end in view and no practical application.
- **Applied research** is original investigation directed towards a specific practical aim/objective.
- **Development** is the use of scientific/technical knowledge in order to produce new/substantially improved **materials**, **devices**, **processes** etc.

Accounting treatment

- **Pure and applied research** should be **written off** as incurred.
- **Development expenditure** should be **written off** in year of expenditure, *except* in certain circumstances when it *may* be **deferred to future periods**.

S	Separately defined project
E	Expenditure separately identifiable
C	Commercially viable
T	Technically feasible
O	Overall profit expected
R	Resources exist to complete the project

- Show deferred development costs as an **intangible asset amortised** from the beginning of commercial production, **systematically** by reference to sales, etc.
- Deferred costs should be **reviewed annually**; where the above criteria no longer apply, write off the cost immediately.
- Development expenditure previously written off **can be reinstated** if the **uncertainties** which led to it being written off **no longer apply**.
- **R & D fixed assets** should be **capitalised** and **written off** over their estimated **economic lives**.
- Deferral of costs should be **applied consistently** to all projects.
- SSAP 13 does not apply to:
  - Fixed assets used for R&D (except amortisation)
  - The cost of locating mineral deposits in extractive industries
  - Expenditure where there is a firm contract for reimbursement

Disclosure

- R & D activities should be disclosed in the **directors' report**.
- **Private companies** outside groups which include a plc are **exempt** from disclosing R & D expenditures (except amortisation) if they would meet the **criteria** for a **medium-sized company × 10**.
- *Disclose:*
  - **Movements** on deferred development expenditure
  - **R & D charged** to the P & L a/c analysed between **current year expenditure** and **amortisation**
  - An accounting **policy** note

The importance of R & D disclosures was emphasised in another **survey** of what **users really needed** in financial statements.

(a) UK institutional investors said the **top requirement** was **future prospects and plans** (84%). R & D is seen to form a crucial quantitative element of prospects and plans.

(b) When specifically asked about R & D, 64% of UK investors said the data was very, or extremely, important to them.

Unfortunately, the top companies analysed failed dismally to provide the information required. There is a wide variety of treatment and information given on R & D and improvements are required in the reporting of R & D.

Question

Research and development

In connection with SSAP 13 *Accounting for research and development*:

(a) Define 'applied research' and 'development'.

(b) Explain why it is considered necessary to distinguish between applied research and development expenditure and how this distinction affects the accounting treatment.

(c) State whether the following items are included within the SSAP 13 definition of research and development, and give your reasons:

(i) Market research
(ii) Testing of pre-production prototypes
(iii) Operational research
(iv) Testing in search of process alternatives

Answer

(a) *Applied research* expenditure is expenditure on **original investigations** which are carried out in order to gain **new scientific or technical knowledge**, but which also have a specific practical aim or objective. An example might be research into a disease with the intention of finding a cure or a vaccine.

Development expenditure is expenditure on the application of existing scientific or technical knowledge in order to produce **new or substantially improved materials, devices, products, processes, systems or services** prior to the commencement of **commercial production**. The costs of developing a prototype would be development expenditure.

(b) SSAP 13 considers that:

'pure and **applied research** can be regarded as part of a **continuing operation** required to maintain a company's business and its competitive position. In general, **no one particular period** rather than any other will be expected to **benefit** and **therefore** it is appropriate that these **costs** should be **written off** as they are **incurred**.'

This has the affect that applied research costs must be written off as incurred but **development expenditure can be deferred** (that is, capitalised as an intangible asset) and **amortised** over the life of the product, service, process or system developed. This treatment is only permissible if the project meets **certain criteria** designed to ensure that deferral is prudent.

(c) (i) **Market research** is **not normally** considered to be **research and development** activity. It is **specifically excluded in the SSAP**. This is presumably because it does not depart from routine activity and it does not contain an appreciable element of innovation.

(ii)   **Testing of prototypes** is included in SSAP 13's list of activities normally to be considered as **research and development**. A prototype must be constructed and tested before full-scale production can be risked and so it is an **essential stage** in the **development process**.

(iii)   '**Operational research not tied** to a **specific research** and development activity' is an activity which SSAP 13 considers should **not normally** be **included in research and development**. 'Operational research' is presumably used here to denote the **branch of applied mathematics** which includes techniques such as linear programming and network analysis. The implication is that routine use of such techniques (to improve production efficiency, for example) does **not fall within the ambit of SSAP 13**, in spite of the use of the word 'research'.

(iv)   'Testing in search for, or evaluation of, product, service or process alternatives' is considered to be research and development work by SSAP 13. It would fall within the definition of applied research.

Question   Development expenditure

R.U. Welle Pharmaceuticals plc incurs the following expenditure in years 20X4-20X8.

	Research £'000	Development £'000
20X4	40	65
20X5	45	70
20X6	49	–
20X7	41	–
20X8	43	–

You are told that R.U. Welle Pharmaceuticals plc capitalises development expenditure when appropriate. The item developed in 20X4 and 20X5 goes on sale on 1 January 20X6 and it will be three years from then until any competitor is expected to have a similar product on the market.

Required

Show the profit and loss account and balance sheet extracts for all five years.

Answer

PROFIT AND LOSS ACCOUNT (EXTRACTS)

	20X4 £'000	20X5 £'000	20X6 £'000	20X7 £'000	20X8 £'000
Research expenditure	40	45	49	41	43
Amortisation of development costs	–	–	45	45	45

BALANCE SHEET (EXTRACT)

	20X4 £'000	20X5 £'000	20X6 £'000	20X7 £'000	20X8 £'000
Intangible fixed assets					
Development costs	65	135	135	135	135
Amortisation	–	–	(45)	(90)	(135)
Net book value	65	135	90	45	–

3 Goodwill: Introduction

3.1 Nature of goodwill

By definition, goodwill is an asset which **cannot be realised separately** from the **business as a whole**.

Key term

> **Goodwill** is the difference between:
>
> (a)   the aggregate fair value of the net assets of a business
>
> (b)   the value of the business as a whole.

3.2 Potential factors giving rise to goodwill

There are many factors which may explain why goodwill arises. Examples are:

(a)   skilled management team

(b)   good labour relations

(c)   strategic location

(d)   good customer relations

These factors are **intangible** and it is **difficult** to place a **money value** on them. Until **recently**, it was **not usual** to show **goodwill** as an **asset** in the balance sheet. Any **amount** at which it was valued was **considered** to be **arbitrary** and **subject to fluctuations**.

3.3 Inherent goodwill and purchased goodwill

Exam focus point

> FRS 10 *Goodwill and intangible assets* is an attractive area for examiners.

Some form of goodwill is likely to exist in every business. However, the **only circumstances** when **goodwill** is **valued** and may be **disclosed** as an **asset** in the balance sheet is when one **business acquires another as a going concern**. This is because there is then a **positive indication** available of the **value of goodwill acquired**. This is known as **purchased goodwill.**

Goodwill which is presumed to exist, but which has not been evidenced in a purchases transaction, is called non purchased or inherent goodwill.

3.4 Accounting treatment of inherent goodwill

FRS 10 stipulates that **inherent goodwill** should **not be recognised** in the financial statements. Its **value cannot** be **measured** with sufficient **reliability** because of the **subjectivity** involved. **It should therefore be ignored.**

3.5 Accounting treatment of purchased goodwill

(a)   Goodwill is an asset which at the **date of acquisition** has a **definite value to the business**.

(b)   This asset is a measure of the extent to which the **earnings** of the **purchased business** will **exceed** those which could be **expected** from the **use of its identifiable assets**. Consequently, it should be **capitalised and amortised** so as to **match costs against income** (the accruals concept). This is the view adopted by FRS 10 *Goodwill and intangible assets*.

<table>
<tr><td>Basic requirements</td><td>(a)   Purchased goodwill should be capitalised and classified as an asset on the balance sheet.
(b)   It should be amortised on a systematic basis over its useful economic life.</td></tr>
</table>

3.6 Negative goodwill

Negative goodwill arises when the price paid for a business is less than the fair value of the separable net assets acquired, for example, if the vendor **needed cash quickly** and was forced to sell at a **bargain price**.

4 FRS 10 Goodwill and intangible assets

FAST FORWARD

> FRS 10 states that **purchased, positive goodwill** and purchased intangible assets or internally-developed intangible assets which have a **readily ascertainable market value** should be capitalised and amortised over their **useful economic life**.

4.1 Overview

FRS 10 *Goodwill and intangible assets* was published in December 1997. The requirements of the FRS **apply to all intangible assets except those specifically addressed by another accounting standard**, eg SSAP 13. Oil and gas exploration and development costs are also exempt.

FRS 10 applies to **all financial statements except** those entities applying the Financial Reporting Standard for Smaller Entities **(FRSSE)** which do not prepare consolidated accounts.

Although FRS 10 is framed around the purchase of a subsidiary undertaking, it also applies to the acquisition of unincorporated entities.

4.2 Objective of FRS 10

The objectives stated by FRS 10 are to ensure that:

(a)   **Capitalised goodwill** and **intangible assets** are charged in the **P&L account** as far as possible in the **periods** in which they are **depleted.**

(b)   **Sufficient information** is **disclosed** in the financial statements to enable users to **determine** the **impact of goodwill** and **intangible assets** on the **financial position** and **performance** of the **reporting entity.**

4.3 Definitions

FRS 10 introduces a variety of new definitions, some of which relate to terms used above.

Key terms

- **Class of intangible assets**: a group of intangible assets that have **similar nature** or **function** in the business of the entity.

- **Identifiable assets and liabilities**: the assets and liabilities of an entity that are capable of being **disposed** of or **settled separately**, without disposing of a business of the entity.

- **Purchased goodwill**: the **difference** between:
    - the fair value of the consideration paid for an acquired entity
    - the aggregate of the fair values of that entity's identifiable assets and liabilities.

- **Residual value**: the **net realisable value** of an asset at the **end of its useful economic life**. Residual values are based on prices at the date of acquisition (or revaluation) of the asset and **do not take account** of **expected future price changes**.

Key terms

- **Useful economic life:** the useful economic life of an **intangible asset** is the **period** over which the entity expects to **derive economic benefit** from that asset.

  The useful economic life of **purchased goodwill** is the period over which the **value** of the **underlying business** is expected to **exceed** the values of its **identifiable net assets**.   *(FRS 10)*

4.4 Ascertaining goodwill

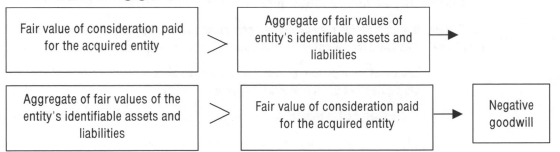

4.5 Example

AJ Limited acquires 80% of VJ Limited at 31 December 20X8.

AJ Limited originally made an initial offer of £75,000 which was rejected. A subsequent offer of £95,000 was however accepted. The total value of VJ Limited is £100,000. Identify the goodwill arising under these two scenarios.

Solution

	Scenario 1 £	Scenario 2 £
Fair value of consideration	75,000	95,000
Fair value of VJ Limited's net assets – 80% of £100,000	(80,000)	80,000
Negative goodwill	5,000	
Positive goodwill		15,000

FRS 10 also includes definitions of the following terms, which are also defined in FRS 11.

(a)   Impairment
(b)   Intangible assets
(c)   Net realisable value
(d)   Readily ascertainable market value
(e)   Recoverable amount
(f)   Value in use

Purchased goodwill is also defined by FRS 11, but the definition given here is fuller.

4.6 Initial recognition and measurement

4.6.1 Goodwill

Positive purchased goodwill should be capitalised and classified as an asset on the balance sheet.

Internally generated goodwill should not be capitalised..

4.6.2 Intangible assets

An intangible asset **purchased separately** from a business should be **capitalised at cost**. Examples of such assets include patents, copyrights and licences.

Where an **intangible** asset is **acquired as part of the acquisition of a business** the treatment **depends** on whether its **value** can be **measured reliably** on its initial recognition.

(a)   If its value **can be measured reliably**, it should initially be **recorded at its fair value**. (The fair value should **not create** or **increase** any **negative goodwill** arising on the acquisition **unless** the asset has a **readily ascertainable market value**.)

(b)   If the value of the asset cannot be measured reliably, the intangible asset must be subsumed within the amount of the purchase price attributed to goodwill.

4.6.3 Internally developed intangibles

FRS 10 states that companies may **capitalise non-purchased** ('internally-developed') **intangibles** but **only if they have a** 'readily ascertainable market value'. This is an important definition that **requires that:**

(a)   The asset belongs to **a group of homogenous assets** (ie they are all of the same kind), that are **equivalent** in **all material respects**.

(b)   There is an **active market** for that **group of assets**, evidenced by **frequent transactions**.

Examples given by FRS 10 of intangibles that may meet these conditions include certain **operating licences**, **franchises** and **quotas**.

FRS 10 also suggests **certain intangibles** that are **not equivalent** in all material aspects, are **indeed unique** and so **do not have readily identifiable market values**.

(a)   Brands
(b)   Publishing titles
(c)   Patented drugs
(d)   Engineering design patents

Hence, FRS 10 effectively precludes the recognition of most internally developed intangibles in financial accounts.

Once they have passed the tests for recognition, FRS 10 requires that intangible assets be treated in exactly the way as goodwill.

4.7 Approach to amortisation and impairment

The FRS 10 approach to amortisation reflects the wish to charge the profit and loss account only to the extent that the **carrying value** of the asset is **not supported** by the **current value** of the asset **within the acquired business**.

The approach is based on a **combination** of:

(a)   **Amortising** over a **limited period** on a **systematic basis**
(b)   An **annual impairment review** (see later coverage)

The first task is to **decide whether** or not the **goodwill** or **intangible** has a **limited useful economic life**.

You may find the following diagram helpful in clarifying the approach outlined above.

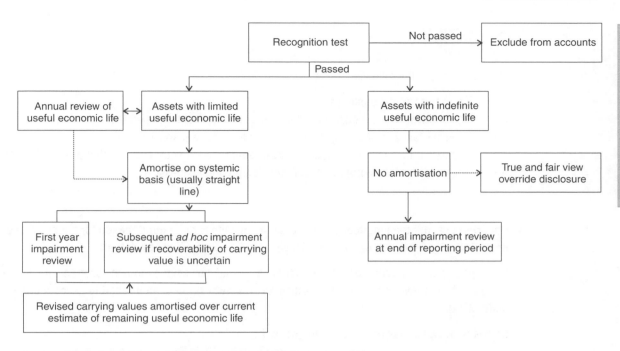

4.8 Assets with a limited useful economic life

4.8.1 Amortisation

FRS 10 states that, where goodwill and intangible assets are regarded as having **limited useful economic lives** they should be **amortised on a systematic basis over those lives**.

FRS 10 gives **little guidance** on how to **predict** an asset's **useful economic life**, which can be very difficult for goodwill and intangibles as it is **impossible** to **see** them **actually wearing out**. It does, however, give **examples** of **relevant considerations**, which include certain **economic** and **legal factors** relating to the asset. An intangible may, for example, be linked to a product with a **specific lifespan**, or there may be time periods attached to **legal rights** (eg patents). It may also be necessary to look at the nature of the business and of the market in which it operates.

There is a **basic assumption** that the **useful economic lives** of **purchased goodwill** and **intangible assets** are limited to periods of **20 years or less**. However, this **presumption** may be **rebutted** and a useful economic life regarded as a longer period or indefinite only if:

(a)   The **durability** of the **acquired business** or **intangible asset** can be demonstrated and justifies estimating the **useful economic life** to **exceed 20 years**.

(b)   The goodwill or intangible asset is capable of **continued measurement** (so that annual impairment reviews will be feasible).

| Question | Goodwill |

The circumstances where an indefinite useful economic life longer than 20 years may be legitimately presumed are limited. What factors determine the durability of goodwill?

Answer

FRS 10 mentions the following.

(a) The **nature** of the business
(b) The **stability** of the industry in which the acquired business operates
(c) Typical **lifespans** of the products to which the goodwill attaches
(d) The extent to which the acquisition **overcomes** market entry **barriers** that will continue to exist
(e) The expected future **impact** of **competition** on the business

Uncertainty about the **length** of the **useful economic** life is **not a good reason** for choosing one that is **unrealistically short** or for adopting a **20 year** useful economic life **by default**.

In amortising an **intangible asset**, a **residual value** may be assigned to that asset only if such residual value can be **measured reliably**. In practice, the **residual value** of an **intangible asset** is **often insignificant**.

No residual value may be assigned to **goodwill**.

The method of amortisation should be chosen to reflect the **expected pattern of depletion** of the goodwill or intangible asset. A **straight-line method should be chosen unless another method can be demonstrated to be more appropriate**.

Whatever the **useful economic life** chosen, the company should be able to justify it. It **should be reviewed annually and revised if appropriate**.

4.8.2 Impairment review

In addition to the amortisation, the asset should be reviewed for impairment:

(a) At the end of the first full financial year following the acquisition ('**the first year review**').

(b) In **other periods** if events or changes in **circumstances** indicate that the **carrying values may not be recoverable**.

If an impairment is identified at the time of the first year review, this impairment is likely to reflect:

(a) An **overpayment**

(b) An **event** that occurred **between** the **acquisition** and the **first year review**

(c) **Depletion** of the acquired goodwill or intangible asset between the acquisition and the first year review that exceeds the amount recognised through amortisation

The requirements of FRS 10 are such that the recognition of an **impairment loss** must be **justified** in the same way as the absence of an impairment loss, is by looking at **expected future cash flows**.

Goodwill and intangible assets that are **amortised** over a period **exceeding 20 years** from the date of acquisition should be **reviewed for impairment at the end of each reporting period**.

Where the **impairment review** indicates a **diminution** in **value**, the goodwill and intangible assets must be **written down accordingly**. The **revised carrying value** should be **amortised** over the current estimate of the **remaining useful economic life**.

4.9 Assets with an indefinite useful economic life

4.9.1 No amortisation

Where goodwill and intangible assets are regarded as having **indefinite useful economic lives**, they **should not be amortised**.

'Indefinite' is not the same as 'infinite', it means merely that no limit can be fixed for it.

Important

> If the option not to amortise is taken, this constitutes a departure from the Companies Act and will need to be justified by invoking the **true and fair override**.

4.9.2 Impairment review

Goodwill and intangible assets that are **not amortised** (because their useful economic life is deemed to be indefinite) should be **reviewed for impairment at the end of each reporting period**.

If an **impairment loss** is **recognised**, the **revised carrying value**, if being amortised, should be **amortised** over the **current estimate** of the **remaining useful economic life**.

If **goodwill** arising on **consolidation** is found to be **impaired**, the carrying amount of the **investment** held in the accounts of the **parent undertaking** should also be **reviewed for impairment**.

The emphasis on impairment reviews is a key feature of FRS 10. The ASB believes that a formal requirement to monitor the value of acquired goodwill and intangible assets using standardised methods and to report any losses in the financial statements will **enhance** the **quality** of the **information** provided to **users of financial statements**.

4.9.3 Reversal of impairment

Normally, once an impairment review has identified a loss, this cannot be restored at a later date. However, **if the loss was caused by an *external* event that later reversed in a way that was not foreseen, the original impairment loss may be restored.** An example of this might be: if a direct competitor came on to the market, leading to an impairment loss, and then the competitor did not survive or produced a different product from the one originally envisaged.

4.9.4 Updating of impairment reviews

After the first period, the reviews need only be updated. If expectations of **future cash flows** and **discount rates** have **not changed significantly**, the updating procedure will be **relatively quick** to **perform**.

If there have been **no adverse changes** in the **key assumptions** and **variables**, or if there was previously substantial leeway between the carrying value and estimated value in use, it **may** even **be possible** to ascertain immediately that an **income generating unit** is **not impaired**.

4.10 Revaluation of goodwill

Goodwill may not be revalued, except in the circumstances described above, ie the **reversal of an impairment**.

If an **intangible asset** has a **readily ascertainable market value**, it may be **revalued** to its **market value**.

Future amortisation should always be made on the revalued amount, just like depreciation for a revalued tangible fixed asset.

Question

Honeybun Ltd has a business unit with the following details:

(a) Carrying value of £4,000,000 at 31 December 20X7. This carrying value comprises £1,000,000 relating to goodwill and £3,000,000 relating to net assets.

(b) The goodwill is not being amortised as its useful life is believed to be indefinite.

(c) In 20X8, changes in the regulatory framework surrounding its business mean that the business unit has a value in use of £3,200,000. As a result of losses, net assets have decreased to £2,800,000 reducing the total carrying value of the unit to £3,800,000 which has thus suffered an impairment loss of £600,000. This is charged to the profit and loss account. The carrying value of goodwill is reduced to £400,000.

(d) In 20X9 the company develops a new product with the result that the value in use of the business unit is now £3,400,000. Net tangible assets have remained at £2,800,000.

Can all or any of the impairment loss be reversed?

Answer

No. Despite the value in use of the business unit now being £3,400,000 compared to its carrying value of £3,200,000, it is not possible to reverse £200,000 of the prior year's impairment loss of £600,000 since the reason for the increase in value of the business unit (the launch of the new product) is not the same as the reason for the original impairment loss (the change in the regulatory environment in which the business operates).

4.11 Negative goodwill

4.11.1 How negative goodwill arises

As mentioned earlier, negative goodwill arises when the fair value of the net assets acquired is more than the fair value of the consideration. In other words, the investor has got a bargain.

4.11.2 Subsequent accounting treatment

FRS 10 states that to ensure that any negative goodwill is justified:

(a) **The investee's assets should be checked for impairment**

(b) **The liabilities checked for understatement**.

   If indeed any negative goodwill remains after these tests, it needs to be disclosed consistently with positive goodwill.

Rather than being shown on the bottom half of the balance sheet as a capital reserve – as was required by SSAP 22 – **it is now disclosed in the intangible fixed assets category, directly under positive goodwill, ie as a 'negative asset'.** A sub-total of the net amount of positive and negative goodwill should be shown on the face of the balance sheet.

This presentation may seem a little odd. However, the ASB argues that negative goodwill does not meet the definition of a liability under the *Statement of Principles* and that this treatment is consistent with that of positive goodwill.

4.12 Transfers to profit and loss account

Negative goodwill should be **recognised in the profit and loss account in the periods when the non-monetary assets acquired are depreciated or sold.**

There are two important points to note.

(a)   It would be strange for the investor to pay less than its fair value for the monetary items acquired. The value of cash, for example, is pretty universal. Therefore, it is more **likely that the negative goodwill represents a shortfall in the value of the non-monetary items**.

(b)   The **benefit** of the 'bargain' of getting these non-monetary items at less than fair value **will only be realised when the non-monetary items themselves are realised**.

[ie it is the non-monetary assets (fixed assets, stock etc) that have been bought on the cheap, effectively at a discount (negative goodwill). Therefore, carry the discount (negative goodwill) in the balance sheet until the relevant assets are sold, or depreciated. Then transfer the relevant chunk of discount (negative goodwill) from the balance sheet to the profit and loss account.]

Hence, any negative goodwill should be credited to the **profit and loss account** only when the **non-monetary assets themselves** are realised, and this is when they are either **depreciated or sold**.

FRS 10 also requires any **remaining goodwill** in **excess** of fair values of the non-monetary assets acquired should be recognised in the **profit and loss account** in the **periods expected to be benefited**.

Question	Negative goodwill

Kewcumber plc acquired its investment in Marrow Ltd during the year ended 31 December 20X8. The goodwill on acquisition was calculated as follows.

	£'000	£'000
Cost of investment		400
Fair value of net assets acquired (remaining useful life – 7 years)		
Fixed assets	700	
Stock	100	
Non-monetary assets	800	
Net monetary assets	200	
		(1,000)
Negative goodwill		(600)

Required

Calculate the amount relating to negative goodwill as reflected in the profit and loss account and balance sheet for the year ended 31 December 20X8.

Answer

Amortisation in the profit and loss account for 20X8

Non-monetary assets recognised through the profit and loss account for the year ended 31 December 20X8:

	£'000
Stock (all sold)	100
Depreciation (£700,000 ÷ 7)	100
Non-monetary assets recognised this year	200
Total non-monetary assets at acquisition	800
∴ Proportion recognised this year	¼

Hence:

	£'000
Negative goodwill arising on acquisition	600
Proportion released to profit and loss account for year to 31.12.X8 (¼)	(150)
Balance at 31.12.X8, shown on balance sheet as deduction from positive goodwill	450

The balance of £450,000 will be carried forward and released into the profit and loss account over the next 6 years at £75,000 per annum, ie in the periods expected to be benefited. (Note: it is assumed that the stock at acquisition was all realised in the year to 31.12.X8.)

4.13 Disclosures

FRS 10 requires various disclosures relating to the following.

- (a) Recognition and measurement
- (b) Amortisation of positive goodwill and intangible assets
- (c) Revaluation
- (d) Negative goodwill
- (e) Impairment (see next section).

The **disclosure requirements are the same as for any other fixed asset**, including the table showing a reconciliation of movements during the year, for every category of intangible assets (including goodwill), details of revaluations, accounting policies and details of amortisation charged.

Significant **additional disclosure** requirements include requirements to explain:

- (a) The **bases of valuation** of intangible assets
- (b) The **grounds for believing a useful economic life to exceed 20 years** or to be indefinite
- (c) The **treatment adopted of negative goodwill**

4.14 Section summary

- (a) **Purchased goodwill** and **intangible assets** will both be **capitalised** as assets in the balance sheet. The option for goodwill of immediate write off to reserves, by-passing the profit and loss account, will no longer be available as it was under SSAP 22.

- (b) Where goodwill and intangible assets have **limited lives** they will be **amortised** to the profit and loss account over their **expected lives**.

- (c) Amortisation will not be required for assets that can be justified as having **indefinite lives**. They need to be **written down only if their values drop below those in the balance sheet**.

- (d) There is a **general presumption** that the **lives** of goodwill and intangible assets will be **no more than 20 years**. **A longer or indefinite life** may be assigned only if the **durability** of the asset can be demonstrated and if it is **possible to remeasure** its value **each year** to **identify any reduction**.

- (e) **Impairment reviews** must be **performed annually** where **lives** of **more than 20 years** are chosen. For **lives of less than 20 years**, they are required only in the **year after acquisition**, and in **other years** if there is some **indication** that the asset's **value might have fallen below its recorded value**.

Chapter Roundup

- The Companies Act sets out the **statutory accounting requirements** relating to **intangible fixed assets** and **investments**. These requirements are supplemented in the case of **development costs** by SSAP 13, in the case of **goodwill** by FRS 10 and in the case of **impairment** by FRS 11.

- SSAP 13 is a standard which has been around for some time and is generally accepted and well understood. It distinguishes between research expenditure and development expenditure and lays down strict criteria for the capitalisation of development expenditure.

- By definition, goodwill is an asset which **cannot be realised separately** from the **business as a whole**.

- FRS 10 states that **purchased, positive goodwill** and purchased intangible assets or internally-developed intangible assets which have a **readily ascertainable market value** should be capitalised and amortised over their **useful economic life**.

Quick Quiz

1   Patents can only be treated as assets in a company's accounts if they are:

- .... for valuable consideration

- .... by the company itself

2   What are the criteria which must be met before development expenditure can be deferred?

- S.....................
- C.....................
- O.....................

- E.....................
- T.....................
- R.....................

3   Development expenditure written off may be reinstated if the uncertainties which led to the write-off no longer apply.

True ☐

False ☐

4   How should negative goodwill be accounted for under FRS10?

5   FRS 11 excludes purchased goodwill.

True ☐

False ☐

Answers to Quick Quiz

1   Acquired, created

2   **S**eparately defined project. **E**xpenses identifiable. **C**ommercially viable, **T**echnically feasible, **O**verall profitability, **R**esources to complete it

3   True

4   It should be disclosed in the intangible fixed assets category

5   False. It excludes non-purchased goodwill

Impairment of assets

6

Topic list	Syllabus reference
1 FRS 11 *Impairment of fixed assets and goodwill*	C8
2 Income generating units	C8
3 Goodwill and the impairment of assets	C8
4 Reversal of past impairments	C8

Introduction

In this chapter we deal with impairment of assets. This applies to both tangible and intangible assets.

Study guide

		Intellectual level
8	**Impairment of assets**	
(a)	Define an impairment loss.	2
(b)	Identify the circumstances that may indicate impairments to assets.	2
(c)	Describe what is meant by an income generating unit.	2
(d)	State the basis on which impairment losses should be allocated, and allocate an impairment loss to the assets of an income generating unit.	2

Exam guide

Impairment could come up as part of an accounts preparation question or could feature in Question 4 or 5.

1 FRS 11 Impairment of fixed assets and goodwill

FAST FORWARD

FRS 11 deals with impairment losses relating to **tangible fixed assets, intangible fixed assets** and **goodwill**. Where the **recoverable amount** of an asset falls below the amount at which it is carried in the financial statements, an **impairment loss** has occurred.

Exam focus point

Impairment is a very examinable area as it ties in well with both FRS 15 and FRS 10.

It is accepted practice that a **fixed asset** should **not be carried in the financial statements at more than its recoverable amount**, ie the higher of the amount for which it could be sold and the amount recoverable from its future use. FRS 11 has been produced to address impairment of fixed assets and goodwill but first we will review the Companies Act requirements.

1.1 Companies Act requirements

Under the Companies Act the treatment of diminutions in value is as follows.

(a) **Assets held at cost**

 (i) **Temporary diminutions** are **not recognised**.
 (ii) **Permanent diminutions** are **recognised** and **charged to the profit and loss account**.

(b) **Assets held at valuation**

 (i) **Temporary diminutions** are **recognised** and **debited to reserves**.
 (ii) **Permanent diminutions** are **recognised** and charged to the **asset's previous surplus in reserves** and **then to the profit and loss account** for the year.

Further points to note are as follows.

(a) Where the increase in value relates to the **reversal of a permanent diminution** in value previously charged to the profit and loss account, the increase will be posted to the profit and loss account for the year.

(b) Any changes in value taken **directly to reserves** must be disclosed in the STRGL.

1.2 FRS 11 Impairment of fixed assets and goodwill

1.2.1 Overview

While statute provides some guidance, it provides none on how the **recoverable amount** should be **measured** and **when impairment losses** should be **recognised**. In consequence, **practice** might be **inconsistent** and perhaps some impairments may **not** be **recognised** on a **timely basis**.

The need for a standard on impairment was increased by the requirement in FRS 10 *Goodwill and intangible assets* (see Section 4) that, where goodwill and intangible assets have a useful life in excess of twenty years or one that is indefinite, the recoverable amount of the goodwill and intangible assets should be reviewed every year.

1.2.2 Objective

The objective of FRS 11 is to ensure that:

(a)   Fixed assets and goodwill are **recorded** in the financial statements at **no more than** their **recoverable amount**.

(b)   Any resulting impairment loss is measured and recognised on a consistent basis.

(c)   **Sufficient information** is **disclosed** in the financial statements to enable users to **understand** the **impact** of the **impairment** on the **financial position** and **performance** of the reporting entity.

1.2.3 Scope

FRS 11 **excludes**:

(a)   Non-purchased goodwill.

(b)   Fixed assets which are governed by the ASB's standard on *Derivatives and financial instruments* (FRS 13 see Chapter 12).

(c)   Investment properties as defined in SSAP 19.

(d)   Shares held by an ESOP.

(e)   Cost capitalised pending determination under the Oil Industry Accounting Committee's SORP.

FRS 11 applies to subsidiary undertakings, associates and joint ventures.

Basic requirement	A **review for impairment** of a fixed asset or goodwill should be carried out if **events** or **changes** in **circumstances** indicate that the **carrying amount** of the fixed asset or goodwill **may not be recoverable**.
Key term	**Impairment**: a **reduction** in the **recoverable amount** of a fixed asset or goodwill **below** its **carrying amount**. (FRS 11)
Exam focus point	In the exam you may be required to: (a) define an impairment loss and explain why companies should carry out a review for impairment of fixed assets and goodwill. (b) describe the circumstances that might indicate that a company's assets may have become impaired.

Impairment occurs due to *either*:

(a)   Something happening to the **fixed asset** itself.

(b)   Something occurring in the **environment** within which the asset operates.

1.3 Indicators of impairment

FRS 11 provides **indicators of impairment** to help determine when an **impairment review** is **required**. Examples of such **events** and **changes** in **circumstances** include the following.

(a)   There is a **current period operating loss** or **net cash outflow** from **operating activities**, combined with *either*:

    (i)   **Past operating losses** or **net cash outflows** from operating activities

    (ii)   An expectation of **continuing operating losses** or **net cash outflows** from operating activities.

(b)   A **fixed asset's market value has declined significantly** during the period.

(c)   Evidence is available of **obsolescence or physical damage** to the fixed asset.

(d)   There is a **significant adverse change** in any of the following.

    (i)   Either the **business or the market** in which the fixed asset or goodwill is involved, such as the entrance of a **major competitor**.

    (ii)   The **statutory or other regulatory environment** in which the business operates.

    (iii)   Any **indicator of value** (eg multiples of turnover) used to measure the fair value of a fixed asset on acquisition.

(e)   A **commitment** by management to undertake a **significant reorganisation**.

(f)   A major loss of **key employees**.

(g)   **Market interest rates** or other market rates of return have **increased significantly**, and these increases are likely to **affect materially** the fixed asset's **recoverable amount**.

Where any of the above (or similar) **triggers** occur, then an impairment review should be carried out. In the case of **tangible fixed assets**, if there is **no cause** to suspect **any impairment**, then **no impairment review** is necessary. **Intangible assets** and **goodwill may**, however, **still require review**.

Key terms

> **Intangible assets: non-financial** fixed assets that do **not have physical substance** but are **identifiable** and **controlled** by the entity through **custody** or **legal rights**.
>
> **Purchased goodwill**: the **difference** between the **cost** of an acquired entity **and** the aggregate of the **fair values** of that entity's identifiable assets and liabilities.
>
> **Tangible fixed assets**: assets that have **physical substance** and are held for **use** in the **production** or **supply of goods or services**, for **rental** to others, or for **administrative purposes** on a **continuing basis** in the reporting entity's activities.
>
> *(FRS 11)*

1.4 Impairment review

Basic requirements

FRS 11 specifies the process for conducting an impairment review.

- The impairment review will consist of a **comparison** of the **carrying amount** of the fixed asset or goodwill with its **recoverable amount** (the higher of net realisable value, if known, and value in use).

- To the extent that the **carrying amount exceeds** the **recoverable amount**, the fixed asset or goodwill is **impaired** and should be **written down**.

Key terms

- The impairment loss should be recognised in the profit and loss account unless it arises on a previously revalued fixed asset.

- **Recoverable amount**: the **higher of net realisable value** and **value in use**.

- **Net realisable value**: the **amount** at which an asset **could be disposed** of, **less** any **direct selling costs**.

- **Value in use**: the **present value** of the **future cash flows** obtainable as a result of an asset's continued use, including those resulting from its **ultimate disposal**.

The issues can be summarised by the following diagram.

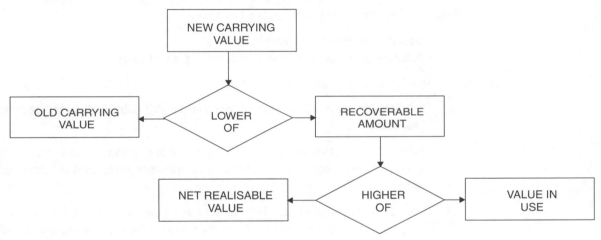

Question   Impairment loss

Determine the impairment loss relating to one of Viegeets Limited's fixed assets for the following four scenarios.

	Scenario 1 £'000	Scenario 2 £'000	Scenario 3 £'000	Scenario 4 £'000
• Carrying amount	750	750	900	900
• Net realisable value *	800	600	800	600
• Value in use **	600	800	600	800

Answer

	Scenario 1	Scenario 2	Scenario 3	Scenario 4
• Recoverable amount	* 800	** 800	* 800	** 800
• Carrying amount	750	750	900	900
• Impairment	Nil	Nil	100	100

Note the following **rules** here.

    (a)   If either NRV *or* value in use is higher than the carrying amount, there is no impairment.

    (b)   If a reliable estimate of NRV cannot be made, the recoverable amount is its value in use.

    (c)   If NRV is less than the carrying amount, then value in use must be found to see if it is higher still. If it is higher, recoverable amount is based on value in use, not NRV.

Basic requirements

- When an **impairment loss** on a fixed asset or goodwill is recognised, the **remaining useful economic life** should be **reviewed** and **revised if necessary**.

- The **revised carrying amount** should be **depreciated** over the **revised estimate of the useful economic life**.

1.5 Calculation of net realisable value

The net realisable value of an asset that is **traded on an active market** will be based on **market value**. Disposal costs should include **only** the **essential selling costs** of the fixed asset and *not* any **costs** of reducing or **reorganising** the **business**.

1.6 Calculation of value in use

The process for computing value in use has **two basic** steps.

    (a)   **Develop projections** of future cash flows.
    (b)   **Discount** projected cash flows to **determine present value**.

In practice, value in use is **not always easy** to estimate.

    (a)   The **value in use** of a fixed asset should be estimated **individually** where **reasonably practicable**.

    (b)   Where it is not reasonably practicable to develop **projected cash flows** arising from an individual fixed asset, value in use should be calculated at the **level of income-generating units**.

    (c)   The **carrying amount of each income-generating unit** containing the fixed asset or goodwill under review should be compared with the **higher of the value in use and the net realisable value** (if it can be measured reliably) of the unit.

2 Income generating units

FAST FORWARD

When it is not possible to calculate the recoverable amount of a single asset, then that of if its **income generating unit** should be measured instead.

Key term

An **income generating unit** is defined as a group of assets, liabilities and associated goodwill that generates income that is largely independent of the reporting entity's other income streams. The assets and liabilities include those already involved in generating the income and an appropriate portion of those used to generate more than one income stream.

Because it is necessary to **identify only material impairments**, in some cases it may be acceptable to consider a **group of income generating units together** rather than on an individual basis.

In some cases a detailed calculation of value in use will not be necessary. A **simple estimate** may be **sufficient** to **demonstrate** that either **value in use is higher than carrying value**, in which case there is no impairment, or value in use is lower than net realisable value, in which case impairment is measured by reference to net realisable value.

2.1 Identification of income generating units

FRS 11 specifies that income generating units should be identified by **dividing** the **total income** of the **entity** into as many largely **independent income streams** as is **reasonably practicable**. Each of the entity's identifiable assets and liabilities should be attributed to, or apportioned between, one or more income generating unit(s). However, the following are **excluded**.

- Deferred tax balances
- Interest bearing debt
- Dividends payable
- Other financing items

In general terms, the income streams identified are likely to **follow** the way in which **management** monitors and makes **decisions** about **continuing** or **closing** the **different lines of business** of the entity. **Unique intangible assets**, such as **brands** and **mastheads**, are generally seen to **generate income independently** of each other and are usually **monitored separately**. Hence they can often be used to identify income-generating units. **Other income streams** may be identified by **reference to major products or services**.

2.2 Example: identification of income generating units

Saferail Limited runs a rail network comprising stations fed by a number of routes. Decisions about continuing or closing the routes are not based on the returns generated by the routes in isolation but on the contribution made to the returns generated by the stations.

Solution

An income-generating unit comprises a station plus the routes associated with it because the cash inflows generated by the station's activities are not independent of the routes.

Question   Income generating unit

Identify the income generating unit in the following cases.

(a)   Supasheds Limited, manufactures garden sheds at a number of different sites. Not all the sites are used to full capacity and the manufacturer can choose how much to make at each site. However, there is not enough surplus capacity to enable any one site to be closed. The cash inflows generated by any one site therefore depend on the allocation of production across all sites.

(b)   Dian Xin Limited has a large number of restaurants across the country. The cash inflows of each restaurants can be individually monitored and sensible allocations of costs to each restaurants can be made.

Answer

(a)   The income-generating unit comprises all the sites at which the sheds can be made.

(b)   Each restaurant is an income-generating unit by itself. However, any impairment of individual restaurants is unlikely to be material. A material impairment is likely to occur only when a number of restaurants are affected together by the same economic factors. It may therefore be acceptable to consider groupings of restaurants affected by the same economic factors rather than each individual restaurants.

To perform impairment reviews as accurately as possible:

(a) The **groups of assets and liabilities** that are considered together should be **as small as is reasonably practicable**, but

(b) The **income stream** underlying the **future cash flows** of one group should be **largely independent** of other income streams of the entity and should be **capable** of being **monitored separately**.

Income-generating units are therefore identified by dividing the total income of the business into as many largely independent income streams as is reasonably practicable in the light of the information available to management.

2.3 Central assets

In practice, businesses may have assets and liabilities that are not directly involved in the production and distribution of individual products therefore not attributed directly to one unit. **Central assets**, such as group or regional **head offices** and **working capital** may have to be **apportioned across** the **units** as on a **logical** and **systematic basis**. In such cases, the **sum of the carrying amounts of the units must equal the carrying amount of the net assets (excluding tax and financing items) of the entity as a whole**.

There may be circumstances where it is not **possible** to **apportion certain central assets** meaningfully **across the income generating units** to which they contribute. Such assets **may be excluded from** the **individual income generating units**.

(a) An **additional impairment review** should be performed on the **excluded central assets**.

(b) The **income generating units** to which the **central assets contribute** should be combined and their **combined carrying amount** (including that of the central assets) should be **compared** with their **combined value in use**.

2.4 Working capital

If there is any working capital in the balance sheet that will generate cash flows equal to its carrying amount, the carrying amount of the working capital may be excluded from the income-generating units and the cash flows arising from its realisation/settlement excluded from the value in use calculation.

2.5 Capitalised goodwill

This **should be attributed to income generating** units or groups of similar units, in the same way as are the assets and liabilities of the entity.

2.6 Cash flows

2.6.1 Basis of cash flows

The **expected future cash flows** of the income generating unit, including any allocation of central overheads but excluding cash flows relating to financing and tax, should be:

(a) Based on **reasonable** and **supportable assumptions**.

(b) **Consistent** with the most up-to-date **budgets** and **plans** that have been **formally approved by management**.

(c)   Assume a **steady** or **declining growth** rate for the **period beyond** that covered by formal budgets and plans.

Only in **exceptional circumstances** should:

(a)   The **period** before the steady or declining growth rate is assumed **extend** to **more than five years**.

(b)   The **steady or declining growth rate exceed** the **long-term average growth rate** for the country or **countries** in which the business operates.

2.6.2 Projections of future cash flows

Future cash flows must be estimated for income generating units in their **current condition**, **ie exclude**:

(a)   **Benefits** expected to arise from a **future reorganisation** for which provision has not been made.

(b)   **Future capital expenditure** that will improve or **enhance** the income generating units **more than the originally assessed standard of performance**.

2.6.3 Subsequent monitoring of cash flows

For the **five years** following each impairment review where the recoverable amount has been based on value in use, **actual cash flows should be compared with forecast cash flows**.

There may be instances where **actual cash flows** are **significantly less** than forecast. This may **suggest** that the **income** generating **unit might** have required recognition of an **impairment** in **previous periods**. In such cases, the original **impairment calculations should be re-performed** using the actual cash flows. Any **impairment** identified should be **recognised** in the **current period** unless the impairment has reversed.

2.7 Discount rate

The **present value** of the income-generating unit under review should be calculated by **discounting** the expected future cash flows of the unit.

(a)   The discount rate used should be an **estimate** of the **rate** that the **market would expect** on an **equally risky investment**.

(b)   It should **exclude** the **effects** of **any risk** for which the **cash flows** have **been adjusted** and should be calculated on a **pre-tax basis**.

3 Goodwill and the impairment of assets

3.1 Allocation of impairment loss

Exam focus point

You may be required to allocate the impairment loss relating to an income generating unit.

Allocation of any impairment loss calculated (ie where carrying amount exceeds value in use) should be allocated:

(a)   First, to any **goodwill** in the unit.
(b)   Thereafter to any **capitalised intangible asset** in the unit.
(c)   Finally, to the **tangible assets** in the unit (pro-rata or other method).

The rationale behind the above allocation is to write down the assets with the most subjective valuations first.

No **intangible asset** with a **readily ascertainable market value** should be written down to **below NRV**. Similarly, **no tangible asset** with a reliably measured net realisable value should be written down **below its NRV**.

Question — Loss allocation

Nutrinitious Foods Limited has suffered an impairment loss of £90,000 on one of its income generating units because low market entry barriers has enabled competitors to develop and successfully market rival products.

The carrying value of net assets in the income generating unit, before adjusting for the impairment loss are as follows:

	£'000
Goodwill	50
Patent (with no market value)	10
Land and buildings	120
Plant and machinery	60
	240

Demonstrate how the impairment loss of £90,000 should be allocated.

Answer

	£'000
Remember the batting order is:	
• Goodwill	50
• Capitalised intangible fixed assets	10
• Tangible fixed assets, on a pro-rata basis	30
	90

Hence:

	Pre-impairment £'000	Impairment loss £'000	Post-impairment £'000
Goodwill	50	(50)	–
Patent	10	(10)	–
Land and buildings ($30 \times \frac{120}{180}$)	120	(20)	100
Plant and machinery ($30 \times \frac{60}{180}$)	60	(10)	50
	240	(90)	150

4 Reversal of past impairments

Tangible fixed assets and investments are treated differently from goodwill and intangible assets.

4.1 Tangible fixed assets and investments

There may be circumstances where, in subsequent periods after an impairment loss has been recognised, the **recoverable amount** of a tangible fixed asset or investment (in subsidiaries, associates and joint ventures) **increases because of an improvement in economic conditions.**

In such instances, the resulting **reversal** of the impairment loss should be **recognised in the current period**. However, recognition is *only* **to the extent that it increases the carrying amount of the fixed asset up to the amount that it would have been had the original impairment not occurred**.

The reversal of the impairment loss should be recognised in the **profit and loss account unless** it arises on a **previously revalued fixed asset.**

The recognition of an increase in the recoverable amount of a tangible fixed asset above the amount that its carrying amount would have been had the original impairment not occurred is a revaluation, not a reversal of an impairment.

The circumstances we are looking at are those given above (Paragraph 5.9) which would **originally** have **triggered** an **impairment review**. Also, **increases** in value arising as a result of the **passage of time** or through the passing of cash outflows are **not circumstances** that would **give rise** to the **reversal of an impairment loss**.

4.2 Goodwill and intangible assets

The reversal of an impairment loss on intangible assets and goodwill should be **recognised in the current period if, and only if**:

(a) An **external event caused** the **recognition** of the impairment loss in **previous periods**, and **subsequent external events** clearly and demonstrably **reverse** the effects of that event in a way that was **not foreseen in** the **original impairment calculations**.

(b) The impairment loss related to an intangible asset with a **readily ascertainable market value** and the **net realisable value based on that market value** has increased **to above the intangible asset's impaired carrying amount**.

The reversal of the impairment loss should be **recognised to the extent that it increases the carrying amount of the goodwill or intangible asset up to the amount that it would have been had the original impairment not occurred**.

The recognition of an increase in the recoverable amount of an intangible asset above the amount that its carrying amount would have been had the original impairment not occurred is a revaluation.

Key term

Readily ascertainable market value, in relation to an intangible asset, is the value that is established by reference to a market where:

(a) The asset belongs to a homogeneous population of assets that are equivalent in all material respects.
(b) An active market, evidenced by frequent transactions, exists for that population of assets. *(FRS 11)*

 Question   Reversal

Exeler 8 Limited has an income-generating unit comprising a factory, plant and equipment etc and associated purchased goodwill which has become impaired because the product has been overtaken by a technologically more advanced model produced by a competitor. The recoverable amount of the income-generating unit has fallen to £50m, resulting in an impairment loss of £100m, allocated as follows.

	Carrying amounts before impairment £m	Carrying amounts after impairment £m
Goodwill	45	–
Patent (with no market value)	15	–
Tangible fixed assets	90	50
Total	150	50

After three years, Exeler 8 Limited makes a technological breakthrough of its own, and the recoverable amount of the income-generating unit increases to £100m. The carrying amount of the tangible fixed assets had the impairment not occurred would have been £70m.

Required

Calculate the reversal of the impairment loss.

Answer

The reversal of the impairment loss is recognised to the extent that it increases the carrying amount of the tangible fixed assets to what it would have been had the impairment not taken place, ie a reversal of the impairment loss of £20m is recognised and the tangible fixed assets written back to £70m.

Reversal of the impairment is not recognised in relation to the goodwill and patent because the effect of the external event that caused the original impairment has not reversed – the original product is still overtaken by a more advanced model.

4.3 Impairment losses on revalued fixed assets

The general rule is that impairment losses on **revalued fixed assets** should be recognised in the **statement of total recognised gains and losses** until the carrying value of the asset falls **below depreciated historical** cost.

However, there may be specific circumstances where the impairment is clearly caused by a **consumption of economic benefits** eg damage, in which case the loss is recognised in the **profit and loss account**. ie such impairments are regarded as additional depreciation rather than as a decline in value.

Impairments **below depreciated historical** cost are recognised in the **profit and loss account**.

Question
                                                                        Revalued asset: impairment loss

Rollakoastas Limited has a fixed asset with the following details:

		£
•	Carrying value at 1 January 20X8 based on its revalued amount	£50,000
•	Depreciated historical cost at 1 January 20X8	£36,000
•	Impairment loss owing to entry of a new competitor	£20,000

Explain how this impairment loss should be accounted for in the financial statements for the year ended 31 December 20X8.

Answer

		£
•	Recognised in statement of total gains and losses	14,000
•	Recognised in profit and loss account	6,000

Workings

	£
Carrying value at 1.1.X8	50,000
Write off to STRGL	(14,000)
Depreciated historical cost	36,000
Write off to profit and loss account	(6,000)
Revised carrying value at 31.12.X8	30,000

4.4 Presentation

Impairment losses recognised in the profit and loss account should be included within **operating profit** under the **appropriate statutory heading**, and disclosed as an exceptional item if appropriate. Impairment losses recognised in the STRGL should be **disclosed separately** on the face of that statement.

In **the notes** to the financial statements in **accounting periods after the impairment**, the impairment loss should be treated as follows.

(a) For assets held on a **historical cost basis**, the impairment loss should be included **within cumulative depreciation**: the cost of the asset should not be reduced.

(b) For **revalued assets held at a market value** (eg existing use value or open market value), the impairment loss should be included **within the revalued carrying amount**.

(c) For **revalued assets held at depreciated replacement** cost, an impairment loss **charged to the profit and loss account** should be included **within cumulative depreciation**: the carrying amount of the asset should not be reduced; an **impairment loss charged to the STRGL** should be **deducted from the carrying amount** of the asset.

4.5 Section summary

The main aspects of FRS 11 to remember are:

(a) **Indications** of impairment
(b) Identification of **income-generating** unit
(c) How an **impairment review** is carried out
(d) **Restoration of past losses** (tangibles vs intangibles)
(e) Impairment and restoration of **revalued fixed assets**

Chapter Roundup

- FRS 11 deals with impairment losses relating to **tangible fixed assets, intangible fixed assets** and **goodwill**. Where the **recoverable amount** of an asset falls below the amount at which it is carried in the financial statements, an **impairment loss** has occurred.

- When it is not possible to calculate the recoverable amount of a single asset, then that of if its **income generating unit** should be measured instead

Quick Quiz

1   How is impairment on a revalued fixed asset which has been caused by consumption of economic benefit accounted for?

2   Define **recoverable amount**.

3   In what order is an impairment loss allocated to the assets in a cash-generating unit?

Answers to Quick Quiz

1   It is disclosed in the profit and loss account

2   The **higher** of **net realisable value** and **value in use**.

3   1.   To any goodwill
    2.   To any intangible assets
    3.   Pro-rata to any tangible assets

Now try the question below from the Exam Question Bank

Number	Level	Marks	Time
Q8	Examination	10	18 mins

BPP
LEARNING MEDIA

Reporting financial performance

7

Topic list	Syllabus reference
1 FRS 3 *Reporting financial performance*	C11
2 FRS 3 Statements and notes	C11

Introduction

FRS 3 *Reporting financial performance* introduced radical changes to the format of the profit and loss account and the associated notes to the accounts. Of major importance are the definitions of extraordinary and exceptional items and prior year adjustments. You may be asked to produce a statement of total recognised gains and losses.

Remember that you will appreciate the contents of this chapter far more if you obtain and examine some company reports (those of *public companies* are required in this case).

Study guide

		Intellectual level
C	**FINANCIAL STATEMENTS**	
11	**Reporting financial performance**	
(a)	Discuss the importance of identifying and reporting the results of continuing and discontinued operations.	2
(b)	Define and account for discontinued operations	2
(c)	Indicate the circumstances where separate disclosure of exceptional items is required	2
(d)	prepare and explain the contents and purpose of the statement of total recognised gains and losses and of reporting change in equity	2
(e)	Prepare statements for the reconciliation and movement in shareholder funds (changes in equity).	2

Exam guide

Revenue recognition is a particularly important area. It is fairly straightforward especially if you take time to relate the concepts to real life situations as you work through the material

1 FRS 3 Reporting financial performance

FAST FORWARD

FRS 3 *Reporting financial performance* has introduced radical **changes to the profit and loss** account of large and medium sized companies.

You must know the **FRS 3 definitions** of:

– **Extraordinary items**
– **Exceptional items**
– **Prior year adjustments**
– **Discontinued operations**
– **Total recognised gains and losses**

Exam focus point

This is an extremely popular exam topic. All recent papers have had a single company accounts preparation question. Make sure that you familiarise yourself fully with the contents of this standard.

FRS 3 represents an attempt by the ASB to improve the quality of financial information provided to shareholders. In particular it was **an attempt to move away from the high profile of the earnings per share**. The main elements of the FRS are as follows.

(a) New structure of the profit and loss account
(b) Extraordinary items
(c) Statement of total recognised gains and losses
(d) Other new disclosures
(e) Earnings per share

Exam focus point

A key way of developing familiarity with this topic is to look at published financial reports. See FT share page for details of free service.

1.1 Exceptional and extraordinary items

A company may experience events or undertake transactions which are 'out of the ordinary', ie they are not the same as what the company normally does.

FRS 3 lays down the rules for dealing with 'out of the ordinary' items in the P & L account and restricts the way companies can manipulate these figures.

1.1.1 Exceptional items

Key terms

> FRS 3 defines **exceptional items** as: 'Material items which derive from events or transactions that fall within the ordinary activities of the reporting entity and which individually or, if of a similar type, in aggregate, need to be disclosed by virtue of their *size or incidence* if the financial statements are to give a true and fair view.'
>
> The definition of **ordinary activities** is important.
>
> > 'Any activities which are undertaken by a reporting entity as **part of its business** and such related activities in which the reporting entity engages in furtherance of, incidental to, or arising from these activities. Ordinary activities include the effects on the reporting entity of any event in the various environments in which it operates including the political, regulatory, economic and geographical environments irrespective of the frequency or unusual nature of the event.'

There are **two** types of exceptional items and their accounting treatment is as follows.

(a)   Firstly there are **three categories of exceptional items,** so called **super exceptionals, which must be shown separately on the face of the profit and loss account** after operating profit and before interest and allocated appropriately to discontinued and continued activities.

       (i)   **Profit or loss on the sale or termination** of an operation

       (ii)   **Costs of a fundamental reorganisation** or restructuring that has a material effect on the nature and focus of the reporting entity's operations

       (iii)   **Profit or loss on disposal of fixed assets**

       For both items (i) and (iii) profit and losses may not be offset within categories.

(b)   **All other items should be allocated to the appropriate statutory format heading** and attributed to **continuing** or **discounted** operations as appropriate. If the item is **sufficiently material** that it is needed to show a **true and fair view** it must be disclosed on the **face of the profit and loss account**.

In both (a) and (b) an adequate description must be given in the notes to the accounts to enable its nature to be understood.

FRS 3 does not give examples of the type of transaction which is likely to be treated as exceptional. However, its predecessor on the subject, SSAP 6, gave a useful list of examples of items which if of a sufficient size might normally be treated as exceptional.

(a)   Abnormal charges for bad debts and write-offs of stock and work in progress.

(b)   Abnormal provisions for losses on long-term contracts.

(c)   Settlement of insurance claims.

1.1.2 Extraordinary items

The ASB publicly stated that it does not envisage extraordinary items appearing on a company's profit and loss account after the introduction of FRS 3. Its decline in importance has been achieved by tightening of the definition of an extraordinary item.

Key term

> **Extraordinary items** are defined as material items possessing a high degree of abnormality which arise from events or transactions that fall outside the ordinary activities of the reporting entity and which are not expected to recur.

An example given by the chairman of the ASB was that 'if the Martians landed and destroyed a company's factory, that could be treated as an extraordinary item'. Extraordinary items are therefore very rare!

Extraordinary items should be shown on the face of profit and loss account before dividends and other minority interests (for group accounts). Tax and minority interest in the extraordinary item should be shown separately. A description of the extraordinary items should be given in the notes to the accounts.

1.2 Structure of the profit and loss account

All statutory headings from turnover to operating profit must be subdivided between that arising from continuing operations and that arising from discontinued operations. In addition, turnover and operating profit must be further analysed between that from existing and that from newly acquired operations.

Only figures for turnover and operating profit need be shown on the face of the P & L account; all additional information regarding costs may be relegated to a note.

PROFIT AND LOSS
EXAMPLE 1 (as shown in FRS 3)

	1993 £m	1993 £m	1992 as restated £m
Turnover			
Continuing operations	550		500
Acquisitions	50		
	600		
Discontinued operations	175		190
		775	690
Cost of sales		(620)	(555)
Gross profit		155	135
Net operating expenses		(104)	(83)
Operating profit			
Continuing operations	50		40
Acquisitions	6		
	56		
Discontinued operations	(15)		12
Less 1992 provision	10		
		51	52
Profit on sale of properties in continuing operations		9	6
Provision for loss on operations to be discontinued			(30)
Loss on disposal of discontinued operations	(17)		
Less 1992 provision	20		
		3	—
Profit on ordinary activities before interest		63	28
Interest payable		(18)	(15)
Profit on ordinary activities before taxation		45	13
Tax on profit on ordinary activities		(14)	(4)
Profit on ordinary activities after taxation		31	9
Minority interests		(2)	(2)
Profit before extraordinary items		29	7
Extraordinary items – included only to show positioning		–	–
Profit for the financial year		29	7
Earnings per share		39p	10p
Adjustments (to be itemised and an adequate description to be given)		Xp	Xp
Adjusted earnings per share		Yp	Yp

Note. Reason for calculating the adjusted earnings per share to be given.

PROFIT AND LOSS ACCOUNT EXAMPLE 2 (to operating profit line)

	Continuing Operations 1993 £m	Acquisitions 1993 £m	Discontinued of operations 1993 £m	Total 1993 £m	Total 1992 as restated £m
Turnover	550	50	175	775	690
Cost of sales	(415)	(40)	(165)	(620)	(555)
Gross profit	135	10	10	155	135
Net operating expenses	(85)	(4)	(25)	(114)	(83)
Less 1992 provision			10	10	
Operating profit	50	6	(5)	51	52
Profit on sale of properties	9			9	6
Provision for loss on operations to be discontinued					(30)
Loss on disposal of the discontinued operations			(17)	(17)	
Less 1992 provision			20	20	
Profit on ordinary activities before interest	59	6	(2)	63	28

Thereafter example 2 is the same as example 1.

NOTES TO THE FINANCIAL STATEMENTS

Note required in respect of profit and loss account example 1

	1993 Continuing £m	1993 Discontinued £m	1993 Total £m	1992 (as restated) Continuing £m	1992 (as restated) Discontinued £m	1992 (as restated) Total £m
Cost of sales	455	165	620	385	170	555
Net operating expenses						
Distribution costs	56	13	69	46	5	51
Administrative expenses	41	12	53	34	3	37
Other operating income	(8)	0	(8)	(5)	0	(5)
	89	25	114	75	8	83
Less 1992 provision	0	(10)	(10)			
	89	15	104			

The total figures for continuing operations in 1993 include the following amounts relating to acquisitions: cost of sales £40 million and net operating expenses £4 million (namely distribution costs £3 million, administrative expenses £3 million and other operating income £2 million).

Note required in respect of profit and loss account example 2

	1993 Continuing £m	1993 Discontinued £m	1993 Total £m	1992 (as restated) Continuing £m	1992 (as restated) Discontinued £m	1992 (as restated) Total £m
Turnover				500	190	690
Cost of sales				385	170	555
Net operating expenses						
Distribution costs	56	13	69	46	5	51
Administrative expenses	41	12	53	34	3	37
Other operating income	(8)	0	(8)	(5)	0	(5)
	89	25	114	75	8	83
Operating profit				40	12	52

The total figure of net operating expenses for continuing operations in 1993 includes £4 million in respect of acquisitions (namely distribution costs £3 million, administrative expenses £3 million and other operating income £2 million).

1.2.1 Discontinued operations

A **discontinued operation** is one which **meets all of the following conditions.**

(a) The sale or termination must have been **completed** before the earlier of 3 months after the year end or the date the financial statements are approved. (Terminations not completed by this date may be disclosed in the notes.)

(b) Former activity must have **ceased permanently**.

(c) The sale or termination has a **material effect** on the nature and focus of the entity's operations and represents a material reduction in its operating facilities resulting either from:

(i) Its withdrawal from a particular market (class of business or geographical); or from
(ii) A material reduction in turnover in its continuing markets.

(d) The assets, liabilities, results of operations and activities are **clearly distinguishable**, physically, operationally and for financial reporting purposes.

1.2.2 Accounting for the discontinuation

(a) **Results**

The results of the discontinued operation up to the date of sale or termination or the balance sheet date should be shown **under each of the relevant profit and loss account headings**.

(b) **Profit/loss on discontinuation**

The profit or loss on discontinuation or costs of discontinuation should be **disclosed separately** as an exceptional item after operating profit and before interest.

(c) **Comparative figures**

Figures for the previous year **must be adjusted for** any **activities** which have become **discontinued in the current year.**

1.3 Acquisitions

Acquisitions include **most holdings acquired by a group**, **as well as unincorporated businesses purchased**. However, start-ups are not acquisitions.

Question	Profit and loss account

Feelgoode plc's profit and loss account for the year ended 31 December 20X2, with comparatives, is as follows.

	20X2 £m	20X1 £m
Turnover	200	180
Cost of sales	(60)	(80)
Gross profit	140	100
Distribution costs	(25)	(20)
Administration expenses	(50)	(45)
Operating profit	65	35

During the year the company sold a material business operation with all activities ceasing on 14 February 20X3. The loss on the sale of the operation amounted to £2.2m and this is included under administration expenses.. The results of the operation for 20X1 and 20X2 were as follows.

	20X2 £m	20X1 £m
Turnover	22	26
Profit/(loss)	(7)	(6)

In addition, the company acquired a business which contributed £7m to turnover and an operating profit of £1.5m.

Required

Prepare the profit and loss account and related notes for the year ended 31 December 20X2 complying with the requirements of FRS 3 as far as possible.

Answer

	20X2 £m	20X2 £m	20X1 £m	20X1 £m
Turnover				
Continuing operations				
(200 – 22 – 7)/(180 – 26)		171.0		154
Acquisitions		7.0		–
		178.0		154
Discontinued		22.0		26
		200.0		180
Cost of sales		(60.0)		(80)
Gross profit		140.0		100
Distribution costs		(25.0)		(20)
Administration expenses (50 – 2.2)		(47.8)		(45)
Operating profit				
Continuing operations* (bal)	72.7		41	
Acquisitions	1.5		–	
	74.2		41	
Discontinued	(7.0)		(6)	
		67.2		35
Exceptional item		(2.2)		–
		65.0		35

* ie 65.0 + 2.2 + 7.0 – 1.5 = 72.7; 35 + 6 = 41

Note to the profit and loss account

	20X2 Continuing £m	20X2 Discontinued £m	20X2 Total £m	20X1 (as restated) Continuing £m	20X1 (as restated) Discontinued £m	20X1 (as restated) Total £m
Cost of sales	X	X	60.0	X	X	80
Net operating expenses						
Distribution costs	X	X	25.0	X	X	20
Administration expenses	X	X	47.8	X	X	45
	X	X	72.8	X	X	65

2 FRS 3 Statements and notes

FRS 3 introduced a new statement and a variety of new notes to expand the information required in published accounts which we saw in Chapter 3.

Exam focus point

You may get an accounts preparation question which requires a STRGL.

2.1 Statement of total recognised gains and losses

FAST FORWARD

You must know the format of the **statement of total recognised gains and losses** and understand its contents.

This is required by FRS 3 to be presented with the same prominence as the P & L account, balance sheet and cash flow statement, ie as a **primary statement**.

The statement will include all gains and losses occurring during the period and so would typically include the following.

	£
Profit for the year (per the profit and loss account)	X
Items taken directly to reserves (not goodwill written off to reserves)	
Surplus on revaluation of fixed assets	X
Surplus/deficit on revaluation of investment properties	X
Total recognised gains and losses for the year	X
Prior period adjustments (see later)	(X)
Total gains and losses recognised since last annual report	X

At a glance, it seems that all this new statement does is to reconcile the opening and closing net assets of a business. This is, however, not so since FRS 3 requires that **transactions with shareholders are to be excluded**, ie:

(a) Dividends paid
(b) Share issues and redemptions

since these transactions do not represent either gains or losses.

In the case of goodwill, which is capitalised and amortised under FRS 10, the amortisation charge will appear indirectly (as part of the results for the year) in the statement.

Where the profit or loss for the year is the only recognised gain or loss, a **statement to that effect should be given** immediately below the profit and loss account.

The profit and loss account and the STRGL taken together report **all** gains and losses other than those arising from transactions with equity holders. This concept of **all** gains and losses is sometimes referred to as **'comprehensive income'** and future developments may lead to a single statement of comprehensive income. This is explained further in Chapter 18.

2.2 Realised and distributable profits

At this point it may be worth pointing out that just because gains and losses are 'recognised' in this statement, they are, **not necessarily 'realised'** (described below, or **'distributable'**, ie as a dividend).

2.3 Reconciliation of movements in shareholders' funds

This reconciliation is required by FRS 3 to be included in the notes to the accounts. What the statement aims to do is to **pull together financial performance** of the entity as is reflected in:

(a)   The profit and loss account.

(b)   Other movements in shareholders' funds as determined by the statement of total recognised gains and losses.

(c)   All other changes in shareholders funds not recognised in either of the above such as goodwill immediately written off to reserves.

The typical contents of the reconciliation would be as follows.

	£
Profit for the financial year	X
* Dividends	(X)
	X
Other recognised gains and losses (per statement of total recognised gains and losses)	X
* New share capital	X
Net addition to shareholders' funds	X
Opening shareholders' funds	X
Closing shareholders' funds	X

* Items not appearing in the statement of recognised gains and losses

STRGL

Extracts from Zoe Ltd's profit and loss account for the year ended 31 December 20X1 were as follows.

	£'000
Profit after tax	512
Dividend	(120)
Retained profit	392

During the year the following important events took place.

(a)   Assets were revalued upward by £110,000.

(b)   £300,000 share capital was issued during the year.

(c)   Certain stock items were written down by £45,000.

(d)   Opening shareholders' funds at 1 January 20X1 were £3,100,000.

Show how the events for the year would be shown in the statement of total recognised gains and losses and the reconciliation of movements in shareholders' funds.

Answer

STATEMENT OF TOTAL RECOGNISED GAINS AND LOSSES

	£'000
Profit after tax	512
Asset revaluation	110
	622

RECONCILIATION OF MOVEMENTS IN SHAREHOLDERS' FUNDS

	£'000
Profit after tax	512
Dividend	(120)
	392
Other recognised gains and losses (622 – 512)	110
New share capital	300
Net addition to shareholders' funds	802
Opening shareholders' funds	3,100
Closing shareholders' funds	3,902

2.4 Note of historical cost profits and losses

If a company has adopted any of the alternative accounting rules as regards revaluation of assets then the reported profit figure per the profit and loss account may deviate from the historical cost profit figure. If this deviation is material then the financial statements must include a reconciliation statement after the statement of recognised gains and losses or the profit and loss account. The profit figure to be reconciled is profit before tax; however, the retained profit for the year must also be restated.

Note that **FRS 3 requires the profit or loss on the disposal of a revalued asset to be calculated by reference to the difference between proceeds and the net carrying amount** (revalued figure less depreciation). The profit or loss based on historical cost will appear in the note of historical cost profits.

Question   Note of historical cost profits and losses

Faiza Ltd reported a profit before tax of £162,000 for the year ended 31 December 20X8. During the year the following transactions in fixed assets took place.

(a)   An asset with a book value of £40,000 was revalued to £75,000. The remaining useful life is estimated to be five years.

(b)   An asset (with a five year useful life at the date of revaluation) was revalued by £20,000 (to carrying value £30,000) was sold one year after revaluation for £48,000.

Show the reconciliation of profit to historical cost profit for the year ended 31 December 20X8.

Answer

RECONCILIATION OF PROFIT TO HISTORICAL COST PROFIT
FOR THE YEAR ENDED 31 DECEMBER 20X8

	£'000
Reported profit on ordinary activities before taxation	162
Realisation of property revaluation gains*	20
Difference between historical cost depreciation charge and the actual depreciation charge of the year calculated on the revalued amount (75,000 – 40,000)/5	7
	189

* By interpretation of the question, the asset was revalued last year with £20,000 being credited to revaluation reserve. With the asset being sold this year, this gain becomes realised. It is assumed that there has been no annual transfer from revaluation reserve to profit and loss account.

2.5 Prior period adjustments

When the financial statements of a company are compiled, certain items (eg accruals, provisions) represent best estimates at a point in time. Further evidence received in the following year may suggest that previous estimates were incorrect. In most cases the 'error' will not be significant in size and so as a result the difference should be dealt with in the current year's accounts.

There are **two situations where a prior period adjustment is necessary:**

(a) **Fundamental errors** – evidence is found to suggest last year's accounts were wrong.

(b) A **change in accounting policy** (see FRS 18 in Chapter 3).

Exam focus point

> Given the upheaval globally in company reporting, many companies have had to admit to fundamental errors, so do consider the likelihood of being examined on the treatment of errors discovered.

The following accounting treatment should be used.

(a) Restate prior year profit and loss account and balance sheet.

(b) Restate opening reserves balance.

(c) Include the adjustment in the reconciliation of movements in shareholders' funds.

(d) Include a note at the foot of the statement of total recognised gains and losses of the current period.

Prior period adjustments are therefore defined by FRS 3 as follows.

Key term

> **Prior period adjustments** are: 'Material adjustments applicable to prior periods arising from changes in accounting policy or from the correction of fundamental errors. They do not include normal recurring adjustments or corrections of accounting estimates made in prior periods.'

A **fundamental error** is an error which is **so significant that the truth and fairness of the financial statements is not achieved.**

A **change in accounting policy requires a prior period adjustment based on the accounting concept of consistency**. For users of the financial statements to make meaningful comparisons of a company's results it is important that the current year's and the last year's comparatives are prepared on the same basis. Therefore if for any reason a company changes its accounting policy they must go back and represent last year's accounts on the same basis.

Reasons for a change in accounting policy are discussed in Chapter 3.

A prior period adjustment will be shown in the **statement of movements in reserves**.

The format of the statement is as follows:

	Share premium account	Revaluation reserve	Other reserve	Profit and loss account	Total
Balance at beginning of year	X	X	X	X	X
Prior year adjustment	–	–	–	(X)	(X)
Balance at beginning of year restated	X	X	X	X	X
Premium on issue of shares	X				X
Goodwill impairment				(X)	(X)
Profit (loss) for the year				X	X
Transfer of realised profits		(X)		X	–
Decrease in value of investments		(X)			(X)
At end of year	X	X	X	X	X

Exam focus point

The June 2003 old syllabus paper required candidates to deal with the discovery of a fraud that had been perpetrated in the previous year.

Question

Deferred development expenditure

Jenny Ltd was established on 1 January 20X0. In the first three years' accounts deferred development expenditure was carried forward as an asset in the balance sheet. During 20X3 the directors decided that for the current and future years, all development expenditure should be written off as it is incurred. This decision has not resulted from any change in the expected outcome of development projects on hand, but rather from a desire to favour the prudence concept. The following information is available.

(a)   Movements on the deferred development account.

Year	Deferred development expenditure incurred during year £'000	Transfer from deferred development expenditure account to P & L account £'000
20X0	525	–
20X1	780	215
20X2	995	360

(b)   The 20X2 accounts showed the following.

	£'000
Retained reserves b/f	2,955
Retained profit for the year	1,825
Retained profits carried forward	4,780

(c)   The retained profit for 20X3 after charging the actual development expenditure for the year was £2,030,000.

Required

Show how the change in accounting policy should be reflected in the statement of movements in reserves in the company's 20X3 accounts.

Ignore taxation.

Answer

If the new accounting policy had been adopted since the company was incorporated, the additional profit and loss account charges for development expenditure would have been:

	£'000
20X0	525
20X1 (780 – 215)	565
	1,090
20X2 (995 – 360)	635
	1,725

This means that the reserves brought forward at 1 January 20X3 would have been £1,725,000 less than the reported figure of £4,780,000; while the reserves brought forward at 1 January 20X2 would have been £1,090,000 less than the reported figure of £2,955,000.

The statement of movement in reserves in Jenny Ltd's 20X3 accounts should, therefore, appear as follows.

STATEMENT OF MOVEMENTS IN RESERVES (EXTRACT)

	Total 20X3 £'000	Comparative (previous year) figures 20X2 £'000
Retained profits at the beginning of year		
Previously reported	4,780	2,955
Prior year adjustment (note 1)	1,725	1,090
Restated	3,055	1,865
Retained profits for the year	2,030	1,190 (note 2)
Retained profits at the end of the year	5,085	3,055

Notes

1   The accounts should include a note explaining the reasons for and consequences of the changes in accounting policy. (See above workings for 20X3 and 20X2.)

2   The retained profit shown for 20X2 is after charging the additional development expenditure of £635,000.

2.6 Potential problems with FRS 3

FRS 3 was designed to put an end to various abuses, for example extraordinary items. The latter have now been effectively prohibited.

Other aspects of FRS 3 have remained problematic. Two aspects may be highlighted.

2.6.1 Discontinued operations

Companies may take advantage of the requirement to analyse operations into continuing and discontinued and **use the analysis to hide 'bad news'.** A discontinued operation is likely to be a poor performer so it is in the company's interests to remove it from the rest of the results.

Careful consideration should be made as to whether the FRS 3 criteria for classification of an operation as continuing or discontinued have been met. The following should be singled out for close consideration.

   (a)   Have sales and costs relating to the discontinued activity been identified? The directors may wish to include sales in continuing operations if possible and costs in discontinued operation if possible.

   (b)   Provisions for profits or (more likely) losses on discontinuance must be considered carefully, as there is scope for manipulation.

2.6.2 Lack of consensus

FRS 3 was the first manifestation of the ASB's **balance sheet approach** to income recognition as outlined in the Board's *Statement of Principles*. This was highlighted through the introduction into UK GAAP of an `additional primary statement of financial performance – the statement of total recognised gains and losses – which focuses on changes in wealth as the means of performance measurement, rather than traditional historical cost profit and loss.

Concern has been expressed that the ASB seems to be entrenching into an accounting standard a conceptual approach which has not been the subject of due process, has no general agreement and which is still only at an early stage of development and discussion. In fact, one of the most crucial chapters of the ASB's framework – that dealing with measurement – had not even been issued in draft form by the time FRS 3 was issued.

Chapter Roundup

- FRS 3 *Reporting financial performance* has introduced radical **changes to the profit and loss** account of large and medium sized companies.

- You must know the **FRS 3 definitions** of:
  - **Extraordinary items**
  - **Exceptional items**
  - **Prior year adjustments**
  - **Discontinued operations**
  - **Total recognised gains and losses**

- You must know the format of the **statement of total recognised gains and losses** and understand its contents.

Quick Quiz

1   Which of the following exceptional items must be shown on the face of the profit and loss account per FRS 3?

    A   Loss on disposal of manufacturing equipment

    B   Profit on the sale of a branch

    C   A significant insurance claim settlement

    D   The cost of restructuring the entity so that its focus and the nature of its operations are materially different

    E   A write off of 40% of the year end stock due to unforeseen obsolescence

    F   A provision for a major loss on a long term contract

2   A company's year end is 31 December 20X1. The financial statements are approved on 10 February 20X2. A large foreign operation is sold on the 11th February. Should the operation be treated as a discontinued operation?

3   How should a discontinued activity be accounted for?

4   Draw up a proforma statement of total recognised gains and losses.

5   The movement in the reconciliation of movements in shareholders' funds is:

$$\text{Profit /loss for the financial year} + \text{Other recognised gains/losses} - \text{Dividends} + \text{New share capital}$$

    True ☐

    False ☐

6   The following accounting treatment should be used to make a prior period adjustment.

- Restate the prior year .... and ....
- Restate the .... balance.
- Include the adjustment in the ....
- Include a .... at the foot of the statement ....
  ....

Answers to Quick Quiz

1   All of them.

2   No. The sale is after the accounts were approved. Disclosure in a note can be made.

3   The **results** of the discontinued activity should be shown along with profit/loss on discontinuation (exceptional item) and comparatives.

4   Compare yours to that in Paragraph 2.1.

5   True

6   • Restate the prior year **profit and loss account** and **balance sheet**

    • Restate the **opening reserves** balance

    • Include the adjustment in the **reconciliation of movements in shareholders' funds**

    • Include a **note** at the foot of the **statement of total recognised gains and losses of the current period**

Now try the question below from the Exam Question Bank

Number	Level	Marks	Time
Q5	Examination	25	45 mins

Introduction to groups

Topic list	Syllabus reference
1 Definitions	D1
2 Exclusion of subsidiary undertakings from group accounts	D1
3 Exemption from the requirement to prepare group accounts	D1
4 Content of group accounts	D1
5 Group structure	D1
6 Group accounts: the related parties issue	D2

Introduction

In this chapter we will look at the major definitions in consolidation and the relevant statutory requirements and accounting standards. These matters are fundamental to your comprehension of group accounts, so make sure you can understand them and then learn them.

The next two chapters deal with the basic techniques of consolidation, and then we move on to more complex aspects in the following chapters.

In all these chapters, make sure that you work through each example and question properly.

Study guide

		Intellectual level
D	**BUSINESS COMBINATIONS**	
1	**The concept and principles of a group**	
(a)	Describe the concept of a group as a single economic unit.	2
(b)	Explain and apply the definition of a subsidiary within relevant accounting standards.	2
(c)	Describe why directors may not wish to consolidate a subsidiary and the circumstances where this is permitted.	2
(d)	Explain the need for using coterminous year ends and uniform accounting policies when preparing consolidated financial statements.	2
2	**The concept of consolidated financial statements**	
(a)	Explain the objective of consolidated financial statements.	2
(b)	Indicate the effect that the related party relationship between a parent and subsidiary may have on the subsidiary's entity statements and the consolidated financial statements.	2

Exam guide

Group accounts and consolidation are an extremely important area of your syllabus as **you are almost certain to face a large compulsory consolidation question in the examination.**

The key to consolidation questions in the examination is to adopt a logical approach and to practise as many questions as possible beforehand.

1 Definitions

FAST FORWARD

A **group** consists of a **parent undertaking** and one or more **subsidiary undertakings.**.

There are many reasons for businesses to operate as groups; for the goodwill associated with the names of the subsidiaries, for tax or legal purposes and so forth. Company law requires that the results of a group should be presented as a whole. Unfortunately, it is not possible simply to add all the results together and this chapter and those following will teach you how to **consolidate** all the results of companies within a group.

Exam focus point

If you are revising, go straight to the summary at the end of this section.

There are **two definitions of a group in company law. One** uses the terms 'holding company' and 'subsidiary' and applies **for general purposes. The other** is wider and applies **only for accounting purposes**. It **uses the terms 'parent undertaking' and 'subsidiary undertaking'**. The purpose of this widening of the group for accounting purposes was to curb the practice of structuring a group in such a way that not all companies or ventures within it had to be consolidated. This is an example of **off balance sheet financing** and has been used extensively to make consolidated accounts look better than is actually justified (see Chapter 15).

We are only really interested in the accounting definitions of parent and subsidiary undertaking here: they automatically include 'holding companies' and 'subsidiaries' under the general definition.

Exam focus point

You may be required to suggest why reliance on the entity financial statements of a subsidiary may mislead a potential purchaser of the company.

1.1 Parent and subsidiary undertakings: definition

FRS 2 states that an undertaking is the **parent undertaking** of another undertaking (**a subsidiary undertaking**) if any of the following apply.

Key term

Parent undertaking

(a) It holds a **majority of the voting rights** in the undertaking.

(b) It **is a member of the undertaking and has the right to appoint or remove directors** holding a majority of the voting rights at meetings of the board on all, or substantially all, matters.

(c) **It has the right to exercise a dominant influence over the undertaking**:

    (i) By virtue of provisions contained in the undertaking's memorandum or articles.

    (ii) By virtue of a control contract (in writing, authorised by the memorandum or articles of the controlled undertaking, permitted by law).

(d) **It is a member of the undertaking and controls alone**, under an agreement with other shareholders or members, **a majority of the voting rights in the undertaking.**

(e) (i) It actually exercises a dominant influence over the undertaking; ir
    (ii) It and the undertaking are managed on a unified basis

(f) A parent undertaking is **also treated as the parent undertaking of the subsidiary undertakings of its subsidiary undertakings.**

This replaced the previous criterion of owning a majority of equity with one of holding a majority of voting rights. **Also, the board is considered to be controlled if the holding company has the right to appoint directors with a majority of the voting rights on the board** (not just to appoint a simple majority of the directors, regardless of their voting rights).

1.1.1 Dominant influence

Key term

FRS 2 defines **dominant influence** as influence that can be exercised to achieve the operating and financial policies desired by the holder of the influence, notwithstanding the rights or influence of any other party.

The standard then distinguishes between the two different situations involving dominant influence.

(a) **The right to exercise a dominant influence** means that the holder has **a right to give directions** with respect to the operating and financial policies of another undertaking with which its directors are obliged to comply, whether or not they are for the benefit of that undertaking.

(b) **The actual exercise of dominant influence** is the exercise of an influence that achieves the result that the operating and financial policies of the undertaking influenced are set in accordance with the wishes of the holder of the influence and for the holder's benefit whether or not those wishes are explicit. The actual exercise of dominant influence is identified by its effect in practice rather than by the way in which it is exercised.

There are four other important definitions.

Key terms

(a) **Control** is the ability of an undertaking to direct the financial and operating policies of another undertaking with a view to gaining economic benefits from its activities.

(b) An **interest held on a long-term basis** is an interest which is held other than exclusively with a view to subsequent resale.

(c) An **interest held exclusively with a view to subsequent resale** is either:

   (i) An interest for which a purchaser has been identified or is being sought, and which is reasonably expected to be disposed of within approximately one year of its date of acquisition.

   (ii) An interest that was acquired as a result of the enforcement of a security, unless the interest has become part of the continuing activities of the group or the holder acts as if it intends the interest to become so.

(d) **Managed on a unified basis:** two or more undertakings are managed on a unified basis if the whole of the operations of the undertakings are integrated and they are managed as a single unit. Unified management does not arise solely because one undertaking manages another.

Other definitions from the standard will be introduced where relevant over the next few chapters.

1.2 The requirement to consolidate

FRS 2 requires a parent undertaking to prepare consolidated financial statements for its group unless it uses one of the exemptions available in the standard.

Key term

Consolidation is defined as: 'The process of adjusting and combining financial information from the individual financial statements of a parent undertaking and its subsidiary undertaking to prepare consolidated financial statements that present financial information for the group as a single economic entity.'

1.3 Associated undertakings

Another important definition, which applies only for the purposes of preparing group accounts, is that of an 'associated undertaking'.

Key term

'An '**associated undertaking**' means an undertaking in which an undertaking included in the consolidation has a participating interest and over whose operating and financial policy it exercises a significant influence, and which is not:

(a) A subsidiary undertaking of the parent company
(b) A joint venture'

'Where an undertaking holds 20% or more of the voting rights in another undertaking, it shall be presumed to exercise such an influence over it unless the contrary is shown.'

An undertaking **S is a subsidiary undertaking of H if:**

   (a) H is a member of S and *either* holds or **controls > 50% of the voting rights** *or* controls the board; *OR*

   (b) S is a **subsidiary** of P (ie S is a sub-subsidiary); *OR*

   (c) H has the right to exercise a **dominant influence** over S (laid down in the memorandum or articles or a control contract); *OR*

(d)   H **actually** exercises a **dominant influence** over S *or* P and S are managed on a unified basis.

∴ Special treatment: consolidate

An undertaking A is an **associated undertaking** of P if:

(a)   P and/or one or more of its subsidiary undertakings **either** hold more than **20%** of the voting rights **or** can otherwise be demonstrated to exercise a **significant** influence over A's operating and financial policy

(b)   A is not a subsidiary undertaking of P nor is it a joint venture.

∴ **Special treatment: equity accounting**

2 Exclusion of subsidiary undertakings from group accounts

FAST FORWARD An entity may have one or more subsidiaries which it would **like** to exclude from the consolidation, for instance they may be loss-making. For this reason, FRS 2 sets out the exact circumstances in which a subsidiary may be excluded.

The Companies Act **specifies circumstances** where a **subsidiary** undertaking is **allowed or required** to be **omitted** from **group accounts.**

(a)   Immateriality   (d)   Severe long-term restrictions
(b)   Held exclusively with a view to subsequent resale   (e)   Disproportionate expense and delay
(c)   Different activities

Where **all the subsidiary undertakings** of parent undertaking fall within **one of these exclusions, no group accounts are required** under the Companies Act. **However, this is modified by the provisions of FRS 2**.

2.1 Immateriality

The Companies Act allows an individual subsidiary to be excluded from consolidation if its inclusion is **not material** for the **purposes** of giving a **true and fair view**.

Where **two or more subsidiaries** are involved, these may be excluded only if they are not material, **taken together**.

FRS 2 states that it does not deal with immaterial items and hence this ground for exclusion is not covered by its requirements.

2.2 Held exclusively with a view to subsequent resale

The **Companies Act allows exclusion** from consolidation where:

'The **interest** of the parent is **held exclusively** with a view to **subsequent resale**.'

FRS 2 reiterates the Companies Act terms relating to this exclusion but **makes it mandatory**. So if the **conditions are met**, the relevant subsidiary undertaking **must be excluded** from consolidation. It specifies that this exclusion applies only to subsidiary undertaking which have not previously been consolidated.

FRS 2 however, sets a **tough test for achieving exclusion** via the **held exclusively for subsequent resale route**.

(a)   A **purchaser** has been **identified** or is being **sought**.

(b)   The interest is **reasonably expected** to be **sold** in approximately **one year of its acquisition**.

A **temporary investment** should be shown under **current assets** in the consolidation balance sheet at the **lower of cost and net realisable value**.

2.3 Severe long term restrictions

The **Companies Act allows** a subsidiary undertaking to be excluded from consolidation where severe long-tem restrictions **consistently hinder the exercise of the rights of the parent company** over the **assets** or **management** of that undertaking.

FRS 2 stiffens this Companies Act permissible exclusion to a **mandatory exclusion**. However, the explanatory notes to FRS 2 suggest that severe long-term restrictions justify excluding a subsidiary undertaking only where the **impact** of those restrictions is to **prevent** the parent undertaking from **controlling** its **subsidiary undertaking**, ie the test is harder to pass but once it is passed, the exclusion is mandatory.

Generally, **restrictions** are **better dealt** with by making **appropriate disclosures** rather than going down the exclusion from consolidation route.

Subsidiary undertakings **excluded** from consolidation **because of severe long-term restrictions** are to be **treated as fixed asset investments**. They should be included at their carrying amount when the restrictions came into force, subject to any write-down for impairment, and no further accruals are to be made for profits or losses of those subsidiary undertakings, unless the parent undertaking still exercises significant influence. In the latter case they are to be treated as associated undertakings.

The following information should be **disclosed** in the group accounts.

(a)   Its **net assets**.

(b)   Its **profit or loss** for the period.

(c)   Any amounts included in the **consolidated profit and loss account** in respect of:

(i)   **Dividends received** by the holding company from the subsidiary

(ii)   **Writing down the value of the investment**

2.4 Disproportionate expense and delay

The **Companies Act allows** a subsidiary company to be excluded from consolidation where the **information** necessary for the preparation of group accounts cannot be obtained without **disproportionate expense** or **undue delay**.

However, **FRS 2 effectively negates** any **scope to exclude** a subsidiary undertaking from consolidation, by stating:

'**Neither disproportionate expense** nor **undue delay** in obtaining the information necessary for the preparation of consolidated financial statements can **justify excluding** from consolidation subsidiary undertakings that are **individually or collectively material** in the **context** of the **group**.'

2.5 Dissimilar activities

The Companies Act allows exclusion where the activities of the subsidiary are so different for the activities of other members of the group that its consolidation is incomparable with the obligation to give a true and fair view.

FRS 2 takes the view that cases of this sort are exceptional and that dissimilar activities are **not** grounds for non-consolidation.

2.6 General disclosure requirements

In all cases given above, FRS 2 states that the consolidated accounts should show:

(a) The **reasons** for exclusion.
(b) The **names** of subsidiaries excluded.
(c) The **premium or discount on acquisition** not written off.
(d) **Anything else required** by the Companies Acts.

The Companies Act requires that when **consolidated group accounts** are **not prepared**, or if **any subsidiaries** are **excluded** from the group accounts (for any of the reasons given above), **a note to the accounts should be given:**

(a) To explain the **reasons** why the subsidiaries are not dealt with in group accounts
(b) To disclose any **auditors' qualifications** in the accounts of the **excluded subsidiaries**

A **note** to the (holding) company's accounts (or the consolidated accounts, if any) should **also state**, for **subsidiaries** which are **not consolidated** in group accounts, the aggregate value of the **total investment** of the **holding company** in the subsidiaries, by way of the **'equity method' of valuation**.

2.7 Section summary

The following table summaries the rules relating to exclusion of a subsidiary.

Reason for exclusion	Companies Act	FRS 2	Classification	Accounting treatment
• Immateriality	Optional	Does not deal with immaterial items	–	–
• Temporary control	Optional	Mandatory	Current asset investment	Lower of cost and NRV
• Severe long-term restrictions	Optional	Mandatory	Fixed asset investment	• Record at carrying amount when restrictions come into force, less any impairment. • Where parent exercises significant influence, treat as associate and apply equity accounting
• Disproportionate expense and delay	Optional	Not allowed	–	–
• Dissimilar activities	Optional	Not allowed	-	• If inclusion *does* violate 'true and fair' should be included using equity method.

3 Exemption from the requirement to prepare group accounts

The CA 1989 introduced a completely new provision exempting some groups from preparing consolidated accounts. There are two grounds.

(a) **Smaller groups** can claim exemptions on grounds of size (see below).

(b) **Parent companies** (*except* for listed companies) **whose immediate parent produces accounts in accordance with IFRS** need not prepare consolidated accounts. The accounts must give the name and country of incorporation of the parent and state the fact of the exemption. In addition, a copy of the audited consolidated accounts of the parent must be filed with the UK company's accounts. Minority shareholders can, however, require that consolidated accounts are prepared.

FRS 2 adds that exemption may be gained if all of the parent's subsidiary undertakings gain exemption under the Companies Act.

The **exemption** from preparing consolidated accounts is **not available to:**

(a) Public companies.
(b) Banking and insurance companies.
(c) Authorised persons under the Financial Services Act 1986.
(d) Companies belonging to a group containing a member of the above classes of undertaking.

Any two of the following **size criteria** for small and medium-sized groups must be met.

	Small	**Medium-sized**
Aggregate turnover	≤ £5.6 million net/ £6.72 million gross	≤ £22.8 million net/ £27.36 million gross
Aggregate gross assets	≤ £2.8 million net/ £3.36 million gross	≤ £11.4 million net/ £13.68 million gross
Aggregate number of employees (average monthly)	≤ 50	≤ 250

The aggregates can be calculated either before (gross) or after (net) consolidation adjustments for intra-group sales, unrealised profit on stock and so on (see following chapters). The qualifying conditions **must be met**:

(a) **In the case of the parent's first financial year, in that year**
(b) **In the case of any subsequent financial year, in that year and the preceding year**

If the qualifying conditions were met in the preceding year but not in the current year, the exemption can be claimed. If, in the subsequent year, the conditions are met again, the exemption can still be claimed, but if they are not met, then the exemption is lost until the conditions are again met for the second of two successive years.

When the exemption is claimed, but the auditors believe that the company is not entitled to it, then they must state in their report that the company is in their opinion not entitled to the exemption and this report must be attached to the individual accounts of the company (ie no report is required when the company *is* entitled to the exemption).

4 Content of group accounts

Group accounts comprise a consolidated profit and loss account, balance sheet and cash flow statement. Each of these financial statements presents the financial position and results of the group as if they were the financial position and results of a single entity.

The information contained in the individual accounts of a holding company and each of its subsidiaries does not give a picture of the group's activities as those of a single entity. To do this, a separate set of accounts can be prepared from the individual accounts. *Note*. **Remember that a group has no separate (legal) existence, except for accounting purposes.**

There is more than one way of amalgamating the information in the individual accounts into a set of group accounts, but the most common way (and now the legally required way) is to prepare consolidated accounts. **Consolidated accounts are one form of group accounts which combines the information contained in the separate accounts of a holding company and its subsidiaries as if they were the accounts of a single entity.** 'Group accounts' and 'consolidated accounts' are often used synonymously, and now that UK law *requires* group accounts to be consolidated accounts, this tendency will no doubt increase.

In simple terms a set of consolidated accounts is prepared by **adding together** the assets and liabilities of the holding company and each subsidiary. The **whole of the assets and liabilities of each company** are included, **even though some subsidiaries may be only partly owned**. The 'capital and reserves' side of the balance sheet will indicate how much of the net assets are attributable to the group and how much to outside investors in partly owned subsidiaries. These **outside investors** are known as **minority interests**.

The CA 1985 requires that group accounts should be prepared whenever a company:

    (a)   Is a parent company at the end of its financial year
    (b)   Is not itself a wholly owned subsidiary of a company incorporated in Great Britain

Most parent companies present their own individual accounts and their group accounts in a single **package**. The package typically comprises a:

    (a)   **Parent company balance sheet**, which will include 'investments in subsidiary undertakings' as an asset.

    (b)   **Consolidated balance sheet**.

    (c)   **Consolidated profit and loss** account.

    (d)   **Consolidated cash flow statement**.

It is not necessary to publish a parent company profit and loss account (s 230 CA 1985), provided the consolidated profit and loss account contains a note stating the profit or loss for the financial year dealt with in the accounts of the parent company and the fact that the statutory exemption is being relied on.

Exam focus point

If you are in a hurry skim or skip the rest of Section 4.

4.1 Co-terminous accounting periods

The Companies Act requires that the directors of the holding company **should ensure that the financial year of each of the subsidiaries in the group shall coincide with the financial year of the holding company.** This is to prevent any possible 'window dressing' (although financial years need not coincide if the directors hold the opinion that there are reasons against it).

If the financial year end of a subsidiary does not coincide with the financial year of the holding company, the appropriate results to include in the group accounts for the subsidiary will be those for its year ending before the year end of the holding company; or if this ended more than three months previously, from interim accounts prepared as at the holding company's year end. These two provisions are included in FRS 2.

Additionally, FRS 2 requires that a note to the group accounts should disclose the:

(a)   Reasons why the directors consider that coinciding dates are not appropriate.

(b)   Name(s) of the subsidiary(ies) concerned.

(c)   Accounting date and length of the accounting period of each relevant subsidiary.

4.2 Disclosure of subsidiaries

The Companies Act requires that a parent company disclose, by note:

(a)   The name of each subsidiary undertaking.

(b)   Its country of incorporation (or, if unincorporated, address of principal place of business).

(c)   The identity and proportion of the nominal value of each class of shares held (distinguishing between direct and indirect holdings).

(d)   The reason for treating a subsidiary undertaking as such *unless* a majority of the voting rights are held and the proportion is the same as that of shares held.

FRS 2 confirms these provisions and also requires that the nature of each subsidiary's business should be indicated.

(*Note*. A subsidiary company must show, in its own accounts, its ultimate holding company's name and country of incorporation.)

4.3 Further provisions of FRS 2

FRS 2 also requires the following.

(a)   **Uniform accounting policies should be applied by all companies in the group,** or if this is not done, appropriate adjustments should be made in the consolidated accounts to achieve uniformity. (If, in exceptional cases, such adjustments are impractical, the different accounting policies used, the effect of the difference on the results and net assets, and the reason for the different treatment should all be disclosed). This is also required by the Companies Act.

(b)   **Where there are material additions to the group there should be disclosure of the extent to which the results of the group are affected by profits and losses** of subsidiaries brought in for the first time. This is also now required by the Companies Act.

(c)   **Outside or minority interests in the share capital and reserves of companies consolidated should be disclosed separately in the consolidated balance sheet** (also required by the Companies Act). Debit balances should be shown only if there is a binding obligation on minority shareholders to make good any losses. Similarly, the profits and losses of such companies attributable to outside interests should be shown separately in the consolidated profit and loss account after arriving at group profit or loss after tax.

(d)   Changes in membership of a group occur on the date control passes, whether by a transaction or other event. **Changes in the membership of the group during the period should be disclosed.**

(e)   When a subsidiary undertaking is acquired the FRS requires its **identifiable assets and liabilities to be brought into the consolidation at their fair values at the date that undertaking becomes a subsidiary** undertaking, even if the acquisition has been made in stages. When a group increases its interest in an undertaking that is already its subsidiary undertaking, the identifiable assets and liabilities of that subsidiary undertaking should be calculated by reference to that fair value. This revaluation is not required if the difference between fair values and carrying amounts of the identifiable assets and liabilities attributable to the increase in stake is not material.

(f) The effect of consolidating the parent and its subsidiary undertakings may be that aggregation obscures useful information about the different undertakings and activities included in the consolidated financial statements. Parent undertakings are encouraged to give **segmental analysis to provide** readers of consolidated financial statements with **useful information on the different risks and rewards, growth and prospects of the different parts of the group.**

5 Group structure

FAST FORWARD

> The first issue to look at is always the **structure** of the group. This shows which companies should be included in the consolidation.

With the difficulties of definition and disclosure dealt with, let us now look at group structures. The simplest are those in which a holding company has only a direct interest in the shares of its subsidiary companies. For example:

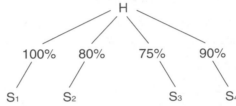

S_1 Ltd is a wholly owned subsidiary of H Ltd. S_2 Ltd, S_3 Ltd and S_4 Ltd are partly owned subsidiaries; a proportion of the shares in these companies is held by outside investors.

Often a holding company will have indirect holdings in its subsidiary companies. This can lead to more complex group structures.

(a)

H
|
51%
|
S
|
51%
|
SS

H Ltd owns 51% of the equity shares in S Ltd, which is therefore its subsidiary. S Ltd in its turn owns 51% of the equity shares in SS Ltd. SS Ltd is therefore a subsidiary of S Ltd and consequently a subsidiary of H Ltd. SS Ltd would describe S Ltd as its **parent** (or holding) company and H Ltd as its **ultimate parent** (or holding) company.

Note that although H Ltd can control the assets and business of SS Ltd by virtue of the chain of control, its interest in the assets of SS Ltd is only 26%. This can be seen by considering a dividend of £100 paid by SS Ltd: as a 51% shareholder, S Ltd would receive £51; H Ltd would have an interest in 51% of this £51 = £26.01.

(b)

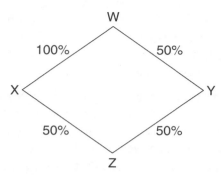

W Ltd owns 100% of the equity of X Ltd and 50% of the equity of Y Ltd. X Ltd and Y Ltd each own 50% of the equity of Z Ltd. Assume that:

(i)   W Ltd does not control the composition of Y Ltd's board; and

(ii)   W Ltd does not hold or control more than 50% of the *voting rights* in Y Ltd; and

(iii)   W Ltd does not have the right to exercise a dominant influence over Y Ltd by virtue of its memorandum, articles or a control contract; and

(iv)   W Ltd and Y Ltd are not managed on a unified basis; and

(v)   W Ltd does not actually exercise a dominant influence over Y Ltd; and

(vi)   none of the above apply to either X Ltd's or Y Ltd's holdings in Z Ltd.

In other words, because W Ltd is not in co-operation with the holder(s) of the other 50% of the shares in Y Ltd, neither Y nor Z can be considered subsidiaries.

In that case:

(i)   X Ltd is a subsidiary of W Ltd;

(ii)   Y Ltd is not a subsidiary of W Ltd;

(iii)   Z Ltd is not a subsidiary of either X Ltd or Y Ltd. Consequently, it is not a subsidiary of W Ltd.

If Z Ltd pays a dividend of £100, X Ltd and Y Ltd will each receive £50. The interest of W Ltd in this dividend is as follows.

	£
Through X Ltd (100% × £50)	50
Through Y Ltd (50% × £50)	25
	75

Although W Ltd has an interest in 75% of Z Ltd's assets, Z Ltd is not a subsidiary of W Ltd.

(c)

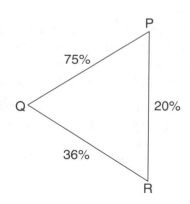

Q Ltd is a subsidiary of P Ltd. P Ltd therefore has indirect control over 36% of R Ltd's equity. P Ltd also has direct control over 20% of R Ltd's equity. R Ltd is therefore a subsidiary of P Ltd, although P Ltd's interest in R Ltd's assets is only 20% + (75% × 36%) = 47%.

Examples (b) and (c) illustrate an important point in company law: in deciding whether a company A holds more than 50% of the equity (or equivalent) of an undertaking B it is necessary to aggregate:

(i)   Shares (or equivalent) in B held directly by A
(ii)   Shares (or equivalent) in B held by undertakings which are subsidiaries of A

Question	Published accounts

During the time until your examination you should obtain as many sets of the published accounts of top quoted companies as possible. Examine the accounting policies in relation to subsidiary and associated companies and consider how these policies are shown in the accounting and consolidation treatment. Consider the effect of any disposals during the year. Also, look at all the disclosures made relating to fair values, goodwill etc and match them to the disclosure requirements outlined in this chapter and in subsequent chapters on FRSs 6 and 7.

Alternatively (or additionally) you should attempt to obtain such information from the financial press.

6 Group accounts: the related parties issue

FAST FORWARD

Parent companies and subsidiaries are **related parties** as per FRS 8. Bear in mind that this relationship can be exploited.

FRS 8 draws attention to the significance of related party relationships and transactions – that transactions between the parties may not be 'at arm's length' and that users of the accounts must be made aware of this, as it may affect their view of the financial statements.

6.1 Individual company accounts

The relationship between a parent and a subsidiary is the most obvious example of a related party relationship and it offers a number of opportunities for manipulating results. Some of these may be aimed at improving the parent's individual financial statements.

Any of the following could take place:

(a)   The subsidiary sells goods to the parent company at an artificially low price. This increases parent company profit while reducing profit in the subsidiary, thus increasing profit available for distribution to parent company shareholders at the expense of the minority.

(b)   The parent sells goods to the subsidiary at an artificially high price. This has the same result as above.

(c)   The subsidiary makes a loan to the parent at an artificially low rate of interest or the parent makes a loan to the subsidiary at an artificially high rate of interest. The loans will be cancelled on consolidation but the interest payments will transfer profits from the subsidiary to the parent.

(d)   The parent can sell an asset to the subsidiary at an amount in excess of its carrying amount. This again serves to transfer profit (and cash) to the parent.

6.2 Consolidated accounts

The transactions above seek to improve the **individual** parent company accounts at the expense of the individual subsidiary accounts. Dividends are paid to shareholders on the basis of these individual company financial statements, not the consolidated financial statements.

The tightening up of the opportunities for excluding a subsidiary from consolidation under FRS 2 have reduced the opportunities for improving the appearance of the **consolidated** financial statements. Prior to this, a number of possibilities could be exploited:

(a) A group could obtain loans via a subsidiary, which was not then consolidated. The loan would not appear in the consolidated balance sheet and group gearing (% of capital provided by loans) would appear lower than it actually was.

(b) Sale and leaseback transactions could be carried out in which assets were sold to a non-consolidated subsidiary and leased back under an operating lease. This enabled the asset and its associated borrowings to be removed from the balance sheet.

6.3 Disposal of subsidiaries

While the situations above are all concerned with improving the appearance of the parent company or group financial statements at the expense of those of the subsidiary, there may be occasions where the **opposite** is the intention.

For instance, when a parent company has decided to dispose of its shares in a poorly-performing subsidiary, it may seek to enhance the results of that subsidiary for the purpose of selling at a profit. In this case, transactions such as those at 6.1 above may be undertaken in the other direction – to transfer profit from the **parent** to the **subsidiary**.

6.4 Effect on trading

Even where no related party transactions have taken place, the parent/subsidiary relationship can still affect how the parties do business. For instance if, prior to acquisition by the parent, the subsidiary had a major customer or supplier who was a competitor of the parent, that trading arrangement can be expected to cease. The subsidiary may itself have been a competitor of the parent, in which case it may now have had to withdraw from certain markets in favour of the parent.

Look out for any of these issues in a consolidated accounts question.

Chapter Roundup

- A **group** consists of a **parent undertaking** and one or more **subsidiary undertakings**.

- An entity may have one or more subsidiaries which it would **like** to exclude from the consolidation, for instance they may be loss-making. For this reason, FRS 2 sets out the exact circumstances in which a subsidiary may be excluded.

- Group accounts comprise a consolidated profit and loss account, balance sheet and cash flow statement. Each of these financial statements presents the financial position and results of the group as if they were the financial position and results of a single entity.

- The first issue to look at is always the **structure** of the group. This shows which companies should be included in the consolidation.

- Parent companies and subsidiaries are **related parties** as per FRS 8. Bear in mind that this relationship can be exploited.

Quick Quiz

1 *Fill in the blanks* in the statements below, using the words in the box.

Per FRS 2, A is a parent of B if:

(a) A holds (1) ……………….. in B

(b) A can appoint or remove (2) ………………..

(c) A has the right to exercise (3) ……………….. over B

(d) B is a (4) ……………….. of A

Sub-subsidiary	Dominant influence
Directors holding a majority of the voting rights	A majority of the voting rights

2 What is dominant influence?

3 How should a subsidiary excluded on the grounds of temporary control be accounted for in the consolidated balance sheet?

4 It is not necessary for a parent company to publish its profit and loss account.

True ☐

False ☐

Answers to Quick Quiz

1 (a) A majority of the voting rights
    (b) Directors holding a majority of the voting rights
    (c) Significant influence
    (d) Sub-subsidiary

2 Influence that can be exercised to achieve the operating and financial policies desired by the holder of the influence, notwithstanding the rights or influence of any other party.

3 It should be included under current assets at the lower of cost and NRV.

4 True. The parent company's balance sheet must be published but there is an exemption for its profit and loss account.

The consolidated balance sheet

Topic list	Syllabus reference
1 Cancellation and part cancellation	D1
2 Minority interests	D3
3 Dividends paid by a subsidiary	D1
4 Goodwill arising on consolidation	D2
5 Inter-company trading	D1
6 Inter-company sales of fixed assets	D1
7 Summary: consolidated balance sheet	D3
8 Acquisition of a subsidiary during its accounting period	D3
9 Dividends and pre-acquisition profits	D3
10 FRS 7 *Fair values in acquisition accounting*	D2

Introduction

This chapter introduces the *basic procedures* required in consolidation and gives a formal step plan for carrying out a balance sheet consolidation. This step procedure should be useful to you as a starting guide for answering any question, but remember that you cannot rely on it to answer the question for you.

The method of consolidation shown here uses schedules for workings (reserves, minority interests etc) rather than the ledger accounts used in some other texts. This is because we believe that ledger accounts lead students to 'learn' the consolidation journals without thinking about what they are doing - always a dangerous practice in consolidation questions.

There are plenty of questions in this chapter - work through *all* of them carefully.

Study guide

		Intellectual level
D	**BUSINESS COMBINATIONS**	
1	**The concept and principles of a group**	
(e)	Explain why it is necessary to eliminate intra-group transactions.	2
2	**The concept of consolidated financial statements**.	2
(a)	Describe and apply the required accounting treatment of consolidated goodwill	
(e)	Explain why it is necessary to use fair values for the consideration of an investment in a subsidiary together with the fair values of a subsidiary's identifiable assets and liabilities when preparing consolidated financial statements.	2
3	**Preparation of consolidated financial statements including an associate**	
(a)	Prepare a consolidated balance sheet for a simple group (parent and one subsidiary) dealing with pre and post acquisition profits, minority interests and consolidated goodwill.	2
(b)	Explain and account for other reserves (eg share premium and revaluation reserves).	1
(c)	Account for the effects (in the income statement and balance sheet) of intra-group trading.	2
(d)	Account for the effects of fair value adjustments (including their effect on consolidated goodwill) to:	2
	(i) Depreciating and non-depreciating non-current assets	
	(ii) Stock	
	(iii) Monetary liabilities	
	(iv) Assets and liabilities not included in the subsidiary's own balance sheet, including contingent assets and liabilities.	
(e)	Account for goodwill impairment.	2

Exam guide

Each question must be approached and answered on its own merits. Examiners often put small extra or different problems in because, as they are always reminding students, it is not possible to 'rote-learn' consolidation.

1 Cancellation and part cancellation

1.1 Basic process

FAST FORWARD

The preparation of a consolidated balance sheet, in a very simple form, consists of two procedures.

(a)   Take the individual accounts of the holding company and each subsidiary and **cancel out items which appear as an asset in one company and a liability in another.**

(b)   **Add together all the uncancelled assets** and liabilities throughout the group.

1.2 Cancellation

Items requiring cancellation may include the following.

(a)   The asset **'shares in subsidiary companies'** which appears in the parent company's accounts will be matched with the liability 'share capital' in the subsidiaries' accounts.

(b)   There may be **inter-company trading** within the group. For example, S Ltd may sell goods to P Ltd. P Ltd would then be a debtor in the accounts of S Ltd, while S Ltd would be a creditor in the accounts of P Ltd.

1.3 Example: cancellation

Peach Ltd regularly sells goods to its one subsidiary company, Strawberry Ltd. The balance sheets of the two companies on 31 December 20X6 are given below.

PEACH LIMITED
BALANCE SHEET AS AT 31 DECEMBER 20X6

	£	£	£
Fixed assets			
Tangible assets			35,000
40,000 £1 shares in Strawberry Ltd at cost			40,000
			75,000
Current assets			
Stocks		16,000	
Debtors: Strawberry Ltd	2,000		
Other	6,000		
		8,000	
Cash at bank		1,000	
		25,000	
Current liabilities			
Creditors		14,000	
			11,000
			86,000
Capital and reserves			
70,000 £1 ordinary shares			70,000
Reserves			16,000
			86,000

STRAWBERRY LIMITED
BALANCE SHEET AS AT 31 DECEMBER 20X6

	£	£	£
Fixed assets			
Tangible assets			45,000
Current assets			
Stocks		12,000	
Debtors		9,000	
		21,000	
Current liabilities			
Bank overdraft		3,000	
Creditors: Peach Ltd	2,000		
Other	2,000		
		4,000	
		7,000	
			14,000
			59,000
Capital and reserves			
40,000 £1 ordinary shares			40,000
Reserves			19,000
			59,000

Prepare the consolidated balance sheet of Peach Ltd.

Solution

The cancelling items are:

(a)   Peach Ltd's asset 'investment in shares of Strawberry Ltd' (£40,000) cancels with Strawberry Ltd's liability 'share capital' (£40,000);

(b)   Peach Ltd's asset 'debtors: Strawberry Ltd' (£2,000) cancels with Strawberry Ltd's liability 'creditors: Peach Ltd' (£2,000).

The remaining assets and liabilities are added together to produce the following consolidated balance sheet.

PEACH LIMITED
CONSOLIDATED BALANCE SHEET AS AT 31 DECEMBER 20X6

	£	£
Fixed assets		
Tangible assets		80,000
Current assets		
Stocks	28,000	
Debtors	15,000	
Cash at bank	1,000	
	44,000	
Current liabilities		
Bank overdraft	3,000	
Creditors	16,000	
	19,000	
		25,000
		105,000
Capital and reserves		
70,000 £1 ordinary shares		70,000
Reserves		35,000
		105,000

1.3.1 Notes on the example

(a)   Peach Ltd's bank balance is not netted off with Strawberry Ltd's bank overdraft. To offset one against the other would be less informative and would conflict with the statutory principle that assets and liabilities should not be netted off.

(b)   The share capital in the consolidated balance sheet is the share capital of the parent company alone. This must *always* be the case, no matter how complex the consolidation, because the share capital of subsidiary companies must *always* be a wholly cancelling item.

1.4 Part cancellation

An item may appear in the balance sheets of a parent company and its subsidiary, but not at the same amounts.

(a)   **The parent company may have acquired shares in the subsidiary at a price greater or less than their nominal value**. The asset will appear in the parent company's accounts at cost, while the liability will appear in the subsidiary's accounts at nominal value. **This raises the issue of goodwill**, which is dealt with later in this chapter.

(b)   Even if the parent company acquired shares at nominal value, it **may not have acquired all the shares of the subsidiary** (so the subsidiary may be only partly owned). This **raises the issue of minority interests**, which are also dealt with later in this chapter.

(c)   The inter-company trading balances may be out of step because of **goods or cash in transit**.

(d)   One company may have **issued loan stock of which a proportion only is taken up** by the other company.

The following example illustrates the techniques needed to deal with the second two items. The procedure is to **cancel as far as possible. The remaining uncancelled amounts will appear in the consolidated balance sheet.**

(a)   Uncancelled loan stock will appear as a liability of the group.

(b)   Uncancelled balances on inter-company accounts represent goods or cash in transit, which will appear in the consolidated balance sheet.

Question

Consolidated balance sheet 1

The balance sheets of Parrot Ltd and of its subsidiary Swallow Ltd have been made up to 30 June. Parrot Ltd has owned all the ordinary shares and 40% of the loan stock of Swallow Ltd since its incorporation.

PARROT LIMITED
BALANCE SHEET AS AT 30 JUNE

	£	£
Fixed assets		
Tangible assets		120,000
Investment in Swallow Ltd, at cost		
80,000 ordinary shares of £1 each		80,000
£20,000 of 12% loan stock in Swallow Ltd		20,000
		220,000
Current assets		
Stocks	50,000	
Debtors	40,000	
Current account with Swallow Ltd	18,000	
Cash	4,000	
	112,000	
Creditors: amounts falling due within one year		
Creditors	47,000	
Taxation	15,000	
	62,000	
Net current assets		50,000
		270,000
Creditors: amounts falling due after more than one year		
10% loan stock		75,000
		195,000
Capital and reserves		
Ordinary shares of £1 each, fully paid		100,000
Reserves		95,000
		195,000

SWALLOW LIMITED
BALANCE SHEET AS AT 30 JUNE

	£	£
Tangible fixed assets		100,000
Current assets		
Stocks	60,000	
Debtors	30,000	
Cash	6,000	
	96,000	
Creditors: amounts falling due within one year		
Creditors	16,000	
Taxation	10,000	
Current account with Parrot Ltd	12,000	
	38,000	
		58,000
		158,000
Creditors: amounts falling due after more than one year		
12% Loan stock		50,000
		108,000
Capital and reserves		
80,000 ordinary shares of £1 each, fully paid		80,000
Reserves		28,000
		108,000

The difference on current account arises because of goods in transit. Prepare the consolidated balance sheet of Parrot Ltd.

Answer

PARROT LIMITED
CONSOLIDATED BALANCE SHEET AS AT 30 JUNE

	£	£
Tangible fixed assets (120,000 + 100,000)		220,000
Current assets		
Stocks (50000 + 60,000)	110,000	
Goods in transit (18,000 − 12,000)	6,000	
Debtors (40,000 + 30,000)	70,000	
Cash (4,400 + 6,000)	10,000	
	196,000	
Creditors: amounts falling due within one year		
Creditors (47,000 + 16,000)	63,000	
Taxation (15,000 + 10,000)	25,000	
	88,000	
		108,000
		328,000
Creditors: amounts falling due after more than one year		
10% loan stock	75,000	
12% loan stock (50,000 × 60%)	30,000	
		105,000
		223,000
Capital and reserves		
Ordinary shares of £1 each, fully paid (parent)		100,000
Reserves (95,000 + 28,000)		123,000
		223,000

Note especially how:

(a)   The uncancelled loan stock in Swallow Ltd becomes a liability of the group
(b)   The goods in transit is the difference between the current accounts (£18,000 – £12,000)
(c)   The investment in Swallow Lt's shares is cancelled against Swallow Ltd's share capital

2 Minority interests

Where the parent does not own 100% of the shares in the subsidiary, the other shares are held by **minority** shareholders. The proportion of share capital and reserves attributable to this **minority interest** must be shown in the consolidated balance sheet.

Exam focus point

All F7 papers will include a group accounts question which is more than likely to involve calculating minority interests.

It was mentioned earlier that the total assets and liabilities of subsidiary companies are included in the consolidated balance sheet, even in the case of subsidiaries which are only partly owned. A proportion of the net assets of such subsidiaries in fact belongs to investors from outside the group (minority interests).

Key term

FRS 2 defines **minority interest** in a subsidiary undertaking as the 'interest in a subsidiary undertaking included in the consolidation that is attributable to the shares held by or on behalf of persons other than the parent undertaking and its subsidiary undertakings'.

In the consolidated balance sheet it is necessary to distinguish this proportion from those assets attributable to the group and financed by shareholders' funds.

The net assets of a company are financed by share capital and reserves. The consolidation procedure for dealing with partly owned subsidiaries is to **calculate the proportion of ordinary shares, preference shares and reserves attributable to minority interests.**

2.1 Example: minority interests

Peppa Ltd has owned 75% of the share capital of Salt Ltd since the date of Salt Ltd's incorporation. Their latest balance sheets are given below.

PEPPA LIMITED – BALANCE SHEET

	£
Fixed assets	
Tangible assets	50,000
30,000 £1 ordinary shares in Salt Ltd at cost	30,000
	80,000
Net current assets	25,000
Net assets	105,000
Capital and reserves	
80,000 £1 ordinary shares	80,000
Reserves	25,000
	105,000

SALT LIMITED BALANCE SHEET

	£
Tangible fixed assets	35,000
Net current assets	15,000
Net assets	50,000
Capital and reserves	
40,000 £1 ordinary shares	40,000
Reserves	10,000
	50,000

Prepare the consolidated balance sheet.

Solution

All of Salt Ltd's net assets are consolidated despite the fact that the company is only 75% owned. The amount of net assets attributable to minority interests is calculated as follows.

	£
Minority share of share capital (25% × £40,000)	10,000
Minority share of reserves (25% × £10,000)	2,500
	12,500

Of Salt Ltd's share capital of £40,000, £10,000 is included in the figure for minority interest, while £30,000 is cancelled with Peppa Ltd's asset 'investment in Salt Limited'.

The consolidated balance sheet can now be prepared.

PEPPA GROUP
CONSOLIDATED BALANCE SHEET

	£
Tangible fixed assets	85,000
Net current assets	40,000
	125,000
Share capital	80,000
Reserves £(25,000 + (75% × 10,000))	32,500
Shareholders' funds	112,500
Minority interest (W)	12,500
	125,000

In this example we have shown minority interest on the 'capital and reserves' side of the balance sheet to illustrate how some of Salt Ltd's net assets are financed by shareholders' funds, while some are financed by outside investors. You may see minority interest as a deduction from the other side of the balance sheet. The second half of the balance sheet will then consist entirely of shareholders' funds. The Companies Act 1985 permits either of the above presentations, but **FRS 4 seems to require the disclosure shown above**.

Exam focus point

In more complicated examples the following technique is recommended for dealing with minority interests.

Step 1 Cancel common items in the draft balance sheets. If there is a minority interest, the subsidiary company's share capital will be a partly cancelled item. Ascertain the proportion of shares held by the minority.

BPP
LEARNING MEDIA

Step 2   Produce a working for the minority interest. Add in the amount of share capital calculated in step 1: this completes the cancellation of the subsidiary's share capital.

Add also the minority's share of each reserve in the subsidiary company. Reserves belong to equity shareholders; the proportion attributable to minority interests therefore depends on their percentage holding of ordinary shares.

Step 3   Produce a separate working for each reserve (capital, revenue etc) found in the subsidiary company's balance sheet. The initial balances on these accounts will be taken straight from the draft balance sheets of the parent and subsidiary company.

Step 4   The closing balances in these workings can be entered directly onto the consolidated balance sheet.

Question

Consolidated balance sheet 2

Set out below are the draft balance sheets of Plug Ltd and its subsidiary Socket Ltd. You are required to prepare the consolidated balance sheet.

PLUG LIMITED

	£	£
Fixed assets		
Tangible assets		31,000
Investment in Socket Ltd		
12,000 £1 ordinary shares at cost	12,000	
£8,000 10% debentures at cost	8,000	
		20,000
		51,000
Net current assets		11,000
		62,000
Capital and reserves		
Ordinary shares of £1 each		40,000
Revenue reserve		22,000
		62,000

SOCKET LIMITED

	£
Tangible fixed assets	34,000
Net current assets	22,000
	56,000
Long-term liability	
10% debentures	26,000
	30,000
Capital and reserves	
Ordinary shares of £1 each	20,000
Capital reserve	6,000
Revenue reserve	4,000
	30,000

Answer

Partly cancelling items are the components of Plug Ltd's investment in Socket Ltd, ie ordinary shares and debentures. Minorities have an interest in 40% (8,000/20,000) of Socket Ltd's equity, including reserves.

You should now produce workings for minority interests, capital reserve and revenue reserve as follows.
Workings

1   *Minority interests*

		£
Ordinary share capital (40% of 20,000)		8,000
Reserves: capital (40% × 6,000)		2,400
revenue (40% × 4,000)		1,600
		12,000

2   *Capital reserve*

	Plug Ltd £	Socket Ltd £
Per question		6,000
Group share in Socket Ltd (6,000 × 60%)	3,600	
Group capital reserves	3,600	

3   *Revenue reserve*

	Plug Ltd £	Socket Ltd £
Per question	22,000	4,000
Group share in Socket Ltd (4,000 × 60%)	2,400	
Group revenue reserves	24,400	

The results of the workings are now used to construct the consolidated balance sheet (CBS).

PLUG GROUP
CONSOLIDATED BALANCE SHEET

	£
Tangible fixed assets	65,000
Net current assets	33,000
	98,000
Long-term liability	
10% debentures (26,000 − 8,000)	(18,000)
	80,000
Capital and reserves	
Ordinary shares of £1 each	40,000
Capital reserve (W2)	3,600
Revenue reserve (W3)	24,400
Shareholders' funds	68,000
Minority interests (W1)	12,000
	80,000

Notes

(a)   Socket Ltd is a subsidiary of Plug Ltd because Plug Ltd owns 60% of its equity capital.

(b)   As always, the share capital in the consolidated balance sheet is that of the parent company alone. The share capital in Socket Ltd's balance sheet was partly cancelled against the investment shown in Plug Ltd's balance sheet, while the uncancelled portion was credited to minority interest.

(c)   The figure for minority interest comprises the interest of outside investors in the share capital and reserves of the subsidiary. The uncancelled portion of Socket Ltd's debentures is not shown as part of minority interest but is disclosed separately as a liability of the group.

3 Dividends paid by a subsidiary

FAST FORWARD

When dealing with dividends paid by a subsidiary, make sure that the entry has been made in the accounts of both the **paying** company and the **receiving** company.

When a subsidiary company pays a dividend during the year the accounting treatment is not difficult. Suppose Silva Ltd, a 60% subsidiary of Pink Ltd, pays a dividend of £1,000 on the last day of its accounting period. Its total reserves before paying the dividend stood at £5,000.

(a)   £400 of the dividend is paid to minority shareholders. The cash leaves the group and will not appear anywhere in the consolidated balance sheet.

(b)   The parent company receives £600 of the dividend, debiting cash and crediting profit and loss account.

(c)   The remaining balance of reserves in Silva Ltd's balance sheet (£4,000) will be consolidated in the normal way. The group's share (60% × £4,000 = £2,400) will be included in group reserves in the balance sheet; the minority share (40% × £4,000 = £1,600) is credited to the minority interest account.

Exam focus point

Dividends *proposed* by a subsidiary do not appear in the accounts and will not be examined.

Note. When a subsidiary pays a dividend out of **pre-acquisition profits** the dividend is accounted for differently. This is explained in the next chapter.

4 Goodwill arising on consolidation

FAST FORWARD

When a company acquires shares in another company for an amount which exceeds the value of that proportion of the fair value of its assets, it has paid a 'premium', which is called **goodwill**. This appears as an **intangible fixed asset** in the consolidated balance sheet and is then **amortised** over its useful life.

In the examples we have looked at so far the cost of shares acquired by the parent company has always been equal to the nominal value of those shares. This is seldom the case in practice and we must now consider some more complicated examples. To begin with, **we will examine the entries made by the parent company in its own balance sheet when it acquires shares.**

When a company P Ltd wishes to **purchase shares** in a company S Ltd it must pay the previous owners of those shares. The most obvious form of payment would be in **cash**. Suppose P Ltd purchases all 40,000 £1 shares in S Ltd and pays £60,000 cash to the previous shareholders in consideration. The entries in P Ltd's books would be:

DEBIT	Investment in S Ltd at cost	£60,000	
CREDIT	Bank		£60,000

However, the previous shareholders might be prepared to accept some other form of consideration. For example, they might accept an agreed number of **shares** in P Ltd. P Ltd would then issue new shares in the agreed number and allot them to the former shareholders of S Ltd. This kind of deal might be attractive to P Ltd since it avoids the need for a heavy cash outlay. The former shareholders of S Ltd would retain an indirect interest in that company's profitability via their new holding in its parent company.

Continuing the example, suppose the shareholders of S Ltd agreed to accept one £1 ordinary share in P Ltd for every two £1 ordinary shares in S Ltd. P Ltd would then need to issue and allot 20,000 new £1 shares. How would this transaction be recorded in the books of P Ltd?

The simplest method would be as follows.

DEBIT	Investment in S Ltd	£20,000	
CREDIT	Share capital		£20,000

However, if the 40,000 £1 shares acquired in S Ltd are thought to have a value of £60,000 this would be misleading. The former shareholders of S Ltd have presumably agreed to accept 20,000 shares in P Ltd because they consider each of those shares to have a value of £3. This view of the matter suggests the following method of recording the transaction in P Ltd's books.

DEBIT	Investment in S Ltd	£60,000	
CREDIT	Share capital		£20,000
	Share premium account		£40,000

The second method is the one which the Companies Act 1985 requires should normally be used in preparing consolidated accounts.

The amount which P Ltd records in its books as the cost of its investment in S Ltd may be more or less than the book value of the assets it acquires. Suppose that S Ltd in the previous example has nil reserves, so that its share capital of £40,000 is balanced by net assets with a book value of £40,000. For simplicity, assume that the book value of S Ltd's assets is the same as their market or fair value.

Now when the directors of P Ltd agree to pay £60,000 for a 100% investment in S Ltd they must believe that, in addition to its tangible assets of £40,000, S Ltd must also have intangible assets worth £20,000. This amount of £20,000 paid over and above the value of the tangible assets acquired is called **goodwill arising on consolidation** (sometimes **premium on acquisition**).

Following the normal cancellation procedure the £40,000 share capital in S Ltd's balance sheet could be cancelled against £40,000 of the 'investment in S Limited' in the balance sheet of P Ltd. This would leave a £20,000 debit uncancelled in the parent company's accounts and this £20,000 would appear in the consolidated balance sheet under the caption 'Intangible fixed assets. Goodwill arising on consolidation' (although see below for FRS 10's requirements on this type of goodwill).

4.1 Goodwill and pre-acquisition profits

Up to now we have assumed that S Ltd had nil reserves when its shares were purchased by P Ltd. Assuming instead that S Ltd had earned profits of £8,000 in the period before acquisition, its balance sheet just before the purchase would look as follows.

	£
Net tangible assets	48,000
Share capital	40,000
Reserves	8,000
	48,000

If P Ltd now purchases all the shares in S Ltd it will acquire net tangible assets worth £48,000 at a cost of £60,000. Clearly in this case S Ltd's intangible assets (goodwill) are being valued at £12,000. It should be apparent that **any reserves earned by the subsidiary prior to its acquisition by the parent company must be incorporated in the cancellation process so as to arrive at a figure for goodwill arising on consolidation.** In other words, not only S Ltd's share capital, but also its pre-acquisition reserves, must be cancelled against the asset 'investment in S Ltd' in the accounts of the parent company. The uncancelled balance of £12,000 appears in the consolidated balance sheet.

The consequence of this is that any pre-acquisition reserves of a subsidiary company are not aggregated with the parent company's reserves in the consolidated balance sheet. **The figure of consolidated reserves comprises the reserves of the parent company plus the post-acquisition reserves only of subsidiary companies. The post-acquisition reserves are simply reserves at the consolidation date less reserves at acquisition.**

4.2 Example: goodwill and pre-acquisition profits

Pace Ltd acquired the ordinary shares of Speed Ltd on 31 March when the draft balance sheets of each company were as follows.

PACE LIMITED
BALANCE SHEET AS AT 31 MARCH

	£
Fixed assets	
Investment in 50,000 shares of Speed Ltd at cost	80,000
Net current assets	40,000
	120,000
Capital and reserves	
Ordinary shares	75,000
Revenue reserves	45,000
	120,000

SPEED LIMITED
BALANCE SHEET AS AT 31 MARCH

	£
Net current assets	60,000
Share capital and reserves	
50,000 ordinary shares of £1 each	50,000
Revenue reserves	10,000
	60,000

Prepare the consolidated balance sheet as at 31 March.

Solution

The technique to adopt here is to produce a new working: 'Goodwill'. A proforma working is set out below.

Goodwill

	£	£
Cost of investment		X
Share of net assets acquired as represented by:		
Ordinary share capital	X	
Share premium	X	
Reserves on acquisition	X	
Group share%		(X)
Goodwill		X

Applying this to our example the working will look like this.

	£	£
Cost of investment		80,000
Share of net assets acquired as represented by:		
Ordinary share capital	50,000	
Revenue reserves on acquisition	10,000	
	60,000	
Group share 100%		60,000
Goodwill		20,000

PACE LIMITED
CONSOLIDATED BALANCE SHEET AS AT 31 MARCH

	£
Fixed assets	20,000
Goodwill arising on consolidation	100,000
Net current assets	120,000
Capital and reserves	
Ordinary shares	75,000
Revenue reserves	45,000
	120,000

4.3 FRS 10 Goodwill and intangible assets

Goodwill arising on consolidation is one form of **purchased goodwill**, and is therefore governed by FRS 10. As explained in an earlier chapter FRS 10 requires that purchased goodwill should be capitalised and classified as an asset on the balance sheet. It is then eliminated from the accounts by **amortisation** through the profit and loss account.

A consolidation adjustment will be required each year as follows.

DEBIT   Consolidated P&L account
CREDIT   Provision for amortisation of goodwill

The **unamortised portion** will be included in the consolidated balance sheet under **fixed assets**.

Goodwill arising on consolidation is the difference between the cost of an acquisition and the value of the subsidiary's net assets acquired. This difference can be **negative**: the aggregate of the fair values of the separable net assets acquired may exceed what the holding company paid for them. This 'negative goodwill', also sometimes called 'discount arising on consolidation', is required by FRS 10 to be disclosed in the intangible fixed assets category, directly under positive goodwill, ie as a 'negative asset'. It is then released to the profit and loss account as the assets on which it is based are consumed (eg depreciated).

4.4 Forms of consideration

The consideration paid by the parent for the shares in the subsidiary can take different forms and this will affect the calculation of goodwill. Here are some examples:

4.4.1 Contingent consideration

The parent acquired 60% of the subsidiary's £100m share capital on 1 Jan 20X6 for a cash payment of £150m and a further payment of £50m on 31 March 20X7 if the subsidiary's post acquisition profits have exceeded an agreed figure by that date.

In the financial statements for the year to 31 December 20X6, three scenarios are possible:
The amount has already been exceeded.
It is probable that the amount will be exceeded by 31 March and this can reliably measured.

It is not probable that the amount will be exceeded.

In the case of (a) and (b), the cost of the combination will be £200m (150 + 50)
In the case of (c) the cost of combination will be £150m. (We have ignored discounting in this example).

4.4.2 Deferred consideration

The parent acquired 75% of the subsidiary's 80m £1 shares on 1 Jan 20X6. It paid £3.50 per share and agreed to pay a further £108m on 1 Jan 20X8.
The parent company's cost of capital is 8%.

In the financial statements for the year to 31 December 20X6 the cost of the combination will be as follows:

	£m
80m shares × 75% × £3.50	210
Deferred consideration:	
£108m × 1/1.08	100
Total consideration	310

At 31 December 20X7, the cost of the combination will be:

	£m
80m shares × 75% × £3.50	210
Due on 1 Jan: £108m	108
Total consideration	318

The increase arises from the **unwinding of the discount**.

4.4.3 Share exchange

The parent has acquired 12,000 £1 shares in the subsidiary by issuing 5 of its own £1 shares for every 4 shares in the subsidiary. The market value of the parent company's shares is £6.

Cost of the combination:

	£
12,000 × 5/4 × £6	90,000

Note that this is credited to the share capital and share premium of the parent company as follows:

	DR	CR
Investment in subsidiary	90,000	
Share capital (£12,000 × 5/4)		15,000
Share premium (£12,000 × 5/4 × 5)		75,000

4.4.4 Expenses and issue costs

Expenses of the combination, such as lawyers and accountants fees are added to the cost of the combination. However, the costs of issuing equity are treated as a deduction from the proceeds of the equity issue **not** as part of the cost of the combination. Share issue costs will therefore be debited to the share premium account.

4.5 Adjustments to goodwill

At the date of acquisition the parent recognises the assets, liabilities and contingent liabilities of the subsidiary at their fair value at the date when control is acquired. It may be that some of these assets or liabilities had not previously been recognised by the acquiree.

For instance, the subsidiary may have tax losses brought forward, but had not recognised these as an asset because it could not forsee future profits against which they could be offset. If it later appears that taxable profits will be forthcoming, the deferred tax asset can be recognised.

An entity has acquired a 60% interest in another entity which has brought forward tax losses unutilised of £200,000. The tax losses can now be utilised.

The adjustment will be:

	DR	CR
Deferred tax	200,000	
Minority interest		80,000
Goodwill		120,000

5 Inter-company trading

Where **inter-company trading** has taken place and goods which have been sold at a profit by one group company are still held in stock by another group company, an adjustment must be made to remove the element of **unrealised profit**. The entry will be: **DR Group reserves CR Group stock**. A similar adjustment is made to account for inter-company sales of fixed assets.

We have already come across cases where one company in a group engages in trading with another group company. Any debtor/creditor balances outstanding between the companies are cancelled on consolidation. No further problem arises if all such intra-group transactions are undertaken at cost, without any mark-up for profit.

However, each company in a group is a separate trading entity and may wish to treat other group companies in the same way as any other customer. In this case, a company (say A Ltd) may buy goods at one price and sell them at a higher price to another group company (B Ltd). The accounts of A Ltd will quite properly include the profit earned on sales to B Ltd; and similarly B Ltd's balance sheet will include stocks at their cost to B Ltd at the amount at which they were purchased from A Ltd.

This gives rise to **two problems.**

  (a)   Although A Ltd makes a profit as soon as it sells goods to B Ltd, the group does not make a sale or achieve a profit until an outside customer buys the goods from B Ltd.

  (b)   Any purchases from A Ltd which remain unsold by B Ltd at the year end will be included in B Ltd's stock. Their balance sheet value will be their cost to B Ltd, which is not the same as their cost to the group.

The objective of consolidated accounts is to present the financial position of several connected companies as that of a single entity, the group. This means that **in a consolidated balance sheet the only profits recognised should be those earned by the group** in providing goods or services to outsiders; and similarly, stock in the consolidated balance sheet should be valued at cost to the group.

Suppose that a parent company P Ltd buys goods for £1,600 and sells them to a wholly owned subsidiary S Ltd for £2,000. The goods are in S Ltd's stock at the year end and appear in S Ltd's balance sheet at £2,000. In this case, P Ltd will record a profit of £400 in its individual accounts, but from the group's point of view the figures are:

Cost	£1,600
External sales	nil
Closing stock at cost	£1,600
Profit/loss	nil

If we add together the figures for retained reserves and stock in the individual balance sheets of P Ltd and S Ltd the resulting figures for consolidated reserves and consolidated stock will each be overstated by £400. A **consolidation adjustment** is therefore necessary as follows.

DEBIT   **Group reserves**
CREDIT   **Group stock (balance sheet)**

with the amount of profit unrealised by the group.

| | Question | | | | | | Consolidated balance sheet 3 |

Pasta Ltd acquired all the shares in Spaghetti Ltd when the reserves of Spaghetti Ltd stood at £10,000. Draft balance sheets for each company are as follows.

	Pasta Ltd		Spaghetti Ltd	
	£	£	£	£
Fixed assets				
Tangible assets		80,000		40,000
Investment in Spaghetti Ltd at cost		46,000		
		126,000		
Current assets	40,000		30,000	
Current liabilities	21,000		18,000	
		19,000		12,000
		145,000		52,000
Capital and reserves				
Ordinary shares of £1 each		100,000		30,000
Reserves		45,000		22,000
		145,000		52,000

During the year Spaghetti Ltd sold goods to Pasta Ltd for £50,000, the profit to Spaghetti Ltd being 20% of selling price. At the balance sheet date, £15,000 of these goods remained unsold in the stocks of Pasta Ltd. At the same date, Pasta Ltd owed Spaghetti Ltd £12,000 for goods bought and this debt is included in the creditors of Pasta Ltd and the debtors of Spaghetti Ltd.

Note. Goodwill is deemed to have an indefinite useful life and is therefore to remain in the balance sheet.

Required

Prepare a draft consolidated balance sheet for Pasta Ltd.

| | Answer |

1   Goodwill

	£	£
Cost of investment		46,000
Share of net assets acquired as represented by		
Share capital	30,000	
Reserves	10,000	
	40,000	
Group share (100%)		40,000
Goodwill		6,000

2   Reserves

	Pasta Ltd	Spaghetti Ltd
	£	£
As per question	45,000	22,000
Pre acquisition		(10,000)
		12,000
Pasta share in Spaghetti (100%)	12,000	
Unrealised profit in stock £5,000 × 20%	(3,000)	
Group reserves	54,000	

PASTA LIMITED
CONSOLIDATED BALANCE SHEET

	£	£
Intangible fixed assets: goodwill		6,000
Tangible fixed assets		120,000
		126,000
Current assets (W1)	55,000	
Current liabilities (W2)	27,000	
		28,000
		154,000
Capital and reserves		
Ordinary shares of £1 each		100,000
Reserves		54,000
		154,000

Workings

1	*Current assets*	£	£
	In Pasta Ltd's balance sheet		40,000
	In Spaghetti Ltd's balance sheet	30,000	
	Spaghetti Ltd's current account with Pasta Ltd cancelled	(12,000)	
			18,000
			58,000
	Unrealised profit excluded from stock valuation		(3,000)
			55,000

2	*Current liabilities*		£
	In Pasta Ltd's balance sheet		21,000
	Less Pasta Ltd's current account with Spaghetti Ltd cancelled		12,000
			9,000
	In Spaghetti Ltd's balance sheet		18,000
			27,000

5.1 Minority interests in unrealised inter-company profits

A further problem occurs where a subsidiary company which is not wholly owned is involved in inter-company trading within the group. If a subsidiary S Ltd is 75% owned and sells goods to the parent company for £16,000 cost plus £4,000 profit, ie for £20,000 and if these stocks are unsold by P Ltd at the balance sheet date, the 'unrealised' profit of £4,000 earned by S Ltd and charged to P Ltd will be partly owned by the minority interest of S Ltd. As far as the minority interest of S Ltd is concerned, their share (25% of £4,000) amounting to £1,000 of profit on the sale of goods would appear to have been fully realised. It is only the group that has not yet made a profit on the sale.

However, FRS 2 requires elimination in full.

Basic requirement

> The elimination of profits or losses relating to inter-group transactions should be set against the interests held by the group and the minority interest in **respective proportion** to their **holdings in the undertaking whose individual statements record the eliminated profits or losses.**

The FRS 2 indicates two scenarios regarding unrealised profits in closing stocks.

(a) **Parent sold the stock to subsidiary.** The **unrealised profits sits in the parent's records** and relates to the **whole group**. Therefore the **entire unrealised profit** is **eliminated** from parent's accounts.

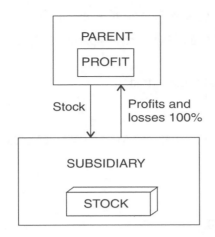

Profit sits in the parent and is attributable to its shareholders. Therefore eliminate 100% of unrealised profit against group profits.

(b) **Subsidiary sold the stock to the parent**. The **unrealised profit sits in the subsidiary's** records and relates to the subsidiary. Hence, the **minority** will have to **bear** its **share** of the elimination.

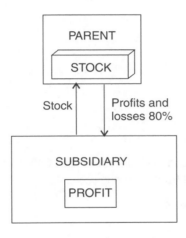

Minority shares in 20% profits and losses of subsidiary. Therefore minority must suffer its 20% share of the elimination of unrealised profit, with balance 80% borne by the group.

5.2 Example: minority interests and inter-company profits

Pie Ltd has owned 75% of the shares of Sandwich Ltd since the incorporation of that company. Draft balance sheets of each company at 31 December 20X4 were as follows.

	Pie Limited		Sandwich Limited	
	£	£	£	£
Fixed assets				
Tangible assets		125,000		120,000
Investment: 75,000 shares in Sandwich Ltd at cost		75,000		–
		200,000		120,000
Current assets				
Stocks	50,000		48,000	
Trade debtors	20,000		16,000	
	70,000		64,000	
Creditors	40,000		24,000	
		30,000		40,000
		230,000		160,000
Capital and reserves				
Ordinary shares of £1 each fully paid		80,000		100,000
Reserves		150,000		60,000
		230,000		160,000

Prepare the draft consolidated balance sheet of Pie Ltd where during the year:

(a) Pie Ltd sold goods costing £16,000 to Sandwich at a price of £20,000 and these goods were still unsold at the year end.

(b) Sandwich Ltd sold the goods to Pie Ltd instead.

Solution

(a) PIE LTD CONSOLIDATED BALANCE SHEET AS AT 31 DECEMBER 20X4

	£	£
Tangible fixed assets		245,000
Current assets		
Stocks (50,000 + 48,000 – 4,000)	94,000	
Trade debtors	36,000	
	130,000	
Creditors	64,000	
Net current assets		66,000
		311,000
Capital and reserves		
Ordinary shares of £1 each		80,000
Reserves (W3)		191,000
Shareholders' funds		271,000
Minority interest (W2)		40,000
		311,000

Workings

1 The unrealised profit sitting in Pie Ltd's books is £4,000. This relates to the group and should be eliminated in full from the group accounts.

2 *Minority interests in Sandwich*

	£
Share capital	100,000
Reserves	60,000
	160,000
Minority share (25%)	40,000

2 *Goodwill*

	£	£
Cost of investment in Sandwich		75,000
Net assets of Sandwich at acquisition		
Share capital	100,000	
Group share	75%	75,000
Goodwill arising on acquisition		NIL

3 *Group reserves*

	Pie Ltd	Sandwich Ltd
	£	£
As per accounts	150,000	60,000
Group share in Sandwich Ltd (60,000 × 75%)	45,000	
Elimination of unrealised profit in stocks (20,000 – 16,000) (W1)	(4,000)	
	191,000	

(b)   PIE LIMITED
       CONSOLIDATED BALANCE SHEET AS AT 31 DECEMBER 20X4

	£	£
Tangible fixed assets		245,000
Current assets		
Stocks £(50,000 + 48,000 – 4,000)	94,000	
Trade debtors	36,000	
	130,000	
Creditors	64,000	
Net current assets		66,000
		311,000
Capital and reserves		
Ordinary shares of £1 each		80,000
Reserves (W3)		192,000
Shareholders' funds		272,000
Minority interest (W2)		39,000
		311,000

Workings

1   The unrealised profit of £4,000 sits in the books of Sandwich Ltd, a subsidiary. This relates to both the group and also the minority shareholders of Sandwich Ltd. The group as well as the minority must suffer their appropriate share of the elimination of unrealised profit.

2   *Goodwill*

	£	£
Cost of investment in Sandwich		75,000
Net assets of Sandwich at acquisition		
Share capital	100,000	
Group share	75%	75,000
Goodwill arising on acquisition		NIL

3   *Group reserves*

	Pie Ltd £	Sandwich Ltd £
As per accounts	150,000	60,000
Unrealised profit in stocks (20,000 – 16,000) (W1)		(4,000)
		56,000
Group share in Sandwich Ltd (56,000 × 75%)	42,000	
	192,000	

Note: Compare these workings with those for scenario (a).

Exam focus point

> Adjustment for unrealised profit in stock is a hardy perennial in financial reporting exams. Make sure you identify which direction the sale is made, the profit involved and how much is left on hand at year end. Most importantly, be careful to identify correctly whether the profit sits in the parent or in a subsidiary.

6 Inter-company sales of fixed assets

As well as engaging in trading activities with each other, **group companies** may on occasion wish to **transfer fixed assets.** In their individual accounts the companies concerned will treat the transfer just like a sale between unconnected parties:

(a)   The **selling company** will record a profit or loss on sale;

(b)   The **purchasing company** will record the asset at the **amount paid** to acquire it

(c)   That amount paid will be used as the basis for calculating **depreciation**

On **consolidation**, the usual **'group entity' principle** applies. The consolidated balance sheet must show **assets** at their **cost to the group**, and any depreciation charged must be based on that cost. Two consolidation adjustments will usually be needed to achieve this.

(a)   An **adjustment** to alter **reserves** and **fixed assets** cost so as to **remove** any element of **unrealised profit or loss**. This is **similar** to the adjustment required in respect of **unrealised profit in stock**.

(b)   An **adjustment** to alter **reserves** and **accumulated depreciation** is made so that **consolidated depreciation** is based on the asset's **cost to the group**.

In practice this can be done simply by one journal entry. The **net** unrealised profit (total profit on the sale less cumulative 'excess' depreciation charges) is eliminated from the carrying amount of the asset and from the profit of the company making the sale.

6.1 Example: parent sells fixed asset to subsidiary

(a)   Potato Ltd owns 60% of Shallot Ltd
(b)   On 1 January 20X8 Potato Ltd sells goods costing £10,000 to Shallot Ltd for £12,500
(c)   Shallot Ltd uses these goods as fixed assets
(d)   Depreciation is 10% straight line.

Identify the necessary consolidation adjustments.

Solution

The **net** unrealised profit is £2,250. (£2,500 unrealised profit less £250 excess depreciation.) This is adjusted as follows:

	Dr	Cr
	£	£
Fixed assets		2,250
Profit and loss account – Potato	2,250	

Note that the value of the fixed asset in the group accounts now becomes:

	£
Sale value	12,500
Net unrealised profit	(2,250)
Depreciation (in Shallot's books)	(1,250)
	9,000

This would have been the carrying value of the asset if it has been transferred at cost (£10,000) and depreciated at 10%.

6.2 Example: subsidiary sells fixed asset to parent

(a)   Parmesan Ltd owns 60% of Stilton Ltd
(b)   On 1 January 20X8, Stilton Ltd sells goods costing £10,000 to Parmesan Ltd for £12,500
(c)   Parmesan Ltd uses these goods as fixed assets
(d)   Depreciation is at 10% straight line

Identify the necessary consolidation adjustments.

Solution

	Dr	Cr
	£	£
Fixed assets (2,500 – 10%)		2,250
Profit and loss account – Stilton	2,250	

Note that, as the net unrealised profit has been debited to the profit and loss account of the subsidiary, part of this cost will be borne by the minority.

7 Summary: consolidated balance sheet

Purpose	To show the net assets which P controls and the ownership of those assets.
Net assets	Always 100% P plus 100% S providing P holds a majority of voting rights.
Share capital	P only.
Reason	Simply reporting to the holding company's shareholders in another form.
Reserves	100% P plus group share of post-acquisition retained reserves of S less consolidation adjustments.
Reason	To show the extent to which the group actually owns net assets included in the top half of the balance sheet.
Minority interest	MI share of S's consolidated net assets.
Reason	To show the extent to which other parties own net assets that are under the control of the holding company.

8 Acquisition of a subsidiary during its accounting period

FAST FORWARD

When a subsidiary is acquired **during its accounting period**, it will be necessary to distinguish between **pre-acquisition** and **post-acquisition** profits.

In the absence of information to the contrary, the profits earned during the period may be assumed to have **accrued evenly** and should be allocated accordingly.

Exam focus point

An acquisition of a subsidiary part way through a year may come up in your exam. If necessary, draw a time line to help you picture what happened when.

When a holding company acquires a subsidiary during its accounting period the only accounting entries will be those recording the cost of acquisition in the holding company's books. As we have already seen, at the end of the accounting year it will be necessary to prepare consolidated accounts.

The subsidiary company's accounts to be consolidated will show the subsidiary's profit or loss for the whole year. **For consolidation** purposes, however, it will be necessary to **distinguish between:**

(a)   **Profits earned before acquisition**
(b)   **Profits earned after acquisition**

In practice, a subsidiary company's profit may not accrue evenly over the year; for example, the subsidiary might be engaged in a trade, such as toy sales, with marked seasonal fluctuations. Nevertheless, statute permits the **assumption** to be made **that profits accrue evenly** whenever it is impracticable to arrive at an accurate split of pre– and post-acquisition profits.

Once the amount of pre-acquisition profit has been established the appropriate consolidation workings (goodwill, reserves) can be produced.

Bear in mind that **in calculating minority interests the distinction between pre- and post-acquisition profits is irrelevant.** The minority shareholders are simply credited with their share of the subsidiary's total reserves at the balance sheet date.

It is worthwhile to summarise what happens on consolidation to the reserves figures extracted from a subsidiary's balance sheet. Suppose the accounts of S Ltd, a 60% subsidiary of P Ltd, show reserves of £20,000 at the balance sheet date, of which £14,000 were earned prior to acquisition. The figure of £20,000 will appear in the consolidated balance sheet as follows.

	£
Minority interests working: their share of total reserves at balance sheet date (40% × £20,000)	8,000
Goodwill working: group share of pre-acquisition profits (60% × £14,000)	8,400
Consolidated reserves working: group share of post-acquisition profits (60% × £6,000)	3,600
	20,000

Question

Consolidated balance sheet

Prawn Ltd acquired 80% of the ordinary shares of Shrimp Ltd on 1 April 20X5. On 31 December 20X4 Shrimp Ltd's accounts showed a share premium account of £4,000 and revenue reserves of £15,000. The balance sheets of the two companies at 31 December 20X5 are set out below. Neither company has paid dividends during the year.

You are required to prepare the consolidated balance sheet of Prawn Ltd at 31 December 20X5.

Note. Goodwill is to be amortised over 25 years. A full year's amortisation is charged in the year of acquisition.

PRAWN LIMITED
BALANCE SHEET AS AT 31 DECEMBER 20X5

	£
Fixed assets	
Tangible assets	32,000
16,000 ordinary shares of 50p each in Shrimp Ltd	50,000
	82,000
Net current assets	65,000
	147,000
Ordinary shares of £1 each	100,000
Share premium account	7,000
Revenue reserves	40,000
	147,000

SHRIMP LIMITED
BALANCE SHEET AS AT 31 DECEMBER 20X5

	£
Tangible fixed assets	30,000
Net current assets	23,000
	53,000
Capital and reserves	
20,000 ordinary shares of 50p each	10,000
Share premium account	4,000
Revenue reserves	39,000
	53,000

Answer

Shrimp Ltd has made a profit of £24,000 (£39,000 – £15,000) for the year. In the absence of any direction to the contrary, this should be assumed to have arisen evenly over the year; £6,000 in the three months to 31 March and £18,000 in the nine months after acquisition. The company's pre-acquisition revenue reserves are therefore as follows.

	£
Balance at 31 December 20X4	15,000
Profit for three months to 31 March 20X5	6,000
Pre-acquisition revenue reserves	21,000

The balance of £4,000 on share premium account is all pre-acquisition.

The consolidation workings can now be drawn up.

1   *Minority interest*

	£
Ordinary share capital (20% × £10,000)	2,000
Revenue reserves (20% × £39,000) (pre-acquisition)	7,800
Share premium (20% × £4,000)	800
	10,600

2   *Goodwill*

	£	£
Cost of investment		50,000
Share of net assets acquired represented by		
Ordinary share capital	10,000	
Revenue reserves (pre-acquisition) (W3)	21,000	
Share premium	4,000	
	35,000	
Group share (80%)		28,000
Goodwill		22,000
Amortisation (22,000 ÷ 25 (W3)		880
Unamortised goodwill		21,200

3   *Revenue reserves*

	Prawn Ltd £	Shrimp Ltd £
As per question	40,000	39,000
Pre-acquisition reserves (W2)		21,000
		18,000
Group share in Shrimp Ltd post-acquisition reserves (18,000 × 80%)	14,400	
Amortisation of goodwill in Shrimp Ltd (W2)	(880)	
Group revenue reserves	53,520	

4   *Share premium account*

	£
Prawn Ltd	7,000

PRAWN LIMITED
CONSOLIDATED BALANCE SHEET AS AT 31 DECEMBER 20X5

	£
Intangible fixed assets: goodwill	21,120
Tangible fixed assets	62,000
Net current assets	88,000
	171,120
Capital and reserves	
Ordinary shares of £1 each	100,000
Reserves	
Share premium account	7,000
Revenue reserves	53,520
Shareholders' funds	160,520
Minority interest	10,600
	171,120

Exam focus point

Remember not to show the share premium of the subsidiary together with the parent company share premium. It must always be set off against the cost of investment or allocated accordingly to minority interest.

8.1 Example: pre-acquisition losses of a subsidiary

As an illustration of the entries arising when a subsidiary has pre-acquisition *losses*, suppose P Ltd acquired all 50,000 £1 ordinary shares in S Ltd for £20,000 on 1 January 20X1 when there was a debit balance of £35,000 on S Ltd's revenue reserves. In the years 20X1 to 20X4 S Ltd makes profits of £40,000 in total, leaving a credit balance of £5,000 on revenue reserves at 31 December 20X4. P Ltd's reserves at the same date are £70,000. Any goodwill is deemed to have an indefinite useful life and should be held in the balance sheet.

The consolidation workings would appear as follows.

1   *Goodwill*

	£	£
Cost of investment		20,000
Share of net assets acquired		
as represented by		
Ordinary share capital	50,000	
Pre-acquisition revenue reserves (W2)	(35,000)	
	15,000	
Group share (100%)		15,000
Goodwill		5,000

2   *Revenue reserve*

	P Ltd	S Ltd
	£	£
As per question	70,000	5,000
Pre-acquisition debit balance 1.1.X1 (W1)		35,000
		40,000
Group share in S Ltd (40,000 × 100%)	40,000	
Group reserves	110,000	

9 Dividends and pre-acquisition profits

FAST FORWARD

Dividends paid by a subsidiary to its parent company may only be **credited to the parent's profit and loss account** to the extent that they are paid from **post-acquisition profits**.

Dividends received by the holding company **from pre-acquisition profits** should be credited to 'investment in subsidiary' account and treated as **reducing the cost of the shares** acquired.

A further problem in consolidation occurs when a subsidiary pays out a dividend soon after acquisition. The holding company, as a member of the subsidiary, is entitled to its share of the dividends paid but it is necessary to decide whether or not these dividends come out of the pre-acquisition profits of the subsidiary.

If the dividends come from post-acquisition profits there is no problem. **The holding company simply credits the relevant amount to its own profit and loss account**, as with any other dividend income. The double entry is **quite different**, however, **if the dividend is paid from pre-acquisition profits**, being as follows.

DEBIT   Cash
CREDIT   Investment in subsidiary

The holding company's balance sheet would then disclose the investment as 'Investment in subsidiary at cost less amounts written down'.

Why do we make this distinction? If we consider the situation of a holding company deciding whether to invest in a subsidiary we can see the significance of a dividend paid from pre-acquisition profits. If the prospective subsidiary's financial statements disclose that it proposes to pay a dividend in the near future, the prospective holding company knows that if it invests in the shares some of its investment will be returned to it very soon. Also, a dividend paid out of pre-acquisition profits cannot be regarded as a return on the holding company's investment because it relates to the period before the investment was made. So we treat it as what it effectively is – a reduction in the cost of the investment.

9.1 Example: dividends and pre-acquisition profits

Planet Ltd acquired 8,000 of the 10,000 £1 ordinary shares of Star Ltd on 1 January 20X5 for £25,000. Star Ltd's balance sheet at 31 December 20X4 showed retained reserves of £12,000. The balance sheets of the two companies at 31 December 20X5 are given below. During 20X5 Star Ltd paid a dividend of £4,000 which was deemed to be from pre-acquisition profits..

PLANET LIMITED
BALANCE SHEET AS AT 31 DECEMBER 20X5

	£
Fixed assets	
Tangible assets	35,000
Investment in Star Ltd at cost less	
amounts written down	21,800
	56,800
Net current assets	27,000
	83,800
Capital and reserves	
Ordinary shares of £1 each	50,000
Retained reserves	33,800
	83,800

STAR LIMITED
BALANCE SHEET AS AT 31 DECEMBER 20X5

	£
Tangible fixed assets	14,500
Net current assets	12,500
	27,000
Capital and reserves	
Ordinary shares of £1 each	10,000
Retained reserves	17,000
	27,000

Required

Prepare the consolidated balance sheet of Planet Ltd at 31 December 20X5.

Note. Goodwill is deemed to have a useful life of 10 years and is therefore to be amortised over that period.

Solution

During the year Star Ltd has paid £4,000 dividend. This will be paid out of profits earned in 20X4. Planet Ltd's share (80% × £4,000 = £3,200) has been correctly credited by that company to its 'investment in Star Ltd' account. That account appears in the books of Planet Ltd as follows.

INVESTMENT IN STAR LIMITED

	£		£
Bank: purchase of 8,000		Bank: dividend received from	
£1 ordinary shares	25,000	pre-acquisition profits	3,200
		Balance c/f	21,800
	25,000		25,000

If Planet Ltd had incorrectly credited the pre-acquisition dividend to its own profit and loss account, it would have been necessary to make the following adjustments in Planet Ltd's accounts before proceeding to the consolidation.

DEBIT	Retained reserves	£3,200	
CREDIT	Investment in Star Ltd		£3,200

This procedure is sometimes necessary in examination questions.

The consolidation workings can be drawn up as follows.

1 *Minority interest*

	£
Share capital (20% × £10,000)	2,000
Reserves (20% × £17,000)	3,400
	5,400

2 *Goodwill*

	£	£
Cost of investment		25,000
Share of pre-acquisition dividend (80% × £4,000)		(3,200)
		21,800
Share of net assets acquired as represented by		
Ordinary share capital	10,000	
Pre-acquisition reserves	12,000	
	22,000	
Group share (80%)		(17,600)
Goodwill		4,200
Amortisation (4,200 ÷ 10)		(420)
Unamortised goodwill		3,780

3   *Reserves*

	Planet Ltd £	Star Ltd £
As per question	33,800	17,000
Pre-acquisition reserves		(12,000)
		5,000
Group share in Star Ltd (5,000 × 80%)	4,000	
Goodwill amortisation (W2)	(420)	
Group reserves	37,380	

PLANET LIMITED
CONSOLIDATED BALANCE SHEET AS AT 31 DECEMBER 20X5

	£
Intangible fixed assets	3,780
Tangible fixed assets	49,500
Net current assets	39,500
	92,780
Capital and reserves	
Ordinary shares of £1 each	50,000
Retained reserves	37,380
Shareholders' funds	87,380
Minority interest	5,400
	92,780

9.2 Is the dividend paid from pre-acquisition profits?

We need next to consider how it is decided whether a dividend is paid from pre-acquisition profits. In the example above there was no difficulty: Planet Ltd acquired shares in Star Ltd on the first day of an accounting period and the dividend was in respect of the previous accounting period. Clearly, the dividend was paid from profits earned in the period before acquisition.

The position is less straightforward if shares are acquired during the subsidiary's accounting period. In this case, the dividend will have to be time-apportioned over the year. Part of the dividend will be pre-acquisition and part of it will be post-acquisition.

10 FRS 7 Fair values in acquisition accounting

FAST FORWARD

Goodwill arising on consolidation is the difference between the purchase consideration and the **fair value** of net assets acquired. **Goodwill** should be calculated **after revaluing** the subsidiary company's assets. If the subsidiary does not incorporate the revaluation in its own accounts, it should be done as a **consolidation adjustment**. The accounting requirements and disclosures of the **fair value exercise** are covered by **FRS 7**.

FRS 10 *Goodwill and intangible assets* **defines goodwill as the difference between the purchase consideration paid by the acquiring company and the aggregate of the 'fair values' of the identifiable assets and liabilities acquired.** The balance sheet of a subsidiary company at the date it is acquired may not be a guide to the fair value of its net assets. For example, the market value of a freehold building may have risen greatly since it was acquired, but it may appear in the balance sheet at historical cost less accumulated depreciation.

Exam focus point

The group accounts question is likely to include a fair value adjustment.

10.1 Fair value adjustment calculations

Until now we have calculated goodwill as the difference between the cost of the investment and the **book value** of net assets acquired by the group. If this calculation is to comply with the definition in FRS 10 we **must ensure that the book value of the subsidiary's net assets is the same as their fair value.**

There are **two possible ways** of achieving this.

(a) **The subsidiary company might incorporate any necessary revaluations in its own books of account.** In this case, we can proceed directly to the consolidation, taking asset values and reserves figures straight from the subsidiary company's balance sheet.

(b) **The revaluations may be made as a consolidation adjustment without being incorporated in the subsidiary company's books.** In this case, we must make the necessary adjustments to the subsidiary's balance sheet as a working. Only then can we proceed to the consolidation.

Note. Remember that when depreciating assets are revalued there may be a corresponding alteration in the amount of depreciation charged and accumulated.

10.2 Example: fair value adjustments

Panache Ltd acquired 75% of the ordinary shares of Style Ltd on 1 September 20X5. At that date the fair value of Style Ltd's fixed assets was £23,000 greater than their net book value, and the balance of retained profits was £21,000. The balance sheets of both companies at 31 August 20X6 are given below. Style Ltd has not incorporated any revaluation in its books of account.

PANACHE LIMITED
BALANCE SHEET AS AT 31 AUGUST 20X6

	£
Fixed assets	
Tangible assets	63,000
Investment in Style Ltd at cost	51,000
	114,000
Net current assets	62,000
	176,000
Capital and reserves	
Ordinary shares of £1 each	80,000
Retained profits	96,000
	176,000

STYLE LIMITED
BALANCE SHEET AS AT 31 AUGUST 20X6

	£
Tangible fixed assets	28,000
Net current assets	33,000
	61,000
Capital and reserves	
Ordinary shares of £1 each	20,000
Retained profits	41,000
	61,000

If Style Ltd had revalued its fixed assets at 1 September 20X5, an addition of £3,000 would have been made to the depreciation charged in the profit and loss account for 20X5/X6.

Required

Prepare Panache Ltd's consolidated balance sheet as at 31 August 20X6.

Note. Goodwill is deemed to have a useful life of 5 years and is to be amortised over that period.

Solution

Style Ltd has not incorporated the revaluation in its draft balance sheet. Before beginning the consolidation workings we must therefore adjust the company's balance of profits at the date of acquisition and at the balance sheet date.

In the consolidated balance sheet, Style Ltd's fixed assets will appear at their revalued amount: £(28,000 + 23,000 – 3,000) = £48,000. The consolidation workings can now be drawn up.

1   *Minority interest*

	£
Share capital (25% × £20,000)	5,000
Revenue reserves (25% × £41,000)	10,250
Fair value adjustment less depreciation (25% × (23,000 – 3,000))	5,000
	20,250

2   *Goodwill*

	£	£
Cost of investment		51,000
Share of net assets acquired as represented by		
Ordinary share capital	20,000	
Revenue reserves (pre-acquisition) (W3)	21,000	
Fair value adjustment (W4)	23,000	
	64,000	
Group share (75%)		48,000
Goodwill		3,000
Amortisation (3,000 ÷ 5)		(600)
Unamortised goodwill		2,400

3   *Revenue reserves*

	Panache Ltd	Style Ltd
	£	£
As per question	96,000	41,000
Pre-acquisition reserves (W2)		(21,000)
Depreciation on FV adjustment (W4)		(3,000)
		17,000
Group share in Style Ltd (17,000 × 75%)	12,750	
Goodwill amortisation (W2)	(600)	
Group revenue reserves	108,150	

4   *Fixed assets*

	£	£
Panache per accounts		63,000
Style		
Per accounts	28,000	
FV adjustment (W2)	23,000	
Depreciation adjustment (W3)	(3,000)	
		48,000
		111,000

PANACHE LIMITED CONSOLIDATED BALANCE SHEET AS AT 31 AUGUST 20X6

	£
Intangible fixed assets: goodwill (W2)	2,400
Tangible fixed assets £(63,000 + 48,000) (W4)	111,000
Net current assets	95,000
	208,400

Capital and reserves

Ordinary shares of £1 each	80,000
Retained profits (W3)	108,150
Shareholders' funds	188,150
Minority interest (W1)	20,250
	208,400

Question

Fair value

An asset is recorded in Shark Ltd's books at its historical cost of £4,000. On 1 January 20X1 Porpoise Ltd bought 80% of Shark Ltd's equity. Its directors attributed a fair value of £3,000 to the asset as at that date. It had been depreciated for two years out of an expected life of four years on the straight line basis. There was no expected residual value. On 30 June 20X1 the asset was sold for £2,600. What is the profit or loss on disposal of this asset to be recorded in Shark Ltd's accounts and in Porpoise Ltd's consolidated accounts for the year ended 31 December 20X1?

Answer

Shark Ltd: NBV at disposal (at historical cost) = £4,000 × 1½/4 = £1,500

∴ Profit on disposal = £1,100 (depreciation charge for the year = £500)

Porpoise Ltd: NBV at disposal (at fair value) = £3,000 × 1½/2 = £2,250

∴ Profit on disposal for consolidation = £350 (depreciation for the year = £750). The minority would be credited with 20% of both items as part of the one line entry in the profit and loss account.

10.3 FRS 7 Fair values in acquisition accounting

Key term

The basic principles stated by FRS 7 are that:

(a)   **All identifiable assets and liabilities** should be **recognised** which are in existence **at the date of acquisition**.

(b)   Such recognised assets and liabilities should be **measured at fair values** which reflect the conditions existing at the date of acquisition.

Fair values should not reflect either the acquirer's intentions or events subsequent to the acquisition.

In addition any **changes** to the acquired assets and liabilities, and the resulting gains and losses, that arise **after control** of the acquired entity has passed to the acquirer should be reported as part of the **post-acquisition profits** of the group.

FRS 7 also sets out specific rules on how fair values should be determined for the main categories of asset and liability. The underlying principle remains that **fair values should reflect the price at which an asset or liability could be exchanged in an arm's length transaction.** For long-term monetary assets and liabilities, fair values may be derived by discounting.

The standard also describes how the value attributed to the consideration given for the acquisition should be determined, and the acquisition expenses that may be included as part of the cost.

10.4 Definitions

The following definitions are given by FRS 7. They are self explanatory except for the highlighted terms.

(a) Acquisition
(b) Business combination
(c) Date of acquisition
(d) **Fair value**

(e) Identifiable assets and liabilities
(f) **Recoverable amount**
(g) **Value in use**

Key terms

(a) In particular note the definition of **fair value**: 'The amount at which an asset or liability could be exchanged in an arm's length transaction between informed and willing parties, other than in a forced or liquidation sale.'

(b) **Recoverable amount** is the greater of the net realisable value of an asset and, when appropriate, the amount recoverable from its further use.

(c) **Value in use** is the present value of the future cash flows obtainable as a result of an asset's continued use, including those resulting from the ultimate disposal of the asset.

10.5 Scope

FRS 7 applies to all financial statements that are intended to give a true and fair view. Although the FRS is framed in terms of the acquisition of a subsidiary undertaking by a parent company that prepares consolidated financial statements, it **also applies where an individual company entity acquires a business other than a subsidiary undertaking**. This last point means that companies cannot avoid the provisions of FRS 7 when taking over an unincorporated entity or joint venture vehicle.

10.6 Determining the fair values of identifiable assets and liabilities acquired

Most importantly, the FRS lists those **items which do not affect fair values** at the date of acquisition, and **which are therefore to be treated as post-acquisition items**:

(a) Changes resulting from the **acquirer's intentions or future actions.**

(b) **Impairments** or other changes, resulting from events subsequent to the acquisition.

(c) **Provisions or accruals for future operating losses** or for reorganisation and integration costs expected to be incurred as a result of the acquisition, whether they relate to the acquired entity or to the acquirer.

10.6.1 Assessing fair value of major categories

In general terms, fair values should be determined in accordance with the acquirer's accounting policies for similar assets and liabilities. The standard does, however, go on to describe how the major categories of assets and liabilities should be assessed for fair values.

(a) **Tangible assets: fair value based on:**

(i) **Market value**, if similar assets are sold on the open market.
(ii) **Depreciated replacement cost**, reflecting normal business practice.

However, **fair value ≤ replacement cost**.

(b) **Intangible assets**, where recognised: **fair value should be based on replacement costs,** which will normally be estimated market value.

(c) **Stocks and work in progress**

   (i)   For stocks which are replaced by purchasing in a **ready market** (commodities, dealing stock etc), the fair value is **market value**.

   (ii)   For other stocks, with **no ready market** (most manufacturing stocks), fair value is represented by the **current cost** to the acquired company of reproducing the stocks.

(d) **Quoted investments:** value at **market price**, adjusted where necessary for unusual price fluctuations or the size of the holding.

(e) **Monetary assets and liabilities:** fair values should take into account the **amounts expected to be received or paid** and their timing. Reference should be made to market prices (where available) or to the current price if acquiring similar assets or entering into similar obligations, or to the discounted present value.

(f) **Contingencies: reasonable estimates** of the expected outcome may be used.

(g) **Pensions and other post-retirement benefits:** the **fair value of a deficiency, a surplus** (to the extent it is expected to be realised) or accrued obligation should be **recognised** as an asset/liability of the acquiring group. Any changes on acquisition should be treated as post-acquisition items.

(h) **Deferred tax** recognised in a fair value exercise should be measured in accordance with the requirements of FRS 19. Thus deferred tax would not be recognised on an adjustment to recognise a non-monetary asset acquired with the business at its fair value on acquisition.

10.7 Business sold or held with a view to subsequent resale

The fair value exercise for such an entity, 'sold as a single unit, within approximately one year of acquisition', should be carried out on the basis of a **single asset investment**.

> 'Its fair value should be based on the **net proceeds of the sale**, **adjusted for the fair value of any assets or liabilities transferred** into or out of the business, unless such adjusted net proceeds are demonstrably different from the fair value at the date of acquisition as a result of a post-acquisition event.'

Any relevant part of the business can be treated in this way if it is separately identifiable, ie it does not have to be a separate subsidiary undertaking.

Where the first financial statements after the date of acquisition come for approval, but the business has not been sold, the above treatment can still be applied if:

(a)   A purchaser has been identified or is being sought.

(b)   The disposal is expected to occur within one year of the date of acquisition.

The interest (or its assets) should be shown in current assets. On determination of the sales price, the original estimate of fair value should be adjusted to reflect the actual sales proceeds.

10.8 Investigation period and goodwill adjustments

FRS 7 states that:

> '**The recognition and measurement of assets and liabilities acquired should be completed, if possible, by the date on which the first post-acquisition financial statements of the acquirer are approved by the directors.**'

Where this has not been possible, provisional valuations should be made, amended if necessary in the next financial statements with a corresponding adjustment to goodwill. Such adjustments should be incorporated into the financial statements in the full year following acquisition. After that, any adjustments (except for the correction of fundamental errors by prior year adjustment) should be recognised as profits or losses as they are identified.

10.9 Determining the fair value of purchase consideration

The cost of acquisition is the amount of cash paid and the fair value of other purchase consideration given by the acquirer, together with the expenses of the acquisition.

The main likely components of purchase consideration are as follows.

(a) *Ordinary shares*

    (i) **Quoted shares** should be valued at **market price** on the date of acquisition.

    (ii) Where there is **no suitable market**, estimate the value using:

        (1) The value of **similar quoted securities**
        (2) The **present value of the future cash** flows of the instrument used
        (3) Any **cash alternative** which was offered

(b) **Other securities:** the value should be based on similar principles to those given in (a).

(c) **Cash or monetary amounts:** value at the **amount paid or payable**.

(d) **Non-monetary assets:** value at **market price**, estimated realisable value, independent valuation or based on other available evidence.

(e) **Deferred consideration: discount** the amounts calculated on the above principles (in (a) to (d)). An appropriate discount rate is that which the acquirer could obtain for a similar borrowing.

(f) **Contingent consideration:** use the **probable** amount. When the actual amount is known, it should be recorded in the financial statements and goodwill adjusted accordingly.

Acquisition cost (the fees and expenses mentioned above) should be **included in the cost of the investment**. Internal costs and the costs of issuing capital instruments should *not* be capitalised, according to the provisions of FRS 4, ie they must be written off to the profit and loss account.

10.10 Summary and assessment

The most important effect of FRS 7 is the ban it imposes on making provisions for future trading losses of acquired companies and the costs of any related rationalisation or reorganisation, unless outgoing management had already incurred those liabilities. This is a controversial area, demonstrated by the dissenting view of one member of the ASB.

Some commentators argued that the ASB's approach ignores the commercial reality of the transaction by treating as an expense the costs of reorganisation that the acquirer regards as part of the capital cost of the acquisition; and that within defined limits a provision for planned post-acquisition expenditure should be permitted to be included in the net assets acquired.

 Case Study

The Hundred Group of finance directors gave an example. If you buy a house for, say £100,000 that you know needs £50,000 spent on it to bring it into good condition and make it equivalent to a property that sells for £150,000, then you would treat the £50,000 renovation expense as part of the cost of the house and not as part of ordinary outgoings. The group states that FRS 7 goes beyond standards set in other countries, including the US. It also recommends that abuses in this area should be dealt with by tightening existing accounting standards and through 'proper policing' by external auditors (the standard is seen to undermine the professional judgement of the auditor) and 'not by distorting accounting concepts'.

The ASB rejected this view, saying that an intention to incur revenue expenditure subsequent to the acquisition could not properly be regarded as a liability of the acquired business at the date of acquisition.

'Acquisition accounting should reflect the business that is acquired as it stands at the date of acquisition and ought not to take account of the changes that an acquirer might intend to make subsequently. Nor could the ASB accept the proposition that some of the inadequacies of the present system could be met by better disclosure. In the ASB's view deficient accounting cannot be put right by disclosure alone.'

This is still an open area of debate and you should keep track of the arguments in the financial and accountancy press.

Question	Goodwill

Prune plc prepares accounts to 31 December. On 1 September 20X7 Prune plc acquired 6 million £1 shares in Sultana plc at £2.00 per share. The purchase was financed by an additional issue of loan stock at an interest rate of 10%. At that date Sultana plc produced the following interim financial statements.

	£m		£m
Tangible fixed assets (note 1)	16.0	Trade creditors	3.2
Stocks (note 2)	4.0	Taxation	0.6
Debtors	2.9	Bank overdraft	3.9
Cash in hand	1.2	Long-term loans (note 6)	4.0
		Share capital (£1 shares)	8.0
		Profit and loss account	4.4
	24.1		24.1

Notes

1 The following information relates to the tangible fixed assets of Sultana plc at 1 September 20X7.

	£m
Gross replacement cost	28.4
Net replacement cost (gross replacement cost less depreciation)	16.6
Economic value	18.0
Net realisable value	8.0

The fixed assets of Sultana plc at 1 September 20X7 had a total purchase cost to Sultana plc of £27.0 million. They were all being depreciated at 25% per annum pro rata on that cost. This policy is also appropriate for the consolidated financial statements of Prune plc. No fixed assets of Sultana plc which were included in the interim financial statements drawn up as at 1 September 19X7 were disposed of by Sultana plc prior to 31 December 20X7. No fixed asset was fully depreciated by 31 December 20X7.

2 The stocks of Sultana plc which were shown in the interim financial statements at cost to Sultana plc of £4 million would have cost £4.2 million to replace at 1 September 20X7 and had an estimated net realisable value at that date of £4.8 million. Of the stock of Sultana plc in hand at 1 September 20X7, goods costing Sultana plc £3.0 million were sold for £3.6 million between 1 September 20X7 and 31 December 20X7.

3 On 1 September 20X7 Prune plc took a decision to rationalise the group so as to integrate Sultana plc. The costs of the rationalisation (which were to be borne by Prune plc) were estimated to total £3.0 million and the process was due to start on 1 March 20X8. No provision for these costs has been made in any of the financial statements given above.

Required

Compute the goodwill on consolidation of Sultana plc that will be included in the consolidated financial statements of the Prune plc group for the year ended 31 December 20X7, explaining your treatment of the items mentioned above. You should refer to the provisions of relevant accounting standards.

Answer

Goodwill on consolidation of Sultana Ltd

	£m	£m
Consideration (£2.00 × 6m)		12.0
Group share of fair value of net assets acquired		
Share capital	8.0	
Pre-acquisition reserves	4.4	
Fair value adjustments		
Tangible fixed assets (16.6 – 16.0)	0.6	
Stocks (4.2 – 4.0)	0.2	
	13.2	
Group share	75%	9.9
Goodwill		2.1

Notes on treatment

(a)   It is assumed that the market value (ie fair value) of the loan stock issued to fund the purchase of the shares in Sultana plc is equal to the price of £12.0m. FRS 2 *Accounting for subsidiary undertakings* requires goodwill to be calculated by comparing the fair value of the consideration given with the fair value of the separable net assets of the acquired business or company.

(b)   Share capital and pre-acquisition profits represent the book value of the net assets of Sultana plc at the date of acquisition. Adjustments are then required to this book value in order to give the fair value of the net assets at the date of acquisition. For short-term monetary items, fair value is their carrying value on acquisition.

(c)   FRS 7 *Fair values in acquisition accounting* states that the fair value of tangible fixed assets should be determined by market value or, if information on a market price is not available (as is the case here), then by reference to depreciated replacement cost, reflecting normal business practice. The net replacement cost (ie £16.6m) represents the gross replacement cost less depreciation based on that amount, and so further adjustment for extra depreciation is unnecessary.

(d)   FRS 7 also states that stocks which cannot be replaced by purchasing in a ready market (eg commodities) should be valued at current cost to the acquired company of reproducing the stocks. In this case that amount is £4.2m.

(e)   The rationalisation costs must be reported in post-acquisition results under FRS 7 *Fair values in acquisition accounting*, so no adjustment is required in the goodwill calculation.

Chapter Roundup

- The preparation of a consolidated balance sheet, in a very simple form, consists of two procedures.

    - Take the individual accounts of the holding company and each subsidiary and **cancel out items which appear as an asset in one company and a liability in another**.

    - **Add together** all the **uncancelled** assets and liabilities throughout the group.

- Where the parent does not own 100% of the shares in the subsidiary, the other shares are held by **minority** shareholders. The proportion of share capital and reserves attributable to this **minority interest** must be shown in the consolidated balance sheet.

- When dealing with dividends paid by a subsidiary, make sure that the entry ahs been made in the accounts of both the **paying** company and the **receiving** company.

- When a company acquires shares in another company for an amount which exceeds the value of that proportion of the fair value of its assets, it has paid a 'premium', which is called **goodwill**. This appears as an **intangible fixed asset** in the consolidated balance sheet and is then **amortised** over its useful life.

- Where **inter-company trading** has taken place and goods which have been sold at a profit by one group company are still held in stock by another group company, an adjustment must be made to remove the element of **unrealised profit**. The entry will be: **DR Group reserves CR Group stock**. A similar adjustment is made to account for inter-company sales of fixed assets.

- When a subsidiary is acquired **during its accounting period**, it will be necessary to distinguish between **pre-acquisition** and **post-acquisition** profits.

- In the absence of information to the contrary, the profits earned during the period may be assumed to have **accrued evenly** and should be allocated accordingly.

- **Dividends** paid by a subsidiary to its parent company may only be **credited to the parent's profit and loss account** to the extent that they are paid from **post-acquisition profits**.

- **Dividends** received by the holding company **from pre-acquisition profits** should be credited to 'investment in subsidiary' account and treated as **reducing the cost of the shares** acquired.

- **Goodwill arising on consolidation** is the difference between the purchase consideration and the **fair value** of net assets acquired. **Goodwill** should be calculated **after revaluing** the subsidiary company's assets. If the subsidiary does not incorporate the revaluation in its own accounts, it should be done as a **consolidation adjustment**. The accounting requirements and disclosures of the **fair value exercise** are covered by **FRS 7**.

Quick Quiz

1   What are the components making up the figure of minority interest in a consolidated balance sheet?

2   The following diagram shows the structure of the Aubergine group.

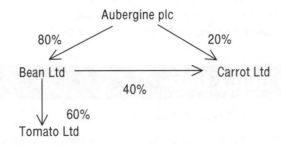

Which are the subsidiaries of Aubergine plc?

A   Bean Ltd
B   Bean Ltd and Tomato Ltd
C   Bean Ltd and Carrot Ltd
D   Bean Ltd, Tomato Ltd and Carrot Ltd

3   Goodwill is always positive. True or false?

4   The following figures relate to Phlox plc and its subsidiary Spirea Ltd for the year ended 31 December 20X9.

	Phlox plc £	Spirea Ltd £
Turnover	600,000	300,000
Cost of sales	(400,000)	(200,000)
Gross profit	200,000	100,000

During the year, Phlox plc sold goods to Spirea Ltd for £20,000 making a profit of £5,000. These goods were all sold by Spirea Ltd before the year end.

What are the amounts for turnover and gross profit in the consolidated profit and loss accounts of Phlox plc for the year ended 31 December 20X9?

5   A holding company can assume that, for a subsidiary acquired during its accounting period, profits accrue evenly during the year. *True or false?*

6   What entries are made in the holding company's accounts to record a dividend received from a subsidiary's pre-acquisition profits? *Fill in the blanks.*

DEBIT
CREDIT

7   How is 'fair value' defined by FRS 7?

8   Which items does FRS 7 state *must* be treated as post-acquisition?

9   How is the cost of an acquisition made up?

10   On 31 March, Plant Ltd purchased 1,800,000 of the 2,000,000 ordinary shares of £1 each in Seed Ltd paying £1.20 per share.

At that date the values of the separable net assets of Seed Ltd were:
Aggregate book value£1,800,000
Aggregate fair value   £1,700,000

What is the values of the goodwill on consolidation as at 31 March?

11   On 31 March, Plant Ltd purchased 1,800,000 of the 2,000,000 ordinary shares of £1 each in Seed Ltd paying £1.20 per share.

At that date the value of the separable net assets of Seed Ltd were:
Aggregate book value   £1,800,000
Aggregate fair value   £1,700,000
What is the value of the minority interest as at 31 March?

Answers to Quick Quiz

1   The minority's share of ordinary shares and reserves.

2   D   Aubergine has control over Bean's 40% holding in Carrot and has a 20% direct holding. Thus Carrot is a subsidiary.

3   False. Goodwill can be negative if the purchaser has 'got a bargain'.

4
	£'000
Turnover (600 + 300 − 20)	880
Cost of sales (400 +200 − 20)	580
Gross profit	300

5   False in practice, true for the purposes of your exam (unless you are told otherwise).

6   DEBIT   Cash
     CREDIT   Investment in subsidiary

7   The amount at which an asset or liability could be exchanged in an arm's length transaction between informed and willing parties other than in forced liquidation sale.

8   • Changes resulting from the acquirer's intentions or future actions
     • Impairments due to subsequent events
     • Provisions for future losses

9   The amount of cash paid
     The fair value of other purchase consideration given by the acquirer
     The expenses of the acquisition

10
	£'000	
Cost	2,160	
Fair value of separable net assets acquired		
90% × 1,700,000	1,530	
	630	(Section 3)

11   10% × £1,700,000 = £170,000.

Now try the questions below from the Exam Question Bank

Number	Level	Marks	Time
Q9	Introductory	15	27 mins
Q10	Introductory	15	27 mins
Q11	Examination	25	45 mins

10

The consolidated profit and loss account

Topic list	Syllabus reference
1 The consolidated profit and loss account	D3
2 FRS 6 *Acquisitions and mergers*	D3

Introduction

This chapter covers the consolidated profit and loss account and Chapter 11 deals with accounting for associated undertakings.

Study guide

		Intellectual level
D	**BUSINESS COMBINATIONS**	
3	**Preparation of consolidated financial statements including an associate**	
(b)	Prepare a consolidated profit and loss account for simple group dealing with an acquisition in the period and minority interest.	2
(d)	account for the effects (in the profit and loss and balance sheet) of intra-group trading.	2

1 The consolidated profit and loss account

FAST FORWARD

The **consolidated profit and loss account** combines the profit and loss accounts of each group company. Adjustments must be made for:

- inter-group trading
- unrealised profit
- minority interest
- inter-group dividends
- elimination of pre-acquisition profits

As always, the source of the consolidated statement is the individual accounts of the separate companies in the group. **It is customary in practice to prepare a working paper** (known as a **consolidation schedule**) **on which the individual profit and loss accounts are set out side by side and totalled to form the basis of the consolidated profit and loss account.**

Exam focus point

In an examination it is very much quicker not to do this. Use workings to show the calculation of complex figures such as the minority interest and show the derivation of others on the face of the profit and loss account, as shown in our examples.

1.1 Consolidated profit and loss account: simple example

Pappadum Ltd acquired 75% of the ordinary shares of Samosa Ltd on that company's incorporation in 20X3. The summarised profit and loss accounts of the two companies for the year ending 31 December 20X6 are set out below.

	Pappadum Ltd £	Samosa Ltd £
Turnover	75,000	38,000
Cost of sales	30,000	20,000
Gross profit	45,000	18,000
Administrative expenses	14,000	8,000
Profit before taxation	31,000	10,000
Taxation	10,000	2,000
Profit for the year	21,000	8,000
Retained profits brought forward	87,000	17,000
Retained profits carried forward	108,000	25,000

BPP LEARNING MEDIA

Required

Prepare the consolidated profit and loss account.

Solution

PAPPADUM LIMITED
CONSOLIDATED PROFIT AND LOSS ACCOUNT
FOR THE YEAR ENDED 31 DECEMBER 20X6

	£
Turnover (75 + 38)	113,000
Cost of sales (30 + 20)	50,000
Gross profit	63,000
Administrative expenses (14 + 8)	22,000
Profit before taxation	41,000
Taxation (10 + 2)	12,000
Profit after taxation	29,000
Minority interest (25% × £8,000)	2,000
Group retained profit for the year	27,000
Retained profits brought forward	
(group share: 87 + (17 × 75%))	99,750
Retained profits carried forward	126,750

Notice how the minority interest is dealt with.

(a) **Down to the line 'profit after taxation' the whole of Samosa Ltd's results is included without reference to group share or minority share. A one-line adjustment is then inserted to deduct the minority's share of Samosa Ltd's profit after taxation.**

(b) **The minority's share** (£4,250) **of Samosa Ltd's retained profits brought forward is excluded.** This means that the carried forward figure of £126,750 is the figure which would appear in the balance sheet for group retained reserves.

This last point may be clearer if we revert to our balance sheet technique and construct the working for group reserves.

Group reserves

	Pappadum Ltd £	Samosa Ltd £
As per question	108,000	25,000
Group share in Samosa Ltd (25,000 × 75%)	18,750	
Group reserves	126,750	

The minority share of Samosa Ltd's reserves comprises the minority interest in the £17,000 profits brought forward plus the minority interest (£2,000) in £8,000 retained profits for the year.

Notice that a consolidated profit and loss account links up with a consolidated balance sheet exactly as in the case of an individual company's accounts: the figure of retained profits carried forward at the bottom of the profit and loss account appears as the figure for retained profits in the balance sheet.

We will now look at the **complications introduced by inter-company trading and pre-acquisition profits in the subsidiary.**

1.2 Inter-company trading

Like the consolidated balance sheet, the consolidated profit and loss account should deal with the results of the group as those of a single entity. When one company in a group sells goods to another an identical amount is added to the turnover of the first company and to the cost of sales of the second. Yet as far as the entity's dealings with outsiders are concerned no sale has taken place.

The consolidated figures for turnover and cost of sales should represent sales to, and purchases from, outsiders. An adjustment is therefore necessary to reduce the turnover and cost of sales figures by the value of inter-company sales during the year.

We have also seen in an earlier chapter that any **unrealised profits on inter-company trading should be excluded** from the figure of group profits. This will occur whenever goods sold at a profit within the group remain in the stock of the purchasing company at the year end. The best way to deal with this is to **calculate the unrealised profit** on **unsold stocks at the year end and reduce consolidated gross profit by this amount**. Cost of sales will be the balancing figure.

1.3 Example: inter-company trading

Suppose in our earlier example that Samosa Ltd had recorded sales of £5,000 to Pappadum Ltd during 20X6. Samosa Ltd had purchased these goods from outside suppliers at a cost of £3,000. One half of the goods remained in Pappadum Ltd's stock at 31 December 20X6.

Solution

The consolidated profit and loss account for the year ended 31 December 20X6 would now be as follows.

	Group £
Turnover (75 + 38 – 5)	108,000
Cost of sales (balancing figure)	46,000
Gross profit (45 + 18 – 1*)	62,000
Administrative expenses	(22,000)
Profit before taxation	40,000
Taxation	(12,000)
	28,000
Minority interest (25% × (£8,000 – £1,000*))	1,750
Group profit for the year	26,250
Retained profits brought forward	99,750
Retained profits carried forward	126,000

*Provision for unrealised profit: ½ × (£5,000 – £3,000)

A provision will be made for the unrealised profit against the stock figure in the consolidated balance sheet.

1.4 Pre-acquisition profits

As explained above, the figure for retained profits at the bottom of the consolidated profit and loss account must be the same as the figure for retained profits in the consolidated balance sheet. We have seen in previous chapters that **retained profits in the consolidated balance sheet comprise:**

(a)   **The whole of the parent company's retained profits,**

(b)   Plus a proportion of the subsidiary company's retained profits. The proportion is **the group's share of post-acquisition retained profits in the subsidiary**. From the total retained profits of the subsidiary we must therefore exclude both the minority's share of total retained profits and the group's share of pre-acquisition retained profits.

A **similar procedure is necessary in the consolidated profit and loss account** if it is to link up with the consolidated balance sheet. Previous examples have shown how the minority share of profits is excluded in the profit and loss account: their share of profits for the year is deducted from profit after tax; while the figure for profits brought forward in the consolidation schedule includes only the group's proportion of the subsidiary's profits.

In the same way, when considering examples which include pre-acquisition profits in a subsidiary, the figure for profits brought forward should include only the group's share of the post-acquisition retained profits. If the subsidiary is acquired *during* the accounting year, it is therefore necessary to apportion its profit for the year between pre-acquisition and post-acquisition elements.

The entire profit and loss account of the subsidiary is split between pre-acquisition and post-acquisition proportions. Only the post-acquisition figures are included in the profit and loss account. **This method is more usual** than the whole-year method and is the one which will be used in this Study Text.

Question

Consolidated profit and loss account 1

Pine Ltd acquired 60% of the equity of Spruce Ltd on 1 April 20X5. The profit and loss accounts and retained earnings of the two companies for the year ended 31 December 20X5 are set out below.

	Pine Ltd £	Spruce Ltd £	Spruce Ltd (9/12) £
Turnover	170,000	80,000	60,000
Cost of sales	65,000	36,000	27,000
Gross profit	105,000	44,000	33,000
Administrative expenses	43,000	12,000	9,000
Profit before tax	62,000	32,000	24,000
Taxation	23,000	8,000	6,000
Profit after tax	39,000	24,000	18,000
Movement on reserves			
Profit for the year	39,000	24,000	
Dividends (paid 31 December)	(12,000)	(6,000)	
Retained profits brought forward	81,000	40,000	
Retained profits carried forward	108,000	58,000	

Pine Ltd has not yet accounted for the dividends received from Spruce Ltd.

Prepare the consolidated profit and loss account.

Answer

The shares in Spruce Ltd were acquired three months into the year. Only the post-acquisition proportion (9/12ths) of Spruce Ltd's P & L account is included in the consolidated profit and loss account. This is shown above for convenience.

PINE LIMITED CONSOLIDATED PROFIT AND LOSS ACCOUNT
FOR THE YEAR ENDED 31 DECEMBER 20X5

	£
Turnover (170 + 60)	230,000
Cost of sales (65 + 27)	92,000
Gross profit	138,000
Administrative expenses (43 + 9)	52,000
Profit before tax	86,000
Taxation (23 + 6)	29,000
Profit after tax	57,000
Minority interest (40% × £18,000)	7,200
Group profit for the year	49,800
Movement on reserves	
Profit for the year	49,800
Dividends (Pine Ltd only)	12,000
Retained profits brought forward*	81,000
Retained profits carried forward	118,800

* All of Spruce Ltd's profits brought forward are pre-acquisition.

1.5 Disclosure requirements

S 230 CA 1985 allows a parent company to dispense with the need to publish its own individual profit and loss account.

(a) Companies taking advantage of this dispensation are obliged to state in their consolidated profit and loss account how much of the group's profit for the financial year is dealt with in the parent company's own profit and loss account.

(b) For internal purposes, of course, it will still be necessary to prepare the parent company's profit and loss account and the profit or loss shown there is the figure to be shown in the note to the group accounts.

(c) This is a point which has been clarified by the CA 1989. In the example above, P Ltd should disclose its own profit after adjustment for its share of the S Ltd dividend (from post-acquisition profits – remember that the pre-acquisition element should be credited to the cost of P's investment in S Ltd).

Where there are **extraordinary items** (now very rare) in the profit and loss account of a group company the **group share only** of such items should be included, after minority interest and the adjustment for inter-company dividends but before dividends payable by the parent company.

If you are required to prepare a consolidated profit and loss account in statutory form, you may need to disclose a figure for **directors' emoluments**. The figure should represent the emoluments of **parent company directors only**, whether those emoluments are paid by the parent company or by subsidiary companies. The emoluments of directors of subsidiary companies should be excluded, unless they are also directors of the parent company.

The movement on reserves statement may be required to show a transfer from the profit and loss account to other reserves. Where this transfer occurs in a subsidiary, only the group's (post-acquisition) share of the transfer will be recorded in the movement on reserves statement. Any minority interest or pre-acquisition profits would be excluded.

BPP
LEARNING MEDIA

MOVEMENT ON RESERVES (EXTRACT)

	Total
	£
Profit and loss account brought forward	X
Add retained profit for the year	X
	X
Less transfer to reserves (all of parent company transfers plus the group share of transfers in a subsidiary)	(X)
Profit and loss account carried forward	X

Section summary

The table below summaries the main points about the consolidated profit and loss account.

Summary: consolidated P & L account

Purpose	To show the results of the group for an accounting period as if it were a single entity.
Turnover to profit after tax	100% P + 100% S (excluding dividend receivable from subsidiary and adjustments for inter-company transactions).
Reason	To show the results of the group which were controlled by the holding company.
Inter-company sales	Strip out inter-company activity from both turnover and cost sales.
Unrealised profit on inter-company sales	(a) Goods sold by P Ltd. Increase cost of sales by unrealised profit. (b) Goods sold by S Ltd. Increase cost of sales by full amount of unrealised profit and decrease minority interest by their share of unrealised profit.
Depreciation	If the value of S Ltd's fixed assets have been subjected to a fair value uplift then any additional depreciation must be charged in the consolidated profit and loss account. The minority interest will need to be adjusted for their share.
Transfer of fixed assets	Any profit on the transfer, less excess depreciation is eliminated from the carrying value of the asset and the profit of the company making the transfer.

Minority interests	S's profit after tax (PAT) X
	 Less: * unrealised profit (X)
	      * profit on disposal of fixed assets (net of additional depreciation) (X)
	      X
	 MI% X
	 * Only applicable if sales of goods and fixed assets made by a subsidiary.

Reason	To show the extent to which profits generated through H's control are in fact owned by other parties.
Retained reserves	As per the balance sheet calculations.

2 FRS 6 Acquisitions and mergers

2.1 Acquisitions and mergers

Merger accounting is not in the syllabus. This was to be expected, as it is no longer allowed under international standards. FRS 6 is still applicable, but you do not need to study the FRS 6 requirements for merger accounting.

However FRS 6 has a number of provisions relating to acquisition accounting.

2.2 Acquisitions

In relation to the consideration:

'The composition and fair value of the consideration given by the acquiring company and its subsidiary undertakings should be disclosed. The nature of any deferred or contingent purchase consideration should be stated, including, for contingent consideration, the range of possible outcomes and the principal factors that affect the outcome.'

A contingent purchase consideration could be where the acquiring company pays a certain amount for the shares and agrees to pay a further amount at a later date if the acquired company reaches a certain level of profit.

FRS 6 also interacts with FRS 3:

'As required by FRS 3, in the period of acquisition the post-acquisition results of the acquired entity should be shown as a component of continuing operations in the profit and loss account, other than those that are also discontinued in the same period.'

If it is not possible to determine the post-acquisition results to the end of the period of acquisition, an indication of the entity's contribution to turnover and operating results should be given; if not, the reason should be explained.

Also in relation to FRS 3:

'Any exceptional profit or loss in periods following the acquisition that is determined using the fair values recognised on acquisition should be disclosed in accordance with the requirements of FRS 3, and identified as relating to the acquisition.'

FRS 6 makes it very clear that any **costs incurred post-acquisition** for **reorganising, restructuring and integrating the acquisition should be shown in the profit and loss account of that period (ie post acquisition).** Such costs are described as those that:

(a)   'Would not have been incurred had the acquisition not taken place.

(b)   Relate to a project identified and controlled by management as part of a reorganisation or integration programme set up at the time of acquisition or as a direct consequence of an immediate post-acquisition review.'

In other words, such costs **cannot be treated as movements on reserves.**

The cash flow impact of the acquisition should be disclosed according to FRS 1 *Cash flow statements* (Group cash flow statements are not in your syllabus).

Chapter Roundup

- The **consolidated profit and loss account** combines the profit and loss accounts of each group company. Adjustments must be made for:

    - inter-group trading
    - unrealised profit
    - minority interest
    - inter-group dividends
    - elimination of pre-acquisition profits

Quick Quiz

1   At what stage in the consolidated profit and loss account does the figure for minority interests appear?

2   What dispensation is granted to a parent company by s 230 CA 1985?

3   Barley Ltd has owned 100% of the issued share capital of Oats Ltd for many years. Barley Ltd sells goods to Oats Ltd at cost plus 20%. The following information is available for the year:

Turnover   – Barley Ltd   £460,000
            – Oats Ltd   £120,000

During the year Barley Ltd sold goods to Oats Ltd for £60,000 of which £18,000 were still held in stock by Oats at the year end.

At what amount should turnover appear in the consolidated profit and loss account?

4   Chicken plc owns 80% of Duck plc. Duck plc sells goods to Chicken plc at cost plus 50%. The total invoiced sales to Chicken plc by Duck plc in the year ended 31 December 20X9 were £900,000 and, of these sales, goods which had been invoiced at £60,000 were held in stock by Chicken plc at 31 December 20X9. What is the reduction in aggregate group gross profit?

5   Pavlova Ltd, which makes up its accounts to 31 December, has an 80% owned subsidiary Sponge Ltd. Sponge Ltd sells goods to Pavlova Ltd at a mark-up on cost of 33.33%. At 31 December 20X8, Pavlova had £12,000 of such goods in stock and at 31 December 20X9 had £15,000 of such goods in stock.

What is a permissible amount by which the consolidated profit attributable to Pavlova Ltd's shareholders should be adjusted in respect of the above?

Ignore taxation

A   £1,000 Debit
B   £800 Credit
C   £750 Credit
D   £600 Debit

Answers to Quick Quiz

1. Down to the line 'profit after taxation', the whole of the subsidiary's results is included. A one line adjustment is then inserted to deduct the minority's share of the subsidiary's PAT.

2. The parent company can choose to not publish its own individual profit and loss account.

3. Turnover: 460 + 120 − 60 = 520.

4. $£60,000 \times \dfrac{50}{150} = £20,000$

5. D $(15,000 - 12,000) \times \dfrac{33.3}{133.3} \times 80\%$

Now try the questions below from the Exam Question Bank

Number	Level	Marks	Time
Q12	Introductory	15	27 mins
Q13	Introductory	20	36 mins

11

Accounting for associates

Topic list	Syllabus reference
1 Background	D3
2 FRS 9 *Associates and joint ventures*	D3
3 Associates	D3

Introduction

Some investments which do not satisfy the criteria for classification as subsidiaries may nevertheless be much more than trade investments. The most important of these are associates and joint ventures which are the subject of this chapter and of FRS 9 *Associates and joint ventures.*

Study guide

		Intellectual level
D	**BUSINESS COMBINATIONS**	
3	**Preparation of consolidated financial statements including an associate**	
(g)	Define an associate and explain the principles and reasoning for the use of equity accounting.	2
(h)	Prepare consolidated financial statements to include a single subsidiary and an associate.	2

1 Background

In the 1960s it became increasingly common for companies to trade through companies in which a **substantial but not a controlling interest** was held. Traditionally such companies were accounted for in the same way as trade investments. In other words the income from associated companies was only included in the investing company's accounts to the extent of the dividends received and receivable up to its balance sheet date. However, it was felt that this treatment did not reflect the reality of the investment, not least because the investor could in many cases influence the investee's dividend policy. The need thus arose for an **intermediate form of accounting for those investments which lie between full subsidiary and trade investment status**.

1.1 Equity accounting and the Companies Act 1985

The intermediate form of accounting developed for this purpose is known as **equity accounting.** The full, up-to-date (FRS 9) definition of equity accounting will be given later in this chapter. For now, think of it as follows.

Key term

> **Equity accounting** is a modified form of consolidation of the results and assets of the investee where the investor has significant influence but not control. Rather than full, line by line consolidation, it involves incorporating the investor's share of the profit/loss and assets of the investee **in one line** in the investor's profit and loss account and balance sheet.

Equity accounting was first recognised in UK accounting literature in SSAP 1 *Accounting for associated companies* (now superseded by FRS 9). **Parent companies are also required by law to use equity accounting to account for holdings in associated undertakings, defined as follows.**

Key term

> 'An "**associated undertaking**" means an undertaking in which an undertaking included in the consolidation has a participating interest and over whose operating and financial policy it exercises a significant influence, and which is not:
>
> (a)   A subsidiary undertaking of the parent company
> (b)   A joint venture'. (s 20(1) Sch 4A, CA 1985)
>
> 'Where an undertaking holds 20% or more of the voting rights in another undertaking, it shall be presumed to exercise such an influence over it unless the contrary is shown.'   (s 20(2) Sch 4A, CA 1985)

2 FRS 9 Associates and joint ventures

Associates and **joint ventures** are entities in which an investor holds a **substantial but not controlling interest**. They are the subject of an accounting standard: **FRS 9** *Associates and joint ventures.*

FRS 9 *Associates and joint ventures* was issued in November 1997. It sets out the definition and accounting treatments for associates and joint ventures, two types of interests that a reporting entity may have in other entities. The definitions and treatments prescribed have been developed to be consistent with the Accounting Standards Board's approach to accounting for subsidiaries (dealt with in FRS 2 *Accounting for subsidiary undertakings*). The requirements are consistent with companies legislation.

Note that joint ventures are **not** in your syllabus.

2.1 Objective

The objective of FRS 9 is **to reflect the effect on an investor's financial position and performance of** its interest in two special kinds of investments – **associates and joint ventures**. The investor is partly accountable for the activities of these investments because of the closeness of its involvement.

(a)   It is closely involved in **associates** as a result of its **participating interest** and **significant influence**.

(b)   Its close involvement with **joint ventures** arises as a result of its **long-term interest** and **joint control**.

Joint ventures and other types of joint arrangement are not in the F7 syllabus, so we will be dealing only with associates.

The table below, taken from the FRS, describes the **different approaches to accounting for subsidiaries, associates and simple investments.**

Entity/ arrangement	Nature of relationship	Description of the defining relationship – the full definitions are given in the FRS
Subsidiary	Investor controls its investee	Control is the ability of an entity to direct the operating and financial policies of another entity with a view to gaining economic benefits from its activities. To have control an entity must have both: (a) The ability to deploy the economic resources of the investee or to direct it. (b) The ability to ensure that any resulting benefits accrue to itself (with corresponding exposure to losses) and to restrict the access of others to those benefits.
* Associate	Investor exercises significant influence	The investor has a long-term interest and is actively involved, and influential, in the direction of its investee through its participation in policy decisions covering the aspects of policy relevant to the investor, including decisions on strategic issues such as: (i) The expansion or contraction of the business, participation in other entities or changes in products, markets and activities of its investee. (ii) Determining the balance between dividend and reinvestment.
Simple investment		The investor's interest does not quality the investee as an associate, a joint venture or a subsidiary because the investor has limited influence or its interest is not long-term.

The table below, also taken from the FRS, sets out the **treatments in consolidated financial statements** for the different interests that a reporting entity may have in other entities.

Type of investment	Treatment in consolidated financial statements
Subsidiaries	The investor should consolidate the assets, liabilities, results and cash flows of its subsidiaries.
Associates	The investor should include its associates in its consolidated financial statements using the equity method. In the investor's consolidated profit and loss account the investor's share of its associates' operating results should be included immediately after group operating results. From the level of profit before tax, the investor's share of the relevant amounts for associates should be included within the amounts for the group. In the consolidated statement of total recognised gains and losses the investor's share of the total recognised gains and losses of its associates should be included, shown separately under each heading, if material. In the balance sheet the investor's share of the net assets of its associates should be included and separately disclosed. The cash flow statement should include the cash flows between the investor and its associates. Goodwill arising on the investor's acquisition of its associates, less any amortisation or write-down, should be included in the carrying amount for the associates but should be disclosed separately. In the profit and loss account the amortisation or write-down of such goodwill should be separately disclosed as part of the investor's share of its associates' results.
Simple investments	The investor includes its interests as investments at either cost or valuation.

2.2 Example: consolidated financial statements

The following example of consolidated financial statements is taken from Appendix IV of FRS 9. Study it for an overview and come back to it when you have finished the chapter.

The format is illustrative only.

CONSOLIDATED PROFIT AND LOSS ACCOUNT

	£m	£m
Group turnover		200
Cost of sales		(120)
Gross profit		80
Administrative expenses		(40)
Group operating profit		40
Share of operating profit in associates		54
		94
Interest receivable (group)		6
Interest payable		
Group	(26)	
Associates	(22)	
		(48)
Profit on ordinary activities before tax		52
Tax on profit on ordinary activities *		(12)
Profit on ordinary activities after tax		40
Minority interests		(6)
Profit on ordinary activities after taxation and minority interest		34

*Tax relates to the following:	Parent and subsidiaries	(5)
	Associates	(7)

CONSOLIDATED BALANCE SHEET

	£m	£m	£m
Fixed assets			
Tangible assets		480	
Investments			
Investments in associates		70	
			550
Current assets			
Stock		15	
Debtors		75	
Cash at bank and in hand		10	
		100	
Creditors (due within one year)		(50)	
Net current assets			50
Total assets less current liabilities			600
Creditors (due after more than one year)			(250)
Provisions for liabilities			(10)
Equity minority interest			(40)
			300

	£m
Capital and reserves	
Called up share capital	50
Share premium account	150
Profit and loss account	100
Shareholders' funds (all equity)	300

3 Associates

FAST FORWARD

> **Associates** are to be included in the investor's consolidated financial statements using the **equity method**. The investor's share of its associates' results should be included immediately after group operating profit.

Exam focus point

Your compulsory consolidation question is likely to include an associate.

Associated undertakings **should be included** by an entity **in its consolidated financial statements using the equity method. In the investor's individual statements**, the interest in associates is **shown as a fixed asset investment**, at cost (less any amounts written off) or valuation.

3.1 Definitions

The most important definitions relate to the **identification** of associates.

Key terms

- **Associate**: an entity (other than a subsidiary) over whose operating and financial policies the investor exercises a **significant influence**.

- **Control** the ability of an entity to direct the operating and financial policies of another entity with a view to gaining economic benefits from its activities.

- **Entity**: a body corporate, a partnership or an unincorporated association carrying on a trade or business with or without a view to profit. *(FRS 9)*

3.2 Long-term interest

This definition relates to a participating interest.

Key term

> **Interest held on a long-term basis**: an interest that is held other than exclusively with a view to subsequent resale. An interest held exclusively with a view to subsequent resale is:
>
> - An interest for which a purchaser has been identified or is being sought, and which is reasonably expected to be disposed or within approximately one year of its date of acquisition.
>
> - An interest that was acquired as a result of the enforcement of a security, unless the interest has become part of the continuing activities of the group or the holder acts as if it intends the interest to become so. *(FRS 9)*

This definition is extremely important.

Key term

> **Exercise of significant influence**: the exercise of a degree of influence by an investor over the operating and financial policies of its investee that results in the following conditions being fulfilled.
>
> (a) The investor is actively involved and is influential in the direction of its investee through its participation in policy decisions covering all aspects of policy relevant to the investor, including decisions on strategic issues such as:
>
>   (i) The expansion or contraction of the business, participation in other entities, changes in products, markets and activities of its investee.
>
>   (ii) Determining the balance between dividend and reinvestment.
>
> (b) Over time, the investee generally implements policies that are consistent with the strategy of the investor and avoids implementing policies that are contrary to the investor's interests. *(FRS 9)*

Significant influence is **usually wielded through nomination to the board of directors**, although it may be achieved in other ways. It presupposes an agreement (formal or informal) between the investor and investee.

The 20% rule is followed here, so that a holding of 20% or more of the voting rights suggests (but does not guarantee) that the investor exercises significant influence. At 20% the presumption of the exercise of significant influence can be rebutted if the criteria above are not fulfilled. The holdings of both parent and subsidiaries in the entity should be taken into account.

3.3 Accounting for associates

Following FRS 9, a reporting entity that prepares **consolidated financial statements** should include its associates in those statements using the **equity method in all the primary statements**. In the investor's **individual financial statements**, its interests in associates should be treated as **fixed asset investments** and shown either **at cost less any amounts written off or at valuation**.

The equity method is discussed here in more detail with regard to each of the primary statements.

3.3.1 Consolidated profit and loss account

FRS 9 stipulates the following.

(a) The investor's **share of its associates' operating results** should be **included immediately after group operating result** (but after the investor's share of the results of its joint ventures, if any).

(b) Any **amortisation** or write-down **of goodwill** arising on acquiring the associates should be **charged** at this point **and disclosed.**

(c)   The **investor's share of any exceptional items** included after operating profit (paragraph 20 of FRS 3) or of interest should be **shown separately** from the amounts for the group.

(d)   **At and below the level of profit before tax**, the **investor's share** of the relevant amounts for associates should be **included within the amounts for the group**, although for items **below this level**, such as taxation, the **amounts relating to associates should be disclosed.**

3.3.2 Consolidated balance sheet

FRS 9 requires the following.

(a)   The investor's **consolidated balance sheet should include as a fixed asset investment the investor's share of the net assets of its associates** shown as a separate item.

(b)   **Goodwill** arising on the investor's acquisition of its associates, less any amortisation or write-down, should be **included in the carrying amount for the associates but should be disclosed separately**.

3.4 Example: associated company in investor's own accounts

Pumpkin Ltd, a company with subsidiaries, acquires 25,000 of the 100,000 £1 ordinary shares in Asparagus Ltd for £60,000 on 1 January 20X0. Asparagus Ltd meets the FRS 9 definitions of an associate. In the year to 31 December 20X0, Asparagus Ltd earns profits after tax of £24,000, from which it declares a dividend of £6,000.

How will Asparagus Ltd's results be accounted for in the individual and consolidated accounts of Pumpkin Ltd for the year ended 31 December 20X0?

Solution

In the individual accounts of Pumpkin Ltd, the investment will be recorded on 1 January 20X0 at cost. Unless there is a permanent diminution in the value of the investment, this amount will remain in the individual balance sheet of Pumpkin Ltd permanently. The only entry in Pumpkin Ltd's individual profit and loss account will be to record dividends received. For the year ended 31 December 20X0, Pumpkin Ltd will:

DEBIT	Cash	£1,500	
CREDIT	Income from shares in associated companies		£1,500

3.5 Consolidated profit and loss account

A consolidation schedule may be used to prepare the consolidated profit and loss account of a group with associates. The treatment of the associate's profits in the following example should be studied carefully.

3.6 Example: associated company in consolidated accounts

The following consolidation schedule relates to the Pisces Ltd group, consisting of the parent company, an 80% owned subsidiary Sagitarius Ltd and an associate Aries Ltd in which the group has a 30% interest.

CONSOLIDATION SCHEDULE

	Group £'000	Pisces Ltd £'000	Sagitarius Ltd £'000	Aries Ltd £'000
Turnover	1,400	600	800	300
Cost of sales	770	370	400	120
Gross profit	630	230	400	180
Distribution costs and administrative expenses (including depreciation, directors' emoluments etc)	290	110	180	80
Group operating profit	340	120	220	100
Share of operating profit in associate	30	–	–	30% 30
	370	120	220	30
Interest receivable (group)	30	30	–	–
	400	150	220	30
Interest payable (group)	(20)	–	(20)	–
Profit on before tax	380	150	200	30
Taxation				
Pisces Ltd	(150)	(60)	(90)	
Associate	(12)	–	–	(12)
Profit after taxation	218	90	110	18
Minority interest	(22)		(22)	
Profit for the period	196	90	88	18

Notes

(a) **Group turnover, group gross profit and costs** such as depreciation etc **exclude** the turnover, gross profit and costs etc of **associates**.

(b) The **group share of the associate's operating profit is credited** to the group profit and loss account (here, 30% of £100,000 = £30,000). If the associated company has been acquired during the year, it would be necessary to deduct the pre-acquisition profits.

(c) **Taxation** consists of:

    (i) Taxation **on the parent company and subsidiaries in total.**

    (ii) Only the **group's share of the tax charge of the associated company**; Aries Ltd tax would be £40,000, so that the group share is £40,000 × 30% = £12,000.

(d) The **minority interest will only ever apply to subsidiary companies.**

(e) **Inter-company dividends** from subsidiaries and associated companies **should all be recorded**.

(f) **Dividends** paid **relate to the holding company only**.

3.7 Pro-forma consolidated profit and loss account

The following is a **suggested layout** (using the figures given in the illustration above) for a profit and loss account for a company having subsidiaries as well as associates. It follows the FRS 9 example given in Section 2 of this chapter.

	£'000	£'000
Turnover		1,400
Cost of sales		770
Gross profit		630
Distribution costs and administrative expenses		290
Group operating profit		340
Share of operating profit in associate		30
		370
Interest and similar income receivable (group)		30
		400
Interest payable and similar charges (group)		(20)
Profit before tax		380
Taxation		162
Profit after taxation		218
Minority interest (in the current year post tax profits of subsidiary)		(22)
Profit for the financial year attributable to the group (of which £110,000 has been dealt with in the accounts of the holding company)		196
Earnings per share		Xp

3.8 Consolidated balance sheet

As explained earlier, the consolidated balance sheet will contain an **asset 'Investment in associates'**. The amount at which this asset is stated will be its original cost plus the group's share of any **profits earned since acquisition** which have not been distributed as dividends.

3.9 Example: consolidated balance sheet

On 1 January 20X6 the net tangible assets of Almond Ltd amount to £220,000, financed by 100,000 £1 ordinary shares and revenue reserves of £120,000. Peanut Ltd, a company with subsidiaries, acquires 30,000 of the shares in Almond Ltd for £75,000. During the year ended 31 December 20X6 Almond Ltd's profit after tax is £30,000, from which dividends of £12,000 are paid.

Show how Peanut Ltd's investment in Almond Ltd would appear in the consolidated balance sheet at 31 December 20X6.

Solution

CONSOLIDATED BALANCE SHEET
AS AT 31 DECEMBER 20X6 (extract)

	£
Fixed assets	
Investment in associate	80,400

This figure of £80,400 is the sum of:

(a) The group's share of Almond Ltd's net assets at 31 December 20X6.
(b) The premium paid over net book value for the shares acquired (goodwill).

This can be shown as follows.

(a) Almond Ltd's net assets at 31 December 20X6:

	£	£
Net assets at 1 January 20X6	220,000	
Retained profit for year	18,000	
Net assets at 31 December 20X6	238,000	
Group share (30%)		71,400

(b) Premium on acquisition (goodwill):

	£	£
Net assets acquired by group on 1 Jan 20X6		
(30% × £220,000)	66,000	
Price paid for shares	75,000	
Premium on acquisition (goodwill)		9,000
Investment in associate per balance sheet		80,400

The reason why this is important is because FRS 9 requires the investment in associated companies to be analysed in this way, ie:

(a) Group share of associate's net assets

(b) Goodwill arising on acquisition of associate less any amortisation or write down is included in (a) but disclosed separately

Fair values should be attributed to the associate's underlying assets and liabilities. These will provide the basis for subsequent depreciation. Both the consideration paid in the acquisition and the goodwill arising should be calculated in the same way as on the acquisition of a subsidiary. The associate's assets should not include any goodwill earned in the balance sheet of the associate.

The goodwill should be treated in accordance with the provisions of FRS 10 *Goodwill and intangible assets.* The usual treatment would therefore be to capitalise and amortise. (Our example assumes for simplicity that the goodwill has an indefinite life and there is no amortisation.)

Question

Associated company

How should a holding company treat the following items in the financial statements for an associated company, when preparing group accounts:

(a) Turnover?
(b) Inter-company profits?
(c) Goodwill?

Answer

(a) The holding company should not aggregate the turnover of an associated company with its own turnover.

(b) Wherever the effect is material, adjustments similar to those adopted for the purpose of presenting consolidated financial statements should be made to exclude from the investing group's consolidated financial statements such items as unrealised profits on stocks transferred to or from associated companies. The adjustments are based on the parents **share** of the associate.

(c) The investing group's balance sheet should disclose 'interest in associated companies'. The amount disclosed under this heading should include both the investing group's share of any goodwill in the associated companies' own financial statements and any premium paid on acquisition of the interests in the associated companies in so far as it has not already been written off or amortised.

![pencil icon] **Question**   **Consolidated balance sheet**

The balance sheets of J plc and its investee companies, P Ltd and S Ltd, at 31 December 20X5 are shown below.

BALANCE SHEETS AS AT 31 DECEMBER 20X5

	J plc £'000	£'000	P Ltd £'000	£'000	S Ltd £'000	£'000
Tangible fixed assets						
Freehold property	1,950		1,250		500	
Plant and machinery	795		375		285	
		2,745		1,625		785
Investments		1,500		–		–
Current assets						
Stock	575		300		265	
Trade debtors	330		290		370	
Cash	50		120		20	
	955		710		655	
Creditors: due within one year						
Bank overdraft	560		–		–	
Trade creditors	680		350		300	
	1,240		350		300	
Net current (liabilities)/assets		(285)		360		355
Creditors: due after one year						
12% debentures		(500)		(100)		–
		3,460		1,885		1,140
Share capital (£1 ordinary shares)		2,000		1,000		750
Profit and loss account		1,460		885		390
		3,460		1,885		1,140

Additional information

(a)   J plc acquired 600,000 ordinary shares in P Ltd on 1 January 20X0 for £1,000,000 when the reserves of P Ltd were £200,000.

(b)   At the date of acquisition of P Ltd, the fair value of its freehold property was considered to be £400,000 greater than its value in P Ltd's balance sheet. P Ltd had acquired the property in January 20W0 and the buildings element (comprising 50% of the total value) is depreciated on cost over 50 years.

(c)   J plc acquired 225,000 ordinary shares in S Ltd on 1 January 20X4 for £500,000 when the reserves of S Ltd were £150,000.

(d)   P Ltd manufactures a component used by both J plc and S Ltd. Transfers are made by P Ltd at cost plus 25%. J plc held £100,000 stock of these components at 31 December 20X5 and S Ltd held £80,000 at the same date.

(e)   It is the policy of J plc to write off goodwill over a period of five years.

Required

Prepare, in a format suitable for inclusion in the annual report of the J Group, the consolidated balance sheet at 31 December 20X5.

Answer

J GROUP CONSOLIDATED BALANCE SHEET AS AT 31 DECEMBER 20X5

	£'000	£'000
Fixed assets		
Tangible assets		
Freehold property (W2)	3,570.00	
Plant and machinery (795 + 375)	1,170.00	
		4,740.00
Investment in associate (W8)		475.20
		5,215.20
Current assets		
Stock (W3)	855.00	
Debtors (W4)	620.00	
Cash at bank and in hand (50 + 120)	170.00	
	1,645.00	
Creditors: amounts falling due within one year (W5)	1,590.00	
Net current assets		55.00
Total assets less current liabilities		5,270.20
Creditors: amounts falling due after more than one year		
(500 + 100)		600.00
		4,670.20
Capital and reserves		
Called up share capital		2,000.00
Profit and loss account (W9)		1,778.12
Shareholders' funds		3,778.12
Minority interests (W6)		892.08
		4,670.20

Workings

1 Group structure

		£'000
J plc		1,950
P Ltd		1,250
Fair value adjustment		400
Additional depreciation (400 × 50% ÷ 40) × 6 years (20X0-20X5)		(30)
		3,570

3 Stock

		£'000
J plc		575
P Ltd		300
PUP (100 × $^{25}/_{125}$)		(20)
		855

4   *Debtors*

		£'000
J plc		330
P Ltd		290
		620

5   *Creditors due < 1 year*

		£'000
J plc:	bank overdraft	560
	trade creditors	680
P Ltd:	trade creditors	350
		1,590

6   *Minority interest*

	£'000
Net assets of P Ltd	1,885.0
Fair value adjustment (W11)	370.0
Less PUP: sales to J plc	(20.0)
sales to S Ltd $(80 \times {}^{25}/_{125} \times 30\%)$	(4.8)
	2,230.2
Minority interest (40%)	892.08

7   *Goodwill*

	£'000	£'000
P Ltd		
Cost of investment		1,000
Share of net assets acquired		
Share capital	1,000	
Reserves	200	
Fair value adjustment	400	
	1,600	
Group share 60%		(960)
Fully amortised		40
S Ltd		
Cost of investment		500
Share of net assets acquired		
Share capital	750	
Reserves	150	
	900	
Group share 30%		(270)
		230
		92

$$\text{Amortisation} = \frac{230}{5} \times 2 =$$

8   *Investment in associate*

	£'000
Share of net assets (30% × 1,140)	342.0
Less PUP	(4.8)
Add unamortised goodwill (230 − 92)	138.0
	475.2

9   *Profit and loss account*

	J £'000	P £'000	S £'000
Reserves per question	1,460.0	885.0	390.0
Adjustments			
Unrealised profit (W10)		(24.8)	
Fair value adjustments (W11)		(30.0)	
		830.2	390.0
Less pre-acquisition reserves		(200.0)	(150.0)
	1,460.0	630.2	240.0
P: 60% × 630.2	378.1		
S: 30% × 240	72.0		
Less amortisation of goodwill: P	(40.0)		
S	(92.0)		
	1,778.1		

10   *Unrealised profit (PUP)*

	£'000
On sales to J (parent co) 100 × 25/125	20.0
On sales to S (associate) 80 × 25/125 × 30%	4.8
	24.8

11   *Fair value adjustments*

	Difference at acquisition £'000	Difference now £'000
Property	400	400
Additional depreciation: 200 × 6/40	–	(30)
	400	370

∴ Charge £30,000 to P&L

Chapter Roundup

- **Associates** and **joint ventures** are entities in which an investor holds a **substantial but not controlling interest**. They are the subject of an accounting standard: **FRS 9** *Associates and joint ventures.*

- **Associates** are to be included in the investor's consolidated financial statements using the **equity method**. The investor's share of its associates' results should be included immediately after group operating profit.

Quick Quiz

1   How does FRS 9 define associate?

2   A group of companies has the following shareholdings.

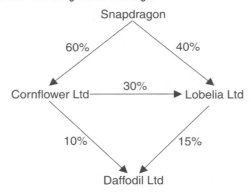

For consolidation purposes what, prima facie, is the relationship of Lobelia Ltd and Daffodil Ltd to Snapdragon plc?

3   Constable plc owns 40% of Turner plc which it treats as an associated company in accordance with FRS 9. Constable plc also owns 60% of Whistler Ltd. Constable has held both of these shareholdings for more than one year. Turnover of each company for the year ended 30 June 20X0 was as follows.

	£m
Constable	400
Turner	200
Whistler	100

What figure should be shown as turnover in the consolidated profit and loss account of Constable plc?

Answers to Quick Quiz

1   An entity over whose operating and financial policies the investor exerts a significant influence.

2   Lobelia Ltd **subsidiary**; Daffodil Ltd **associate**

Shares held by subsidiary companies count in full. Snapdragon has control of Cornflower's 30% holding in Lobelia. It owns 40% itself, 40 + 30 gives control. Snapdragon therefore controls Lobelia's 15% in Daffodil and Cornflower's 10% in Daffodil (10 + 15 = 25 = associate).

3   Turnover will be 100% H + 100% S only. Associates are introduced in to the consolidated profit and loss account as a share of their operating profits in the first instance.

	£m
Constable	400
Whistler (subsidiary)	100
	500

Now try the questions below from the Exam Question Bank

Number	Level	Marks	Time
Q14	Examination	25	45 mins

Stocks and long-term contracts

12

Topic list	Syllabus reference
1 Stocks and short-term work in progress	C4
2 Long-term contract work in progress	C4

Introduction

You have encountered stocks and stock valuation in your earlier studies. Stock valuation has a direct impact on a company's gross profit and it is usually a material item in any company's accounts. This is therefore an important subject area. If you have any doubts about accounting for stocks and methods of stock valuation you would be advised to go back to your lower level study material and revise this topic.

Section 1 of this chapter goes over some of this ground again, concentrating on the effect of SSAP 9. Section 2 goes on to discuss a new area, long-term contract work in progress.

Study guide

		Intellectual level
C	**FINANCIAL STATEMENTS**	
4	**Inventory**	
(a)	Describe and apply the principles of inventory valuation.	2
(b)	Define a long-term contract and discuss the role of accounting concepts in the recognition of profit.	2
(c)	Describe the acceptable methods of determining the stage (percentage) of completion of a long-term contract.	2
(d)	Prepare financial statement extracts for long-term contracts.	2

Exam guide

You should find long-term contracts fairly logical as long as you work through the examples and exercise carefully.

1 Stocks and short-term work in progress

FAST FORWARD

Stocks comprise:

Raw materials and consumables
Work in progress
Finished goods and goods for resale
Payments on account (of purchases)

They must be revalued at **lower of cost and net realisable value**.

FIFO and **weighted average** are the accepted means of valuation under SSAP 9.

Exam focus point

Stock is most likely to appear as an item in an accounts preparation question.

In most businesses the value put on stock is an important factor in the determination of profit. Stock valuation is, however, a highly subjective exercise and consequently there is a wide variety of different methods used in practice.

The Companies Act 1985 regulations and SSAP 9 *Stocks and long-term contracts* requirements were developed to achieve greater uniformity in the valuation methods used and in the disclosure in financial statements prepared under the historical cost convention.

SSAP 9 defines stocks and work in progress as:

(a) Goods or other assets purchased for resale.
(b) Consumable stores.
(c) Raw materials and components purchased for incorporation into products for sale.
(d) Products and services in intermediate stages of completion.
(e) Long-term contract balances.
(f) Finished goods.

In published accounts, the Companies Act 1985 requires that these stock categories should be grouped and disclosed under the following headings:

(a)   Raw materials and consumables ((c) and (b) above).

(b)   Work in progress ((d) and (e) above).

(c)   Finished goods and goods for resale ((f) and (a) above).

(d)   Payments on account (presumably intended to cover the case of a company which has paid for stock items but not yet received them into stock).

A distinction is also made in SSAP 9 between:

(a)   Stocks and work in progress other than long-term contract work in progress.
(b)   Long-term contract work in progress.

We will look at long-term contracts later in the chapter. Stocks and short-term work in progress are revised briefly here.

Knowledge brought forward from earlier studies

SSAP 9 Stock and long-term contracts (Stock and short-term WIP)

Under the matching concept costs must be allocated between the cost of goods sold (matched against current revenues) and closing stock (matched against future revenues).

- Stock should be valued at the **lower of cost and net realisable value** (NRV).

- **Costs** should include those incurred in the **normal course of business** in bringing a product or service to its **present location and condition**.

- Costs include direct costs (labour, materials), production overheads and other attributable overheads. Exclude all 'abnormal' overheads, eg exceptional spoilage.

- CA 1985 also allows the inclusion of interest payable on capital borrowed to finance the production of the asset (allowed by SSAP 9 under 'other attributable overheads').

- **NRV is the actual or estimated selling price less further costs to be incurred in marketing, selling and distribution.**

- The method used in allocating costs to stock should produce the fairest approximation to the expenditure incurred.

- Methods include (per CA 1985): average cost, base stock, current cost, FIFO, LIFO, replacement cost, standard cost, unit cost; however, base stock and LIFO are not allowed under SSAP 9.

- The principal situation where NRV will be less than cost will be where:
  - There have been increases in the costs or falls in selling price
  - Physical deterioration of stock has occurred
  - Products have become obsolescent
  - The company has decided to make and sell a product at a loss
  - There are errors in production or purchasing

The following question is a very simple reminder of how FIFO operates.

Question

Digby Pillay, a retailer commenced business on 1 January 20X5, with a capital of £500. He decided to specialise in a single product line and by the end of June 20X5, his purchases and sales of this product were as follows.

	Purchases		Sales	
	Units	Unit price	Units	Unit price
		£		£
January	30	5.00	20	7.00
February	–	–	5	7.20
April	40	6.00	25	8.00
May	25	6.50	30	8.50
June	20	7.00	20	9.00
	115		100	

Required

(a) Ascertain Digby Pillay's gross profit for the period using FIFO.

(b) Assuming that all purchases and sales are made for cash and that there are no other transactions for the period, draw up a balance sheet as at 30 June 20X5.

Answer

(a)

	£	£
Sales		811.00
Purchases	692.50	
Less closing stock (15 @ £7.00)	105.00	
		587.50
		223.50

(b) BALANCE SHEET AS AT 30 JUNE 20X5

	£
Original capital	500.00
Profit	223.50
	723.50
Stock	105.00
Cash	618.50
	723.50

2 Long-term contract work in progress

2.1 Introduction

The most controversial aspect of SSAP 9 is its approach to the valuation of work in progress for incomplete long-term contracts.

Key term

> A **long-term contract** is defined as: 'a contract entered into for the design, manufacture or construction of a **single substantial asset** or the provision of a service (or of a combination of assets or services which together constitute a **single project**) where the time taken substantially to complete the contract is such that the **contract activity** falls into **different accounting periods**.'

Usually long-term contracts will **exceed one year** in duration, although a **sufficiently material contract** whose activity **straddles a balance sheet date** should still be accounted for as a **long-term contract even if it will last in total less than a year**. This is to ensure that the accounts for **both accounting periods** involved will still give a **true and fair view** of the activities of the company.

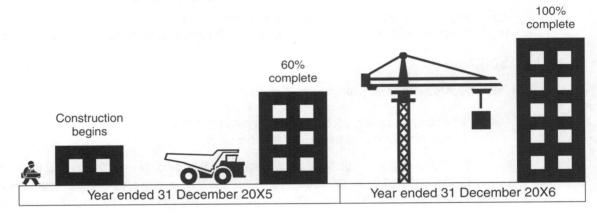

The existence of a proper **contract** is **important**, because it provides a basis of **reasonable certainty** whereby it is nevertheless **prudent** to **allow recognition** of **profits before completion of work**.

2.2 The underlying problem

FAST FORWARD

> Turnover and profit should be recognised throughout the duration of the contract. Any foreseeable loss should be recognised immediately.

It is the following requirement which causes the greatest controversy around SSAP 9.

'Separate consideration needs to be given to long-term contracts. Owing to the **length of time** taken to complete such contracts, to defer recording turnover and taking profit into account until completion may result in the profit and loss account reflecting not so much a **fair view** of the results of the **activity** of the company **during the year** but rather the results relating to contracts that have been completed in the year. It is therefore appropriate to take **credit** for **ascertainable turnover** and **profit** while contracts are **in progress ....'**

Some companies might prefer to value work in progress on long-term contracts at cost, and to **defer taking any profit** on the contract into the profit and loss account **until the contract had been completed**. This policy may be considered **prudent**, but there may be an **underlying management motive** to **defer profits** and **tax liabilities.**

2.3 Example: Long-term contracts

Jianzhu Construction Ltd started a contract on 1 January 20X5, with an estimated completion date of 31 December 20X6. In the first year, to 31 December 20X5:

(a)   Costs incurred amounted to £900,000.

(b)   Sixty per cent of the work on the contract was completed.

(c)   The final contract price is £2,000,000.

(d)   Certificates of work completed have been issued, to the value of £1,200,000. (*Note*. It is usual, in a long-term contract, for a qualified person such as an architect or engineer to inspect the work completed, and if it is satisfactory, to issue certificates. This will then be the notification to the customer that progress payments are now due to the contractor. Progress payments are commonly the amount of valuation on the work certificates issued, minus a precautionary retention of 10%.).

(e)   It is estimated with reasonable certainty that further costs to completion in 20X6 will be £600,000.

What is the contract profit in 20X5, and what entries would be made for the contract at 31 December 20X5 if:

(a)   Profits are deferred until the completion of the contract?
(b)   A proportion of the estimated turnover and profit is credited to the profit and loss account in 20X5?

Solution

(a)   *Profits deferred until completion of contract*

	£
• Turnover and profits recognised on the contract in 20X5	Nil
• Value of work in progress at 31 December 20X5	900,000

SSAP 9 takes the view that this policy is unreasonable, because in 20X6, the total profit of £500,000 [2,000,000 – (900,000 + 600,000)] would be recorded. Since the contract revenues are earned throughout 20X5 and 20X6, a profit of nil in 20X5 and £500,000 in 20X6 would be contrary to the accruals basis of accounting.

(b)   It is fairer to recognise turnover and profit throughout the duration of the contract.

As at 31 December 20X5 turnover of £1,200,000 should be matched with cost of sales of £900,000 [(900,000 + 600,000) × 60%] in the profit and loss account, leaving an attributable profit for 20X5 of £300,000.

The only balance sheet entry as at 31 December 20X5 is a debtor of £1,200,000 recognising that the company is owed this amount for work done to date. No balance remains for stock, the whole £900,000 having been recognised in cost of sales.

2.4 Definitions

SSAP 9 gives some other important definitions, as well as that of long-term contracts themselves given above.

Key terms

'**Attributable profit**. That part of the **total profit** currently estimated to arise over the **duration** of the **contract**, after allowing for **estimated remedial** and **maintenance costs** and increases in costs so far as **not recoverable** under the terms of the contract, that fairly reflects the profit attributable to that part of the **work performed** at the accounting date. (There can be no attributable profit until the **profitable outcome** of the contract can be assessed with **reasonable certainty**.)

Foreseeable losses. Losses which are currently estimated to arise over the **duration** of the **contract** (after allowing for **estimated remedial** and **maintenance costs** and increases in costs so far as **not recoverable** under the terms of the contract). This estimate is required irrespective of:

(a)   Whether or not work has yet **commenced** on such contracts
(b)   The **proportion** of work **carried out** at the accounting date
(c)   The amount of **profits expected** to arise on other contracts

Payments on account. All amounts **received** and **receivable** at the accounting date in respect of contracts in progress.'

2.5 Approach for calculating turnover and profit to be taken

The SSAP 9 guidelines for calculating the turnover and profit to be taken on incomplete long-term contracts follow directly from the definitions given above.

- (a) **Turnover and profit**

  - (i) Must reflect the **proportion** of **work carried** out at the **accounting date**.

  - (ii) Must take into account any **known inequalities of profitability** in the **various stages** of a contract.

  - (iii) Must be ascertained in a **manner appropriate** to the **industry** in which the **company operates**.

- (b) **Situations where the outcome of a contract cannot be assessed with reasonable certainty**.

  - (i) Generally no profit should be taken up in the profit and loss, especially where the contract is in its early stages.

  - (ii) If no loss is expected, it may be appropriate to include in turnover, a proportion of the total contract value using a zero estimate of profit.

- (c) **Situations where there is an expected loss on a contract as a whole**

  Provision must be made for the whole of the loss as soon as it is foreseen, ie, none of the loss should be deferred.

  This has the effect of reducing the value of WIP to its net realisable value. For example, if a contract is 75% complete, and:

  - (i) Costs incurred to date are £300,000
  - (ii) Further costs to completion are expected to be £100,000
  - (iii) The contract price is £360,000

In addition to a **suitable proportion of costs incurred**, then the **full expected loss of £40,000** should be **charged against profit** in the current period.

This approach must be applied consistently between different contracts over time.

2.6 Treatment of other costs

The **estimated future costs** must take into account **estimated costs of rectification and guarantee work** and any possible increases in wages, prices of raw materials etc, so far as these are **not recoverable** from the **customer** under the terms of the contract.

Interest payable for finance etc must be **excluded** from **costs unless specifically attributable** to the **contract**.

2.7 Estimating attributable profit

FAST FORWARD

There are generally two alternative formulae for determining the estimated attributable profit for the year.

- Work certified basis
- Costs incurred basis

(a) Attributable profit = $\dfrac{\text{Work certified to date}}{\text{Total contract price}} \times \text{Estimated total profit}$

(b) Attributable profit = $\dfrac{\text{Cost of work completed to date}}{\text{Total costs}} \times \text{Estimated total profit}$

Care should be exercised in adopting a costs incurred basis eg if there is high initial outlay or perhaps the expensive items only go in towards the end of the contract. The examiner may therefore provide a tailored formula for the specific exam question which you will need to interpret and apply on the day.

2.8 Available guidance

SSAP 9 does not provide any guidance on how to work out cost of sales, but focuses instead on the approach to determining attributable profit.

The amount of turnover and profit on a long-term contract to be recognised in an accounting period is found using a cumulative approach ie deduct figure total at end of last year from total at end of this year to get figure for the current year.

	£
Cumulative turnover/attributable profit	X
Less any turnover/attributable profit taken into account in previous years	X
Turnover/profit to be recognised in current period	X

Estimates of total profit may change from one year to another. Therefore, attributable profits have to be **recalculated** at the end of **each period**. Remember that at an **early stage** in the contract, in order to show a **true and fair view** of activity in the period, an **appropriate proportion of turnover** should be recorded in the profit and loss account but, on grounds of **prudence**, **no profit** should be recorded until the overall result of the contract is more certain.

2.9 Using a step-by-step approach

FAST FORWARD

Long-term contract WIP can be calculated as:	
Costs to date	X
Less Costs transferred to cost of sales	(X)
Less Foreseeable losses	(X)
Less Payments on account in excess of turnover	(X)
WIP	X

In valuing long-term WIP and implementing the other disclosures required under SSAP 9, you may find a step-by-step approach to be helpful. The following suggested process should assist you to tackle the problem in an ordered way.

STEP 1

Calculate the expected total profit or loss on the contract.

	£
Contract value	X
Less: Costs incurred to date	(X)
Expected further costs to complete	(X)
Expected total profit/(loss)	X/(X)

(a) If the contract is expected to make a profit, recognise attributable profit, if outcome is reasonably certain.

(b) If a loss is foreseen (that is, if the costs to date plus estimated costs to completion exceed the contract value) then it must be charged against profits.

(c) If a loss has already been charged in previous years, then only the difference between the loss as previously and currently estimated need be charged (or credited).

STEP 2

Using the percentage certified/completed to date (or other formula given in the question), calculate turnover attributable to the contract for the period.

	£
Total contract value × percentage certified (or formula given in the question)	X
Less Turnover recognised in previous period	(X)
Turnover attributable to current period	X

STEP 3

Calculate the cost of sales attributable to the contract for the period.

	£
Total contract costs × percentage certified (or formula given in question)	X
Less Any costs charged in previous periods	(X)
	X
Add Foreseeable losses in full (not previously charged)	X
Cost of sales attributable to current period	X

STEP 4

Review the balance on work in progress

(a) A debit balance for WIP will remain on the balance sheet

(b) A credit balance on WIP should be shown under provision for liabilities and charges.

STEP 5

Calculate cumulative turnover on the contract (the total turnover recorded in respect of the contract in the profit and loss accounts of all accounting periods since the inception of the contract). Compare this with total progress payments to date.

(a) If turnover exceeds payments on account (from customers), an 'amount recoverable on contracts' is established and separately disclosed within debtors.

(b) If payments on account (from customers) exceed cumulative turnover then the excess is:

   (i) First deducted from any remaining balance on work in progress

   (ii) Any balance is disclosed within creditors

These steps must be done for each contract individually. Only when the amounts under each heading, in respect of contract, have been determined, should they be added together for presentation in the accounts.

2.10 Double entry

The accounting double entry for a long-term contract is as follows.

(a) *During the year*

   (i)   DEBIT   Contract costs account (WIP)
            CREDIT   Bank/creditors
            Being costs incurred on contract

   (ii)   DEBIT   Trade debtors
            CREDIT   Progress payments account
            Being progress payments invoiced to customers

   (iii) DEBIT   Bank
            CREDIT   Trade debtors
            Being cash received from customers

(b) *At year end*

   (i)   DEBIT   Progress payments account
            CREDIT   Turnover (P&L)
            Being turnover recognised in respect of certified work

   (ii)   DEBIT   Cost of sales (P&L)
            CREDIT   Contract costs account (WIP)
            Being costs matched against turnover

   (iii) DEBIT   Provisions on long-term contracts (P&L)
            CREDIT   Provision for future losses (B/S)
            Being a provision for future losses

2.11 Summary of accounting treatment

The following is a handy summary of the accounting treatment for long-term contracts.

2.11.1 Profit and loss account

(a) **Turnover and costs**

   (i)   Turnover and associated costs should be recorded in the profit and loss account 'as contract activity progresses'.

   (ii)   Include an 'appropriate proportion of total contract value as turnover' in the profit and loss account.

   (iii) The costs incurred in reaching that stage of completion are matched with this turnover, resulting in the reporting of results which can be attributed to the proportion of work completed.

   (iv) Turnover is the 'value of work carried out to date'.

(b) **Attributable profit**

   (i)   It must reflect the proportion of work carried out.

   (ii)   It should take into account any known inequalities in profitability in the various stages of a contract.

Balance sheet

(a) **Stocks**

	£
Costs to date	X
Less Transfer to profit and loss account	(X)
	X
Less Foreseeable losses	(X)
	X
Less Payments on account in excess of turnover	(X)
Work in progress	X

(b) **Debtors**

	£
Amounts recoverable on contracts	X
Progress payments receivable (trade debtors)	X

(c) **Creditors**. Where payments on account exceed both cumulative turnover and net WIP the excess should be included in creditors under 'payments on account'.

(d) **Provisions**. To the extent foreseeable future losses exceed WIP, the losses should be provided.

Question

The main business of Fenix Projex Ltd is construction contracts for civil engineering projects such as dams and bridges. At the end of September 20X3 there is an uncompleted contract on the books, for a bridge over River X, details of which are as follows.

CONTRACT	River X
Date commenced	1.4.X1
Expected completed date	23.12.X3
	£
Final contract price	290,000
Costs to 30.9.X3	210,450
Value of work certified to 30.9.X3	230,000
Progress payments invoiced to 30.9.X3	210,000
Cash received to 30.9.X3	194,000
Estimated costs to completion at 30.9.X3	20,600

Required

Prepare calculations showing the amounts to be included in the balance sheet at 30 September 20X3 in respect of the above contract. Fenix estimates profit on the basis of work certified.

Answer

- *River X* is a long-term contract and will be accounted for using long-term contract accounting.

Estimated final profit

	£
Contract value	290,000
Less: Costs incurred to date	(210,450)
Estimated future costs	(20,600)
Expected total profit	58,950

Attributable profit

Estimated final profit $\times$ $\dfrac{\text{Work certified}}{\text{Total contract value}}$

£58,950 $\times$ $\dfrac{230,000}{290,000}$

Attributable profit   £46,753

Profit and loss account (extract)

	£
Turnover	230,000
Cost of sales (W2)	(183,247)
	46,753

Balance sheet (extract)

	£
Stock: long term contracts (W1)	27,203
Debtors:	
Amounts recoverable on contracts (W1)	20,000
Progress payments invoiced less cash received (W1)	16,000

Workings

1

CONTRACT X (WIP)

	£		£
Costs to 30.9.X3	210,450	Tfr to cost of sales	183,247
		Balance c/d	27,203
	210,450		210,450
Balance b/d	27,203		

TRADE DEBTORS

	£		£
Invoices; progress payments	210,000	Cash received	194,000
		Balance c/d	16,000
	210,000		210,000
Balance b/d	16,000		

PROGRESS PAYMENTS – CONTRACT X (Amount recoverable on contract)

	£		£
Work certified	230,000	Invoices; progress payments	210,000
		Balance c/d	20,000
	230,000		230,000
Balance c/d	20,000		

TURNOVER

	£		£
		Work certified	230,000

COST OF SALES

	£		£
Tfr from WIP	183,247		

2

	£
Work certified	230,000
Cost of sales (balancing figure)	(183,247)
Attributable profit	46,753

2.12 Profitable and loss-making contracts

Students sometimes find accounting for long-term contracts quite confusing, particularly where contracts are loss-making. We can look at the differences between profitable and loss-making contracts in more depth.

2.12.1 Profitable contracts

PROFIT AND LOSS ACCOUNT (EXTRACT)

	£
Turnover	X
Cost of sales	(X)
Attributable profit	X

BALANCE SHEET (EXTRACT)

	£
Current assets	
Stock: Long-term contracts	
Costs to date	X
Less P&L a/c cost of sales	(X)
Less Excess payments on accounts	(X)
	X
Debtors: amounts recoverable on contracts	
Turnover, work certified	X
Less Progress payments invoiced	(X)
	X
Debtors: trade debtors	
Progress payments invoiced less cash received	X
Current liabilities	
Payments on account (when payments received in excess of turnover which	
cannot be offset against stock balance)	X

2.12.2 Loss-making contracts

PROFIT AND LOSS ACCOUNT (EXTRACT)

	£
Turnover	X
Cost of sales	(X)
	(X)
Provision for loss (balancing figure)	(X)
Total foreseeable loss	(X)

BALANCE SHEET (EXTRACT)

	£
Current assets	
Stock: long-term contracts	
Costs incurred	X
Less Cost of sales	(X)
Less Provision for loss	(X)
Less Negative debtors balance	(X)
Positive/nil balance	X
Debtors: amounts recoverable on contracts	
Turnover; work certified	X
Less Progress payments invoiced	(X)
Positive/nil balance	X
Debtors: trade debtors	
Progress payments invoiced less cash received	X
Current liabilities	
Payments on account	
Negative debtor balance not relieved against stock	X
Provision for liabilities	
Provision for loss not offset against stock balance	X

Exam focus point

> A question is more likely to be set on long-term contracts than on stock or short term WIP, simply because stock and short term WIP were covered in depth at lower level papers.

The following comprehensive question should make things clearer.

Question
Contracts

Znowhyatt plc has two contracts in progress, the details of which are as follows.

	Happy (profitable) £'000	Grumpy (loss-making) £'000
Total contract price	300	300
Costs incurred to date	90	150
Estimated costs to completion	110	225
Progress payments invoiced and received	116	116

Required

Show extracts from the profit and loss account and the balance sheet for each contract, assuming they are both:

(a)   40% complete; and
(b)   36% complete.

Answer

(a)   *Happy contract*

(i)   *40% complete*

	£'000
Profit and loss account	
Turnover (40% × 300)	120
Cost of sales (40% × 200)	(80)
Gross profit	40
Balance sheet	
Debtors (120 – 116)	4
WIP (90 – 80)	10

(ii)   *36% complete*

	£'000
Profit and loss account	
Turnover (36% × 300)	108
Cost of sales (36% × 200)	(72)
Gross profit	36
Balance sheet	
Debtors (108 – 116 = –8)	–
WIP (90 – 72 – 8*) =	10

* Set off excess payments on account against WIP.

(b)   *Grumpy contract*

(i)   *40% complete*

Working

	£'000	£'000
Total contract price		300
Less: costs to date	150	
estimated costs to completion	225	
		375
Foreseeable loss		(75)

	£'000
Profit and loss account	
Turnover (40% × 300)	120
Cost of sales (40% × 375)	(150)
	(30)
Provision for future losses (bal fig)	(45)
Gross loss	(75)

	£'000
Balance sheet	
Debtors (120 – 116)	4
WIP (150 – 150)	–
Provision for future losses	(45)

(ii)   *36% complete*

	£'000
Profit and loss account	
Turnover (36% × 300)	108
Cost of sales (36% × 375)	(135)
	(27)
Provision for future losses (balancing figure)	(48)
Gross loss	(75)
Balance sheet	
Debtors (108 – 116 = –8)	–
WIP (150 – 135 – 48* = –33)	–
Creditors: payments on account	8
Provisions: provisions for future losses	33

* Set off provision for losses before excess payments on account.

2.13 Scope for profit smoothing

At the beginning of this section on long term contract accounting, the problems associated with taking profits only on completion of a long term contract were identified.

However, the reference provided by **SSAP 9**, whereby **turnover** and **prudently calculated attributable profit** are **recognised** as the **contract progresses**, might create a **different** set of **financial reporting issues**, particularly in terms of the **scope for profit smoothing**.

(a)   The scope for adopting **various formulae** or methods for calculating attributable profit can provide opportunities for profit smoothing. There is **no prescribed formula** provided in **SSAP 9**.

(b)   Given the adoption of a particular formula for determining attributable profit, a company could '**manage**' the **underlying transactions** to provide the desired year by year profit profile over the duration of a long-term contract.

  (i)   **Cost incurred basis**. Actual expenditure could be incurred in a manner that gives the desired level of profit to be taken for a particular year. Eg. putting in an expensive piece of equipment to accelerate profit recognition.

  (ii)   **Work certified basis**. Here, scope for influencing the level of attributable profits recognised, depends on the arrangements for raising certificates.

  (iii)   **Other basis**. There may be other industry or company specific methods that give a particular outcome. The formula may be a basis that ensures a smooth profile of attributable profit but this does not necessarily accord with the underlying commercial reality. The method should be scrutinised to see whether it will produce figures that meet the true and fair criteria.

(c)   The process of determining attributable profits includes potentially subjective estimates eg. costs to complete the contract.

(d)   SSAP 9 specifies that **profit** on a contract should be recognised only when the **outcome can be foreseen** with **reasonable certainty**. SSAP 9 does not provide any guidance on how this assessment can be quantified. Professional judgement has therefore to be used and commonly used rules of thumb can vary between 25% to 30% of contract completion.

2.14 Example

Kikabout Konstruction Ltd is building a new £4,000,000 football stadium for a newly promoted club Willesden Wanderers. The contract commenced on 1 June 20X4 and is planned to be completed by 31 July 20X6 in time for the new 20X6/X7 season.

- Costs incurred by Kikabout Konstruction Ltd on the contract to year end 30 December 20X4 amounted to £1,040,000.

- During the year, Kikabout Konstruction issued two invoices for progress payments:

Progress payment 1   £600,000

Progress payment 2   £520,000

- Work certified by architects for the year amounts to £1,240,000.
- The estimated costs to completion on 31 July 20X6 are £1,960,000.

Show how the above transactions should be accounted for in the profit and loss account and balance sheet of Kikabout Konstruction Ltd in the year ended 31 December 20X6. Percentage of completion is calculated on the basis of work certified.

Solution

Calculation of contract profitability

		£
Contract value		4,000,000
Costs incurred to date	1,040,000	
Expected further costs to complete	1,960,000	3,000,000
Expected total profit		1,000,000

Percentage completed

$$\frac{\text{Work certified}}{\text{Contract value}} = \frac{£1,240,000}{£4,000,000} = 31\%$$

	Estimated total £	Certified 31% £	Recognised previous period £	Recognised this period £
Turnover	4,000,000	1,240,000	–	1,240,000
Cost of sales (balancing figure)	3,000,000	930,000	–	930,000
Gross profit	1,000,000	310,000	–	310,000

Profit and loss account	£
Turnover	1,240,000
Cost of sales	930,000
Gross profit	310,000

Balance sheet	£
Current assets	
WIP (W1)	110,000
Amounts recoverable on contracts (W2)	120,000

Workings

1   WIP

	£
Costs to date	1,040,000
Transferred to cost of sales	(930,000)
	110,000

2   *Amounts recoverable on contracts*

	£
Work certified	1,240,000
Less progress payments invoiced (600 + 520)	(1,120,000)
	120,000

The WIP account shows costs incurred of £1,040,000 less costs of £930,000 transferred to profit and loss account, via cost of sales. The WIP balance should be disclosed as 'long-term contract balances' and disclosed separately under the heading stocks.

The progress payments account provides a record of the extent to which work certified by the architects has been invoiced to the customer. The debit of £1,240,000 is the work certified, with credits of £600,000 and £520,000, in respect of invoices sent to the customer.

The debit balance on the progress payment account reflects unbilled work. The debit balance should be disclosed separately as 'Amounts recoverable on contracts' under debtors.

Chapter Roundup

- **Stocks** comprise:

  Raw materials and consumables
  Work in progress
  Finished goods and goods for resale
  Payments on account (of purchases)

  They must be revalued at **lower of cost and net realisable value**.

  FIFO and **weighted average** are the accepted means of valuation under SSAP 9.

- The most controversial aspect of SSAP 9 is its approach to the valuation of work in progress for incomplete long-term contracts.

- Turnover and profit should be recognised throughout the duration of the contract. Any foreseeable loss should be recognised immediately.

- There are generally two alternative formulae for determining the estimated attributable profit for the year.

  – Work certified basis
  – Costs incurred basis

- Long-term contract WIP can be calculated as:

Costs to date	X
Less Costs transferred to cost of sales	(X)
Less Foreseeable losses	(X)
Less Payments on account in excess of turnover	(X)
WIP	X

Quick Quiz

1   Net realisable value = Selling price **less** .... **less** ....

2   Which stock costing methods are permissible under SSAP 9?

    A   FIFO, LIFO, average cost, unit cost
    B   Unit cost, job cost, batch cost, LIFO
    C   Process costing, unit cost LIFO, average cost
    D   Job costing, average cost, FIFO, unit cost.

3   Any expected loss on a long-term contract must be recognised, in full, in the year it was identified.

    True   ☐

    False   ☐

4   List the five steps to be taken when valuing long-term contracts.

5   Which items in the profit and loss and balance sheet are potentially affected by long term contracts?

Answers to Quick Quiz

1   Net realisable value = selling price **less** costs to completion **less** costs to market, sell and distribute. (See Para 1.)

2   D, LIFO is not an acceptable costing method .

3   True

4   1   Calculate the expected profit or loss
     2   Calculate turnover for the period
     3   Calculate cost of sales
     4   Review balance on WIP
     5   Compare cumulative turnover with payments on account (2.9)

5   Profit and loss: turnover and cost of sales. Balance sheet: stocks, debtors, creditors and provisions

Now try the question below from the Exam Question Bank

Number	Level	Marks	Time
Q15	Examination	10	18 mins
Q16	Examination	15	27 mins

Provisions, contingent liabilities and contingent assets

13

Topic list	Syllabus reference
1 FRS 12 *Provisions, contingent liabilities and contingent assets*	C7
2 Restructuring and provisions	C7
3 Contingent liabilities and contingent assets	C7

Introduction

FRS 12 *Provisions, contingent liabilities and contingent assets* is very important as it can affect many items in the accounts. Make sure you learn all the relevant definitions and understand the standard accounting treatment.

There are various disclosures relating to creditors, provisions and reserves, and share capital which it is convenient to mention here. The profit and loss disclosures are additional to the FRS 3 disclosures mentioned earlier.

Study guide

		Intellectual level
C	**FINANCIAL STATEMENTS**	
7	**Provisions, contingent liabilities and contingent assets**	
(a)	Explain why an accounting standard on provisions is necessary	2
(b)	Distinguish between legal and constructive obligations.	2
(c)	State when provisions may and may not be made and demonstrate how they should be accounted for.	2
(d)	Explain how provisions should be measured.	1
(e)	Define contingent assets and liabilities and describe their accounting treatment.	2
(f)	Identify and account for:	2
	(i) Warranties/guarantees	
	(ii) Onerous contracts	
	(iii) Environmental and similar provisions	
	(iv) Provisions for future repairs or refurbishments	

1 FRS 12 Provisions, contingent liabilities and contingent assets

FAST FORWARD

Under FRS 12, a **provision** should be recognised

- When an entity has a **present obligation**, legal or constructive
- It is probable that a **transfer of economic benefits** will be required to settle it
- A **reliable estimate** can be made of its amount

As we have seen, financial statements must include **all the information necessary for an understanding of the company's financial position**.

Provisions, contingent liabilities and contingent assets are 'uncertainties' that must be accounted for consistently if are to achieve this understanding.

1.1 Objective

FRS 12 *Provisions, contingent liabilities and contingent assets* aims to ensure that appropriate **recognition criteria** and **measurement bases** are applied to provisions, contingent liabilities and contingent assets and that **sufficient information** is disclosed in the **notes** to the financial statements to enable users to understand their nature, timing and amount.

1.2 Provisions

Before FRS 12, there was no accounting standard dealing with provisions. Companies wanting to show their results in the most favourable light used to make large **'one off' provisions** in years where a high level of underlying profits was generated. These provisions, often known as **'big bath'** provisions, were then available to shield expenditure in future years when perhaps the underlying profits were not as good.

In other words, **provisions were used for profit smoothing**. Profit smoothing is misleading.

Important

The key aim of FRS 12 is to ensure that provisions are made only where there are valid grounds for them.

FRS 12 views a provision as a **liability**.

Key terms

A **provision** is a **liability** of uncertain timing or amount.

A **liability** is an obligation of an entity to transfer economic benefits as a result of past transactions or events.   *(FRS 12)*

The FRS distinguishes provisions from other liabilities such as trade creditors and accruals. This is on the basis that for a provision there is **uncertainty** about the timing or amount of the future expenditure. Whilst uncertainty is clearly present in the case of certain accruals, the uncertainty is generally much less than for provisions.

1.3 Recognition

FRS 12 states that a provision should be **recognised** as a liability in the financial statements when:

(a)   An entity has a **present obligation** (legal or constructive) as a result of a past event.

(b)   It is probable that a **transfer of economic benefits** will be required to settle the obligation.

(c)   A **reliable estimate** can be made of the obligation.

1.4 Meaning of obligation

It is fairly clear what a legal obligation is. However, you may not know what a **constructive obligation** is.

Key term

FRS 12 defines a **constructive obligation** as

'An obligation that derives from an entity's actions where:

- By an established pattern of past practice, published policies or a sufficiently specific current statement the entity has indicated to other parties that it will accept certain responsibilities.

- As a result, the entity has created a valid expectation on the part of those other parties that it will discharge those responsibilities.'

Question   Provisions 1

In which of the following circumstances might a provision be recognised?

(a)   On 13 December 20X9 the board of an entity decided to close down a division. The accounting date of the company is 31 December. Before 31 December 20X9 the decision was not communicated to any of those affected and no other steps were taken to implement the decision.

(b)   The board agreed a detailed closure plan on 20 December 20X9 and details were given to customers and employees.

(c)   A company is obliged to incur clean up costs for environmental damage (that has already been caused).

(d)   A company intends to carry out future expenditure to operate in a particular way in the future.

Answer

(a) No provision would be recognised as the decision has not been communicated.

(b) A provision would be made in the 20X9 financial statements.

(c) A provision for such costs is appropriate.

(d) No present obligation exists and under FRS 12 no provision would be appropriate. This is because the entity could avoid the future expenditure by its future actions, maybe by changing its method of operation.

1.4.1 Probable transfer of economic benefits

For the purpose of the FRS, a transfer of economic benefits is regarded as **'probable'** if the event is **more likely than not** to occur. This appears to indicate a probability of more than 50%. However, the standard makes it clear that where there is a number of similar obligations the probability should be based on considering the population as a whole, rather than one single item.

1.5 Example: Transfer of economic benefits

If a company has entered into a warranty obligation then the probability of transfer of economic benefits may well be extremely small in respect of one specific item. However, when considering the population as a whole the probability of some transfer of economic benefits is quite likely to be much higher. If there is a **greater than 50% probability** of some transfer of economic benefits then a **provision** should be made for the **expected amount**.

1.5.1 Measurement of provisions

Important!

> The amount recognised as a provision should be the best estimate of the expenditure required to settle the present obligation at the balance sheet date.

The estimates will be determined by the **judgement** of the entity's management supplemented by the experience of similar transactions.

Allowance is made for **uncertainty**. Where the provision being measured involves a large population of items, the obligation is estimated by weighting all possible outcomes by their discounted probabilities, ie **expected value**.

Question

Expected value

Patel plc sells goods with a warranty under which customers are covered for the cost of repairs of any manufacturing defect that becomes apparent within the first six months of purchase. The company's past experience and future expectations indicate the following pattern of likely repairs.

% of goods sold	Defects	Cost of repairs
		£m
75	None	–
20	Minor	1.0
5	Major	4.0

What is the expected cost of repairs?

Answer

The cost is found using 'expected values' (75% × £nil) + (20% × £1.0m) + (5% × £4.0m) = £400,000.

Where the **time value of money** is material, the amount of a provision should be the **present value** of the expenditure required to settle the obligation. An appropriate **discount** rate should be used.

1.6 Example

A company knows that when it ceases a certain operation in 5 years time it will have to pay environmental cleanup costs of £5m.

The provision to be made now will be the **present value** of £5m in 5 years time.

The relevant discount rate in this case is 10%.

Therefore a provision will be made for:

	£
£5m × 0.62092 (discount rate for 5 year's time at 10%)	3,104,600
The following year the provision will be:	
£5m × 0.68301 (4 years time at 10%)	3,415,050
Increase	310,450

The increase in the second year of £310,450 will be charged to the profit and loss account. It is referred to as the **unwinding** of the discount.

1.6.1 Future events

Future events which are reasonably expected to occur (eg new legislation, changes in technology) may affect the amount required to settle the entity's obligation and should be taken into account.

1.6.2 Expected disposal of assets

Gains from the expected disposal of assets should not be taken into account in measuring a provision.

1.6.3 Reimbursements

Some or all of the expenditure needed to settle a provision may be expected to be recovered from a third party. If so, the **reimbursement should be recognised only when it is virtually certain that reimbursement will be received if the entity settles the obligation**.

(a)   The reimbursement should be treated as a separate asset, and the amount recognised should not be greater than the provision itself.

(b)   The provision and the amount recognised for reimbursement may be netted off in the profit and loss account.

1.6.4 Changes in provisions

Provisions should be renewed at each balance sheet date and adjusted to reflect the current best estimate. If it is no longer probable that a transfer of economic benefits will be required to settle the obligation, the provision should be reversed.

1.6.5 Use of provisions

A provision should be used only for expenditures for which the provision was originally recognised. Setting expenditures against a provision that was originally recognised for another purpose would conceal the impact of two different events.

1.6.6 Recognising an asset when recognising a provision

Normally the setting up of a provision should be charged immediately to the profit and loss account. But **if the incurring of the present obligation recognised as a provision gives access to future economic benefits an asset should be recognised.**

1.7 Example: Recognising an asset

An obligation for decommissioning costs is incurred by commissioning an oil rig. At the same time, the commissioning gives access to oil reserves over the years of the oil rig's operation. Therefore an asset representing future access to oil reserves is recognised at the same time as the provision for decommissioning costs.

1.7.1 Future operating losses

Provisions should not be recognised for future operating losses. They do not meet the definition of a liability and the general recognition criteria set out in the standard.

1.7.2 Onerous contracts

If an entity has a contract that is onerous, the present obligation under the contract **should be recognised and measured** as a provision. An example might be vacant leasehold property. The entity is under an obligation to maintain the property but is receiving no income from it.

Key term

> An **onerous contract** is a contract entered into with another party under which the unavoidable costs of fulfilling the terms of the contract exceed any revenues expected to be received from the goods or services supplied or purchased directly or indirectly under the contract and where the entity would have to compensate the other party if it did not fulfil the terms of the contract.

1.8 Examples of possible provisions

It is easier to see what FRS 12 is driving at if you look at examples of those items which are possible provisions under this standard. Some of these we have already touched on.

- **Warranties**. These are argued to be genuine provisions as on past experience it is probable, ie more likely than not, that some claims will emerge. The provision must be estimated, however, on the basis of the class as a whole and not on individual claims. There is a clear legal obligation in this case.

- **Major repairs**. In the past it has been quite popular for companies to provide for expenditure on a major overhaul to be accrued gradually over the intervening years between overhauls. Under FRS 12 this will no longer be possible as FRS 12 would argue that this is a mere intention to carry out repairs, not an obligation. The entity can always sell the asset in the meantime. The only solution is to treat major assets such as aircraft, ships, furnaces etc as a series of smaller assets where each part is depreciated over shorter lives. Thus any major overhaul may be argued to be replacement and therefore capital rather than revenue expenditure.

- **Self insurance**. A number of companies have created a provision for self insurance based on the expected cost of making good fire damage etc instead of paying premiums to an insurance company. Under FRS 12 this provision would no longer be justifiable as the entity has no obligation until a fire or accident occurs. No obligation exists until that time.

- **Environmental contamination**. If the company has an environment policy such that other parties would expect the company to clean up any contamination or if the company has broken current environmental legislation then a provision for environmental damage must be made.

- **Decommissioning or abandonment costs**. When an oil company initially purchases an oilfield it is put under a legal obligation to decommission the site at the end of its life. Prior to FRS 12 most oil companies applied the SORP on *Accounting for abandonment costs* published by the Oil Industry Accounting Committee and they built up the provision gradually over the life of the field so that no one year would be unduly burdened with the cost.

  FRS 12, however, insists that a legal obligation exists on the initial expenditure on the field and therefore a liability exists immediately. This would appear to result in a large charge to profit and loss in the first year of operation of the field. However, the FRS takes the view that the cost of purchasing the field in the first place is not only the cost of the field itself but also the costs of putting it right again. Thus all the costs of abandonment may be capitalised.

- **Restructuring**. This is considered in detail below.

2 Restructuring provisions

2.1 Provisions for restructuring

One of the main purposes of FRS 12 was to target abuses of provisions for restructuring. Accordingly, FRS 12 lays down **strict criteria** to determine when such a provision can be made.

Key term

> FRS 12 defines a **restructuring** as:
>
> A programme that is planned and is controlled by management and materially changes either:
>
> - The scope of a business undertaken by an entity
> - The manner in which that business is conducted

The FRS gives the following **examples** of events that may fall under the definition of restructuring.

- The **sale or termination** of a line of business

- The **closure of business locations** in a country or region or the **relocation** of business activities from one country region to another

- **Changes in management structure**, for example, the elimination of a layer of management

- **Fundamental reorganisations** that have a material effect on the **nature and focus** of the entity's operations

The question is whether or not an entity has an obligation – legal or constructive – at the balance sheet date.

- An entity must have a **detailed formal plan** for the restructuring.

- It must have **raised a valid expectation** in those affected that it will carry out the restructuring by starting to implement that plan or announcing its main features to those affected by it

Important!

> **A mere management decision is not normally sufficient**. Management decisions may sometimes trigger off recognition, but only if earlier events such as negotiations with employee representatives and other interested parties have been concluded subject only to management approval.

Where the restructuring involves the **sale of an operation** then FRS 12 states that no obligation arises until the entity has entered into a **binding sale agreement**. This is because until this has occurred the entity will be able to change its mind and withdraw from the sale even if its intentions have been announced publicly.

2.2 Costs to be included within a restructuring provision

The FRS states that a restructuring provision should include only the **direct expenditures** arising from the restructuring, which are those that are both:

- **Necessarily entailed** by the restructuring; and
- Not associated with the **ongoing activities** of the entity.

The following costs should specifically **not** be included within a restructuring provision.

- **Retraining** or relocating continuing staff
- **Marketing**
- **Investment in new systems** and distribution networks

2.3 Disclosure

Disclosures for provisions fall into two parts.

- Disclosure of details of the **change in carrying value** of a provision from the beginning to the end of the year

- Disclosure of the **background** to the making of the provision and the uncertainties affecting its outcome

3 Contingent liabilities and contingent assets

3.1 Contingent liabilities

FAST FORWARD

> An entity should not recognise a contingent asset or liability, but they should be disclosed.

Now you understand provisions it will be easier to understand contingent assets and liabilities.

Key term

> FRS 12 defines a **contingent liability** as:
>
> - A possible obligation that arises from past events and whose existence will be confirmed only by the occurrence or non-occurrence of one or more uncertain future events not wholly within the entity's control; or
>
> - A present obligation that arises from past events but is not recognised because:
>   - It is not probable that a transfer of economic benefits will be required to settle the obligation
>   - The amount of the obligation cannot be measured with sufficient reliability

As a rule of thumb, probable means more than 50% likely. **If an obligation is probable, it is not a contingent liability** – instead, a **provision is needed**.

3.1.1 Treatment of contingent liabilities

Contingent liabilities **should not be recognised in financial statements** but they **should be disclosed**. The required disclosures are:

- A brief description of the nature of the contingent liability
- An estimate of its financial effect
- An indication of the uncertainties that exist
- The possibility of any reimbursement

3.2 Contingent assets

Key term

> FRS 12 defines a **contingent asset** as:
>
> A possible asset that arises from past events and whose existence will be confirmed by the occurrence of one or more uncertain future events not wholly within the entity's control.

A contingent asset must not be recognised. Only when the realisation of the related economic benefits is **virtually certain** should recognition take place. At that point, **the asset is no longer a contingent asset**!

3.2.1 Disclosure: contingent liabilities

A **brief description** must be provided of all material contingent liabilities unless they are likely to be remote. In addition, provide

- An estimate of their **financial effect**
- Details of **any uncertainties**

Disclosure: contingent assets

Contingent assets must only be disclosed in the notes if they are **probable**. In that case a brief description of the contingent asset should be provided along with an estimate of its likely financial effect.

3.2.2 'Let out'

FRS 12 permits reporting entities to avoid disclosure requirements relating to provisions, contingent liabilities and contingent assets if they would be expected to **seriously prejudice** the position of the entity in dispute with other parties. However, this should only be employed in **extremely rare** cases. Details of the general nature of the provision/contingencies must still be provided, together with an explanation of why it has not been disclosed.

You must practise the questions below to get the hang of FRS 12. But first, study the flow chart, taken from FRS 12, which is a good summary of its requirements.

Exam focus point

> If you learn this flow chart you should be able to deal with most of the questions you are likely to meet in the exam.

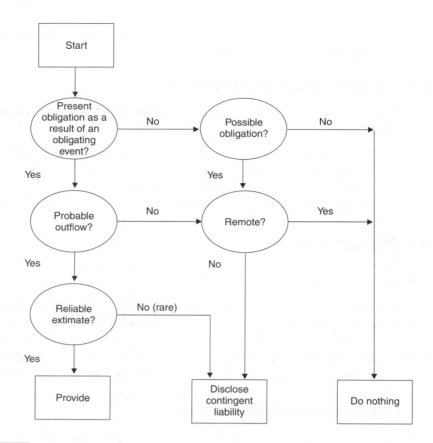

 Question

During 20X9 Avocado Ltd gives a guarantee of certain borrowings of Banana Ltd, whose financial condition at that time is sound. During 20Y0, the financial condition of Banana Ltd deteriorates and at 30 June 20Y0 Banana Ltd goes into administration.

What accounting treatment is required:

(a)   At 31 December 20X9?
(b)   At 31 December 20Y0?

Answer

(a)   *At 31 December 20X9*

There is a present obligation as a result of a past obligating event. The obligating event is the giving of the guarantee, which gives rise to a legal obligation. However, at 31 December 20X9 no transfer of economic benefits is probable in settlement of the obligation.

No provision is recognised. The guarantee is disclosed as a contingent liability unless the probability of any transfer is regarded as remote.

(b)   *At 31 December 20Y0*

As above, there is a present obligation as a result of a past obligating event, namely the giving of the guarantee.

At 31 December 20Y0 it is probable that a transfer of economic events will be required to settle the obligation. A provision is therefore recognised for the best estimate of the obligation.

Question

Super Produx Ltd gives warranties at the time of sale to purchasers of its products. Under the terms of the warranty the manufacturer undertakes to make good, by repair or replacement, manufacturing defects that become apparent within a period of three years from the date of the sale. Should a provision be recognised?

Answer

Super Produx Ltd **cannot avoid** the cost of repairing or replacing all items of product that manifest manufacturing defects in respect of which warranties are given before the balance sheet date, and a provision for the cost of this should therefore be made.

Super Produx Ltd is obliged to repair or replace items that fail within the entire warranty period. Therefore, in respect of **this year's sales**, the obligation provided for at the balance sheet date should be the cost of making good items for which defects have been notified but not yet processed, **plus** an estimate of costs in respect of the other items sold for which there is sufficient evidence that manufacturing defects **will** manifest themselves during their remaining periods of warranty cover.

Question

After a wedding in 20X0 ten people died, possibly as a result of food poisoning from products sold by Crippen Ltd. Legal proceedings are started seeking damages from Crippen but it disputes liability. Up to the date of approval of the financial statements for the year to 31 December 20X0, Crippen's lawyers advise that it is probable that it will not be found liable. However, when Crippen prepares the financial statements for the year to 31 December 20X1 its lawyers advise that, owing to developments in the case, it is probable that it will be found liable.

What is the required accounting treatment:

(a)   At 31 December 20X0?

(b)   At 31 December 20X1?

Answer

(a)   *At 31 December 20X0*

On the basis of the evidence available when the financial statements were approved, there is no obligation as a result of past events. No provision is recognised. The matter is disclosed as a contingent liability unless the probability of any transfer is regarded as remote.

(b)   *At 31 December 20X1*

On the basis of the evidence available, there is a present obligation. A transfer of economic benefits in settlement is probable.

A provision is recognised for the best estimate of the amount needed to settle the present obligation.

3.3 Section summary

(a)   The objective of FRS 12 is to ensure that appropriate recognition criteria and measurement bases are applied to provisions and contingencies and that sufficient information is disclosed.

(b)   The FRS seeks to ensure that provisions are only recognised when a measurable obligation exists. It includes detailed rules that can be used to ascertain when an obligation exists and how to measure the obligation.

(c)   The standard attempts to eliminate the 'profit smoothing' which has gone on before it was issued.

Chapter Roundup

- Under FRS 12, a **provision** should be recognised

  - When an entity has a **present obligation**, legal or constructive
  - It is probable that a **transfer of economic benefits** will be required to settle it
  - A **reliable estimate** can be made of its amount

- An entity should not recognise a contingent asset or liability, but they should be disclosed.

Quick Quiz

1   A provision is a .... of .... timing or amount.

2   A programme is undertaken by management which converts the previously wholly owned chain of restaurants they ran into franchises. Is this restructuring?

3   Define contingent asset and contingent liability.

4   How should decommissioning costs be accounted for under FRS 12?

5   'Provisions for major overhauls should be accrued for over the period between overhauls'. Is this correct?

Answers to Quick Quiz

1   Liability of uncertain timing or amount.

2   Yes. The manner in which the business is conducted has changed.

3   A contingent asset is a possible asset that arises from past events and whose existence will be confirmed by the occurrence of one or more uncertain future events not wholly within the entity's control.

   A contingent liability is a possible obligation that arises from past events and whose existence will be confirmed by the occurrence of one or more uncertain future events not wholly within the entity's control.

4   They should be capitalised as part of the initial expenditure on the oilfield.

5   No. It is not correct. See paragraph 1.7.

Now try the question below from the Exam Question Bank

Number	Level	Marks	Time
Q17	Examination	25	45 mins

Financial assets and liabilities

Topic list	Syllabus reference
1 Financial instruments	C5
2 Presentation of financial instruments	C5
3 Disclosure of financial instruments	C5
4 Recognition of financial instruments	C5
5 Measurement of financial instruments	C5

Introduction

The debate over **measurement and recognition** of financial instruments is very closely connected to the **off balance sheet finance debate**. Before the issue of FRS 25 and FRS 26 many financial instruments were not recognised or disclosed in financial statements at all.

The issues of disclosure and presentation are addressed in **FRS 25 and 29**. Recognition and measurement issues are dealt with in **FRS 26**.

Study guide

		Intellectual level
C	**FINANCIAL STATEMENTS**	
5	**Financial assets and financial liabilities**	
(a)	Explain the need for an accounting standard on financial instruments.	1
(b)	Define financial instruments in terms of financial assets and financial liabilities.	1
(c)	Indicate for the following categories of financial instruments how they should be measured and how any gains and losses from subsequent measurement should be treated in the financial statements:	1
	(i) Fair value through profit and loss	
	(ii) Held to maturity (use of amortised cost, interest to income)	
	(iii) Available for sale (carried at fair value with changes to equity, but dividends to income)	
	(iv) Loans and receivables	
(d)	Distinguish between debt and equity capital.	2
(e)	Apply the requirements of relevant accounting standards to the issue and finance costs of:	2
	(i) Equity	
	(ii) Redeemable preference shares and debt instruments with no conversion rights (principle of amortised cost).	

Exam guide

This is a highly controversial topic and therefore likely to be examined.

Exam focus point

> You will not be expected to deal with derivatives but you should known what they are.

1 Financial instruments

FAST FORWARD

> Financial instruments can be very complex, particularly **derivative instruments**, although **primary instruments** are more straightforward.

If you read the financial press you will probably be aware of **rapid international expansion** in the use of financial instruments. These vary from straightforward, traditional instruments, eg bonds, through to various forms of so-called 'derivative instruments'

We can perhaps summarise the reasons why a project on financial instruments was considered necessary as follows.

(a)   The **significant growth of financial instruments** over recent years has outstripped the development of guidance for their accounting.

(b)   The topic is of **international concern**, other national standard-setters are involved as well as the IASB.

(c) There have been recent **high-profile disasters** involving derivatives (eg Barings) which, while not caused by accounting failures, have raised questions about accounting and disclosure practices.

There are three standards on financial instruments, all issued as part of the ASB's convergence programme, and all of which implement IAS.

(a) FRS 25 *Financial instruments: presentation*, which deals with:

(i) The classification of financial instruments between liabilities and equity
(ii) Presentation of certain compound instruments

(b) FRS 29 *Financial instruments: disclosures,* which revised, simplified and incorporated disclosure requirements previously in FRS 25.

(c) FRS 26 *Financial Instruments: recognition and measurement*, which deals with:

(i) Recognition and derecognition
(ii) The measurement of financial instruments
(iii) Hedge accounting

Note: The recognition and derecognition rules were introduced in April 2006 by an amendment.

1.1 Definitions

FAST FORWARD

The important definitions to learn are:

- **Financial asset**
- **Financial liability**
- **Equity instrument**

The most important definitions are common to all three standards.

Key terms

Financial instrument. Any contract that gives rise to both a financial asset of one entity and a financial liability or equity instrument of another entity.

Financial asset. Any asset that is:

(a) Cash

(b) An equity instrument of another entity

(c) A contractual right to receive cash or another financial asset from another entity; or to exchange financial instruments with another entity under conditions that are potentially favourable to the entity

Financial liability. Any liability that is:

(a) A contractual obligation:

(i) To deliver cash or another financial asset to another entity, or

(ii) To exchange financial instruments with another entity under conditions that are potentially unfavourable

Equity instrument. Any contract that evidences a residual interest in the assets of an entity after deducting all of its liabilities.

Fair value is the amount for which an asset could be exchanged, or a liability settled, between knowledgeable, willing parties in an arm's length transaction   *(FRS 25, FRS 26 and FRS 29)*

1.1.1 More detail

We should clarify some points arising from these definitions. Firstly, one or two terms above should be themselves defined.

(a)   A '**contract**' need not be in writing, but it must comprise an agreement that has 'clear economic consequences' and which the parties to it cannot avoid, usually because the agreement is enforceable in law.

(b)   An '**entity**' here could be an individual, partnership, incorporated body or government agency.

The definitions of **financial assets and financial liabilities** may seem rather circular, referring as they do to the terms financial asset and financial instrument. The point is that there may be a chain of contractual rights and obligations, but it will lead ultimately to the receipt or payment of cash *or* the acquisition or issue of an equity instrument.

Examples of **financial assets** include:

(a)   Trade debtors
(b)   Options
(c)   Shares (when used as an investment)

Examples of **financial liabilities** include:

(a)   Trade creditors
(b)   Debenture loans payable
(c)   Redeemable preference (non-equity) shares
(d)   Forward contracts standing at a loss

FRS 25 makes it clear that the following items are *not* financial instruments.

(a)   **Physical assets**, eg stocks, property, plant and equipment, leased assets and intangible assets (patents, trademarks etc)

(b)   **Prepaid expenses**, deferred revenue and most warranty obligations

(c)   Liabilities or assets that are **not contractual** in nature

(d)   Contractual rights/obligations that **do not involve transfer of a financial asset**, eg commodity futures contracts, operating leases

Question   Financial instruments

Can you give the reasons why the first two items listed above do not qualify as financial instruments?

Answer

Refer to the definitions of financial assets and liabilities given above.

(a)   **Physical assets**: control of these creates an opportunity to generate an inflow of cash or other assets, but it does not give rise to a present right to receive cash or other financial assets.

(b)   **Prepaid expenses, etc**: the future economic benefit is the receipt of goods/services rather than the right to receive cash or other financial assets.

(c)   **Deferred revenue, warranty obligations**: the probable outflow of economic benefits is the delivery of goods/services rather than cash or another financial asset.

Contingent rights and obligations meet the definition of financial assets and financial liabilities respectively, even though many do not qualify for recognition in financial statements. This is because the contractual rights or obligations exist because of a past transaction or event (eg assumption of a guarantee).

1.2 Section summary

- Three accounting standards are relevant:

    - FRS 25 *Financial instruments: presentation*
    - FRS 26 *Financial instruments: recognition and measurement*
    - FRS 29 *Financial instruments: disclosures*

- The definitions of **financial asset, financial liability** and **equity instrument** are fundamental to FRS 25, FRS 26 and FRS 29.

2 Presentation of financial instruments

The objective of FRS 25 is:

'to enhance financial statement users' understanding of the significance of on-balance-sheet and off-balance-sheet financial instruments to an entity's financial position, performance and cash flows.'

2.1 Scope

FRS 25 should be applied in the presentation and disclosure of **all types of financial instruments**, whether recognised or unrecognised.

Certain items are **excluded**.

- Interests in subsidiaries (FRS 2, FRS 5)

- Interests in associates (FRS 9)

- Interests in joint ventures (FRS 9)

- Pensions and other post-retirement benefits (FRS 17)

- Insurance contracts

- Contracts for contingent consideration in a business combination

- Contracts that require a payment based on climatic, geographic or other physical variables

- Financial instruments, contracts and obligations under share-based payment transactions (FRS 20)

2.2 Liabilities and equity

FAST FORWARD

Financial instruments must be classified as **liabilities** or **equity** according to their **substance**.

The main thrust of FRS 25 here is that financial instruments should be presented according to their **substance, not merely their legal form**. In particular, entities which issue financial instruments should classify them (or their component parts) as **either financial liabilities, or equity**.

The classification of a financial instrument as a liability or as equity depends on the following.

(a)   The **substance of the contractual arrangement** on initial recognition

(b)   The definitions of a financial liability and an equity instrument

The critical feature of a financial liability is the **contractual obligation to deliver cash** or another financial instrument.

How should a **financial liability be distinguished from an equity instrument**? The critical feature of a **liability** is an **obligation** to transfer economic benefit. Therefore a financial instrument is a financial liability if there is a **contractual obligation** on the issuer either to deliver cash or another financial asset to the holder or to exchange another financial instrument with the holder under potentially unfavourable conditions to the issuer.

The financial liability exists **regardless of the way in which the contractual obligation will be settled**. The issuer's ability to satisfy an obligation may be restricted, eg by lack of access to foreign currency, but this is irrelevant as it does not remove the issuer's obligation or the holder's right under the instrument.

Where the above critical feature is *not* met, then the financial instrument is an **equity instrument**. FRS 25 explains that although the holder of an equity instrument may be entitled to a *pro rata* share of any distributions out of equity, the issuer does *not* have a contractual obligation to make such a distribution.

Although substance and legal form are often **consistent with each other**, this is not always the case. In particular, a financial instrument may have the legal form of equity, but in substance it is in fact a liability. Other instruments may combine features of both equity instruments and financial liabilities.

For example, many entities issue **preference shares** which must be **redeemed** by the issuer for a fixed (or determinable) amount at a fixed (or determinable) future date. Alternatively, the holder may have the right to require the issuer to redeem the shares at or after a certain date for a fixed amount. In such cases, the issuer has an **obligation**. Therefore the instrument is a **financial liability** and should be classified as such.

The classification of the financial instrument is made when it is **first recognised** and this classification will continue until the financial instrument is removed from the entity's balance sheet.

2.3 Compound financial instruments

Compound instruments are split into **equity** and **liability** components and presented in the balance sheet accordingly.

Some financial instruments contain both a liability and an equity element. In such cases, FRS 25 requires the component parts of the instrument to be **classified separately**, according to the substance of the contractual arrangement and the definitions of a financial liability and an equity instrument.

One of the most common types of compound instrument is **convertible debt**. This creates a primary financial liability of the issuer and grants an option to the holder of the instrument to convert it into an equity instrument (usually ordinary shares) of the issuer. This is the economic equivalent of the issue of conventional debt plus a warrant to acquire shares in the future.

Although in theory there are several possible ways of calculating the split, FRS 25 requires the following method:

(a)   Calculate the value for the liability component.

(b)   Deduct this from the instrument as a whole to leave a residual value for the equity component.

The reasoning behind this approach is that an entity's equity is its residual interest in its assets amount after deducting all its liabilities.

The **sum of the carrying amounts** assigned to liability and equity will always be equal to the carrying amount that would be ascribed to the instrument **as a whole**.

2.4 Example: Valuation of compound instruments

Rathbone Co issues 2,000 convertible bonds at the start of 20X2. The bonds have a three year term, and are issued at par with a face value of £1,000 per bond, giving total proceeds of £2,000,000. Interest is payable annually in arrears at a nominal annual interest rate of 6%. Each bond is convertible at any time up to maturity into 250 common shares.

When the bonds are issued, the prevailing market interest rate for similar debt without conversion options is 9%. At the issue date, the market price of one common share is £3. The dividends expected over the three year term of the bonds amount to 14p per share at the end of each year. The risk-free annual interest rate for a three year term is 5%.

Required

What is the value of the equity component in the bond?

Solution

The liability component is valued first, and the difference between the proceeds of the bond issue and the fair value of the liability is assigned to the equity component. The present value of the liability component is calculated using a discount rate of 9%, the market interest rate for similar bonds having no conversion rights, as shown.

	£
Present value of the principal: £2,000,000 payable at the end of three years	
(£2m ×0.772)*	1,544,00
Present value of the interest: £120,000 payable annually in arrears for three years	
(£120,000 ×2.531)*	303,720
Total liability component	1,847,720
Equity component (balancing figure)	152,280
Proceeds of the bond issue	2,000,000

* These figures can be obtained from discount and annuity tables.

The split between the liability and equity components remains the same throughout the term of the instrument, even if there are changes in the **likelihood of the option being exercised.** This is because it is not always possible to predict how a holder will behave. The issuer continues to have an obligation to make future payments until conversion, maturity of the instrument or some other relevant transaction takes place.

2.5 Interest, dividends, losses and gains

As well as looking at balance sheet presentation, FRS 25 considers how financial instruments affect the profit and loss account (and movements in equity). The treatment varies according to whether interest, dividends, losses or gains relate to a financial liability or an equity instrument.

(a)   Interest, dividends, losses and gains relating to a financial instrument (or component part) classified as a **financial liability** should be recognised as **income or expense** in profit or loss.

(b)   Distributions to holders of a financial instrument classified as an **equity instrument** should be **debited directly to equity** by the issuer.

(c)   **Transaction costs** of an equity transaction shall be accounted for as a **deduction from equity** (unless they are directly attributable to the acquisition of a business, in which case they are accounted for under FRS 2).

2.6 Section summary

(a) Financial instruments must be classified as **liabilities** or **equity**

(b) The **substance** of the financial instrument is more important than its **legal form**

(c) The **critical feature of a financial liability** is the contractual obligation to deliver cash or another financial instrument

(d) **Compound instruments** are split into equity and liability parts and presented accordingly

(e) **Interest, dividends, losses and gains** are treated according to whether they relate to a financial asset or a financial liability

(f) Rules apply stating whether liabilities should be classified as **current or non current**

3 Disclosure of financial instruments

FAST FORWARD

FRS 29 specifies the **disclosures** required for financial instruments. The standard requires qualitative and quantitative disclosures about exposure to risks arising from financial instruments and specifies minimum disclosures about credit risk, liquidity risk and market risk.

The IASB and ASB maintain that users of financial instruments need information about an entity's exposures to risks and how those risks are managed, as this information can **influence a user's assessment of the financial position and financial performance of an entity** or of the amount, timing and uncertainty of its **future cash flows.**

There have been new techniques and approaches to measuring risk management, which highlighted the need for guidance.

Accordingly, FRS 29 *Financial instruments: disclosures* was issued in December 2005. This embodies IFRS 7 of the same name, amended for UK entities.

3.1 Objective

The objective of the standard is to require entities to provide disclosures in their financial statements that enable users to evaluate:

(a) The significance of financial instruments for the entity's financial position and performance

(b) The nature and extent of risks arising from financial instruments to which the entity is exposed during the period and at the reporting date, and how the entity manages those risks.

The principles in FRS 29 complement the principles for recognising, measuring and presenting financial assets and financial liabilities in FRS 25 *Financial instruments: presentation* and FRS 26 *Financial instruments: recognition and measurement.*

3.2 Classes of financial instruments and levels of disclosure

The entity must group financial instruments into classes **appropriate to the nature of the information disclosed**. An entity must decide in the light of its circumstances how much detail it provides. Sufficient information must be provided to permit reconciliation to the line items presented in the balance sheet.

3.2.1 Balance sheet

The following must be disclosed.

(a)   **Carrying amount** of financial assets and liabilities by FRS 26 category

(b)   **Reason for any reclassification** between fair value and amortised cost (and vice versa)

3.2.2 Profit and loss account

The entity must disclose the following **items of income, expense, gains or losses**, either on the face of the financial statements or in the notes.

(a)   Net gains/losses by FRS 26 category (broken down as appropriate: eg interest, fair value changes, dividend income)

(b)   Interest income/expense

(c)   Impairments losses by class of financial asset

3.3 Nature and extent of risks arising from financial instruments

In undertaking transactions in financial instruments, an entity may assume or transfer to another party one or more of **different types of financial risk**. The disclosures required by the standard show the extent to which an entity is exposed to these different types of risk, relating to both recognised and unrecognised financial instruments.

The examiner has stated that you will **not** be examined on the **financial risks** of financial instruments.

4 Recognition of financial instruments

FAST FORWARD

> FRS 26 *Financial instruments: recognition and measurement* establishes principles for recognising and measuring financial assets and financial liabilities.

4.1 Scope

FRS 26 applies to **all entities** and to **all types of financial instruments** except those specifically excluded, for example investments in subsidiaries, associates and joint ventures.

4.2 Initial recognition

Financial instruments should be recognised in the balance sheet when the entity becomes a party to the **contractual provisions of the instrument**.

Notice that this is **different** from the recognition criteria in the ASB *Statement of Principles* and in most other standards. Items are normally recognised when there is a probable inflow or outflow of resources and the item has a cost or value that can be measured reliably.

4.3 Example: initial recognition

An entity has entered into two separate contracts.

(a)   A firm commitment (an order) to buy a specific quantity of iron

(b)   A forward contract to buy a specific quantity of iron at a specified price on a specified date.

Contract (a) is a **normal trading contract**. The entity does not recognise a liability for the iron until the goods have actually been delivered. (Note that this contract is not a financial instrument because it involves a physical asset, rather than a financial asset.)

Contract (b) is a **financial instrument**. Under FRS 26 the entity recognises a financial liability (an obligation to deliver cash) on the **commitment date**, rather than waiting for the closing date on which the exchange takes place.

Note that planned future transactions, no matter how likely, are not assets and liabilities of an entity – the entity has not yet become a party to the contract.

4.4 Derecognition

Derecognition is the removal of a previously recognised financial instrument from an entity's balance sheet.

An entity should derecognise a **financial asset** when:

(a)   The **contractual rights** to the cash flows from the financial asset **expire**, or

(b)   The entity **transfers substantially all the risks and rewards of ownership** of the financial asset to another party.

An entity should derecognise a **financial liability** when it is **extinguished** – ie, when the obligation specified in the contract is discharged or cancelled or expires.

On derecognition, the amount to be included in net profit or loss for the period is calculated as follows:

Formula to learn

	£	£
Carrying amount of asset/liability (or the portion of asset/liability) transferred		X
Less: Proceeds received/paid	X	
Any cumulative gain or loss reported in equity	X	
		(X)
Difference to net profit/loss		X

4.5 Section summary

(a)   **All financial assets** and **liabilities** should be **recognised on the balance sheet**.

(b)   Financial assets should be derecognised when the **rights to the cash flows** from the asset **expire** or where **substantially all the risks and rewards of ownership are transferred** to another party.

(c)   Financial liabilities should be derecognised when they are **extinguished**.

5 Measurement of financial instruments

FRS 26 *Financial instruments: recognition and measurement* was published in 2004, and amended in 2006 to include the IAS 39 rules on recognition and derecognition. It applies to listed entities or entities whose financial statements are prepared in accordance with the fair value accounting rules of CA 85. Entities applying the FRSSE are exempt.

5.1 Initial measurement

Financial instruments are initially measured at the **fair value** of the consideration given or received (ie, **cost**) **plus** (in most cases) **transaction costs** that are **directly attributable** to the acquisition or issue of the financial instrument.

The **exception** to this rule is where a financial instrument is designated as **at fair value through profit or loss** (this term is explained below). In this case, **transaction costs** are **not** added to fair value at initial recognition.

The fair value of the consideration is normally the transaction price or market prices. If market prices are not reliable, the fair value may be **estimated** using a valuation technique (for example, by discounting cash flows).

5.2 Subsequent measurement

For the purposes of measuring a financial asset held subsequent to initial recognition, FRS 26 classifies financial assets into four categories defined here.

Key terms

A financial asset or liability at fair value through profit or loss meets either of the following conditions:

(a)   It is classified as held for trading. A financial instrument is classified as held for trading if it is:

    (i)   Acquired or incurred principally for the purpose of selling or repurchasing it in the near term

    (ii)   Part of a portfolio of identified financial instruments that are managed together and for which there is evidence of a recent actual pattern of short-term profit-taking

(b)   Upon initial recognition it is designated by the entity as at fair value through profit or loss. Any financial instrument may be so designated when it is initially recognised except for investments in equity instruments that do not have a quoted market price in an active market and whose fair value cannot be reliably measured.

Held-to-maturity investments are non-derivative financial assets with fixed or determinable payments and fixed maturity that an entity has the positive intent and ability to hold to maturity other than:

(a)   Those that the entity upon initial recognition designates as at fair value through profit or loss
(b)   Those that the entity designates as available for sale and
(c)   Those that meet the definition of loans and receivables.

Key terms

Loans and receivables are non-derivative financial assets with fixed or determinable payments that are not quoted in an active market, other than:

(a)   Those that the entity intends to sell immediately or in the near term, which should be classified as held for trading and those that the entity upon initial recognition designates as at fair value through profit or loss

(b)   Those that the entity upon initial recognition designates as available-for-sale or

(c)   Those for which the holder may not recover substantially all of the initial investment, other than because of credit deterioration, which shall be classified as available for sale

An interest acquired in a pool of assets that are not loans or receivables (for example, an interest in a mutual fund or a similar fund) is not a loan or a receivable.

Available-for-sale financial assets are those financial assets that are not:

(a)   Loans and receivables originated by the entity,
(b)   Held-to-maturity investments, or
(c)   Financial assets at fair value through profit or loss. *(FRS 26)*

FAST FORWARD

Subsequently they should be **re-measured to fair value** except for

(a)   Loans and receivables not held for trading
(b)   Other **held-to-maturity investments**
(c)   **Financial assets** whose value **cannot be reliably measured**

After initial recognition, all financial assets should be **remeasured to fair value**, without any deduction for transaction costs that may be incurred on sale of other disposal, except for:

(a) **Loans and receivables**

(b) **Held to maturity investments**

(c) Investments in **equity instruments** that do not have a quoted market price in an active market and whose **fair value cannot be reliably measured** and derivatives that are linked to and must be settled by delivery of such unquoted equity instruments

Loans and receivables and **held to maturity investments** should be measured at **amortised cost using the effective interest method**.

Key term

> Amortised cost of a financial asset or financial liability is the amount at which the financial asset or liability is measured at initial recognition minus principal repayments, plus or minus the cumulative amortisation of any difference between that initial amount and the maturity amount, and minus any write-down (directly or through the use of an allowance account) for impairment or uncollectability.
>
> The **effective interest method** is a method of calculating the amortised cost of a financial instrument and of allocating the interest income or interest expense over the relevant period.
>
> The **effective interest rate** is the rate that exactly discounts estimated future cash payments or receipts through the expected life of the financial instrument. *(FRS 26)*

5.3 Example: Amortised cost

On 1 January 20X1 Abacus Co purchases a debt instrument for its fair value of £1,000. The debt instrument is due to mature on 31 December 20X5. The instrument has a principal amount of £1,250 and the instrument carries fixed interest at 4.72% that is paid annually. The effective interest rate is 10%.

How should Abacus Co account for the debt instrument over its five year term?

Solution

Abacus Co will receive interest of £59 (1,250 × 4.72%) each year and £1,250 when the instrument matures.

Abacus must allocate the discount of £250 and the interest receivable over the five year term at a constant rate on the carrying amount of the debt. To do this, it must apply the effective interest rate of 10%.

The following table shows the allocation over the years:

Year	Amortised cost at beginning of year	Profit and loss account: Interest income for year (@10%)	Interest received during year (cash inflow)	Amortised cost at end of year
	£	£	£	£
20X1	1,000	100	(59)	1,041
20X2	1,041	104	(59)	1,086
20X3	1,086	109	(59)	1,136
20X4	1,136	113	(59)	1,190
20X5	1,190	119	(1,250+59)	–

Each year the carrying amount of the financial asset is increased by the interest income for the year and reduced by the interest actually received during the year.

Investments whose **fair value cannot be reliably measured** should be measured at **cost**.

5.4 Classification

On initial recognition, certain financial instruments must be designated at fair value through profit and loss.

In contrast, it is quite difficult for an entity **not** to remeasure financial instruments to fair value.

For a financial instrument to be held to maturity it must meet several extremely narrow criteria. The entity must have a **positive intent** and a **demonstrated ability** to hold the investment to maturity. These conditions are not met if:

(a)   The entity intends to hold the financial asset for an undefined period

(b)   The entity stands ready to sell the financial asset in response to changes in interest rates or risks, liquidity needs and similar factors (unless these situations could not possibly have been reasonably anticipated)

(c)   The issuer has the right to settle the financial asset at an amount significantly below its amortised cost (because this right will almost certainly be exercised)

(d)   It does not have the financial resources available to continue to finance the investment until maturity

(e)   It is subject to an existing legal or other constraint that could frustrate its intention to hold the financial asset to maturity

In addition, an **equity** instrument is **unlikely** to meet the criteria for classification as held to maturity.

There is a **penalty** for selling or reclassifying a 'held-to-maturity' investment other than in certain very tightly defined circumstances. If this has occurred during the **current** financial year or during the **two preceding** financial years **no** financial asset can be classified as held-to-maturity.

If an entity can no longer hold an investment to maturity, it is no longer appropriate to use amortised cost and the asset must be re-measured to fair value. **All** remaining held-to-maturity investments must also be re-measured to fair value and classified as available-for-sale (see above).

5.5 Subsequent measurement of financial liabilities

After initial recognition, all financial liabilities should be measured at **amortised cost**, with the exception of financial liabilities at fair value through profit or loss (including most derivatives). These should be measured at **fair value**, but where the fair value **is not capable of reliable measurement**, they should be measured at **cost**.

Question

Deep discount bond

Galaxy plc issues a bond for £503,778 on 1 January 20X2. No interest is payable on the bond, but it will be redeemed on 31 December 20X4 for £600,000. The bond has **not** been designated as at fair value through profit or loss. The effective interest rate is 6%.

Required

Calculate the charge to the profit and loss account of Galaxy plc for the year ended 31 December 20X2 and the balance outstanding at 31 December 20X2.

Answer

The bond is a 'deep discount' bond and is a financial liability of Galaxy plc. It is measured at amortised cost. Although there is no interest as such, the difference between the initial cost of the bond and the price at which it will be redeemed is a finance cost. This must be allocated over the term of the bond at a constant rate on the carrying amount.

The charge to the profit and loss account is £30,226 (503,778 × 6%)

The balance outstanding at 31 December 20X2 is £534,004 (503,778 + 30,226)

5.6 Gains and losses

Instruments at **fair value through profit or loss**: gains and losses are recognised **in profit or loss** (ie, in the profit and loss account).

Available for sale financial assets: gains and losses are recognised **in the statement of total recognised gains and losses.** When the asset is derecognised the cumulative gain or loss previously recognised in the STRGL should be recognised in profit and loss.

Financial instruments carried at **amortised cost**: gains and losses are recognised **in profit and loss** as a result of the amortisation process and when the asset is derecognised.

Question

Gains and losses

Ellesmere plc entered into the following transactions during the year ended 31 December 20X3:

(1) Purchased 6% debentures in FG Ltd on 1 January 20X1 (their issue date) for £150,000 as an investment. Ellesmere plc intends to hold the debentures until their redemption at a premium in 5 year's time. The effective rate of interest of the bond is 8.0%.

(2) Purchased 50,000 shares in ST Ltd on 1 July 20X3 for £3.50 each as an investment. The share price on 31 December 20X3 was £3.75.

Required

Show the accounting treatment and relevant extracts from the financial statements for the year ended 31 December 20X3.

Answer

BALANCE SHEET EXTRACTS

	£
Financial assets:	
4% debentures in FG Ltd (W1)	153,000
Shares in ST Ltd (W2)	187,500

PROFIT AND LOSS ACCOUNT EXTRACTS

	£
Finance income:	
Effective interest on 6% debentures (W1)	12,000

Workings

1   Debentures

On the basis of the information provided, this can be treated as a held-to-maturity investment.

Initial measurement (at cost):

DEBIT	Financial asset	£150,000	
CREDIT	Cash		£150,000

At 31.12.20X3 (amortised cost):

DEBIT	Financial asset (150,000 × 8%)	£12,000	
CREDIT	Finance income		£12,000
DEBIT	Cash (150,000 × 6%)	£9,000	
CREDIT	Financial asset		£9,000

Amortised cost at 31.12.20X3:

| (150,000 + 12,000 – 9,000) | £153,000 |

2   *Shares*

These are treated as an available for sale financial asset (shares cannot normally be held to maturity and they are clearly not loans or receivables).

Initial measurement (at cost):

| DEBIT | Financial asset (50,000 × £3.50) | £175,000 | |
| CREDIT | Cash | | £175,000 |

At 31.12.20X3 (re-measured to fair value):

| DEBIT | Financial asset ((50,000 × £3.75) – £175,000)) | £12,500 | |
| CREDIT | Statement of total recognised gains and losses | | £12,500 |

5.7 Impairment and uncollectability of financial assets

At each balance sheet date, an entity should assess whether there is any objective evidence that a financial asset or group of assets is impaired.

Question

Impairment

Give examples of indications that a financial asset or group of assets may be impaired.

Answer

FRS 26 lists the following:

(a)   Significant financial difficulty of the issuer

(b)   A breach of contract, such as a default in interest or principal payments

(c)   The lender granting a concession to the borrower that the lender would not otherwise consider, for reasons relating to the borrower's financial difficulty

(d)   It becomes probable that the borrower will enter bankruptcy

(e)   The disappearance of an active market for that financial asset because of financial difficulties

Where there is objective evidence of impairment, the entity should **determine the amount** of any impairment loss.

5.7.1 Financial assets carried at amortised cost

The impairment loss is the **difference** between the asset's **carrying amount** and its **recoverable amount**. The asset's recoverable amount is the present value of estimated future cash flows, discounted at the financial instrument's **original** effective interest rate.

The amount of the loss should be **recognised in profit or loss.**

If the impairment loss decreases at a later date (and the decrease relates to an event occurring **after** the impairment was recognised) the reversal is recognised in profit or loss. The carrying amount of the asset must not exceed the original amortised cost.

5.7.2 Financial assets carried at cost

Unquoted equity instruments are carried at cost if their fair value cannot be reliably measured. The impairment loss is the difference between the asset's **carrying amount** and the **present value of estimated future cash flows**, discounted at the current market rate of return for a similar financial instrument. Such impairment losses cannot be reversed.

5.7.3 Available for sale financial assets

Available for sale financial assets are carried at fair value and gains and losses are recognised in the statement of total recognised gains and losses. Any impairment loss on an available for sale financial asset should be **removed from statement of total recognised gains and losses** and **recognised in net profit or loss for the period** even though the financial asset has not been derecognised.

The impairment loss is the difference between its **acquisition cost** (net of any principal repayment and amortisation) and **current fair value** (for equity instruments) or recoverable amount (for debt instruments), less any impairment loss on that asset previously recognised in profit or loss.

Impairment losses relating to equity instruments cannot be reversed. Impairment losses relating to debt instruments may be reversed if, in a later period, the fair value of the instrument increases and the increase can be objectively related to an event occurring after the loss was recognised.

5.8 Example: Impairment

Broadfield plc purchased 5% debentures in X Ltd at 1 January 20X3 (their issue date) for £100,000. The term of the debentures was 5 years and the maturity value is £130,525. The effective rate of interest on the debentures is 10% and the company has classified them as a held-to-maturity financial asset.

At the end of 20X4 X Ltd went into liquidation. All interest had been paid until that date. On 31 December 20X4 the liquidator of X Ltd announced that no further interest would be paid and only 80% of the maturity value would be repaid, on the original repayment date.

The market interest rate on similar bonds is 8% on that date.

Required

(a) What value should the debentures have been stated at just before the impairment became apparent?

(b) At what value should the debentures be stated at 31 December 20X4, after the impairment?

(c) How will the impairment be reported in the financial statements for the year ended 31 December 20X4?

Solution

(a) The debentures are classified as a held-to-maturity financial asset and so they would have been stated at amortised cost:

	£
Initial cost	100,000
Interest at 10%	10,000
Cash at 5%	(5,000)
At 31 December 20X3	105,000
Interest at 10%	10,500
Cash at 5%	(5,000)
At 31 December 20X4	110,500

(b) After the impairment, the debentures are stated at their recoverable amount (using the **original** effective interest rate of 10%, which, from tables, gives a discount factor of 0.751):

80% × £130,525 × 0.751 = £78,419

(c) The impairment of £32,081 (£110,500 − £78,419) should be recorded:

DEBIT Profit and loss account	£32,081	
CREDIT Financial asset		£32,081

5.9 Section summary

(a) On initial recognition, financial instruments are measured at **cost**.

(b) Subsequent measurement depends on how a financial asset is **classified**.

(c) Financial assets at **fair value through profit or loss** are measured at **fair value**; gains and losses are recognised in **profit or loss**.

(d) **Available for sale** assets are measured at **fair value**; gains and losses are taken to **the STRGL**.

(e) **Loans and receivables** and **held to maturity** investments are measured at **amortised cost**; gains and losses are recognised in **profit or loss**.

(f) Financial **liabilities** are normally measured at **amortised cost**, unless they have been classified as at fair value through profit and loss.

Chapter Roundup

- The important definitions to learn are:

  - **Financial asset**
  - **Financial liability**
  - **Equity instrument**

- Financial instruments must be classified as **liabilities** or **equity** according to their **substance**.

- The critical feature of a financial liability is the **contractual obligation to deliver cash** or another financial instrument. On this basis **redeemable preferences** shares are clarified as a liability, not as equity.

- **Compound instruments** are split into **equity** and **liability** components and presented in the balance sheet accordingly.

- **FRS 29** Specifies the **disclosures** required for financial instruments. The standard requires quantitative and qualitative disclosures about exposure to risks arising from financial instruments.

- **FRS 26** *Financial instruments: measurement* has been amended to include the recognition and derecognition rules of IAS 39.

- **Financial assets** should **initially** be measured at **cost = fair value**.

- Subsequently they should be **re-measured to fair value** except for

  (a) Loans and receivables not held for trading
  (b) Other **held-to-maturity investments**
  (c) **Financial assets** whose value **cannot be reliably measured**

Quick Quiz

1 A **financial liability** involves an obligation to ....

2 How are redeemable preference shares classified?

3 How should financial assets be initially measured?

4 What is the effective interest rate?

Answers to quick quiz

1 A financial liability involves an obligation to deliver cash or another financial asset to another entity, or to exchange financial instruments with another entity under conditions that are potentially unfavourable.

2 As financial liabilities.

3 Financial assets should be initially measured at fair value or cost.

4 The rate that exactly discounts estimated future cash payments or receipts through the expected life of the financial instrument.

Now try the questions below from the Exam Question Bank

Number	Level	Marks	Time
21	–	10	18 mins

15

The legal versus the commercial view of accounting

Topic list	Syllabus reference
1 Substance over form	A4
2 Off balance sheet finance	A4
3 Revenue recognition	A3

Introduction

This is a very topical area and has been for some time. Companies (and other entities) have in the past used the **legal form** of a transaction to determine its accounting treatment when in fact the substance of the transaction has been very different. We will look at the question of **substance over form** and the kind of transactions it gives rise to.

FRS 5 *Reporting the substance of transactions* is a key standard which you need to understand. Make sure you get to grips with why such a standard was put together.

Study guide

		Intellectual level
A	**CONCEPTUAL FRAMEWORK FOR FINANCIAL REPORTING**	
3	**Recognition and measurement**	
(d)	Demonstrate the role of the principle of substance over form in relation to recognising sales revenue.	2
4	**The legal versus the commercial view of accounting**	
(a)	Explain the importance of recording the commercial substance rather than the legal form of transactions – give examples of previous abuses in this area.	2
(b)	Describe the features which may indicate that the substance of transactions differs from their legal form.	2
(c)	Apply the principle of substance over form to the recognition and derecognition of assets and liabilities.	2
(d)	Recognise the substance of transactions in general, and specifically account for the following types of transactions:	2
	(i) Goods sold on sale or return/consignment stock	
	(ii) Sale and repurchase/leaseback agreements	
	(iii) Factoring of debtors.	

Exam guide

Substance over form has been highlighted as a key area in the syllabus.

1 Substance over form

FAST FORWARD

Transactions must be accounted for according to their **substance**, **not** just their legal **form.**

There are a number of '**creative accounting**' techniques, the purpose of which is to manipulate figures for a desired result.

Exam focus point

You may be asked to discuss the importance of recording the substance rather than the legal form of transactions and describe what might indicate that the substance of a transaction is different from its legal form.

Or you may be given a scenario and were required to discuss which party bears the risks and rewards and to arrive at a conclusion on how the transactions involved should be treated by each party.

'Substance over form' is a very important concept and it **has been used to determine accounting treatment in financial statements through accounting standards and so prevent off balance sheet transactions**. The following paragraphs give examples of where the principle of substance over form is enforced, particularly in accounting standards.

1.1 SSAP 21 Accounting for leases and hire purchase contracts

In SSAP 21 there is an explicit requirement that if the lessor transfers substantially all the risks and rewards of ownership to the lessee then, even though the legal title has not passed, the item being leased should be shown as an asset in the balance sheet of the lessee and the amount due to the lessor should be shown as a liability.

1.2 FRS 8 Related party disclosures

FRS 8 requires financial statements to disclose fully material transactions undertaken with a related party by the reporting entity, regardless of any price charged.

1.3 SSAP 9 Stocks and long-term contracts

In SSAP 9 there is a requirement to account for attributable profits on long-term contracts under the accruals convention. However, there may be a problem with realisation, since it is arguable whether we should account for profit which, although attributable to the work done, may not have yet been invoiced to the customer. It is argued that the convention of substance over form is applied to justify ignoring the strict legal position.

1.4 FRS 2 Accounting for subsidiary undertakings

This is perhaps the most important area of off balance sheet finance which has been prevented by the application of the substance over form concept.

The use of quasi-subsidiaries was very common in the 1980s. A **quasi-subsidiary** is defined by FRS 5: in effect it **is a vehicle which does not fulfil the definition of a subsidiary, but it operates just like a subsidiary.**

The main off balance sheet transactions involving quasi-subsidiaries were as follows.

(a) **Sale of assets**. The sale of assets to a quasi-subsidiary was carried out to remove the associated borrowings from the balance sheet and so reduce gearing; or perhaps so that the company could credit a profit in such a transaction. The asset could then be rented back to the vendor company under an operating lease (no capitalisation required by the lessee).

(b) **Purchase of companies or assets**. One reason for such a purchase through a quasi-subsidiary is if the acquired entity is expected to make losses in the near future. Post-acquisition losses can be avoided by postponing the date of acquisition to the date the holding company acquires the purchase from the quasi-subsidiary.

(c) **Business activities conducted outside the group**. Such a subsidiary might have been excluded through a quasi-subsidiary or not consolidated on the grounds of 'dissimilar activities'. Exclusion from consolidation might be undertaken because the activities are high risk and have high gearing.

CA 1989 introduced a new definition of a subsidiary based on *control* rather than just ownership rights and this definition (along with other related matters) was incorporated into FRS 2, thus substantially reducing the effectiveness of this method of off-balance sheet finance.

An amendment to FRS 2 by way of statutory instrument 2947 in 2004 removed the need for a parent company to have a 'participating interest' in a subsidiary, ie a 20% shareholding. Instead, the criterion is '… it has the power to exercise, or actually exercises, dominant influence or control over it.' So this moves the definition of a subsidiary away from 'interest' (shareholding) to 'control'. This parallels the situation with a 'quasi-subsidiary' and should have the effect of brining certain types of quasi-subsidiaries into group accounts.

1.5 Creative accounting

Creative accounting, the **manipulation of figures for a desired result**, takes many forms. Off balance sheet finance is a major type of creative accounting and it probably has the most serious implications. Before we look at some of the other types of creative accounting, we should consider some important points.

Firstly, **it is very rare for a company, its directors or employees to manipulate results for the purpose of fraud. The major consideration is usually the effect the results will have on the share price of the company**. If the share price falls, the company becomes vulnerable to takeover.

Analysts, brokers and economists, whose opinions affect the stock markets, are often perceived as having an outlook which is both short-term and superficial. Consequently, **companies will attempt to produce the results the market expects or wants.** The companies will aim for steady progress in a few key numbers and ratios and they will aim to meet the market's stated expectation.

Another point to consider, particularly when you approach this topic in an examination, is that the **number of methods** available for creative accounting and the determination and imagination of those who wish to perpetrate such acts are **endless**. It has been seen in the past that, wherever an accounting standard or law closes a loophole, another one is found. This has produced a change of approach in regulators and standard setters, towards general principles rather than detailed rules.

Let us now examine some examples of creative accounting, the reaction of the standard setters and possible actions in the future which may halt or change such practices. Remember that this list is not comprehensive and that the frequency and materiality of the use of each method will vary a great deal. Remember also that we have already covered several methods in our examination of off balance sheet finance.

1.5.1 Income recognition and cut-off

Manipulation of cut-off is relatively straightforward. A company may issue invoices before the year end and inflate sales for the year when in fact they have not received firm orders for the goods. Income recognition can be manipulated in a variety of ways.

One example is where a company sells software under contract. The sales contracts will only be realised in full over a period of time, but the company might recognise the full sales value of the contract once it has been secured, even though some payments from clients will fall due over several years. This is clearly imprudent, but the company might justify it by pointing to the irrevocable nature of the contract. But what if a customer should go in to liquidation? No income would be forthcoming from the contract under such circumstances.

1.5.2 Reserves

Reserves are often used to manipulate figures, avoiding any impact on the profit and loss account. This occurs particularly in situations where an accounting standard allows a choice of treatments.

1.5.3 Revaluations

The optional nature of the revaluation of fixed assets leaves such practices open to manipulation. The choice of whether to revalue can have a significant impact on a company's balance sheet. Companies which carried out such revaluations would expect to suffer a much higher depreciation charge as a result. However, many companies charged depreciation in the profit and loss account based on the historical cost only. The rest of the depreciation charge (on the excess of the revalued amount over cost) was transferred to reserves and offset against the revaluation reserve.

Again, this is an abuse of the use of reserves and it was outlawed by the revised SSAP 12 (now superseded by FRS 15). Companies must now charge depreciation on the revalued amount and pass the whole charge through the profit and loss account.

1.5.4 Other creative accounting techniques

The examples given above are some of the major 'abuses' in accounting over recent years. A few more are mentioned here and you should aim to think up as many examples of each as you can. You may also know of other creative accounting techniques which we have not mentioned here.

(a) **Window dressing**. This is where transactions are passed through the books at the year end to make figures look better, but in fact they have not taken place and are often reversed after the year end. An example is where cheques are written to creditors, entered in the cash book, but not sent out until well after the year end.

(b) **Change of accounting policies**. This tends to be a last resort because companies which change accounting policies know they will not be able to do so again for some time. The effect in the year of change can be substantial and prime candidates for such treatment are depreciation, stock valuation, changes from current cost to historical cost (practised frequently by privatised public utilities) and foreign currency losses.

(c) **Manipulation of accruals, prepayments and contingencies**. These figures can often be very subjective, particularly contingencies. In the case of impending legal action, for example, a contingent liability is difficult to estimate, the case may be far off and the solicitors cannot give any indication of likely success, or failure. In such cases companies will often only disclose the possibility of such a liability, even though the eventual costs may be substantial.

Question	Creative accounting

Creative accounting, off balance sheet finance and related matters (in particular how ratio analysis can be used to discover these practices) often come up in articles in, for example, the *Financial Times* and *The Economist*. Find a library, preferably a good technical library, which can provide you with copies of back issues of such newspapers or journals and look for articles on creative accounting. Alternatively you may have access to the Internet and could therefore search the relevant websites.

2 Off balance sheet finance

FAST FORWARD

The subject of **off balance sheet finance** is complex and difficult to understand. In practice, off balance sheet finance schemes are often very sophisticated and they are beyond the range of this syllabus.

Key term

Off balance sheet finance has been described as 'the funding or refinancing of a company's operations in such a way that, under legal requirements and existing accounting conventions, some or all of the finance may not be shown on its balance sheet.'

Off balance sheet transactions' is the term used for transactions which meet the above objective. These transactions may involve the removal of assets from the balance sheet, as well as liabilities, and they are likely to have a significant impact on the profit and loss account.

2.1 The off balance sheet finance problem

The result of the use of increasingly sophisticated off balance sheet finance transactions is a situation where the users of financial statements do not have a proper or clear view of the state of the company's affairs. The disclosures required by company law and current accounting standards do not provide sufficient rules for disclosure of off balance sheet finance transactions and so very little of the true nature of the transaction is exposed.

Whatever the purpose of such transactions, insufficient disclosure creates a problem. This problem has been debated over the years by the accountancy profession and other interested parties and some progress has been made (see the later sections of this chapter).

The incidence of company collapses over the last few years has risen due to the recession and a great many of these have revealed much higher borrowings than originally thought, because part of the borrowing was off balance sheet.

The main argument used for disallowing off balance sheet finance is that the true substance of the transactions should be shown, not merely the legal form, particularly when it is exacerbated by poor disclosure.

2.2 ASB initiatives

Although the ASB wanted to give the old exposure draft on this subject priority in its work programme, there were problems. A general problem was how to ensure that any new standard was consistent with the revised *Statement of Principles*. There was also a specific problem with securitisation because of opposition from the banking industry. All these aspects are discussed below.

Two chapters of the *Statement of Principles* affect the question of off balance sheet finance: *The elements of financial statements* and *The recognition of items in financial statements*.

The definitions are as follows.

Key terms

> (a) **Assets** are defined as 'rights or other access to future economic benefits controlled by an entity as a result of past transactions or events'.
>
> (b) **Liabilities** are defined as 'an entity's obligations to transfer economic benefits as a result of past transactions or events'.

This chapter also lays out the **criteria for recognition** and derecognition of assets and liabilities.

    (a) An item should be recognised in financial statements if:

        (i) The item meets the definition of an element of financial statements (such as an asset or a liability).

        (ii) There is enough evidence that the change in assets or liabilities inherent in the item has occurred (including evidence that a future inflow or outflow of benefit will occur).

        (iii) The item can be measured in monetary terms with sufficient reliability.

    (b) An item should cease to be recognised as an asset or liability if:

        (i) The item no longer meets the definition of the relevant element of financial statements.

        (ii) There is no longer enough evidence that the entity has access to future economic benefits or an obligation to transfer economic benefits.

2.3 FRS 5 Reporting the substance of transactions

After many years' work on the subject of off balance sheet finance (some of it detailed above), the ASB has finally published FRS 5 *Reporting the substance of transactions*. It is a daunting document, running to well over 100 pages, although the standard section itself is relatively short.

2.3.1 Scope and exclusions

FRS 5 applies to all entities whose accounts are intended to give a true and fair view, with no exemptions for any particular type or size of companies. However, it excludes a number of transactions from its scope, unless they are part of a larger series of transactions that is within the scope of the standard. These exclusions are:

(a) **Forward contracts and futures** (such as those for foreign currencies or commodities).

(b) **Foreign exchange and interest rate swaps**.

(c) contracts where a net amount will be paid or received based on the movement in a price or an index (sometimes referred to as **'contracts for differences'**).

(d) **Expenditure commitments** (such as purchase commitments) and orders placed, until the earlier of delivery or payment.

(e) **Employment contracts**.

2.3.2 Relationship to other standards

The interaction of FRS 5 with other standards and statutory requirements is also an important issue; **whichever rules are the more specific should be applied**. Leasing provides a good example (as we will see in the next chapter): straightforward leases which fall squarely within the terms of SSAP 21 should continue to be accounted for without any need to refer to FRS 5, but where their terms are more complex, or the lease is only one element in a larger series of transactions, then FRS 5 comes into play.

In addition, the standard requires that its general principle of substance over form should apply to the application of other existing rules.

Exam focus point

A full question on FRS 5, covering both knowledge and application could be set.

2.3.3 Application notes

FRS 5 deals with certain specific aspects of off balance sheet finance in detailed **application notes**. The topics covered are:

(a) **Consignment stock**
(b) **Sale and repurchase agreements**
(c) **Factoring of debts**
(d) **Securitised assets**
(e) **Loan transfers**
(f) **Private Finance Initiative and similar contracts**
(g) **Revenue recognition**

The application notes explain how to apply the standard to the particular transactions which they describe, and also contain specific disclosure requirements in relation to those transactions. The application notes are not exhaustive and they do not override the general principles of the standard itself, but they are regarded as authoritative insofar as they assist in interpreting it. The notes are discussed in more detail in the next section.

2.3.4 Basic principles

FRS 5's fundamental principle is that the substance of an entity's transactions should be reflected in its accounts. The key considerations are whether a transaction has given rise to new assets and liabilities, and whether it has changed any existing assets and liabilities. Definitions of assets and liabilities and rules for their recognition and derecognition are discussed below.

Sometimes there will be a series of connected transactions to be evaluated, not just a single transaction. It is necessary to identify and account for the substance of the series of transactions as a whole, rather than addressing each transaction individually.

2.3.5 Definitions of assets and liabilities

According to the standard:

'**Assets** are rights or other access to future economic benefits controlled by an entity as a result of past transactions or events.'

'**Liabilities** are an entity's obligations to transfer economic benefits as a result of past transactions or events.'

The standard goes on to say that identification of who has the risks relating to an asset will generally indicate who has the benefits and hence who has the asset. It also says that if an entity is in certain circumstances unable to avoid an outflow of benefits, this will provide evidence that it has a liability. The various risks and benefits relating to particular assets and liabilities are discussed in the application notes.

2.3.6 Recognition

The next key question is deciding **when** something which satisfies the definition of an asset or liability has to be recognised in the balance. sheet. The standard seeks to answer this by saying that:

'where a transaction results in an item that meets the definition of an asset or liability, that item should be recognised in the balance sheet if:

(a)   There is sufficient evidence of the existence of the item (including, where appropriate, evidence that a future inflow or outflow of benefit will occur), and

(b)   The item can be measured at a monetary amount with sufficient reliability.'

2.3.7 Derecognition

As the name suggests, derecognition is the opposite of recognition. It **concerns the question of when to remove from the balance sheet the assets and liabilities which have previously been recognised**. FRS 5 addresses this issue only in relation to assets, not liabilities, and its rules are designed to determine one of three outcomes, discussed below: complete derecognition, no derecognition, and the in-between case, partial derecognition.

The issue of derecognition is perhaps one of the most common aspects of off balance sheet transactions; has an asset been sold or has it been used to secure borrowings? The concept of partial derecognition is a new addition to FRS 5 and attempts to deal with the in-between situation of where sufficient benefits and risks have been transferred to warrant at least some derecognition of an asset.

2.3.8 Complete derecognition

In the simplest case, where a transaction results in the transfer to another party of all the significant benefits and risks relating to an asset, the entire asset should cease to be recognised. In this context, the word 'significant' is explained further: it should not be judged in relation to all the conceivable benefits and risks that could exist, but only in relation to those that are likely to occur in practice. This means that the importance of the risk retained must be assessed in relation to the magnitude of the total realistic risk which exists.

2.3.9 No derecognition

At the other end of the spectrum, **where a transaction results in no significant change to the benefits or to the risks relating to the asset in question, no sale can be recorded and the entire asset should continue to be recognised.** Retaining *either* the benefits or the risks is sufficient to keep the asset on the balance sheet. This means that the elimination of risk by financing the asset on a non-recourse basis will not remove it from the balance sheet; it would be necessary to dispose of the upside as well in order to justify recording a sale. (A further possible treatment, the special case of a 'linked presentation', is discussed below.)

The standard says that **any transaction that is 'in substance a financing' will not qualify for derecognition**; the item will therefore stay on the balance sheet, and the finance will be introduced as a liability.

2.3.10 Partial derecognition

As can be seen, the above criteria are relatively restrictive. The standard therefore goes on to deal with circumstances where, although not all significant benefits and risks have been transferred, the transaction is more than a mere financing and has transferred enough of the benefits and risks to warrant at least some derecognition of the asset. It addresses three such cases.

(a) **Where an asset has been subdivided**

Where an identifiable part of an asset is separated and sold off, with the remainder being retained, the asset should be split and a partial sale recorded. Examples include the sale of a proportionate part of a loan receivable, where all future receipts are shared equally between the parties, or the stripping of interest payments from the principal of a loan instrument.

(b) **Where an item is sold for less than its full life**

This exception arises where the seller retains a residual value risk by offering to buy the asset back at a predetermined price at a later stage in the asset's life. Such an arrangement is sometimes offered in relation to commercial vehicles, aircraft, and so on. The standard says that in such cases the original asset will have been replaced by a residual interest in the asset together with a liability for its obligation to pay the repurchase price.

(c) **Where an item is transferred for its full life but some risk or benefit is retained**

This may arise, for example, where a company gives a warranty or residual value guarantee in relation to the product being sold. Under the standard, this does not preclude the recording of the sale so long as the exposure under the warranty or guarantee can be assessed and provided for if necessary. Companies may also sometimes retain the possibility of an upward adjustment to the sale price of an asset based on its future performance, for example, when a business is sold subject to an earn-out clause, but again this should not preclude the recognition of the sale.

In all of these cases of partial disposals, the amount of the initial profit or loss may be uncertain. **FRS 5 says that the normal rules of prudence should be applied, but also that the uncertainty should be disclosed if it could have a material effect on the accounts.**

2.3.11 Linked presentation

FAST FORWARD

You need to understand **linked presentation**. This was originally an FRS 5 Application Note and is now part of FRS 26.

This requires **non-recourse finance** to be **shown on the face of the balance sheet as a deduction from the asset to which it relates** (rather than in the liabilities section of the balance sheet), provided certain stringent criteria are met. This is really a question of how, rather than whether, to show the asset and liability in the balance sheet, so it is not the same as derecognition of these items, although there are some similarities in the result. This is an issue to consider in regard to debt factoring.

Linked presentation should be used when an asset is financed in such a way that:

(a)   The finance will be repaid only from proceeds generated by the specific item it finances (or by transfer of the item itself) and there is no possibility whatsoever of a claim on the entity being established other than against funds generated by that item (or against the item itself).

(b)   There is no provision whereby the entity may either keep the item on repayment of the finance or reacquire it at any time.

2.3.12 Consolidation of other entities

The Companies Act definition of a 'subsidiary undertaking' means that the consolidation of other entities is based largely on *de facto* control. However, FRS 5 takes the view that this is not conclusive in determining which entities are to be included in consolidated accounts. It envisages that there will be occasions where the need to give a true and fair view will require the inclusion of **'quasi subsidiaries'**. FRS 5 defines a quasi subsidiary in these terms.

Key term

> 'A **quasi subsidiary** of a reporting entity is a company, trust, partnership or other vehicle that, though not fulfilling the definition of a subsidiary, is directly or indirectly controlled by the reporting entity and gives rise to benefits for that entity that are in substance no different from those that would arise were the vehicle a subsidiary.'

Statutory instrument 2947 has brought some quasi subsidiaries into the net for consolidation – see 1.4 above.

2.3.13 Disclosure

FRS 5 has a general requirement to **disclose transactions in sufficient detail to enable the reader to understand their commercial effect**, whether or not they have given rise to the recognition of assets and liabilities. This means that where transactions or schemes give rise to assets and liabilities which are *not* recognised in the accounts, disclosure of their nature and effects still has to be considered in order to ensure that the accounts give a true and fair view.

A second general principle is that an **explanation** should be given **where there are any assets or liabilities whose nature is different from that which the reader might expect** of assets or liabilities appearing in the accounts under that description. The standard also calls for specific disclosures in relation to the use of the linked presentation, the inclusion of quasi subsidiaries in the accounts, and the various transactions dealt with in the application notes.

2.4 Common forms of off balance sheet finance

The application notes attached to FRS 5 are intended to clarify and develop the methods of applying the proposed standard to the particular transactions which they describe and to provide guidance on how to interpret it in relation to other similar transactions. These transactions are the more common types.

2.4.1 Consignment stock

Consignment stock is an arrangement where stock is **held by one party** (say a distributor) but is **owned by another party** (for example a manufacturer or a finance company). Consignment stock is common in the motor trade and is similar to goods sold on a 'sale or return' basis.

To identify the correct treatment, it is necessary to identify the point at which the distributor acquired the benefits of the asset (the stock) **rather than the point at which legal title was acquired**. If the manufacturer has the right to require the return of the stock, and if that right is likely to be exercised, then the stock is not an asset of the dealer. If the dealer is rarely required to return the stock, then this part of the transaction will have little commercial effect in practice and should be ignored for accounting purposes. The potential liability would need to be disclosed in the accounts.

2.4.2 Sale and repurchase transactions

These are arrangements under which the company sells an asset to another person on terms that allow the company to repurchase the assets in certain circumstances. **The key question is whether the transaction is a straightforward sale, or whether it is, in effect, a secured loan**. It is necessary to look at the arrangement to determine who has the rights to the economic benefits that the asset generates, and the terms on which the asset is to be repurchased.

If the seller has the right to the benefits of the use of the asset, and the repurchase terms are such that the repurchase is likely to take place, the transaction should be accounted for as a **loan**.

2.4.3 Sale and leaseback transactions

A sale and leaseback transaction involves the sale of an asset and the leasing back of the same asset. The lease payment and the sale price are usually negotiated as a package.

The accounting treatment depends upon the type of lease involved. If the transaction results in a **finance lease**, then it is in substance a loan from the lessor to the lessee, with the asset as security. In this case, any 'profit' on the sale should not be recognised as such, but should be deferred and amortised over the lease term. The asset remains on the balance sheet.

If the transaction results in an **operating lease** and the transaction has been conducted at fair value, then it can be regarded as a normal sale transaction. The asset is derecognised and any profit on the sale is recognised. The operating lease instalments are treated as lease payments, rather than repayment of capital plus interest.

This will become clearer when you have covered Chapter 15 and you may want to return to it at that point.

2.4.4 Factoring of debts

Where debts are factored, the original creditor sells the debts to the factor. The sales price may be fixed at the outset or may be adjusted later. It is also common for the factor to offer a credit facility that allows the seller to draw upon a proportion of the amounts owed.

In order to determine the correct accounting treatment it is **necessary to consider whether the benefit of the debts has been passed on to the factor, or whether the factor is, in effect, providing a loan on the security of the debtors.** If the seller has to pay interest on the difference between the amounts advanced to him and the amounts that the factor has received, and if the seller bears the risks of non-payment by the debtor, then the indications would be that the transaction is, in effect, a loan. Depending on the circumstances, either a linked presentation or separate presentation may be appropriate.

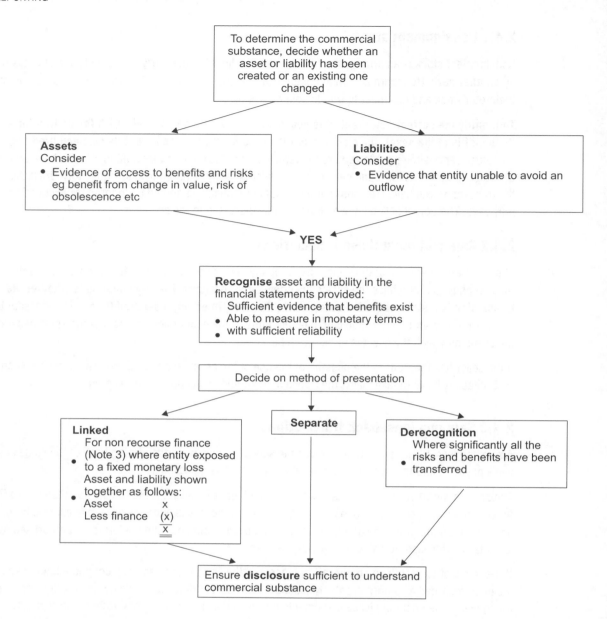

3 Revenue recognition

FAST FORWARD

Revenue recognition is straightforward in most business transactions, but some situations are more complicated. It is necessary to determine the **substance of each transaction, rather than the legal form**.

Generally revenue is recognised when the entity has transferred to the buyer the **significant risks and rewards of ownership** and when the revenue can be **measured reliably**.

Exam focus point

You may be asked to explain the implications that the ASB's *Statement of Principles* and the application of substance over form have on the recognition of income and to provide examples of how this may conflict with traditional practice and some accounting standards.

3.1 ASB balance sheet driven approach

FAST FORWARD

You should learn the conditions for revenue recognition for all transactions. You should also bear in mind the ASB's **balance sheet driven** approach to revenue recognition.

Accruals accounting is based on the requirement that the **non-cash impact** of transactions are recognised in the **period of occurrence** rather than in the period any cash is received or paid. It is crucially important under this convention that we can establish the **point** at which **revenue may be recognised** and **related costs** treated as an **asset**, being representative of a **right** to **future economic benefits**. For example, the costs of producing an item of finished goods should be carried as an asset in the balance sheet until such time as it is sold; they should then be derecognised as an asset and written off as a charge to the trading account. The treatment which should be applied cannot be decided upon until it is clear at what moment the sale of the item takes place; when one form of **right to economic benefits** is **replaced** by **another form** of **right to economic benefits**, ie **stock replaced by a debtor**.

The decision has a direct impact on profit since under the prudence concept, where there is **uncertainty** regarding the **right to receive economic** benefits, **appropriate caution** must be **exercised in recognising revenue** and **profit** from a sale.

Exam focus point

Given the current USA controversies over the reporting of earnings by public companies there, consider how you might respond to a proposition by a director to accelerate revenue recognition.

3.2 Point of sale

Revenue is generally recognised as earned at the point of sale, because at that point four criteria will generally have been met.

(a) The product or service has been **provided** to the buyer.

(b) The buyer has **recognised** his **liability** to **pay** for the goods or services provided. The converse of this is that the seller has **recognised** that **ownership** of **goods** has **passed** from himself to the buyer.

(c) The buyer has indicated his **willingness** to **hand over cash** or other assets in **settlement** of his liability.

(d) The **monetary value** of the goods or services has been **established**.

At **earlier points** in the **business cycle** there will not in general be firm evidence that the above criteria will be met. **Until work** on a product is **complete**, there is a **risk** that some flaw in the manufacturing process will necessitate its **writing off**; even when the product is complete there is no guarantee that it will find a buyer, ie there is **uncertainty** whether the **stock** will **yield future economic benefits**, and the stock might need to be derecognised from the balance sheet.

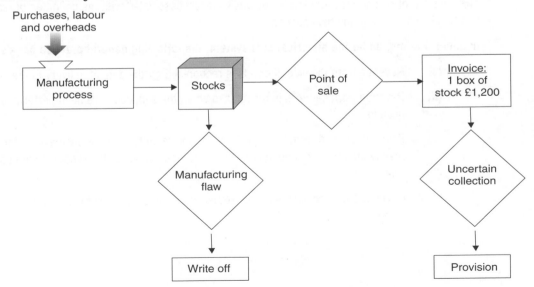

At later points in the business cycle, for example when cash is received for the sale, the recognition of revenue may occur in a period later than that in which the related costs were charged. Revenue recognition would then depend on **fortuitous circumstances**, such as the **cash flow** of a company's **debtors**, and might **fluctuate** misleadingly from one period to another. Again if collection of payment from any debtors is uncertain, they may need to be derecognised from the balance sheet.

3.3 Times other than point of sale

However, **occasionally revenue is recognised at other times** than at the completion of a sale.

(a) **Recognition of profit on long-term contract work in progress**. Under SSAP 9 *Stocks and long-term contracts*, credit is taken in the profit and loss account for 'that part of the total profit currently estimated to arise over the duration of the contract which fairly reflects the profit attributable to that part of the work performed at the accounting date'.

   (i) Owing to the length of time taken to complete such contracts, to defer taking profit into account until completion may result in the profit and loss account reflecting not so much a fair view of the activity of the company during the year but rather the results relating to contracts which have been completed by the year end.

   (ii) Revenue in this case is recognised when production on, say, a section of the total contract is complete, even though no sale can be made until the whole is complete.

(b) **Sale on hire purchase.** Title to goods provided on hire purchase terms does not pass until the last payment is made, at which point the sale is complete.

   (i) To defer the recognition of revenue until that point, however, would be to distort the nature of the revenue earned.

   (ii) The profits of an HP retailer in effect represent the interest charged on finance provided and such interest arises over the course of the HP agreement rather than at its completion. Revenue in this case is recognised when each instalment of cash is received.

The determination of whether revenue should be recognised is based partly on the accruals concept, but also on the often conflicting accounting concept of prudence. Under the prudence concept revenue and profits are not anticipated and anticipated losses are provided for as soon as they are foreseen (preventing costs being deferred if there is doubt as to their recoverability).

The question of revenue recognition is obviously closely associated with the definition of realised profits, and this is discussed in the next section.

In general terms, under the historical cost system, the following general practice has developed.

(a) Revenue from the sale of goods is recognised on the date of delivery to the customer.

(b) Revenue from services is recognised when the services have been performed and are billable.

(c) Revenue derived from letting others use the resources of the businesses (for example royalty income, rent and interest) is recognised either as the resources are used or on a time basis.

(d) Revenue from the sale of assets (other than products of the business) is recognised at the date of the sale.

3.4 Problem areas

The problem with revenue recognition is that there are some areas where accounting standards have not (yet) been issued which deal with all types of transaction. We will not go into too much detail here about these situations, but you should be aware of them, and a list is given below (the list is not comprehensive).

(a) **Receipt of initial fees**, at the beginning of a service, may not have been 'earned' and it is often difficult to determine what they represent.

(b) **Franchise fees** can be incurred in complex franchise agreements and no standard form of agreement has allowed an accepted accounting practice to develop. Each agreement must be dealt with on its own merits.

(c) **Advance royalty or licence receipts** would normally be dealt with as deferred income and released to the profit and loss account when earned under the agreement. In some businesses, however, such advances consist of a number of different components which require different accounting treatments, for example in the record industry.

(d) **Loan arrangement fees** could be recognised in the year the loan is arranged or spread over the life of the loan.

(e) **Credit card fees** charged by credit card companies on their cardholders might be recognised on receipt or spread over the period that the fee allows the cardholder to use the card.

3.5 Revenue

Revenue recognition should be when it is probable that **future economic benefits** will flow to the entity and when these benefits can be **measured reliably**.

Income includes both revenues and gains. Revenue is income arising in the ordinary course of an entity's activities and it may be called different names, such as sales, fees, interest, dividends or royalties.

Interest, royalties and dividends are included as income because they arise from the use of an entity's assets by other parties.

Key terms

> **Interest** is the charge for the use of cash or cash equivalents or amounts due to the entity.
>
> **Royalties** are charges for the use of non-current assets of the entity, eg patents, computer software and trademarks.
>
> **Dividends** are distributions of profit to holders of equity investments, in proportion with their holdings, of each relevant class of capital.

3.6 Definitions

Key terms

> **Revenue** is the gross inflow of economic benefits during the period arising in the course of the ordinary activities of an entity when those inflows result in increases in equity, other than increases relating to contributions from equity participants.
>
> **Fair value** is the amount for which an asset could be exchanged, or a liability settled, between knowledgeable, willing parties in an arm's length transaction.

Revenue **does not include** sales taxes, value added taxes or goods and service taxes which are only collected for third parties, because these do not represent an economic benefit flowing to the entity. The same is true for revenues collected by an agent on behalf of a principal. Revenue for the agent is only the commission receive for acting as agent.

3.7 UITF Abstract 40

In November 2003 revenue recognition by professional firms (mainly law and accountancy firms) was further regulated by application note G to FRS 5 *Reporting the Substance of Transactions*.

Under the application note, **unbilled fee income**, which would previously have been classified as WIP in the financial statements and valued at cost in accordance with SSAP 9, should now be classified as **accrued income** and valued at expected recovery value, where the point has been reached at which the firm is contractually allowed to raise a fee note.

This has the effect of accelerating the revenue recognised by the firm and accelerating its taxation charge. It will not ultimately increase the amount of tax payable, but it will require it to be paid in an earlier period, so this is a cash management issue for professional firms.

The real impact will be felt by **retiring partners**. It makes a difference to a retiring partner whether unbilled income in his final year is classified as WIP or as accrued income. If it is accounted for as accrued income, he will receive a share of the profit. If it is accounted for as WIP, it will be income the following year, and he will not receive a share of the profit.

In March 2005 UITF Abstract 40 *Revenue recognition and service contracts* was issued. This applied the provisions of Application Note G to *all* contracts for services.

Where there are distinguishable phases of a single contract it may be appropriate to account for the contract as two or more separate transactions, provided the value of each phase can be reliably estimated.

Contracts for services should not be accounted for as long-term contracts unless they involve the provision of a single service, or a number of services that constitute a single project.

A contract for services should be accounted for as a long-term contract where contract activity falls into different accounting periods and the effect of this is material. Revenue accrued should reflect the value of the work performed as the contract progresses.

Where the substance of a contract is that a right to consideration does not arise until the occurrence of a critical event, revenue is not recognised until that event occurs.

3.8 Measurement of revenue

When a transaction takes place, the amount of revenue is usually decided by the **agreement of the buyer and seller**. The revenue is actually measured, however, as the **fair value of the consideration received**, which will take account of any trade discounts and volume rebates.

3.9 Identification of the transaction

Normally, each transaction can be looked at **as a whole**. Sometimes, however, transactions are more complicated, and it is necessary to break a transaction down into its **component parts**. For example, a sale may include the transfer of goods and the provision of future servicing, the revenue for which should be deferred over the period the service is performed.

At the other end of the scale, **seemingly separate transactions must be considered together** if apart they lose their commercial meaning. An example would be to sell an asset with an agreement to buy it back at a later date. The second transaction cancels the first and so both must be considered together.

3.10 Sale of goods

Revenue from the sale of goods should only be recognised when *all* these conditions are satisfied.

    (a)   The entity has transferred the **significant risks and rewards** of ownership of the goods to the buyer

    (b)   The entity has **no continuing managerial involvement** to the degree usually associated with ownership, and no longer has effective control over the goods sold

    (c)   The amount of revenue can be **measured reliably**

    (d)   It is probable that the **economic benefits** associated with the transaction will flow to the entity

    (e)   The **costs incurred** in respect of the transaction can be measured reliably

The transfer of risks and rewards can only be decided by examining each transaction. Mainly, the transfer occurs at the same time as either the **transfer of legal title**, or the **passing of possession** to the buyer – this is what happens when you buy something in a shop.

If **significant risks and rewards remain with the seller**, then the transaction is *not* a sale and revenue cannot be recognised, for example if the receipt of the revenue from a particular sale depends on the buyer receiving revenue from his own sale of the goods.

It is possible for the seller to retain only an **'insignificant' risk of ownership** and for the sale and revenue to be recognised. The main example here is where the seller retains title only to ensure collection of what is owed on the goods. This is a common commercial situation, and when it arises the revenue should be recognised on the date of sale.

The probability of the entity receiving the revenue arising from a transaction must be assessed. It may only become probable that the economic benefits will be received when an uncertainty is removed, for example government permission for funds to be received from another country. Only when the uncertainty is removed should the revenue be recognised. This is in contrast with the situation where revenue has already been recognised but where the **collectability of the cash** is brought into doubt. Where recovery has ceased to be probable, the amount should be recognised as an expense, *not* an adjustment of the revenue previously recognised. These points also refer to services and interest, royalties and dividends below.

The traditional approach is that **matching** should take place, ie the revenue and expenses relating to the same transaction should be recognised at the same time. It is usually easy to estimate expenses at the date of sale (eg warranty costs, shipment costs, etc). Where they cannot be estimated reliably, then revenue cannot be recognised; any consideration which has already been received is treated as a liability.

3.11 Rendering of services

When the outcome of a transaction involving the rendering of services can be estimated reliably, the associated revenue should be recognised by reference to the **stage of completion of the transaction** at the balance sheet date. The outcome of a transaction can be estimated reliably when *all* these conditions are satisfied.

    (a)   The amount of revenue can be **measured reliably**

    (b)   It is probable that the **economic benefits** associated with the transaction will flow to the entity

    (c)   The **stage of completion** of the transaction at the balance sheet date can be measured reliably

    (d)   The **costs incurred** for the transaction and the costs to complete the transaction can be measured reliably

The parties to the transaction will normally have to agree the following before an entity can make reliable estimates.

    (a)   Each party's **enforceable rights** regarding the service to be provided and received by the parties

    (b)   The **consideration** to be exchanged

    (c)   The **manner and terms of settlement**

There are various methods of determining the stage of completion of a transaction, but for practical purposes, when services are performed by an indeterminate number of acts over a period of time, revenue should be recognised on a **straight line basis** over the period, unless there is evidence for the use of a more appropriate method. If one act is of more significance than the others, then the significant act should be carried out *before* revenue is recognised.

In uncertain situations, when the outcome of the transaction involving the rendering of services cannot be estimated reliably, then it may be appropriate to adopt a **no loss/no gain approach**. Revenue is recognised only to the extent of the expenses recognised that are recoverable.

This is particularly likely during the **early stages of a transaction**, but it is still probable that the entity will recover the costs incurred. So the revenue recognised in such a period will be equal to the expenses incurred, with no profit.

Obviously, if the costs are not likely to be reimbursed, then they must be recognised as an expense immediately. **When the uncertainties cease to exist**, revenue should be recognised as laid out in above.

3.12 Interest, royalties and dividends

When others use the entity's assets yielding interest, royalties and dividends, the revenue should be recognised on the bases set out below when:

    (a)   It is probable that the **economic benefits** associated with the transaction will flow to the entity

    (b)   The amount of the revenue can be **measured reliably**

The revenue is recognised on the following bases.

    (a)   **Interest** is recognised on a time proportion basis that takes into account the effective yield on the asset

    (b)   **Royalties** are recognised on an accruals basis in accordance with the substance of the relevant agreement

    (c)   **Dividends** are recognised when the shareholder's right to receive payment is established

It is unlikely that you would be asked about anything as complex as this in the exam, but you should be aware of the basics. The **effective yield** on an asset mentioned above is the rate of interest required to discount the stream of future cash receipts expected over the life of the asset to equate to the initial carrying amount of the asset.

Royalties are usually recognised on the same basis that they accrue **under the relevant agreement**. Sometimes the true substance of the agreement may require some other systematic and rational method of recognition.

Once again, the points made above about **probability and collectability** on sale of goods also apply here.

Exam focus point

Because of the recent financial reporting scandals, revenue recognition is very topical and you should be prepared for a question on it.

Question

Revenue recognition

Given that prudence is the main consideration, discuss under what circumstances, if any, revenue might be recognised at the following stages of a sale.

(a)   Goods are acquired by the business which it confidently expects to resell very quickly.

(b)   A customer places a firm order for goods.

(c)   Goods are delivered to the customer.

(d)   The customer is invoiced for goods.

(e)   The customer pays for the goods.

(f)   The customer's cheque in payment for the goods has been cleared by the bank.

Answer

(a)   A sale must never be recognised before the goods have even been ordered by a customer. There is no certainty about the value of the sale, nor when it will take place, even if it is virtually certain that goods will be sold.

(b)   A sale must never be recognised when the customer places an order. Even though the order will be for a specific quantity of goods at a specific price, it is not yet certain that the sale transaction will go through. The customer may cancel the order, the supplier might be unable to deliver the goods as ordered or it may be decided that the customer is not a good credit risk.

(c)   A sale will be recognised when delivery of the goods is made only when:

   (i)   The sale is for cash, and so the cash is received at the same time

   (ii)   Or the sale is on credit and the customer accepts delivery (eg by signing a delivery note)

(d)   The critical event for a credit sale is usually the despatch of an invoice to the customer. There is then a legally enforceable debt, payable on specified terms, for a completed sale transaction.

(e)   The critical event for a cash sale is when delivery takes place and when cash is received; both take place at the same time.

   It would be too cautious or 'prudent' to await cash payment for a credit sale transaction before recognising the sale, unless the customer is a high credit risk and there is a serious doubt about his ability or intention to pay.

(f)   It would again be over-cautious to wait for clearance of the customer's cheques before recognising sales revenue. Such a precaution would only be justified in cases where there is a very high risk of the bank refusing to honour the cheque.

Chapter Roundup

- Transactions must be accounted for according to their **substance**, **not** just their legal **form.**

- There are a number of **'creative accounting'** techniques, the purpose of which is to manipulate figures for a desired result.

- The subject of **off balance sheet finance** is complex and difficult to understand. In practice, off balance sheet finance schemes are often very sophisticated and they are beyond the range of this syllabus.

- You need to understand the methods of presentation described in FRS 5, particularly **linked presentation**.

- **Revenue recognition** is straightforward in most business transactions, but some situations are more complicated. It is necessary to determine the **substance of each transaction, rather than the legal form**.

- Generally revenue is recognised when the entity has transferred to the buyer the **significant risks and rewards of ownership** and when the revenue can be **measured reliably**.

- You should learn the conditions for revenue recognition for all transactions. You should also bear in mind the ASB's **balance sheet driven** approach to revenue recognition.

Quick Quiz

1   What is meant by 'substance over form'?

2   How are assets and liabilities defined in the *Statement of Principles*?

3   Describe 'linked presentation' as set out in FRS 5.

4   What topics does FRS 5 discuss in the application notes?

5   Generally, revenue is recognised at the ....

6   When will revenue be recognised at other times than on the completion of a sale?

7   What are the general procedures for recognising revenue under the historical cost system?

8   Define 'revenue'.

Answers to Quick Quiz

1   Transactions should be accounted for in accordance with their substance and financial reality, not their legal form

2   Assets are defined as 'rights or other access to future economic benefits controlled by an entity as a result of past transactions or events'.

Liabilities are defined as 'an entity's obligations to transfer economic benefits as a result of past transactions or events'.

3   Refer to Paragraph 2.3.11.

4   Consignment stock, sale and leaseback transactions, factoring of debts, revenue recognition and service contracts.

5   At the point of sale

6   Long term contracts and hire purchase

7   The general procedures are as follows:

Sale of goods – revenue recognised at date of delivery
Services – revenue recognised when services have been performed
Rent, interest, royalties – recognised as resources used, or on time basis
Sale of assets – date of sale

8   The gross inflow of economic benefits during the period resulting in an increase in equity, other than contributions from equity holders.

Now try the question below from the Exam Question Bank

Number	Level	Marks	Time
Q18	Examination	25	45 mins
Q19	Examination	15	27 mins

Leasing

16

Topic list	Syllabus reference
1 Types of leases	C6
2 Accounting for a finance lease	C6

Introduction

Leasing transactions are extremely common so this is an important practical subject. **Lease accounting is regulated by SSAP 21**, which was introduced because of abuses in the use of lease accounting by companies.

These companies effectively 'owned' an asset and 'owed' a debt for its purchase, but showed neither the asset nor the liability on the balance sheet because they were not required to do so. This is called **'off balance sheet finance',** a term which you will recognise from the previous chapter.

Study guide

		Intellectual level
C	**FINANCIAL STATEMENTS**	
6	**Leases**	
(a)	Explain why recording the legal form of a finance lease can be misleading to users (referring to the commercial substance of such leases).	2
(b)	Describe and apply the method of determining a lease type (ie an operating or finance lease).	2
(c)	Discuss the effect on the financial statements of a finance lease being incorrectly treated as an operating lease.	2
(d)	Account for assets financed by finance leases in the records of the lessee.	2
(e)	Account for operating leases in the records of the lessee.	2

Exam guide

You must learn how to deal with leases. Make sure you can cope with the numbers.

1 Types of leases

FAST FORWARD

Finance leases are like HP contracts. In both cases:

- Assets acquired should be capitalised
- Interest element of instalments should be charged against profit.

1.1 Definitions

SSAP 21 recognises two types of lease.

Key terms

A **finance lease** transfers substantially all the risks and rewards of ownership to the lessee. Although strictly the leased asset remains the property of the lessor, in substance the lessee may be considered to have acquired the asset and to have financed the acquisition by obtaining a loan from the lessor.

An **operating lease** is any lease which is not a finance lease. An operating lease has the character of a rental agreement with the lessor usually being responsible for repairs and maintenance of the asset. Often these are relatively short-term agreements with the same asset being leased, in succession, to different lessees.

A *finance lease* is very similar in substance to a *hire purchase agreement*. (The difference in law is that under a hire purchase agreement the customer eventually, after paying an agreed number of instalments, becomes entitled to exercise an option to purchase the asset. Under a leasing agreement, ownership remains forever with the lessor.)

In this chapter the **user** of an asset will often be referred to simply as the **lessee**, and the **supplier** as the **lessor**. You should bear in mind that identical requirements apply in the case of hirers and vendors respectively under hire purchase agreements.

1.2 Ninety per cent rule

Transfer of risks and ownership can be presumed if at the inception of a lease the present value of the minimum lease payments amounts to substantially all (normally 90% or more) of the fair value of the leased asset.

The present value should be calculated by using the **interest rate implicit in the lease**.

The **minimum lease payments** are the minimum payments over the remaining part of the lease term plus any residual amounts guaranteed by the lessee or by a party related to the lessee.

Fair value is the price at which an asset could be exchanged in an arm's length transaction.

The **interest rate implicit in the lease** is the discount rate that, at the inception of a lease, when applied to the amounts which the lessor expects to receive and retain, produces an amount equal to the fair value of the leased asset.

The **lease term** is the period for which the lessee has contracted to lease the asset and any further terms for which the lessee has the option to continue to lease the asset, with or without further payment, which option it is reasonably certain at the inception of the lease that the lessee will exercise.

1.3 Operating leases

Operating leases are **rental agreements** and all instalments are charged against profit.

Operating leases do not really pose an accounting problem.

- In the books of the lessee payments are debited to the profit and loss account
- In the books of the lessor, the asset is recorded in fixed assets and receipts from the lessee are credited to profit and loss account

1.4 Finance leases

For assets held **under finance leases or hire purchase** the above accounting treatment would not disclose the reality of the situation. From a **lessor's perspective,** if an asset is leased out on a finance lease, the asset will probably never be seen on his premises or used in his business again. It would be inappropriate for a lessor to record such an asset as a fixed asset. In reality, **the asset is a debtor rather than a fixed asset.**

Similarly, from the lessee's point of view, a finance lease may be used to fund the 'acquisition' of a major asset which he will then use in his business perhaps for many years. **The substance of the transaction is that the lessee has acquired a fixed asset, and this is reflected in the accounting treatment prescribed by SSAP 21**, even though in law the lessee never becomes the owner of the asset.

Questions on leasing could involve a discussion of the reasons for the different accounting treatments of operating and finance leases. We only deal with the accounts of the **lessee.**

Practical questions could involve preparation of the relevant ledger accounts and/or extracts from the financial statements.

2 Accounting for a finance lease

You must learn how to apply actuarial method of **interest allocation**.

2.1 Accounting treatment

In light of the above, **SSAP 21 requires that, when an asset changes hands under a finance lease or HP agreement, lessor and lessee should account for the transaction as though it were a credit sale.** In the lessee's books therefore:

DEBIT   Asset account
CREDIT   Lessor (liability) account

The amount to be recorded in this way is the capital cost or fair value of the asset. This may be taken as the amount which the lessee might expect to pay for it in a cash transaction.

The asset should be depreciated over the shorter of:

    (a)   The lease term
    (b)   Its useful life

2.2 Apportionment of rental payments

When the lessee makes **a rental payment** it **will comprise two elements.**

    (a)   **An interest charge on the finance provided by the lessor**. This proportion of each payment is interest payable and interest receivable in the profit and loss accounts of the lessee and lessor respectively.

    (b)   **A repayment of part of the capital cost of the asset.** In the lessee's books this proportion of each rental payment must be debited to the lessor's account to reduce the outstanding liability. In the lessor's books, it must be credited to the lessee's account to reduce the amount owing (the debit of course is to cash).

The accounting problem is to decide what proportion of each instalment paid by the lessee **represents interest, and what proportion represents a repayment of the capital** advanced by the lessor. There are **three methods** you may encounter:

    (a)   The **level spread method**.
    (b)   The **actuarial method**.
    (c)   The **sum-of-the-digits method**.

Exam focus point

> The examiner has said that he will not examine the sum-of-the-digits method. So you will be expected to use the actuarial method.

The level spread method is based on the assumption that finance charges accrue evenly over the term of the lease agreement. For example, if an asset with a fair value of £3,000 is being 'acquired' on a finance lease for five payments of £700 each, the total interest is £(3,500 – 3,000) = £500. This is assumed to accrue evenly and therefore there is £100 interest comprised in each rental payment, the £600 balance of each instalment being the capital repayment.

The level spread method is quite **unscientific and takes no account of the commercial realities of the transaction.** You should use it in the examination only if you are specifically instructed to or if there is insufficient information to use another method.

The actuarial method is the best and most scientific method. It derives from the commonsense assumption that the **interest charged by a lessor company will equal the rate of return desired by the company, multiplied by the amount of capital it has invested.**

(a)   At the beginning of the lease the capital invested is equal to the fair value of the asset (less any initial deposit paid by the lessee).

(b)   This amount reduces as each instalment is paid. It follows that the interest accruing is greatest in the early part of the lease term, and gradually reduces as capital is repaid. In this section, we will look at a simple example of the actuarial method.

2.3 Example: Apportionment

On 1 January 20X0 Bacchus Ltd, wine merchants, obtains a small bottling and labelling machine from Silenus Limited under a finance lease. The cash price of the machine was £7,710 while the total amount of the instalment was £10,000. The agreement required the immediate payment of a £2,000 deposit with the balance being settled in four equal annual instalments commencing on 31 December 20X0. The charge of £2,290 represents interest of 15% per annum, calculated on the remaining balance of the liability during each accounting period. Depreciation on the plant is to be provided for at the rate of 20% per annum on a straight line basis assuming a residual value of nil.

Solution

Interest is calculated as 15% of the outstanding *capital* balance at the beginning of each year. The outstanding capital balance reduces each year by the capital element comprised in each instalment. The outstanding capital balance at 1 January 20X0 is £5,710 (£7,710 fair value less £2,000 deposit).

	£
Balance 1 January 20X0	5,710
Interest 15%	856
Instalment 31 December 20X0	(2,000)
Balance outstanding 1 January 20X1	4,566
Interest 15%	685
Instalment 31 December 20X1	(2,000)
Balance outstanding 1 January 20X2	3,251
Interest 15%	488
Instalment 31 December 20X2	(2,000)
Balance outstanding 1 January 29X3	1,739
Interest 15%	261
Instalment 31 December 20X3	(2,000)
	-

Note. You will not be required to do this whole calculation in an exam. You will probably have to calculate the first few instalments in order to obtain figures for current and non-current liabilities (as in 2.4).

Exam focus point

Where you get a numerical question, make sure you provide clear workings. In the words of the examiner, where workings are not shown:

'If an answer is wrong, it is unlikely that any marks can be awarded, as the marker will not be able to determine how the answer was arrived at.'

2.4 Disclosure requirements for lessees

SSAP 21 requires lessees to disclose the following information.

(a)   The **gross amounts of assets held under finance leases* together with the related accumulated depreciation, analysed by class of asset**. This information may be consolidated with the corresponding information for owned assets, and not shown separately. In that case, the net amount of assets held under finance leases included in the overall total should also be disclosed.

(b) The **amounts of obligations related to finance leases (net of finance charges allocated to future periods).** These should be disclosed separately from other obligations and liabilities and should be analysed between amounts payable in the next year, amounts payable in the second to fifth years inclusive from the balance sheet date and the aggregate amounts payable thereafter.

(c) The **aggregate finance charges allocated for the period** in respect of finance leases.

These disclosure requirements will be illustrated for Bacchus Ltd (above example). We will assume that Bacchus Ltd makes up its accounts to 31 December and uses the actuarial method to apportion finance charges. The company's accounts for the first year of the finance lease, the year ended 31 December 20X0, would include the information given below.

BALANCE SHEET AS AT 31 DECEMBER 20X0 (EXTRACTS)

	£	£
Fixed assets		
Tangible assets held under finance leases		
Plant and machinery at cost	7,710	
Less accumulated depreciation (25% × £7,710)	1,927	
		5,783
Creditors: amounts falling due within one year		
Obligations under finance leases (2,000 − 685)		1,315
Creditors: amounts falling due after more than one year		
Obligations under finance leases, falling due		
within two to five years £(4,566 + 1,315)		3,251

(Notice that only the outstanding *capital* element is disclosed under creditors. That is what is meant by the phrase 'net of finance charges allocated to future periods' in Paragraph 2.4(b) above.)

PROFIT AND LOSS ACCOUNT
FOR THE YEAR ENDED 31 DECEMBER 20X0

	£
Interest payable and similar charges	
Lease finance charges	856

As noted above, SSAP 21 requires that **leased assets should be depreciated over the shorter of the lease term and their useful lives**. Bacchus should therefore depreciate the machine over four years.

For operating leases the disclosure is simpler.

(a) The **total of operating lease rentals** charged as an expense in the profit and loss account should be disclosed, distinguishing between rentals payable for hire of plant and machinery and other rentals.

(b) Disclosure should be made of **payments to which the lessee is committed** under operating leases, analysed between those in which the commitment expires:

(i) **Within a year** from the balance sheet date
(ii) In the **second to fifth** years inclusive
(iii) **Later than five years** from the balance sheet date

Commitments in respect of land and buildings should be shown separately from other commitments.

Chapter Roundup

- **Finance leases** are like HP contracts. In both cases:
  - Assets acquired should be capitalised
  - Interest element of instalments should be charged against profit.
- **Operating leases** are **rental agreements** and all instalments are charged against profit.
- You must learn how to apply the actuarial method of **interest allocation**.
- You must also learn the **disclosure requirements of SSAP 21** for lessees.

Quick Quiz

1   (a)   ....leases transfer substantially the risks and rewards of ownership.

    (b)   ....leases are usually short-term rental agreements with the lessor being responsible for the repairs and maintenance of the asset.

2   The present value of the minimum lease payments is equal to 89% of the fair value of the leased asset. What type of lease is this likely to be?

3   A business acquires an asset under a finance lease. What is the double entry?

    DEBIT
    CREDIT

4   A lorry has an expected useful life of six years. It is acquired under a four year finance lease. Over which period should it be depreciated?

5   A company leases a photocopier under an operating lease which expires in June 20X2. Its office is leased under an operating lease due to expire in January 20X3. How should past and future operating leases be disclosed in its 31 December 20X1 accounts?

Answers to Quick Quiz

1 (a) Finance leases
   (b) Operating leases

2 Per SSAP 21, an operating lease

3 DEBIT Asset account
   CREDIT Lessor account

4 Over four years (the shorter of lease tem and useful life).

5 The total operating lease rentals charged though the profit and loss should be disclosed. The payments committed to should be disclosed, analysing them between those falling due in the next year and the second to fifth years.

Now try the question below from the Exam Question Bank

Number	Level	Marks	Time
Q20	Examination	10	18 mins
Q22	Examination	10	18 mins

Accounting for taxation

Introduction

Tax is a straightforward area. There are plenty of exercises here - make sure that you attempt each one yourself without referring to the solution immediately.

In relation to corporation tax you must be able to calculate the relevant tax figures *and* know how they should be disclosed in the accounts according to FRS 16.

Deferred taxation is probably the most difficult topic in this chapter. Concentrate on trying to understand the logic behind the adjustment and the reasons why the FRS 19 approach has been adopted.

Study guide

		Intellectual level
C	**FINANCIAL STATEMENTS**	
9	**Taxation**	
(a)	Account for current taxation in accordance with relevant accounting standards.	2
(b)	Record entries relating to income tax in the accounting records.	2
(c)	Explain the effect of timing differences on accounting and taxable profits.	2
(d)	Compute and record deferred tax amounts in the financial statements.	2

Exam guide

Learn the disclosures, they are bound to come up in an accounts preparation question

1 FRS 16 current tax

FAST FORWARD

> The **FRS 16 requirements** relating to company taxation are straightforward but **must be learned**. The best way is to practise on past exam questions.

Companies pay corporation tax, usually nine months after the year end. FRS 16 *Current tax*, which was published in December 1999, specifies how current tax should be reflected in the financial statements. This should be done in a **'consistent and transparent manner'**.

Specifically, the FRS deals with **tax credits** and **withholding tax**. Consider these definitions.

Key terms

- **Current tax**. The amount of tax estimated to be payable or recoverable in respect of the taxable profit or loss for a period, along with adjustments to estimates in respect of previous periods.

- **Withholding tax**. Tax on dividends or other income that is deducted by the payer of the income and paid to the tax authorities wholly on behalf of the recipient.

- **Tax credit**. The tax credit given under UK tax legislation to the recipient of a dividend from a UK company. The credit is given to acknowledge that the income out of which the dividend has been paid has already been charged to tax, rather than because any withholding tax has been deducted at source. The tax credit may discharge or reduce the recipient's liability to tax on the dividend. Non-taxpayers may or may not be able to recover the tax credit.

You can see from these definitions that a tax credit is different from a withholding tax.

- A tax credit **gives credit for** tax paid by a company
- A **withholding tax withholds** the taxable part of the income

Accordingly, the tax credit and the withholding tax are treated differently in the financial statements.

1.1 Treatment in financial statements

Learn this treatment.

Outgoing dividends paid, interest or other amounts payable

- Include withholding tax
- Exclude tax credit

Incoming dividends, interest or other amounts payable

- Include withholding tax
- Exclude tax credit
- Include the effect of withholding tax suffered as part of the tax charge

---

1.2 Example: current tax

Taxus Ltd made a profit of £1,000,000. It received a dividend of £80,000 on which there was a tax credit of £20,000. From an overseas company it received a dividend of £3,000 on which 25% withholding tax had been deducted. The corporation tax charge was £300,000.

Required

Show how this information would be presented in the financial statements in accordance with FRS 16 *Current tax*.

Solution

	£
Operating profit	1,000,000
Income from fixed asset investments	
UK (note 1)	80,000
Foreign (note 2)	4,000
Profit before tax	1,084,000
Taxation (note 3)	301,000
Profit after tax	783,000

Notes

1   Excludes tax credit

2   Includes withholding tax: £3,000 + £1,000 = £4,000. Read the question carefully – 25% had been deducted already

3   Add back withholding tax of £1,000

1.2.1 Other requirements of FRS 16

Current tax should be recognised in the **profit and loss account**. But if it is attributable to a gain or loss that has been recognised in the statement of total recognised gains and losses it should be recognised in that statement.

Current tax should be measured using tax rates and laws that have been enacted or substantially enacted by the balance sheet date.

Generally (apart from the treatment of withholding tax) income and expenses are **not adjusted** to reflect a **notional amount** of tax that would have been paid or received if the transaction had been taxable or allowable on a different basis. Income and expenses are included in pre-tax results on the basis of amounts **actually receivable or payable**.

1.2.2 Income tax withheld

If a company reasonably believes the receipt of payments of annual interest, royalties or annuities is chargeable to corporation tax on the payment, with effect from 1 April 2001, the paying company is not required to withhold income tax on the payment. However, such payments made to individuals, partnerships etc (ie non-companies) are still made under deduction of income tax.

1.2.3 Tax disclosure in the notes

This example, taken from the appendix to FRS 16, illustrates one method of showing by way of a note the tax items required to be disclosed under CA 1985 and the FRS.

	£'000	£'000
UK corporation tax		
Current tax on income for the period	X	
Adjustments in respect of prior periods	X	
	X	
Double taxation relief*	(X)	
		X
Foreign tax		
Current tax on income for the period	X	
Adjustments in respect of prior periods	X	
		X
Tax on profit on ordinary activities		X

*Don't worry about this – it's unlikely to come up in your exam.

2 FRS 19 Deferred tax

FAST FORWARD

FRS 19 requires full provision for **deferred** tax. It is unlikely that complicated numerical questions will be set in the exam so concentrate on **understanding** deferred tax.

Exam focus point

A deferred tax adjustment is likely to be part of an accounts preparation question.

You may already be aware from your studies of taxation that accounting profits and taxable profits are not the same. There are several reasons for this but they may conveniently be considered under two headings.

(a) **Permanent differences** arise because certain expenditure, such as entertainment of UK customers, is not allowed as a deduction for tax purposes although it is quite properly deducted in arriving at accounting profit. Similarly, certain income (such as UK dividend income) is not subject to corporation tax, although it forms part of accounting profit.

(b) **Timing differences** arise because certain items are included in the accounts of a period which is different from that in which they are dealt with for taxation purposes.

Deferred taxation is the tax attributable to timing differences.

Key term

Deferred tax. Estimated future tax consequences of transactions and events recognised in the financial statements of the current and previous periods.

Deferred taxation is therefore a means of ironing out the tax inequalities arising from timing differences.

(a) In years when **corporation tax is saved** by timing differences such as accelerated capital allowances, a charge for deferred taxation is made in the P&L account and a provision set up in the balance sheet.

(b)   In years when **timing differences reverse**, because the depreciation charge exceeds the capital allowances available, a deferred tax credit is made in the P&L account and the balance sheet provision is reduced.

Deferred tax is the subject of a new standard, FRS 19 *Deferred tax*. Before we look at the detailed requirements of FRS 19, we will explore some of the issues surrounding deferred tax.

You should be clear in your mind that the tax actually payable to the Inland Revenue is the **corporation tax liability**. The credit balance on the deferred taxation account represents an estimate of tax saved because of timing differences but expected ultimately to become payable when those differences reverse.

FRS 19 identifies the main categories in which timing differences can occur.

(a)   **Accelerated capital allowances.** Tax deductions for the cost of a fixed asset are accelerated or decelerated, ie received before or after the cost of the fixed asset is recognised in the profit and loss account.

(b)   **Pension liabilities** are accrued in the financial statements but are allowed for tax purposes only when paid or contributed at a later date (pensions are not in the paper 2.5 syllabus).

(c)   **Interest charges or development costs** are capitalised on the balance sheet but are treated as revenue expenditure and allowed as incurred for tax purposes.

(d)   **Intragroup profits in stock**, unrealised at group level, are reversed on consolidation.

(e)   **Revaluations.** An asset is revalued in the financial statements but the revaluation gain becomes taxable only if and when the asset is sold.

(f)   **Unrelieved tax losses.** A tax loss is not relieved against past or present taxable profits but can be carried forward to reduce future taxable profits.

(g)   **Unremitted earnings of subsidiaries.** The unremitted earnings of subsidiary and associated undertakings and joint ventures are recognised in the group results but will be subject to further taxation only if and when remitted to the parent undertaking.

Deferred taxation is therefore an accounting convention which is introduced in order to apply the accruals concept to income reporting where timing differences occur. However, **deferred tax assets** are not included in accounts as a rule, because it would not be prudent, given that the recovery of the tax is uncertain.

2.1 Basis of provision

A comprehensive tax allocation system is one in which deferred taxation is computed for every instance of timing differences: **full provision**. The opposite extreme would be the **nil provision** approach ('**flow through** method'), where only the tax payable in the period would be charged to that period.

The **full provision method** has the **advantage** that it is consistent with general international practice. It also recognises that each timing difference at the balance sheet date has an effect on future tax payments. If a company claims an accelerated capital allowance on an item of plant, future tax assessments will be bigger than they would have been otherwise. Future transactions may well affect those assessments still further, but that is not relevant in assessing the position at the balance sheet date. The **disadvantage** of full provision is that, under certain types of tax system, it gives rise to large liabilities that may fall due only far in the future. The **full provision** method is the one prescribed by **FRS 19**.

Exam focus point

> You need to understand the concept of deferred tax, it is unlikely that you will need to perform detailed calculations.

It is important that you understand the issues properly so consider the example below.

2.2 Example: deferred tax

Suppose that Pamella plc begins trading on 1 January 20X7. In its first year it makes profits of £5m, the depreciation charge is £1m and the capital allowances on those assets is £1.5m. The rate of corporation tax is 33%.

Solution: Full provision

The tax liability is £1.485m again, but the debit in the P&L account is increased by the deferred tax liability of 33% × £0.5m = £165,000. The total charge to the P&L account is therefore £1,650,000 which is an effective tax rate of 33% on accounting profits (ie 33% × £5.0m).

2.3 Objective

The objective of FRS 19 is to ensure that:

(a) Future tax consequences of past transactions and events are recognised as liabilities or assets in the financial statements

(b) The financial statements disclose any other special circumstances that may have an effect on future tax charges.

2.4 Scope

The FRS applies **to all financial statements that are intended to give a true and fair view** of a reporting entity's financial position and profit or loss (or income and expenditure) for a period. The FRS applies to taxes calculated on the basis of taxable profits, including withholding taxes paid on behalf of the reporting entity.

Reporting entities applying the Financial Reporting Standard for Smaller Entities **(FRSSE)** currently applicable are **exempt** from the FRS.

2.5 Recognition of deferred tax assets and liabilities

Remember!

> **Deferred tax** should be recognised in respect of **all timing differences that have originated but not reversed by the balance sheet date**.
>
> Deferred tax should **not be recognised on permanent differences**.

Question   Timing differences

Can you remember some examples of timing differences?

Answer

(a) Accelerated capital allowances
(b) Pension liabilities accrued but taxed when paid
(c) Interest charges and development costs capitalised but allowed for tax purposes when incurred
(d) Unrealised intra-group stock profits reversed on consolidation
(e) Revaluation gains
(f) Tax losses
(g) Unremitted earnings of subsidiaries and associates recognised in group results.

Key term

> **Permanent differences.** Differences between an entity's taxable profits and its results as stated in the financial statements that arise because certain types of income and expenditure are non-taxable or disallowable, or because certain tax charges or allowances have no corresponding amount in the financial statements.

2.5.1 Allowances for fixed asset expenditure

Deferred tax **should be recognised** when the **allowances** for the cost of a fixed asset are **received before or after the cost of the fixed asset is recognised in the profit and loss account.** However, if and when **all conditions** for retaining the allowances have been met, the **deferred tax should be reversed.**

If an asset is not being depreciated (and has not otherwise been written down to a carrying value less than cost), the timing difference is the amount of capital allowances received.

Most capital allowances are received on a **conditional basis**, ie they are repayable (for example, via a balancing charge) if the assets to which they relate are sold for more than their tax written-down value. However, some, such as industrial buildings allowances, are repayable only if the assets to which they relate are sold within a specified period. Once that period has expired, all conditions for retaining the allowance have been met. At that point, deferred tax that has been recognised (ie on the excess of the allowance over any depreciation) is reversed.

Question

Tax allowances

An industrial building qualifies for an IBA when purchased in 20X1. The building is still held by the company in 20Z6. What happens to the deferred tax?

Answer

All the conditions for retaining tax allowances have been met. This means that the timing differences have become permanent and the deferred tax recognised should be reversed. Before the 25 year period has passed, deferred tax should be provided on the difference between the amount of the industrial building allowance and any depreciation charged on the asset.

2.5.2 Revaluation of fixed assets

Revaluation of a fixed asset does not create an unavoidable tax liability and so does not affect the deferred tax provision. The exception to this is where an agreement has been entered into to dispose of the asset at the revalued amount, and the gains and losses expected to arise on the sale have been recognised at the balance sheet date. In this case, FRS 19 requires deferred tax to be recognised on the timing difference. As the revaluation gain will be shown under reserves in the statement of total recognised gains and losses, the deferred tax on the revaluation gain or loss will also be adjusted directly in the revaluation reserve.

2.5.3 Example:

Z Ltd owns a property which has a carrying value at the beginning of 20X9 of £1,500,000. At the year end, it has entered into a contract to sell the property for £1,800,000. The tax rate is 30%. How will this be shown in the financial statements?

Solution

STATEMENT OF TOTAL RECOGNISED GAINS AND LOSSES

	£'000
Profit for the financial year	X
Unrealised surplus on revaluation of property	(300)
Deferred tax on revaluation surplus	(90)
Total gains and losses relating to year	X

The journal entries will be as follows:

	Dr £'000	Cr £'000
Property	300	
Deferred tax		90
Revaluation reserve		210

Question

Current and deferred tax

Jonquil Co buys equipment for £50,000 on 1 January 20X1 and depreciates it on a straight line basis over its expected useful life of five years. For tax purposes, the equipment is depreciated at 25% per annum on a straight line basis. Tax losses may be carried back against taxable profit of the previous five years. In year 20X0, the entity's taxable profit was £25,000. The tax rate is 40%.

Required

Assuming nil profits/losses after depreciation in years 20X1 to 20X5 show the current and deferred tax impact in years 20X1 to 20X5 of the acquisition of the equipment.

Answer

Jonquil Co will recover the carrying amount of the equipment by using it to manufacture goods for resale. Therefore, the entity's current tax computation is as follows.

(1)

	Year				
	20X1	20X2	20X3	20X4	20X5
	£	£	£	£	£
Taxable income*	10,000	10,000	10,000	10,000	10,000
Depreciation for tax purposes	12,500	12,500	12,500	12,500	0
Taxable profit (tax loss)	(2,500)	(2,500)	(2,500)	(2,500)	10,000
Current tax expense (income) at 40%	(1,000)	(1,000)	(1,000)	(1,000)	4,000

* ie nil profit plus $50,000 ÷ 5 depreciation add-back.

The entity recognises a current tax asset at the end of years 20X1 to 20X4 because it recovers the benefit of the tax loss against the taxable profit of year 20X5.

The temporary differences associated with the equipment and the resulting deferred tax asset and liability and deferred tax expense and income are as follows.

(2)

	Year				
	20X1	20X2	20X3	20X4	20X5
	£	£	£	£	£
Depreciation	10,000	20,000	30,000	40,000	50,000
Capital allowances	12,500	25,000	37,500	50,000	50,000
Taxable temporary difference	2,500	5,000	7,500	10,000	0
Opening deferred tax liability @ 40%	0	1,000	2,000	3,000	4,000
Deferred tax expense (income): bal fig	1,000	1,000	1,000	1,000	(4,000)
Closing deferred tax liability @ 40%	1,000	2,000	3,000	4,000	0

The entity recognises the deferred tax liability in years 20X1 to 20X4 because the reversal of the taxable temporary difference will create taxable income in subsequent years. The entity's profit and loss account is as follows.

	Year				
	20X1	20X2	20X3	20X4	20X5
	£	£	£	£	£
Income	10,000	10,000	10,000	10,000	10,000
Depreciation	10,000	10,000	10,000	10,000	10,000
Profit before tax	0	0	0	0	0
Current tax expense (income) as (1) above	(1,000)	(1,000)	(1,000)	(1,000)	4,000
Deferred tax expense (income) as (2) above	1,000	1,000	1,000	1,000	(4,000)
Total tax expense (income)	0	0	0	0	0
Net profit for the period	0	0	0	0	0

2.6 Measurement – discounting

Reporting entities are **permitted but not required** to discount deferred tax assets and liabilities to reflect the time value of money.

The ASB believes that, just as other long-term liabilities such as provisions and debt are discounted, so too in principle should long-term deferred tax balances. The FRS therefore permits discounting and provides guidance on how it should be done. However, the ASB stopped short of making discounting mandatory, acknowledging that there is as yet **no internationally accepted methodology** for discounting deferred tax, and that for some entities **the costs might outweigh the benefits.** Entities are encouraged to select the more appropriate policy, taking account of factors such as materiality and the policies of other entities in their sector.

Question   Discounting

Can you think of a situation where it might be appropriate to discount deferred tax liabilities?

Answer

Where the reversal is fairly slow, for example with industrial buildings allowances.

2.7 Presentation

In the **balance sheet** classify:

- Net deferred tax liabilities as 'provisions for liabilities'

- Net deferred tax assets as debtors, as a separate subhead if material where taxes are levied by the same tax authority or in a group where tax losses of one entity can reduce the taxable profits of another.

Balances are to be **disclosed separately** on the face of the balance sheet **if** so **material** as to distort the financial statements.

In the **profit and loss account** classify as part of **tax on profit or loss on ordinary activities.**

2.8 Problems

FRS 19 has the effect of **increasing the liabilities** reported by entities that at present have **large amounts of unprovided deferred tax** arising from capital allowances in excess of depreciation.

Criticisms that may be made of the FRS 19 approach include the following.

- The provisions on **discounting** are somewhat **confusing**.

- The standard is **complicated,** and there is **scope for manipulation and inconsistency**, since discounting is optional.

- It is **open to question whether deferred tax is a liability** as defined in the *Statement of Principles*. It is not, strictly speaking, a present obligation arising as a result of a past event. However, it is being recognised as such under the FRS.

- Arguably the flow-through or **nil provision method is closer to the ASB definition**, but this method, although much simpler, has been rejected to bring the standard closer to the IAS.

2.9 Section summary

- Deferred tax is tax relating to timing differences.
- Full provision must be made for tax timing differences.
- Discounting is allowed but not required.

Exam focus point

Questions on deferred tax should be fairly straightforward. It is likely to be tested as part of a larger question rather than a question in its own right.

3 Taxation in company accounts

FAST FORWARD

The balance sheet liability for tax payable is the tax charge for the year. In the income statement the tax charge for the year is adjusted for transfers to or from deferred tax and for prior year under– or over-provisions.

We have now looked at the 'ingredients' of taxation in company accounts. There are two aspects to be learned:

(a) Taxation on profits in the profit and loss account.

(b) Taxation payments due, shown as a liability in the balance sheet.

3.1 Taxation in the profit and loss account

The tax on profit on ordinary activities is calculated by **aggregating**:

(a) **Corporation tax** on taxable profits
(b) **Transfers to or from deferred taxation**
(c) Any **under provision or overprovision** of corporation tax on profits of previous years

When corporation tax on profits is calculated for the profit and loss account, **the calculation is only an estimate of what the company thinks its tax liability will be. In subsequent dealings with the Inland Revenue, a different corporation tax charge might eventually be agreed.**

The difference between the estimated tax on profits for one year and the actual tax charge finally agreed for the year is made as an adjustment to taxation on profits in the following year, **resulting in the disclosure of either an underprovision or an overprovision of tax.**

Question
Tax payable

In the accounting year to 31 December 20X3, Neil Down Ltd made an operating profit before taxation of £110,000.

Corporation tax on the operating profit has been estimated as £45,000. In the previous year (20X2) corporation tax on 20X2 profits had been estimated as £38,000 but it was subsequently agreed at £40,500 with the Inland Revenue.

A transfer to the deferred taxation account of £16,000 will be made in 20X3.

Required

(a) Calculate the tax on profits for 20X3 for disclosure in the accounts.
(b) Calculate the amount of mainstream corporation tax payable on 30 September 20X4.

Answer

(a)

	£
Corporation tax on profits	45,000
Deferred taxation	16,000
Underprovision of tax in previous year £(40,500 – 38,000)	2,500
Tax on profits for 20X3	63,500

(b)

	£
Tax payable on 20X3 profits	45,000
Mainstream corporation tax liability	45,000

3.2 Taxation in the balance sheet

It should already be apparent from the previous examples that the corporation tax charge in the profit and loss account will not be the same as corporation tax liabilities in the balance sheet.

In the balance sheet, there are several items which we might expect to find.

(a) **Income tax may be payable** in respect of (say) interest payments paid in the last accounting return period of the year, or accrued.

(b)   If no corporation tax is payable (or very little), then there might be an **income tax recoverable asset** disclosed in current assets (income tax is normally recovered by offset against the tax liability for the year).

(c)   There will usually be a **liability for mainstream corporation tax**, possibly including the amounts due in respect of previous years but not yet paid.

(d)   We may also find a **liability on the deferred taxation account**. Deferred taxation is shown under 'provisions for liabilities' in the balance sheet.

Question   Tax charge

For the year ended 31 July 20X4 Norman Kronkest Ltd made taxable trading profits of £1,200,000 on which corporation tax is payable at 30%.

(a)   A transfer of £20,000 will be made to the deferred taxation account. The balance on this account was £100,000 before making any adjustments for items listed in this paragraph.

(b)   The estimated tax on profits for the year ended 31 July 20X3 was £80,000, but tax has now been agreed with the Inland Revenue at £84,000 and fully paid.

(c)   Mainstream corporation tax on profits for the year to 31 July 20X4 is payable on 1 May 20X5.

(d)   In the year to 31 July 20X4 the company made a capital gain of £60,000 on the sale of some property. This gain is taxable at a rate of 30%.

Required

(a)   Calculate the tax charge for the year to 31 July 20X4.
(b)   Calculate the tax liabilities in the balance sheet of Norman Kronkest as at 31 July 20X4.

Answer

(a)   *Tax charge for the year*

		£
(i)	Tax on trading profits (30% of £1,200,000)	360,000
	Tax on capital gain	18,000
	Deferred taxation	20,000
		398,000
	Underprovision of taxation in previous years £(84,000 – 80,000)	4,000
	Tax charge on ordinary activities	402,000

(ii)   *Note.* The profit and loss account will show the following.

	£
Operating profit (assumed here to be the same as taxable profits)	1,200,000
Profit from sale of asset (exceptional)	60,000
Profit on ordinary activities before taxation	1,260,000
Tax on profit on ordinary activities	402,000
Retained profits for the year	858,000

	£
Deferred taxation	
Balance brought forward	100,000
Transferred from profit and loss account	20,000
Deferred taxation in the balance sheet	120,000

The mainstream corporation tax liability is as follows.

	£
Payable on 1 May 20X5	
Tax on ordinary profits (30% of £1,200,000)	360,000
Tax on capital gain (30% of £60,000)	18,000
Due on 1 May 20X5	378,000

Summary

	£
Creditors: amounts falling due within one year	
Mainstream corporation tax, payable on 1 May 20X5	378,000
Provisions for liabilities	
Deferred taxation	120,000

Note. It may be helpful to show the journal entries for these items.

			£	£
(b)	DEBIT	Tax charge (profit and loss account)	402,000	
	CREDIT	Corporation tax creditor		*382,000
		Deferred tax		20,000

* This account will show a debit balance of £4,000 until the underprovision is recorded, since payment has already been made: (360,000 + 18,000 + 4,000).

4 Disclosure requirements

You must also be able to prepare the **notes to the accounts** on tax for publication. This means mastering the disclosure requirements of FRS 16, FRS 19 and the CA 1985.

The CA 1985 requires that the **'tax on profit or loss on ordinary activities' is disclosed on the face of the profit and loss account or in a note to the accounts.** In addition, the **notes** to the profit and loss account **must state:**

(a) The **basis** on which the charge for UK corporation tax and UK income tax is computed

(b) The **amounts** of the charge for:

    (i) UK corporation tax (showing separately the amount, if greater, of UK corporation tax before any double taxation relief)

    (ii) UK income tax

    (iii) Non-UK taxation on profits, income and capital gains

4.1 FRS 16

FRS 16 *Current Tax* supplements and extends these provisions requiring that a company's *profit and loss account* should disclose separately (if material):

(a) The **amount of the UK corporation** tax specifying:

    (i) **The current charge for corporation tax** on the income of the year (stating the rate used to make the provision).

    (ii) Adjustments in respect of prior periods.

(b)   The **total foreign taxation** specifying:

(i)   The current foreign tax charge on the income of the year.

(ii)   Adjustments in respect of prior periods.

4.2 FRS 19

FRS 19 requires that **deferred** tax relating to the ordinary activities of the entity should be **shown separately** as a part of the tax on profit or loss on ordinary activities, either on the face of the profit and loss account, or by note.

Adjustments to deferred tax arising from changes in tax rates and tax allowances should normally be **disclosed separately** as part of the tax charge for the period.

The **deferred liabilities and assets**, should be **disclosed in the balance sheet or notes**. They should be disclosed separately on the face of the balance sheet if the amounts are so material that the absence of disclosure would affect interpretation of the Financial Statements.

4.3 Companies Acts

Finally, the **Companies Acts requires certain disclosures in respect of deferred tax.**

(a)   Deferred tax should be shown **in the balance sheet under the heading 'provisions for liabilities'** and in the category of provision for 'taxation, including deferred taxation'. The amount of any provision for taxation other than deferred taxation must be disclosed. The provision for taxation is different from tax liabilities which are shown as creditors in the balance sheet.

(b)   **Movements on reserves and provisions** must be disclosed, including provisions for deferred tax:

(i)   The amount of the provision at the beginning of the year and the end of the year

(ii)   The amounts transferred to or from the provision during the year

(iii) The source/application of any amount so transferred

(c)   Information must be disclosed about any **contingent liability** not provided for in the accounts **(such as deferred tax not provided for) and its legal nature**. It is understood that deferred tax not provided for is a contingent liability within the terms of the Act.

(d)   The **basis on which the charge for UK tax is computed** has to be stated. Particulars are required of any special circumstances affecting the tax liability for the financial year or succeeding financial years.

Chapter Roundup

- The **FRS 16 requirements** relating to company taxation are straightforward but **must be learned**. The best way is to practise on past exam questions.

- **FRS 19** requires full provision for **deferred** tax. It is unlikely that complicated numerical questions will be set in the exam so concentrate on **understanding** deferred tax.

- The balance sheet liability for tax payable is the tax charge for the year. In the income statement the tax charge for the year is adjusted for transfers to or from deferred tax and for prior year under– or over-provisions.

- You must also be able to prepare the **notes to the accounts** on tax for publication. This means mastering the disclosure requirements of FRS 16, FRS 19 and the Companies Acts.

Quick Quiz

1   The due date of payment of corporation tax is:

    A   Twelve months after the company's financial statements have been filed at Companies House
    B   Nine months after the end of the relevant accounting period
    C   Nine months after the company's financial statements have been filed at Companies House
    D   Twelve months after the end of the relevant accounting period

2   Which method of computing deferred tax does FRS 19 require to be used?

3   Under FRS 19 deferred tax assets and liabilities may/must be discounted. (*Delete as applicable.*)

4   Tax on profit on ordinary activities is the aggregate of:

    .... + ... + ...

Answers to Quick Quiz

1   B (see Para 1)

2   Full provision

3   May

4   Corporation tax on taxable profits, transfers to/from deferred tax, under/over provisions from previous years

Number	Level	Marks	Time
Q23	Examination	15	27 mins

Now try the question below from the Exam Question Bank

Earnings per share

18

Topic list	Syllabus reference
1 FRS 22 *Earnings per share*	C11
2 Basic EPS	C11
3 Effect on EPS of changes in capital structure	C11
4 Diluted EPS	C11
5 Presentation, disclosure and other matters	C11

Introduction

Section 1 of this chapter involves the description of EPS, the mechanics of its calculation and the disclosure required by FRS 22. EPS is an important indicator of a company's performance.

FRS 22 is a relatively new standard and therefore topical.

The purpose of any earnings yardstick is to achieve as far as possible clarity of meaning, comparability between one company and another and one year and another, and attribution of profits to the equity shares.

FRS 22 *Earnings per share* goes some way to ensuring that all these aims are achieved.

Study guide

		Intellectual level
C	**FINANCIAL STATEMENTS**	
11	**Reporting financial performance**	
(a)	Earnings per share (eps)	
	(i) Calculate the eps in accordance with relevant accounting standards (dealing with bonus issues, full market value issues and rights issues)	2
	(ii) Explain the relevance of the diluted eps and calculate the diluted eps involving convertible debt and share options (warrants)	2
	(iii) Explain why the trend of eps may be a more accurate indicator of performance than a company's profit trend and the importance of eps as a stock market indicator.	2
	(iv) Discuss the limitations of using eps as a performance measure.	2

Exam guide

Both of these standards can appear alongside a requirement to interpret financial statements. You not only need to learn the disclosure but also about the information you arrive at.

1 FRS 22 Earnings per share

FAST FORWARD

FRS 22 has brought the UK's treatment of the EPS calculation into line with international standards.

Earnings per share is a measure of the amount of profits earned by a company for each ordinary share. Earnings are profits after tax and preference dividends.

Exam focus point

You studied earnings per share for earlier papers, so we will skim over basic EPS and spend more time looking at diluted EPS.

FRS 22 *Earnings per share* was published in December 2004 as part of the ASB's convergence programme. It implements IAS 33 of the same name. The objective of FRS 22 is to improve the **comparison** of the performance of different entities in the same period and of the same entity in different accounting periods.

1.1 Definitions

The following definitions are given in FRS 22.

Key terms

- **Ordinary share**: an equity instrument that is subordinate to all other classes of equity instruments.

- **Potential ordinary share:** a financial instrument or other contract that may entitle its holder to ordinary shares.

- **Options, warrants and their equivalents**: financial instruments that give the holder the right to purchase ordinary shares.

- **Contingently issuable ordinary shares** are ordinary shares issuable for little or no cash or other consideration upon the satisfaction of certain conditions in a contingent share agreement.

Key terms

> - **Contingent share agreement:** an agreement to issue shares that is dependent on the satisfaction of specified conditions.
>
> - **Dilution** is a reduction in earnings per share or an increase in loss per share resulting from the assumption that convertible instruments are converted, that options or warrants are exercised, or that ordinary shares are issued upon the satisfaction of certain conditions.
>
> - **Antidilution** is an increase in earnings per share or a reduction in loss per share resulting from the assumption that convertible instruments are converted, that options or warrants are exercised, or that ordinary shares are issued upon the satisfaction of certain conditions. *(FRS 22)*

1.1.1 Ordinary shares

There may be more than one class of ordinary shares, but ordinary shares of the same class will have the same rights to receive dividends. Ordinary shares participate in the net profit for the period **only after other types of shares**, eg preference shares.

1.1.2 Potential ordinary shares

FRS 22 identifies the following examples of financial instrument and other contracts generating potential ordinary shares.

(a) **Debts** (financial liabilities) **or equity instruments**, including preference shares, that are convertible into ordinary shares

(b) **Share warrants and options**

(c) Shares that would be issued upon the satisfaction of **certain conditions** resulting from contractual arrangements, such as the purchase of a business or other assets

1.2 Scope

FRS 22 has the following **scope restrictions**.

(a) Only companies with (potential) ordinary shares which are **publicly traded** need to present EPS (including companies in the process of being listed).

(b) EPS need only be presented on the basis of **consolidated results** where the parent's results are shown as well.

(b) Where companies **choose** to present EPS, even when they have no (potential) ordinary shares which are traded, they must do so according to FRS 22.

(c) Entities applying the Financial Reporting Standard for Smaller Entities (FRSSE) are exempt.

2 Basic EPS

FAST FORWARD

> **Basic EPS** is calculated by dividing the net profit or loss for the period attributable to ordinary shareholders by the weighted average number of ordinary shares outstanding during the period.
>
> You should know how to calculate **basic EPS** and how to deal with related complications (issue of shares for cash, bonus issue, share splits/reverse share splits, rights issues).

Basic EPS should be calculated for **profit or loss attributable to ordinary equity holders** of the parent entity and **profit or loss from continuing operations** attributable to those equity holders (if this is presented).

2.1 Measurement

Basic EPS should be calculated by dividing the **net profit** or loss for the period attributable to ordinary equity holders by the **weighted average number of ordinary shares** outstanding during the period.

$$\frac{\text{Net profit/(loss) attribtable to ordinary shareholders}}{\text{Weighted average number of ordinary shares outstanding during the period}}$$

2.2 Earnings

Earnings includes **all items of income and expense** (including tax and minority interests) *less* net profit attributable to **preference shareholders**, including preference dividends. (In practice most preference dividends are now treated as finance costs and will have been deducted before tax.)

2.3 Per share

The number of ordinary shares used should be the weighted average number of ordinary shares during the period. This figure (for all periods presented) should be **adjusted for events**, other than the conversion of potential ordinary shares, that have changed the number of shares outstanding without a corresponding change in resources.

The **time-weighting factor** is the number of days the shares were outstanding compared with the total number of days in the period. A reasonable approximation is usually adequate.

2.4 Example: weighted average number of shares

Justina Co, a listed company, has the following share transactions during 20X7.

Date	Details	Shares issued
1 January 20X7	Balance at beginning of year	170,000
31 May 20X7	Issue of new shares for cash	80,000
31 December 20X7	Balance at year end	250,000

Required

Calculate the weighted average number of shares outstanding for 20X7.

Solution

The weighted average number of shares can be calculated in two ways.

(a) $(170,000 \times 5/12) + (250,000 \times 7/12) = 216,666$ shares
(b) $(170,000 \times 12/12) + (80,000 \times 7/12) = 216,666$ shares

2.5 Consideration

Shares are usually included in the weighted average number of shares from the **date consideration is receivable** which is usually the date of issue. In other cases consider the specific terms attached to their issue (consider the substance of any contract). The treatment for the issue of ordinary shares in different circumstances is as follows.

Consideration	Start date for inclusion
In exchange for cash	When cash is receivable
As a result of the conversion of a debt instrument to ordinary shares	Date interest ceases accruing
In place of interest or principal on other financial instruments	Date interest ceases accruing
In exchange for the settlement of a liability of the entity	The settlement date
As consideration for the acquisition of an asset other than cash	The date on which the acquisition is recognised
For the rendering of services to the entity	As services are rendered

Ordinary shares issued as **purchase consideration** in an acquisition should be included as of the date of acquisition because the acquired entity's results will also be included from that date.

Ordinary shares that will be issued on the **conversion** of a mandatorily convertible instrument are included in the calculation from the **date the contract is entered into**.

If ordinary shares are **partly paid**, they are treated as a fraction of an ordinary share to the extent they are entitled to dividends relative to fully paid ordinary shares.

Contingently issuable shares (including those subject to recall) are included in the computation when all necessary conditions for issue have been satisfied.

Question

Basic EPS

Flame Ltd is a company with a called up and paid up capital of 100,000 ordinary shares of £1 each and 20,000 10% preference shares of £1 each. The company manufactures gas appliances. During its financial year to 31 December the company had to pay £50,000 compensation and costs arising from an uninsured claim for personal injuries suffered by a customer while on the company premises.

The gross profit was £200,000. Flame Ltd paid the required preference share dividend and declared an ordinary dividend of 42p per share. Assuming an income tax rate of 30% on the given figures show the trading results and EPS of the company.

Answer

FLAME LTD
TRADING RESULTS FOR YEAR TO 31 DECEMBER

	£
Gross profit	200,000
Expense (50,000 + 2,000 preference dividend)	(52,000)
Profit before tax	148,000
Tax at 30%	(44,400)
Profit for the period	103,600

EARNINGS PER SHARE

$$\frac{103,600}{100,000} = 103.6p$$

3 Effect on EPS of changes in capital structure

3.1 New issues/buy backs

When there has been an issue of new shares or a buy-back of shares, the corresponding figures for EPS for the previous year will be comparable with the current year because, as the weighted average of shares has risen or fallen, there has been a **corresponding increase or decrease in resources**. Money has been received when shares were issued, and money has been paid out to repurchase shares. It is assumed that the sale or purchase has been made at full market price.

3.2 Example: earnings per share with a new issue

On 30 September 20X2, Boffin Co made an issue at full market price of 1,000,000 ordinary shares. The company's accounting year runs from 1 January to 31 December. Relevant information for 20X1 and 20X2 is as follows.

	20X2	20X1
Shares in issue as at 31 December	9,000,000	8,000,000
Profits after tax and preference dividend	£3,300,000	£3,280,000

Required

Calculate the EPS for 20X2 and the corresponding figure for 20X1.

Solution

	20X2	20X1
Weighted average number of shares		
8 million × 9/12	6,000,000	
9 million × 9/12	2,250,000	
	8,250,000	8,000,000
Earnings	£3,300,000	£3,280,000
EPS	40 pence	41 pence

In spite of the increase in total earnings by £20,000 in 20X2, the EPS is not as good as in 20X1, because there was extra capital employed for the final 3 months of 20X2.

There are other events, however, which change the number of shares outstanding, **without a corresponding change in resources**. In these circumstances it is necessary to make adjustments so that the current and prior period EPS figures are comparable.

Four such events are considered by IAS 33.

(a) **Capitalisation or bonus issue** (sometimes called a stock dividend)
(b) Bonus element in any other issue, eg a **rights issue** to existing shareholders
(c) **Share split**
(d) **Reverse share split** (consolidation of shares)

There are other events, however, which change the number of shares outstanding, **without a corresponding change in resources**. In these circumstances (four of which are considered by FRS 22) it is necessary to make adjustments so that the current and prior period EPS figures are comparable.

3.3 Capitalisation/bonus issue

In this case, ordinary shares are issued to existing shareholders for **no additional consideration**. The number of ordinary shares has increased without an increase in resources.

This problem is solved by **adjusting the number of ordinary shares outstanding before the event** for the proportionate change in the number of shares outstanding as if the event had occurred at the beginning of the earliest period reported.

3.4 Example: earnings per share with a bonus issue

Greymatter Ltd had 400,000 shares in issue, until on 30 September 20X2 it made a bonus issue of 100,000 shares. Calculate the EPS for 20X2 and the corresponding figure for 20X1 if total earnings were £80,000 in 20X2 and £75,000 in 20X1. The company's accounting year runs from 1 January to 31 December.

Solution

	20X2	20X1
Earnings	£80,000	£75,000
Shares at 1 January	400,000	400,000
Bonus issue	100,000	100,000
	500,000 shares	500,000 shares
EPS	16p	15p

The number of shares for 20X1 must also be adjusted if the figures for EPS are to remain comparable.

3.5 Rights issue

A rights issue of shares is an issue of new shares to existing shareholders **at a price below the current market value**. The offer of new shares is made on the basis of x new shares for every y shares currently held, eg a 1 for 3 rights issue is an offer of 1 new share at the offer price for every 3 shares currently held. This means that there is a bonus element included.

To arrive at figures for EPS when a rights issue is made, we first calculate the **theoretical ex-rights price**. This is a weighted average value per share.

3.6 Example: theoretical ex-rights price

Suppose that Egghead Ltd has 10,000,000 shares in issue. It now proposes to make a 1 for 4 rights issue at a price of £3 per share. The market value of existing shares on the final day before the issue is made is £3.50 (this is the 'with rights' value). What is the theoretical ex-rights price per share?

Solution

	£
Before issue 4 shares, value £3.50 each	14.00
Rights issue 1 share, value £3	3.00
Theoretical value of 5 shares	17.00

Theoretical ex-rights price = $\dfrac{£17.00}{5}$ = £3.40 per share

Note that this calculation can alternatively be performed using the total value and number of outstanding shares.

3.7 Procedures

The procedures for calculating the EPS for the current year and a corresponding figure for the previous year are as follows.

(a) The **EPS for the corresponding previous period** should be multiplied by the following fraction. (*Note.* The market price on the last day of quotation is taken as the fair value immediately prior to exercise of the rights, as required by the standard.)

$$\frac{\text{Fair value per share}}{\text{Fair value per share immediately before the exercise of rights}}$$

(b) To obtain the **EPS for the current year** you should:

(i) multiply the number of shares before the rights issue by the fraction of the year before the date of issue and by the following fraction.

$$\frac{\text{Fair value per share immediately before the exercise of rights}}{\text{Theoretical ex - rights fair value per share}}$$

(ii) multiply the number of shares after the rights issue by the fraction of the year after the date of issue and add to the figure arrived at in (i).

The total earnings should then be divided by the total number of shares so calculated.

3.8 Example: earnings per share with a rights issue

Brains Ltd had 100,000 shares in issue, but then makes a 1 for 5 rights issue on 1 October 20X2 at a price of £1. The market value on the last day of quotation with rights was £1.60.

Calculate the EPS for 20X2 and the corresponding figure for 20X1 given total earnings of £50,000 in 20X2 and £40,000 in 20X1.

Solution

Calculation of theoretical ex-rights price:

	£
Before issue 5 shares, value × £1.60	8.00
Rights issue 1 share, value × £1.00	1.00
Theoretical value of 6 shares	9.00

Theoretical ex-rights price = $\dfrac{£9}{6}$ = £1.50

EPS for 20X1

EPS as calculated before taking into account the rights issue = 40p (£40,000 divided by 100,000 shares).

EPS = $\dfrac{1.50}{1.60}$ × 40p = 37½p

(Remember: this is the corresponding value for 20X1 which will be shown in the financial statements for Brains Ltd at the end of 20X2.)

EPS for 20X2

Number of shares before the rights issue was 100,000. 20,000 shares were issued.

Stage 1: $100,000 \times {}^{9}/_{12} \times \dfrac{1.60}{1.50} =$ 80,000

Stage 2: $120,000 \times {}^{3}/_{12} =$ 30,000

     110,000

$$EPS = \dfrac{£50,000}{110,000} = 45\tfrac{1}{2}p$$

The figure for total earnings is the actual earnings for the year.

Question

Were you awake?

Give the formula for the 'bonus element' of a rights issue.

Answer

$$\dfrac{\text{Actual cum - rights fair value per share}}{\text{Theoretical ex - rights fair value per share}}$$

Question

Basic EPS

Macarone Ltd has produced the following net profit figures.

	£m
20X6	1.1
20X7	1.5
20X8	1.8

On 1 January 20X7 the number of shares outstanding was 500,000. During 20X7 the company announced a rights issue with the following details.

Rights:	1 new share for each 5 outstanding (100,000 new shares in total)
Exercise price:	£5.00
Last date to exercise rights:	1 March 20X7

The market (fair) value of one share in Macarone Ltd immediately prior to exercise on 1 March 20X7 = £11.00.

Required

Calculate the EPS for 20X6, 20X7 and 20X8.

Answer

Computation of theoretical ex-rights price

This computation uses the total fair value and number of shares.

$$\dfrac{\text{Fair value of all outstanding shares + total received from exercise of rights}}{\text{No shares outstanding prior to exercise + no shares issued in exercise}}$$

$$= \dfrac{(£11.00 \times 500,000)+(£5.00 \times 100,000)}{500,000+100,000} = £10.00$$

Computation of EPS

		20X6 £	20X7 £	20X8 £
20X6	EPS as originally reported $\dfrac{£1,100,000}{500,000}$	2.20		
20X6	EPS restated for rights issue = $\dfrac{£1,100,000}{500,000} \times \dfrac{10}{11}$	2.00		
20X7	EPS including effects of rights issue $\dfrac{£1,500,000}{(500,000 \times 2/12 \times 11/10) + (600,000 \times 10/12)}$		2.54	
20X8	EPS = $\dfrac{£1,800,000}{600,000}$			3.00

4 Diluted EPS

FAST FORWARD

Diluted EPS is calculated by adjusting the net profit attributable to ordinary shareholders and the weighted average number of shares outstanding for the effects of all dilutive potential ordinary shares.

You must be able to deal with **options** and all other **dilutive potential ordinary shares**.

At the end of an accounting period, a company may have in issue some **securities** which do not (at present) have any 'claim' to a share of equity earnings, but **may give rise to such a claim in the future**.

(a) A **separate class of equity shares** which at present is not entitled to any dividend, but will be entitled after some future date.

(b) **Convertible loan stock** or **convertible preferred shares** which give their holders the right at some future date to exchange their securities for ordinary shares of the company, at a pre-determined conversion rate.

(c) **Options** or **warrants**.

In such circumstances, the future number of shares ranking for dividend might increase, which in turn results in a fall in the EPS. In other words, a **future increase** in the **number of equity shares will cause a dilution or 'watering down' of equity**, and it is possible to calculate a **diluted earnings per share** (ie the EPS that would have been obtained during the financial period if the dilution had already taken place). This will indicate to investors the possible effects of a future dilution.

4.1 Earnings

The earnings calculated for basic EPS should be adjusted by the **post-tax** (including deferred tax) effect of the following.

(a) Any **dividends** on dilutive potential ordinary shares that were deducted to arrive at earnings for basic EPS.

(b) **Interest recognised** in the period for the dilutive potential ordinary shares.

(c) Any **other changes in income or expenses** (fees or discount) that would result from the conversion of the dilutive potential ordinary shares.

The conversion of some potential ordinary shares may lead to changes in **other income or expenses**. For example, the reduction of interest expense related to potential ordinary shares and the resulting increase in net profit for the period may lead to an increase in the expense relating to a non-discretionary employee profit-sharing plan. When calculating diluted EPS, the net profit or loss for the period is adjusted for any such consequential changes in income or expense.

4.2 Per share

The number of ordinary shares is the weighted average number of ordinary shares calculated for basic EPS plus the weighted average number of ordinary shares that would be issued on the conversion of all the **dilutive potential ordinary shares** into ordinary shares.

It should be assumed that dilutive ordinary shares were converted into ordinary shares at the **beginning of the period** or, if later, at the actual date of issue. There are two other points.

(a)   The computation assumes the most **advantageous conversion rate** or exercise rate from the standpoint of the holder of the potential ordinary shares.

(b)   Potential ordinary shares should be treated as dilutive when, and only when, their conversion to ordinary shares would decrease earnings per share or increase loss per share.

4.3 Example: diluted EPS

In 20X7 Farrah plc had a basic EPS of 105p based on earnings of £105,000 and 100,000 ordinary £1 shares. It also had in issue £40,000 15% Convertible Loan Stock which is convertible in two years' time at the rate of 4 ordinary shares for every £5 of stock. The rate of tax is 30%. In 20X7 net profit of £150,000 was recorded after interest payments of £6,000.

Required

Calculate the diluted EPS.

Solution

Diluted EPS is calculated as follows.

Step 1   **Number of shares**: the additional equity on conversion of the loan stock will be 40,000 × 4/5 = 32,000 shares

Step 2   **Earnings**: Farrah plc will save interest payments of £6,000 but this increase in profits will be taxed. Hence the earnings figure may be recalculated:

	£
Net profit £(150,000 + 6,000)	156,000
Taxation (30%)	46,800
Profit after tax	109,200

Step 3   **Calculation**: Diluted EPS = $\dfrac{£109,200}{132,000}$ = 82.7p

Step 4   **Dilution**: the dilution in earnings would be 105p − 82.7p = 22.3p per share.

Question

Ardent Ltd has 5,000,000 ordinary shares of 25 pence each in issue, and also had in issue in 20X4:

(a) £1,000,000 of 14% convertible debentures, convertible in three years' time at the rate of 2 shares per £10 of debentures.

(b) £2,000,000 of 10% convertible debentures, convertible in one year's time at the rate of 3 shares per £5 of debenture.

The total earnings in 20X4 were £1,750,000.

The rate of income tax is 35%.

Required

Calculate the EPS and diluted EPS.

Answer

(a) Basic EPS = $\dfrac{£1,750,000}{5 \text{ million}}$ = 35 pence

(b) We must decide which of the potential ordinary shares (ie the debentures) are dilutive (ie would decrease the EPS if converted).

For the 14% debentures incremental EPS $= \dfrac{0.65 \times £140,000}{2,000,000 \text{ shares}}$

$= 45.5\text{p}$

For the 10% debentures, incremental EPS $= \dfrac{0.65 \times £200,000}{1.2\text{m shares}}$

$= 10.8\text{p}$

The effect of converting the 14% debentures is therefore to **increase** the EPS figure, since the incremental EPS of 45.5p is greater than the basic EPS of 35p. The 14% debentures are therefore **not dilutive** and are excluded from the diluted EPS calculations.

The 10% debentures are dilutive.

Diluted EPS $= \dfrac{£1.75\text{m} + £0.13\text{m}}{5\text{m} + 1.2\text{m}}$

$= 30.3\text{p}$

4.4 Treatment of options

It should be assumed that options are exercised and that the assumed proceeds would have been received from the issue of shares at **fair value**. Fair value for this purpose is calculated on the basis of the average price of the ordinary shares during the period.

Options and other share purchase arrangements are dilutive when they would result in the issue of ordinary shares for **less than fair value**. The amount of the dilution is fair value less the issue price. In order to calculate diluted EPS, each transaction of this type is treated as consisting of two parts.

(a)   A contract to issue a certain number of ordinary shares at their **average market price** during the period. These shares are fairly priced and are assumed to be neither dilutive nor antidilutive. They are ignored in the computation of diluted earnings per share.

(b)   A contract to issue the remaining ordinary shares for **no consideration**. Such ordinary shares generate no proceeds and have no effect on the net profit attributable to ordinary shares outstanding. Therefore such shares are dilutive and they are added to the number of ordinary shares outstanding in the computation of diluted EPS.

To the extent that **partly paid shares** are not entitled to participate in dividends during the period, they are considered the equivalent of **warrants** or **options**.

Employee share options with fixed or determinable terms (ie, **not performance based**) and outstanding shares are treated as **options** in the calculation of diluted earnings per share. **Performance based** employee share options are treated as **contingently issuable shares** because their issue is contingent upon satisfying specified conditions in addition to the passage of time.

Question   EPS 2

Brand plc has the following results for the year ended 31 December 20X7.

Net profit for year	£1,200,000
Weighted average number of ordinary shares outstanding during year	500,000 shares
Average fair value of one ordinary share during year	£20.00
Weighted average number of shares under option during year	100,000 shares
Exercise price for shares under option during year	£15.00

Required

Calculate both basic and diluted earnings per share.

Answer

	Per share	Earnings £	Shares
Net profit for year		1,200,000	
Weighted average shares outstanding during 20X7			500,000
Basic earnings per share	2.40		
Number of shares under option			100,000
Number of shares that would have been issued At fair value: (100,000 × £15.00/£20.00)			(75,000) *
Diluted earnings per share	2.29	1,200,000	525,000

*   The earnings have not been increased as the total number of shares has been increased only by the number of shares (25,000) deemed for the purpose of the computation to have been issued for no consideration.

4.4.1 Retrospective adjustment

If the number of ordinary or potential ordinary shares outstanding **increases** as a result of a capitalisation, bonus issue or share split, or decreases as a result of a reverse share split, the calculation of basic and diluted EPS for all periods presented should be **adjusted retrospectively**.

If these changes occur **after the balance sheet date** but before issue of the financial statements, the calculations per share for the financial statements and those of any prior period should be based on the **new number of shares** (and this should be disclosed).

In addition, basic and diluted EPS of all periods presented should be adjusted for the effects of **errors**, and adjustments resulting from **changes** in **accounting policies**, accounted for retrospectively.

An entity **does not restate diluted EPS** of any prior period for changes in the assumptions used or for the conversion of potential ordinary shares into ordinary shares outstanding.

5 Presentation, disclosure and other matters

5.1 Presentation

A entity should present on the **face of the profit and loss account** basic and diluted EPS for:

(a)   profit or loss from continuing operations; and
(b)   profit or loss for the period

for each class of ordinary share that has a different right to share in the net profit for the period.

The basic and diluted EPS should be presented with **equal prominence** for all periods presented.

Basic and diluted EPS for any **discontinued operations** must also be presented.

Disclosure must still be made where the EPS figures (basic and/or diluted) are **negative** (ie a loss per share).

5.2 Disclosure

An entity should disclose the following.

(a)   The amounts used as the **numerators** in calculating basic and diluted EPS, and a **reconciliation** of those amounts to the net profit or loss for the period.

(b)   The weighted average number of ordinary shares used as the **denominator** in calculating basic and diluted EPS, and a **reconciliation** of these denominators to each other.

(c)   Instruments that could potentially dilute basic EPS but which were **not included** in the calculation because they were **antidilutive** for the period presented.

An entity should also disclose a description of ordinary share transactions or potential ordinary share transactions, other than capitalisation issues and share splits, which occur **after the balance sheet date** when they are of such importance that non-disclosure would affect the ability of the users of the financial statements to make proper evaluations and decisions. Examples of such transactions include the following.

(a)   Issue of shares for cash

(b)   Issue of shares when the proceeds are used to repay debt or preferred shares outstanding at the balance sheet date

(c)   Redemption of ordinary shares outstanding

(d)   Conversion or exercise of potential ordinary shares, outstanding at the balance sheet date, into ordinary shares

(e)   Issue of warrants, options or convertible securities

(f)   Achievement of conditions that would result in the issue of contingently issuable shares

EPS amounts are not adjusted for such transactions occurring after the balance sheet date because such transactions **do not affect the amount of capital used** to produce the net profit or loss for the period.

5.3 Alternative EPS figures

An entity may present **alternative EPS figures if it wishes**. However, FRS 22 lays out certain rules where this takes place.

(a) The weighted average number of shares as calculated under FRS 22 **must** be used.

(b) A **reconciliation** must be given between the component of profit used in the alternative EPS (if it is not a line item in the income statement) and the line item for profit reported in the income statement.

(c) The entity must indicate the basis on which the **numerator** is determined.

(d) Basic and diluted EPS must be shown with **equal prominence**.

5.4 Significance of earnings per share

Earnings per share (EPS) is one of the most frequently quoted statistics in financial analysis. Because of the widespread use of the price earnings **(P/E) ratio** as a yardstick for investment decisions, it became increasingly important.

Reported and forecast EPS can, through the P/E ratio, have a **significant effect on a company's share price**. Thus, a share price might fall if it looks as if EPS is going to be low. There are a number of reasons why EPS should **not** be used to determine the value of a company's shares. FRS 22 concentrates on the **denominator** of EPS – ie the number of shares. However, it is more difficult to regulate the **numerator** – earnings. Reported earnings can be affected by a number of factors – choice of accounting policy, asset valuation, taxation issues. Directors who want to present favourable EPS can find ways to boost reported earnings, as happened with Enron.

EPS has also served as a means of assessing the **stewardship and management** role performed by company directors and managers. Remuneration packages might be linked to EPS growth, thereby increasing the pressure on management to improve EPS. The danger of this is that management effort may go into distorting results to produce a favourable EPS. It should also be noted that EPS takes no account of other issues that affect whether a company is worth investing in, such as its risk profile and its investment requirements. Nevertheless, the market is sensitive to EPS.

Chapter Roundup

- FRS 22 has brought the UK's treatment of the EPS calculation into line with international standards.

- **Earnings per share** is a measure of the amount of profits earned by a company for each ordinary share. Earnings are profits after tax and preference dividends.

- **Basic EPS** is calculated by dividing the net profit or loss for the period attributable to ordinary shareholders by the weighted average number of ordinary shares outstanding during the period.

  You should know how to calculate **basic EPS** and how to deal with related complications (issue of shares for cash, bonus issue, rights issues).

- **Diluted EPS** is calculated by adjusting the net profit attributable to ordinary shareholders and the weighted average number of ordinary shares outstanding during the period for the effects of all dilutive potential ordinary shares.

Quick Quiz

1   Define earnings per share.

2   Following a rights issue, what is the fraction by which the EPS for the corresponding previous period should be multiplied?

3   What is diluted EPS?

Answers to Quick Quiz

1   EPS is profit in pence attributable to each equity share.

2   $$\frac{\text{Fair value of current shares}}{\text{Theoretical ex - rights value per share}}$$

3   Diluted EPS shows users of the accounts how EPS would appear taking into account the effects of all dilutive potential ordinary shares.

Now try the question below from the Exam Question Bank

Number	Level	Marks	Time
Q24	Examination	25	45 mins

19

Analysing and interpreting financial statements

Topic list	Syllabus reference
1 The broad categories of ratio	E2
2 Profitability and return on capital	E2
3 Liquidity, gearing and working capital	E2
4 Shareholders' investment ratios	E2
5 Presentation of financial performance	E2

Introduction

This chapter looks at **interpretation of accounts**. We deal here with the calculation of ratios, how they can be analysed and interpreted, and how the results should be presented to management.

Study guide

		Intellectual level
2	**Calculation and interpretation of accounting ratios and trends to address users' and stakeholders' needs**	
(a)	define and compute relevant financial ratios.	2
(b)	explain what aspects of performance specific ratios are intended to assess.	2
(c)	analyse and interpret ratios to given an assessment of an entity's performance and financial position in comparison with:	2
(i)	an entity's previous periods' financial statements	
(ii)	another similar entity for the same reporting period	
(iii)	industry average ratios.	
(d)	interpret an entity's financial statements to give advice from the perspectives of different stakeholders.	2
(e)	discuss how the interpretation of current value based financial statements would differ from those using historical cost based accounts.	1

1 The broad categories of ratio

FAST FORWARD

> Your syllabus requires you to **appraise and communicate** the position and prospects of a business based on given and prepared statements and ratios.

If you were to look at a balance sheet or income statement, how would you decide whether the company was doing well or badly? Or whether it was financially strong or financially vulnerable? And what would you be looking at in the figures to help you to make your judgement?

Ratio analysis involves **comparing one figure against another** to produce a ratio, and assessing whether the ratio indicates a weakness or strength in the company's affairs.

1.1 The broad categories of ratios

Broadly speaking, basic ratios can be grouped into five categories.

- Profitability and return
- Long-term solvency and stability
- Short-term solvency and liquidity
- Efficiency (turnover ratios)
- Shareholders' investment ratios

Within each heading we will identify a number of standard measures or ratios that are normally calculated and generally accepted as meaningful indicators. One must stress however that each individual business must be considered separately, and a ratio that is meaningful for a manufacturing company may be completely meaningless for a financial institution. **Try not to be too mechanical** when working out ratios and constantly think about what you are trying to achieve.

The key to obtaining meaningful information from ratio analysis is **comparison**. This may involve comparing ratios over time within the same business to establish whether things are improving or declining, and comparing ratios between similar businesses to see whether the company you are analysing is better or worse than average within its specific business sector.

It must be stressed that ratio analysis on its own is not sufficient for interpreting company accounts, and that there are **other items of information** which should be looked at, for example:

(a)   The content of any **accompanying commentary** on the accounts and other statements

(b)   The age and nature of the **company's assets**

(c)   **Current and future developments** in the company's markets, at home and overseas, recent acquisitions or disposals of a subsidiary by the company

(d)   **Unusual** items separately disclosed in the profit and loss account

(e)   Any other **noticeable features** of the report and accounts, such as events after the balance sheet date, contingent liabilities, a qualified auditors' report, the company's taxation position, and so on

1.2 Example: calculating ratios

To illustrate the calculation of ratios, the following **draft** balance sheet and profit and loss account figures will be used.

FURLONG LTD PROFIT AND LOSS ACCOUNT
FOR THE YEAR ENDED 31 DECEMBER 20X8

	Notes	20X8 £	20X7 £
Turnover	1	3,095,576	1,909,051
Operating profit	1	359,501	244,229
Interest	2	17,371	19,127
Profit before taxation		342,130	225,102
Taxation		74,200	31,272
Profit for the period		267,930	193,830
Earnings per share		12.8p	9.3p

FURLONG LTD BALANCE SHEET
AS AT 31 DECEMBER 20X8

	Notes	20X8 £	20X8 £	20X7 £	20X7 £
Assets					
Fixed assets					
Tangible fixed assets			802,180		656,071
Current assets					
Stock		64,422		86,550	
Debtors	3	1,002,701		853,441	
Cash at bank and in hand		1,327		68,363	
		1,068,450		1,008,354	
Current liabilities	4	860,731		895,656	
Net current assets			207,719		112,698
Total assets less current liabilities			1,009,899		768,769
Long term liabilities					
10% debentures 20X4/20Y0			100,000		100,000
			909,899		668,769
Share capital and reserves					
Ordinary 10p shares	5		210,000		210,000
Share premium account			48,178		48,178
Profit and loss account			651,721		410,591
			909,899		668,769

NOTES TO THE ACCOUNTS

		20X8	20X7
		£	£
1	*Turnover and profit*		
	Turnover	3,095,576	1,909,051
	Cost of sales	2,402,609	1,441,950
	Gross profit	692,967	467,101
	Administration expenses	333,466	222,872
	Operating profit	359,501	244,229
	Depreciation charged	151,107	120,147
2	*Interest*		
	Payable on bank overdrafts and other loans	8,115	11,909
	Payable on debentures	10,000	10,000
		18,115	21,909
	Receivable on short-term deposits	744	2,782
	Net payable	17,371	19,127
3	*Debtors*		
	Amounts falling due within one year		
	Trade debtors	905,679	807,712
	Prepayments and accrued income	97,022	45,729
		1,002,701	853,441
4	*Current liabilities*		
	Trade creditors	627,018	545,340
	Accruals and deferred income	81,279	280,464
	Corporate taxes	108,000	37,200
	Other taxes	44,434	32,652
		860,731	895,656
5	*Called-up share capital*		
	Authorised ordinary shares of 10p each	1,000,000	1,000,000
	Issued and fully paid ordinary shares of 10p each	210,000	210,000
6	Dividends paid	20,000	–

2 Profitability and return on capital

FAST FORWARD

Return on capital employed (ROCE) may be used by the shareholders or the Board to assess the performance of management.

In our example, the company made a profit in both 20X8 and 20X7, and there was an increase in profit between one year and the next:

(a)   Of 52% before taxation
(b)   Of 39% after taxation

Profit before taxation is generally thought to be a better figure to use than profit after taxation, because there might be unusual variations in the tax charge from year to year which would not affect the underlying profitability of the company's operations.

Another profit figure that should be calculated is PBIT, **profit before interest and tax**. This is the amount of profit which the company earned before having to pay interest to the providers of loan capital, such as debentures and medium-term bank loans, which will be shown in the balance sheet as long-term liabilities.

Formula to learn

> **Profit before interest and tax** is therefore:
>
> (a)   the profit on ordinary activities before taxation; **plus**
> (b)   interest charges on loan capital.

Published accounts do not always give sufficient detail on interest payable to determine how much is interest on long-term finance. We will assume in our example that the whole of the interest payable (£18,115, note 2) relates to long-term finance.

PBIT in our example is therefore:

	20X8	20X7
	£	£
Profit on ordinary activities before tax	342,130	225,102
Interest payable	18,115	21,909
PBIT	360,245	247,011

This shows a 46% growth between 20X7 and 20X8.

2.1 Return on capital employed (ROCE)

It is impossible to assess profits or profit growth properly without relating them to the **amount of funds (capital) that were employed in making the profits**. The most important profitability ratio is therefore return on capital employed (ROCE), which states the profit as a percentage of the amount of capital employed.

Formula to learn

$$ROCE = \frac{\text{Profit before interest and taxation}}{\text{Capital employed}} \times 100\%$$

Capital employed = Shareholders' equity plus long-term liabilities (*or* total assets less current liabilities)

The underlying principle is that we must **compare like with like**, and so if capital means share capital and reserves plus long-term liabilities and debt capital, profit must mean the profit earned by all this capital together. This is PBIT, since interest is the return for loan capital.

In our example, capital employed = 20X8 £1,870,630 − £860,731 = £1,009,899
20X7 £1,664,425 − £895,656 = £768,769

These total figures are the total assets less current liabilities figures for 20X8 and 20X7 in the balance sheet.

		20X8	20X7
ROCE	=	$\dfrac{£360,245}{£1,009,899}$	$\dfrac{£247,011}{£768,769}$
	=	35.7%	32%

What does a company's ROCE tell us? What should we be looking for? There are three comparisons that can be made.

(a)   The **change in ROCE from one year to the next** can be examined. In this example, there has been an increase in ROCE by about 4 percentage points from its 20X7 level.

(b)   The **ROCE being earned by other companies**, if this information is available, can be compared with the ROCE of this company. Here the information is not available.

(c)   A comparison of the ROCE with **current market borrowing rates** may be made.

(i) What would be the cost of extra borrowing to the company if it needed more loans, and is it earning a ROCE that suggests it could make profits to make such borrowing worthwhile?

(ii) Is the company making a ROCE which suggests that it is getting value for money from its current borrowing?

(iii) Companies are in a risk business and commercial borrowing rates are a good independent yardstick against which company performance can be judged.

In this example, if we suppose that current market interest rates, say, for medium-term borrowing from banks, are around 10%, then the company's actual ROCE of 36% in 20X8 would not seem low. On the contrary, it might seem high.

However, it is easier to spot a low ROCE than a high one, because there is always a chance that the company's fixed assets, especially property, are **undervalued** in its balance sheet, and so the capital employed figure might be unrealistically low. If the company had earned a ROCE, not of 36%, but of, say only 6%, then its return would have been below current borrowing rates and so disappointingly low.

2.2 Return on equity (ROE)

Return on equity gives a more restricted view of capital than ROCE, but it is based on the same principles.

Formula to learn

$$ROE = \frac{\text{Profit after tax and preference dividend}}{\text{Ordinary share capital and other equity}} \times 100\%$$

In our example, ROE is calculated as follows.

	20X8	20X7
ROE =	$\dfrac{£267{,}930}{£909{,}899} = 29.4\%$	$\dfrac{£193{,}830}{£668{,}769} = 29\%$

ROE is **not a widely-used ratio**, however, because there are more useful ratios that give an indication of the return to shareholders, such as earnings per share, dividend per share, dividend yield and earnings yield, which are described later.

2.3 Analysing profitability and return in more detail: the secondary ratios

We often sub-analyse ROCE, to find out more about why the ROCE is high or low, or better or worse than last year. There are two factors that contribute towards a return on capital employed, both related to sales revenue.

(a) **Profit margin**. A company might make a high or low profit margin on its sales. For example, a company that makes a profit of 25p per £1 of sales is making a bigger return on its revenue than another company making a profit of only 10p per £1 of sales.

(b) **Asset turnover**. Asset turnover is a measure of how well the assets of a business are being used to generate sales. For example, if two companies each have capital employed of £100,000 and Company A makes sales of £400,000 per annum whereas Company B makes sales of only £200,000 per annum, Company A is making a higher turnover from the same amount of assets (twice as much asset turnover as Company B) and this will help A to make a higher return on capital employed than B. Asset turnover is expressed as 'x times' so that assets generate x times their value in annual sales. Here, Company A's asset turnover is 4 times and B's is 2 times.

Profit margin and asset turnover together explain the ROCE and if the ROCE is the primary profitability ratio, these other two are the secondary ratios. The relationship between the three ratios can be shown mathematically.

Formula to learn

Profit margin × Asset turnover = ROCE

$$\therefore \quad \frac{PBIT}{Sales} \times \frac{Sales}{Capital\ employed} = \frac{PBIT}{Capital\ employed}$$

In our example:

		Profit margin		Asset turnover		ROCE
(a)	20X8	$\dfrac{£360,245}{£3,095,576}$	×	$\dfrac{£3,095,576}{£1,009,899}$	=	$\dfrac{£360,245}{£1,009,899}$
		11.64%	×	3.06 times	=	35.6%
(b)	20X7	$\dfrac{£247,011}{£1,909,051}$	×	$\dfrac{£1,909,051}{£768,769}$	=	$\dfrac{£247,011}{£768,769}$
		12.94%	×	2.48 times	=	32.1%

In this example, the company's improvement in ROCE between 20X7 and 20X8 is attributable to a higher asset turnover. Indeed the profit margin has fallen a little, but the higher asset turnover has more than compensated for this.

It is also worth commenting on the change in sales revenue from one year to the next. You may already have noticed that Furlong achieved sales growth of over 60% from £1.9 million to £3.1 million between 20X7 and 20X8. This is very strong growth, and this is certainly one of the most significant items in the profit and loss account and balance sheet.

2.3.1 A warning about comments on profit margin and asset turnover

It might be tempting to think that a high profit margin is good, and a low asset turnover means sluggish trading. In broad terms, this is so. But there is a trade-off between profit margin and asset turnover, and you cannot look at one without allowing for the other.

(a)   A **high profit margin** means a high profit per £1 of sales, but if this also means that sales prices are high, there is a strong possibility that turnover will be depressed, and so asset turnover lower.

(b)   A **high asset turnover** means that the company is generating a lot of sales, but to do this it might have to keep its prices down and so accept a low profit margin per £1 of sales.

Consider the following.

Company A		*Company B*	
Turnover	£1,000,000	Sales turnover	£4,000,000
Capital employed	£1,000,000	Capital employed	£1,000,000
PBIT	£200,000	PBIT	£200,000

These figures would give the following ratios.

ROCE	=	$\dfrac{£200,000}{£1,000,000}$	= 20%	ROCE	=	$\dfrac{£200,000}{£1,000,000}$	= 20%
Profit margin	=	$\dfrac{£200,000}{£1,000,000}$	= 20%	Profit margin	=	$\dfrac{£200,000}{£4,000,000}$	= 5%
Asset turnover	=	$\dfrac{£1,000,000}{£1,000,000}$	= 1	Asset turnover	=	$\dfrac{£4,000,000}{£1,000,000}$	= 4

The companies have the same ROCE, but it is arrived at in a very different fashion. Company A operates with a low asset turnover and a comparatively high profit margin whereas company B carries out much more business, but on a lower profit margin. Company A could be operating at the luxury end of the market, whilst company B is operating at the popular end of the market.

2.4 Gross profit margin, net profit margin and profit analysis

Depending on the format of the profit and loss account, you may be able to calculate the gross profit margin as well as the net profit margin. **Looking at the two together** can be quite informative.

For example, suppose that a company has the following summarised profit and loss account for two consecutive years.

	Year 1 £	Year 2 £
Turnover	70,000	100,000
Cost of sales	42,000	55,000
Gross profit	28,000	45,000
Expenses	21,000	35,000
Net profit	7,000	10,000

Although the net profit margin is the same for both years at 10%, the gross profit margin is not.

In year 1 it is: $\dfrac{£28,000}{£70,000}$ = 40%

and in year 2 it is: $\dfrac{£45,000}{£100,000}$ = 45%

The improved gross profit margin has not led to an improvement in the net profit margin. This is because expenses as a percentage of sales have risen from 30% in year 1 to 35% in year 2.

2.5 Historical vs current cost

In this chapter we are dealing with interpretation of financial statements based on historical cost accounts.

It is worth considering how the analysis would change if we were dealing with financial statements based on some form of current value accounting (which we will go on to look at in Chapter 22).

These are some of the issues that would arise:

- Fixed asset values would probably be stated at fair value. This may be higher than depreciated historical cost. Therefore capital employed would be higher. This would lead to a reduction in ROCE.

- Higher asset values would lead to a higher depreciation charge, which would reduce net profit.

- If opening stock were shown at current value, this would increase cost of sales and reduce net profit.

So you can see that ROCE based on historical cost accounts is probably overstated in real terms.

3 Liquidity, gearing and working capital

> **FAST FORWARD**
>
> Banks and other lenders will be interested in a company's gearing level.

3.1 Long-term solvency: debt and gearing ratios

Debt ratios are concerned with **how much the company owes in relation to its size**, whether it is getting into heavier debt or improving its situation, and whether its debt burden seems heavy or light.

(a) When a company is heavily in debt, banks and other potential lenders may be unwilling to advance further funds.

(b) When a company is earning only a modest profit before interest and tax, and has a heavy debt burden, there will be very little profit left over for shareholders after the interest charges have been paid. And so if interest rates were to go up (on bank overdrafts and so on) or the company were to borrow even more, it might soon be incurring interest charges in excess of PBIT. This might eventually lead to the liquidation of the company.

These are two big reasons why companies should keep their debt burden under control. There are four ratios that are particularly worth looking at, the debt ratio, gearing ratio, interest cover and cash flow ratio.

3.2 Debt ratio

Formula to learn

> The **debt ratio** is the ratio of a company's total debts to its total assets.

(a) Assets consist of fixed assets at their balance sheet value, plus current assets.
(b) Debts consist of all amounts due, whether they are due within one year or after more than one year.

You can ignore other long-term liabilities, such as deferred taxation.

There is no absolute guide to the maximum safe debt ratio, but as a very general guide, you might regard 50% as a safe limit to debt. In practice, many companies operate successfully with a higher debt ratio than this, but 50% is nonetheless a helpful benchmark. In addition, if the debt ratio is over 50% and getting worse, the company's debt position will be worth looking at more carefully.

In the case of Furlong the debt ratio is as follows.

	20X8	20X7
Total debts	£(881,731 + 100,000)	£(912,456 + 100,000)
Total assets	£1,870,630	£1,664,425
	= 52%	= 61%

In this case, the debt ratio is quite high, mainly because of the large amount of current liabilities. However, the debt ratio has fallen from 61% to 52% between 20X7 and 20X8, and so the company appears to be improving its debt position.

3.3 Gearing

Capital gearing is concerned with a company's **long-term capital structure**. We can think of a company as consisting of fixed assets and net current assets (ie working capital, which is current assets minus current liabilities). These assets must be financed by long-term capital of the company, which is one of two things.

(a) Issued share capital which can be divided into:

    (i) Ordinary shares plus other capital (eg reserves)
    (ii) Non-redeemable preference shares (unusual)

(b) Long-term debt including redeemable preference shares.

Preference share capital is normally classified as a long-term liability in accordance with FRS 25, and preference dividends (paid or accrued) are included in interest payable in the profit and loss account.

Non-redeemable preference shares can be classified as capital but would still be regarded as **prior charge capital**, because preference dividends have to be paid before payment of any ordinary dividend.

The **capital gearing ratio** is a measure of the proportion of a company's capital that is prior charge capital. It is measured as follows.

Formula to learn

$$\text{Capital gearing} = \frac{\text{Total prior charge capital}}{\text{Shareholders' equity} + \text{total prior charge capital}} \times 100\%$$

As with the debt ratio, there is **no absolute limit** to what a gearing ratio ought to be. A company with a gearing ratio of more than 50% is said to be high-geared (whereas low gearing means a gearing ratio of less than 50%). Many companies are high geared, but if a high geared company is becoming increasingly high geared, it is likely to have difficulty in the future when it wants to borrow even more, unless it can also boost its shareholders' capital, either with retained profits or by a new share issue.

Note that gearing can be looked at conversely, by calculating the proportion of total assets financed by equity, and which may be called the **equity to assets ratio**. It is calculated as follows.

Formula to learn

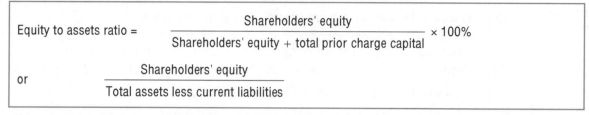

Equity to assets ratio = $\dfrac{\text{Shareholders' equity}}{\text{Shareholders' equity} + \text{total prior charge capital}} \times 100\%$

or $\dfrac{\text{Shareholders' equity}}{\text{Total assets less current liabilities}}$

In the example of Furlong, we find that the company, although having a high debt ratio because of its current liabilities, has a low gearing ratio. It has no preference share capital and its only long-term debt is the 10% debenture. The equity to assets ratio is therefore high.

		20X8	20X7
Gearing ratio	=	£100,000	£100,000
		£1,009,899	£768,769
		= 10%	= 13%
Equity to assets ratio	=	£909,899	£668,769
		£1,009,899	£768,769
		= 90%	= 87%

As you can see, the equity to assets ratio is the mirror image of gearing.

3.4 The implications of high or low gearing

We mentioned earlier that **gearing** is, amongst other things, an attempt to **quantify the degree of risk involved in holding equity shares in a company**, risk both in terms of the company's ability to remain in business and in terms of expected ordinary dividends from the company. The problem with a highly geared company is that by definition there is a lot of debt. Debt generally carries a fixed rate of interest (or fixed rate of dividend if in the form of preference shares), hence there is a given (and large) amount to be paid out from profits to holders of debt before arriving at a residue available for distribution to the holders of equity. The riskiness will perhaps become clearer with the aid of an example.

	Company A	Company B	Company C
	£'000	£'000	£'000
Ordinary shares	600	400	300
Profit and loss account	200	200	200
Revaluation reserve	100	100	100
	900	700	600
6% preference shares	-	-	100
10% debenture	100	300	300
Capital employed	1,000	1,000	1,000
Gearing ratio	10%	30%	40%
Equity to assets ratio	90%	70%	60%

Now suppose that each company makes a profit before interest and tax of £50,000, and the rate of tax on company profits is 30%. Amounts available for distribution to equity shareholders will be as follows.

	Company A £'000	Company B £'000	Company C £'000
Profit before interest and tax	50	50	50
Interest	10	30	30
Taxable profit	40	20	20
Taxation at 30%	12	6	6
Profit after tax	28	14	14
Preference dividend	–	–	6
Available for ordinary shareholders	28	14	8

If in the subsequent year profit before interest and tax falls to £40,000, the amounts available to ordinary shareholders will become as follows.

	Company A £'000	Company B £'000	Company C £'000
Profit before interest and tax	40	40	40
Interest	10	30	30
Taxable profit	30	10	10
Taxation at 30%	9	3	3
Profit after tax	21	7	7
Preference dividend	–	–	6
Available for ordinary shareholders	21	7	1

Note the following.

Gearing ratio	10%	30%	40%
Equity to assets ratio	90%	70%	60%
Change in PBIT	– 20%	– 20%	– 20%
Change in profit available for ordinary shareholders	– 25%	– 50%	– 87.5%

The more highly geared the company, the greater the risk that little (if anything) will be available to distribute by way of dividend to the ordinary shareholders. The example clearly displays this fact in so far as the more highly geared the company, the greater the percentage change in profit available for ordinary shareholders for any given percentage change in profit before interest and tax. The relationship similarly holds when profits increase, and if PBIT had risen by 20% rather than fallen, you would find that once again the largest percentage change in profit available for ordinary shareholders (this means an increase) will be for the highly geared company. This means that there will be greater *volatility* of amounts available for ordinary shareholders, and presumably therefore greater volatility in dividends paid to those shareholders, where a company is highly geared. That is the risk: you may do extremely well or extremely badly without a particularly large movement in the PBIT of the company.

The risk of a company's ability to remain in business was referred to earlier. Gearing or leverage is relevant to this. A highly geared company has a large amount of interest to pay annually (assuming that the debt is external borrowing rather than preference shares). If those borrowings are **'secured'** in any way (and debentures in particular are secured), then the **holders of the debt are perfectly entitled to force the company** to **realise assets to pay their interest** if funds are not available from other sources. Clearly the more highly geared a company the more likely this is to occur when and if profits fall.

3.5 Interest cover

The interest cover ratio shows whether a company is earning enough profits before interest and tax to pay its interest costs comfortably, or whether its interest costs are high in relation to the size of its profits, so that a fall in PBIT would then have a significant effect on profits available for ordinary shareholders.

Formula to learn

$$\text{Interest cover} = \frac{\text{Profit before interest and tax}}{\text{Interest charges}}$$

An interest cover of 2 times or less would be low, and should really exceed 3 times before the company's interest costs are to be considered within acceptable limits.

Returning first to the example of Companies A, B and C, the interest cover was as follows.

		Company A	Company B	Company C
(a)	When PBIT was £50,000 =	£50,000	£50,000	£50,000
		£10,000	£30,000	£30,000
		5 times	1.67 times	1.67 times
(b)	When PBIT was £40,000 =	£40,000	£40,000	£40,000
		£10,000	£30,000	£30,000
		4 times	1.33 times	1.33 times

Both B and C have a low interest cover, which is a warning to ordinary shareholders that their profits are highly vulnerable, in percentage terms, to even small changes in PBIT.

Question

Interest cover

Returning to the example of Furlong in Paragraph 1.2, what is the company's interest cover?

Answer

Interest payments should be taken gross, from the note to the accounts, and not net of interest receipts as shown in the profit and loss account.

	20X8	20X7
PBIT	360,245	247,011
Interest payable	18,115	21,909
	= 20 times	= 11 times

Furlong has more than sufficient interest cover. In view of the company's low gearing, this is not too surprising and so we finally obtain a picture of Furlong as a company that does not seem to have a debt problem, in spite of its high (although declining) debt ratio.

3.6 Cash flow ratio

The cash flow ratio is the ratio of a company's **net cash inflow to its total debts**.

(a) **Net cash inflow** is the amount of cash which the company has coming into the business from its operations. A suitable figure for net cash inflow can be obtained from the cash flow statement.

(b) **Total debts** are short-term and long-term debts, including provisions. A distinction can be made between debts payable within one year and other debts and provisions.

Obviously, a company needs to be earning enough cash from operations to be able to meet its foreseeable debts and future commitments, and the cash flow ratio, and changes in the cash flow ratio from one year to the next, provide a **useful indicator of a company's cash position**.

3.7 Short-term solvency and liquidity

Profitability is of course an important aspect of a company's performance and gearing or leverage is another. Neither, however, addresses directly the key issue of *liquidity*.

Key term

> **Liquidity** is the amount of cash a company can put its hands on quickly to settle its debts (and possibly to meet other unforeseen demands for cash payments too).

Liquid funds consist of:

(a)   Cash

(b)   Short-term investments for which there is a ready market

(c)   Fixed-term deposits with a bank or other financial institution, for example, a six month high-interest deposit with a bank

(d)   Trade debtors (because they will pay what they owe within a reasonably short period of time)

(e)   Bills of exchange receivable (because like ordinary trade debts, these represent amounts of cash due to be received within a relatively short period of time)

In summary, **liquid assets are current asset items that will or could soon be converted into cash, and cash itself.** Two common definitions of liquid assets are:

(a)   All current assets without exception
(b)   All current assets with the exception of stocks

A company can obtain liquid assets from sources other than sales of goods and services, such as the issue of shares for cash, a new loan or the sale of fixed assets. But a company cannot rely on these at all times, and in general, obtaining liquid funds depends on turnover and profits. Even so, profits do not always lead to increases in liquidity. This is mainly because funds generated from trading may be immediately invested in fixed assets or paid out as dividends.

The reason why a company needs liquid assets is so that it can meet its debts when they fall due. Payments are continually made for operating expenses and other costs, and so there is a **cash cycle** from trading activities of cash coming in from sales and cash going out for expenses.

3.8 The cash cycle

To help you to understand liquidity ratios, it is useful to begin with a brief explanation of the cash cycle. The cash cycle describes **the flow of cash out of a business and back into it again as a result of normal trading operations.**

Cash goes out to pay for supplies, wages and salaries and other expenses, although payments can be delayed by taking some credit. A business might hold stock for a while and then sell it. Cash will come back into the business from the sales, although customers might delay payment by themselves taking some credit.

The main points about the cash cycle are as follows.

(a)   The timing of cash flows in and out of a business does not coincide with the time when sales and costs of sales occur. **Cash flows out can be postponed by taking credit. Cash flows in can be delayed by having debtors.**

(b)   **The time between making a purchase and making a sale also affects cash flows**. If stocks are held for a long time, the delay between the cash payment for stock and cash receipts from selling it will also be a long one.

(c) **Holding stocks and having debtors can therefore be seen as two reasons why cash receipts are delayed.** Another way of saying this is that if a company invests in working capital, its cash position will show a corresponding decrease.

(d) Similarly, **taking credit from creditors can be seen as a reason why cash payments are delayed**. The company's liquidity position will worsen when it has to pay creditors, unless it can get more cash in from sales and debtors in the meantime.

The liquidity ratios and working capital turnover ratios are used to test a company's liquidity, length of cash cycle, and investment in working capital.

3.9 Liquidity ratios: current ratio and quick ratio

The 'standard' test of liquidity is the **current ratio**. It can be obtained from the balance sheet.

Formula to learn

$$\text{Current ratio} = \frac{\text{Current assets}}{\text{Current liabilities}}$$

The idea behind this is that a company should have enough current assets that give a promise of 'cash to come' to meet its future commitments to pay off its current liabilities. Obviously, a **ratio in excess of 1 should be expected**. Otherwise, there would be the prospect that the company might be unable to pay its debts on time. In practice, a ratio comfortably in excess of 1 should be expected, but what is 'comfortable' varies between different types of businesses.

Companies are not able to convert all their current assets into cash very quickly. In particular, some manufacturing companies might hold large quantities of raw material stocks, which must be used in production to create finished goods stock. These might be warehoused for a long time, or sold on lengthy credit. In such businesses, where stock turnover is slow, most stocks are not very 'liquid' assets, because the cash cycle is so long. For these reasons, we calculate an additional liquidity ratio, known as the quick ratio or acid test ratio.

The **quick ratio**, or **acid test ratio**, is calculated as follows.

Formula to learn

$$\text{Quick ratio} = \frac{\text{Current assets less stock}}{\text{Current liabilities}}$$

This ratio should ideally be **at least 1** for companies with a slow stock turnover. For companies with a fast stock turnover, a quick ratio can be comfortably less than 1 without suggesting that the company could be in cash flow trouble.

Both the current ratio and the quick ratio offer an indication of the company's liquidity position, but the absolute figures **should not be interpreted too literally**. It is often theorised that an acceptable current ratio is 1.5 and an acceptable quick ratio is 0.8, but these should only be used as a guide. Different businesses operate in very different ways. A supermarket group for example might have a current ratio of 0.52 and a quick ratio of 0.17. Supermarkets have low debtors (people do not buy groceries on credit), low cash (good cash management), medium stocks (high stocks but quick turnover, particularly in view of perishability) and very high creditors.

Compare this with a manufacturing and retail organisation, with a current ratio of 1.44 and a quick ratio of 1.03. Such businesses operate with liquidity ratios closer to the standard.

What is important is the **trend** of these ratios. From this, one can easily ascertain whether liquidity is improving or deteriorating. If a supermarket has traded for the last 10 years (very successfully) with current ratios of 0.52 and quick ratios of 0.17 then it should be supposed that the company can continue in business with those levels of liquidity. If in the following year the current ratio were to fall to 0.38 and the quick ratio to 0.09, then further investigation into the liquidity situation would be appropriate. It is the relative position that is far more important than the absolute figures.

Don't forget the other side of the coin either. A current ratio and a quick ratio can get **bigger than they need to be**. A company that has large volumes of stocks and debtors might be over-investing in working capital, and so tying up more funds in the business than it needs to. This would suggest poor management of debtors (credit) or stocks by the company.

3.10 Efficiency ratios: control of debtors and stock

A rough measure of the average length of time it takes for a company's customers to pay what they owe is the debtors collection period.

Formula to learn

The estimated average debtors collection period is calculated as:

$$\frac{\text{Trade debtors}}{\text{Turnover}} \times 365 \text{ days}$$

The figure for turnover should be taken as the turnover figure in the profit and loss account. The trade debtors are not the total figure for debtors in the balance sheet, which includes prepayments and non-trade debtors. The trade debtors figure will be itemised in an analysis of the total debtors, in a note to the accounts.

The estimate of the debtors collection period is **only approximate**.

(a) The balance sheet value of debtors might be abnormally high or low compared with the 'normal' level the company usually has.

(b) Turnover in the profit and loss account is exclusive of sales taxes, but debtors in the balance sheet are inclusive of sales tax. We are not strictly comparing like with like.

Sales are usually made on 'normal credit terms' of payment within 30 days. A collection period significantly in excess of this might be representative of poor management of funds of a business. However, some companies must allow generous credit terms to win customers. Exporting companies in particular may have to carry large amounts of debtors, and so their average collection period might be well in excess of 30 days.

The **trend of the collection period over time** is probably the best guide. If the collection period is increasing year on year, this is indicative of a poorly managed credit control function (and potentially therefore a poorly managed company).

3.11 Debtors collection period: examples

Using the same types of company as examples, the collection period for each of the companies was as follows.

Company	$\dfrac{\text{Trade debtors}}{\text{Sales}}$	Collection period ($\times$ 365)	Previous year	Collection period ($\times$ 365)
Supermarket	$\dfrac{\text{£5,016K}}{\text{£284,986K}} =$	6.4 days	$\dfrac{\text{£3,977K}}{\text{£290,668K}} =$	5.0 days
Manufacturer	$\dfrac{\text{£458.3m}}{\text{£2,059.5m}} =$	81.2 days	$\dfrac{\text{£272.4m}}{\text{£1,274.2m}} =$	78.0 days
Sugar refiner and seller	$\dfrac{\text{£304.4m}}{\text{£3,817.3m}} =$	29.3 days	$\dfrac{\text{£287.0m}}{\text{£3,366.3m}} =$	31.1 days

The differences in collection period reflect the differences between the types of business. Supermarkets have hardly any trade debtors at all, whereas the manufacturing companies have far more. The collection periods are fairly constant from the previous year for all three companies.

3.12 Stock turnover period

Another ratio worth calculating is the stock turnover period. This is another estimated figure, obtainable from published accounts, which indicates the average number of days that items of stock are held for. As with the average debtors collection period, however, it is only an approximate estimated figure, but one which should be reliable enough for comparing changes year on year.

Formula to learn

The stock turnover period is calculated as:

$$\frac{\text{Stock}}{\text{Cost of sales}} \times 365 \text{ days}$$

This is another measure of how vigorously a business is trading. A lengthening stock turnover period from one year to the next indicates:

(a)   a slowdown in trading; or

(b)   a build-up in stock levels, perhaps suggesting that the investment in stocks is becoming excessive.

Generally the **higher the stock turnover the better**, ie the lower the turnover **period** the better, but several aspects of stock holding policy have to be balanced.

(a)   Lead times

(b)   Seasonal fluctuations in orders

(c)   Alternative uses of warehouse space

(d)   Bulk buying discounts

(e)   Likelihood of stock perishing or becoming obsolete

Presumably if we add together the stock turnover period and debtors collection period, this should give us an indication of how soon stock is converted into cash. Both debtors collection period and stock turnover period therefore give us a further indication of the company's liquidity.

3.13 Stock turnover period: example

The estimated stock turnover periods for a supermarket are as follows.

Company	$\dfrac{\text{Stock}}{\text{Cost of sales}}$	Stock turnover period (days× 365)		Previous year		
Supermarket	$\dfrac{\text{£15,554K}}{\text{£254,571K}}$	22.3 days	$\dfrac{\text{£14,094K}}{\text{£261,368K}}$	×	365	= 19.7 days

3.14 Creditors payment period

Formula to learn

Creditors payment period is ideally calculated by the formula:

$$\frac{\text{Trade creditors}}{\text{Purchases}} \times 365 \text{ days}$$

It is rare to find purchases disclosed in published accounts and so **cost of sales serves as an approximation**. The payment period often helps to assess a company's liquidity; an increase is often a sign of lack of long-term finance or poor management of current assets, resulting in the use of extended credit from suppliers, increased bank overdraft and so on.

Question

Calculate liquidity and working capital ratios from the accounts of TEB Ltd, a business which provides service support (cleaning etc) to customers worldwide. Comment on the results of your calculations.

	20X7 £m	20X6 £m
Turnover	2,176.2	2,344.8
Cost of sales	1,659.0	1,731.5
Gross profit	517.2	613.3
Current assets		
Stocks	42.7	78.0
Debtors (note 1)	378.9	431.4
Short-term deposits and cash	205.2	145.0
	626.8	654.4
Current liabilities		
Loans and overdrafts	32.4	81.1
Tax on profits	67.8	76.7
Accruals	11.7	17.2
Creditors (note 2)	487.2	467.2
	599.1	642.2
Net current assets	27.7	12.2
Notes		
1 Trade debtors	295.2	335.5
2 Trade creditors	190.8	188.1

Answer

	20X7	20X6
Current ratio	$\dfrac{626.8}{599.1} = 1.05$	$\dfrac{654.4}{642.2} = 1.02$
Quick ratio	$\dfrac{584.1}{599.1} = 0.97$	$\dfrac{576.4}{642.2} = 0.90$
Debtors collection period	$\dfrac{295.2}{2,176.2} \times 365 = 49.5 \text{ days}$	$\dfrac{335.5}{2,344.8} \times 365 = 52.2 \text{ days}$
Stock turnover period	$\dfrac{42.7}{1,659.0} \times 365 = 9.4 \text{ days}$	$\dfrac{78.0}{1,731.5} \times 365 = 16.4 \text{ days}$
Creditors payment period	$\dfrac{190.8}{1,659.0} \times 365 = 42.0 \text{ days}$	$\dfrac{188.1}{1,731.5} \times 365 = 40.0 \text{ days}$

The company's current ratio is a little lower than average but its quick ratio is better than average and very little less than the current ratio. This suggests that stock levels are strictly controlled, which is reinforced by the low stock turnover period. It would seem that working capital is tightly managed, to avoid the poor liquidity which could be caused by a long debtors collection period and comparatively high creditors.

The company in the exercise is a service company and hence it would be expected to have very low stock and a very short stock turnover period. The similarity of debtors collection period and creditors payment period means that the company is passing on most of the delay in receiving payment to its suppliers.

Question

(a)   Calculate the operating cycle for Moribund plc for 20X2 on the basis of the following information.

	£
Stock: raw materials	150,000
work in progress	60,000
finished goods	200,000
Purchases	500,000
Trade debtors	230,000
Trade creditors	120,000
Sales	900,000
Cost of goods sold	750,000

Tutorial note. You will need to calculate stock turnover periods (total year end stock over cost of goods sold), debtors as daily sales, and creditors in relation to purchases, all converted into 'days'.

(b)   List the steps which might be taken in order to improve the operating cycle.

Answer

(a)   The operating cycle can be found as follows.

Stock turnover period: $\dfrac{\text{Total closing stock} \times 365}{\text{Cost of goods sold}}$

plus

Debtors collection period: $\dfrac{\text{Closing trade debtors} \times 365}{\text{Sales}}$

less

Creditors payment period: $\dfrac{\text{Closing trade creditors} \times 365}{\text{Purchases}}$

	20X2
Total closing stock (£)	410,000
Cost of goods sold (£)	750,000
Stock turnover period	199.5 days
Closing debtors (£)	230,000
Sales (£)	900,000
Debtors collection period	93.3 days
Closing creditors (£)	120,000
Purchases (£)	500,000
Creditors payment period	(87.6 days)
Length of operating cycle (199.5 + 93.3 − 87.6)	205.2 days

(b)   The steps that could be taken to reduce the operating cycle include the following.

(i)   Reducing the raw material stock turnover period.

(ii)   Reducing the time taken to produce goods. However, the company must ensure that quality is not sacrificed as a result of speeding up the production process.

(iii)   Increasing the period of credit taken from suppliers. The credit period already seems very long – the company is allowed three months credit by its suppliers, and probably could not be increased. If the credit period is extended then the company may lose discounts for prompt payment.

(iv)   Reducing the finished goods stock turnover period.

(v)   Reducing the debtors collection period. The administrative costs of speeding up debt collection and the effect on sales of reducing the credit period allowed must be evaluated. However, the credit period does already seem very long by the standards of most industries. It may be that generous terms have been allowed to secure large contracts and little will be able to be done about this in the short term.

4 Shareholders' investment ratios

These are the ratios which help equity shareholders and other investors to **assess the value and quality of an investment in the ordinary shares of a company.**

They are:

(a)   Earnings per share
(b)   Dividend per share
(c)   Dividend cover
(d)   P/E ratio
(e)   Dividend yield

The value of an investment in ordinary shares in a company **listed on a stock exchange** is its market value, and so investment ratios must have regard not only to information in the company's published accounts, but also to the current price, and ratios (d) and (e) involve using the share price.

4.1 Earnings per share

It is possible to calculate the return on each ordinary share in the year. This is the earnings per share (EPS). Earnings per share is the amount of net profit for the period that is attributable to each ordinary share which is outstanding during all or part of the period (see Chapter 18).

4.2 Dividend per share and dividend cover

The **dividend per share** in pence is self-explanatory, and clearly an item of some interest to shareholders.

Formula to learn

Dividend cover is a ratio of: $\dfrac{\text{Earnings per share}}{\text{Dividend per (ordinary) share}}$

It shows the **proportion of profit for the year that is available for distribution to shareholders that has been paid (or proposed) and what proportion will be retained in the business to finance future growth.** A dividend cover of 2 times would indicate that the company had paid 50% of its distributable profits as dividends, and retained 50% in the business to help to finance future operations. Retained profits are an important source of funds for most companies, and so the dividend cover can in some cases be quite high.

A **significant change** in the dividend cover from one year to the next would be worth looking at closely. For example, if a company's dividend cover were to fall sharply between one year and the next, it could be that its profits had fallen, but the directors wished to pay at least the same amount of dividends as in the previous year, so as to keep shareholder expectations satisfied.

4.3 P/E ratio

Formula to learn

> The **Price/Earnings (P/E) ratio** is the ratio of a company's current share price to the earnings per share.

A high P/E ratio indicates strong shareholder **confidence** in the company and its future, eg in profit growth, and a lower P/E ratio indicates lower confidence.

The P/E ratio of one company can be compared with the P/E ratios of:

(a)   Other companies in the same business sector
(b)   Other companies generally

It is often used in **stock exchange reporting** where prices are readily available.

4.4 Dividend yield

Dividend yield is the return a shareholder is currently expecting on the shares of a company.

Formula to learn

> $$\text{Dividend yield} = \frac{\text{Dividend on the share for the year}}{\text{Current market value of the share (ex div)}} \times 100\%$$

(a)   The dividend per share is taken as the dividend for the previous year.
(b)   Ex-div means that the share price does *not* include the right to the most recent dividend.

Shareholders look for **both dividend yield and capital growth**. Obviously, dividend yield is therefore an important aspect of a share's performance.

Question
Dividend yield

In the year to 30 September 20X8, an advertising agency declares an interim ordinary dividend of 7.4p per share and a final ordinary dividend of 8.6p per share. Assuming an ex div share price of 315 pence, what is the dividend yield?

Answer

The total dividend per share is (7.4 + 8.6) = 16 pence

$$\frac{16}{315} \times 100 = 5.1\%$$

5 Presentation of financial performance

Exam focus point

> Examination questions on financial performance may try to simulate a real life situation. A set of accounts could be presented and you may be asked to prepare a report on them, addressed to a specific interested party, such as a bank.

You should begin your report with a heading showing who it is from, the name of the addressee, the subject of the report and a suitable date.

A good approach is often to head up a **'schedule of ratios and statistics'** which will form an appendix to the main report. Calculate the ratios in a logical sequence, dealing in turn with operating and profitability ratios, use of assets (eg turnover period for stocks, collection period for debtors), liquidity and gearing/leverage.

As you calculate the ratios you are likely to be struck by **significant fluctuations and trends**. These will form the basis of your comments in the body of the report. The report should begin with some introductory comments, setting out the scope of your analysis and mentioning that detailed figures have been included in an appendix. You should then go on to present your analysis under any categories called for by the question (eg separate sections for management, shareholders and creditors, or separate sections for profitability and liquidity).

Finally, look out for opportunities to **suggest remedial action** where trends appear to be unfavourable. Questions sometimes require you specifically to set out your advice and recommendations.

5.1 Planning your answers

This is as good a place as any to stress the importance of planning your answers. This is particularly important for 'wordy' questions. While you may feel like breathing a sigh of relief after all that number crunching, you should not be tempted to 'waffle'. The best way to avoid going off the point is to **prepare an answer plan**. This has the advantage of making you think before you write and structure your answer logically.

The following approach may be adopted when preparing an answer plan.

(a)   Read the question **requirements**.

(b)   **Skim through the question** to see roughly what it is about.

(c)   Read through the question carefully, **underlining any key words**.

(d)   Set out the **headings** for the main parts of your answer. Leave space to insert points within the headings.

(e)   **Jot down points** to make within the main sections, underlining points on which you wish to expand.

(f)   Write your **full answer**.

You should allow yourself the full time allocation for written answers, that is 1.8 minutes per mark. If, however, you run out of time, a clear answer plan with points in note form will earn you more marks than an introductory paragraph written out in full.

Question   Ratios

The following information has been extracted from the recently published accounts of DG.

EXTRACTS FROM THE PROFIT AND LOSS ACCOUNTS TO 30 APRIL

	20X9	20X8
	£'000	£'000
Turnover	11,200	9,750
Cost of sales	8,460	6,825
Net profit before tax	465	320
This is after charging:		
Depreciation	360	280
Debenture interest	80	60
Interest on bank overdraft	15	9
Audit fees	12	10

BALANCE SHEETS AS AT 30 APRIL

	20X9		20X8	
	£'000	£'000	£'000	£'000
Assets				
Fixed assets		1,850		1,430
Current assets				
Stock	640		490	
Debtors	1,230		1,080	
Cash	80		120	
	1,950		1,690	
Current liabilities				
Bank overdraft	110		80	
Creditors	750		690	
Taxation	30		20	
	890		790	
Net current assets		1,060		900
Total assets less current liabilities		2,910		2,330
Long-term liabilities				
10% debentures		800		600
		2,110		1,730
Share capital and reserves				
Ordinary £ shares		800		800
Profit and loss account		1,310		930
		2,110		1,730

The following ratios are those calculated for DG, based on its published accounts for the previous year, and also the latest industry average ratios:

	DG 30 April 20X8	Industry average
ROCE (capital employed = equity and debentures)	16.70%	18.50%
Profit/sales	3.90%	4.73%
Asset turnover	4.29	3.91
Current ratio	2.00	1.90
Quick ratio	1.42	1.27
Gross profit margin	30.00%	35.23%
Debtors collection period	40 days	52 days
Creditors payment period	37 days	49 days
Stock turnover (times)	13.90	18.30
Gearing	26.37%	32.71%

Required

(a)   Calculate comparable ratios (to two decimal places where appropriate) for DG for the year ended 30 April 20X9. All calculations must be clearly shown.

(b)   Write a report to your board of directors analysing the performance of DG, comparing the results against the previous year and against the industry average.

Answer

(a)

	20X8	20X9	Industry average
ROCE	$\dfrac{320+60}{2,330}=16.30\%$	$\dfrac{465+80}{2,910}=18.72\%$	18.50%
Profit/sales	$\dfrac{320+60}{9,750}=3.90\%$	$\dfrac{465+80}{11,200}=4.87\%$	4.73%
Asset turnover	$\dfrac{9,750}{2,330}=4.18x$	$\dfrac{11,200}{2,910}=3.85x$	3.91x
Current ratio	$\dfrac{1,690}{790}=2.10$	$\dfrac{1,950}{890}=2.20$	1.90
Quick ratio	$\dfrac{1,080+120}{790}=1.52$	$\dfrac{1,230+80}{890}=1.47$	1.27
Gross profit margin	$\dfrac{9,750-6,825}{9,750}=30.00\%$	$\dfrac{11,200-8,460}{11,200}=24.46\%$	35.23%
Debtors collection period	$\dfrac{1,080}{9,750}\times 365=40\text{days}$	$\dfrac{1,230}{11,200}\times 365=40\text{days}$	52 days
Creditors payment period	$\dfrac{690}{6,825}\times 365=37\text{days}$	$\dfrac{750}{8,460}\times 365=32\text{days}$	49 days
Stock turnover (times)	$\dfrac{6,825}{490}=13.9x$	$\dfrac{8,460}{640}=13.2x$	18.30x
Gearing	$\dfrac{600}{2,330}=25.75\%$	$\dfrac{800}{2,910}=27.5\%$	32.71%

(b) (i) REPORT

To: Board of Directors
From: Accountant   Date: xx/xx/xx
Subject: Analysis of performance of DG

This report should be read in conjunction with the appendix attached which shows the relevant ratios (from part (a)).

Trading and profitability

Return on capital employed has improved considerably between 20X8 and 20X9 and is now higher than the industry average.

Net income as a proportion of sales has also improved noticeably between the years and is also now marginally ahead of the industry average. Gross margin, however, is considerably lower than in the previous year and is only some 70% of the industry average. This suggests either that there has been a change in the cost structure of DG or that there has been a change in the method of cost allocation between the periods. Either way, this is a marked change that requires investigation. The company may be in a period of transition as sales have increased by nearly 15% over the year and it would appear that new fixed assets have been purchased.

Asset turnover has declined between the periods although the 20X9 figure is in line with the industry average. This reduction might indicate that the efficiency with which assets are used has deteriorated or it might indicate that the assets acquired in 20X9 have not yet fully contributed to the business. A longer term trend would clarify the picture.

(ii)   Liquidity and working capital management

The current ratio has improved slightly over the year and is marginally higher than the industry average. It is also in line with what is generally regarded as satisfactory (2:1).

The quick ratio has declined marginally but is still better than the industry average. This suggests that DG has no short term liquidity problems and should have no difficulty in paying its debts as they become due.

Debtors as a proportion of sales is unchanged from 20X8 and are considerably lower than the industry average. Consequently, there is probably little opportunity to reduce this further and there may be pressure in the future from customers to increase the period of credit given. The period of credit taken from suppliers has fallen from 37 days' purchases to 32 days' and is much lower than the industry average; thus, it may be possible to finance any additional debtors by negotiating better credit terms from suppliers.

Stock turnover has fallen slightly and is much slower than the industry average and this may partly reflect stocking up ahead of a significant increase in sales. Alternatively, there is some danger that the stock could contain certain obsolete items that may require writing off. The relative increase in the level of stock has been financed by an increased overdraft which may reduce if the stock levels can be brought down.

The high levels of stock, overdraft and debtors compared to that of creditors suggests a labour intensive company or one where considerable value is added to bought-in products.

(iii)   Gearing

The level of gearing has increased only slightly over the year and is below the industry average. Since the return on capital employed is nearly twice the rate of interest on the debenture, profitability is likely to be increased by a modest increase in the level of gearing.

Signed: Accountant

Chapter roundup

- This lengthy chapter has gone into quite a lot of detail about basic ratio analysis. The ratios you should be able to calculate and/or comment on are as follows.

  - **Profitability ratios**

    - Return on capital employed
    - Net profit as a percentage of sales
    - Asset turnover ratio
    - Gross profit as a percentage of sales

  - **Debt and gearing ratios**

    - Debt ratio
    - Gearing ratio
    - Interest cover
    - Cash flow ratio

  - **Liquidity and working capital ratios**

    - Current ratio
    - Quick ratio (acid test ratio)
    - Debtors collection period
    - Creditors payment period
    - Stock turnover period

  - **Ordinary shareholders' investment ratios**

    - Earnings per share
    - Dividend cover
    - P/E ratio
    - Dividend yield

- With the exception of the last two ratios, where the share's market price is required, all of these ratios **can be calculated from information in a company's published accounts.**

- Ratios provide information through **comparison**.

  - **Trends** in a company's ratios from **one year to the next**, indicating an improving or worsening position.

  - In some cases, **against a 'norm' or 'standard'**.

  - In some cases, **against the ratios of other companies**, although differences between one company and another should often be expected.

- You must realise that, however many ratios you can find to calculate, **numbers alone will not answer a question**. You *must* interpret all the information available to you and support your interpretation with ratio calculations.

Quick quiz

1   List the main categories of ratio.

2   ROCE is $\dfrac{\text{Profit before interest and tax}}{\text{Capital employed}} \times 100\%$

True ☐

False ☐

3   Company Q has a profit margin of 7%. Briefly comment on this.

4   The debt ratio is a company's long-term debt divided by its net assets.

True ☐

False ☐

5   The cash flow ratio is the ratio of:

A   Gross cash inflow to total debt
B   Gross cash inflow to net debt
C   Net cash inflow to total debt
D   Net cash inflow to net debt

6   List the formulae for:

(a)   Current ratio   (c)   Debtors collection period
(b)   Quick ratio   (d)   Stock turnover period

Answers to quick quiz

1   See Section 1.1.

2   True

3   You should be careful here. You have very little information. This is a low margin but you need to know what industry the company operates in. 7% may be good for a major retailer.

4   False (see Section 3.2)

5   C (see Section 3.6)

6   See Sections 3.9, 3.10 and 3.12.

Now try the questions below from the Exam Question Bank

Number	Level	Marks	Time
25	Examination	25	45 mins

Limitations of financial statements and interpretation techniques

Topic list	Syllabus reference
1 Limitations of financial statements	E1
2 Accounting policies and the limitations of ratio analysis	E3

Introduction

In the last chapter we looked at how we interpret financial statements. In this chapter we take a look at how far we can rely on such interpretation.

Study guide

		Intellectual level
E	**ANALYSING AND INTERPRETING FINANCIAL STATEMENTS**	
1	**Limitations of financial statements**	
(a)	Indicate the problems of using historic information to predict future performance and trends.	2
(b)	Discuss how financial statements may be manipulated to produce a desired effect (creative accounting, window dressing)	2
(c)	Recognise how related party relationships have the potential to mislead users.	2
(d)	Explain why balance sheet figures may not be representative of average values throughout the period for example, due to:	2
	(i) Seasonal trading	
	(ii) Major asset acquisitions near the end of the accounting period.	
3	**Limitations of interpretation techniques**	
(a)	Discuss the limitations in the use of ratio analysis for assessing corporate performance.	2
(b)	Discuss the effect that changes in accounting policies or the use of different accounting policies between entities can have on the ability to interpret performance.	2
(c)	Indicate other information, including non-financial information, that may be of relevance to the assessment of an entity's performance.	1

Exam guide

These issues are unlikely to form a whole question but could well appear in a question on interpretation of accounts.

1 Limitations of financial statements

FAST FORWARD

Financial statements are affected by the obvious shortcomings of historic cost information and are also subject to manipulation.

Financial statements are intended to give a fair presentation of the financial performance of an entity over a period and its financial position at the end of that period. The ASB *Statement of Principles* and the SSAPs/FRSs are there to ensure as far as possible that they do. However, there are a number of reasons why the information in financial statements should not just be taken at its face value.

1.1 Problems of historic cost information

Historic cost information is reliable and can be verified, but it becomes less relevant as time goes by. The value shown for assets carried in the balance sheet at historic cost may bear no relation whatever to what their current value is and what it may cost to replace them. The corresponding depreciation charge will also be low, leading to the overstatement of profits in real terms. The financial statements do not show the real cost of using such assets.

This is particularly misleading when attempting to predict future performance. It could be that a major asset will need to be replaced in two years time, at vastly more than the original cost of the asset currently shown in the balance sheet. This will then entail much higher depreciation and interest payments (if a loan or finance lease is used). In addition, overstatement of profit due to the low depreciation charge can have led to too much profit having been distributed, increasing the likelihood of new asset purchases having to be financed by loans. This information could not have been obtained just from looking at the financial statements.

In a period of inflation, financial statements based on historic cost are subject to an additional distortion. Turnover will be keeping pace with inflation and so will the cost of purchases. However, using FIFO (and to some degree the weighted average method) stock being used will be valued as the earliest (and therefore cheapest) purchases. This leads to understatement of cost of sales and overstatement of profits. This is the result of stock carried at historic cost.

1.2 Creative accounting

Listed companies produce their financial statements with one eye on the stock market and, where possible, they like to produce financial statements which show analysts what they are expecting to see. For instance, a steady rise in profits, with no peaks or troughs, is reassuring to potential investors. Companies could sometimes achieve this by using provisions to smooth out the peaks and troughs. This has been largely outlawed by FRS 12 (see Chapter 12), but companies can still achieve similar effects by delaying or advancing invoicing or manipulating cut-offs or accruals. Directors who are paid performance bonuses will favour the steady rise (enough to secure the bonus each year, rather than up one year, down the next) while those who hold share options may be aiming for one spectacular set of results just before they sell.

An important aspect of improving the appearance of the balance sheet is keeping gearing as low as possible. Investors know that interest payments reduce the amount available for distribution and potential lenders will be less willing to lend to a company which is already highly geared.

A number of creative accounting measures are aimed at reducing gearing. In the past parent companies could find reasons to exclude highly-geared subsidiaries from the consolidation and could obtain loans in the first place via such 'quasi subsidiaries', so that the loan never appeared in the consolidated balance sheet. This loophole has been effectively closed by FRS 2, but other means of keeping debt off the balance sheet exist. Finance leases can be treated as operating leases, so that the asset and the loan are kept off-balance sheet. Assets can be 'sold' under a sale and leaseback agreement, which is in effect a disguised loan. And if all else fails, a last minute piece of 'window dressing' can be undertaken. For instance, a loan can be repaid just before the year end and taken out again at the beginning of the next year.

1.3 The effect of related parties

The objective of FRS 8 is to ensure that an entity's financial statements contain the disclosures necessary to draw attention to the possibility that its financial position and profit or loss may have been affected by the existence of related parties and by transactions and outstanding balances with such parties.

Related parties are a normal feature of business. It is common for entities to carry on activities with or through subsidiaries and associates, or occasionally to engage in transactions with directors or their families. The point is that such transactions cannot be assumed to have been engaged in 'at arm's length' or in the best interests of the entity itself, which is why investors and potential investors need to be made aware of them. Transfer pricing can be used to transfer profit from one company to another and intercompany loans and transfers of fixed assets can also be used in the same way.

Despite FRS 8, companies which wish to disguise a related party relationship can probably still find complex ways to do it (the Enron scandal revealed the existence of numerous related party transactions) and financial statements do not show the unseen effects of such a relationship. For instance, a subsidiary may not have been allowed to tender for a contract in competition with another group company. Its shareholders will never know about such missed opportunities.

1.4 Seasonal trading

This is another issue that can distort reported results. Many companies whose trade is seasonal position their year end after their busy period, to minimise time spent on the stock count. At this point in time, the balance sheet will show a healthy level of cash and/or debtors and a low level of trade creditors, assuming most of them have been paid. Thus the position is reported at the moment when the company is at its most solvent. A balance sheet drawn up a few months earlier, or even perhaps a few months later, when trade is still slack but fixed costs still have to be paid, may give a very different picture.

1.5 Asset acquisitions

Major asset acquisitions just before the end of an accounting period can also distort results. The balance sheet will show an increased level of assets and corresponding liabilities (probably a loan or lease creditor), but the income which will be earned from utilisation of the asset will not yet have materialised. This will adversely affect the company's return on capital employed.

1.6 Events after the balance sheet date

FRS 21 defines events after the balance sheet date as: 'those events, favourable and unfavourable, that occur between the balance sheet date and the date when the financial statements are authorised for issue.'

What has to be considered is whether such events provide evidence of conditions that existed at the balance sheet date (adjusting events) or are indicative of conditions that arose **after** the balance sheet date (non-adjusting events).

Adjusting events require the financial statements to be amended. **Non-adjusting** events are simply disclosed by note.

Adjusting events include:

- Debtors going bankrupt after the balance sheet date
- Changes made to stock valuation
- Outcome of legal cases provided for at the year end

Non-adjusting events can also be very significant as far as users of the financial statements are concerned. If one of the factories was destroyed by fire after the balance sheet date, this is a non-adjusting event, but it has a material effect on the company's position.

2 Accounting policies and the limitations of ratio analysis

FAST FORWARD

Ratios provide information **through comparison**:

- trends in a company's ratios **from one year to the next**
- in some cases, against an industry norm or standard
- comparison with the ratios of other companies in the same industry

But note that the use of different **accounting policies** may distort comparisons between companies.

The choice of accounting policy and the effect of its implementation are almost as important as its disclosure. This is because the results of a company can be altered significantly by the choice of accounting policy.

BPP
LEARNING MEDIA

2.1 The impact of choice of accounting policies

Where accounting standards allow alternative treatment of items in the accounts, then the accounting policy note should declare which policy has been chosen. It should then be applied consistently.

The problem of comparability arises where companies with similar business adopt different policies. In recent years, financial reporting standard have restricted the selection of accounting treatments. However, there are a few areas where preparers are allowed significant choice.

2.2 Development expenditure

Although the criteria for capitalising development expenditure are very strict, the **choice** of whether to **capitalise and amortise or write off such costs** can have a significant impact on profit.

The **capitalisation** of development costs has **various impacts** on the figures used for analysing accounts.

(a) The capitalised development cost will be **amortised annually** and will **hit earnings**, including EPS, **until fully written off**.

(b) The capitalised development costs are included as part of **capital employed** and hence **ROCE will fall**.

(c) The **gearing ratio** will be **reduced** whilst any of the **capitalised development costs** are still **carried in the balance sheet**.

2.3 Capitalisation of finance costs

FRS 15 allows the capitalisation of finance costs that are **directly attributable** to the **construction** of tangible fixed assets. An entity **need not capitalise** finance costs. However, if an entity adopts a **policy of capitalisation** of finance costs, then it should be **applied consistently** to all tangible fixed assets where finance cost fall to be capitalised.

The impacts of capitalising finance costs in relation to tangible fixed assets on the calculation of accounting ratios is **similar** to those outlined above for **capitalised development costs**.

Remember that capitalisation of interest does not impact on interest cover because an appropriate adjustment must be made to include capitalised interest in the interest cover calculation.

2.4 Leases and the ninety per cent test

Companies might use the 90% test in such a way that ensures that leases are classified as **operating leases** and thereby kept **off the balance sheet**. This would entail **various impacts** on the accounting ratios.

(a) The **profit and loss account** would show a **lease charge instead of finance charges and depreciation**.

(b) The **balance sheet** would **not reflect the asset nor the corresponding liability**. **Capital employed** and **ROCE** would remain **roughly the same**.

(c) **Long term debt** will be **less** under an **operating lease scenario** with little impact on equity interests. Hence, the **gearing ratio** is **likely** to **fall significantly**.

2.5 Tangible fixed asset revaluation

Revaluation of fixed affects various figures shown in the accounts.

(a) The total amount of **depreciation written off** through the profit and loss account over the life of the asset **will increase**. **Reported profits** will therefore be **lower**.

(b)   **Distributable profits** are however **not affected**. A **portion of revaluation reserves** may be **transferred to profit and loss reserves** as they become realised as result of additional depreciation of disposal.

(c)   **Shareholder** funds, **capital employed** and **total net assets** will **increase**.

(d)   **Debt** will be **unaffected**.

These changes in accounts balances will have consequential impacts on accounting ratios.

(a)   The **gearing ratio** will **decrease**

(b)   **ROCE** will **fall**

(c)   **EPS** will also **fall**.

2.6 Areas of judgment and estimation

The accounting standards specify detailed requirements in many areas of accounting and financial reporting. However, there still remains **significant scope** for the area of **professional judgement** in preparing accounts.

Accounts area	Scope for professional judgement on:
Tangible fixed assets	Depreciation rates and methods
Stocks	Overhead cost inclusion
	Net realisable value estimate
Long-term contracts	Turnover and profit recognition
	Decision to treat as long-term contract
General provisions	Existence of obligation
	Likelihood of transfer of economic benefit
	Measurement of liability

2.7 Limitations of ratio analysis

The consideration of how accounting policies may be used to massage company results leads us to some of the other limitations of ratio analysis. The most important ones are:

(a)   In a company's first year of trading there will be no comparative figures. So there will be no indication of whether or not a ratio is improving.

(b)   Comparisons against industry averages may not be that revealing. A business may be subject to factors which are not that common in the industry.

(c)   Ratios based on historic cost accounts are subject to the distortions described in 1.1 above. In particular, undervalued assets will distort ROCE and exaggerate gearing.

(d)   Ratios are influenced by the choice of accounting policy. For instance, a company seeking to maintain or increase its ROCE may choose not to revalue its assets.

(e)   Financial statements are subject to manipulation and so are the ratios based on them. Creative accounting is undertaken with key ratios in mind.

(f)   Inflation over a period will distort results and ratios. Net profit, and therefore ROCE, can be inflated where FIFO is applied during an inflationary period.

(g)   No two companies, even operating in the same industry, will have the same financial and business risk profile. For instance, one may have better access to cheap borrowing than the other and so may be able to sustain a higher level of gearing.

2.8 Other issues

Are there other issues which should be looked at when assessing an entity's performance? Factors to consider are:

- How technologically advanced is it? If it is not using the latest equipment and processes it risks being pushed out of the market at some point or having to undertake a high level of capital expenditure.

- What are its environmental policies? Is it in danger of having to pay for cleanup if the law is tightened? Does it appeal to those seeking 'ethical investment'?

- What is the reputation of its management? If it has attracted good people and kept them, that is a positive indicator.

- What is its mission statement? To what degree does it appear to be fulfilling it?

- What is its reputation as an employer? Do people want to work for this company? What are its labour relations like?

- What is the size of its market? Does it trade in just one or two countries or worldwide?

- How strong is its competition? Is it in danger of takeover?

You can probably think of other factors that you would consider important. In some cases you can also look at the quality of the product that a company produces.

Exam focus point

In the exam, always bear these points in mind; you may even be asked to discuss such limitations, but in any case they should have an impact on your analysis of a set of results.

Question

Ratios

The following are a selection of accounting ratios for a range of UK listed public companies in various industries ie

- Furniture
- Recruitment and business services
- Supermarket
- Cruise liner holidays
- Bakery shops

Review the table provided, then have a go at trying to identify which ratios relate to which industry. Write your response into the space provided at the foot of the table.

Standard ratios	Company A	Company B	Company C	Company D	Company E
Gross margin	8.0%	61.3%	49.6%	24.0%	-
ROCE	17.4%	26.3%	11.6%	10.1%	29.2%
Asset turnover	2.9 times	3.4 times	2.5 times	0.7 times	2.7 times
Current ratio	0.8:1	0.7:1	1.4:1	0.7:1	1.1:1
Stock turnover	20.4 days	15.7 days	102.2 days	12.0 days	N/A
Debtors turnover	1.1 days	0.5 days	15.0 days	5.8 days	56.2 days
Creditors turnover	40.0 days	54.7 days	53.7 days	30.2 days	-
Non-standard ratio					
Staff costs per employee	£17,566	£9,211	£22,279	£9,672	£24,646
Report date	1999	2000	2001	2000	2001
Industry involved					

Answer

Company	Industry
A	Supermarket chain
B	Bakery shop chain
C	Furniture retailer
D	Cruise holiday operator
E	Recruitment and business services

Chapter Roundup

- Financial statements are affected by the obvious shortcomings of historic cost information and are also subject to manipulation.

- Ratios provide information **through comparison**:

  - Trends in a company's ratios from one year to the next
  - In some cases against an industry norm or standard
  - Comparison with the ratios of other companies in the same industry

  But note that the use of different **accounting policies** may distort comparisons between companies.

Quick Quiz

1　What is the effect of stock carried at historical cost in a period of inflation?

2　What is 'window dressing'?

3　How can companies attempt to transfer profits from one group company to another?

4　Will two companies in the same industry have the same ROCE?

Answers to Quick Quiz

1　Overstatement of profits (see para 1.1)

2　An accounting adjustment made just before the year end to improve the appearance of the financial statements

3　Transfer pricing, intercompany loans, transfers of fixed assets (see para 1.3)

4　Probably not, there may be many other differences between them

Now try the questions below from the Exam Question Bank

Number	Level	Marks	Time
Q26	Examination	25	45 mins

Cash flow statements

Topic list	Syllabus reference
1 FRS 1 *Cash flow statements*	C1
2 Preparing a cash flow statement	C1
3 Interpretation of cash flow statements	C1

Introduction

You have already covered basic cash flow accounting in your earlier studies. Here, the study of cash flow statement revolves around FRS 1, which governs the content and disclosure of cash flow statements in company accounts.

FRS 1 was the first standard produced by the Accounting Standards Board and it was revised in October 1996.

This chapter adopts a systematic approach to the preparation of cash flow statements in examinations; you should learn this method and you will then be equipped for any problems in the exam itself.

The third section in the chapter looks at the information which is provided by cash flow statements and how it should be analysed.

Study guide

		Intellectual level
C	**FINANCIAL STATEMENTS**	
1	**Cash flow statements**	
(a)	Prepare a cash flow statement for a single entity (not a group) in accordance with relevant accounting standards using the direct and the indirect method.	2
(b)	Compare the usefulness of cash flow information with that of a profit and loss account.	2
(c)	Interpret a cash flow statement (together with other financial information) to assess the performance and financial position of an entity.	2

Exam guide

Preparation and analysis of cash flow statements is identified in the syllabus as a key area so make sure you master both techniques.

1 FRS 1 Cash flow statements

FAST FORWARD

Cash flow statements were made compulsory for companies because it was recognised that accounting profit is not the only indicator of a company's performance.

Cash flow statements concentrate on the **sources** and **uses of cash** and are a useful indicator of a company's **liquidity** and **solvency**.

It has been argued that 'profit' does not always give a useful or meaningful picture of a company's operations. **Readers of a company's financial statements might even be misled by a reported profit figure.**

(a)   Shareholders might believe that if a company makes a profit after tax of, say, £100,000 then this is the amount which it could afford to **pay as a dividend**. Unless the company has **sufficient cash** available to stay in business and also to pay a dividend, the shareholders' expectations would be wrong.

(b)   Employees might believe that if a company makes profits, it can afford to **pay higher wages** next year. This opinion may not be correct: the ability to pay wages depends on the **availability of cash**.

(c)   Survival of a business entity depends not so much on profits as on its **ability to pay its debts when they fall due**. Such payments might include 'profit and loss' items such as material purchases, wages, interest and taxation etc, but also capital payments for new fixed assets and the repayment of loan capital when this falls due (for example on the redemption of debentures).

From these examples, it may be apparent that a company's performance and prospects depend not so much on the 'profits' earned in a period, but more realistically on liquidity or **cash flows**.

The great advantage of a cash flow statement is that it is unambiguous and provides information which is additional to that provided in the rest of the accounts. It also describes to the cash flows of an organisation by activity and not by balance sheet classification.

1.1 FRS 1 Cash flow statements (revised)

FRS 1 sets out the structure of a cash flow statement and it also sets the minimum level of disclosure.
In October 1996 the ASB issued a revised version of FRS 1 *Cash flow statements*. The revision of FRS 1 was part of a normal process of revision, but it also responded to various criticisms of the original FRS 1. Although cash flow statements were found to be useful, some shortcomings were perceived, which we will discuss in Section 3.

Exam focus point

> Examination questions are likely to be computational, but some discussion and interpretation may be required.

1.2 Objective

The FRS begins with the following statement.

> 'The objective of this FRS is to ensure that reporting entities falling within its scope:
>
> (a)   Report their cash generation and cash absorption for a period by highlighting the significant components of cash flow in a way that facilitates comparison of the cash flow performance of different businesses
>
> (b)   Provide information that assists in the assessment of their liquidity, solvency and financial adaptability.'

1.3 Scope

The FRS applies to all financial statements intended to give a true and fair view of the financial position and profit or loss (or income and expenditure), except those of various exempt bodies in group accounts situations or where the content of the financial statement is governed by other statutes or regulatory regimes. In addition, **small entities are excluded** as defined by companies legislation.

1.4 Format of the cash flow statement

An example is given of the format of a cash flow statement for a single company and this is reproduced below.

A cash flow statement should list its cash flows for the period classified under the following **standard headings**.

> **Standard headings**
>
> (a)   Operating activities (using either the direct or indirect method)
> (b)   Returns on investments and servicing of finance
> (c)   Taxation
> (d)   Capital expenditure and financial investment
> (e)   Acquisitions and disposals
> (f)   Equity dividends paid
> (g)   Management of liquid resources
> (h)   Financing

The last two headings can be shown in a single section provided a subtotal is given for each heading. Acquisitions and disposals are not on your syllabus; the heading is included here for completeness.

Individual categories of inflows and outflows under the standard headings should be disclosed separately either in the cash flow statements or in a note to it unless they are allowed to be shown net. Cash inflows and outflows may be shown net if they relate to the management of liquid resources or financing and the inflows and outflows either:

    (a)   Relate in substance to a single financing transaction (unlikely to be a concern in Paper 2.5)

    (b)   Are due to short maturities and high turnover occurring from rollover or reissue (for example, short-term deposits).

The requirement to show cash inflows and outflows separately does not apply to cash flows relating to operating activities.

Each cash flow should be classified according to the substance of the transaction giving rise to it.

1.5 Links to other primary statements

Because the information given by a cash flow statement is best appreciated in the context of the information given by the other primary statements, the FRS requires **two reconciliations**, between:

    (a)   **Operating profit and the net cash flow from operating activities**.
    (b)   The **movement in cash in the period and the movement in net debt**.

Neither reconciliation forms part of the cash flow statement but each may be given either adjoining the statement or in a separate note.

The **movement in net debt** should identify the following components and reconcile these to the opening and closing balance sheet amount:

    (a)   The **cash flows** of the entity.
    (b)   **Other non-cash changes**.
    (c)   The recognition of **changes in market value** and **exchange rate movements**.

1.6 Definitions

The FRS includes the following **important definitions** (only those of direct concern to your syllabus are included here). Note particularly the definitions of cash and liquid resources.

    (a)   An **active market** is a market of sufficient depth to absorb the investment held without a significant effect on the price. (This definition affects the definition of liquid resources below.)

    (b)   **Cash** is cash in hand and deposits repayable on demand with any qualifying financial institution, less overdrafts from any qualifying financial institution repayable on demand. Deposits are repayable on demand if they can be withdrawn at any time without notice and without penalty or if a maturity or period of notice of not more than 24 hours or one working day has been agreed. Cash includes cash in hand and deposit denominated in foreign currencies.

    (c)   **Cash flow** is an increase or decrease in an amount of cash.

    (d)   **Liquid resources** are current asset investments held as readily disposable stores of value. A readily disposable investment is one that:

        (i)   Is disposable by the reporting entity without curtailing or disrupting its business.
        (ii)   Is either:

            (1)   Readily convertible into known amounts of cash at or close to its carrying amount.

            (2)   Traded in an active market.

(e)   **Net debt** is the borrowings of the reporting entity less cash and liquid resources. Where cash and liquid resources exceed the borrowings of the entity reference should be to 'net funds' rather than to 'net debt'.

(f)   **Overdraft** is a borrowing facility repayable on demand that is used by drawing on a current account with a qualifying financial institution.

1.7 Classification of cash flows by standard heading

The FRS looks at each of the cash flow categories in turn.

Exam focus point

If you are in a hurry or revising skim through these definitions, taking in the highlighted words and go straight to the example in Paragraph 1.12.

1.7.1 Operating activities

Cash flows from operating activities are in general the **cash effects of transactions** and other events **relating to operating or trading activities**, normally shown in the profit and loss account in arriving at operating profit. They include cash flows in respect of operating items relating to provisions, whether or not the provision was included in operating profit.

A **reconciliation** between the operating profit reported in the profit and loss account and the net cash flow from operating activities should be given **either adjoining the cash flow statement or as a note**. The reconciliation is not part of the cash flow statement: if adjoining the cash flow statement, it should be clearly labelled and kept separate. The reconciliation should disclose separately the movements in stocks, debtors and creditors related to operating activities and other differences between cash flows and profits.

1.7.2 Returns on investments and servicing of finance

These are **receipts resulting from the ownership of an investment and payments to providers of finance and non-equity shareholders** (eg the holders of preference shares).

Cash inflows from returns on investments and servicing of finance include:

(a)   **Interest received**, including any related tax recovered.

(b)   **Dividends received**, net of any tax credits.

Cash outflows from returns on investments and servicing of finance include:

(a)   **Interest paid** (even if capitalised), including any tax deducted and paid to the relevant tax authority.

(b)   Cash flows that are treated as **finance costs** (this will include issue costs on debt and non-equity share capital).

(c)   The **interest element of finance lease rental** payments.

(d)   **Dividends paid on non-equity shares** of the entity.

1.7.3 Taxation

These are cash flows to or from taxation authorities in respect of the reporting entity's revenue and capital profits. VAT and other sales taxes are discussed later.

(a)   Taxation cash **inflows** include **cash receipts** from the relevant tax authority of tax rebates, claims or returns of overpayments.

(b)   Taxation cash **outflows** include **cash payments** to the relevant tax authority of tax, including payments of advance corporation tax.

1.7.4 Capital expenditure and financial investment

These **cash flows** are those **related to the acquisition or disposal of any fixed asset** other than one required to be classified under 'acquisitions and disposals' (discussed below), **and any current asset investment** not included in liquid resources (also dealt with below). If no cash flows relating to financial investment fall to be included under this heading the caption may be reduced to 'capital expenditure'.

The **cash inflows** here include:

(a)   **Receipts from sales or disposals** of property, plant or equipment.

(b)   **Receipts from the repayment of** the reporting entity's **loans** to other entities.

Cash outflows in this category include:

(a)   **Payments to acquire property**, plant or equipment.

(b)   **Loans made** by the reporting entity.

1.7.5 Acquisitions and disposals

These cash flows are related to the acquisition or disposal of any trade or business, or of an investment in an entity that is either an associate, a joint venture, or a subsidiary undertaking (these group matters are beyond the scope of your syllabus).

(a)   Cash **inflows** here include **receipts from sales of trades or businesses**.

(b)   Cash **outflows** here include **payments to acquire trades or businesses**.

1.7.6 Equity dividends paid

The cash outflows are **dividends paid on** the reporting entity's **equity shares**.

1.7.7 Management of liquid resources

This section should include cash flows in respect of liquid resources as defined above. Each entity should explain what it includes as liquid resources and any changes in its policy. The cash flows in this section can be shown in a single section with those under 'financing' provided that separate subtotals for each are given.

Cash inflows include:

(a)   **Withdrawals from short-term deposits** not qualifying as cash.

(b)   Inflows from **disposal or redemption** of any other investments held as liquid resources.

Cash outflows include:

(a)   **Payments into short-term deposits** not qualifying as cash.

(b)   Outflows to **acquire any other investments** held as liquid resources.

1.7.8 Financing

Financing cash flows comprise receipts or repayments of principal from or to external providers of finance. The cash flows in this section can be shown in a single section with those under 'management of liquid resources' provided that separate subtotals for each are given.

Financing **cash inflows** include receipts **from issuing**:

(a)   **Shares** or other equity instruments.

(b)   **Debentures**, loans and from other long-term and short-term borrowings (other than overdrafts).

Financing cash **outflows** include:

(a)   **Repayments of amounts borrowed** (other than overdrafts).
(b)   The **capital element of finance lease rental** payments.
(c)   Payments to **reacquire or redeem the entity's shares**.
(d)   Payments of **expenses or commission on any issue of equity shares**.

1.8 Exceptional and extraordinary items and cash flows

Where cash flows relate to items that are classified as exceptional or extraordinary in the profit and loss account they **should be shown under the appropriate standard headings according to the nature of each item**. The cash flows relating to exceptional or extraordinary items should be identified in the cash flow statement or a note to it and the relationship between the cash flows and the originating exceptional or extraordinary item should be explained.

Where cash flows are exceptional because of their size or incidence but are not related to items that are treated as exceptional or extraordinary in the profit and loss account, **sufficient disclosure should be given to explain their cause and nature.**

1.9 Value added tax and other taxes

Cash flows should be shown net of any attributable value added tax or other sale tax unless the tax is irrecoverable by the reporting entity. The net movement on the amount payable to, or receivable from the taxing authority should be allocated to cash flows from operating activities unless a different treatment is more appropriate in the particular circumstances concerned. Where restrictions apply to the recoverability of such taxes, the irrecoverable amount should be allocated to those expenditures affected by the restrictions. If this is impracticable, the irrecoverable tax should be included under the most appropriate standard heading.

Taxation cash flows other than those in respect of the reporting entity's revenue and capital profits and value added tax, or other sales tax, **should be included within the cash flow statement** under the same standard heading as the cash flow that gave rise to the taxation cash flow, unless a different treatment is more appropriate in the particular circumstances concerned.

1.10 Material non-cash transactions

Material transactions not resulting in movements of cash of the reporting entity **should be disclosed in the notes** to the cash flow statement if disclosure is necessary for an understanding of the underlying transactions.

1.11 Comparative figures

Comparative figures **should be given for all items in the cash flow statement** and such notes thereto as are required by the FRS with the exception of the note to the statement that analyses changes in the balance sheet amount making up net debt.

1.12 Example: Single company

The following example is provided by the standard for a single company.

XYZ LIMITED
CASH FLOW STATEMENT FOR THE YEAR ENDED 31 DECEMBER 20X6

Reconciliation of operating profit to net cash inflow from operating activities

	£'000
Operating profit	6,022
Depreciation charges	899
Increase in stocks	(194)
Increase in debtors	(72)
Increase in creditors	234
Net cash inflow from operating activities	6,889

CASH FLOW STATEMENT

	£'000
Net cash inflow from operating activities	6,889
Returns on investments and servicing of finance (note 1)	2,999
Taxation	(2,922)
Capital expenditure (note 1)	(1,525)
	5,441
Equity dividends paid	(2,417)
	3,024
Management of liquid resources (note 1)	(450)
Financing (note 1)	57
Increase in cash	2,631

The reconciliation of operating profit to net cash flow from operating activities can be shown in a note.

NOTES TO THE CASH FLOW STATEMENT

1   *Gross cash flows*

	£'000	£'000
Returns on investments and servicing of finance		
Interest received	3,011	
Interest paid	(12)	
		2,999
Capital expenditure		
Payments to acquire intangible fixed assets	(71)	
Payments to acquire tangible fixed assets	(1,496)	
Receipts from sales of tangible fixed assets	42	
		(1,525)
Management of liquid resources		
Purchase of treasury bills	(650)	
Sale of treasury bills	200	
		(450)
Financing		
Issue of ordinary share capital	211	
Repurchase of debenture loan	(149)	
Expenses paid in connection with share issues	(5)	
		57

Note. These gross cash flows can be shown on the face of the cash flow statement, but it may sometimes be neater to show them as a note like this.

 **Question** | Cash flow statement format

Close the book for a moment and jot down the format of the cash flow statement.

2 Preparing a cash flow statement

You need to learn the **format** of the statement – this is the essential first stage in preparation. Always use the step-by-step procedure.

Exam focus point

In essence, preparing a cash flow statement is very straightforward. You should therefore simply learn the format given above and apply the steps noted in the example below. Note that the following items are treated in a way that might seem confusing, but the treatment is logical if you think in terms of **cash**.

(a) **Increase in stock** is treated as **negative** (in brackets). This is because it represents a cash **outflow**; cash is being spent on stock.

(b) An **increase in debtors** would be treated as **negative** for the same reasons; more debtors means less cash.

(c) By contrast an **increase in creditors** is **positive** because cash is being retained and not used to pay off creditors. There is therefore more of it.

2.1 Example: Preparation of a cash flow statement

Kitty Ltd's profit and loss account for the year ended 31 December 20X2 and balance sheets at 31 December 20X1 and 31 December 20X2 were as follows.

KITTY LIMITED
PROFIT AND LOSS ACCOUNT FOR THE YEAR ENDED 31 DECEMBER 20X2

	£'000	£'000
Sales		720
Raw materials consumed	70	
Staff costs	94	
Depreciation	118	
Loss on disposal	18	
		300
Operating profit		420
Interest payable		28
Profit before tax		392
Taxation		124
Profit after tax		268

KITTY LIMITED
BALANCE SHEETS AS AT 31 DECEMBER

	20X2		20X1	
	£'000	£'000	£'000	£'000
Fixed assets				
Cost		1,596		1,560
Depreciation		318		224
		1,278		1,336
Current assets				
Stock	24		20	
Trade debtors	76		58	
Bank	48		56	
	148		134	
Current liabilities				
Trade creditors	12		6	
Taxation	102		86	
	114		92	
Working capital		34		42
		1,312		1,378
Long-term liabilities				
Long-term loans		200		500
		1,112		878
Share capital		360		340
Share premium		36		24
Profit and loss		716		514
		1,112		878

During the year, the company paid £90,000 for a new piece of machinery.

Dividends paid amounted to £66,000.

Required

Prepare a cash flow statement for Kitty Ltd for the year ended 31 December 20X2 in accordance with the requirements of FRS 1 (revised).

Solution

STEP 1

Set out the proforma cash flow statement with all the headings required by FRS 1 (revised). You should leave plenty of space. Ideally, use three or more sheets of paper, one for the main statement, one for the notes (particularly if you have a separate note for the gross cash flows) and one for your workings. It is obviously essential to know the formats very well.

STEP 2

Complete the reconciliation of operating profit to net cash inflow as far as possible. When preparing the statement from balance sheets, you will usually have to calculate such items as depreciation, loss on sale of fixed assets and profit for the year (see Step 4).

STEP 3

Calculate the figures for tax paid, dividends paid, purchase or sale of fixed assets, issue of shares and repayment of loans if these are not already given to you (as they may be). Note that you may not be given the tax charge in the profit loss account. You will then have to assume that the tax paid in the year is last year's year-end provision and calculate the charge as the balancing figure.

STEP 4

If you are not given the profit figure, open up a working for the profit and loss account. Using the opening and closing balances, the taxation charge and dividends paid, you will be able to calculate profit for the year as the balancing figure to put in the statement.

STEP 5

Complete note 1, the gross cash flows. Alternatively this information may go straight into the statement.

STEP 6

You will now be able to complete the statement by slotting in the figures given or calculated.

KITTY LIMITED
CASH FLOW STATEMENT FOR THE YEAR ENDED 31 DECEMBER 20X2

Reconciliation of operating profit to net cash inflow

	£'000	£'000
Operating profit		420
Depreciation		118
Loss on sale of tangible fixed assets		18
Increase in stocks		(4)
Increase in debtors		(18)
Increase in creditors		6
Net cash inflow from operating activities		540

CASH FLOW STATEMENT

Net cash flows from operating activities		540
Returns on investment and servicing of finance		
Interest paid		(28)
Taxation		
Corporation tax paid (W1)		(108)
Capital expenditure		
Payments to acquire tangible fixed assets (W2)	(90)	
Receipts from sales of tangible fixed assets (W2)	12	
Net cash outflow from capital expenditure		(78)
		326
Equity dividends paid		(66)
		260
Financing		
Issues of share capital (360 + 36 – 340 – 24)	32	
Long-term loans repaid (500 – 200)	(300)	
Net cash outflow from financing		(268)
Decrease in cash		(8)

Workings

1 *Corporation tax paid*

	£'000
Opening CT payable	86
Charge for year	124
Net CT payable at 31.12.X2	(102)
Paid	108

2 *Fixed asset disposals*

COST

	£'000		£'000
At 1.1.X2	1,560	At 31.12.X2	1,596
Purchases	90	Disposals	54
	1,650		1,650

ACCUMULATED DEPRECIATION

	£'000		£'000
At 31.1.X2	318	At 1.1.X2	224
Depreciation on disposals	24	Charge for year	118
	342		342

	£'000
NBV of disposals	30
Net loss reported	(18)
Proceeds of disposals	12

2.2 Alternative methods

FRS 1 allows two possible layouts for cash flow statement in respect of operating activities:

(a) The **indirect method**, which is the one we have used so far

(b) The **direct method**.

Under the **direct method** the operating element of the cash flow statement should be shown as follows.

	£'000
Operating activities	
Cash received from customers	X
Cash payments to suppliers	(X)
Cash paid to and on behalf of employees	(X)
Other cash payments	(X)
Net cash flow from operating activities	X

Points to note are as follows.

(a) The **reconciliation** of operating profits and cash flows is **still required** (by note).

(b) **Cash received from customers** represents cash flows received during the accounting period in respect of sales.

(c) **Cash payments to suppliers** represents cash flows made during the accounting period in respect of goods and services.

(d) **Cash payments to and on behalf of employees** represents amounts paid to employees including the associated tax and national insurance. It will, therefore, comprise gross salaries, employer's National Insurance and any other benefits (eg pension contributions).

The direct method is, in effect, an analysis of the cash book. This information does not appear directly in the rest of the financial statements and so many companies might find it difficult to collect the information. Problems might include the need to reanalyse the cash book, to collate results from different cash sources and so on. The indirect method may be easier as it draws on figures which can be obtained from the financial statements fairly easily.

Question — Cash flow statement

The summarised accounts of Rene plc for the year ended 31 December 20X8 are as follows.

RENE PLC
BALANCE SHEET AS AT 31 DECEMBER 20X8

	20X8 £'000	20X8 £'000	20X7 £'000	20X7 £'000
Fixed assets				
Tangible assets		628		514
Current assets				
Stocks	214		210	
Debtors	168		147	
Cash	7		–	
	389		357	
Creditors: amounts falling due within one year				
Trade creditors	136		121	
Tax payable	39		28	
Overdraft	–		14	
	175		163	
Net current assets		214		194
Total assets less current liabilities		842		708
Creditors: amounts falling due after more than one year				
10% debentures		(80)		(50)
		762		658

Capital and reserves

Share capital (£1 ords)	250	200
Share premium account	70	60
Revaluation reserve	110	100
Profit and loss account	332	298
	762	658

RENE PLC
PROFIT AND LOSS ACCOUNT
FOR THE YEAR ENDED 31 DECEMBER 20X8

	£'000
Sales	600
Cost of sales	(319)
Gross profit	281
Other expenses (including depreciation of £42,000)	(194)
Profit before tax	87
Tax	(31)
Profit after tax	56

You are additionally informed that there have been no disposals of fixed assets during the year. New debentures were issued on 1 January 20X8. Wages for the year amounted to £86,000. Dividends paid were £22,000.

Required

Produce a cash flow statement using the direct method suitable for inclusion in the financial statements, as per FRS 1.

Answer

RENE PLC
CASH FLOW STATEMENT
FOR THE YEAR ENDED 31 DECEMBER 20X8

	£'000	£'000
Operating activities		
Cash received from customers (W1)	579	
Cash payments to suppliers (W2)	(366)	
Cash payments to and on behalf of employees	(86)	
		127
Returns on investments and servicing of finance		
Interest paid		(8)
Taxation		
UK corporation tax paid (W4)		(20)
Capital expenditure		
Purchase of tangible fixed assets (W5)	(146)	
Net cash outflow from capital expenditure		(146)
		(47)
Equity dividends paid		(22)
Financing		
Issue of share capital	60	
Issue of debentures	30	
Net cash inflow from financing		90
Increase in cash		21

NOTE TO THE CASHFLOW STATEMENT

1   *Reconciliation of operating profit to net cash inflow from operating activities*

	£'000
Operating profit (87 + 8)	95
Depreciation	42
Increase in stock	(4)
Increase in debtors	(21)
Increase in creditors	15
	127

Workings

1   *Cash received from customers*

DEBTORS CONTROL ACCOUNT

	£'000		£'000
B/f	147	Cash received (bal)	579
Sales	600	C/f	168
	747		747

2   *Cash paid to suppliers*

CREDITORS CONTROL ACCOUNT

	£'000		£'000
Cash paid (bal)	366	B/f	121
C/f	136	Purchases (W3)	381
	502		502

3   *Purchases*

	£'000
Cost of sales	319
Opening stock	(210)
Closing stock	214
Expenses (194 – 42 – 86 – 8 debenture interest)	58
	381

4   *Taxation*

TAXATION

	£'000		£'000
∴ Tax paid	20	Balance b/f	28
Balance c/f	39	Charge for year	31
	59		59

5   *Purchase of fixed assets*

	£'000
Opening fixed assets	514
Less depreciation	(42)
Add revaluation (110 – 100)	10
	482
Closing fixed assets	628
Difference = additions	146

Note: In the exam you may have a number of issues to deal with in the cash flow statement. Examples are:

•   Share capital issues. The proceeds will be split between share capital and share premium.

•   Bonus issues. These do *not* involve cash.

- Revaluation of fixed assets. This must be taken into account in calculating acquisitions and disposals.

- Movement on deferred tax. This must be taken into account in calculating tax paid.

- Finance leases. Assets acquired under finance leases must be adjusted for in your fixed asset calculations, and the amount paid under the finance lease must appear as a cash flow.

Make sure you attempt Question 27 in the question bank which includes a finance lease.

3 Interpretation of cash flow statements

FAST FORWARD

Cash flow statements provide **useful information** about a company which is not provided elsewhere in the accounts. Note that you may be expected to **analyse** or **interpret** a cash flow statement.

FRS 1 *Cash flow statements* was introduced on the basis that it would provide better, more comprehensive and more useful information than its predecessor standard. So what kind of information does the cash flow statement, along with its notes, provide?

Some of the **main areas where FRS 1 should provide information not found elsewhere in the accounts are as follows.**

- The **relationships between profit and cash** can be seen clearly and analysed accordingly.

- **Management of liquid resources** is highlighted, giving a better picture of the liquidity of the company.

- **Financing inflows and outflows must be shown, rather than simply passed through reserves**.

One of the most important things to realise at this point is that, as the ASB is always keen to emphasise, it is wrong to try to assess the health or predict the death of a reporting entity solely on the basis of a single indicator. When analysing cash flow data, the **comparison should not just be between cash flows and profit, but also between cash flows over a period of time** (say three to five years).

Cash is not synonymous with profit on an annual basis, but you should also remember that the 'behaviour' of profit and cash flows will be very different. **Profit is smoothed out** through accruals, prepayments, provisions and other accounting conventions. This does not apply to cash, so the **cash flow figures are likely to be 'lumpy' in comparison**. You must distinguish between this 'lumpiness' and the trends which will appear over time.

The **relationship between profit and cash flows will vary constantly**. Note that healthy companies do not always have reported profits exceeding operating cash flows. Similarly, unhealthy companies can have operating cash flows well in excess of reported profit. The value of comparing them is in determining the extent to which earned profits are being converted into the necessary cash flows.

Profit is not as important as the extent to which a company can convert its profits into cash on a continuing basis. This process should be judged over a period longer than one year. The cash flows should be compared with profits over the same periods to decide how successfully the reporting entity has converted earnings into cash.

Cash flow figures should also be considered in terms of their specific relationships with each other over time. A form of **'cash flow gearing' can** be determined by comparing operating cash flows and financing flows, particularly borrowing, to **establish the extent of dependence of the reporting entity on external funding**.

Other relationships can be examined.

(a) Operating cash flows and investment flows can be related to match cash recovery from investment to investment.

(b) Investment can be compared to distribution to indicate the proportion of total cash outflow designated specifically to investor return and reinstatement.

(c) A comparison of tax outflow to operating cash flow minus investment flow will establish a 'cash basis tax rate'.

The 'ratios' mentioned above can be monitored inter– and intra-firm and the analyses can be undertaken in monetary, general price-level adjusted, or percentage terms.

3.1 The advantages of cash flow accounting

The advantages of cash flow accounting are as follows.

(a) Survival in business depends on the **ability to generate** cash. Cash flow accounting directs attention towards this critical issue.

(b) Cash flow is **more comprehensive** than 'profit' which is dependent on accounting conventions and concepts.

(c) **Creditors** (long and short-term) **are more interested in an entity's ability to repay them than in its profitability**. Whereas 'profits' might indicate that cash is likely to be available, cash flow accounting is more direct with its message.

(d) Cash flow reporting provides a **better means of comparing the results** of different companies than traditional profit reporting.

(e) Cash flow reporting satisfies the needs of all users better.

    (i) For **management**, it provides the sort of information on which decisions should be taken: (in management accounting, 'relevant costs' to a decision are future cash flows); traditional profit accounting does not help with decision-making.

    (ii) For **shareholders and auditors**, cash flow accounting can provide a satisfactory basis for stewardship accounting.

    (iii) As described previously, the information needs of **creditors and employees** will be better served by cash flow accounting.

(f) Cash flow forecasts are **easier to prepare**, as well as more useful, than profit forecasts.

(g) They can in some respects be **audited more easily** than accounts based on the accruals concept.

(h) The accruals concept is confusing, and cash flows are **more easily understood**.

(i) Cash flow accounting should be both retrospective, and also include a forecast for the future. This is of **great information value** to all users of accounting information.

(j) **Forecasts** can subsequently be **monitored** by the publication of variance statements which compare actual cash flows against the forecast.

 Question   Disadvantages

Can you think of some possible disadvantages of cash flow accounting?

Answer

The main disadvantages of cash accounting are essentially the advantages of accruals accounting (proper matching of related items). There is also the practical problem that few businesses keep historical cash flow information in the form needed to prepare a historical cash flow statement and so extra record keeping is likely to be necessary.

Exam focus point

A cash flow statement is very likely to come up as Question 3 in your exam. In this chapter we give you the basics, but you should also do as many as possible of the cash flow statement questions from the Practice and Revision Kit. These will give you practice at the various items that you may have to deal with in a cash flow question.

Chapter Roundup

- **Cash flow statements** were made compulsory for companies because it was recognised that accounting profit is not the only indicator of a company's performance.

- Cash flow statements concentrate on the **sources** and **uses of cash** and are a useful indicator of a company's **liquidity** and **solvency**.

- You need to learn the **format** of the statement – this is the essential first stage in preparation. Always use the step-by-step procedure.

- Cash flow statements provide **useful information** about a company which is not provided elsewhere in the accounts. Note that you may be expected to **analyse** or **interpret** a cash flow statement.

Quick Quiz

1 List the aims of a cash flow statement.

2 The standard headings in the FRS1 cash flow statement are:

- O... a...

- R.. on i....................................... and s.. of f..

- T...

- C.. e... and f... i...

  - A................................... and d...................................

  - E.................................. d.................................. p....................................

  - M.................................. of l.................................. r...................................

  - F...................................

3 Liquid resources are current asset investments which will mature or can be redeemed within three months of the year end.

True ☐

False ☐

4 Why are you more likely to encounter the indirect method as opposed to the direct method?

5 List five advantages of cash flow accounting.

Answers to Quick Quiz

1   Comparability and assessment of liquidity, solvency and financial adaptability.

2   See Paragraph 1.4.

3   False. See the definition in Paragraph 1.6 if you are not sure about this.

4   The indirect method utilises figures which appear in the financial statements. The figures required for the direct method may not be readily available.

5   See Paragraph 3.1 for ten advantages.

Now try the question below from the Exam Question Bank

Number	Level	Marks	Time
Q27	Introductory	15	27 mins
Q28	Examination	25	45 mins

BPP LEARNING MEDIA

Alternative models and practices

22

Topic list	Syllabus reference
1 Historical cost versus current value	A5
2 Concepts of capital and capital maintenance	A5
3 Current purchasing power (CPP)	A5
4 Current cost accounting (CCA)	A5

Introduction

In this chapter we look at the alternatives to historical cost accounting.

Study guide

		Intellectual level
A	**A CONCEPTUAL FRAMEWORK FOR FINANCIAL REPORTING**	
5	**Alternative models and practices**	
(a)	Describe the advantages and disadvantages of the use of historical cost accounting.	2
(b)	Discuss whether the use of current value accounting overcomes the problems of historical cost accounting.	2
(c)	Describe the concept of financial and physical capital maintenance and how this affects the determination of profits.	1

Exam guide

In this chapter we will be looking in more detail at historical cost accounting, its advantages and disadvantages, and the possible alternatives.

1 Historical cost versus current value

FAST FORWARD

A number of alternatives to historical cost accounting are presently under discussion, some progress has been made and more can be expected in the future.

1.1 Advantages of historical cost accounting

As we are still using historical cost accounting, it may be supposed to have a number of advantages. The most important ones are:

- Amounts used are objective and free from bias

- Amounts are reliable; they can always be verified, they exist on invoices and documents

- Balance sheet amounts can be matched perfectly with amounts in the cash flow statement

- Opportunities for creative accounting are less than under systems which allow management to apply their judgement to the valuation of assets

- It has been used for centuries and is easily understood

1.2 Disadvantages of historical cost accounting

Historical cost accounting has a number of distinct disadvantages. They arise as particular problems in periods if inflation. The main ones are:

- It can lead to understatement of assets on the balance sheet. A building purchased 50 years ago will appear at the price that was paid for it 50 years ago.

- Because assets are understated, depreciation will also be understated. While the purpose of depreciation is not to set aside funds for replacement of assets, if an asset has to be replaced at twice the price that was paid for its predecessor, the company may decide that it may have been prudent to make some provision for this in earlier years.

BPP
LEARNING MEDIA

- When prices are rising, and when the company is operating a FIFO system, the cheapest stocks are being charged to cost of sales and the most expensive are being designated as closing stock on the balance sheet. This leads to understatement of cost of sales.

- An organisation selling in an inflationary market will see its turnover and profits rise, but this is 'paper profit', distorted by the understated depreciation and cost of sales.

From these disadvantages various issues arise:

- Understatement of assets will depress a company's share price and make it vulnerable to takeover. In practice, listed companies avoid this by revaluing land and buildings in line with market values.

- Understated depreciation and understated cost of sales lead to overstatement of profits, compounded by price inflation.

- Overstated profits can lead to too much being distributed to shareholders, leaving insufficient amounts for investment.

- Overstated profits will lead shareholders to expect higher dividends and employees to demand higher wages.

- Overstated profits lead to overstated tax bills

During periods where price inflation is low, profit overstatement will be marginal. The disadvantages of historical cost accounting become most apparent in periods of inflation. It was during the inflationary period of the 70s that alternatives were sought and that an attempt was made to introduce Current Cost Accounting (CCA). As inflation came back under control, the debate died down, but it is becoming increasingly recognised that historical cost accounting has shortcomings which need to be addressed.

1.3 Current value accounting

The move towards current value accounting has already taken a number of steps. Entities are now permitted to revalue fixed assets such as land and buildings in line with market value and financial assets and liabilities such as securities and investments can be carried at **fair value**, defined in FRS 26 as: 'the amount for which an asset could be exchanged, or a liability settled, between knowledgeable, willing parties in an arm's length transaction'.

These developments, and the use of fair values in acquisition accounting (to measure the assets of the subsidiary and thus arrive at a realistic goodwill valuation) are relatively uncontroversial. However there are those who would like fair value to be used more widely as a system of current value. The European Central Bank recently produced a paper on the possible use of Full Fair Value Accounting (FFVA) in the banking industry.

In the US a similar move is being advocated towards Current Value Accounting (CVA). Under CVA the original cost of an asset would be replaced with its discounted present value ie. the present value of its future cash flows. This is obviously suitable for monetary items such as debtors and creditors. The expected inflows and outflows would be discounted to present value using an interest rate which reflects the current time value of money. For assets such as vehicles, which do not yield a pre-determined future cash flow, current cost would be a more applicable measure – based either on the current cost of the original asset or on its replacement by a more up-to-date version. For stocks, current replacement cost or NRV would be indicated. Under this measurement basis, the LIFO/FIFO distinction would no longer apply.

1.4 Historical cost accounting; does it have a future?

Investment analysts have argued that historical cost information is out of date and not relevant and that fair value information, where based on active market prices, is the best available measure of future cash flows which an asset can be expected to generate.

This is heard increasingly in the US, where investors are the most highly-regarded user group for financial information, and the issue is likely to arise in the context of the IASB/FASB discussions on a joint conceptual framework. In due course this will impact upon the ASB, probably leading to a revised *Statement of Principles*.

We will now go on to look at two alternative systems which have sought in the past to address the shortcomings of historical cost accounting – **Current purchasing power (CPP)** and **Current cost accounting (CCA)**. We begin by looking at the fundamental difference between these two systems – a different concept of capital maintenance and therefore of profit.

2 Concepts of capital and capital maintenance

FAST FORWARD ❯❯ The concept of capital selected should be appropriate to the needs of the users of an entity's financial statements.

Most entities use a **financial concept of capital** when preparing their financial statements.

2.1 Concepts of capital maintenance and the determination of profit

First of all, we need to define the different concepts of capital.

Key term

> **Capital**. Under a **financial concept of capital**, such as invested money or invested purchasing power, capital is the net assets or equity of the entity. The financial concept of capital is adopted by most entities.
>
> Under a **physical concept of capital**, such as operating capability, capital is the productive capacity of the entity based on, for example, units of output per day.

The definition of profit is also important.

Key term

> **Profit**. The residual amount that remains after expenses (including capital maintenance adjustments, where appropriate) have been deducted from income. Any amount over and above that required to maintain the capital at the beginning of the period is profit.

The main difference between the two concepts of capital maintenance is the treatment of the **effects of changes in the prices of assets and liabilities** of the entity. In general terms, an entity has maintained its capital if it has as much capital at the end of the period as it had at the beginning of the period. Any amount over and above that required to maintain the capital at the beginning of the period is profit.

(a) **Financial capital maintenance**: profit is the increase in nominal money capital over the period. This is the concept used in CPP, and used under historical cost accounting.

(b) **Physical capital maintenance**: profit is the increase in the physical productive capacity over the period. This is the concept used in CCA.

2.2 Capital maintenance in times of inflation

Profit can be measured as the **difference between how wealthy a company is at the beginning and at the end of an accounting period.**

(a) This wealth can be expressed in terms of the capital of a company as shown in its opening and closing balance sheets.

(b) A business which maintains its capital unchanged during an accounting period can be said to have broken even.

(c)   **Once capital has been maintained, anything achieved in excess represents profit.**

For this analysis to be of any use, we must be able to draw up a company's balance sheet at the beginning and at the end of a period, so as to place a value on the opening and closing capital. There are particular difficulties in doing this during a period of rising prices.

In conventional historical cost accounts, assets are stated in the balance sheet at the amount it cost to acquire them (less any amounts written off in respect of depreciation or diminution in value). Capital is simply the difference between assets and liabilities.

Important!

> If prices are rising, it is possible for a company to show a profit in its historical cost accounts despite having identical physical assets and owing identical liabilities at the beginning and end of its accounting period.

For example, consider the following opening and closing balance sheets of a company.

	Opening £	Closing £
Stock (100 items at cost)	500	600
Other net assets	1,000	1,000
Capital	1,500	1,600

Assuming that no new capital has been introduced during the year, and no capital has been distributed as dividends, the profit shown in historical cost accounts would be £100, being the excess of closing capital over opening capital. And yet in physical terms the company is no better off: it still has 100 units of stock (which cost £5 each at the beginning of the period, but £6 each at the end) and its other net assets are identical. The 'profit' earned has merely enabled the company to keep pace with inflation.

An alternative to the concept of capital maintenance based on historical costs is to express capital in physical terms. On this basis, no profit would be recognised in the example above because the physical substance of the company is unchanged over the accounting period. In the UK, a system of accounting (called **current cost accounting** or CCA) was introduced in 1980 by SSAP 16 (now withdrawn) and had as its basis a concept of capital maintenance based on 'operating capability'.

Capital is maintained if at the end of the period the company is in a position to achieve the same physical output as it was at the beginning of the period.

You should bear in mind that financial definitions of capital maintenance are not the only ones possible; in theory at least, there is no reason why profit should not be measured as the increase in a company's *physical* capital over an accounting period.

3 Current purchasing power (CPP)

3.1 The unit of measurement

Another way to tackle the problems of capital maintenance in times of rising prices is to look at the unit of measurement in which accounting values are expressed.

It is an axiom of **conventional accounting**, as it has developed over the years, that value should be measured in terms of money. It is also **implicitly assumed that money values are stable**, so that £1 at the start of the financial year has the same value as £1 at the end of that year. **But when prices are rising, this assumption is invalid: £1 at the end of the year has less value (less purchasing power) than it had one year previously.**

This **leads to problems when aggregating amounts which have arisen at different times.** For example, a company's fixed assets may include items bought at different times over a period of many years. They will each have been recorded in £s, but the value of £1 will have varied over the period. In effect the fixed asset figure in a historical cost balance sheet is an aggregate of a number of items expressed in different units. It **could be argued that such a figure is meaningless.**

Faced with this argument, one possibility would be to re-state all accounts items in terms of a stable monetary unit. There would be difficulties in practice, but in theory there is no reason why a stable unit (£ CPP = £s of current purchasing power) should not be devised. In this section we will look at a system of accounting (current purchasing power accounting, or CPP) based on precisely this idea.

3.2 Specific and general price changes

We can identify two different types of price inflation.

When prices are rising, it is likely that the current value of assets will also rise, but not necessarily by the general rate of inflation. For example, if the replacement cost of a machine on 1 January 20X2 was £5,000, and the general rate of inflation in 20X2 was 8%, we would not necessarily expect the replacement cost of the machine at 31 December 20X2 to be £5,000 plus 8% = £5,400. The rate of price increase on the machinery might have been less than 8% or more than 8%. (Conceivably, in spite of general inflation, the replacement cost of the machinery might have gone down.)

(a)   There is **specific price inflation,** which **measures price changes over time for a specific asset or group of assets.**

(b)   There is **general price inflation,** which **is the average rate of inflation, which reduces the general purchasing power of money.**

To counter the problems of specific price inflation some system of current value accounting may be used (for example, the system of current cost accounting described in the following chapter). The capital maintenance concepts underlying current value systems do not attempt to allow for the maintenance of real value in money terms.

Current purchasing power (CPP) accounting is based on a different concept of capital maintenance.

> **CPP** measures profits as the increase in the current purchasing power of equity. Profits are therefore stated after allowing for the declining purchasing power of money due to price inflation.

In Britain attempts to introduce CPP accounting have been in a combination with historical cost accounting, and it is on this aspect that this section will concentrate.

When applied to historical cost accounting, **CPP is a system of accounting which makes adjustments to income and capital values to allow for the general rate of price inflation.** An attempt to introduce such a system was made in 1974 with the publication of a Provisional Statement of Standard Accounting Practice, PSSAP 7 *Accounting for changes in the purchasing power of money*. Although it was withdrawn after a year, and was then superseded by SSAP 16, it remains a topic of debate and **some knowledge of CPP accounting is necessary to understand the diversity of views currently held on inflation accounting in general.**

3.3 Monetary and non-monetary items

It is obvious that during a period of inflation borrowers benefit at the expense of lenders. A sum borrowed at the beginning of the year will cost less to repay at the end of the year (although lenders will seek to allow for this in higher interest charges). Similarly, debtors benefit at the expense of creditors. CPP accounting seeks to remove this element of 'holding gain'.

Monetary items (cash, debts, creditors) cannot be restated, as their amount is fixed. Non-monetary items (fixed assets and stocks) are restated in line with the general price index (at £C) and the balancing figure is equity.

3.4 Example: CPP

Rice and Price set up in business on 1 January 20X5 with no fixed assets, and cash of £5,000. On 1 January they acquired some stocks for the full £5,000 which they sold on 30 June 19X5 for £6,000. On 30 November they obtained a further £2,100 of stock on credit. The index of the general price level gives the following index figures.

Date	Index
1 January 20X5	300
30 June 20X5	330
30 November 20X5	350
31 December 20X5	360

Calculate the CPP profits (or losses) of Rice and Price for the year to 31 December 20X5.

Solution

The approach is to prepare a CPP profit and loss account.

	£c	£c
Sales (6,000 × 360/330)		6,545
Less cost of goods sold (5,000 × 360/300)		6,000
		545
Loss on holding cash for 6 months*	(545)	
Gain by having creditor for 1 month**	60	
		485
CPP profit		60

* (£6,000 × 360/330) − £6,000 = £c 545
**(£2,100 × 360/350) − £2,100 = £c 60

Note that under historic cost accounting the gross profit would be £1,000 (£6,000 − £5,000)

3.5 The advantages and disadvantages of CPP accounting

3.5.1 Advantages

(a) The **restatement of asset values in terms of a stable money value provides a more meaningful basis of comparison** with other companies. Similarly, provided that previous years' profits are re-valued into CPP terms, it is also possible to compare the current year's results with past performance.

(b) Profit is measured in 'real' terms and excludes 'inflationary value increments'. This **enables better forecasts of future prospects to be made.**

(c) CPP **avoids the subjective valuations** of current value accounting, because a single price index is applied to all non-monetary assets.

(d) CPP **provides a stable monetary unit** with which to value profit and capital; ie £c.

(e) Since it is based on historical cost accounting, **raw data is easily verified**, and measurements of value can be readily audited.

3.5.2 Disadvantages

(a) It is **not clear what £c means**. 'Generalised purchasing power' as measured by the Retail Price Index, or indeed any other general price index, has no obvious practical significance.

'Generalised purchasing power has no relevance to any person or entity because no such thing exists in reality, except as a statistician's computation.'   (T A Lee)

(b) The use of indices **inevitably involves approximations** in the measurements of value.

(c) **The value of assets in a CPP balance sheet has less meaning than a current value balance sheet**. It cannot be supposed that the CPP value of net assets reflects:

　(i) The general goods and services that could be bought if the assets were released.

　(ii) The consumption of general goods and services that would have to be forgone to replace those assets.

In this respect, a CPP balance sheet has similar drawbacks to an historical cost balance sheet.

4 Current cost accounting (CCA)

FAST FORWARD

CCA is an alternative to the historical cost convention which attempts to overcome the problems of accounting for **specific price inflation**. Unlike CPP accounting, it does not attempt to cope with general inflation. CCA is based on a physical concept or **capital maintenance**. Profit is recognised after the operating capability of the business has been maintained.

4.1 Value to the business (deprival value)

The **conceptual basis of CCA is that the value of assets consumed or sold, and the value of assets in the balance sheet, should be stated at their value to the business** (also known as 'deprival value').

A system of current cost accounting was introduced into the UK by SSAP 16 *Current cost accounting* in March 1980. This was the culmination of a long process of research into the problems of accounting in times of inflation. SSAP 16 encountered heavy criticism and was finally withdrawn in April 1988.

In CCA, a physical rather than financial definition of capital is used: capital maintenance is measured by the ability of the business entity to keep up the same level of operating capability.

Key term

The **deprival value** of an asset is the loss which a business entity would suffer if it were deprived of the use of the asset.

Value to the business, or deprival value, can be any of the following values.

(a) **Replacement cost**. In the case of fixed assets, it is assumed that the replacement cost of an asset would be its net replacement cost (NRC), its gross replacement cost minus an appropriate provision for depreciation to reflect the amount of its life already 'used up'.

(b) **Net realisable value** (NRV); what the asset could be sold for, net of any disposal costs.

(c) **Economic value** (EV), or utility; what the existing asset will be worth to the company over the rest of its useful life.

The choice of deprival value from one of the three values listed will depend on circumstances. The decision tree on the next page illustrates the principles involved in the choice, but in simple terms you should remember that in **CCA deprival value is nearly always replacement cost**.

If the asset is worth replacing, its deprival value will always be net replacement cost. If the asset is not worth replacing, it might be disposed of straight away, or else it might be kept in operation until the end of its useful life.

You may therefore come across a statement that deprival value is the **lower of**:

(a)   **Net replacement cost** (NRC)
(b)   The **higher of net realisable value and economic value**

We have already seen that if an asset is not worth replacing at the end of its life, the deprival value will be NRV or EV. However, there are many assets which will not be replaced either:

(a)   Because the asset is technologically obsolete, and has been (or will be) superseded by more modern equipment.

(b)   Because the business is changing the nature of its operations and will not want to continue in the same line of business once the asset has been used up.

Such assets, even though there are reasons not to replace them, would still be valued (usually) at net replacement cost, because this 'deprival value' still provides an estimate of the operating capability of the company.

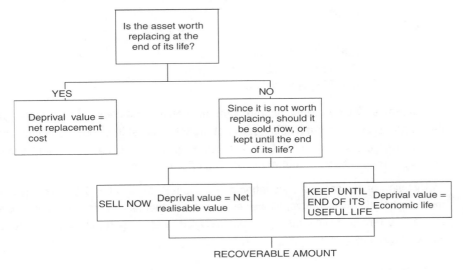

4.2 CCA profits and deprival value

The deprival value of assets is reflected in the CCA profit and loss account by the following means.

(a)   **Depreciation** is **charged** on fixed assets **on the basis of gross replacement cost** of the asset (where NRC is the deprival value).

(b)   Where **NRV or EV** is the deprival value, the **charge against CCA profits will be the loss in value of the asset during the accounting period**; ie from its previous balance sheet value to its current NRV or EV.

(c)   **Goods sold are charged at their replacement cost**. Thus if an item of stock cost £15 to produce, and sells for £20, by which time its replacement cost has risen to £17, the CCA profit would be £3.

	£
Sales	20
Less replacement cost of goods sold	17
Current cost profit	3

4.3 Example:

It is useful to explain the distinction here between CCA and accounting for inflation, and a simple example may help to describe the difference. Suppose that Arthur Smith Ltd buys an asset on 1 January for £10,000. The estimated life of the asset is 5 years, and straight line depreciation is charged. At 31 December the gross replacement cost of the asset is £10,500 (5% higher than on 1 January) but general inflation during the year, as measured by the retail price index, has risen 20%.

(a) To maintain the value of the business against inflation, the asset should be revalued as follows.

	£
Gross (£10,000 × 120%)	12,000
Depreciation charge for the year (@ 20%)	2,400
Net value in the balance sheet	9,600

(b) In CCA, the business maintains its operating capability if we revalue the asset as follows.

	£
Gross replacement cost	10,500
Depreciation charge for the year (note)	2,100
NRC; balance sheet value	8,400

Note	£
Historical cost depreciation	2,000
CCA depreciation adjustment (5%)	100
Total CCA depreciation cost	2,100

CCA preserves the operating capability of the company but does not necessarily preserve it against the declining value in the purchasing power of money (against inflation). As mentioned in the previous chapter, CCA is a system which takes account of specific price inflation (changes in the prices of specific assets or groups of assets) but not of general price inflation.

A strict view of current cost accounting might suggest that a set of CCA accounts should be prepared from the outset on the basis of deprival values. In practice that has not been the procedure adopted in the UK. Instead, current cost accounts have been prepared by starting from historical cost accounts and making appropriate adjustments.

4.4 CCA accounts

CCA accounts will include the following adjustments:

1. **Depreciation adjustment** – to amend depreciation in line with the gross replacement cost of the asset

2. **Cost of sales adjustment** – to take account of increases in stock prices and remove any element of profit based on this

3. **Working capital adjustment** – to remove any element of profit or loss based on having debtors or creditors in a period of inflation

You do not need to know how to do these adjustments, but you can see that they attempt to deal with the areas where inflation can lead to 'holding gains.'

Exam focus point

This topic will probably be dealt with in a general discussion question in the exam. It is not a 'core' topic and you are unlikely to have to deal with any calculations.

4.5 The advantages and disadvantages of current cost accounting

4.5.1 Advantages

(a)   By excluding holding gains from profit, CCA **can be used to indicate whether** the **dividends** paid to shareholders (which by UK law can exceed the size of the CCA profit) **will reduce the operating capability** of the business.

(b)   Assets are valued after management has considered the **opportunity cost** of holding them, and the expected benefits from their future use. CCA is therefore **a useful guide for management in deciding whether to hold or sell assets.**

(c)   It is **relevant to the needs of information users** in:

   (i)   Assessing the stability of the business entity.

   (ii)   Assessing the vulnerability of the business (eg to a takeover), or the liquidity of the business.

   (iii)   Evaluating the performance of management in maintaining and increasing the business substance.

   (iv)   Judging future prospects.

(d)   It can be **implemented fairly easily** in practice, by making simple adjustments to the historical cost accounting profits. A current cost balance sheet can also be prepared with reasonable simplicity.

4.5.2 Disadvantages

(a)   It is impossible to make valuations of EV or NRV without subjective judgements. The **measurements used are** therefore **not objective.**

(b)   There are **several problems to be overcome in deciding how to provide an estimate of replacement costs for fixed assets.**

(c)   The **mixed value approach** to valuation **means** that some assets will be valued at replacement cost, but others will be valued at net realisable value or economic value. It is arguable that the **total assets** will, therefore, have an **aggregate value** which is **not particularly meaningful** because of this mixture of different concepts.

(d)   It can be argued that **'deprival value' is an unrealistic concept, because the business entity has not been deprived of the use of the asset.** This argument is one which would seem to reject the fundamental approach to 'capital maintenance' on which CCA is based.

Chapter Roundup

- A number of alternatives to historical cost accounting are presently under discussion, some progress has been made and more can be expected in the future,

- **CPP accounting** is a method of accounting for general (not specific) inflation. It does so by expressing asset values in a stable monetary unit, the £c or £ of current purchasing power.

- In the **CPP balance sheet**, **monetary items** are stated at their **face value**. **Non-monetary items** are stated at their **current purchasing power** as at the balance sheet date.

- **CCA** is an alternative to the historical cost convention which attempts to overcome the problems of accounting for **specific price inflation**. Unlike CPP accounting, it does not attempt to cope with general inflation.

- CCA is based on a **physical concept of capital maintenance**. Profit is recognised after the operating capability of the business has been maintained.

- The current cost profit and loss account is constructed by taking **historical cost** profit before interest and taxation as a starting point.

  - Current cost **operating adjustments** in respect of **cost of sales**, **monetary working capital** and **depreciation** are made so as to arrive at **current cost operating profit**.

Quick Quiz

1   Stock is a non-monetary item.

    True   ☐

    False ☐

2   List the advantages and disadvantages of CPP as a method of accounting.

3   *Fill in the three blanks.*

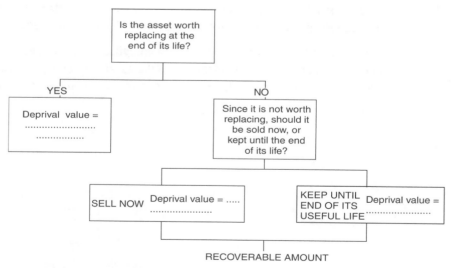

4   List the advantages and disadvantages of CCA.

BPP
LEARNING MEDIA

Answers to Quick Quiz

1   True

2   See Paragraph 3.5

3   Answers (from left to right) net replacement cost, net realisable value and economic value

4   Refer to Paragraph 4.5.

Now try the question below from the Exam Question Bank

Number	Level	Marks	Time
Q29	Examination	15	27 mins

Specialised, not-for-profit and public sector entities

Topic list	Syllabus reference
1 Primary aims	B3
2 Regulatory framework	B3
3 Performance measurement	E4

Introduction

In this chapter we look at the applicant of accounting rules and performance measurement for not-for-profit and public sector entities.

Study guide

		Intellectual level
B	**A REGULATORY FRAMEWORK FOR FINANCIAL REPORTING**	
3	**Specialised, not-for-profit and public sector entities**	
(a)	Distinguish between the primary aims of not-for-profit and public sector entities and those of profit oriented entities.	1
(b)	Discuss the extent to which International Financial Reporting Standards (FRSs) are relevant to specialised, not-for-profit and public sector entities.	1
E	**ANALYSING AND INTERPRETING FINANCIAL STATEMENTS**	
4	**Specialised, not-for-profit and public sector entities**	
(a)	Discuss the different approaches that may be required when assessing the performance of specialised, not-for-profit and public sector organisations.	1

1 Primary aims

FAST FORWARD

> The accounting requirements for not-for-profit and public sector entities are moving closer to those required for profit-making entities. However, they do have different goals and purposes.

What organisations do we have in mind when we refer to **Not-for-profit and public sector entities**? These are the most obvious examples:

(a) Central government departments and agencies

(b) Local or federal government departments

(c) Publicly-funded bodies providing healthcare (in the UK this would be the NHS) and social housing

(d) Further and higher education institutions

(e) Charitable bodies

The first four are **public sector entities**. Charities are **private** not-for-profit entities.

Not-for-profit entities have different goals and purposes to profit-making entities and are responsible to different stakeholders. However, they are dealing in very large sums of money and it is important that they are properly managed and that their accounts present fairly the results of their operations.

Until recently, **public sector** accounts were prepared on a **cash basis**. A transition is still in progress which will get them operating on an **accruals basis**, in line with normal practice in the private sector.

1.1 Conceptual framework for not-for profit entities

The IASB and the FASB are currently in a project to produce a new, improved conceptual framework for financial reporting, entitled: *The Objective of Financial Reporting and Qualitative Characteristics of Decision-Useful Financial Reporting Information*. This project is being undertaken in phases. Phase G is entitled *Application to not-for-profit entities in the private and public sector*. A monitoring group, including ASB members, set up to advise on this has made the following points:

(a) Not-for profit entities have different objectives, different operating environments and other different characteristics to private sector businesses.

(b)   The following issues exist regarding application of the proposals to not-for-profit entities:

- Insufficient emphasis on accountability/stewardship
- A need to broaden the definition of users and user groups
- The emphasis on future cash flows is inappropriate to not-for-profit entities
- Insufficient emphasis on budgeting

1.2 Accountability/stewardship

Not-for-profit entities are not reporting to shareholders, but it is very important that they can account for funds received and show how they have been spent. In some cases, resources may be contributed for specific purposes and management is required to show that they have been utilised for that purpose. Perhaps most importantly, taxpayers are entitled to see how the government is spending their money.

1.3 Users and user groups

The primary user group for not-for-profit entities is providers of funds. In the case of public bodies, such as government departments, this primary group will consist of taxpayers. In the case of private bodies such as charities it will be financial supporters, and also potential future financial supporters. There is also a case for saying that a second primary user group should be recognised, being the recipients of the goods and services provided by the not-for-profit entity.

1.4 Cash flow focus

The new framework, like the existing framework, emphasises the need to provide information which will enable users to assess an entity's ability to generate net cash inflows. Not-for-profit entities also need to generate cash flows, but other aspects are generally more significant – for instance, the resources the entity has available to deliver future goods and services, the cost and effectiveness of those it has delivered in the past and the degree to which it is meeting its objectives.

1.5 Budgeting

The IASB has decided to leave consideration of whether financial reporting should include forecast information until later in the project. However, for not-for-profit entities, budgets and variance analyses are more important. In some cases, funding is supplied on the basis of a formal, published budget.

2 Regulatory framework

FAST FORWARD

There is a general move to get public bodies reporting under the accruals system. Many private not-for-profit organisations still use cash accounting.

Regulation of public not-for-profit entities, principally local and national governments and governmental agencies, is by the **ASB**, assisted by two specialist advisory committees – the Financial Sector and Other Special Industries Committee (FSOSIC) and the Committee on Accounting for Public Benefit Entities (CAPE). These bodies advise the ASB on proposals for Statements of Recommended Practice (SORPs) put forward by specialist bodies developing accounting practice for their sectors.

The ASB gives approval to bodies which wish to develop SORPs. They are developed in accordance with ASB guidelines and the ASB will then give a statement granting approval to the SORP.

These are some SORPs prepared by independent bodies to which the ASB has given its statement:

Authorised Unit Trust Schemes and Authorised Open-Ended Investment Companies
The Investment Management Association

Derivatives
British Bankers Association

Accounting and Reporting by Charities
Charity Commission for England and Wales

Accounting for Further and Higher Education
Universities UK

Accounting for Insurance Business
Association of British Insurers

Limited Liability Partnerships
The Consultative Committee of Accountancy Bodies

Accounting by Registered Social Landlords
National Housing Federation

Code of Practice on Local Authority Accounting in the UK
Chartered Institute of Public Finance and Accountancy

You do not need to remember any of these, but this gives you some idea of the bodies which prepare SORPs. The ASB approval signifies that the SORP complies with current UK accounting standards, the ASB's Statement of Principles and GAAP, apart from any departures arising from the Government's requirements.

2.1 Characteristics of Not-for-profit Entities

As part of its preliminary report on the new Framework, the IASB, advised by the ASB, sets out some of the characteristics of not-for-profit entities as follows:

2.2 Private Sector

Not-for-profit entities in the private sector have the following characteristics:

- Their objective is to provide goods and services to various recipients and not to make a profit

- They are generally characterised by the absence of defined ownership interests (shares) that can be sold, transferred or redeemed

- They may have a wide group of stakeholders to consider (including the public at large in some cases)

- Their revenues generally arise from contributions (donations or membership dues) rather than sales

- Their capital assets are typically acquired and held to deliver services without the intention of earning a return on them

2.3 Public sector

Nor-for-profit entities in the public sector have similar key characteristics to those in the private sector. They are typically established by legislation and:

- Their objective is to provide goods and services to various recipients or to develop or implement policy on behalf of governments and not to make a profit

- They are characterised by the absence of defined ownership interests that can be sold, transferred or redeemed

- They typically have a wide group of stakeholders to consider (including the public at large)

- Their revenues are generally derived from taxes or other similar contributions obtained through the exercise of coercive powers

- Their capital assets are typically acquired and held to deliver services without the intention of earning a return on them

2.4 Not-for-profit entities – specific issues

While the general trend is to get not-for-profit entities producing accounts which are based as far as possible on the provisions of FRSs and which are generally comparable to those produced for profit-making entities, there are two issues which have yet to be resolved.

2.5 Cost of transition

While there has been a general assumption that for public sector entities the move to the accruals basis will result in more relevant and better quality financial reporting, no actual cost-benefit analysis has been undertaken on this.

One of the arguments in favour of the adoption of the accruals basis is that it will be possible to compare the cost of providing a service against the same cost in the private sector. It will then be possible to see how goods and services can be most cheaply sourced.

However, it is questionable whether governments get a good deal anyway when they involve themselves with the private sector and the move to accruals accounting has not gained universal acceptance. The governments of Germany, Italy and Holland have so far made no plans for the transition and the governments of China, Japan, Malaysia and Singapore have decided against it. The main issue is the huge cost involved in terms of the number of qualified accountants required. For developing countries this cost is considered to be prohibitive.

2.6 Definition of a liability

The *Statement of Principles* defines a liability as 'a present obligation of the entity arising from past events, the settlement of which is expected to result in an outflow from the entity of resources embodying economic benefits'. A liability is recognised when the amount of the outflow can be reliably measured.

Public benefit entities are subject to a commitment to provide public benefits, but there is an issue to be resolved over whether this commitment meets the definition of a liability. In this situation there has been no 'exchange'. The entity has not received any goods or services for which it is required to make 'settlement'. A distinction can be drawn between 'general commitments to provide public benefits' and 'specific commitments to provide public benefits'. The specific commitment can be regarded as a 'present obligation', but it can be argued that the obligation only arises when the entity formally undertakes to provide something such as a non-performance-related grant. (If the grant were performance-related, the entity would be able to withdraw from the agreement if the performance targets were not reached.)

There is also the issue of 'reliable measurement'. Governments in particular often find themselves funding projects which go a long way over budget, suggesting that reliable measurement was not obtained at the outset.

This issue is still being debated by the CAPE. It is of major importance in the financial reporting of the social policies of governments.

2.7 Charities

Financial reporting by UK charities is regulated by a Statement of Recommended Practice (SORP), which was last revised in 2005, generally referred to as SORP 2005. This SORP is the work of the Charity Commission, and they review it each year, taking into account changes in the financial environment.

2.7.1 SORP 2005

SORP 2005 is a summary of how accounting standards, charity law and company law impact on charity financial reporting. UK charities are not currently allowed to adopt IFRS. They are required to report under UK standards. The Charities SORP will continue to be reviewed to take into account changes in UK standards, including those arising from the convergence process with IFRS. The SORP deals with accruals-based accounts, although smaller charities with a gross income of below £100,000 per annum are still allowed to prepare cash-based receipts and payments accounts.

2.7.2 Statement of Financial Activities

In addition to a balance sheet, charities also produce a Statement of Financial Activities (SOFA), an Annual Report to the Charity Commission and sometimes an income and expenditure account. The Statement of Financial Activities is the primary statement showing the results of the charity's activities for the period.

The SoFA shows **Incoming resources**, **Resources expended**, and the resultant **Net movement in funds**. Under incoming resources, income from all sources of funds are listed. These can include:

- Subscription or membership fees
- Public donations
- Donations from patrons
- Government grants
- Income from sale of goods
- Investment income
- Publication sales
- Royalties

The resources expended will show the amount spent directly in furtherance of the Charity's objects. It will also show items which form part of any profit and loss account, such as salaries, depreciation, travelling and entertaining, audit and other professional fees. These items can be very substantial.

Charities, especially the larger charities, now operate very much in the way that profit-making entities do. They run high-profile campaigns which cost money and they employ professional people who have to be paid. At the same time, their stakeholders will want to see that most of their donation is not going on running the business, rather than achieving the aims for which funds were donated.

One of the problems charities experience is that, even although the accruals basis is being applied, they will still have income and expenditure recognised in different periods, due to the difficulty of correlating them. The extreme example is a campaign to persuade people to leave money to the charity in their will. The costs will have to be recognised, but there is no way to predict when the income will arise.

3 Performance measurement

FAST FORWARD

Not-for-profit and public sector entities are required to manage their funds efficiently but are not expected to show a profit. Their performance is measured in terms of achievement of their stated purpose.

Not-for-profit and public sector entities produce financial statements in the same way as profit-making entities do but, while they are expected to remain solvent, their performance cannot be measured simply by the bottom line.

A public sector entity is not expected to show a profit or to underspend its budget. In practice, government and local government departments know that if they underspend the budget, next year's allocation will be correspondingly reduced. This leads to a rash of digging up the roads and other expenditure just before the end of the financial year as councils strive to spend any remaining funds.

Private and public sector entities are judged principally on the basis of what they have achieved, not how much or how little they have spent in achieving it. So how is performance measured?

3.1 Public sector entities

These will have performance measures laid down by government. The emphasis is on economy, efficiency and effectiveness. Departments and local councils have to show how they have spent public money and what level of service they have achieved. Performance measurement will be based on Key Performance Indicators (KPIs). Examples of these for a local council could be:

- Number of homeless people rehoused
- % of rubbish collections made on time
- Number of children in care adopted

Public sector entities use the services of outside contractors for a variety of functions. They then have to be able to show that they have obtained the best possible value for what they have spent on outside services. This principle is usually referred to as Value For Money (VFM). In the UK, local authorities are required to report under a system known as Best Value. They have to show that they applied 'fair competition' in awarding contracts.

Best Value is based on the principle of the 'four Cs':

1   **Challenging** why, how and by whom a service is provided
2   **Comparing** performance against other local authorities
3   **Consulting** service users, the local community etc.
4   Using fair **Competition** to secure efficient and effective services

3.2 Charities

While charities must demonstrate that they have made proper use of whatever funds they have received, their stakeholders will be more interested in what they have achieved in terms of their stated mission. People who donate money to a relief fund for earthquake victims will want to know what help has been given to survivors, before enquiring how well the organisation has managed its funds. Although it must be said that any mismanagement of funds by a charity is taken very seriously by the donating public.

Some charities produce 'impact reports' which highlight what the charity set out to achieve, what it has achieved and what it has yet to do. Stakeholders should know what the organisation is aiming to achieve and how it is succeeding. Each charity will have its own performance indicators which enable it to measure this.

Question | Performance measurement

Choose a charity with which you are familiar and produce a possible set of performance indicators for it.

Exam focus point

The examiner has indicated that question 3(c) In the pilot paper is typical of how he will examine this topic.

Chapter Roundup

- The accounting requirements for not-for-profit and public sector entities are moving closer to those required for profit-making entities. However, they do have different goals and purposes.

- There is a general move to get public bodies reporting under the accruals system. Many private not-for-profit organisations still use cash accounting.

- Not-for-profit and public sector entities are required to manage their funds efficiently but are not expected to show a profit. Their performance is measured in terms of achievement of their stated purpose.

Quick Quiz

1   Give some examples of not-for-profit and public sector entities.

2   What are some of the characteristics of **private sector** not-for-profit entities?

3   What are the 'four Cs'?

Answers to Quick Quiz

1   Central and local government departments, schools, hospitals, charities.

2   See paragraph 2.2

3   See paragraph 3.1

Now try the question below from the Exam Question Bank

Number	Level	Marks	Time
Q3 (b)	–	5	9 mins

Exam question bank

1 Conceptual framework

(a) Explain and give an example of the effect on a set of published financial statements if the going concern convention is held not to apply.

(b) Explain in general terms what the ASB *Statement* is trying to achieve.

(10 marks)

2 Regulators

State three different regulatory influences on the preparation of the published accounts of UK quoted companies and briefly explain the role of each one. Comment briefly on the effectiveness of this regulatory system. **(10 marks)**

3 Standard setters

There are those who suggest that any standard setting body is redundant because accounting standards are unnecessary. Other people feel that such standards should be produced, but by the government, so that they are a legal requirement.

Required

(a) Discuss the statement that accounting standards are unnecessary for the purpose of regulating financial statements.

(b) Discuss whether or not the financial statements of not-for-profit entities should be subject to regulation. **(10 marks)**

4 Polymer

The following trial balance has been prepared by Polymer Ltd, plastics manufacturers, on 31 May 20X8, which is the end of the company's accounting period:

	£	£
Authorised and issued 300,000 ordinary shares of £1 each, fully paid		300,000
100,000 8.4% cumulative preference shares of £1 each, fully paid		100,000
Revaluation reserve		50,000
Share premium account		100,000
General reserve		50,000
Profit and loss reserve – 31 May 20X7		283,500
Patents and trademarks	215,500	
Freehold land at cost	250,000	
Leasehold property at cost	75,000	
Amortisation of leasehold property – 31 May 20X7		15,000
Factory plant and machinery at cost	150,000	
Accumulated depreciation – plant and machinery – 31 May 20X7		68,500
Furniture and fixtures at cost	50,000	
Accumulated depreciation – furniture and fixtures – 31 May 20X7		15,750
Motor vehicles at cost	75,000	
Accumulated depreciation – motor vehicles – 31 May 20X7		25,000
10% debentures (20Y0 – 20Y5)		100,000
Trade debtors/ trade creditors	177,630	97,500
Bank overdraft		51,250
Stocks – raw materials at cost – 31 May 20X7	108,400	
Purchases – raw materials	750,600	
Carriage inwards – raw materials	10,500	
Manufacturing wages	250,000	
Manufacturing overheads	125,000	
Cash	5,120	
Work in progress – 31 May 20X7	32,750	
Sales		1,526,750
Administrative expenses	158,100	
Selling and distribution expenses	116,800	
Legal and professional expenses	54,100	
Allowance for debtors – 31 May 20X8		5,750
Stocks – finished goods – 31 May 20X7	184,500	
	2,789,000	2,789,000

Additional information:

(1)   Stocks at 31 May 20X8 were:

	£
Raw materials	112,600
Finished goods	275,350
Work in progress	37,800

(2)   Depreciation for the year is to be charged as follows:

Plant and machinery	8% on cost – charged to production
Furniture and fixtures	10% on cost – charged to admin
Motor vehicles	20% on reducing value – 25% admin
	– 75% selling and distribution

(3)   Financial, legal and professional expenses include:

Solicitors' fees for purchase of freehold property during year   5,000

(4)   Provision is to be made for a full year's interest on the debentures.

(5)   Corporation tax on the profits for the year is estimated at £40,000 and is due for payment on 28 February 20X9.

(6)   The directors recommended on 30 June that a dividend of 3.5p per share be paid on the ordinary share capital. No ordinary dividend was paid during the year ended 31 May 20X7.

(7)   The leasehold land and buildings are held on a 50 year lease, acquired ten years ago.

Required

From the information given above, prepare the profit and loss account of Polymer Ltd for the year to 31 May 20X8 and a balance sheet at that date for publication in accordance with UK GAAP.

You should also show a statement of the movement in the profit and loss reserve.

Notes to the financial statements are *not* required.   **(25 marks)**

5 Winger

The following trial balance relates to Winger plc at 31 March 20X1:

	£'000	£'000
Turnover (note (i))		358,450
Cost of sales	185,050	
Distribution costs	28,700	
Administration expenses	15,000	
Lease rentals (note (ii))	20,000	
Debenture interest paid	2,000	
Dividends paid	12,000	
Land and buildings – cost (note (iii))	200,000	
Plant and equipment – cost	154,800	
Depreciation 1 April 20X0 – plant and equipment		34,800
Development expenditure (note (iv))	30,000	
Profit on disposal of fixed assets (note (iii))		45,000
Trade debtors	55,000	
Stocks – 31 March 20X1	28,240	
Cash and bank	10,660	
Trade creditors		29,400
Taxation – over provision in year to 31 March 20X0		2,200
Ordinary shares of 25p each		150,000
8% Debenture (issued in 20W8)		50,000
Profit and loss reserve 1 April 20X0		71,600
	741,450	741,450

The following notes are relevant:

(i)   Included in the turnover is £27 million, which relates to sales made to customers under sale or return agreements. The expiry date for the return of these goods is 30 April 20X1. Winger plc has charged a mark-up of 20% on cost for these sales.

(ii)   A lease rental of £20 million was paid on 1 April 20X0. It is the first of five annual payments in advance for the rental of an item of equipment that has a cash purchase price of £80 million. The auditors have advised that this is a finance lease and have calculated the implicit interest rate in the lease as 12% per annum. Leased assets should be depreciated on a straight-line basis over the life of the lease.

(iii)   On 1 April 20X0 Winger plc acquired new land and building at a cost of £200 million. For the purpose of calculating depreciation only, the asset has been separated into the following elements:

Separate asset	Cost	Life
	£'000	
Land	50,000	Freehold
Heating system	20,000	10 years
Lifts	30,000	15 years
Building	100,000	50 years

The depreciation of the elements of the building should be calculated on a straight-line basis. The new building replaced an existing building that was sold on the same date for £95 million. It had cost £50 million and had a carrying value of £80 million at the date of sale. The profit on this building has been calculated on the original cost. It had not been depreciated on the basis that the depreciation charge would not be material.

Plant and machinery is depreciated at 20% on the reducing balance basis.

(iv)   The figure for development expenditure in the trial balance represents the amounts capitalised in previous years in respect of the development of a new product. Unfortunately, during the current year, the Government has introduced legislation which effectively bans this type of product. As a consequence of this the project has been abandoned. The directors of Winger plc are of the opinion that writing off the development expenditure, as opposed to its previous capitalisation, represents a change of accounting policy and therefore wish to treat the write off as a prior adjustment.

(v)   A provision for corporation tax for the year to 31 March 20X1 of £15 million is required.

(vi)   The finance cost on the debentures is £4,000 per annum.

Required

(a)   Prepare the profit and loss account of Winger plc for the year to 31 March 20X1.   **(9 marks)**

(b)   Prepare a balance sheet as at 31 March 20X1 in accordance with the Companies Acts and current Accounting Standards so far as the information permits.   **(11 marks)**

Notes to the financial statements are not required.

(c)   Discuss the current acceptability of the company's previous policy in respect of non-depreciation of buildings and the proposed treatment of the deferred development expenditure.   **(5 marks)**

(Total = 25 marks)

6 Hewlett

Hewlett is a quoted company reporting under UK GAAP. During the year end 31 December 20X2, the company changed its accounting policy with respect to property valuation. There are also a number of other issues that need to be finalised before the financial statements can be published.

Hewlett's trial balance from the general ledger at 31 December 20X2 showed the following balances:

	£'m	£'m
Revenue		2,648
Debenture interest paid	3	
Purchases	1,669	
Distribution costs	514	
Administrative expenses	345	
Interim dividend paid	6	
Stocks at 1 January 20X2	444	
Trade debtors	545	
Trade creditors		434
Cash at bank and in hand	28	
50p ordinary shares		100
Share premium account		244
General reserve		570
Profit and loss reserve at 1 January 20X2		349
4% debenture loans repayable 20X8 (issued 20X0)		150
Land and buildings: cost (including £60m land)	380	
accumulated depreciation at 1 January 20X2		64
Plant and machinery: cost	258	
accumulated depreciation at 1 January 20X2		126
Investment properties at 1 January 20X2	548	
Rental income		48
Proceeds from sale of machinery		7
	4,740	4,740

Further information to be taken into account:

(i) Closing stocks were counted and amounted to £388m at cost. However, shortly after the year end out-of-date stocks with a cost of £15m were sold for £8m.

(ii) The company decided to change its accounting policy with respect to its 10 year old land and buildings from depreciated historical cost to revalued amounts. The revalued amounts at 1 January 20X2 were £800m (including £100m for the land). No further revaluation was necessary at 31 December 20X2. The company wishes to treat the revaluation surplus as being realised over the life of the asset.

(iii) Due to a change in the company's product portfolio plans, an item of plant with a carrying value £22m at 31 December 20X1 (after adjusting for depreciation for the year) may be impaired due to a change in use. An impairment test conducted at 31 December, revealed its net selling price to be £16m. The asset is now expected to generate an annual net income stream of £3.8m for the next 5 years at which point the asset would be disposed for £4.2m. An appropriate discount rate is 8%. 5 year discount factors at 8% are:

Simple	Cumulative
0.677	3.993

(iv) The corporation tax liability for the year is estimated at £27m.

(v) An interim dividend of 3p per share was paid on 30 June 20X2. A final dividend of 1.5p per share was declared by the directors on 28 January 20X3.

(vi) During the year, Hewlett Ltd disposed of some malfunctioning machinery for £7m. The machinery had cost £15m and had accumulated depreciation brought forward at 1 January 20X2 of £3m.

There were no other additions or disposal of tangible assets in the year.

(vii) The company treats depreciation on plant and machinery as a cost of sale and on land and buildings as an administration cost. Depreciation rates as per the company's accounting policy note are as follows:

Buildings	2% straight line
Plant and machinery	20% reducing balance

Hewlett's accounting policy is to charge a full year's depreciation in the year of an asset's purchase and none in the year of disposal.

(viii) During the year on 1 July 20X2, Hewlett made a 1 for 3 bonus issue, capitalising its general reserve. This transaction had not yet been accounted for. The fair value of the company's shares on the date of the bonus issue was £7.50 each.

(ix) The fair value of the investment properties at 31 December 20X2 was £586m. No previous revaluations had been necessary.

Required

Prepare the profit and loss account and reconciliation of movement in shareholders' funds for Hewlett Ltd for the year to 31 December 20X2 and a balance sheet at that date in accordance with UK GAAP insofar as the information permits.

Notes to the financial statements are not required, but all workings should be clearly shown.

Work to the nearest £1m. Comparative information is not required. **(25 marks)**

7 Gains

Using the information below prepare the statement of total recognised gains and losses, the reconciliation of shareholders' funds and the reconciliation of profit to historical cost profit for Gains Ltd for the year ended 31 December 20X9.

(a) *Gains Ltd profit and loss account extract*

	£'000
Operating profit	792
Interest receivable	24
Interest payable	(10)
Profit before tax	806
Taxation	(240)
Profit after tax	566

(b) *Fixed assets*

(i) Assets held at cost were impaired by £25,000.

(ii) Freehold land and buildings were revalued to £500,000 (Book value £380,000). The remaining life of the assets is 25 years.

(iii) A previously revalued asset was sold for £60,000.

Details of the revaluation are as follows:

	£
Book value at revaluation	30,000
Revaluation	50,000
	80,000
Depreciation (80,000/10) × 3)	24,000
	56,000

(iv)   Details of investment properties are as follows:

	£
Cost	120,000
Investment revaluation reserve	40,000
Value at 1.1.20X9	160,000

The properties had a valuation on 31 December 20X9 of £110,000. The fall in value is deemed to be temporary.

(c)   *Share capital*

During the year the company had the following changes to its capital structure.

(i)   An issue of £200,000 £1 ordinary bonus shares.
(ii)   An issue of 400,000 £1 ordinary shares (issue price £1.40 per share).

(d)   *Shareholders funds*

The book value of shareholders funds at the start of the year amounted to £6,820,000.

(e)   *Dividends*

Dividends paid during the year amounted to £200,000.

8 Multiplex

On 1 January 20X1 Multiplex plc acquired Steamdays Ltd, a company that operates a scenic railway along the coast of a popular tourist area. The summarised balance sheet at fair values of Steamdays Ltd on 1 January 20X1, reflecting the terms of the acquisition was:

	£'000
Goodwill	200
Operating licence	1,000
Property – train stations and land	250
Rail track and coaches	250
Two steam engines	1,000
Other net assets	300
Purchase consideration	3,000

The operating licence is for ten years. It was renewed on 1 January 20X1 by the transport authority and is stated at the cost of its renewal. The carrying values of the property and rail track and coaches are based on their value in use. The engines, and other net assets are valued at their net selling prices.

On 1 February 20X1 the boiler of one of the steam engines exploded, completely destroying the whole engine. Fortunately no one was injured, but the engine was beyond repair. Due to its age a replacement could not be obtained. Because of the reduced passenger capacity the estimated value in use of the whole of the business after the accident was assessed at £2 million.

Passenger numbers after the accident were below expectations even after allowing for the reduced capacity. A market research report concluded that tourists were not using the railway because of their fear of a similar accident occurring to the remaining engine. In the light of this the value in use of the business was re-assessed on 31 March 20X1 at £1.8 million. On this date Multiplex plc received an offer of £600,000 in respect of the operating licence (it is transferable). The realisable value of the other net assets has not changed significantly.

Required

Calculate the carrying value of the assets of Steamdays Ltd (in Multiplex plc's consolidated balance sheet) at 1 February 20X1 and 31 March 20X1 after recognising the impairment losses.   **(10 marks)**

9 Barcelona and Madrid

Barcelona acquired 60% of Madrid's ordinary share capital on 30 June 20X2 at a price £1.06 per share. The balance on Madrid's retained earnings at that date was £104m and the general reserve stood at £11m.

Their respective balance sheets as at 30 September 20X6 are as follows:

	Barcelona		Madrid	
	£m	£m	£m	£m
Fixed assets				
Patents		45		–
Tangible assets		2,848		354
Investment in Madrid		159		–
		3,052		354
Current assets				
Stocks	895		225	
Debtors	1,348		251	
Cash	212		34	
	2,455		510	
Creditors: amounts falling due within one year				
Trade and other creditors	1,168		183	
Current portion of long-term borrowings	–		23	
	1,168		206	
Net current assets		1,287		304
Total assets less current liabilities		4,339		658
Creditors: amounts falling due after more than one year				
Long-term borrowings		(558)		(168)
		3,781		490
Capital and reserves				
Share capital (20p ordinary shares)		920		50
General reserve		775		46
Profit and loss reserve		2,086		394
		3,781		490

Goodwill is tested annually for impairment. Annual impairment tests have revealed cumulative impairment losses relating to recognised goodwill of £17m to date.

Required

Produce the consolidated balance sheet for the Barcelona Group as at 30 September 20X6. **(15 marks)**

10 Reprise

Reprise plc purchased 75% of Encore Ltd for £2,000,000 on 1 April 20X0 when the balance on its profit and loss reserve was £1,044,000. The balance sheets of the two companies as at 31 March 20X4 are as follows:

	Reprise plc		Encore Ltd	
	£'000	£'000	£'000	£'000
Fixed assets				
Investment in Encore Ltd		2,000		–
Land and buildings		3,350		–
Plant and machinery		1,010		2,210
Motor vehicles		510		345
		6,870		2,555
Current assets				
Stocks	890		352	
Debtors	1,372		514	
Cash at bank and in hand	89		51	
	2,351		917	
Creditors: amounts falling due within one year				
Trade creditors	996		362	
Net current assets		1,355		555
Total assets less current liabilities		8,225		3,110
Creditors: amounts falling due after more than one year				
10% debentures		500		–
		7,725		3,110
Capital and reserves				
Share capital - £1 ordinary shares		1,000		500
Revaluation reserve		2,500		–
Profit and loss reserve		4,225		2,610
		7,725		3,110

The following additional information is available:

(1) Included in debtors of Reprise plc are amounts owed by Encore of £75,000. The current accounts do not at present balance due to a cheque for £39,000 being in transit at the year end from Encore Ltd.

(2) Included in the stocks of Encore Ltd are items purchased from Reprise plc during the year for £31,200. Reprise marks up its goods by 30% to achieve its selling price.

(3) Goodwill is amortised over 8 years.

Required

Prepare the consolidated balance sheet for the Reprise plc group of companies as at 31 March 20X4.

11 War

(a) When an acquisition takes place, the purchase consideration may be in the form of share capital. Where no suitable market price exists (for example, shares in an unquoted company) how may the fair value of the purchase consideration be estimated? **(4 marks)**

(b) On 1 May 20X7, War plc acquired 70% of the ordinary share capital of Peace Ltd by issuing to Peace Co's shareholders 500,000 ordinary £1 shares at a market value of £1.60p per share. The costs associated with the share issue were £50,000.

As at 30 June 20X7, the following financial statements for War plc and Peace Ltd were available.

PROFIT AND LOSS ACCOUNTS
FOR THE YEAR ENDED 30 JUNE 20X7

	War plc	Peace Ltd
	£'000	£'000
Turnover	3,150	1,770
Cost of sales	(1,610)	(1,065)
Gross profit	1,540	705
Distribution costs	(620)	(105)
Administrative expenses	(325)*	(210)
Operating profit	595	390
Interest payable	(70)	(30)
Dividends from Peace Ltd	42	–
Profit on ordinary activities before taxation	567	360
Tax on profit	(283)	(135)
Profit after tax	284	225

*Note. The issue costs of £50,000 on the issue of ordinary share capital are included in this figure.

Dividends paid during the year were: War plc £38,000; Peace Ltd £60,000.

BALANCE SHEETS AS AT 30 JUNE 20X7

	War plc	Peace Ltd
	£'000	£'000
Fixed assets		
Tangible fixed assets	1,750	350
Investment in Peace Ltd	800	–
	2,550	350
Current assets		
Stock	150	450
Debtors	238	213
Cash	187	112
	575	775
Creditors: amounts falling due within one year	(400)	(250)
Net current assets	175	525
Total assets less current liabilities	2,725	875
Creditors: amounts falling due after one year	(1,050)	(175)
	1,675	700
Capital and reserves		
Ordinary shares of £1 each	750	100
Share premium	300	150
Profit and loss account	625	450
	1,675	700

BPP
LEARNING MEDIA

You have been asked to prepare the consolidated financial statements, taking account of the following further information.

(i) Any goodwill arising on acquisition is to be amortised over 5 years on a straight line basis, with a full year's amortisation charged in the year of acquisition. The charge is to be included in administrative expenses.

(ii) War plc accounts for pre-acquisition dividends by treating them as a deduction from the cost of the investment. Peace Ltd paid an ordinary dividend of 60p per share on 1 June 20X7. No dividends were proposed as at 30 June 20X7.

(iii) The profit of Peace Ltd may be assumed to accrue evenly over the year.

(iv) The tangible fixed assets of Peace Ltd had a net realisable value of £400,000 at the date of acquisition. Their open market value was £500,000. It has been decided that, as Peace Ltd was acquired so close to the year end, no depreciation adjustment will be made in the group accounts; the year end value will be taken as the carrying value of the tangible fixed assets in the accounts of Peace Ltd. The remaining assets and liabilities of Peace Ltd were all stated at their fair value as at 1 May 20X7.

(v) Peace Ltd did not issue any shares between the date of acquisition and the year end.

(vi) There were no intercompany transactions during the year.

Required

Prepare the consolidated balance sheet and the consolidated profit and loss account of the War Group plc for the year ended 30 June 20X7. You should work to the nearest £'000. You do not need to prepare notes to the accounts. **(21 marks)**

(Total = 25 marks)

12 Fallowfield and Rusholme

Fallowfield plc acquired a 60% holding in Rusholme Limited three years ago when Rusholme's profit and loss reserve balance stood at £16,000. Both businesses have been very successful since the acquisition and their respective profit and loss accounts for the year ended 30 June 20X8 are as follows:

	Fallowfield plc £	Rusholme Ltd £
Turnover	403,400	193,000
Cost of sales	(201,400)	(92,600)
Gross profit	202,000	100,400
Distribution costs	(16,000)	(14,600)
Administrative expenses	(24,250)	(17,800)
Operating profit	161,750	68,000
Dividends from Rusholme	15,000	–
Profit before tax	176,750	68,000
Tax	(61,750)	(22,000)
Profit after tax	115,000	46,000

Reconciliation of movement in the profit and loss reserve

	£	£
Profit and loss reserve b/fwd	163,000	61,000
Profit after tax	115,000	46,000
Dividends paid	(40,000)	(25,000)
Profit and loss reserve c/fwd	238,000	82,000

Additional information

1. During the year Rusholme sold some goods to Fallowfield for £40,000, including 25% mark up. Half of these items were still in stock at the year-end.

Required

Produce the consolidated profit and loss account of Fallowfield plc and its subsidiary undertaking for the year ended 30 June 20X8, and a reconciliation of the movement in the consolidated profit and loss reserve. (Ignore goodwill.)

(15 marks)

13 Panther Group

Panther operated as a single company, but in 20X4 decided to expand its operations. Panther acquired a 60% interest in Sabre on 1 July 20X4 for £2,000,000.

The profit and loss accounts of Panther and Sabre for the year ended 31 December 20X4 are as follows:

	Panther	Sabre
	£'000	£'000
Turnover	22,800	4,300
Cost of sales	(13,600)	(2,600)
Gross profit	9,200	1,700
Distribution costs	(2,900)	(500)
Administrative expenses	(1,800)	(300)
Operating profit	4,500	900
Interest payable	(200)	(70)
Interest receivable	50	–
Profit before tax	4,350	830
Tax	(1,300)	(220)
Profit after tax	3,050	610

Since acquisition, Panther purchased £320,000 of goods from Sabre. Of these, £60,000 remained in stocks at the year end. Sabre makes a mark-up on cost of 20% under the transfer pricing agreement between the two companies. The fair value of the identifiable net assets of Sabre on purchase were £200,000 greater than their book value. The difference relates to properties with a remaining useful life of 20 years.

On the acquisition date Panther advanced a loan to Sabre amounting to £800,000 at an interest rate of 5%. The loan is due for repayment in 20X9.

Reserves (extracts) for the two companies:

	Panther Profit & loss reserve	Sabre Profit & loss reserve
	£'000	£'000
Balance at 1 January 20X9	12,750	2,480
Profit after tax	3,050	610
Dividends paid	(900)	–
Balance at 31 December 20X9	14,900	3,090

Panther and Sabre had £400,000 and £150,000 of share capital in issue throughout the period respectively.

Required

Prepare the consolidated profit and loss account and reconciliation of the movement in the consolidated profit and loss reserve for the Panther Group for the year ended 31 December 20X4.

Goodwill is tested annually for impairment. No adjustments for impairment losses were necessary in the group financial statements.

Assume revenue and expenses (other than intragroup items) accrue evenly. **(20 marks)**

14 Hever

Hever plc has held shares in two companies, Spiro Ltd and Aldridge plc, for a number of years. As at 31 December 20X4 they have the following balance sheets:

	Hever plc		Spiro Ltd		Aldridge Plc	
	£'000	£'000	£'000	£'000	£'000	£'000
Fixed assets						
Tangible assets		370		190		260
Investments		218		–		–
		588		190		260
Current assets						
Stocks	160		100		180	
Trade debtors	170		90		100	
Cash	50		40		10	
	380		230		290	
Creditors						
Trade creditors	100		60		70	
Net current assets		280		170		220
		868		360		480
Capital and reserves						
Share capital (£1 ords)		200		80		50
Share premium		100		80		30
Profit and loss reserve		568		200		400
		868		360		480

You ascertain the following additional information:

(1) The 'investments' in the balance sheet comprise solely Hever plc's investment in Spiro Ltd (£128,000) and in Aldridge plc (£90,000).

(2) The 48,000 shares in Spiro Ltd were acquired when Spiro's profit and loss reserve balance stood at £20,000.

The 15,000 shares in Aldridge plc were acquired when that company had a profit and loss reserve balance of £150,000.

(3) When Hever acquired its shares in Spiro the fair value of Spiro's net assets equalled their book values with the following exceptions:

	£'000	
Tangible assets	50	higher
Stocks	20	lower (sold during 20X4)

Depreciation arising on the fair value adjustment to fixed assets since this date is £5,000.

(4) During the year, Hever sold stocks to Spiro Ltd for £16,000, which originally cost Hever £10,000. Three-quarters of these stocks has subsequently been sold by Spiro.

(5) Goodwill is to be kept in the balance sheet without amortisation. No impairment of goodwill has occurred.

Required

Produce the consolidated balance sheet for the Hever plc group (incorporating the associate). **(25 marks)**

15 Trontacc

Trontacc plc is a company whose activities are in the field of major construction projects. During the year ended 30 September 20X7, it enters into three separate long-term contracts, each with a fixed contract price of £1,000,000. The following information relates to these contracts at 30 September 20X7:

	Contract A £'000	B £'000	C £'000
Payments on account (including amounts receivable)	540	475	400
Costs incurred to date	500	550	320
Estimate costs to complete the contract	300	550	580
Estimate percentage of work completed	60%	50%	35%

Required

(a) Show how each contract would be reflected in the balance sheet of Trontacc plc at 30 September 20X7 under SSAP 9 (revised).

(b) Show how each contract would be reflected in the profit and loss account of Trontacc plc for the year ended 30 September 20X7 under SSAP 9 (revised). **(10 marks)**

16 C plc

C plc is a civil engineering company. It started work on two long-term contracts during the year ended 31 December 20X0. The following figures relate to those projects at the balance sheet date.

	Maryhill bypass £'000	Rottenrow Centre £'000
Contract price	9,000	8,000
Costs incurred to date	1,400	2,900
Estimated costs to completion	5,600	5,200
Value of work certified to date	2,800	3,000
Payments on account	2,600	3,400

An old mineshaft has been discovered under the site for the Rottenrow Centre and the costs of dealing with this have been taken into account in the calculation of estimated costs to completion. C plc's lawyers are reasonably confident that the customer will have to bear the additional costs which will be incurred in stabilising the land. If negotiations are successful then the contract price will increase to £10m.

C plc recognises turnover and profits on long-term contracts on the basis of work certified to date.

Required

(a) Calculate the figures which would appear in C plc's financial statements in respect of these two projects.

(b) It has been suggested that profit on long-term contracts should not be recognised until the contract is completed. Briefly explain whether you believe that this suggestion would improve the quality of financial reporting for long-term contracts. **(15 marks)**

17 Provisions

FRS 12 *Provisions, contingent liabilities and contingent assets* was issued in September 1998. Prior to its publication, there was no Accounting Standard that dealt with the general subject of accounting for provisions.

Extract plc prepares its financial statements to 31 December each year. During the years ended 31 December 20X0 and 31 December 20X1, the following event occurred.

Extract plc is involved in extracting minerals in a number of different countries. The process typically involves some contamination of the site from which the minerals are extracted. Extract plc makes good this contamination only where legally required to do so by legislation passed in the relevant country.

The company has been extracting minerals in Copperland since January 20W8 and expects its site to produce output until 31 December 20X5. On 23 December 20X0, it came to the attention of the directors of Extract plc that the government of Copperland was virtually certain to pass legislation requiring the making good of mineral extraction sites. The legislation was duly passed on 15 March 20X1. The directors of Extract plc estimate that the cost of making good the site in Copperland will be £2 million. This estimate is of the actual cash expenditure that will be incurred on 31 December 20X5.

Required

(a) Explain why there was a need for an accounting standard dealing with provisions, and summarise the criteria that need to be satisfied before a provision is recognised. **(12 marks)**

(b) Compute the effect of the estimated cost of making good the site on the financial statements of Extract plc for **both** of the years ended 31 December 20X0 and 20X1. Give full explanations of the figures you compute.

The annual discount rate to be used in any relevant calculations is 10%.

The relevant discount factors at 10% are:

Year 4 at 10%   0.683
Year 5 at 10%   0.621   **(13 marks)**

(Total = 25 marks)

18 Alpha

In producing the Statement of Principles and FRS 5, the Accounting Standards Board (ASB) has sought to address the potential problem that the management of some companies may choose to adopt inappropriate accounting policies. These could have the effect of portraying an entity's financial position in a favourable manner. In some countries this is referred to as 'creative accounting'. Included in the statement and FRS 5, is the application of the principle of 'substance over form'.

Required

(a) Describe in broad terms common ways in which management can manipulate financial statements to indulge in 'creative accounting' and why they would wish to do so. **(7 marks)**

(b) Explain the principle of substance over form and how it limits the above practice; and for each of the following areas of accounting describe an example of the application of substance over form.

   (i)   Group accounting
   (ii)   Financing fixed assets
   (iii) Measurement and disclosure of current assets   **(8 marks)**

(c) Alpha plc is considering how it should raise £10 million of finance which is required for a major and vital fixed asset renewal scheme that will be undertaken during the current year to 31 December 20X6. Alpha is particularly concerned about how analysts are likely to react to its financial statements for the year to 31 December 20X6. Present forecasts suggest that Alpha's earnings per share and its financial gearing ratios may be worse than market expectations. Mr Wong, Alpha's Finance Director, is in favour of raising the finance by issuing a convertible debenture. He has suggested that the coupon (interest) rate on the debenture should be 5%; this is below the current market rate of 9% for this type of debenture. In order to make the debenture attractive to investors the terms of conversion into equity would be very favourable to compensate for the low interest rate.

Required

(i) Explain why the Finance Director believes the above scheme may favourably improve Alpha's earnings per share and gearing.

(ii) Describe how the requirements of FRS 22 *Earnings per share* and FRS 25 *Financial instruments: presentation* are intended to prevent the above effects. **(10 marks)**

(Total = 25 marks)

19 Jenson

The timing of revenue (income) recognition has long been an area of debate and inconsistency in accounting. Industry practice in relation to revenue recognition varies widely, the following are examples of different points in the operating cycle of businesses that revenue and profit can be recognised.

- On the acquisition of goods
- During the manufacture or production of goods
- On delivery/acceptance of goods
- When certain conditions have been satisfied after the goods have been delivered
- Receipt of payment for credit sales
- On the expiry of a guarantee or warranty

In the past the 'critical event' approach has been used to determine the timing of revenue recognition. The Accounting Standards Board (ASB) in its 'Statement of Principles for Financial Reporting' has defined the 'elements' of financial statements, and it uses these to determine when a gain or loss occurs.

Required

(a) Explain what is meant by the critical event in relation to revenue recognition and discuss the criteria used in the Statement of Principles for determining when a gain or loss arises. **(5 marks)**

(b) For each of the stages of the operating cycle identified above, explain why it may be an appropriate point to recognise revenue and, where possible, give a practical example of an industry where it occurs. **(12 marks)**

(c) Jenson plc has entered into the following transactions/agreements in the year to 31 March 20X1:

(i) Goods, which had cost £20,000 were sold to Wholesaler plc for £35,000 on 1 June 20X0. Jenson plc has an option to repurchase the goods from Wholesaler plc at any time within the next two years. The repurchase price will be £35,000 plus interest charged at 12% per annum from the date of sale to the date of repurchase. It is expected that Jenson plc will repurchase the goods.

(ii) Jenson plc owns the rights to a fast food franchise. On 1 April 20X0 it sold the right to open a new outlet to Mr Cody. The franchise is for five years. Jenson plc received an initial fee of £50,000 for the first year and will receive £5,000 per annum thereafter. Jenson plc has continuing service obligations on its franchise for advertising and product development that amount to approximately £8,000 per annum per franchised outlet. A reasonable profit margin on the provision of the continuing services is deemed to be 20% of revenues received.

(iii)   On 1 September 20X0 Jenson plc received total subscriptions in advance of £240,000. The subscriptions are for 24 monthly publications of a magazine produced by Jenson plc. At the year end Jenson plc had produced and despatched six of the 24 publications. The total cost of producing the magazine is estimated at £192,000 with each publication costing a broadly similar amount.

Required

Describe how Jenson plc should treat each of the above examples in its financial statements in the year to 31 March 20X1.   **(8 marks)**

(Total = 25 marks)

20 Bulwell

Bulwell Aggregates Ltd wish to expand their transport fleet and purchased three heavy lorries with a list price of £18,000 each. Robert Bulwell has negotiated lease purchase finance to fund this expansion, and the company has entered into a lease purchase agreement with Granby Garages plc on 1 January 20X1. The agreement states that Bulwell Aggregates will pay a deposit of £9,000 on 1 January 20X1, and two annual instalments of £24,000 on 31 December 20X1, 20X2 and a final instalment of £20,391 on 31 December 20X3.

Interest is to be calculated at 25% on the balance outstanding on 1 January each year and paid on 31 December each year.

The depreciation policy of Bulwell Aggregates Ltd is to write off the vehicles over a four year period using the straight line method and assuming a scrap value of £1,333 for each vehicle at the end of its useful life.

The cost of the vehicles to Granby Garages is £14,400 each.

Required

Show the entries in the profit and loss account and balance sheet for the years 20X1, 20X2, 20X3. This is the only leasing transaction undertaken by this company.

Calculations to the nearest £.   **(10 marks)**

21 Financial assets and liabilities

(a)   On 1 January 2005, an entity issued a debt instrument with a coupon rate of 3.5% at a par value of £6,000,000. The directly attributable costs of issue were £120,000. The debt instrument is repayable on 31 December 2011 at a premium of £1,100,000.

What is the total amount of the finance cost associated with the debt instrument?   **(3 marks)**

(b)   On 1 January 20X3 Deferred issued £600,000 debentures. Issue costs were £200. The debentures do not carry interest, but are redeemable at a premium of £152,389 on 31 December 20X4. The effective finance cost of the debentures is 12%.

What is the finance cost in respect of the debentures for the year ended 31 December 20X4?
(3 marks)

(c)   On 1 January 20X1, EFG issued 10,000 5% convertible bonds at their par value of £50 each. The bonds will be redeemed on 1 January 20X6. Each bond is convertible to equity shares at the option of the holder at any time during the five year period. Interest on the bond will be paid annually in arrears.

The prevailing market interest rate for similar debt without conversion options at the date of issue was 6%.

The discount factors for 6% at year 5 is 0.747.

The cumulative discount factor for years 1-5 at 6% is 4.212.

At what value should the equity element of the financial instrument be recognised in the financial statements at EFG at the date of issue? **(4 marks)**

(Total = 10 marks)

22 Lis

On 1 January 20X3 Lis Ltd entered into a lease agreement to rent an asset for a 6 year period with annual payments of £18,420 made in advance. The market price of the asset on the same date was £86,000. The present value of minimum lease payments amounts to £84,000, discounted at the implicit interest rate shown in the lease agreement of 12.5%.

Lis Ltd intends to use the asset for 5 years which is its expected useful life.

Required

Explain how the above lease would be accounted for the year ending 31 December 20X3 including producing relevant extracts from the profit and loss account and balance sheet.

You are not required to prepare the notes to the financial statements. **(10 marks)**

23 Carpati

The following information relates to Carpati Ltd:

(1)   The net book value of plant and machinery at 30 September 20X6 is £1,185,000.

(2)   The tax written down value of plant and machinery at 1 October 20X5 was £405,000.

(3)   During the year ended 30 September 20X6, the company bought plant and machinery of £290,000, which is eligible for capital allowances.

(4)   Carpati Ltd bought its freehold property in 20W5 for £600,000, which it uses and plans to continue to use as its head office. It was revalued in the 20X6 accounts to £1,500,000. Ignore depreciation on buildings. No capital allowances were available to Carpati Ltd on the buildings, but the gain will be taxable on sale.

Required

Draft the balance sheet note at 30 September 20X6 omitting comparatives, in respect of deferred tax. Work to the nearest £'000. Assume a current tax rate of 30%. Capital allowances are at 25% on a reducing balance basis. The current tax rate enacted for 20X7 is 28%. **(15 marks)**

BPP
LEARNING MEDIA

24 Pilum

The draft profit and loss account of Pilum plc for the year ended 31 December 20X4 is set out below:

DRAFT PROFIT AND LOSS ACCOUNT FOR YEAR ENDED 31 DECEMBER 20X4

	£	£
Profit before tax		2,530,000
Less taxation:		
Corporation tax		1,127,000
		1,403,000
Transfer to reserves		230,000
Dividends:		
Paid preference interim dividend	138,000	
Paid ordinary interim divided	184,000	
Declared preference final dividend	138,000	
Declared ordinary final dividend	230,000	
		690,000
Retained		483,000

On 1 January 20X4 the issued share capital of Pilum plc was 4,600,000 6% preference shares of £1 each and 4,120,000 ordinary shares of £1 each.

Required

Calculate the earnings per share (on basic and diluted basis) in respect of the year ended 31 December 20X4 for each of the following circumstances. (Each of the three circumstances (a) to (c) is to be dealt with separately):

(a) On the basis that there was no change in the issued share capital of the company during the year ended 31 December 20X4.

(b) On the basis that the company made a rights issue of £1 ordinary shares on 1 October 20X4 in the proportion of 1 for every 5 shares held, at a price of £1.20. the middle market price for the shares on the last day of quotation cum rights was £1.78 per share.

(c) On the basis that the company made no new issue of shares during the year ended 31 December 20X4 but on that date it had in issue £1,500,000 10% convertible loan stock 20X8 – 20Y1. This loan stock will be convertible into ordinary £1 shares as follows:

20X8 90 £1 shares for £100 nominal value loan stock
20X9 85 £1 shares for £100 nominal value loan stock
20Y0 80 £1 shares for £100 nominal value loan stock
20Y1 75 £1 shares for £100 nominal value loan stock

Assume where appropriate that the corporation tax rate is 30%.

25 Biggerbuys

Biggerbuys has carried on business for a number of years as a retailer of a wide variety of consumer products. The entity operates from a number of stores around the country. In recent years the entity has found it necessary to provide credit facilities to its customers in order to maintain growth in turnover. As a result of this decision the liability to its bankers has increased substantially. The statutory financial statements for the year ended 30 June 20X9 have recently been published and extracts are provided below, together with comparative figures for the previous two years.

PROFIT AND LOSS ACCOUNT FOR THE YEARS ENDED 30 JUNE

	20X7	20X8	20X9
	£m	£m	£m
Turnover	1,850	2,200	2,500
Cost of sales	(1,250)	(1,500)	(1,750)
Gross profit	600	700	750
Other operating costs	(550)	(640)	(700)
Operating profit	50	60	50
Interest from credit sales	45	60	90
Interest payable	(25)	(60)	(110)
Profit before taxation	70	60	30
Tax payable	(23)	(20)	(10)
Profit after taxation	47	40	20

BALANCE SHEETS AT 30 JUNE

	20X7	20X8	20X9
	£m	£m	£m
Tangible fixed assets	278	290	322
Current assets			
Stocks	400	540	620
Trade debtors	492	550	633
Cash	12	12	15
	904	1,102	1,268
Current liabilities			
Trade creditors	270	270	280
Tax payable	20	20	8
	290	290	288
Net current assets	614	812	980
Net assets	892	1,102	1,302
Bank loans	(320)	(520)	(610)
Other interest bearing borrowings	(200)	(200)	(320)
	372	382	372
Capital and reserves			
Share capital	90	90	90
Reserves	282	292	282
	372	382	372

Other information

(1)   Depreciation charged for the three years in question was as follows.

Year ended 30 June	20X7	20X8	20X9
	£m	£m	£m
	55	60	70

(2)   The other interest bearing borrowings are secured by a floating charge over the assets of Biggerbuys. Their repayment is due on 30 June 20Y9.

(3)   Dividends of £30m were paid in 20X7 and 20X8. A dividend of £20m has been proposed.

(4)   The bank loans are unsecured. The maximum lending facility the bank will provide is £630m.

(5)   Over the past three years the level of credit sales has been:

Year ended 30 June	20X7	20X8	20X9
	£m	£m	£m
	300	400	600

The entity offers extended credit terms for certain products to maintain market share in a highly competitive environment.

Given the steady increase in the level of bank loans which has taken place in recent years, the entity has recently written to its bankers to request an increase in the lending facility. The request was received by the bank on 15 October 20X9, two weeks after the financial statements were published. The bank is concerned at the steep escalation in the level of the loans and has asked for a report on the financial performance of Biggerbuys for the last three years.

Required

As a consultant management accountant employed by the bankers of Biggerbuys, prepare a report to the bank which analyses the financial performance of the company for the period covered by the financial statements. Your report may take any form you wish, but you are aware of the particular concern of the bank regarding the rapidly increasing level of lending. Therefore it may be appropriate to include aspects of prior performance that could have contributed to the increase in the level of bank lending.   **(25 marks)**

26 Webster

Webster plc is a diversified holding company that is looking to acquire a suitable engineering company. Two private limited engineering companies, Cole Ltd and Darwin Ltd, are available for sale. The summarised financial statements for the year to 31 March 20X1 of both companies are as follows:

PROFIT AND LOSS ACCOUNTS

	Cole Limited		Darwin Limited	
	£'000	£'000	£'000	£'000
Sales (note (i))		3,000		4,400
Opening stock	450		720	
Purchases (note (ii))	2,030		3,080	
	2,480		3,800	
Closing stock	(540)		(850)	
		(1,940)		(2,950)
Gross profit		1,060		1,450
Operating expenses	480		964	
Debenture interest	80		nil	
Overdraft interest (note (v))	nil		10	
		(560)		(974)
Net profit		500		476

BALANCE SHEETS

	Cole Limited		Darwin Limited	
	£'000	£'000	£'000	£'000
Fixed assets				
Premises (note iii)		1,140		1,900
Plant (note iv)		1,200		1,200
		2,340		3,100
Current assets				
Stock	540		850	
Debtors	522		750	
Bank	20		nil	
	1,082		1,600	
Current liabilities				
Creditors	438		562	
Overdraft	nil		550	
	(438)		(1,112)	
		644		488
Net current assets		2,984		3,588
10% Debenture		(800)		nil
Net assets		2,184		3,588
Share capital and reserves				
Ordinary shares of £1 each		1,000		500
Reserves				
Revaluation reserve		nil		700
Profit and loss – 1 April 20X0	684		1,912	
Profit for year to 31 March 20X1	500		476	
		1,184		2,388
		2,184		3,588

Webster plc bases its preliminary assessment of target companies on certain key ratios. These are listed below together with the relevant figures for Cole Ltd and Darwin Ltd calculated from the above financial statements:

	Cole Limited		Darwin Limited	
Return on capital employed				
$(500 + 80)/(2,184 + 800) \times 100$	19.4%	$(476/3,588) \times 100$	13.3%	
Asset turnover (3,000/2,984)	1.01 times	(4,400/3,588)	1.23 times	
Gross profit margin	35.3%		33.0%	
Net profit margin	16.7%		10.8%	
Debtors collection period	64 days		62 days	
Creditors payment period	79 days		67 days	

Note. Capital employed is defined as shareholders' funds plus long-term, debt at the year end; asset turnover is sales revenues divided by gross assets less current liabilities.

The following additional information has been obtained.

(i)   Cole Ltd is part of the Velox Group. On 1 March 20X1 it was permitted by its holding company to sell goods at a price of £500,000 to Brander Ltd, a fellow subsidiary. Cole Ltd's normal selling price for these goods would have been £375,000. In addition Brander Ltd was instructed to pay for the goods immediately. Cole Ltd normally allows three months credit.

(ii)   On 1 January 20X1 Cole Ltd purchased £275,000 (cost price to Cole Ltd) of its materials from Advent Ltd, another member of the Velox Group. Advent Ltd was also instructed to depart from its normal trading terms that would have resulted in a charge of £300,000 to Cole Ltd for these goods. The Group's finance director also authorised a four-month credit period on this sale. Normal credit terms for this industry are two months credit from suppliers. Cole Ltd had sold all of these goods at the year-end.

(iii)   Fixed assets:

Details relating to the two companies' fixed assets at 31 March 20X1 are:

		Cost/revaluation £'000	Depreciation £'000	Book value £'000
Cole Ltd	– property	3,000	1,860	1,140
	– plant	6,000	4,800	1,200
				2,340
Darwin Ltd	– property	2,000	100	1,900
	– plant	3,000	1,800	1,200
				3,100

Both companies own very similar properties. Darwin Ltd's property was revalued to £2,000,000 at the beginning of the current year (ie 1 April 20X0). On this date Cole Ltd's property, which is carried at cost less depreciation, had a book value of £1,200,000. Its current value (on the same basis as Darwin Ltd's property) was also £2,000,000. On this date (1 April 20X0) both properties had the same remaining life of 20 years.

(iv)   Darwin Ltd purchased new plant costing £600,000 in February 20X1. In line with company policy a full year's depreciation at 20% per annum has been charged on all plant owned at the year-end. The plant is still being tested and will not come on-stream until next year. The purchase of the plant was largely financed by an overdraft facility that resulted in the interest cost shown in the profit and loss account. Both companies depreciate plant over a five-year life.

(v)   The bank overdraft that would have been required but for the favourable treatment towards Cole Ltd in respect of the items in (i) and (ii) above, would have attracted interest of £15,000 in the year to 31 March 20X1.

Required

(a)   Restate the financial statements of Cole Ltd and Darwin Ltd for the year to 31 March 20X1 in order that they may be considered comparable for decision making purposes. State any assumptions you make.
(10 marks)

(b)   Recalculate the key ratios used by Webster plc and, together with any other relevant points, comment on how the revised ratios may affect the relative assessment of the two companies.
(10 marks)

(c)   Discuss whether the information in notes (i) to (v) above would be publicly available, and if so, describe its source(s).
(5 marks)

(Total = 25 marks)

27 Dundee

The summarised accounts of Dundee plc for the year ended 31 March 20X7 are as follows.

BALANCE SHEETS AT 31 MARCH

	20X7		20X6	
	£m	£m	£m	£m
Fixed assets				
Tangible fixed assets		4,200		3,700
Current assets				
Stocks	1,500		1,600	
Debtors	2,200		1,800	
	3,700		3,400	
Creditors: amounts falling due within one year				
Trade creditors	1,250		1,090	
Taxation	225		205	
Obligations under finance leases	500		450	
Bank overdraft	155		205	
	2,130		1,950	
		1,570		1,450
Creditors: amounts falling due after more than one year				
Obligations under finance leases		(1,300)		(1,200)
Provisions for liabilities				
Deferred taxation		(1,070)		(850)
		3,400		3,100
Capital and reserves				
Called-up share capital		1,200		1,200
Profit and loss reserve		2,200		1,900
		3,400		3,100

PROFIT AND LOSS ACCOUNT FOR THE YEAR ENDED 31 MARCH 20X7

	£m
Turnover	4,300
Cost of sales	(2,000)
Gross profit	2,300
Operating expenses	(1,000)
Operating profit	1,300
Interest payable	(250)
Profit before tax	1,050
Taxation	(450)
Profit after tax	600
Dividends paid in the period	300

Notes

1   Depreciation charged for the period totalled £970 million. There were no disposals of fixed assets in the period.

2   There was no accrual of interest at the beginning or at the end of the year.

3 Dundee plc finances a number (but not all) of its fixed asset purchases using finance leases. In the period, fixed assets which would have cost £600 million to purchase outright were acquired under finance leases.

Required

Prepare the cash flow statement for Dundee plc for the year ended 31 March 20X7 as per FRS 1.

(15 marks)

28 Elmgrove

As financial accountant for Elmgrove plc, you are responsible for the preparation of a cash flow statement for the year ended 31 March 20X9.

The following information is available:

ELMGROVE PLC
BALANCE SHEET AS AT 31 MARCH 20X9

	20X9		20X8	
	£m	£m	£m	£m
Fixed assets				
Tangible assets		327		264
Current assets				
Stocks	123		176	
Debtors	95		87	
Short term investments	65		30	
Cash at bank and in hand	29		–	
	312		293	
Creditors: amounts falling due within one year	(172)		(149)	
Net current assets		140		144
Total assets less current liabilities		467		408
Creditors: amounts falling due after more than one year				
10% debentures		(150)		(150)
		317		258
Capital and reserves				
Ordinary £1 shares		150		120
Share premium account		30		–
Revaluation reserve		66		97
Profit and loss reserve		71		41
		317		258

ELMGROVE PLC
PROFIT AND LOSS ACCOUNT
FOR THE YEAR ENDED 31 MARCH 20X9

	£m
Turnover	473
Cost of sales	(229)
Gross profit	244
Distribution costs	(76)
Administrative expenses	(48)
Operating profit	120
Interest payable	(17)
Interest receivable	6
Profit before taxation	109
Taxation	(47)
Profit after taxation	62
Dividends paid in the period	32

The following notes are also relevant.

1 *Tangible assets*

Tangible assets held by Elmgrove plc are items of plant and machinery and freehold premises. During the year to 31 March 20X9 items of plant and machinery which originally cost £40m were disposed of, resulting in a loss of £6m. These items had a net book value of £28m at the date of disposal.

2 *Short term Investments*

The short term investments meet the definition of liquid resources per FRS 1.

3 *Creditors: amounts falling due within one year*

The total creditors figure breaks down as follows:

	20X9	20X8
	£m	£m
Bank overdraft	–	22
Trade creditors	126	70
Interest payable	7	3
Current tax payable	39	54
	172	149

4 *Depreciation*

The depreciation charge for the year, included in the profit and loss account, was £43m.

Required:

(a) Using the information provided, prepare a cash flow statement for Elmgrove plc for the year ended 31 March 20X9, together with relevant notes. **(20 marks)**

(b) Write a memorandum to a director of Elmgrove plc which summarises the major benefits which it is claimed a user receives from a published cash flow statement. **(5 marks)**

(Total: 25 marks)

29 CPP and CCA

(a) 'It is important that management and other users of financial accounts should be in a position to appreciate the effects of inflation on the business with which they are concerned.'

Required

Consider the above statement and explain how inflation obscures the meaning of accounts prepared by the traditional historical cost convention, and discuss the contribution which CPP accounting could make to providing a more satisfactory system of accounting for inflation.

(b) Compare the general principles underlying CPP and CCA accounting.

(c) Define the term 'realised holding gain'.   **(15 marks)**

Exam answer bank

1 Conceptual framework

(a)   The **going concern assumption** is that an entity will continue in operational existence for the foreseeable future. This means that the financial statements of an entity are prepared on the assumption that the entity will **continue** trading. If this were not the case, various adjustments would have to be made to the accounts: provisions for losses; revaluation of assets to their possible market value; all fixed assets and long-term liabilities would be reclassified as current; and so forth.

Unless it can be assumed that the business is a going concern, other accounting assumptions cannot apply.

For example, it is meaningless to speak of consistency from one accounting period to the next when this is the final accounting period.

The **accruals basis** of accounting states that items are recognised as assets, liabilities, equity, income and expenses when they satisfy the definitions and recognition criteria in the *Statement*. The effect of this is that revenue and expenses which are related to each other are matched, so as to be dealt with in the same accounting period, without regard to when the cash is actually paid or received. This is particularly relevant to the purchase of fixed assets. The cost of a fixed asset is spread over the accounting periods expected to benefit from it, thus matching costs and revenues. In the absence of the going concern convention, this cannot happen, as an example will illustrate.

Suppose a company has a machine which cost £10,000 two years ago and now has a net book value of £6,000. The machine can be used for another three years, but as it is highly specialised, there is no possibility of selling it, and so it has no market value.

If the going concern assumption applies, the machine will be shown at **cost less depreciation** in the accounts (ie £6,000), as it still has a part to play in the continued life of the entity. However, if the assumption cannot be applied, the machine will be given a nil value and other assets and liabilities will be similarly revalued on the basis of winding down the company's operations.

(b)   One of the ideas behind the *Statement* is to **avoid the fire-fighting approach**, which has characterised the development of accounting standards in the past, and instead develop an underlying philosophy as a basis for consistent accounting principles so that each standard fits into the whole framework. Research began from an analysis of the fundamental objectives of accounting and their relationship to the information needs of accounts users. The *Statement* has gone behind the requirements of existing accounting standards, which define accounting treatments for particular assets, liabilities, income and expenditure, to define the nature of assets, liabilities, income and expenditure.

2 Regulators

> **Tutorial note.** It is best to use headings to divide up your answer, as we do here.

The Stock Exchange

The shares of a quoted company are listed on the Stock Exchange. In order to have its shares listed a company must conform to the Stock Exchange regulations contained in the Yellow Book. The company is then committed to abiding by the procedures and standards of the Stock Exchange, including requirements for the disclosure of accounting information which are more stringent than those included in the Companies Act. Failure to abide by these requirements can lead to securities no longer being listed. This is a very powerful regulatory influence on a quoted company's accounts.

The Companies Acts

UK quoted companies must of course comply with the Companies Act 2006. However, the regulations concerning financial statements remain as laid down under the Companies Act 1985, amended by the Companies Act 1989. The Companies Acts require the preparation of a profit and loss account and balance sheet and lay down standard formats, and requirements regarding the notes. The Companies Acts also require the preparation of group accounts and give legal backing to accounting standards.

The ASB

The role of the ASB is to issue accounting standards based on its Statement of Principles. Accounting standards are held to apply to all financial statements intended to give a 'true and fair' view and compliance with accounting standards is required by the Stock Exchange for listed companies. Auditors are required to state in their opinion that the financial statements are in accordance with applicable accounting standards. Departures from accounting standards, or from the requirements of the Companies Acts can be investigated by the Financial Reporting Review Panel and a court order obtained requiring the preparation of revised accounts.

This regulatory system is reasonably effective because there are quite a few sanctions in place for quoted companies who do not keep to the regulations. They can be put to the expense of having to revise their financial statements, they can be threatened with a qualified audit report or they can run the risk of having their listing withdrawn.

3 Standard setters

(a)   The users of financial information – creditors, management, employees, business contacts, financial specialists, government and the general public – are entitled to information about a business entity to a greater or lesser degree. However, the needs and expectations of these groups will vary.

The preparers of the financial information often find themselves in the position of having to reconcile the interests of different groups in the best way for the business entity. For example whilst shareholders are looking for increased profits to support higher dividends, employees will expect higher wage increases; and yet higher profits without corresponding higher tax allowances (increased capital allowances for example) will result in a larger tax bill.

Without accounting standards to prescribe how certain transactions should be treated, preparers would be tempted to produce financial information which meets the expectations of the favoured user group. For example creative accounting methods, such as off balance sheet finance could be used to enhance a company's balance sheet to make it more attractive to investors/lenders.

The aim of accounting standards is that they should regulate financial information in order that it shows the following characteristics.

(i)   Relevance
(ii)   Reliability
(iii)   Understandability
(iv)   Comparability

(b)   A number of reasons could be advanced why the financial statements of not-for-profit entities should not be subject to regulation.

(i)   They do not have shares that are being traded, so their financial statements are not produced with a share price in mind.

(ii)   They do not have chief executives with share options seeking to present favourable figures to the market.

(iii) They are not seeking to make a profit, so whether they have or not is perhaps irrelevant.

(iv) They are perceived to be on slightly higher moral ground than profit-making entities, so are less in need of regulation.

However a closer look at this brings up the following points.

(i) Charities may not be invested in by the general public, but they are funded by the public, often through direct debits.

(ii) Charities are big business. In addition to regular public donations they receive large donations from high-profile backers.

(iii) They employ staff and executives at market rates and have heavy administrative costs. Supporters are entitled to know how much of their donation has gone on administration.

(iv) Any misappropriation of funds is serious in two ways. It is taking money from the donating public, who thought they were donating to a good cause, and it is diverting resources from the people who should have been helped.

(v) Not all charities are *bona fide*. For instance, some are thought to be connected to terrorism.

For these reasons, it is important that the financial statements of not-for-profit entities are subject to regulation.

4 Polymer

POLYMER LTD: PROFIT AND LOSS ACCOUNT FOR THE YEAR ENDED 31 MAY 20X8

	£
Turnover	1,526,750
Cost of sales (W3)	(1,048,000)
Gross profit	478,750
Distribution costs (W4)	(124,300)
Administrative expenses (W5)	(216,200)
Operating profit	138,250
Finance costs (W6)	(18,400)
Profit before tax	119,850
Tax on profit	(40,000)
Profit after tax	79,850

Note. the directors have proposed a dividend of 3.5p per share.

POLYMER LTD: BALANCE SHEET AS AT 31 MAY 20X8

	£	£
Fixed assets		
Intangible assets		215,500
Tangible assets(W7)		452,250
		667,750
Current assets		
Stocks (W8)	425,750	
Debtors (W9)	171,880	
Cash at bank and in hand	5,120	
	602,750	
Creditors: amounts falling due within one year		
Trade and other creditors (W10)	155,900	
Bank overdraft	51,250	
	207,150	
Net current assets		395,600
Total assets less current liabilities		1,063,350
Creditors: amounts falling due after more than one year		
10% debentures		(100,000)
8.4% cumulative preference shares		(100,000)
		863,350
Capital and reserves		
Called up share capital		300,000
Share premium account		100,000
Revaluation reserve		50,000
General reserve		50,000
Profit and loss reserve (283,500 + 79,850)		363,350
		863,350

Workings

1   *Depreciation*

		£
Cost of sales:	8% × 150,000	12,000
Administration:	10% × 50,000	5,000
	1/4 × 20% × 50,000	2,500
		7,500
Distribution:	3/4 × 20% × 50,000	7,500

2   *Depreciation (amortisation) of lease*

£75,000 × 1/50	1,500

3   *Cost of sales*

	£
Opening stocks (108,400 + 32,750 + 184,500)	325,650
Purchases	750,600
Carriage inwards	10,500
Manufacturing wages	250,000
Manufacturing overheads	125,000
Depreciation of plant (W1)	12,000
Closing stocks (W8)	(425,750)
	1,048,000

4   *Distribution costs*

	£
Per question	116,800
Depreciation (W1)	7,500
	124,300

5   *Administrative expenses*

		£
Per question		158,100
Legal expenses	54,100	
less: solicitors' fees capitalised	5,000	
		49,100
Depreciation (W1)		7,500
Amortisation of lease (W2)		1,500
		216,200

6   *Finance costs*

	£
Interest expense on debenture loans (£100,000 × 10%)	10,000
Preference dividend	8,400
	18,400

7   *Tangible assets*

	Freehold land £	Leasehold property £	Plant & machinery £	Furniture & fixtures £	Motor vehicles £	Total £
NBV per TB						
Cost or valuation	250,000	75,000	150,000	50,000	75,000	
Accumulated dep'n	–	(15,000)	(68,500)	(15,750)	(25,000)	
Net book value	250,000	60,000	81,500	34,250	50,000	
Solicitor's fees	5,000					
Depreciation charge	–	(1,500)	(12,000)	(5,000)	(10,000)	
NBV 31 May 20X8	255,000	58,500	69,500	29,250	40,000	452,250

8   *Stocks*

	£
Raw materials	112,600
Work in progress	37,800
Finished goods	275,350
	425,750

9   *Debtors*

	£
Trade debtors (177,630 – 5,750 allowance for doubtful debts)	171,880

11   *Trade and other creditors*

	£
Trade creditors	97,500
Current tax payable	40,000
Loan interest payable	10,000
Preference dividend payable	8,400
	155,900

5 Winger

(a) WINGER PLC
PROFIT AND LOSS ACCOUNT FOR THE
YEAR ENDED 31 MARCH 20X1

	£'000
Turnover (358,450 – 27,000)	331,450
Cost of sales (W1)	(208,550)
Gross profit	122,900
Distribution expenses	(28,700)
Administration expenses	(15,000)
Operating profit	79,200
Exceptional items	
Profit on disposal of land and buildings (95,000 – 80,000)	15,000
Loss on abandonment of research project	(30,000)
Profit on ordinary activities before interest	64,200
Interest expense (W3)	(11,200)
Profit before tax	53,000
Taxation (15,000 – 2,200)	(12,800)
Profit after tax	40,200

(b) BALANCE SHEET AS AT 31 MARCH 20X1

	£'000	£'000
Fixed assets: tangible		
Land and buildings (200,000 – 6,000 (W2))		194,000
Plant and machinery (W5)		160,000
		354,000
Current assets		
Stock (28,240 + 22,500 (W1))	50,740	
Debtors (55,000 – 27,000 (W1))	28,000	
Cash	10,660	
	89,400	
Creditors due within one year		
Trade and other creditors (W6)	51,400	
Taxation	15,000	
	66,400	
Net current assets		23,000
Total assets less current liabilities		377,000
Creditors due after one year		
Lease creditor (W7)		(47,200)
8% debentures		(50,000)
Net assets		279,800
Capital and reserves		
Ordinary shares 25p each		150,000
Profit and loss account (W4)		129,800
Shareholders' funds		279,800

Workings

		£'000
1	*Cost of sales*	
	Per question	185,050
	Less sale/return goods (27,000 × 100/120)	(22,500)
	Add depreciation (W2)	46,000
		208,550

2	Depreciation	£'000
	Building (100,000 ÷ 50)	2,000
	Heating system (20,000 ÷ 10)	2,000
	Lifts (30,000 ÷ 15)	2,000
		6,000
	Leased plant (80,000 × 20%)	16,000
	Owned plant (154,800 − 34,800) × 20%	24,000
		46,000

3	Interest expense	£'000
	Debenture interest (50,000 × 8%)	4,000
	Finance lease (80,000 − 20,000) × 12%	7,200
		11,200

4	Profit and loss reserve	£'000
	B/f 1 April 20X0	71,600
	Transfer to profit and loss of revaluation surplus on building sold 1 April 20X0	30,000
	Profit for the year	40,200
	Dividend paid	(12,000)
		129,800

5	Plant and machinery	£'000
	Cost: owned plant	154,800
	leased plant	80,000
		234,800
	Depreciation: owned plant (34,800 + 24,000 (W2))	(58,800)
	leased plant (80,000 × 20%)	(16,000)
		160,000

6	Trade and other creditors	£'000
	Trial balance	29,400
	Lease creditor (W7)	20,000
	Accrued debenture interest	2,000
		51,400

7	Lease creditor	£'000
	Total payments due	80,000
	Less amount paid	(20,000)
		60,000
	Add accrued interest (60,000 × 12%)	7,200
	Total creditor	67,200
	Due within one year	20,000
	Due after one year	47,200

(c) Prior to the issue of FRS 15 *Tangible fixed assets*, companies often used to justify the non-depreciation of buildings on several grounds, including:

(i) That the current value of the buildings was **higher than cost**.

(ii) That the level of **maintenance** meant that no deterioration or consumption had taken place.

(iii) That the depreciation charge would **not be material**.

FRS 15 dismisses the first two of them as being **insufficient grounds** for a policy of non-depreciation. Depreciation is **not** a valuation model; rather it is a means of **allocating the depreciable amount** of the asset to accounting periods.

However, it is still permissible not to charge depreciation on the grounds of non-materiality, but only when **both** the depreciation charge for the period **and** the accumulated depreciation that would have been charged against the value of the asset at that point in time, are immaterial. Thus assets with very long lives and/or high residual values may fall not to be depreciated. FRS 15 also requires that, for depreciation to be classed as immaterial:

(i)   There must be a policy of **regular maintenance**.

(ii)   The asset is unlikely to **suffer obsolescence**.

(iii)   There is a policy **and** practice of disposing of similar assets long **before** the **end of their useful lives** at proceeds not materially less than their carrying amounts.

An annual **test for impairment** is also required (except for land).

On the facts given, Winger's policy may have complied with FRS 15.

6 Hewlett

HEWLETT LTD – PROFIT AND LOSS ACCOUNT
FOR THE YEAR ENDED 31 DECEMBER 20X2

	£m
Turnover	2,648
Cost of sales (W1)	(1,765)
Gross profit	883
Distribution costs (W1)	(514)
Administrative expenses (W1)	(359)
Operating profit	10
Income from fixed asset investments	48
Interest payable (4% × 150)	(6)
Profit before tax	52
Tax on profit (note iv)	(27)
Profit after tax	25

BALANCE SHEET AS AT 31 DECEMBER 20X2

		£m
Fixed assets		
Tangible assets (W2)		878
Investment properties (note ix)		586
		1,464
Current assets		
Stocks (388 – (15 – 8))	381	
Trade debtors	545	
Cash	28	
	954	
Creditors: amounts falling due within one year		
Trade creditors	434	
Current tax payable (note v)	27	
Interest payable ((4% × 150) – 3)	3	
	464	
Net current assets		490
Total assets less current liabilities		1,954
Creditors: amounts falling due after more than one year		
4% debentures 20X8		(150)
		1,804

	£m
Capital and reserves	
Share capital	133
Share premium account	244
Revaluation reserve	473
Investment revaluation reserve (586 – 548)	38
General reserve	537
Profit and loss reserve	379
	1,804

RECONCILIATION OF MOVEMENT IN SHAREHOLDERS' FUNDS
FOR THE YEAR ENDED 31 DECEMBER 20X2

	£m
Profit for the financial year	25
Dividends (W5)	(6)
Retained profit	19
Other recognised gains and losses relating to the year (586 – 548)	38
New share capital subscribed (none – bonus issue)	–
Net addition to shareholders' funds	57
Opening shareholders' funds at 1 January 20X2 (originally (W6) £1,263m before adding prior year adjustment of (W2) £484m)	1,747
Closing shareholders' funds at 31 December 20X2	1,804

Workings

1   *Expenses*

	Cost of sales £m	Distribution £m	Admin £m
Per TB	1,669	514	345
Opening stocks	444		
Depreciation of buildings (W2)			14
Depreciation of plant and machinery (W2)	24		
Impairment loss on plant (W3)	4		
Loss on sale of machinery (12 – 7)	5		
Closing stocks (388 – (15 – 8))	(381)		
	1,765	514	359

2   *Tangible assets*

	Land & buildings £m	Plant & machinery £m	Total £m
Cost	380	258	
Accumulated depreciation	(64)	(126)	
NBV at 1 January 20X2	316	132	
Change in accounting policy (bal)	484		
	800	132	
Disposal of machinery (15 – 3)		(12)	
	800	120	
Depreciation during year			
Buildings ((£800m – £100m) × 2%)	(14)		
Plant & machinery (£120m × 20%)		(24)	
Impairment loss on plant (W3)		(4)	
NBV at 31 December 20X2	786	92	878

505

3   *Impairment loss on plant*

	£m
Carrying value	22
Recoverable amount (Value in use: $(3.8m \times 3.993) + (4.2m \times 0.677)$)	(18)
	(4)

Recoverable amount is the higher of value in use (£18m) and fair value less costs to sell (£16m).

4   *Bonus issue*

Dr General reserve (£100m /£0.50 × 1/3 = 66.667m shares × £0.50)	£33.333m
Cr Share capital	£33.333m

5   *Dividends*

	£m
Interim (£100m /£0.50 = 200m shares × £0.03)	6 per trial balance

The final dividend has not been paid and is not a liability of the company at the year end.

6   *Opening shareholders' funds*

	£m
Share capital	100
Share premium	244
General reserve	570
Profit and loss reserve	349
	1,263

7 Gains

(a)   **Statement of total recognised gains and losses**

	20X9
	£'000
Profit for the financial year	566
Surplus on revaluation of freehold land and buildings	120
Deficit on revaluation of investment properties	(50)
	636

(b)   **Reconciliation of movements in shareholders funds**

	20X9
	£'000
Profit for the financial year	566
Dividend	(200)
	366
Other recognised gains (120 – 50)	70
New share capital subscribed (400 × £1.40)	560
Net addition to shareholders' funds	996
Opening shareholders funds	6,820
Closing shareholders funds	7,816

(c) **Note of historical cost profits for the period**

	£'000
Reported profit before tax	806
Realisation of property revaluation gains of previous years (W1)	35
Difference between an historical cost depreciation charge and the actual depreciation charge of the year calculated on the revalued amount ((500,000 − 380,000)/25))	4.8
	845.8
Historical cost retained profit for the year (366 + 35 + 4.8)	405.8

Workings

1	£'000	£'000
Actual gain (60,0000 − 56,000)		4
HC gain		
Proceeds	60	
NBV (30,000 − (30,000/10 × 3))	(21)	
		39
Difference		35

8 Multiplex

The impairment losses are allocated as required by FRS 11 *Impairment of fixed assets and goodwill.*

	Asset at 1.1.20X1 £'000	1st provision (W1) £'000	Assets at 1.2.20X1 £'000	2nd provision (W2) £'000	Revised asset £'000
Goodwill	200	(200)	–	–	–
Operating licence	1,000	(300)	700	(100)	600
Property: stations/land	250	–	250	(50)	200
Rail track/coaches	250	–	250	(50)	200
Steam engines	1,000	(500)	500	–	500
Other net assets	300	–	300	–	300
	3,000	(1,000)	2,000	(200)	1,800

Workings

1   *First provision*

£500,000 relates directly to an engine and its recoverable amount can be assessed directly (ie zero).

FRS 11 then requires goodwill to be written off. Any further impairment must be written off intangible assets.

2   *Second provision*

The first £100,000 of the impairment loss is applied to the operating licence to write it down to NRV.

The remainder is applied pro rata to assets carried at other than their net selling prices.

9 Barcelona and Madrid

CONSOLIDATED BALANCE SHEET AS AT 30 SEPTEMBER 20X6

	£m	£m
Fixed assets		
Patents		45
Goodwill (W2)		43
Tangible assets (2,848 + 354)		3,202
		3,290
Current assets		
Stocks (895 + 225)	1,120	
Debtors (1,348 + 251)	1,599	
Cash (212 + 34)	246	
	2,965	
Creditors: amounts falling due within one year		
Trade and other creditors (1,168 + 183)	1,351	
Current portion of long-term borrowings	23	
	1,374	
Net current assets		1,591
Total assets less current liabilities		4,881
Creditors: amounts falling due after more than one year		
Long-term borrowings (558 + 168)		(726)
		4,155
Capital and reserves		
Share capital		920
General reserve (W4)		796
Profit and loss reserve (W3)		2,243
		3,959
Minority interest (490 × 40%)		196
		4,155

Workings

1   *Group structure*

Barcelona

| 60% (30.6.X2)

Madrid

2   *Goodwill*

	£m	£m
Cost of acquired entity		159
Net assets at acquisition:		
Share capital	50	
General reserve	11	
Profit and loss reserve	104	
	165	
Group share (60%)		99
Goodwill at acquisition		60
Impairment losses to date		(17)
Goodwill at balance sheet date		43

3   *Profit and loss reserve*

	Barcelona £m	Madrid £m
Per question	2,086	394
Pre-acquisition	–	(104)
	2,086	290
Madrid – share of post acquisition P&L reserve (290 × 60%)	174	
Less: goodwill impairment losses to date	(17)	
	2,243	

4   *General reserve*

	Barcelona £m	Madrid £m
Per question	775	46
Pre-acquisition	–	(11)
	775	35
Madrid – share of post acquisition general reserve (35 × 60%)	21	
	796	

10 Reprise

REPRISE PLC
CONSOLIDATED BALANCE SHEET AS AT 31 MARCH 20X4

	£'000	£'000
Fixed assets		
Intangible asset (W4)		421
Land and buildings		3,350
Plant and machinery (1,010 + 2,210)		3,220
Motor vehicles (510 + 345)		855
		7,846
Current assets		
Stocks (890 + 352 – (W2) 7.2)	1,234.8	
Debtors (1,372 + 514 – 39 – (W3) 36)	1,811	
Cash at bank and in hand (89 + 39 + 51)	179	
	3,224.8	
Creditors: amounts falling due within one year		
Trade creditors (996 + 362 – (W3) 36)	1,322	
Net current assets		1,902.8
Total assets less current liabilities		9,748.8
Creditors: amounts falling due after more than one year		
10% debentures		(500)
		9,248.8

Capital and reserves

Share capital	1,000
Revaluation reserve	2,500
Profit and loss reserve (W6)	4,971.3
	8,471.3
Minority interests (W5)	777.5
	9,248.8

Workings

1   *Group structure*

1.4.X0   R → E   75%   ∴ minority interest = 25%

2   *Unrealised profit on stocks*

Unrealised profit included in stocks is:

$$£31,200 \times \frac{30}{130} = £7,200$$

3   *Debtors/creditors*

Intragroup balance of £75,000 is reduced to £36,000 once cash-in-transit of £39,000 is followed through to its ultimate destination.

4   *Goodwill*

	£'000	£'000
Cost of acquired entity		2,000
Net assets acquired as represented by:		
Share capital	500	
Profit and loss reserve	1,044	
	1,544	
Group's share 75%		1,158
Goodwill at acquisition		842
Goodwill amortisation (4/8)		(421)
Goodwill at balance sheet date		421

5   *Minority interests*

	£'000
Share of Encore's net assets at 31 March 20X4	777.5
(3,110 × 25%)	

6   *Consolidated profit and loss reserve*

	Reprise £'000	Encore £'000
Per question	4,225	2,610
PUP	(7.2)	
Pre-acquisition		(1,044)
	4,217.8	1,566
Share of Encore post acquisition P&L reserve (1,566 × 75%)	1,174.5	
Less: goodwill amortisation to date (W4)	(421)	
	4,971.3	

11 War

> **Tutorial note.** This question may look intimidating because it involves an acquisition part of the way through the year, some FRS 7 issues and both the consolidated profit and loss account and balance sheet. It is, however, fairly straightforward. You should not have overlooked FRS 3 aspects in the consolidated profit and loss account.

(a)   FRS 7 *Fair values in acquisition accounting* states that quoted shares should be valued at market price on the date of acquisition. However, the standard acknowledges that the market price may be difficult to determine if it is unreliable because of an inactive market. In particular, where the shares are not quoted, there may be no suitable market. In such cases the value must be estimated using:

(i)   The value of similar quoted securities
(ii)   The present value of the cash flows of the shares
(iii)   Any cash alternative which was offered
(iv)   The value of any underlying security into which there is an option to convert

It may be necessary to undertake a valuation of the company in question should none of the above methods prove feasible.

(b)   WAR GROUP PLC
CONSOLIDATED BALANCE SHEET AS AT 30 JUNE 20X7

	£'000	£'000
Fixed assets		
Tangible assets (1,750 + 500)		2,250
Goodwill (W3)		151
		2,401
Current assets		
Stocks	600	
Debtors	451	
Cash at bank and in hand	299	
	1,350	
Creditors: amounts falling due within one year	(650)	
Net current assets		700
Total assets less current liabilities		3,101
Creditors: amounts falling due after one year		(1,225)
		1,876

Capital and reserves

Ordinary share capital	750
Share premium (W6)	250
Profit and loss account (W5)	621
	1,621
Minority interests (W4)	255
	1,876

WAR GROUP PLC
CONSOLIDATED PROFIT AND LOSS ACCOUNT
FOR THE YEAR ENDED 30 JUNE 20X7

	£'000	£'000
Turnover (3,150 + (1,770 × 2/12))		3,445
Cost of sales		(1,788)
Gross profit		1,657
Distribution costs	638	
Administrative expenses (W7)	348	
		(986)
Operating profit		671
Interest payable		(75)
Profit on ordinary activities before taxation		596
Tax on profit on ordinary activities		(306)
Profit after tax		290
Minority interests (equity) (W8)		(11)
Profit for the financial year		279

Workings

1   *Fair value adjustment*

	£'000
Peace Ltd: tangible fixed assets at market value	500
Carrying value	350
Fair value adjustment	150

FRS 7 *Fair values in acquisition accounting* states that open market values should be used to value tangible fixed assets, and it is this figure which is compared with the carrying value here, rather than the net realisable value. The latter is lower because the costs of realisation are deducted. However, as the group does not intend to dispose of the asset, the market value is more appropriate.

2   *Pre-acquisition dividend*

Dividend paid by Peace to War: £42,000
Pre-acquisition element $^{10}/_{12}$ × £42,000 = £35,000

3   *Goodwill*

	£'000	£'000
Cost of investment		800
Pre-acquisition dividend (W2)		(35)
		765
Share capital	100	
Share premium	150	
Fair value adjustment (W1)	150	
Profit and loss account		
Prior year: 450 – 165	285	
Current year: $^{10}/_{12} \times 165$	138	
	823	
Group share: 70%		576
Goodwill		189
Amortisation for period (189 × 1/5)		(38)
Unamortised goodwill		151

4   *Minority interests (balance sheet)*

	£'000
Share capital	100
Share premium	150
Fair value adjustment (W1)	150
Profit and loss account	450
	850

MI = £850,000 × 30% = £255,000.

5   *Profit and loss account*

	War Ltd	Peace Ltd
	£	£
As per accounts	625	450
Adj pre-acquisition dividend (W2)	(35)	
Adj issue costs (W7)	50	
Pre-acquisition profit Prior year (W3)		(285)
Current year (W3)		(138)
Group share in Peace Ltd (27 × 70%)	19	27
Goodwill amortised (W3)	(38)	
	621	

6   *Share premium account*

	£'000
War plc	300
Less issue costs	(50)
	250

7   *Administrative expenses*

	£'000
War plc	325
Peace Ltd ($^{2}/_{12} \times 210$)	35
Goodwill written off	38
	398
Issue costs	(50)
	348

8   Minority interest (P&L)
     $225 \times {}^{2}/_{12} \times 30\% = £11,250$

12 Fallowfield and Rusholme

CONSOLIDATED PROFIT AND LOSS ACCOUNT
FOR THE YEAR ENDED 30 JUNE 20X8

	£
Turnover (403,400 + 193,000 – 40,000)	556,400
Cost of sales (201,400 + 92,600 – 40,000 + 4,000)	(258,000)
Gross profit	298,400
Distribution costs (16,000 + 14,600)	(30,600)
Administrative expenses (24,250 + 17,800)	(42,050)
Profit before tax	225,750
Tax (61,750 + 22,000)	(83,750)
Profit after tax	142,000
Minority interest (W2)	(16,800)
Profit after tax and minority interest	125,200

RECONCILIATION OF MOVEMENT IN THE PROFIT AND LOSS RESERVE

	£
Profit and loss reserve brought forward (W3)	190,000
Profit after tax and minority interest	125,200
Dividends	(40,000)
Profit and loss reserve carried forward (W4)	275,200

Workings

1 *Group structure*

Fallowfield

> 60%   3 years ago
> Pre-acquisition P&L reserve: £16,000

Rusholme

2 *Minority interest*

	£
Rusholme – profit after tax	46,000
Less: PUP (40,000 × ½ × 25/125)	4,000
	42,000
Minority share 40%	16,800

3 *Profit and loss reserve brought forward*

	Fallowfield £	Rusholme £
Per question	163,000	61,000
Pre-acquisition P&L reserve	–	(16,000)
	163,000	45,000
Rusholme – share of post acquisition P&L reserve (45,000 × 60%)	27,000	
	190,000	

4   *Profit and loss reserve carried forward*

	Fallowfield £	Rusholme £
Per question	238,000	82,000
PUP	–	(4,000)
Pre-acquisition P&L reserve		(16,000)
	238,000	62,000
Rusholme – share of post acquisition P&L reserve		
(62,000 × 60%)	37,200	
	275,200	

13 Panther Group

PANTHER GROUP
CONSOLIDATED PROFIT AND LOSS ACCOUNT FOR THE YEAR ENDED 31 DECEMBER 20X4

	£'000
Turnover [22,800 + (4,300 × 6/12) – 320]	24,630
Cost of sales [13,600 + (2,600 × 6/12) –320 + (W2) 10 + (W4) 5]	(14,595)
Gross profit	10,035
Distribution costs (2,900 + (500 × 6/12))	(3,150)
Administrative expenses (1,800 + (300 × 6/12))	(1,950)
Operating profit	4,935
Interest payable [200 + ((70 – (W3) 20) × 6/12)]	(225)
Interest receivable (50 – (W3) 20)	30
Profit before tax	4,740
Tax [1,300 + (220 × 6/12)]	(1,410)
Profit after tax	3,330
Minority interest (W5)	(112)
Profit after tax and minority interest	3,218

RECONCILIATION OF THE MOVEMENT IN THE CONSOLIDATED PROFIT AND LOSS RESERVE FOR THE YEAR ENDED 31 DECEMBER 20X4

	£'000
Balance at 1 January 20X9 (Panther only)	12,750
Profit after tax and minority interest	3,218
Dividends paid	(900)
Balance at 31 December 20X9 (W4)	15,068

Workings

1   *Timeline*

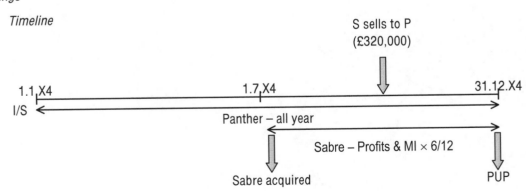

2   *Unrealised profit on intragroup trading*

Sabre to Panther = £60,000 × $\frac{20\%}{120\%}$ = £10,000

Adjust minority interest in books of seller (Sabre).

3   *Interest on intragroup loan*

£800,000 × 5% × 6/12 = £20,000
Cancel in books of Panther and Sabre.

4   *Fair value adjustments*

	At acq'n 1.7.X4 £'000	Movement	£'000	At B/S date 31.12.X4 £'000
Property	200	(200/20 × 6/12)	(5)	195

5   *Minority interest*

	£'000
Profit for the period ((610 + (W3)20*) × 6/12)	315
Less: Post-acquisition interest* (W3)	(20)
Less: PUP (W2)	(10)
Additional depreciation on fair value adjustment (W4)	(5)
	280
Minority share 40%	112

* The interest on the loan is specific to the post-acquisition period. Therefore, it is added back before time-apportioning the remainder of the profits and then deducted in full as it is a post-acquisition expense.

6   *Group P&L reserve carried forward (proof)*

	Panther £'000	Sabre £'000
Per question	14,900	3,090
PUP (W2)		(10)
Fair value change (W3)		(5)
Pre acquisition P&L reserve [2,480 + ((610 + (W3) 20) × 6/12)]		(2,795)
		280
Sabre – share of post acquisition P&L reserve (280 × 60%)	168	
	15,068	

14 Hever

CONSOLIDATED BALANCE SHEET AS AT 31 DECEMBER 20X4

	£'000	£'000
Fixed assets		
Intangible fixed assets (W4)		2
Tangible assets (370 + 190 + (W3) 45)		605
Investment in associate (W5)		165
		772
Current assets		
Stocks (160 + 100 − (W2) 1.5)	258.5	
Trade debtors (170 + 90)	260	
Cash (50 + 40)	90	
	608.5	
Creditors		
Trade creditors (100 + 60)	160	
Net current assets		448.5
		1,220.5
Capital and reserves		
Share capital		200
Share premium		100
Profit and loss reserve (W7)		758.5
		1,058.5
Minority interest (W6)		162
		1,220.5

Workings

1   *Group structure*

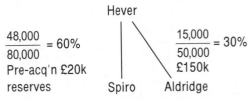

$$\frac{48,000}{80,000} = 60\%$$

Pre-acq'n £20k reserves

$$\frac{15,000}{50,000} = 30\%$$

£150k

∴ In the absence of information to the contrary, Spiro is a subsidiary, and Aldridge an associate of Hever.

2   *Unrealised profit on stocks*

Mark-up = 6,000 ∴ ¼ × 6,000 = £1,500

3   *Fair values – adjustment to net assets*

	At Acquisition	Movement	At balance sheet date
Tangible assets	50	(5)	45
Stocks	(20)	20	0
	30	15	45

4   *Goodwill on consolidation – Spiro*

	£'000	£'000
Cost of acquired entity		128
Net assets at acquisition		
Share capital	80	
Profit and loss reserve	20	
Share premium	80	
Fair value adjustments (W3)	30	
	210	
Group share (60%)		(126)
		2

Goodwill on consolidation – Aldridge

	£'000	£'000
Cost of acquired entity		90
Net assets at acquisition		
Share capital	50	
Profit and loss reserve	150	
Share premium	30	
	230	
Group share (30%)		(69)
		21

5   *Investment in associate*

	£'000
Share of associate's net assets at balance sheet date (480 × 30%)	144
Unamortised goodwill (W4)	21
	165

6   *Minority interest*

	£'000	£'000
Net assets	360	
Fair value adjustment (W3)	45	
	405	
Group share (40%)		162

7   *Profit and loss reserve*

	Hever £'000	Spiro £'000	Aldridge £'000
Per question	568	200	400
PUP (W2)	(1.5)	–	–
Fair value adjustment (W3)		15	
Pre-acquisition profit and loss reserve		(20)	(150)
		195	250
Spiro – share of post acquisition P&L reserve (195 × 60%)	117		
Aldridge – share of post acquisition P&L reserve (250 × 30%)	75		
Less: goodwill amortisation to date	(0)		
	758.5		

15 Trontacc

(a)   **Treatment of long-term contracts in the balance sheet of Trontacc plc at 30 September 20X7**

	£'000
Contract A (W1)	
Stocks – long-term contract WIP	20
Debtors – amounts recoverable on contracts	60
Contract B (W2)	
Debtors – amounts recoverable on contracts	25
Provision for losses on long-term contracts	(50)
Contract C (W3)	
Creditors – payments on account	(45)

(b)   **Treatment of long-term contracts in the profit and loss account of Trontacc plc for the year ended 30 September 20X7**

		Contract	
	A	B	C
	£'000	£'000	£'000
	(W1)	(W2)	(W3)
Turnover	600	500	350
Cost of sales	480	550	315
Gross profit	120	(50)	35
Provision for future loss	–	(50)	–
	120	(100)	35

Workings

			£'000
1	*Contract A*		
	(i)	Profit and loss account	
		Turnover (1,000 × 60%)	600
		Cost of sales	480
		Gross profit	120
	(ii)	Debtors: Amounts recoverable on contracts	
		Turnover recognised	600
		Less: payments on account	540
			60
	(iii)	Work-in-progress	
		Costs to date	500
		Less: recognised in P&L	480
			20

			£'000
2	*Contract B*		
	(i)	Profit and loss account	
		Turnover (1,000 × 50%)	500
		Cost of sales (all costs to date)	550
		Gross profit	(50)
		Provision for future losses	(50)
			(100)

(ii)	Debtors: Amounts recoverable on contracts		
		Turnover recognised	500
		Less: payments on account	475
			25
(iii)	Work-in-progress		
		Costs to date	550
		Less: recognised in P&L	550
			–
(iv)	Provision for losses (per P&L)		(50)

3 *Contract C* £'000

(i)	Profit and loss account		
		Turnover (1,000 × 35%)	350
		Cost of sales	315
		Gross profit (W1)	35
(ii)	Debtors: Amounts recoverable on contracts		
		Turnover recognised	350
		Less: payments on account	400
		Excess payments on account	(50)
(iii)	Work-in-progress		
		Costs to date	320
		Less: recognised in P&L	315
			5
		Less: excess payments on account (per (ii))	50
		Excess payments on account	(45)
(iv)	Creditors – payments on account (per (iii))		(45)

16 C plc

(a) **Maryhill bypass**

£'000

Profit and loss account

Turnover (work certified)	2,800
Cost of sales (balancing figure)	2,178
Gross profit (W)	622

Balance sheet
Debtor: amount recoverable on contract

Turnover recognised	2,800
Less: payments on account	2,600
	200

Working

Total expected profit (9,000 – 1,400 – 5,600)	2,000
Profit recognised to date (2,000 × $\frac{2,800}{9,000}$)	622

Rottenrow centre

	£'000
Profit and loss account	
Turnover (work certified)	3,000
Cost of sales (balancing figure)	3,100
Loss (W)	(100)
Balance sheet	
Creditor: payments on account	
Turnover recognised	3,000
Less: payments on account	3,400
	400
Working	
Expected loss (8,000 – 2,900 – 5,200)	(100)

(b) Long-term contracts are recognised as such when they cover at **least two accounting periods**. If they were not to be treated as they are under SSAP 9, then the costs incurred during the early years of the contract would be recognised but with no corresponding revenue. This would lead to several years of losses then one year of high profits regardless of how profitable the contract really was. The advantage of this approach however would be that there would be no need to use estimates and forecasts.

The current treatment **matches an element of the revenue to the costs incurred**. There is an attempt to maintain **prudence** by ensuring that any **foreseeable** losses are **accounted for immediately**. This gives a fairer representation of the underlying financial substance of the transaction and makes it easier for the user of the accounts to assess the financial position of the company.

17 Provisions

(a) **Why there was a need for an accounting standard dealing with provisions**

FRS 12 *Provisions, contingent liabilities and contingent assets* was issued to prevent entities from using provisions for creative accounting. It was common for entities to recognise material provisions for items such as future losses, restructuring costs or even expected future expenditure on repairs and maintenance of assets. These could be combined in one large provision (sometimes known as the 'big bath'). Although these provisions reduced profits in the period in which they were recognised (and were often separately disclosed on grounds of materiality), they were then released to enhance profits in subsequent periods. To make matters worse, provisions were often recognised where there was no firm commitment to incur expenditure. For example, an entity might set up a provision for restructuring costs and then withdraw from the plan, leaving the provision available for profit smoothing.

The criteria that need to be satisfied before a provision is recognised

FRS 12 states that a provision should not be recognised unless:

(i) An entity has a present obligation to transfer economic benefits as a result of a past transaction or event, and

(ii) It is probable that a transfer of economic benefits will be required to settle the obligation, and

(iii) A reliable estimate can be made of the amount of the obligation.

An obligation can be legal or constructive. An entity has a constructive obligation if:

(i)   It has indicated to other parties that it will accept certain responsibilities (by an established pattern of past practice or published policies), and

(ii) As a result, it has created a valid expectation on the part of those other parties that it will discharge those responsibilities.

(b)   Extract plc should recognise a provision for the estimated costs of making good the site because:

(i)   It has a present obligation to incur the expenditure as a result of a past event. In this case the obligating event occurred when it became virtually certain that the legislation would be passed. Therefore the obligation existed at 31 December 20X0, and

(ii) A transfer of economic benefits is probable, and

(iii) It is possible to make a reliable estimate of the amount.

Effect on the financial statements

For the year ended 31 December 20X0:

- A provision of £1,242,000 (2,000,000 × 0.621) is reported as a liability under provisions.

- A fixed asset of £1,242,000 is also recognised. The provision results in a corresponding asset because the expenditure gives the company access to future economic benefits; there is no effect on the profit and loss account for the year.

For the year ended 31 December 20X1:

- Depreciation of £248,400 (1,242,000 × 20%) is charged to the profit and loss account. The fixed asset is depreciated over its remaining useful economic life of 5 years from 31 December 20X0 (the site will cease to produce output on 31 December 20X5).

- Therefore at 31 December 20X1 the net book value of the fixed asset will be £993,600 (1,242,000 − 248,400).

- At 31 December 20X1 the provision will be £1,366,000 (2,000,000 × 0.683).

- The increase in the provision of £124,000 (1,366,000 − 1,242,000) is recognised in the profit and loss account as a finance cost. This arises due to the unwinding of the discount.

18 Alpha

Tutorial note. Creative accounting and substance over form are important concepts. You must relate your answer to the situation given in part (c) of the question and not just write a general essay. One or two examples would be enough in (a).

(a)   **Creative accounting**, the manipulation of figures for a desired result, takes many forms. Off-balance sheet finance is a major type of creative accounting and it probably has the most serious implications.

It is very rare for a company, its directors or employees to manipulate results for the purpose of fraud. The major consideration is usually the effect the results will have on the share price of the company. If the share price falls, the company becomes vulnerable to takeover. Analysts, brokers and economists, whose opinions affect the stock markets, are often perceived as having an outlook which is both short-term and superficial. Consequently, companies will attempt to produce the results the market expects or wants. The companies will aim for steady progress in a few key numbers and ratios and they will aim to meet the market's stated expectation.

The number of methods available for creative accounting and the determination and imagination of those who wish to perpetrate such acts are endless. It has been seen in the past that, wherever an accounting standard or law closes a loophole, another one is found. This has produced a change of approach in regulators and standard setters, towards general principles rather than detailed rules.

Here are a few examples of creative accounting.

(i) **Income recognition and cut-off**

Manipulation of cut-off is relatively straightforward. For instance, a company may delay invoicing in order to move revenue into the following year.

(ii) **Revaluations**

The optional nature of the revaluation of fixed assets leaves such practices open to manipulation. The choice of whether to revalue can have a significant impact on a company's balance sheet.

(iii) **Window dressing**

This is where transactions are passed through the books at the year end to make figures look better, but in fact they have not taken place and are often reversed after the year end. An example is where cheques are written to creditors, entered in the cash book, but not sent out until well after the year end.

(iv) **Change of accounting policies**

This tends to be a last resort because companies which change accounting policies know they will not be able to do so again for some time. The effect in the year of change can be substantial and prime candidates for such treatment are depreciation, stock valuation, changes from current cost to historical cost (practised frequently by privatised public utilities) and foreign currency losses.

(v) **Manipulation of accruals, prepayments and contingencies**

These figures can often be very subjective, particularly contingencies. In the case of impending legal action, for example, a contingent liability is difficult to estimate, the case may be far off and the lawyers cannot give any indication of likely success, or failure. In such cases companies will often only disclose the possibility of such a liability, even though the eventual costs may be substantial.

(b) The phrase 'substance over form' is defined in FRS 5.

'Transactions and other events should be accounted for and presented in accordance with their substance and financial reality and not merely with their legal form.'

This is a very important concept. FRS 5 also goes on to define assets and liabilities and set out the recognition criteria. In these situations it has to be decided whether or not an asset or liability should be recognised or derecognised.

(i) **Group accounting** is perhaps the most important area of off balance sheet finance which has been prevented by the application of the substance over form concept.

The most important point is that the definition of a subsidiary (under FRS 2) is based upon the **principle of control rather than purely ownership.** Where an entity is controlled by another, the controlling entity can ensure that the benefits accrue to itself and not to other parties. Similarly, one of the circumstances where a subsidiary may be excluded from consolidation is where there are severe long-term restrictions that prevent effective control.

(ii) Finance leases and their accounting treatment under SSAP 21 are an example of the application of substance over form.

Operating leases do not really pose an accounting problem. The lessee pays amounts periodically to the lessor and these are charged to the profit and loss account. The lessor treats the leased asset as a fixed asset and depreciates it in the normal way. Rentals received from the lessee are credited to the profit and loss account in the lessor's books.

For assets held under **finance leases** this accounting treatment would not disclose the reality of the situation. If a lessor leases out an asset on a finance lease, the asset will probably never be seen on his premises or used in his business again. It would be inappropriate for a lessor to record such an asset as a fixed asset. In reality, what he owns is a stream of cash flows receivable from the lessee. The asset is a debtor rather than a fixed asset.

Similarly, a lessee may use a finance lease to fund the 'acquisition' of a major asset which he will then use in his business perhaps for many years. The substance of the transaction is that he has acquired a fixed asset, and this is reflected in the accounting treatment prescribed by SSAP 21, even though in law the lessee may never become the owner of the asset.

(iii) With regard to **measurement or disclosure of current assets**, a common example where substance over form is relevant are sale and repurchase agreements. There are arrangements under which the company sells an asset to another person on terms that allow the company to repurchase the asset in certain circumstances. A common example of such a transaction is the sale and repurchase of maturing whisky stocks. The key question is whether the transaction is a straightforward sale, or whether it is, in effect, a secured loan. It is necessary to look at the arrangement to determine who has the rights to the economic benefits that the asset generates, and the terms on which the asset is to be repurchased.

If the seller has the right to the benefits of the use of the asset, and the repurchase terms are such that the repurchase is likely to take place, the transaction should be accounted for as a loan.

Another example is the factoring of **trade debtors**. Where debts are factored, the original creditor sells the debts to the factor. The sales price may be fixed at the outset or may be adjusted later. It is also common for the factor to offer a credit facility that allows the seller to draw upon a proportion of the amounts owed.

In order to determine the correct accounting treatment it is necessary to consider whether the benefit of the debts has been passed on to the factor, or whether the factor is, in effect, providing a loan on the security of the debts. If the seller has to pay interest on the difference between the amounts advanced to him and the amounts that the factor has received, and if the seller bears the risks of non-payment by the debtor, then the indications would be that the transaction is, in effect, a loan.

(c) (i) The Finance Director may be right in believing that renewing the fixed assets of the company will contribute to generating higher earnings and hence improved earnings per share. However, this will not happen immediately as the assets will need to have been in operation for at least a year for results to be apparent. Earnings will be higher because of the loan being at a commercially unrealistic rate, namely 5% instead of 9%.

As regards gearing, the Finance Director may well wish to classify the convertible debenture as equity rather than debt; thus gearing will be lower. He may argue that because the loan is very likely to be converted into shares, the finance should be treated as equity rather than as debt.

(ii) FRS 22 *Earnings per share* requires the calculation of **basic earnings per share**. The Finance Director believes that the convertible loan he is proposing will not affect EPS and that an interest cost of 5% will not impact heavily on gearing.

However, FRS 25 will require the interest cost to be based on 9% and FRS 22 also requires the calculation and disclosure of **diluted EPS**.

The need to disclose diluted earnings per share arose because of the limited value of a basic EPS figure when a company is financed partly by convertible debt. Because the right to convert carries benefits, it is usual that the interest rate on the debt is lower than on straight debt. Calculation of EPS on the assumption that the debt is non-convertible can, therefore, be misleading since:

(1)   Current EPS is higher than it would be under straight debt

(2)   On conversion, EPS will fall – diluted EPS provides some information about the extent of this future reduction, and warns shareholders of the reduction which will happen in the future

FRS 25 *Financial instruments: presentation* affects the proposed scheme in that FRS 25 requires that convertible loans such as this should be split on the balance sheet and presented partly as equity and partly as debt. Thus the company's gearing will probably increase as the convertible loan cannot be 'hidden' in equity.

19 Jenson

(a)   In revenue recognition, the 'critical event' is the point in the earnings process or operating cycle at which the transaction is deemed to have been **sufficiently completed** to allow the **profit** arising from the transaction, or a distinct component part of it, to be **recognised** in income in a particular period. This has to be addressed in order to allocate transactions and their effects to different accounting periods and is a direct result of the episodic nature of financial reporting. For most companies the **normal earnings cycle** is the purchase of raw materials which are transformed through a manufacturing process into saleable goods, for which orders are subsequently received, delivery is made and then payment received.

In the past the approach has been to **match costs with revenues** and record both once the critical event has passed; in most systems this critical event has been full or near **full performance of the transaction**, so that no material uncertainties surround either the transaction being completed or the amounts arising from the transaction. This is encompassed in the notion of prudence, so that revenue is recognised only in cash or near cash form. However, any point in the cycle could be deemed to be the critical event. This approach leaves the balance sheet as a statement of uncompleted transaction balances, comprising unexpired costs and undischarged liabilities.

UITF abstract 40 has been published as an amendment to FRS 5 and changes how revenue is recognised by professional firms. Work that was unbilled at the year end would previously have been classified as WIP. Now, when work is unbilled at the year end for which a fee note could be raised, it is treated as revenue and valued at its estimated sales value.

In contrast, the *Statement of Principles* defines gains and losses (or income and expenses) in terms of **changes** in assets and liabilities other than those arising from transactions with owners as owners, not in terms of an earnings or matching process. The balance sheet thus assumes primary importance in the recognition of earnings and profits. A gain **can only be recognised** if there is an **increase** in the **ownership interest** (ie net assets) of an entity not resulting from contributions from owners. Similarly, a loss is recognised if there is a **decrease** in the ownership interest of an entity not resulting from distributions to owners. Thus gains arise from recognition of assets and derecognition of liabilities, and losses arise from derecognition of assets and recognition of liabilities. The Statement explains that it is not possible to reverse this definitional process, ie by defining assets and liabilities in terms of gains and losses, because it has not been possible to formulate robust enough base definitions of gains and losses (partly because the choice of critical event can be subjective). Nevertheless the two approaches are linked by the Statement, which says that '**sufficient evidence**' for recognition or derecognition will be met at the critical event in the operating cycle.

(b) *On the acquisition of goods*

This would be **unlikely** to be a critical event for most businesses. However, for some the acquisition of the raw materials is the most important part of the process, eg extraction of gold from a mine, or the harvesting of coffee beans. Only where the goods in question could be **sold immediately in a liquid market** would it be appropriate to recognise revenue, ie they would have to have a **commodity value**.

During the manufacture or production of goods

This is also **unlikely** to be the critical event for most businesses because **too many uncertainties** remain, eg of damaged goods or overproduction leading to obsolete stock. An **exception** would be **long-term contracts** for the construction of specific assets, which tend to earn the constructing company revenues over the length of the contract, usually in stages, ie there is a **series of critical events** in the operating cycle (according to the *Statement of Principles*). It would **not** be appropriate to recognise all the revenue at the end of the contract, because this would reflect profit earned in past periods as well as the present period. Profit is therefore recognised during manufacture or production, usually through certification of a qualified valuer. Some would argue that this is not really a critical event approach, but rather an 'accretion approach'.

On delivery/acceptance of goods

Goods are frequently sold on **credit**, whereby the vendor hands over the inventory asset and receives in its place a **financial asset of a debt** due for the price of the goods. At that point legal title passes and **full performance** has taken place. In general, the bulk of the risks of the transaction have gone and the only ones remaining relate to the creditworthiness of the purchaser and any outstanding warranty over the goods. Many trade sales take place in this way, with periods of credit allowed for goods delivered, eg 30 days. This therefore tends to be the critical event for many types of business operating cycles.

Where certain conditions have been satisfied after the goods have been delivered

In these situations the customer had a right of return of the goods without reason or penalty, but usually within a time and non-use condition. A good example is clothes retailers who allow **non-faulty goods to be returned**. Another example is that the goods need only be paid for once they are sold on to a third party. Traditionally, recognition of revenue is delayed until, eg the **deadline to allowed return passes**. However, in circumstances where goods are never returned, it might be argued that the substance of the transaction is a sale on delivery.

Receipt or payment for credit sales

Once payment is received, only warranty risk remains. A company may wait until this point to recognise income if receipt is considered uncertain, eg when goods have been sold to a company resident in a country that has **exchange controls**. It would otherwise be **rare** to delay recognition until payment.

On the expiry of a guarantee or warranty

Many businesses may feel unable to recognise revenue in full because of **outstanding warranties**, eg a construction company which is subject to fee retention until some time after completion of the contract. Other businesses, such as car manufacturers, may make a **general provision** for goods returned under warranty as it will not be possible to judge likely warranty costs under individual contracts.

(c) (i) This agreement is worded as a **sale**, but it is fairly obvious from the terms and assessed substance that it is in fact a **secured loan**. Jensen should therefore continue to recognise the stock on balance sheet and should treat the receipt from Wholesaler as a loan, not revenue. Finance costs will be charged to the profit and loss account, of £35,000 × 12% × 9/12 = £3,150.

(ii) Years 2 to 5 of the franchise contract would be **loss making** for Jensen and hence part of the initial fee of £50,000 should be **deferred over the life of the contract**. Since Jensen should be making a profit margin of 20% on this type of arrangement, revenues of £10,000 will be required to match against the costs of £8,000. The company will receive £5,000 pa and so a further £5,000 × 4 = £20,000 of the initial fee should be deferred, leaving £50,000 − £20,000 = £30,000 to be recognised in the first year. However, this may not represent a liability under FRS 12 *Provisions, contingent liabilities and contingent assets*, where a liability is defined as an obligation to transfer economic benefits as a result of past transactions or events. It will be necessary to consider the terms of the initial fee and whether it is returnable.

(iii) The cost of the first 6 months' publications is £192,000 ÷ 24 × 6 = £48,000. On an accruals basis, income of £240,000 ÷ 24 × 6 = 60,000 should be recognised. This would leave deferred income of £240,000 − £60,000 = £180,000 in Jensen's balance sheet (ie as a liability). As in (ii), however, this may not represent a liability. In fact, the liability of the company may only extend to the cost of the future publications, ie £192,000 − £48,000 = £144,000. This would allow Jensen to **recognise all the profit** on the publications **immediately**. In want of an accounting standard on revenue recognition, it will be necessary to consider the extent of Jensen's commitments under this arrangement.

20 Bulwell

PROFIT AND LOSS ACCOUNTS (EXTRACTS)

	20X1 £	20X2 £	20X3 £	20X4 £
Finance lease interest	11,250	8,063	4,078	
Depreciation on lorries	12,500	12,500	12,500	12,500

BALANCE SHEETS AT 31 DECEMBER (EXTRACTS)

	20X1 £	20X2 £	20X3 £	20X4 £
Fixed assets				
Lorries: at cost	54,000	54,000	54,000	54,000
depreciation	12,500	25,000	37,500	50,000
	41,500	29,000	16,500	4,000
Current liabilities				
Obligations under finance lease	15,937	16,313	–	–
Long-term liabilities				
Obligations under finance lease	16,313	–	–	–

Working

Apportionment of instalments between interest and capital repayment.

	20X1 £	20X2 £	20X3 £
Opening liability (after deposit)	45,000	32,250	16,313
Interest at 25%	11,250	8,063	4,078
	56,250	40,313	20,391
Instalment	(24,000)	(24,000)	(20,391)
Closing liability	32,250	16,313	Nil
Interest element as above	11,250	8,063	4,078
∴ Capital repayment	12,750	15,937	16,313
Total instalment	24,000	24,000	20,391

21 Financial assets and liabilities

(a)

	£
Issue costs	120,000
Interest £6,000,000 × 3.5% × 7	1,470,000
Premium on redemption	1,100,000
Total finance cost	2,690,000

(b)   The premium on redemption of the debentures represents a finance cost. The effective rate of interest must be applied so that the debt is measured at amortised cost.

At the time of issue, the debentures are recognised at their net proceeds of £599,800 (600,000 – 200).

The finance cost for the year ended 31 December 20X4 is calculated as follows:

	£
1.1.20X3 Proceeds of issue (600,000 – 200)	599,800
Interest at 12%	71,976
Balance at 31.12.20X3	671,776
Interest at 12%	80,613
Balance at 31.12.20X4	752,389

The finance cost for the year ended 31.12.20X4 is $80,613.

(c)

> **Top tip.** The method to use here is to find the present value of the principal value of the bond, £500,000 (10,000 × £50) and the interest payments of £25,000 annually (5% × £500,000) at the market rate for non-convertible bonds of 6%, using the discount factors. The difference between this total and the principal amount of £500,000 is the equity element.

	£
Present value of principal £500,000 × 0.747	373,500
Present value of interest £25,000 × 4.212	105,300
Liability value	478,800
Principal amount	500,000
Equity element	21,200

22 Lis

The lease appears to be a finance lease for the following reasons:

(a)   title will be transferred at the end of the lease term.

(b)   the present value of minimum lease payments amounts to 98% (£84,000/£86,000) of the fair value of the asset at inception of the lease, which can be regarded as 'substantially all'.

(c)   the asset will be used by Lis Ltd for the whole of its economic life as it will be scrapped by the lessor at the end of the lease.

Consequently the asset should be capitalised in the balance sheet. The asset should be depreciated over the shorter of its useful life (5 years) and the lease term (6 years).

A lease liability will be shown in the balance sheet, reduced by lease payments made in advance and increased by interest calculated using the interest rate implicit in the lease, 12.5%.

Both the asset and lease liability will initially be recognised at £84,000, the present value of minimum lease payments, as this is lower than the fair value of the asset, so it would not be appropriate to substitute fair value as an approximation. In present value terms the lessor is making a £2,000 loss by not selling the asset at its market value of £86,000, but may have reasons for doing so or the market may be illiquid.

FINANCIAL STATEMENT EXTRACTS

	£
Profit and loss account (extract)	
Depreciation (W1)	16,800
Interest payable (W2)	8,198
Balance sheet (extract)	
Fixed assets	
Leased assets (W1)	67,200
Creditors: amounts falling due within one year	
Finance lease obligation (W2) (73,778 – 55,358)	18,420
Creditors: amounts falling due after more than one year	
Finance lease obligation (W2)	55,358

Workings

1   *Net book value of leased asset*

	£
Depreciation of asset: £84,000/5 years useful life	16,800
Net book value at year end (£84,000 – £16,800)	67,200

2   *Finance lease*

		£
1.1:X3	Present value of minimum lease payments	84,000
1.1.X3	Payment in advance	(18,420)
		65,580
1.1.X3 – 31.12.X3	Interest at 12.5% (£65,580 × 12.5%)	8,198
31.12.X3	**Finance lease obligation c/d**	**73,778**
1.1.X4	Payment in advance	(18,420)
1.1.X4	**Finance lease obligation c/d after next instalment**	**55,358**

The interest element (£8,198) of the current liability can also be shown separately as interest payable.

23 Carpati

Provision for deferred tax

	20X6
	£'000
Accelerated tax depreciation (W1)	186
Revaluation (W2)	0
	186

Workings

1   *Tax depreciation*

	£'000	£'000
At 30 September 20X6:		
Carrying value		1,185
Tax written down value:		
At 1 October 20X5	405	
Expenditure in year	290	
	695	
Less: capital allowance (25%)	(174)	
		(521)
Cumulative timing difference		664
	@ 28%=	186

2   *Revaluation surplus*

The revaluation gain of £252,000 (£1,500,000 – £600,000) will only become taxable if Carpati sells its head office building, which it does not intend to do at the present time.

Accordingly, FRS 19 *Deferred Tax* only requires/permits deferred tax to be recognised on such revaluations when:

(a)   the company has entered into a binding sale agreement to sell the revalued asset, and
(b)   it has recognised the gains and losses expected to arise on sale.

Only (b) has been met in this instance and so no deferred tax provision is made.

24 Pilum

(a)   Earnings per share

	£
Profit before tax	2,530,000
Less taxation	(1,127,000)
Profit after tax	1,403,000
Less preference dividends	(276,000)
Earnings	1,127,000
Earnings per share =	1,127,000
	4,120,000
	27.4p

(b)   The first step is to calculate the theoretical ex-rights price. Consider the holder of 5 shares.

	No	£
Before rights issue	5	8.90
Rights issue	1	1.20
After rights issue	6	10.10

The theoretical ex-rights price is therefore £10.10/6 = £1.68.

The number of shares in issue before the rights issue must be multiplied by the fraction:

$$\frac{\text{Fair value immediately before exercise of rights}}{\text{theoretical ex - rights price}} = \frac{£1.78}{£1.68}$$

Weighted average number of shares in issue during the year:

Date	Narrative	Shares	Time period	Fraction	Total
1.1.X4	b/d	4,120,000	× 9/12	1.78/1.68	3,273,929
1.10.X4	Rights issue	824,000			
		4,944,000	× 3/12		1,236,000
					4,509,929

$$\text{EPS} = \frac{1,127,000}{4,509,929}$$

$$= 25.0p$$

(c) The maximum number of shares into which the loan stock could be converted is 90% × 1,500,000 = 1,350,000. The calculation of diluted EPS should be based on the assumption that such a conversion actually took place on 1 January 20X4. Shares in issue during the year would then have numbered (4,120,000 + 1,350,000) = 5,470,000 and revised earnings would be as follows:

	£	£
Earnings from (a) above		1,127,000
Interest saved by conversion (1,500,000x10%)	150,000	
Less attributable taxation (150,000x30%)	(45,000)	
		105,000
		1,232,000

$$\therefore \text{Diluted EPS} = \frac{1,232,000}{5,470,000}$$

$$= 22.5p$$

25 Biggerbuys

REPORT

To: The bankers of Biggerbuys
From: Consultant management accountant
Subject: Financial performance 20X7 – 20X9
Date: 30 October 20X9

1 Introduction

1.1 In accordance with your instructions, I set out below a review of the entity's financial performance over the last three years.

1.2 The main focus of this report is on the reasons for the increase in the level of bank loans.

1.3 Appropriate accounting ratios are included in the attached appendix.

2 Bank lending

2.1 The main reason for the steep increase in bank lending is due to the entity not generating sufficient cash from its operating activities over the past three years.

2.2 For the year ended 30 June 20X8, the entity had a **net cash deficiency on operating activities** of £18m.

2.3 In addition, for at least the past two years, the cash generated from operating activities has not been sufficient to cover interest payable. Therefore those payments, together with tax and dividends, have had to be covered by borrowings.

2.4 As at 30 June 20X9, bank borrowings were £610m out of a total facility of £630m. Payment of the proposed dividends alone would increase the borrowings to the limit.

3 Operating review

3.1 Although turnover has been rising steadily over the period, operating profit has remained almost static.

3.2 Over this period the profit margin has risen, but not as much as would be expected. The cost of sales have risen in almost the same proportion as sales. This may be due to increased costs of raw materials, as stocks have risen steeply; but the turnover of stock has been falling or static over the same period.

3.3 There has also been a large increase in trade debtors. Both the increase in stock and trade debtors have had to be financed out of operating activities leading to the present pressure on borrowings.

3.4 Although the number of days sales in trade debtors has fallen steadily over the period, the trade debtors at the end of June 20X9 still represent nearly a year's credit sales. This is excessive and seems to imply a poor credit control policy, even taking into account the extended credit terms being granted by the company.

4 Recommendations

4.1 The entity needs to undertake an urgent review of its credit terms in order to reduce the levels of trade debtors.

4.2 Stock levels are also extremely high (representing over four months' sales) and should be reviewed.

4.3 Operating costs also need to be kept under control in order to generate more cash from sales.

Please contact me if you need any further information.

Signed: An Accountant

Appendix: Accounting ratios

		20X7	20X8	20X9
1	Profit margin $\dfrac{\text{Profit before interest}}{\text{Turnover}} \times 100$	$\dfrac{(50+45)}{1,850} \times 100\%$ $= 5.1\%$	$\dfrac{(60+60)}{2,200} \times 100\%$ $= 5.5\%$	$\dfrac{(50+90)}{2,500} \times 100\%$ $= 5.6\%$
2	Operating costs $\dfrac{\text{Other operating costs}}{\text{Turnover}} \times 100$	$\dfrac{550}{1,850} \times 100\%$ $= 29.7\%$	$\dfrac{640}{2,200} \times 100\%$ $= 29.1\%$	$\dfrac{700}{2,500} \times 100\%$ $= 28.0\%$
3	Stock turnover $\dfrac{\text{Cost of sales}}{\text{Stock}}$	$\dfrac{1,250}{400}$ $= 3.1 \text{ times}$	$\dfrac{1,500}{540}$ $= 2.8 \text{ times}$	$\dfrac{1,750}{620}$ $= 2.8 \text{ times}$
4	Trade debtors turnover $\dfrac{\text{Trade debtors}}{\text{Credit sales}} \times 365$	$\dfrac{492}{(300+45)} \times 365$ $= 523 \text{ days}$	$\dfrac{550}{(400+60)} \times 365$ $= 436 \text{ days}$	$\dfrac{633}{(600+90)} \times 365$ $= 334 \text{ days}$

		20X7	20X8	20X9
5	*Cash generated from operations*			
			20X8	20X9
			£m	£m
	Profit before interest		120	140
	Depreciation		60	70
	Increase in stock		(140)	(80)
	Increase in trade debtors		(58)	(83)
	Increase in trade creditors		–	10
			(18)	57

		20X7	20X8	20X9
6	*ROCE*			

$$\frac{\text{Profit before interest}}{\text{Net assets} + \text{borrowings}} \times 100\%$$

		20X7	20X8	20X9
		$\frac{95}{(372+520)} \times 100\%$	$\frac{120}{(382+720)} \times 100\%$	$\frac{140}{(372+930)} \times 100\%$
		= 10.6%	= 10.9%	= 10.7%

7	Interest cover			
	$\dfrac{\text{Profit before interest}}{\text{Interest payable}}$	$\dfrac{95}{25}$	$\dfrac{120}{60}$	$\dfrac{140}{110}$
		= 3.8	= 2.0	= 1.3

8	Gearing			
	$\dfrac{\text{Borrowings}}{\text{Net assets} + \text{borrowings}}$	$\dfrac{520}{892}$	$\dfrac{720}{1,102}$	$\dfrac{930}{1,302}$
		= 58.3%	= 65.3%	= 71.4%

9	Asset turnover			
	$\dfrac{\text{Turnover}}{\text{Net assets} + \text{borrowings}}$	$\dfrac{1,850}{892}$	$\dfrac{2,200}{1,102}$	$\dfrac{2,500}{1,302}$
		= 2.1 times	= 2.0 times	= 1.9 times

26 Webster

(a) PROFIT AND LOSS ACCOUNTS (Restated)

	Cole Ltd		Darwin Ltd	
	£'000	£'000	£'000	£'000
Sales (W1)		2,875		4,400
Opening stock	450		720	
Purchases (W2)	2,055		3,080	
	2,505		3,800	
Closing stock	(540)		(850)	
		(1,965)		(2,950)
Gross profit		910		1,450
Operating expenses (W3)	520		844	
Debenture interest	80		–	
Overdraft interest	15		–	
		(615)		(844)
Net profit		295		606

BALANCE SHEETS (restated)

	Cole Ltd		Darwin Ltd	
	£'000	£'000	£'000	£'000
Fixed assets (W4)				
Premises		1,900		1,900
Plant		1,200		720
		3,100		2,620
Current assets				
Sales	540		850	
Debtors (522 + 375)	897		750	
Bank (W5)	–		60	
	1,437		1,660	
Current liabilities				
Creditors (438 – 275)	163		562	
Overdraft (W5)	795		–	
	958		562	
Net current assets		479		1,098
		3,579		3,718
10% debenture		(800)		–
Net assets		2,779		3,718
Share capital and reserves				
Ordinary shares £1 each		1,000		500
Revaluation reserve (800 – 40)		760		700
Profit and loss account		1,019		2,518
(684 + 295 + 40)/(1,912 + 606)		2,779		3,718

Workings

			£'000
1	*Cole's sales*		
	Per P&L account		3,000
	Over-priced intra group sales (500 – 375)		(125)
			2,875

			£'000
2	*Cole's purchases*		
	Per P&L account		2,030
	Under-priced intra group sales (300 – 275)		25
			2,055

			£'000
3	*Operating expenses*		
	Cole: as if property is revalued		
	Per P&L account		480
	Additional depreciation (2,000 – 1,200) ÷ 20		40
			520
	Darwin's as if plant not yet acquired		£'000
	Per P&L account		964
	Depreciation on plant (600 × 20%)		(120)
			844

		Cole	Darwin
4	*Fixed asset balance*	£'000	£'000
	Property	2,000	2,000
	Depreciation	(100)	(100)
		1,900	1,900
	Plant	1,200	1,200
	Plant not on stream (600 – (600 × 20%))	–	(480)
		1,200	720

			£'000
5	*Bank balances*		
	Cole		
	Per balance sheet		20
	Intra group sale		(500)
	Intra group purchase		(300)
	Overdraft interest		(15)
			(795)
	Darwin		
	Per balance sheet		(550)
	Plant purchase reversed		600
	Overdraft interest reversed		10
			60

(b)   Ratios

	Cole Limited		Darwin Limited	
	Original	*Restated*	*Original*	*Restated*
ROCE (W1)	19.4%	10.5%	13.3%	16.3%
Asset turnover (W2)	1.01 times	0.80 times	1.23 times	1.18 times
Gross profit margin (W30	35.3%	31.7%	33.0%	33.0%
Net profit margin (W4)	16.7%	10.3%	10.8%	13.8%
Debtors collection period (W5)	64 days	114 days	62 days	62 days
Creditors payment period (W6)	79 days	29 days	67 days	67 days

Workings

1   ROCE

$$\text{Cole} \quad = \quad \frac{295 + 80}{2,779 + 800} \quad = \quad 10.5\%$$

$$\text{Darwin} \quad = \quad \frac{606}{3,718} \quad = \quad 16.3\%$$

2   *Asset turnover*

$$\text{Cole} \quad = \quad \frac{2,875}{3,579} \quad = \quad 0.80 \text{ times}$$

$$\text{Darwin} \quad = \quad \frac{4,400}{3,718} \quad = \quad 1.18 \text{ times}$$

3   *Gross profit margin*

$$\text{Cole} \quad = \quad \frac{910}{2,875} \quad = \quad 31.7\%$$

4   *Net profit margin*

$$\text{Cole} \quad = \quad \frac{295}{2,875} \quad = \quad 10.3\%$$

$$\text{Darwin} \quad = \quad \frac{606}{4,400} \quad = \quad 13.8\%$$

5   *Debtors collection period*

$$\text{Cole} \quad = \quad \frac{897}{2,875} \times 365 \quad = 114 \text{ days}$$

6   *Creditors payments period*

$$\text{Cole} \quad = \quad \frac{163}{2,055} \times 365 \quad = 29 \text{ days}$$

The general effect of the restatement is to **improve Darwin's results** in comparison to Cole's. Once the impact of the **beneficial intra-group purchases** and sales are removed, Cole is shown to have a **poorer gross profit margin** than Darwin. This has fed through to the net margin, which is also affected in Cole's case by the impact of a **higher depreciation charge**. The **cash flow** situation for Cole is significantly **worse**, thus increasing interest payable which also impacts on net profit margin.

Darwin's **return on capital** has been **improved** by removing the asset that had yet to make a contribution to the company's profitability. It is significant that the revaluation of Cole's property along the same lines as Darwin has **failed to compensate** for the increase in depreciation and the decrease in gross margin caused by the adjustments to the intra-group transactions.

These adjustments have also had a marked effect on **Cole's collection periods**; whereas these are evenly matched between debtors and creditors by Darwin; Cole's figures indicate an **imbalance**, with far longer taken to pay by debtors than Cole can take to pay its own debts to creditors.

In summary, **Darwin** looks much the **better investment opportunity**. However, Webster will also have to consider:

(i) The relative **asking prices** of the companies.

(ii) The likelihood that the **historical results** are a **true reflection** of future profitability (eg what is the likely effect of Darwin's new machinery coming on stream?).

(c) **Some** but **not all** of the **information** is likely to be available, although each company may disclose voluntarily beyond that required by legislation or standards.

Items (i) and (ii)

FRS 8 Related party transactions requires the disclosure of transactions and balances, between **related parties**. These would be included, but may be aggregated with other similar transactions, as permitted by the standard. Further, if Cole is 90% + owned by Velox, then an exemption from disclosure is permitted.

Item (iii)

Companies that do not follow a policy of revaluation are **not required** to state **market values**, other than in the Directors' Report, where considered significant. However, those that **do revalue** are required to give **historical cost information**; in any case, the additional depreciation would appear in the note of historical cost profits and losses.

Item (iv)

The company's **depreciation policy** would be disclosed, but not necessarily that a certain asset is yet to come on-line, nor how the purchase had been financed.

Item (v)

Without the information in (i) and (ii), it would **not** be possible to work out how much overdraft interest Cole would have to pay.

27 Dundee

CASH FLOW STATEMENT FOR THE YEAR ENDED 31 MARCH 20X7

	£m
Cash flow from operating activities (note)	2,130
Returns on investment and servicing of finance	
Interest paid	(250)
Taxation paid (W2)	(210)
Capital expenditure	
Payments to acquire tangible fixed assets (W1)	(870)
Equity dividends paid	(300)
Financing	
Repayment of finance lease obligations (W3)	(450)
Increase in cash	50

Note – Reconciliation of operating profit to cash flows from operating activities

	£m
Operating profit	1,300
Decrease in stock (1,600 – 1,500)	100
Increase in debtors (2,200 – 1,800)	(400)
Increase in creditors (1,250 – 1,090)	160
Depreciation	970
	2,130

Workings

1   *Payments to acquire tangible fixed assets*

TANGIBLE FIXED ASSETS

	£		£
b/d	3,700	Depreciation	970
Addition – finance leases	600		
∴ Additions – cash	870	c/d	4,200
	5,170		5,170

2   *Taxation paid*

TAXATION PAYABLE

		£			£
∴ paid		210	b/d	CT	205
c/d	CT	225		DT	850
	DT	1,070	P&L		450
		1,505			1,505

3   *Repayments of finance lease obligations*

OBLIGATIONS UNDER FINANCE LEASES

		£			£
∴ paid		450	b/d	< 1 yr	450
c/d	< 1 yr	400		> 1 yr	1,200
	> 1 yr	1,300	Fixed assets		600
		2,250			2,250

28 Elmgrove

Marking scheme

		Marks	
(a)	Net cash inflow from operating activities (½ per item)	3	
	Interest paid	2	
	Interest received	1	
	Taxation	2	
	Purchase of fixed assets	2	
	Sale of fixed assets	1	
	Equity dividend paid	1	
	Purchase of ST investment	1	
	Issue of share capital	2	
	Reconciliation of net cash flow to movement in net debt (½ per item)	3	
	Analysis of changes in net debt (½ per item)	2	
	Available/Maximum		20
(b)	Memo format	1	
	Identify users	1	
	Ability to generate cash	1	
	Ability to repay debts	1	
	Helps decision making	1	
	Easier to understand than the P + L a/c	1	
	Aids comparison	1	
	Available	7	
	Maximum		
	Total		5
			25

Suggested solution

(a)   CASH FLOW STATEMENT
FOR THE YEAR ENDED 31 MARCH 20X9

	£m	£m
Net cash inflow from operating activities (note)		270
Returns on investments and servicing of finance		
Interest paid (W2)	(13)	
Interest received	6	
		(7)
Taxation		
Corporation tax paid (W3)		(62)
Capital expenditure		
Purchase of tangible fixed assets (W1)	(165)	
Receipts from sale tangible fixed assets	22	
		(143)
Equity dividend paid		(32)
Management of liquid resources		
Purchase of short term investment		(35)
Financing		
Issue of share capital (W4)		60
Increase in cash		51

NOTE TO THE CASH FLOW STATEMENT

Reconciliation of operating profit to net cash inflow from operating activities

	£m
Operating profit	120
Depreciation	43
Loss on disposal of fixed assets	6
Decrease in stocks (176 – 123)	53
Increase in debtors (95 – 87)	(8)
Increase in creditors (126 – 70)	56
Net cash inflow from operating activities	270

Workings

1   *Tangible assets additions*

TANGIBLE ASSETS

	£m		£m
Balance b/d (NBV)	264	Revaluation reserve	31
		Depreciation	43
		Disposal	28
∴ Additions	165	Balance c/d (NBV)	327
	429		429

2   *Interest paid*

INTEREST PAYABLE

	£m		£m
		Balance b/d	3
∴ Paid	13	P&L	17
Balance c/d	7		
	20		20

3   *Tax paid*

CURRENT TAX PAYABLE

	£m		£m
		Balance b/d	54
∴ Paid	62	P&L	47
Balance c/d	39		
	101		101

4   *Issue of shares*

	£m
Share capital (plus premium) 31/3/20X9	180
Share capital 31/3/20X8	120
Increase	60
Shares issued for cash	60

(b)

MEMO

To: Memorandum to the directors of Elmgrove plc

From: An Accountant

Date: 1 April 20X4

Subject: Major benefits to the users of financial statements from the publication of cash flow statements

1   **Users**

    1.1   The users of financial statements can basically be divided into the following groups.

        (a)   Shareholders
        (b)   Management
        (c)   Creditors and lenders
        (d)   Employers

    1.2   The **needs** of these groups are **not identical** and hence not all the benefits listed below will be applicable to all users.

2   **Benefits**

    2.1   Cash flow statements direct attention to the **survival** of the enterprise which depends on its **ability** to **generate cash**.

    2.2   Cash flow statements indicate the **ability** of an enterprise to **repay its debts**.

    2.3   They give information which can be used in the **decision making** and **stewardship** process.

    2.4   They are more **easily understood** than profit and loss accounts which depend on accounting conventions and concepts.

    2.5   Cash flow statements give a **better** means of **inter-company comparison**.

Signed

An Accountant

29 CPP and CCA

> **Tutorial note.** It is unlikely that a detailed computation will be asked for, but you must have an understanding of the principles of CPP and CCA, the differences between them and the ways in which they try to improve on HCA.

(a)   In accounting, the value of income and capital is measured in terms of money. In simple terms, profit is the difference between the closing and opening balance sheet values (after adjustment for new sources of funds and applications such as dividend distribution). If, because of inflation, the value of assets in the closing balance sheet is shown at a higher monetary amount than assets in the opening balance sheet, a profit has been made. In traditional accounting, it is assumed that a monetary unit of £1 is a stable measurement; inflation removes this stability.

CPP accounting attempts to provide a more satisfactory method of valuing profit and capital by establishing a stable unit of monetary measurement, £1 of current purchasing power, as at the end of the accounting period under review.

A distinction is made between monetary items, and non-monetary items. In a period of inflation, keeping a monetary asset (eg trade debtors) results in a loss of purchasing power as the value of money erodes over time. Non-monetary assets, however, are assumed to maintain 'real' value over time, and these are converted into monetary units of current purchasing power as at the year end, by means of a suitable price index. The equity interest in the balance sheet can be determined as a balancing item.

The profit or deficit for the year in CPP terms is found by converting sales, opening and closing stock, purchases and other expenses into year-end units of £CPP. In addition, a profit on holding net monetary liabilities (or a loss on holding net monetary assets) is computed in arriving at the profit or deficit figure.

CPP arguably provides a more satisfactory system of accounting since transactions are expressed in terms of 'today's money' and similarly, the balance sheet values are adjusted for inflation, so as to give users of financial information a set of figures with which they can:

(i) Decide whether operating profits are satisfactory (profits due to inflation are eliminated)

(ii) Obtain a better appreciation of the size and 'value' of the entity's assets

(b) CPP and CCA accounting are different concepts, in that CPP accounting makes adjustments for general inflationary price changes, whereas CCA makes adjustments to allow for specific price movements (changes in the deprival value of assets). Specific price changes (in CCA) enable a company to determine whether the operating capability of a company has been maintained; it is not a restatement of price levels in terms of a common unit of money measurement. The two conventions use different concepts of capital maintenance (namely operating capability with CCA, and general purchasing power with CPP).

In addition CPP is based on the use of a general price index. In contrast, CCA only makes use of a specific price index where it is not possible to obtain the current value of an asset by other means (eg direct valuation).

(c) In CCA, holding gains represent the difference between the historical cost of an asset and its current cost. If the asset is unsold, and appears in the balance sheet of a company at current cost, there will be an 'unrealised' holding gain, which must be included in a current cost reserve. When the asset is eventually sold, the profit (equal to the sale price minus the historical cost) may be divided into:

(i) An operating profit which would have been made if the cost of the asset were its current value

(ii) A *realised* holding gain which has arisen because of the appreciation in value of the asset between the date of its acquisition and the date of its sale

Pilot paper

Pilot paper

Paper F7

Financial Reporting (United Kingdom)

Time allowed

Reading and planning:	15 minutes
Writing:	3 hours

All FIVE questions are compulsory and MUST be attempted

Do NOT open this paper until instructed by the supervisor.

During reading and planning time only the question paper may be annotated. You must NOT write in your answer booklet until instructed by the supervisor.

This question paper must not be removed from the examination hall.

Warning

The pilot paper cannot cover all of the syllabus nor can it include examples of every type of question that will be included in the actual exam. You may see questions in the exam that you think are more difficult than any you see in the pilot paper.

ALL FIVE questions are compulsory and MUST be attempted

1   On 1 October 2005 Pumice acquired the following fixed asset investments:
-   80% of the equity share capital of Silverton at a cost of £13.6 million
-   50% of Silverton's 10% loan notes at par
-   1.6 million equity shares in Amok at a cost of £6.25 each.

The summarised draft balance sheets of the three companies at 31 March 2006 are:

	Pumice		Silverton		Amok	
	£'000	£'000	£'000	£'000	£'000	£'000
Tangible fixed assets		20,000		8,500		16,500
Investments		26,000		nil		1,500
		46,000		8,500		18,000
Current assets	15,000		8,000		11,000	
Creditors: amounts falling due within one year	(10,000)		(3,500)		(5,000)	
Net current assets		5,000		4,500		6,000
Total assets less current liabilities		51,000		13,000		24,000
Creditors: amounts falling after more than one year						
8% Loan note		(4,000)		nil		nil
10% Loan note		nil		(2,000)		nil
		47,000		11,000		24,000
Capital and reserves						
Equity shares of £1 each		10,000		3,000		4,000
Profit and loss account		37,000		8,000		20,000
		47,000		11,000		24,000

The following information is relevant:

(i)   The fair values of Silverton's assets were equal to their carrying amounts with the exception of land and plant. Silverton's land had a fair value of £400,000 in excess of its carrying amount and plant had a fair value of £1.6 million in excess of its carrying amount. The plant had a remaining life of four years (straight-line depreciation) at the date of acquisition.

(ii)   In the post acquisition period Pumice sold goods to Silverton at a price of £6 million. These goods had cost Pumice £4 million. Half of these goods were still in the stock of Silverton at 31 March 2006. Silverton had a balance of £1.5 million owing to Pumice at 31 March 2006 which agreed with Pumice's records.

(iii)   The net profit after tax for the year ended 31 March 2006 was £2 million for Silverton and £8 million for Amok. Assume profits accrued evenly throughout the year.

(iv)   Consolidated goodwill is to be written off over a five-year life using time apportionment in the year of acquisition.

(v)   No dividends were paid during the year by any of the companies.

Required:

(a) **Discuss how the investments purchased by Pumice on 1 October 2005 should be treated in its consolidated financial statements.**   (5 marks)

(b) **Prepare the consolidated balance sheet for Pumice as at 31 March 2006.**   (20 marks)

(25 marks)

2   The following trial balance relates to Kala, a publicly listed company, at 31 March 2006:

	£'000	£'000
Land and buildings at cost (note (i))	270,000	
Plant – at cost (note (i))	156,000	
Investment properties – valuation at 1 April 2005 (note (i))	90,000	
Purchases	78,200	
Operating expenses	15,500	
Loan interest paid	2,000	
Rental of leased plant (note (ii))	22,000	
Dividends paid	15,000	
Stock at 1 April 2005	37,800	
Trade debtors	53,200	
Turnover		278,400
Income from investment property		4,500
Equity shares of £1 each fully paid		150,000
Profit and loss reserve at 1 April 2005		112,500
Investment property revaluation reserve at 1 April 2005		7,000
8% (actual and effective) loan note (note (iii))		50,000
Accumulated depreciation at 1 April 2005 – buildings		60,000
– plant		26,000
Trade creditors		33,400
Deferred tax		12,500
Bank		5,400
	739,700	739,700

The following notes are relevant:

(i)   The land and buildings were purchased on 1 April 1990. The cost of the land was £70 million. No land and buildings have been purchased by Kala since that date. On 1 April 2005 Kala had its land and buildings professionally valued at £80 million and £175 million respectively. The directors wish to incorporate these values into the financial statements. The estimated life of the buildings was originally 50 years and the remaining life has not changed as a result of the valuation.

Later, the valuers informed Kala that investment properties of the type Kala owned had increased in value by 7% in the year to 31 March 2006.

Plant, other than leased plant (see below), is depreciated at 15% per annum using the reducing balance method. Depreciation of buildings and plant is charged to cost of sales.

(ii)   On 1 April 2005 Kala entered into a lease for an item of plant which had an estimated life of five years. The lease period is also five years with annual rentals of £22 million payable in advance from 1 April 2005. The plant is expected to have a nil residual value at the end of its life. If purchased this plant would have a cost of £92 million and be depreciated on a straight-line basis. The lessor includes a finance cost of 10% per annum when calculating annual rentals. (Note: you are not required to calculate the present value of the minimum lease payments.)

(iii)   The loan note was issued on 1 July 2005 with interest payable six monthly in arrears.

(iv)   The provision for corporation tax for the year to 31 March 2006 has been estimated at £28.3 million. The deferred tax provision at 31 March 2006 is to be adjusted to a credit balance of £14.1 million.

(v)   Stock at 31 March 2006 was valued at £43.2 million.

Required, prepare for Kala:

(a) A profit and loss account for the year ended 31 March 2006.   (9 marks)

(b) A statement of the movement in share capital and reserves for the year ended 31 March 2006.   (5 marks)

(c) A balance sheet as at 31 March 2006.   (11 marks)

(25 marks)

Note: A statement of total recognised gains and losses is NOT required.

3 Reactive is a publicly listed company that assembles domestic electrical goods which it then sells to both wholesale and retail customers. Reactive's management were disappointed in the company's results for the year ended 31 March 2005. In an attempt to improve performance the following measures were taken early in the year ended 31 March 2006:

- a national advertising campaign was undertaken,
- rebates to all wholesale customers purchasing goods above set quantity levels were introduced,
- the assembly of certain lines ceased and was replaced by bought in completed products. This allowed Reactive to dispose of surplus plant.

Reactive's summarised financial statements for the year ended 31 March 2006 are set out below:

Profit and loss account	£million
Turnover (25% cash sales)	4,000
Cost of sales	(3,450)
Gross profit	550
Operating expenses	(370)
Operating profit	180
Profit on disposal of plant (note (i))	40
Finance costs	(20)
Profit before taxation	200
Taxation	(50)
Profit for the financial year	150

Balance Sheet	£million	£million
Tangible fixed assets		
Property		300
Plant and equipment (note (i))		250
		550
Current assets		
Stock	250	
Debtors	360	
Bank	nil	
	610	
Creditors: amounts falling due within one year		
Bank overdraft	10	
Trade creditors	430	
Taxation	40	
	(480)	130
Creditors: amounts falling due after more than one year		
8% loan note		(200)
		480
Capital and reserves		
Equity shares of 25 pence each		100
Profit and loss account reserve		380
		480

Below are ratios calculated for the year ended 31 March 2005.

Return on year end capital employed (profit before interest and tax over total assets less current liabilities)	28.1%
Net asset (equal to capital employed) turnover	4 times
Gross profit margin	17 %
Net profit (before tax) margin	6.3 %
Current ratio	1.6:1
Closing stock holding period	46 days
Debtors' collection period	45 days
Creditors' payment period	55 days
Dividend yield	3.75%
Dividend cover	2 times

Notes:

(i) Reactive received £120 million from the sale of plant that had a carrying amount of £80 million at the date of its sale.

(ii) the market price of Reactive's shares throughout the year averaged £3.75 each.

(iii) there were no issues or redemption of shares or loans during the year.

(iv) dividends paid during the year ended 31 March 2006 amounted to £90 million, maintaining the same dividend paid in the year ended 31 March 2005.

Required:

(a) Calculate ratios for the year ended 31 March 2006 (showing your workings) for Reactive, equivalent to those provided. (10 marks)

(b) Analyse the financial performance and position of Reactive for the year ended 31 March 2006 compared to the previous year. (10 marks)

(c) Explain in what ways your approach to performance appraisal would differ if you were asked to assess the performance of a not-for-profit organisation. (5 marks)

(25 marks)

4 **(a)** The qualitative characteristics of relevance, reliability and comparability identified in the ASB's *Statement of principles for financial reporting* are some of the attributes that make financial information useful to the various users of financial statements.

Required:

Explain what is meant by relevance, reliability and comparability and how they make financial information useful. (9 marks)

(b) During the year ended 31 March 2006, Porto experienced the following transactions or events:

(i) entered into a finance lease to rent an asset for substantially the whole of its useful economic life.

(ii) a decision was made by the Board to change the company's accounting policy from one of expensing the finance costs on building new retail outlets to one of capitalising such costs.

(iii) the company's profit and loss account prepared using historical costs showed a loss from operating its hotels, but the company is aware that that the increase in the value of its properties during the period far outweighed the operating loss.

Required:

Explain how you would treat the items in (i) to (iii) above in Porto's financial statements and indicate on which of the Statement's qualitative characteristics your treatment is based. (6 marks)

(15 marks)

5   SSAP 9 *Stocks and long-term contracts* deals with accounting for long-term contracts whose durations usually span at least two accounting periods.

Required:

(a) Describe the issues of revenue and profit recognition relating to long-term contracts.   (4 marks)

(b) Beetie is a construction company that prepares its financial statements to 31 March each year. During the year ended 31 March 2006 the company commenced two construction contracts that are expected to be completed in the accounting period ended 31 March 2007. The position of each contract at 31 March 2006 is as follows:

Contract	1	2
	£'000	£'000
Agreed contract price	5,500	1,200
Estimated total cost of contract at commencement	4,000	900
Estimated total cost at 31 March 2006	4,000	1250
Certified value of work completed at 31 March 2006	3,300	840
Contract billings invoiced and received at 31 March 2006	3,000	880
Contract costs incurred to 31 March 2006	3,900	720

The certified value of the work completed at 31 March 2006 is considered to be equal to the revenue earned in the year ended 31 March 2006. The percentage of completion is calculated as the value of the work completed to the agreed contract price.

Required:

Calculate the amounts which should appear in the profit and loss account and balance sheet of Beetie at 31 March 2006 in respect of the above contracts.   (6 marks)

(10 marks)

Paper F7 Financial Reporting (UK) Commentary

General

Question 1 is a consolidated balance sheet

Question 2 is an accounts preparation question

Question 3 is on interpretation of accounts

Question 4 is a discursive question on the qualitative characteristics of financial information

Question 5 is a long-term contract

Question 1

Top tips. There are a number of issues to deal with here – fair value adjustments, unrealised profit, an associate – but none of them are that difficult. Note particularly the workings for investment. Start with the goodwill working and set everything out very clearly.

Question 2

Top tips. This is a straightforward accounts preparation question and the most time-consuming workings are fixed assets and the finance lease, so you should do those first. Note that the amount payable on the lease within one year will be paid the next day, so does not include future interest.

Question 3

Top tips. The main point to note in this question was that the ratios had been distorted by the asset disposal. As with all these questions, you must consider **why** a ratio has moved.

Question 4

Top tips. Part (a) was not difficult, but remember to state *how* these attributes apply. Part (b) took a bit more thought as you had to match the characteristic to the scenario. Keep to what the question is asking in any question like this.

Question 5

Top tips. Its usually to be relied upon when you are given two long-term contracts that one of them will be loss-making. Remember that the whole loss must be taken into account.

Pilot Paper F7 (UK) **Answers**
Financial Reporting (United Kingdom)

1 **(a)** As the investment in shares represents 80% of Silverton's equity shares it is likely to give Pumice control of that company. Control is the ability to direct the operating and financial policies of an entity. This would make Silverton a subsidiary of Pumice and require Pumice to prepare group financial statements which would require the consolidation of the results of Silverton from the date of acquisition (1 October 2005). Consolidated financial statements are prepared on the basis that the group is a single economic entity.

The investment of 50% (£1 million) of the 10% loan note in Silverton is effectively a loan from a parent to a subsidiary. On consolidation Pumice's asset of the loan (£1 million) is cancelled out with £1 million of Silverton's total loan note liability of £2 million. This would leave a net liability of £1 million in the consolidated balance sheet.

The investment in Amok of 1.6 million shares represents 40% of that company's equity shares. This is generally regarded as not being sufficient to give Pumice control of Amok, but is likely to give it significant influence over Amok's policy decisions (eg determining the level of dividends paid by Amok). Such investments are generally classified as associates and FRS 9 *Associates and joint ventures* requires the investment to be included in the consolidated financial statements using equity accounting.

(b) Consolidated balance sheet of Pumice at 31 March 2006

		£'000
Intangible fixed assets:		
Goodwill (4,000 – 400 (w (ii)))		3,600
Tangible fixed assets (w (i))		30,300
Investments – associate (w (iii))		11,400
– other ((26,000 – 13,600 – 10,000 – 1,000 intra-group loan note))		1,400
		46,700
Current assets (15,000 + 8,000 – 1,000 (w (iv)) – 1,500 current account)	20,500	
Creditors: amounts falling due within one year (10,000 + 3,500 – 1,500 current account)	(12,000)	
Net current assets		8,500
Total assets less current liabilities		55,200
Creditors: amounts falling due after more than one year		
8% Loan note	(4,000)	
10% Loan note (2,000 – 1,000 intra-group)	(1,000)	(5,000)
		50,200
Capital and reserves:		
Equity shares of £1 each		10,000
Reserves:		
Profit and loss account (w (v))		37,640
		47,640
Minority interest (w (vi))		2,560
		50,200

Workings in £'000

(i) Tangible fixed assets

Pumice		20,000
Silverton		8,500
Fair value – land	400	
– plant	1,600	2,000
Additional depreciation (see below)		(200)
		30,300

The fair value adjustment to plant will create additional depreciation of £400,000 per annum (1,600/4 years) and in the post acquisition period of six months this will be £200,000.

(ii) Goodwill in Silverton:

Investment at cost		13,600
Less – equity shares of Silverton (3,000 x 80%)	(2,400)	
– pre-acquisition reserves (7,000 x 80% (see below))	(5,600)	
– fair value adjustments (2,000 (w (i)) x 80%)	(1,600)	(9,600)
Goodwill on consolidation		4,000

Goodwill amortisation will be £4,000/5 years x 6/12 =   400

The pre-acquisition reserves are:
At 31 March 2006   8,000
Post acquisition (2,000 x 6/12)   (1,000)
                                                                                                   7,000

(iii) Purchase of Amok
       Cost of investment (1,600 x £6.25)   10,000
       Less
       Net assets at 1 October 2005:
       Equity 31 March 2006   24,000
       Profit 1 October 2005 to 31 March 2006 (8,000 x 6/12)   (4,000)
                                                                               20,000 x 40% (8,000)

       Goodwill   2,000

       Carrying amount at 31 March 2006
       Cost   10,000
       Share post acquisition profit (8,000 x 6/12 x 40%)   1,600
       Less goodwill amortisation (2,000/5 years x 6/12)   (200)

       Carrying amount   11,400

(iv) The unrealised profit (URP) in stock is calculated as:
      Intra-group sales are £6 million of which Pumice made a profit of £2 million. Half of these are still in stock, thus there is
      an unrealised profit of £1 million.

(v)   Consolidated reserves:
      Pumice's reserves   37,000
      Silverton's post acquisition (((2,000 x 6/12) - 200 depreciation) x 80%)   640
      Amok's post acquisition profits (8,000 x 6/12 x 40%)   1,600
      URP in stock (see (iv))   (1,000)
      Goodwill amortisation (w (ii)) – Silverton   400
                             (w (iii)) – Amok   200   (600)

                                                                                                   37,640

(vi) Minority interest
      Equity shares of Silverton (3,000 x 20%)   600
      Profit and loss reserve ((8,000 – 200 depreciation) x 20%)   1,560
      Fair value adjustments (2,000 x 20%)   400

                                                                                                   2,560

2 (a) **Kala – Profit and loss account – Year ended 31 March 2006**

	£'000	£'000
Turnover		278,400
Cost of sales (w (i))		(115,700)
Gross profit		162,700
Operating expenses		(15,500)
Operating profit		147,200
Investment income – property rental		4,500
Finance costs – loan (w (ii))	(3,000)	
– lease (w (iii))	(7,000)	(10,000)
Profit on ordinary activities before tax		141,700
Taxation (28,300 + (14,100 – 12,500))		(29,900)
Profit for the financial year		111,800

(b) Kala – Statement of movement in share capital and reserves – Year ended 31 March 2006

	Equity shares £'000	Investment property resv £'000	Land and building revln reserve £'000	Profit and loss account £'000	Total £'000
At 1 April 2005	150,000	7,000	nil	112,500	269,500
Profit for period (see (a))				111,800	111,800
Revaluation (w (iv))		6,300	45,000		51,300
Equity dividends paid				(15,000)	(15,000)
At 31 March 2006	150,000	13,300	45,000	209,300	417,600

(c) Kala – Balance sheet as at 31 March 2006

	£'000	£'000
Tangible fixed assets		
Land and buildings (w (iv))	250,000	
Plant (w (iv))	184,100	434,100
Investment properties (90,000 + (90,000 x 7%))		96,300
		530,400
Current assets		
Stock	43,200	
Trade debtors	53,200	
	96,400	
Creditors: amounts falling due within one year		
Trade creditors	33,400	
Accrued loan interest (w (ii))	1,000	
Bank overdraft	5,400	
Lease obligation (w (iii)) – accrued interest	7,000	
– capital	15,000	
Corporation tax	28,300	
	(90,100)	
Net current assets		6,300
Total assets less current liabilities		536,700
Creditors: amounts falling due after more than one year		
8% loan note	(50,000)	
Lease obligation (w (iii))	(55,000)	(105,000)
Provisions for liabilities		
Deferred tax		(14,100)
		417,600
Capital and reserves (see (b) above):		
Equity shares of £1 each		150,000
Reserves:		
Revaluation reserves – land and buildings	45,000	
– Investment property	13,300	
Profit and loss account	209,300	267,600
		417,600

Workings in brackets in £'000

(i) Cost of sales:	
Opening stock	37,800
Purchases	78,200
Depreciation (w (iv)) – buildings	5,000
– plant: owned	19,500
leased	18,400
Closing stock	(43,200)
	115,700

(ii)   The loan has been in issue for nine months. The total finance cost for this period will be £3 million (50,000 x 8% x 9/12). Kala has paid six months interest of £2 million, thus accrued interest of £1 million should be provided for.

(iii) Finance lease:

	£'000
Net obligation at inception of lease (92,000 – 22,000)	70,000
Accrued interest 10% (current liability)	7,000
Total outstanding at 31 March 2006	77,000

The second payment in the year to 31 March 2007 (made on 1 April 2006) of £22 million will be £7 million for the accrued interest (at 31 March 2006) and £15 million paid of the capital outstanding. Thus the amount outstanding as an obligation over one year is £55 million (77,000 – 22,000).

(iv) Fixed assets/depreciation:
Land and buildings:
At the date of the revaluation the land and buildings have a carrying amount of £210 million (270,000 – 60,000). With a valuation of £255 million this gives a revaluation surplus (to reserves) of £45 million. The accumulated depreciation of £60 million represents 15 years at £4 million per annum (200,000/50 years) and means the remaining life at the date of the revaluation is 35 years. The amount of the revalued building is £175 million, thus depreciation for the year to 31 March 2006 will be £5 million (175,000/35 years). The carrying amount of the land and buildings at 31 March 2006 is £250 million (255,000 – 5,000).

Plant: owned
The carrying amount prior to the current year's depreciation is £130 million (156,000 – 26,000). Depreciation at 15% on the reducing balance basis gives an annual charge of £19.5 million. This gives a carrying amount at 31 March 2006 of £110.5 million (130,000 – 19,500).

Plant: leased
The fair value of the leased plant is £92 million. Depreciation on a straight-line basis over five years would give a depreciation charge of £18.4 million and a carrying amount of £73.6 million.

The carrying amount of all plant in the balance sheet at 31 March 2006 is therefore £184.1 million (110,500 + 73,600)

3 **(a)** Note: figures in the calculations are in £million

Return on year end capital employed	32.3 %	220/(550 + 130) x 100
Net assets turnover	5.9 times	4,000/680
Gross profit margin	13.8 %	(550/4,000) x 100
Net profit (before tax) margin	5.0 %	(200/4,000) x 100
Current ratio	1.3:1	610:480
Closing stock holding period	26 days	250/3,450 x 365
Debtors' collection period	44 days	360/(4,000 – 1,000) x 365
Creditors' payment period (based on cost of sales)	45 days	(430/3,450) x 365
Dividend yield	6.0%	(see below)
Dividend cover	1.67 times	150/90

The dividend per share is 22.5p (90,000/(100,000 x 4 i.e. 25p shares). This is a yield of 6.0% on a share price of £3.75.

(b) Analysis of the comparative financial performance and position of Reactive for the year ended 31 March 2006

Profitability
The measures taken by management appear to have been successful as the overall ROCE (considered as a primary measure of performance) has improved by 15% (32.3 -28.1)/28.1). Looking in more detail at the composition of the ROCE, the reason for the improved profitability is due to increased efficiency in the use of the company's assets (asset turnover), increasing from 4 to 5.9 times (an improvement of 48%). The improvement in the asset turnover has been offset by lower profit margins at both the gross and net level. On the surface, this performance appears to be due both to the company's strategy of offering rebates to wholesale customers if they achieve a set level of orders and also the beneficial impact on sales revenue of the advertising campaign. The rebate would explain the lower gross profit margin, and the cost of the advertising has reduced net profit margin (presumably management expected an increase in sales volume as a compensating factor). The decision to buy complete products rather than assemble them in house has enabled the disposal of some plant which has reduced the asset base. Thus possible increased sales and a lower asset base are the cause of the improvement in the asset turnover which in turn, as stated above, is responsible for the improvement in the ROCE.

The effect of the disposal needs careful consideration. The profit (before tax) includes a profit of £40 million from the disposal. As this is a 'one-off' profit, recalculating the ROCE without its inclusion gives a figure of only 23.7% (180m/(550m + 130m + 80m (the 80m is the carrying amount of plant)) and the fall in the net profit percentage (before tax) would be down even more to only 4.0% (160m/4,000m). On this basis the current year performance is worse than that of the previous year and the reported figures tend to flatter the company's real underlying performance.

Liquidity

The company's liquidity position has deteriorated during the period. An acceptable current ratio of 1.6 has fallen to a worrying 1.3 (1.5 is usually considered as a safe minimum). With the debtors collection period at virtually a constant (45/44 days), the change in liquidity appears to be due to the levels of stock and trade creditors. These give a contradictory picture. The closing stock holding period has decreased markedly (from 46 to 26 days) indicating more efficient stock holding. This is perhaps due to short lead times when ordering bought in products. The change in this ratio has reduced the current ratio, however the creditors' payment period has decreased from 55 to 45 days which has increased the current ratio. This may be due to different terms offered by suppliers of bought in products.

Importantly, the effect of the plant disposal has generated a cash inflow of £120 million, and without this the company's liquidity would look far worse.

Investment ratios

The current year's dividend yield of 6.0% looks impressive when compared with that of the previous year's yield of 3.75%, but as the company has maintained the same dividend (and dividend per share as there is no change in share capital), the 'improvement' in the yield is due to a falling share price. Last year the share price must have been £6.00 to give a yield of 3.75% on a dividend per share of 22.5 pence. It is worth noting that maintaining the dividend at £90 million from profits of £150 million gives a cover of only 1.67 times whereas on the same dividend last year the cover was 2 times (meaning last year's profit (after tax) was £180 million).

Conclusion

Although superficially the company's profitability seems to have improved as a result of the directors' actions at the start of the current year, much, if not all, of the apparent improvement is due to the change in supply policy and the consequent beneficial effects of the disposal of plant. The company's liquidity is now below acceptable levels and would have been even worse had the disposal not occurred. It appears that investors have understood the underlying deterioration in performance as there has been a marked fall in the company's share price.

(c) It is generally assumed that the objective of stock market listed companies is to maximise the wealth of their shareholders. This in turn places an emphasis on profitability and other factors that influence a company's share price. It is true that some companies have other (secondary) aims such as only engaging in ethical activities (eg not producing armaments) or have strong environmental considerations. Clearly by definition not-for-profit organisations are not motivated by the need to produce profits for shareholders, but that does not mean that they should be inefficient. Many areas of assessment of profit oriented companies are perfectly valid for not-for-profit organisations: efficient stock holdings, tight budgetary constraints, use of key performance indicators, prevention of fraud etc.

There are a great variety of not-for-profit organisations; eg public sector health, education, policing and charities. It is difficult to be specific about how to assess the performance of a not-for-profit organisation without knowing what type of organisation it is. In general terms an assessment of performance must be made in the light of the stated objectives of the organisation. Thus for example in a public health service one could look at measures such as treatment waiting times, increasing life expectancy etc, and although such organisations don't have a profit motive requiring efficient operation, they should nonetheless be accountable for the resources they use. Techniques such as 'value for money' and the three Es (economy, efficiency and effectiveness) have been developed and can help to assess the performance of such organisations.

4   (a)   Relevance

Information has the quality of relevance when it can influence users' economic decisions on a timely basis. It helps to evaluate past, present and future events by confirming, or perhaps correcting, past evaluations of economic events. There are many ways of interpreting and applying the concept of relevance, for example, only material information is considered relevant as, by definition, information is material only if its omission or misstatement could influence users. Other common aspects of relevance are the debate as to whether current value information is more relevant than that based on historical cost. An interesting emphasis placed on relevance within the Statement is that relevant information assists in the predictive ability of financial statements. That is not to say the financial statements should be predictive in the sense of forecasts, but that (past) information should be presented in a manner that assists users to assess an entity's ability to take advantage of opportunities and react to adverse situations. A good example of this is the separate presentation of discontinued operations in the profit and loss account. From this users will be better able to assess the parts of the entity that will produce future profits (the continuing operations) and users can judge the merits of the discontinuation ie has the entity sold a profitable part of the business (which would lead users to question why), or has the entity acted to curtail the adverse affect of a loss-making operation.

Reliability

The Statement states that for information to be useful it must be reliable. The quality of reliability is described as being free from material error (accurate) and representing faithfully that which it purports to portray (ie the financial statements are a faithful representation of the entities' underlying transactions). There can be occasions where the legal form of a transaction can be engineered to disguise the economic reality of the transaction. A cornerstone of faithful representation is that transactions must be accounted for according to their substance (ie commercial intent or economic reality) rather than their legal or contrived form. To be reliable information must be free from deliberate or systematic bias (ie it is neutral). Biased information attempts to influence users (to perhaps come to a predetermined decision) by the manner in which it is presented. It is recognised that financial statements cannot be absolutely accurate due to inevitable uncertainties surrounding their preparation. A typical example would be estimating the useful economic lives of fixed assets. This is addressed by the use of prudence which is the exercise of a degree of caution in matters of uncertainty. However, prudence cannot be used to deliberately understate profit or create excessive provisions (this would break the neutrality principle). Reliable information must also be complete; omitted information (that should be reported) will obviously mislead users.

Comparability

Comparability is fundamental to assessing an entity's performance. Users will compare an entity's results over time and also with other similar entities. This is the principal reason why financial statements contain corresponding amounts for previous period(s). Comparability is enhanced by the use (and disclosure) of consistent accounting policies such that users can confirm that comparative information (for calculating trends) is comparable and the disclosure of accounting policies at least informs users if different entities use different policies. That said, comparability should not stand in the way of improved accounting practices (usually through new Standards); it is recognised that there are occasions where it is necessary to adopt new accounting policies if they enhance relevance and reliability.

(b) (i) This item involves the characteristic of reliability and specifically the use of substance over form. As the lease agreement is for substantially the whole of the asset's useful economic life, Porto will experience the same risks and rewards as if it owned the asset. Although the legal form of this transaction is a rental, its substance is the equivalent to acquiring the asset and raising a loan. Thus, in order for the financial statements to be reliable (and comparable to those where an asset is bought from the proceeds of a loan), the transaction should be shown as an asset on Porto's balance sheet with a corresponding liability for the future lease rental payments. The profit and loss account should be charged with depreciation on the asset and a finance charge on the 'loan'.

(ii) This item involves the characteristic of comparability. Changes in accounting policies should generally be avoided in order to preserve comparability. Presumably the directors have good reason to believe the new policy presents a more reliable and relevant view. In order to minimise the adverse effect a change in accounting policy has on comparability, the financial statements (including the corresponding amounts) should be prepared on the basis that the new policy had always been in place (retrospective application). Thus the assets (retail outlets) should include the previously expensed finance costs and profit and loss accounts will no longer show a finance cost (in relation to these assets whilst under construction). Any finance costs relating to periods prior to the policy change (ie for two or more years ago) should be adjusted for by increasing profits brought forward in the profit and loss reserve (equity).

(iii) This item involves the characteristic of relevance. This situation questions whether historical cost accounting is more relevant to users than current value information. Porto's current method of reporting these events using purely historical cost based information (ie showing an operating loss, but not reporting the increases in property values) is perfectly acceptable. However, the company could choose to revalue its hotel properties (which would subject it to other requirements). This option would still report an operating loss (probably an even larger loss than under historical cost if there are increased depreciation charges on the hotels), but the increases in value would also be reported (in equity) arguably giving a more complete picture of performance.

5 (a) The correct timing of when revenue (and profit) should be recognised is an important aspect of a profit and loss account showing a true and fair view. Only realised profits should be included in the profit and loss account. For most types of supply and sale of goods it is generally accepted that a profit is realised when the goods have been manufactured (or obtained) by the supplier and satisfactorily delivered to the customer. The issue with long-term contracts is that the process of completing the project takes a relatively long time and, in particular, will spread across at least one accounting period-end. If such contracts are treated like most sales of goods, it would mean that revenue and profit would not be recognised until the contract is completed (the "completed contracts" basis). This is often described as following the prudence concept. The problem with this approach is that it may not show a true and fair view as all the profit on a contract is included in the period of completion, whereas in reality (a true and fair view), it is being earned, but not reported, throughout the duration of the contract. SSAP 9 remedies this by requiring the recognition of profit on uncompleted contracts in proportion to some measure of the percentage of completion applied to the estimated total contract profit. This is sometimes said to reflect the accruals concept, but it should only be applied where the outcome of the contract is reasonably foreseeable. In the event that a loss on a contract is foreseen, the whole of the loss must be recognised immediately, thereby ensuring the continuing application of prudence.

(b) Beetie

Profit and loss account	Contract 1 £'000	Contract 2 £'000	Total £'000
Turnover	3,300	840	4,140
Cost of sales (balancing figure)	(2,400)	(890)	(3,290)
Attributable profit/(loss) (see working)	900	(50)	850

Balance sheet

Stock: long-term contract balances

	Contract 1 £'000	Contract 2 £'000	Total £'000
Costs to date	3,900	720	4,620
Transferred to cost of sales	(2,400)	(720)	(3,120)
	1,500	nil	1,500
Debtors: amounts recoverable			
Turnover	3,300		3,300
Payments on account	(3,000)		(3,000)
	300		300
Creditors: amounts falling due within one year			
Payments on account (880 – 840)		40	40
Provisions			
Cost incurred and losses to date (890 – 720)		170	170

Workings in £'000

Estimated total profit:

	Contract 1	Contract 2
Agreed contract price	5,500	1,200
Estimated contract cost	(4,000)	(1,250)
Estimated total profit/(loss)	1,500	(50)

Percentage complete:

Work certified at 31 March 2006	3,300
Contract price	5,500
Percentage complete at 31 March 2006 (3,300/5,500 x 100)	60%
Profit to 31 March 2006 (60% x 1,500)	900

At 31 March 2006 the increase in the expected total costs of contract 2 mean that a loss of £50,000 is expected on this contract. In these circumstances, regardless of the percentage completed, the whole of this loss should be recognised immediately.

Pilot Paper F7 (UK)
Financial Reporting (United Kingdom)

This marking scheme is given as a guide in the context of the suggested answers. Scope is given to markers to award marks for alternative approaches to a question, including relevant comment, and where well-reasoned conclusions are provided. This is particularly the case for written answers where there may be more than one acceptable solution.

1	**(a)**	1 mark per relevant point	**5**
	(b)	Balance sheet:	
		goodwill	3½
		tangible fixed assets	2½
		investments – associate	3
		– other	1
		current assets	2
		creditors – 1 year	1
		8% loan notes	½
		10% loan notes	1
		equity shares	1
		profit and loss account	3
		minority interest	1½
			20
		Total for question	**25**

2	**(a)**	Profit and loss account	
		turnover	½
		cost of sales	4½
		operating expenses	½
		investment income	½
		finance costs	1½
		taxation	1½
			9
	(b)	Movement in share capital and reserves	
		brought forward figures	1
		profit for period	1
		revaluation gains	2
		dividends paid	1
			5
	(c)	Balance sheet	
		land and buildings	2
		plant and equipment	2
		investment property	1
		stocks and trade debtors	1
		trade creditors and overdraft	1
		accrued interest	½
		lease obligation: interest and capital one year	1
		capital over one year	1
		corporation tax provision	½
		8% loan	½
		deferred tax	½
			11
		Total for question	**25**

3 **(a)** one mark per ratio   10

     (b) 1 mark per valid point   maximum   10

     (c) 1 mark per valid point   maximum   5

                                                            Total for question   25

4 **(a)** 3 marks each for relevance, reliability and comparability   9

     (b) 2 marks for each transaction ((i) to (iii)) or event   6

                                                            Total for question   15

5 **(a)** one mark per valid point to   maximum   4

     (b) turnover (½ mark for each contract)   1
             profit/loss (½ mark for each contract)   1
             stocks   1
             debtors   1
             payment on account   1
             provision   1

                                                               6
                                            Total for question   10

Index

Note: **Key Terms** and their page references are given in **bold**.

Review Form & Free Prize Draw – Paper F7 Financial Reporting (6/07)

All original review forms from the entire BPP range, completed with genuine comments, will be entered into one of two draws on 31 January 2008 and 31 July 2008. The names on the first four forms picked out on each occasion will be sent a cheque for £50.

Name: _____ Address: _____

_____

_____

How have you used this Text?
(Tick one box only)

☐ Home study (book only)

☐ On a course: college _____

☐ With 'correspondence' package

☐ Other _____

Why did you decide to purchase this Text? *(Tick one box only)*

☐ Have used BPP Texts in the past

☐ Recommendation by friend/colleague

☐ Recommendation by a lecturer at college

☐ Saw advertising

☐ Saw information on BPP website

☐ Other _____

During the past six months do you recall seeing/receiving any of the following?
(Tick as many boxes as are relevant)

☐ Our advertisement in *ACCA Student Accountant*

☐ Our advertisement in *Pass*

☐ Our advertisement in *PQ*

☐ Our brochure with a letter through the post

☐ Our website www.bpp.com

Which (if any) aspects of our advertising do you find useful?
(Tick as many boxes as are relevant)

☐ Prices and publication dates of new editions

☐ Information on Text content

☐ Facility to order books off-the-page

☐ None of the above

Which BPP products have you used?

Text	☑	*Success CD*	☐	*Learn Online*	☐
Kit	☐	*i-Learn*	☐	*Home Study Package*	☐
Passcard	☐	*i-Pass*	☐	*Home Study PLUS*	☐

Your ratings, comments and suggestions would be appreciated on the following areas.

	Very useful	Useful	Not useful
Introductory section (Key study steps, personal study)	☐	☐	☐
Chapter introductions	☐	☐	☐
Key terms	☐	☐	☐
Quality of explanations	☐	☐	☐
Case studies and other examples	☐	☐	☐
Exam focus points	☐	☐	☐
Questions and answers in each chapter	☐	☐	☐
Fast forwards and chapter roundups	☐	☐	☐
Quick quizzes	☐	☐	☐
Question Bank	☐	☐	☐
Answer Bank	☐	☐	☐
Index	☐	☐	☐

Overall opinion of this Study Text	Excellent ☐	Good ☐	Adequate ☐	Poor ☐

Do you intend to continue using BPP products?   Yes ☐   No ☐

On the reverse of this page are noted particular areas of the text about which we would welcome your feedback. The BPP author of this edition can be e-mailed at: marymaclean@bpp.com

Please return this form to: Nick Weller, ACCA Publishing Manager, BPP Learning Media, FREEPOST, London, W12 8BR

Review Form & Free Prize Draw (continued)

TELL US WHAT YOU THINK

Free Prize Draw Rules

1. Closing date for 31 January 2008 draw is 31 December 2007. Closing date for 31 July 2008 draw is 30 June 2008.

2. Restricted to entries with UK and Eire addresses only. BPP employees, their families and business associates are excluded.

3. No purchase necessary. Entry forms are available upon request from BPP Learning Media. No more than one entry per title, per person. Draw restricted to persons aged 16 and over.

4. Winners will be notified by post and receive their cheques not later than 6 weeks after the relevant draw date.

5. The decision of the promoter in all matters is final and binding. No correspondence will be entered into.